THE OCEAN WORLD.

LONDON: PRINTED BY WILLIAM CLOWES AND SONS, STAMFORD STREET AND CHARING CROSS

Plate I.—The Argonaut sailing in the open sea.

THE

OCEAN WORLD:

BEING

A DESCRIPTIVE HISTORY OF THE SEA AND ITS LIVING INHABITANTS.

CHIEFLY TRANSLATED FROM "LA VIE ET LES MŒURS DES ANIMAUX"

BY LOUIS FIGUIER,

AUTHOR OF "THE WORLD BEFORE THE DELUGE," "THE VEGETABLE WORLD," AND OTHER POPULAR WORKS.

ILLUSTRATED BY FOUR HUNDRED AND TWENTY-SEVEN ENGRAVINGS, CHIEFLY DESIGNED UNDER THE DIRECTION OF M. CH. BÉVALET, FROM SPECIMENS IN THE MUSEUMS OF PARIS.

NEW YORK:
D. APPLETON & CO., 445 BROADWAY.
1868.

PREFACE.

"OUR PLANET is surrounded by two great oceans," says Dr. Maury, the eminent American *savant*: "the one visible, the other invisible; one is under foot, the other over head. One entirely envelopes it, the other covers about two-thirds of its surface." It is proposed in "THE OCEAN WORLD" to give a brief record of the Natural History of one of those great oceans and its living inhabitants, with as little of the nomenclature of Science, and as few of the repulsive details of Anatomy, as is consistent with clearness of expression; to describe the ocean in its majestic calm and angry agitation; to delineate its inhabitants in their many metamorphoses: the cunning with which they attack or evade their enemies: their instructive industry: their quarrels, their combats, and their loves.

The learned Schleiden eloquently paints the living wonders of the deep: "If we dive into the liquid crystal of the Indian Ocean, the most wondrous enchantments are opened to us, reminding us of the fairy tales of childhood's dreams. The strangely-branching thickets bear living flowers. Dense masses of *Meandrineas* and *Astreas* contrast with the leafy, cup-shaped expansions of the *Explanarias*, and the variously-branching *Madrepores*, now spread out like fingers, now rising in trunk-like branches, and now displaying an elegant array of interlacing tracery. The colouring surpasses everything; vivid greens alternate with brown and yellow; rich tints, ranging from purple and deepest blue to a pale reddish-brown. Brilliant rose, yellow, or peach-coloured *Nullipores* overgrow the decaying masses: they themselves being interwoven with the pearl-coloured plates of the *Retipores*, rivalling the most delicate ivory carvings. Close by wave the yellow and lilac Sea-fans (*Gorgonia*), perforated like delicate trellis-work. The bright sand of the bottom is covered with a thousand strange forms of sea-urchins and star-fishes. The leaf-like *Flustræ* and *Escharæ* adhere like mosses and lichens to the branches of coral—the yellow, green, and purple-striped limpets clinging to their trunks. The sea-anemones expand their crowns of tentacula upon the rugged rocks or on flat sands, looking like beds of variegated ranunculuses, or sparkling like gigantic cactus blossoms, shining with brightest colours.

"Around the branches of the coral shrubs play the humming-birds of the ocean: little fishes sparkling with red or blue metallic glitter, or gleaming in golden green or brightest silvery lustre; like spirits of the deep, the delicate milk-white jelly-fishes float softly through the charmed world. Here gleam the violet and gold-green Isabelle, and the flaming yellow, black, and vermilion-striped Coquette, as they chase their prey; there the band-fish shoots snake-like through the thicket, resembling a silvery ribbon glittering with rose and azure hue. Then come the fabulous cuttle-fishes, in all the diaphanous colours of the rainbow, but with no definite outline.

"When day declines, with the shades of night this fantastic garden is lighted up with renewed splendour. Millions of microscopic medusæ and crustaceans, like so many glowing sparks, dance through the gloom. The Sea-pen waves in a greenish phosphorescent light. Whatever is beautiful or wondrous among *fishes*, *Echinoderms*, *jelly-fishes* and *polypi* and *molluscs*, is crowded into the warm and crystal waters of the Tropical ocean."

It is stated on the Title-page that "THE OCEAN WORLD" is chiefly translated from M. Louis Figuier's two most recent works. In justice to that gentleman, we must explain this statement. The History of the Ocean is to a large extent, but not wholly, compiled from "La Terre et les Mers," one of the volumes of M. Figuier's "Tableau de la Nature;" but the larger portion of the work is a free translation of that author's latest work, "La Vie et les Mœurs des Animaux;" other chapters, such as "Life in the Ocean," the chapter on Crustaceans, and some others, are compiled from various sources; they will not be found in either of M. Figuier's volumes; but in other respects his text has been pretty closely followed.

M. Figuier's plan is to begin the study of animals with the less perfect beings occupying the lower rounds of the Zoological ladder, his reason for doing so being an impression that the presence of the gradually perfecting animal structure, from the simplest organisms up to the more perfect forms, was specially calculated to attract the reader. "What can be more curious or more interesting to the mind," he asks, "than to examine the successive links in the uninterrupted chain of living beings which commence with the Infusoria and terminate in Man?"

The work, he hopes, is not without the impress of a true character of novelty and originality; at least he knows no work in which the strange habits and special interests of the Zoophytes and Molluscs can be studied, nor any work in which an attempt is made to represent them by means of designs at once scientifically correct and attractive from the picturesque character of the illustrations, most of which have been made from specimens selected by Monsieur Ch. Bévalet from the various museums in Paris.

One of these charming plain-speaking children we sometimes meet with lately said to M. Figuier. "They tell me thou art a vulgariser of Science. What is that?"

He took the child in his arms, and carried it to the window where there was a beautiful rose-tree in blossom, and invited it to pull a rose.

The child gathered the perfumed flower, not without pricking itself cruelly with the spines; then, with its little hands still bleeding, it went to distribute roses to others in the room.

"Thou art now a vulgariser," said he to the child, "for thou takest to thyself the thorns, and givest the flowers to others!"

The parallel, although exaggerated, is not without its basis of truth, and was probably suggested by the criticism some of his works have met with: the critics forgetting apparently that these works are an attempt to render scientific subjects popular, and attractive to the general reader.

W. S. O.

LONDON, *January*, 1868.

CONTENTS.

CHAPTER I.

PAGE

THE OCEAN 3
Depth of the Sea 5
Colour of the Ocean . . . 13
Phosphorescence 14
Local Colour 17

CHAPTER II.

CURRENTS OF THE OCEAN . . 31
Trade-winds 33
Gulf Stream 34
Storms 37
Tides 40
Polar Seas 47
Antarctic Seas 54

CHAPTER III.

LIFE IN THE OCEAN 63

CHAPTER IV.

ZOOPHYTES 71
Foraminifera 78
Infusoria 89

CHAPTER V.

POLYPIFERA 107

CHAPTER VI.

PAGE

CORALLINES 121
Tubiporinæ 122
Gorgonidæ 123
Isidians 126

CHAPTER VII.

ZOANTHARIA 149
Madreporidæ 151
Porites 164
Actiniaria 183
Minyadinians 195

CHAPTER VIII.

ACALEPHÆ 197
Medusæ 215
Rhizostoma 221
Vilelladæ 231
Ctenophora 256

CHAPTER IX.

ECHINODERMATA 261
Asterias 262
Crinoïdea 272
Echinoidæ 282

MOLLUSCA.

PAGE
General Definition 303

CHAPTER X.

Molluscoïda 305
Tunicata 311
Ascidians 312

CHAPTER XI.

Acephalous Mollusca . . . 319
Ostreadæ 324

CHAPTER XII.

Acephalous Mollusca . . . 361
Mytilidæ 361
Cephalous Molluscs 391
Their Characteristics . . . 391

CHAPTER XIII.

Pulmonary Gasteropods . . . 393
Limneans 404

CHAPTER XIV.

Non-pulmonary Gasteropods . 407
Buccinidæ 416
Purpura 426
Pterocera 436

CHAPTER XV.

PAGE
Molluscous Pteropods . . . 441

CHAPTER XVI.

Cephalopodous Mollusca . . 445
Acetabula 445
Tentaculifera 470

CHAPTER XVII.

Crustaceans 473
General Definition 473
Crabs and Crayfish . . . 480
Lobsters 490

FISHES.

General Definition 493

CHAPTER XVIII.

Cartilaginous Fishes . . . 499
Cyclostomata 499
Selachia 501
Sturiona 515

CHAPTER XIX.

Osseous, or Bony Fishes . . 521
Plectognathi 522
Lophobranchii 526
Malacopterygii 528
Abdominales 552
Acanthopterygians . . . 578
Pharyngians 584

ILLUSTRATIONS.

PLATE		PAGE
I.	THE ARGONAUT SAILING BEFORE THE WIND . (*Frontispiece*)	490
II.	SPONGE FISHING ON THE COAST OF SYRIA	115
III.	CORAL FISHING ON THE COAST OF SICILY	140
IV.	CORAL ISLAND IN THE POMOTOUAN ARCHIPELAGO	169
V.	SEA ANEMONES (I.)	189
VI.	SEA ANEMONES (II.)	191
VII.	AGALMA RUBRA	241
VIII.	GALEOLARIA AURANTIACA	246
IX.	SEA URCHINS	292
X.	FISHING FOR HOLOTHURIA	297
XI.	SYNAPTA DUVERNÆA	301
XII.	DREDGING FOR OYSTERS	335
XIII.	OYSTER PARKS ON LAKE FUSARO	337
XIV.	PECTINIDÆ	347
XV.	SPONDYLUS	350
XVI.	ANODONTA	370
XVII.	TRIDACNA GIGANTEA	373
XVIII.	VENUS AND CYTHEREA	378
XIX.	SOLENIDÆ (*Razor-fish*)	380
XX.	TEMPLE OF SERAPIS	384
XXI.	CONUS	417
XXII.	CYPRÆADÆ	418

PLATE PAGE

XXIII. Voluta 423

XXIV. Capture of a Gigantic Cuttle-fish 459

XXV. Shark Fishing 511

XXVI. Sturgeon Fishing on the Volga 518

XXVII. Fishing for Electrical Eels 531

XXVIII. Greenlanders Fishing for Halibut 532

XXIX. The Herring Fishery 568

XXX. A Roman Feast 582

XXXI. Fishing for Tunny in Provence 587

XXXII. Fishing for Mackerel off the Cornwall Coast 590

THE OCEAN WORLD.

CHAPTER I.

THE OCEAN.

Ἄριστον μὲν ὕδωρ—"The best of all things is water."—PINDAR.

WE have said that the sea covers nearly two-thirds of the surface of the earth. The calculation, as given by astronomers, is as follows: The surface of the earth is estimated at 31,625,625$\frac{1}{12}$ square miles, that portion occupied by the waters being about 23,814,121 square miles, and that consisting of continents, peninsulas, and islands being 7,811,504 miles; whence it follows that the surface covered with water is to dry land as 3·8 is to 1·2. The waters thus cover a little more than seven-tenths of the whole surface. "On the surface of the globe," Michelet remarks, "water is the rule, dry land the exception."

Nevertheless, the immensity and depth of the seas are aids rather than obstacles to the intercourse and commerce of nations; the maritime routes are now traversed by ships and steamers conveying cargoes and passengers equal in extent to the land routes. One of the features most characteristic of the ocean is its continuity; for, with the exception of inland seas, such as the Caspian, the Dead Sea, and some others, the ocean is one and indivisible. As the poet says, "it embraces the whole earth with an uninterrupted wave."

Περὶ πᾶσαν θ' εἱλισσομένου
χθόν' ἀκοιμήτῳ ῥεύματι.
ÆSCHYLUS in *Prometheus Vinctus.*

The mean depth of the sea is not very exactly ascertained, but certain phenomena observed in the movement of tides are supposed to be incapable of explanation without admitting a mean depth of three thousand five hundred fathoms. It is true that a great number of deep sea soundings fall short of that limit; but, on the other hand, many others reach seven or eight thousand. Admitting that three thousand fathoms represents the mean depth of the ocean, Sir John Herschel finds that the volume of its waters would exceed three thousand two hundred and seventy-nine million cubic yards.

This vast volume of water is divided by geographers into five great oceans: the Arctic, the Atlantic, Indian, Pacific, and Antarctic Oceans.

The Arctic Ocean extends from the Pole to the Polar Circle; it is situated between Asia, Europe, and America.

The Atlantic Ocean commences at the Polar Circle and reaches Cape Horn. It is situated between America, Europe, and Africa, a length of about nine thousand miles, with a mean breadth of two thousand seven hundred, covering a surface of about twenty-five million square miles, placed between the Old World and the New. Beyond the Cape of Storms, as Cape Horn may be truly called, it is only separated by an imaginary line from the vast seas of the south, in which the waves, which are the principal source of *tides*, have their birth. Here, according to Maury, the young tidal wave, rising in the circumpolar seas of the south, and obedient to the sun and moon, rolls on to the Atlantic, and in twelve hours after passing the parallel of Cape Horn is found pouring its flood into the Bay of Fundy, whence it is projected in great waves across the Atlantic and round the globe, sweeping along its shores and penetrating its gulfs and estuaries, rising and falling in the open sea two or three feet, but along the shore having a range of ten or twelve feet. Sometimes, as at Fundy on the American coast; at Brest on the French coast; and Milford Haven, and the mouth of the Severn in the Bristol Channel, rising and falling thirty or forty feet, "impetuously rushing against the shores, but gently stopping at a given line, and flowing back to its place when the word goes forth, 'Thus far shalt thou go, and no farther.' That which no human power can repel, returns at its appointed time so regularly and surely, that the hour of its approach and the measure of its mass may be predicted with unerring certainty centuries beforehand."

The Indian Ocean, sometimes called Oceania, is bounded on the north by Asia, on the west by Africa, on the east by the peninsula of Molucca, the Sunda Isles, and Australia.

The Pacific, or Great Ocean, stretches from north to south, from the Arctic to the Antarctic Circle, being bounded on one side by Asia, the island of Sunda, and Australia; on the other by the west coast of America. This ocean contrasts in a striking manner with the Atlantic: the one has its greatest length from north to south, the other from east to west; the currents of the Pacific are broad and slow, those of the other narrow and rapid; the waves of this are low, those of the other very high. If we represent the volume of water which falls into the Pacific by one, that received by the Atlantic will be represented by the figure 5. The Pacific is the calmest of seas; the Atlantic Ocean is the most stormy ocean.

The Antarctic Ocean extends from the Antarctic Polar Circle to the South Pole.

It is remarkable that one half of the globe should be entirely covered with water, whilst the other contains less of water than dry land. Moreover, the distribution of land and water, if, in considering the germ of the oceanic basins, we compare the hemispheres separated by the Equator and the northern and southern halves of the globe, is found to be very unequal.

Oceans communicate with continents and islands by coasts, which are said to be scarped when a rocky shore makes a steep and sudden descent to the shore, as in Brittany, Norway, and the west coast of the British islands. In this kind of coast certain rocky indentations encircle it, sometimes above, sometimes under water, forming a labyrinth of islands, as at the Land's End, Cornwall, where the Scilly Islands form a compact group of from one to two hundred rocky islets, rising out of a deep sea, or, in the case of the Channel, on the opposite coast of France, where the coast makes a sudden descent, forming steep cliffs and leaving an open sea. The coast is said to be flat when it consists of soft argillaceous soil descending to the shore with a gentle slope. Of this description of coast there are two, namely, sandy beaches, and hillocks or dunes.

What is the average depth of the sea? It is difficult to give an exact answer to this question, because of the great difficulty met with in taking soundings, caused chiefly by the deviations of submarine currents. No reliable soundings have yet been made in water over five miles in depth.

Laplace found, on astronomical consideration, that the mean depth of the ocean could not be more than ten thousand feet. Alexander von Humboldt adopts the same figures. Dr. Young attributes to the Atlantic a mean depth of a thousand yards, and to the Pacific, four thousand. Mr. Airy, the Astronomer Royal, has laid down a formula, that waves of a given breadth will travel with certain velocities at a given depth, from which it is estimated that the average depth of the North Pacific, between Japan and California, is two thousand one hundred and forty-nine fathoms, or two miles and a half. But these estimates fall far short of the soundings reported by navigators, in which, as we shall see, there are important and only recently discovered elements of error. Du Petit Thouars, during his scientific voyage in the frigate *Venus*, took some very remarkable soundings in the Southern Pacific Ocean: one, without finding bottom at two thousand four hundred and eleven fathoms; another, in the equinoctial region, indicated bottom at three thousand seven hundred and ninety.

In his last expedition, in search of a north-west passage, Captain Ross found soundings at five thousand fathoms. Lieutenant Walsh, of the American Navy, reports a cast of the deep-sea lead, not far from the American coast, at thirty-four thousand feet without bottom. Lieutenant Berryman reported another unsuccessful attempt to fathom mid ocean with a line thirty-nine thousand feet in length. Captain Denman, of H. M. S. *Herald*, reported bottom in the South Atlantic at the depth of forty-six thousand feet; and Lieutenant J. P. Parker, of the United States frigate *Congress*, on attempting soundings near the same region, let go his plummet, after it had run out a line fifty thousand feet long, as though bottom had not been reached. We have the authority of Lieutenant Maury for saying, however, that "there are no such depths as these." The under-currents of the deep sea have power to take the line out long after the plummet has ceased to sink, and it was before this fact was discovered that these great soundings were reported. It has also been discovered that the line, once dragged down into the depths of the ocean, runs out unceasingly. This difficulty was finally overcome by the ingenuity of Midshipman Brooke. Under the judicious patronage of the Secretary to the United States Navy, Mr. Brooke invented the simple and ingenious apparatus (Fig. 1), by which soundings are now made, in a manner which not only establishes the depth, but brings up specimens of the bottom. The sounding-line in this apparatus is attached to a weighty rod of iron, the lower extremity of which contains a hollow cup for the reception of tallow or some other soft substance. This rod is passed through a hole in a thirty-two pound spherical shot, being supported in its position by slings A, which are hooked on to the line by the swivels *a*. When the rod strikes the bottom, the tension on

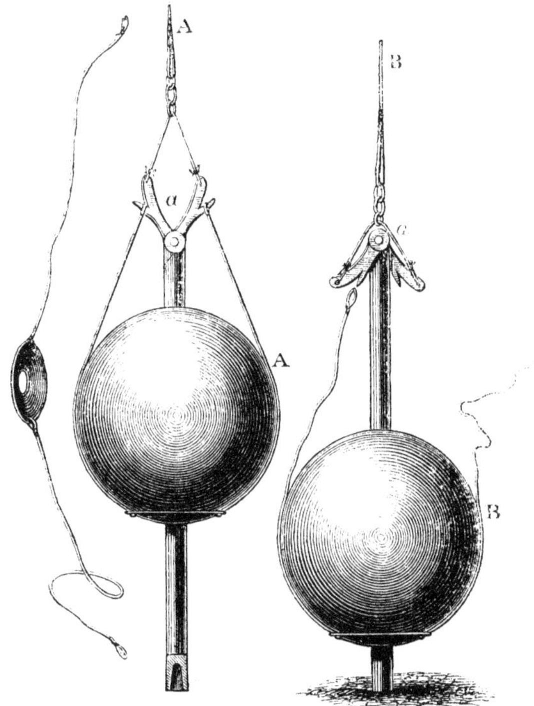

Fig. 1. Brooke's Sounding Apparatus

the line ceases, the swivels are reversed, the slings B are thrown out of the hooks, the ball falls to the ground, and the rod, released from its weight, is easily drawn up, bringing with it portions of the bottom attached to the greasy substance in the cup. By means of this apparatus, specimens of the bottom have been brought up from the depth of four miles.

The greatest depth at which the bottom has been reached with this plummet is in the North Atlantic between the parallels of thirty-five and forty degrees north, and immediately south of the great bank of rocks off Newfoundland. This does not appear to be more than twenty-five thousand feet deep. "The basin of the Atlantic," says Maury, "according to the deep sea soundings in the accompanying diagram, is a long trough separating the Old World from the New, and extending, probably, from pole to pole. In breadth, it contrasts strongly with the Pacific Ocean. From the top of Chimborazo to the bottom of the Atlantic, at the deepest place yet reached by the plummet in that ocean, the distance in a vertical line is nine miles."

"Could the waters of the Atlantic be drawn off, so as to expose to view this great sea gash which separates continents, and extends from the Arctic to the Antarctic Seas, it would present a scene the most rugged, grand, and imposing; the very ribs of the solid earth with the foundations of the sea would be brought to light, and we should have presented to us in one view, in the empty cradle of the ocean, 'a thousand fearful wrecks,' with the array of 'dead men's skulls, great anchors, heaps of pearls, and inestimable stones,' which, in the poet's eye, lie scattered on the bottom of the sea, making it hideous with the sight of ugly death."

The depth of the Mediterranean is comparatively inconsiderable. Between Gibraltar and Ceuta, Captain Smith estimates the depth at about five thousand seven hundred feet, and from one to three thousand in the narrower parts of the straits. Near Nice, Saussure found bottom at three thousand two hundred and fifty. It is said that the bottom is shallower in the Adriatic, and does not exceed a hundred and forty feet between the coast of Dalmatia and the mouths of the Po.

The Baltic Sea is remarkable for its shallow waters, its maximum rarely exceeding six hundred feet.

It thus appears that the sea has similar inequalities to those observed on land; it has its mountains, valleys, hills, and plains.

The Deep Sea Sounding Apparatus of Lieutenant Brooke has already furnished some very remarkable results. Aided by it, Dr. Maury has constructed his fine orographic map of the basin of the Atlantic, which is probably as exact as the maps which represent Africa or Australia.

Dr. Maury has also published many charts, giving the depths of the ocean, the substance of which is given in the accompanying map, which represents the configuration of the Atlantic up to the tenth degree of south latitude, not in figures, as in Dr. Maury's charts, but in tints; diagonal lines from right to left, representing the shores of both hemispheres, indicate a depth of less than a thousand fathoms; from left to right, indicate bottom at one thousand to two thousand; horizontal lines, two to three thousand fathoms; cross lines show an average depth of three to four thousand fathoms; finally, the perpendicular lines indicate a depth of four thousand fathoms and upwards. Solid black

Fig. 2. Chart of the Atlantic Ocean.

indicates continents and islands; waving lines, surrounding both continents at a short distance from the shore, indicate the sands which surround the coast line at a little distance from the shore.

The question is sometimes asked, What useful purpose is served by taking soundings at great depths? To this we may quote the answer of Franklin to a similar question, addressed to aeronauts—"What purpose is served by the birth of a child?" Every fact in physics is interesting in itself; it forms a rallying point, round which, sooner or later, others will meet, in order to establish some useful truth; and the importance of making and recording deep sea soundings is established by the successful immersion of the transatlantic telegraph.

At the bottom of the Atlantic there exists a remarkable plateau, extending from Cape Race in Newfoundland, to Cape Clear in Ireland, a distance of over two thousand miles, with a breadth of four hundred and seventy miles: its mean depth along the whole route is estimated at two miles to two miles and a half. It is upon this telegraphic plateau, as it has been called, that the attempt was made to lay down the cable in 1858, and it is on it that the enterprise has been so successfully completed, during the year 1866. The surface of this plateau had been previously explored by means of Brooke's apparatus, and the bottom was found to be composed chiefly of microscopic calcareous shells (*Foraminifera*), and a few siliceous shells (*Diatomaceæ*). These delicate and fragile shells, which seemed to strew the bottom of the sea, in beds of great thickness, were brought up by the sounding-rod in a state of perfect preservation, which proves that the water is remarkably quiet in these depths,—an inference which is fully borne out by the condition in which the cable of 1858 was found, when picked up in 1866.

The first exploration of this plateau was undertaken by the American brig *Dolphin*, which took a hundred soundings one hundred miles from the coast of Scotland, afterwards taking the direction of the Azores, to the north of which bottom was found, consisting of chalk and yellow sand, at nine thousand six hundred feet. To the south of Newfoundland, the depth was found to be sixteen thousand five hundred feet. In 1856, Lieutenant Berryman, of the American steamer *Arctic*, completed a line of soundings from St. John, Newfoundland, to Valentia, off the Irish coast, and in 1857, Lieutenant Dayman, of the English steamship *Cyclops*, repeated the same operation: this last line of soundings, the result of which is represented in the accompanying section, differed slightly from that followed by Lieutenant Berryman.

Fig. 3. Section of the Atlantic Telegraph.

In the Gulf of Mexico, the depth does not seem to exceed seven thousand feet; the Baltic does not in any place exceed eleven hundred. The depth of the Mediterranean is, as we have said, very variable. At Nice, according to Horace de Saussure, the average depth is three thousand three hundred feet. Between the Dalmatian coast and the mouth of the Po, bottom is found at a hundred and forty feet. Captain Smith found soundings at from one thousand to nine thousand feet in the Straits of Gibraltar, and at ten thousand feet between Gibraltar and Ceuta, where the breadth exceeds sixteen miles. Between Rhodes and Alexandria, the greatest depth is ten thousand feet. Between Alexandria and Candia it is ten thousand three hundred. A hundred and twenty miles east of Malta it is fifteen thousand. The peculiar form of the Mediterranean has led to its being compared to a vast inverted tunnel.

The Arctic Ocean has, probably, no great depth. According to Baron Wrangel, the bottom of the glacial sea, on the north coast of Siberia, forms a gentle slope, and, at the distance of two hundred miles from the shore, it is still only from ninety to a hundred feet. Nevertheless, in Baffin's Bay, Dr. Kane made soundings at eleven thousand six hundred feet.

The inequalities of the basin of the Pacific Ocean are, comparatively, unknown to us. The greatest depth observed by Lieutenant Brooke in the great ocean is two thousand seven hundred fathoms, which he found in fifty-nine degrees north latitude and one hundred and sixty-six degrees east longitude. Applying the theory of waves to the billows propelled from the coast of Japan to California, during the earthquake of the 23rd of December, 1854, Professor Bache calculated that the mean depth of this part of the Pacific is fourteen thousand four hundred feet. In the Pacific Ocean, latitude sixty degrees south and one hundred and sixty degrees east longitude, he found soundings at fourteen thousand six hundred feet—about two miles and a half. Another cast of the lead in the Indian Ocean was made in seven thousand and forty fathoms, but without bringing up any soil from the bottom. Among the fragments brought up from the bottom of the Coral Sea, a remarkable absence of calcareous shells was noted, whilst the siliceous fragments of sponges were found in great quantities. Other soundings made in the Pacific, at a depth of four or five miles, were examined by Ehrenberg, who found a hundred and thirty-five different forms of infusoria represented, and among them twenty-two species new to him. Generally speaking, the composition of the infusoria of the Atlantic are calcareous; those of the Pacific, siliceous. These animalcules draw from the sea the mineral matter with which it is charged—that is, the lime or silica which form their shell. These shells accumulate after the death of the animal, and form the bottom of the ocean. The animals construct their habitations near the surface; when they die, they fall into the depths of the ocean, where they accumulate in myriads, forming mountains and plains in mid ocean. In this manner, we may remark, *en passant*, many of the existing continents had their birth in geological times. The horizontal beds of marine deposits, which are called *sedimentary rocks*, and especially the cretaceous rocks and calcareous beds of the Jurassic and Tertiary periods, all result from such remains.*

The sea level is, in general, the same everywhere. It represents the spherical form of our planet, and is the basis for calculating all terrestrial heights; but many gulfs and inlands open on the east are supposed to be exceptions to this rule: the accumulation of waters, pressed into these receptacles by the general movement of the sea from east to west, it is alleged, may pile up the waters, in some cases, to a greater height than the general level.

It had long been admitted, on the faith of inexact observation, that the level of the Red Sea was higher than that of the Mediterranean. It has also been said that the level of the Pacific Ocean at Panama is higher by about forty inches than the mean level of the Atlantic at Chagres, and that, at the moment of high water, this difference was increased to about thirteen feet, while at low it is over six feet in the opposite direction. This has been proved, so far as the evidence goes, to be error in what concerns the difference in level of the Red Sea and Mediterranean, and the opening of the Suez Canal, which is near at hand, will probably furnish still more convincing proofs. It is probable that errors of measurement have also occurred, so far as the Pacific and Atlantic are concerned.

It has been calculated that all the waters of the several seas gathered together would form a sphere of fifty or sixty leagues in diameter, and, supposing the surface of the globe perfectly level, that

* "World before the Deluge." Second edition.

these waters would submerge it to the depth of more than six hundred feet. Again, admitting the mean depth of the sea to be thirteen thousand feet, its estimated contents ought to be nearly two thousand two hundred and fifty millions of cubic miles of water; and, if the sea could be imagined to be dried up, all the sewers of the earth would require to pour their waters into it for forty thousand years, in order to fill the vast basins anew.

If we could imagine the entire globe to be divided into one thousand seven hundred and eighty-six parts by weight, we should find approximately, according to Sir John Herschel, that the total weight of the oceanic waters is equivalent to one of these parts.

The specific weight of sea water is a little above that of fresh water, the proportion being as a thousand to a thousand and twenty-seven. The Dead Sea, which receives no fresh water into its bosom to maintain itself at the same level as other seas, acquires a higher degree of saltness, and is equal to a thousand and twenty-eight. The specific gravity of sea water is about the same as the milk of a healthy woman.

The colour of the sea is continually varying. According to the testimony of the majority of observers, the ocean, seen by reflection, presents a fine azure blue or ultramarine (*cæruleum mare*). When the air is pure and the surface calm this tint softens insensibly, until it is lost and blended with the blue of the heavens. Near the shore it becomes more of a green or glaucus, and more or less brilliant, according to circumstances. There are some days when the ocean assumes a livid aspect, and others when it becomes a very pure green; at other times, the green is sombre and sad. When the sea is agitated, the green takes a brownish hue. At sunset, the surface of the sea is illumined with tints of every hue of purple and emerald. Placed in a vase, sea water appears perfectly transparent and colourless. According to Scoresby, the Polar Seas are of brilliant ultramarine blue. Castaz says of the Mediterranean, that it is celestial blue, and Tuckey describes the equinoctial Atlantic as being of a vivid blue.

Many local causes influence the colours of marine waters, and give them certain decided and constant shades. A bottom of white sand will communicate a greyish or apple-green colour to the water, if not very deep; when the sand is yellow, the green appears more sombre; the presence of rocks is often announced by the deep colour which the sea takes in their vicinity. In the Bay of Loango the waters appear of a deep red, because the bottom is there naturally red. It appears white in the Gulf of Guinea, yellow on the coast of Japan, green to the west of the Canaries, and black round the Maldive group of islands. The Mediterranean, towards the Archipelago, sometimes becomes more or less red. The White and Black Seas appear to be named after the ice of the one and the tempests to which the other is subject.

At other times, coloured animalcules give to the water a particular tint. The Red Sea owes its colour to a delicate microscopic algæ (*Trychodesmium erythræum*), which was subjected to the microscope by Ehrenberg; but other causes of colouration are suggested. Some microscopists maintain that it is imparted by the shells and other remains of infusoria; others ascribe the colour to the evaporation which goes on unceasingly in that riverless district, producing salt rocks on a great scale all round its shores. In the same manner sea water, concentrated by the action of the solar rays in the salt marshes of the south of France, when they arrive at a certain stage of concentration take a fine red colour, which is due to the presence of some red-shelled animalcules which only appear in sea water of this strength. Strangely enough, these minute creatures die when the waters attain greater density by further concentration, and also if it becomes weaker from the effects of rain.

Navigators often traverse long patches of green, red, white, or yellow coloured water, all of which are due to the presence of microscopic crustaceans, medusæ, zoophytes, and marine plants; the Vermilion Sea on the Californian coasts is entirely due to the latter cause.

The phenomena known as *Phosphorescence of the Sea*, is due to analogous causes. This wonderful sight is observable in all seas, but is most frequent in the Indian Ocean, the Arabian Gulf, and other tropical seas. In the Indian Ocean, Captain Kingman, of the American ship *Shooting Star*, traversed a zone twenty-three miles in length so filled with phosphorescent animalcules that at seven hours forty-five minutes the water was rapidly assuming a white, milky appearance, and during the night it presented the appearance of a vast field of snow. "There was scarcely a cloud in the heavens," he continues, "yet the sky, for about ten degrees above the horizon, appeared as black as if a storm were raging; stars of the first magnitude shone with a feeble light, and the 'Milky Way' of the heavens was almost entirely eclipsed by that through which we were sailing." The animals which produced this appearance were about six inches long, and formed of a gelatinous and translucent matter. At times, the sea was one blaze of light, produced by countless millions of minute globular creatures, called *Noctilucæ*. The motion of a vessel or the plash of an oar will often excite their lucidity, and sometimes, after the ebb of tide, the rocks and seaweed of the coast are glowing with them. Various other tribes of animals there are which contribute to this luminous appearance of the sea. M. Peron thus describes the effect produced by *Pyrosoma Atlanticum*, on his voyage to the Isle of France: "The wind was blowing with great violence, the night was dark, and the vessel was making rapid way, when what appeared to be a vast sheet of phosphorus presented itself floating on the waves, and occupying a great space ahead of the ship. The vessel having passed through this fiery mass, it was discovered that the light was occasioned by animalcules swimming about in the sea at various depths round the ship. Those which were deepest in the water looked like red-hot balls, while those on the surface resembled cylinders of red-hot iron. Some of the latter were caught: they were found to vary in size from three to seven inches. All the exterior of the creatures bristled with long thick tubercles, shining like so many diamonds, and these seemed to be the principal seat of its luminosity. Inside also there appeared to be a multitude of oblong narrow glands, exhibiting a high degree of phosphoric power. The colour of these animals when in repose is an opal yellow, mixed with green; but, on the slightest movement, the animal exhibits a spontaneous contractile power, and assumes a luminous brilliancy, passing through various shades of deep red, orange green, and azure blue."

The phosphorescence of the sea is a spectacle at once imposing and magnificent. The ship, in plunging through the waves, seems to advance through a sea of red and blue flame, which is thrown off by the keel like so much lightning. Myriads of creatures float and play on the surface of the waves, dividing, multiplying, and reuniting, so as to form one vast field of fire. In stormy weather the luminous waves roll and break in a silvery foam. Glittering bodies, which might be taken for fire-fishes, seem to pursue and catch each other —lose their hold, and dart after each other anew. From time immemorial, the phosphorescence of the sea has been observed by navigators. The luminous appearance presents itself on the crest of the waves, which in falling scatters it in all directions. It attaches itself to the rudder and dashes against the bows of the vessel. It plays round the reefs and rocks against which the waves beat, and on silent nights, in the Tropics, its effects are truly magical. This phosphorescence is due chiefly to the presence of a multitude of mollusks and zoophytes which seem to shine by their own light; they emit a fluid so susceptible of expansion, that in the zigzag movement pursued they leave a luminous train upon the water, which spreads with immense rapidity. One of the most remarkable of these minute mollusks is a species of *Pyrosoma*, a sort of mucous sac of an inch long, which, thrown upon the deck of a ship, emits a light like a rod of iron heated to a white heat. Sir John Herschel noted on the surface of calm water a very curious form of this phosphorescence; it was a polygon of rectilinear shape, covering many square feet of surface, and it illuminated the whole region for some moments with a vivid light, which traversed it with great rapidity.

This phosphorescence may also result from another cause. When animal matter is decomposed, it becomes phosphorescent. The bodies of certain fishes, when they become a prey to putrefaction, emit an intense light. MM. Becquerel and Breschet have noted fine phosphorescent effects from this cause in the waters of the Brenta at Venice. Animal matter in a state of decomposition, proceeding from dead fish which floats on the surface of ponds, is capable of producing large patches of oleaginous matter, which, piled upon the water, communicates to a considerable extent the phosphorescent aspect.

Whatever may be the case elsewhere, there are local causes which affect the colour of the waters in certain rivers, and even originate their names. The Guaïnia of the Rio Negro, or Black River, is of a deep brown, which scarcely interferes with the limpidity of its waters. The waters of the Orinoco and the Casiquaire have also a brownish colour. The Ganges is of a muddy brown, while the Djumna, which it receives, is green or blue. The whitish colour belongs to the Rio Bianco, or White River, and to many other rivers. The Ohio in America, the Torgedale, the Goetha, the Traun at Ischl, and most of the Norwegian rivers, are of a delicate limpid green. The Yellow River and the Blue River in China are distinguished by the characteristic tint of their waters. The Arkansas, the Red River, and the Lobregat in Catalonia, are remarkable for their red colour, which, like the Dart and other English rivers, they owe to the earth over which they flow, or which their waters hold in suspension.

The water of the sea is essentially *salt*, of a peculiar flavour, slightly acrid and bitter, and a little nauseous. It has an odour perfectly *sui generis*, and is slightly viscous. In short, it includes a great number of mineral salts and some other compounds, which give it a very disagreeable taste, and render it unfit for domestic use. It contains nearly all the soluble substances which exist on the globe, but principally chloride of sodium, or marine salt, and sulphates of magnesia, of potassium, and of lime.

Pure water is produced by a combination of one volume of oxygen and of two volumes of hydrogen, or in weight 100 oxygen and 12·50 hydrogen. Sea water is composed of the same; but we find there, besides, other elements, the presence of which chemistry reveals to us. In 1000 grains of sea water the following ingredients are found:

Water	962·0
Chloride of sodium	27·1
Chloride of magnesium	5·4
Chloride of potassium	0·4
Bromide of magnesia	0·1
Sulphate of magnesia	1·2
Sulphate of lime	0·8
Carbonate of lime	0·1
Leaving a residuum of	2·9
	1000

consisting of sulphuretted hydrogen, hydrochlorate of ammonia, iodine, iron, copper, and even silver in various quantities and proportions, according to the locality of the specimen. In examining the plates of copper taken from the bottom of a ship at Valparaiso which had been long at sea, distinct traces of silver were found deposited by the sea. Finally, we find dissolved in the ocean a peculiar mucus, which seems of a mixed animal and vegetable nature; organic matter proceeding from the successive decomposition of innumerable generations of animals which have disappeared since the beginning of the world. This matter has been described by the Count Marsigli, who designates it sometimes under the name of *glu*, sometimes as an *unctuosity*. The numerous salts which exist in the sea can neither be deposited in its bed, nor exhaled with the vapour, to be again poured upon the soil in showers of rain. Particular agents retain these salts in solution, transform them, and prevent their accumulation. Hence sea water always maintains a certain degree of saltness and bitterness, and the ocean continues to present the chemical characters which it has exhibited in all times, varying only in certain localities where more or less fresh water is poured into the sea basin from rivers: thus the saltness of the Mediterranean is greater than that of the ocean, probably because it loses more water by evaporation than it receives from its fresh-water affluents. For the opposite reason, the Black and the Caspian Seas are less charged with these salts. The Dead Sea is so strongly impregnated with salt that the body of a man floats on its surface without sinking, like a piece of cork upon fresh water. The supposed cause is excessive evaporation and the absence of rivers of any importance.

The saltness of the sea seems to be generally less towards the Poles than the Equator; but there are exceptions to this law. In the Irish Channel, near the Cumberland coast, the water contains salt equal to the fortieth of its weight; on the coast of France, it is equal to one thirty-second; in the Baltic, it is equal to a thirtieth; at Teneriffe, a twenty-eighth; and off the coast of Spain, to a sixteenth. Again, in many places the sea is less salt at the surface than at the bottom. In the Straits of the Dardanelles, at Constantinople, the proportion is as seventy-two to sixty-two. In the Mediterranean, it is as thirty-two to twenty-nine. It is also stated that as the salt increases at a certain depth, the water becomes less bitter. At the mouth of the great rivers it is scarcely necessary to add that the water is always less saline than on shores which receive no supplies of fresh water; the same remark applies to sea water in the vicinity of polar ice, the melting of which is productive of much fresh water. A recent analysis of the water of the Dead Sea by M. Roux gives about two pounds of salt to one gallon of water. No mineral water, if we except that of the Salt Lake of Utah, is so largely impregnated with saline substances; the quantity of bromide of magnesia is 0·35 grammes to the litre. The water of the Dead Sea is, according to these proportions, the richest natural depository of bromide, which it might be made to furnish abundantly. The waters of the great Lake Utah and Lake Ourmiah in Persia are both highly saline. In Lake Ourmiah, as in the Dead Sea, the proportion of salt is six times greater than in the ocean. Many of our fresh-water lakes were probably salt originally, but have by degrees lost their saline properties by the mingling of their waters with those of the rivers which traverse or flow into them. Among the lakes which appear to have been divested of their saline properties may be mentioned the great lakes ot Canada and the Sea of Baikal, in all of which seals and other marine animals are still found, which have become acclimatized as the water gradually became fresh.

The saltness of sea water increases its density, and at the same time its buoyancy, thus adapting it for bearing ships and other burdens on its bosom; moreover, to abbreviate slightly Dr. Maury's remark, "the brine of the ocean is the ley of the earth." From it the sea derives dynamical power, and its currents their main strength. It is the salt of the sea that imparts to its waters those curious anomalies in the laws of freezing and of thermal dilatation, that assist the rays of heat to penetrate its bosom; the salts of the sea invest it with adaptations which fresh water could not possess. In the latter case, the maximum density would be thirty-nine degrees five seconds instead of twenty-five degrees six seconds, when the dynamical force of the sea would be insufficient to put the Gulf Stream in motion. Nor could it regulate those climates we call marine.

We have said that sea water contains nearly all the soluble substances which exist in the globe. "The water which evaporates from the sea," says Youman, in his "Chemistry," "is nearly pure, containing but very minute traces of salts. Falling as rain upon the land, it washes the soil, percolates through the rocky layers, and becomes charged with saline substances, which are borne seaward by the returning currents. The ocean, therefore, is the great depository of all substances that water can dissolve and carry down from the surface of the continents; and, as there is no channel for their escape, they would constantly accumulate, were it not for the creatures which inhabit the seas, and utilize the material thus brought within their reach." These substances are chloride of sodium or marine salt, sulphates of magnesia, potassa, lime, and other substances which the water of various seas is found to contain.

In the year 1847, I made an analysis of water taken a few leagues from the coast at Havre, which gave the following result, from one litre (1 pint ·760773):*

	Grammes
Chloride of sodium	25·704
Chloride of magnesium	2·905
Sulphate of magnesia	2·462
Sulphate of lime	1·210
Sulphate of potassa	0·094
Carbonate of lime	0·132
Silicate of soda	0·017
Bromide of sodium	0·103
Bromide of magnesium	0·030
Oxide of iron, carbonate and phosphate of magnesia, and oxide of manganese	Only traces.
	32·657

The water of the Mediterranean contains more salts than that of the ocean.

The following are, according to M. Usiglio, who was one of a commission sent to examine the different kinds of salt water in the south of France, the component parts of one hundred gallons of Mediterranean water:

	lbs.
Chloride of sodium	29·524
Chloride of potassium	0·405
Chloride of magnesium	3·219
Sulphate of magnesia	2·477
Chloride of calcium	6·080
Sulphate of lime	1·557
Carbonate of lime	0·114
Bromide of sodium	0·356
Protoxide of iron	0·003
Total . . .	43·735

We conclude, from the quantity of sea salt contained in the water of the ocean, that, if it were spread over the surface of the globe, it would form a layer of more than thirty feet in height.

* Examen Comparatif des Principales eaux Minérales Salines de France et d'Allemagne, par MM. L. Figuier et Mialhe. Read at the Académie de Médecin, 23rd of May, 1848.

The salt contained in sea water gives it a greater density than fresh water; its average specific weight is 1·027. The density of the water of the Mediterranean is, according to M. Usiglio, 1·025 when at the temperature of seventy degrees. But the saltness of the sea varies very much under the influence of a great many local circumstances, among which we must count principally currents, winds favourable to evaporation, rivers coming from the continents, &c.

It has been remarked that the sea is less salt towards the Poles than at the Equator; that the saltness increases, in general, with the distance from land, and the depth of the water; that the interior seas, such as the Baltic, the Black Sea, the White Sea, the Sea of Marmora, and the Yellow Sea, are less salt than the ocean. The Mediterranean is an exception to this last rule; it is, as we have seen, salter than the ocean. This difference is explained by the fact that the quantity of fresh water brought into it by rivers is less than that lost by evaporation. The Mediterranean must therefore grow salter with time, unless its water is discharged into the ocean by a counter current, which would run under the current coming from the Atlantic by the Straits of Gibraltar.

The Black Sea, on the contrary, the water of which has a density of only 1·013, receives from rivers more fresh water than it loses by evaporation. The saltness of this interior sea is only half as intense as that of the ocean.

The Sea of Azov and the Caspian Sea are still less salt than the Black Sea.

The following table shows the relative composition of the water in these three interior seas:

In 100 Gallons of Water.	Black Sea. Density, 1·013.	Sea of Azov. Density, 1·009.	Caspian Sea Density, 1·005.
Chloride of sodium	14·0195	9·6583	3·6731
Chloride of potassium	9·1892	0·1279	0·0761
Chloride of magnesium	1·3045	0·8870	0·6324
Sulphate of magnesia	1·4704	0·7642	1·2389
Sulphate of lime	0·1047	0·2879	0·4903
Bicarbonate of magnesia	0·2086	0·1286	0·0129
Bicarbonate of lime	0·3646	0·0221	0·1705
Bromide of magnesium	0·0052	0·0035	traces
	17·6663	11·8795	6·2942

In lakes without any outlet, as the Dead Sea, and the Lake of Ural, the degree of saltness has considerably augmented. Numerous experiments have proved that the water of the Dead Sea is six times salter than that of the ocean. MM. Boutron and O'Henry analysed, in April, 1850, after the rainy season, some water of the Dead Sea, taken at about two leagues from the mouth of the Jordan; its density was then 1·10.

The saltness of sea water makes it more fitted to carry ships, because its density is increased by the salts which are dissolved in it. Besides this, these salts contribute to prevent what is called the *corruption of water*, caused by decomposition of the organic matter contained in it.

By the table representing the composition of the water of the ocean and of that of the Mediterranean, we see that salts of lime and potassium, as well as iodine and silicium, are only found in infinitely small quantities. Nevertheless, the lime and silicium contained in the sea water are of very great importance, for these quantities, which appear to us so small in the table of a chemical analysis, become enormous in the entire extent of the ocean. The marine plants take in the lime, the silicium, the potassa, and the iodides which are dissolved in the sea water; these mineral substances enter into their textures. It is from the carbonate of lime and silicium that the marine animals form their solid covering, their shell or carapace. The infusoria make use of the lime, silicium, and potassa for the same purpose. It is by the life and habits of the polypi that we explain these *Coral Islands* found in the sea, the existence of which has been a subject of much astonishment, and ought, therefore, to find a place in this chapter.

The Pacific and Indian Oceans are studded with islands in a state of formation, which owe their origin to the polypi and corallines. These zoophytes extract from the sea water the lime and silicium which are found there in the state of soluble salts. In order to grow and develope, they must be continually under water. They are constantly producing calcareous deposits; these deposits rise rapidly, and at last reach the surface of the water. Then the seaweed and rubbish of all kinds that the sea carries along with it, arrested by these emerged masses, cover them with a layer of fertile soil which is soon covered with vegetation, as the birds and the waves bring seeds thither. The Coral Islands of the Pacific are formed in this way.

These islands are in general well wooded. It is almost always the case that the summits of the Coral Islands, which emerge simultaneously round another submarine summit, join and form a circuit in the shape of a ring, the centre of which is a little lake, in which are found large quantities of shells producing pearls and mother-of-pearl. The islands of Oeno and Whitsunday, in the archipelago of Pomotou, are of this kind. With time, this ring grows broader; the openings, which gave access to the interior lagoons, close; and when the little interior lake has been filled or dried up, the island becomes gradually like an ordinary island. The archipelagoes of the Maldives, Chagos, and the Laccadives, in the south of India, are all of *madreporic* origin. Among those islands, designated under the name of *atolls*, there are some so recent that our fathers might have seen them rise from the bed of the ocean.

These aggregations form numerous reefs. The large islands of this archipelago are surrounded by a barrier of reefs, the slow work of the polypi, which, rising at a certain distance from the coast, renders the approach very dangerous. The eastern coast of Australia, between nine and twenty-five degrees of south latitude, is provided with a belt of this sort. The coral bank, called the Great Barrier, is a thousand and sixty-two miles long, and has an average breadth of thirty miles, giving a surface of thirty-one thousand eight hundred and sixty square miles.

The walls formed by the polypi are always perpendicular, and the sea is often of great depth in the neighbourhood of these islands. Sometimes the first plateau is destroyed, and lowered by the action of the water; the polypi then begin their edifice again upon this new base. The island of Tahiti rests on a volcanic shell, the summit of which is about a mile and a quarter above the level of the sea.

Mr. Darwin has given a very interesting description of the atolls of the Sunda group. We borrow from this description some details relative to these extraordinary formations.

It was formerly believed that the circular structure of coral reefs was caused by old volcanic craters, upon which the polypi built up their edifices. But this theory does not accord with fact, and it seems, in general, difficult to believe in a volcanic upheaval of the ground as the base of madreporic formations; for the polypi cannot live under very deep water, and it would be impossible to admit that the bottom of the sea has everywhere risen to the same level. It is, therefore, more probable that the foundations of the Coral Islands are only natural elevations of the bottom of the sea, or submerged mountains, not far from the surface of which the polypi have taken possession, in order to raise their structures. It is a curious fact that the barriers of coral which run parallel to the coast are always separated by a broad canal, analogous to the lagoons in the atolls, and of a breadth varying from one to twelve miles. One of these reefs incloses at times a dozen rocky islands. In the island of Bolabola, the barrier is transformed into dry land; but the white line of enormous reefs, with small islands crowned with cocoa-nut trees scattered here and there, separates the dark ocean from the placid surface of the interior canal, whose limpid water bathes an alluvial soil covered with a tropical vegetation. This many-coloured riband stretches out at the foot of the wild and abrupt mountains of the centre.

In the year 1858, Mr. Darwin explored in particular the island of Keeling, or of cocoa-nuts, to the south of Sumatra. It is formed of a circle of reefs, crowned by a wreath of very narrow islets, which leave towards the north a passage for ships. In the interior of the anchorage the water is a calm and transparent lagoon, so pure that the white and level bottom is clearly seen; this lagoon is many miles broad. Mr. Darwin landed with Captain Fitzroy upon an islet at the farther end of the lagoon, in order to see the waves break on the reefs to windward. The cocoa-nut palms formed festoons of emerald-green, clearly defined, against the deep blue of the sky; the flat. calcareous beach, with scattered blocks of white stone, was bathed by the foaming waves.

Besides the substances named, sea water also contains, in infinitesimally small quantities, metals such as iron, copper, lead, and silver. The old copper collecting round the keels of ships sometimes contains so much silver that it has been thought worth extracting! A curious calculation has been attempted, based on the age of ships and the distance they have gone during all their voyages, to show that the sea contains in solution two million tons of silver.*

* Sir J. Herschel's "Physical Geography," p. 22, gives the basis and details of this calculation.

The following question is one that the uneducated often asks himself without being able to find a satisfactory answer; and the learned have not been more fortunate in their interrogations: Whence comes the salt and other substances held in solution in the ocean? In other terms, what is the cause of the saltness of sea water?

Some persons take delight, very foolishly, in satisfying childish curiosity by silly answers. Born near the shores of the Mediterranean, with the sea always before my eyes, I once, when quite a child, addressed this question to those who were near me. Some persons, who pretended to be very clever, told me that the sea was salt, because certain ships were charged to throw into it regularly large pyramids of salt like those we see heaped up on the banks of our salt-pits. It is not irreverent to say that the theories presented by certain *savants* to account for the saltness of the sea are not much more to the purpose than the naïve explanation with which I was answered in my childhood. Some of them, indeed, state that the salt is engendered spontaneously at the bottom of the sea; others, that the tributary rivers are sufficient to supply it. If our readers will turn back to the first few pages of "The World before the Deluge," they will understand the very simple geological explanation that we are going to give of the origin of different substances dissolved in sea water.

In the first stage of our planet, before the watery vapours contained in the primitive atmosphere were condensed, and before they had begun to fall on the earth in the form of boiling rain, the shell of the earth contained an infinite variety of heterogeneous mineral substances, some soluble in water, others not. When rain fell on the burning surface for the first time, the waters became charged with all the soluble substances, which were reunited and afterwards deposited; accumulating in the large depressions of the soil. The seas of the primitive globe were thus formed of rain water, holding in solution all that the earth had given up, collected in large basins. Chloride of sodium, sulphates of soda, magnesia, potassium, lime, and silicium, in the form of soluble silicate; in a word, every soluble matter that the primitive globe contained formed part of the mineral contingent of this water. If we reflect that through all time up to the present day none of the general laws of nature have changed—if we consider that the soluble substances contained in the water of the primitive seas have remained there, and that the fresh water of the rivers constantly replaces the water which disappears by evaporation—we have the true explanation of the saltness of sea water. "It is a very simple theory, it is true," adds M. Figuier, "but one that we have found nowhere, and the responsibility of which we therefore claim. The chloride of sodium is by no means the only substance dissolved in sea water. It contains, besides, many other mineral substances: in short, every *soluble salt* on the face of the globe, and, along with them, portions of different metals in infinitely small quantities."

The mean temperature of the surface of the sea is nearly the same as the atmosphere, so long as no currents of heat or cold interpose their perturbing influence. In the neighbourhood of the Tropics, it appears that the surface of the water is slightly warmer than the ambient air, but experiments on the temperature of the sea from the surface to the bottom reveal, according to our author,* "some evidence which establishes a curious law. In very deep water a perfectly uniform temperature of four degrees below zero prevails, which corresponds, as physics have established, to the maximum density of water. Under the Equator this temperature exists at the depth of seven thousand feet. In the Polar regions, where water is colder at the surface, this temperature is maintained at four thousand six hundred feet. The isothermal lines of four degrees form a line of demarcation between the Zones, where the surface of the sea is colder, and those where it is warmer than the bed of four degrees below zero." This is more clearly shown in Fig. 4, which represents a section of the ocean, the curved line which touches two points at the surface indicating the depths where the temperature is constantly fixed at four degrees.

Dr. Maury's account of this phenomenon is asserted with less confidence. The existence of an *isothermal floor* of the ocean, as he calls it, was first suggested by the observations of Kotzebue, Admiral Beechey, and Sir James C. Ross. "Its temperature, according to Kotzebue, is thirty-six degrees Fahr., or four degrees Cent.; the depth of this bed, of invariable and uniform temperature, is twelve hundred fathoms at the Equator; thence it gradually rises to the parallel of about fifty-six degrees north and south, when it crops out, and there the temperature of the sea from top to bottom is conjectured

* "La Terre et les Mers," p. 517. Troisième Ed.

to be permanent at thirty-six degrees. The place of this outcrop, no doubt, shifts with the seasons, vibrating north and south, after the manner of the Calm belts. Proceeding onwards to the Frigid zones, this aqueous stratum of an unchanging temperature dips again, and

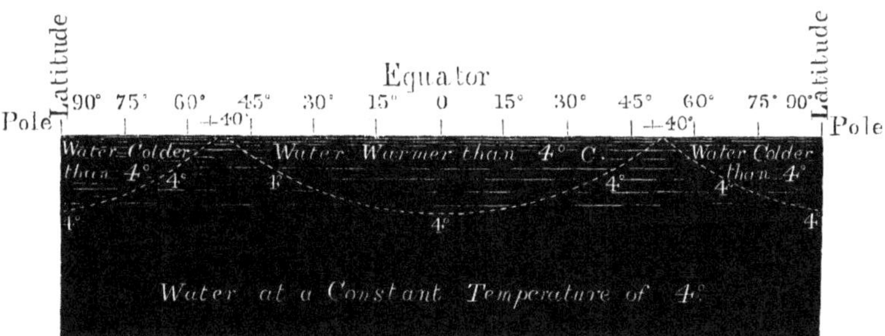

Fig. 4. Thermal Lines of equal Temperature.

continues to incline till it reaches the Poles at the depth of seven hundred and fifty fathoms; so that on the equatorial side of the outcrop the water above the isothermal floor is the warmer, but in Polar seas the supernatant water is the colder."

In the saline properties of sea water Maury discovers one of the principal forces from which currents in the ocean proceed. "The brine of the ocean is the ley of the earth," he says; "from it the sea derives dynamical powers, and its currents their main strength. Hence, to understand the dynamics of the ocean, it is necessary to study the effects of their saltness upon the equilibrium of the waves. Why is the sea made salt? It is the salts of the sea that impart to its waters those curious anomalies in the laws of freezing and of thermal dilatation. It is the salts of the sea that assist the rays of heat to penetrate its bosom." The circulation of the ocean is indispensable to the distribution of temperature—to the maintenance of the meteorological and climatic conditions which rule the development of life; and this circulation could not exist—at least, the character of its waters would be completely changed—if they were fresh in place of salt. "Let us imagine," says M. Julien, "that the sea, now entirely composed of fresh water, of one uniform temperature from the Pole to the Equator, and from the surface to its greatest depths; the solar heat would penetrate the liquid beds nearest to the Equator; it would dilate them, so as to raise them above their primitive level; by the single effect of gravitation, they would glide on the surface towards the polar zones. The absence of all solar radiation would tend, on the contrary, to cool and contract them without this tendency. An exchange would be established from the extremities towards the centre; in other words, a counter current of cold and heavy water, calculated to replace the losses occasioned by the action of solar radiation, would descend from the Poles, but quite maintaining itself beneath the light and warm current from the Equator."

In a like system of general circulation, the physical properties of pure water, which attains its maximum of density four degrees below zero, would produce the most singular consequences. As its temperature rose above that point, the water would become lighter, having, consequently, a tendency to ascend towards the upper beds. After this, the equatorial current, meeting in its progress towards the Poles the cold water, would itself be cooled down; and when its temperature had reached four degrees below zero, being now heavier than the polar current, would change places with it, descending until it reached water equally dense, while the polar current would ascend. Hence would arise a sort of confusion of currents which would give to a fresh-water ocean the strangest results, disarranging every instant the regular circulation of its waters. It could not be so, however, in an ocean of salt water, which attains its maximum specific gravity at two degrees below zero. By evaporation at the surface it is concentrated and precipitated, and thus rendered denser than that immediately below the surface. It consequently sinks, while the lower beds come up to replace, in order to modify it, and in turn to be precipitated in the same manner. "In this manner we find established a continually ascending and descending movement, which carries down into the depths of ocean the water warmed at the surface by the solar rays of the Torrid zone. This double vertical current facilitates and prepares the grand horizontal current which puts these submarine reservoirs of heat in communication with the lower beds of the glacial sea. In the Arctic basin the clouds, the melted snow, and the great rivers, which have their mouths on the north of both continents, produce considerable quantities of fresh water, which, mixing with the waves of the Polar

Sea, form a bed of mean density light enough to maintain itself and flow off towards the Atlantic Ocean. These surface movements determine in the lower regions certain contrary movements, whence originate the powerful counter currents which ascend the Straits from Baffin's Bay and reappear in the mysterious Polynia of Kane, diffusing there its treasure of heat brought from intertropical seas." Dr. Kane, in his interesting Narrative, reports an open sea north of the parallel of eighty-two degrees which he and his party crossed a barrier of ice eighty miles broad to reach, and before he reached it the thermometer marked sixty degrees. Beyond this ice-bound region he found himself on the shores of an iceless sea, extending in an unbroken sheet of water as far as the eye could reach towards the Pole. Its waves were dashing on the beach with the swell of a great ocean; the tides ebbed and flowed. Now the question arises, Where did those tides have their origin? The tidal wave of the Atlantic could not have passed under the icy barrier which De Haven found so firm; therefore they must have been cradled in the cold sea round the Pole; in which case it follows that most, if not all, the unexplored regions about the Pole must be covered with deep water, the only source of strong and regular tides. Seals were sporting and waterfowl feeding in this open sea, as Dr. Kane tells us, and the temperature of the water which rolled in and dashed at his feet with measured beat was thirty-six degrees, while the bottom of the icy barrier of eighty miles was probably hundreds of feet below the surface level.

"The existence of these tides," says Maury, "with the immense flow and drift which annually take place from the Polar Seas and the Atlantic, suggests many conjectures as to the condition of these unexplored regions. Whalemen have always been puzzled as to the breeding place of the great whale. It is a cold-water animal, and, following up the train of thought, the question arises, Is not the nursery for the great whale in this Polar Sea, which is so set about and hemmed in by a hedge of ice that man may not trespass there?"

One or two points worthy of notice may be recorded here. Shallow water, and water near the coast, or covering raised sand-banks, is colder than water in the open sea. Alexander von Humboldt explains this phenomenon by supposing that deep waters of higher temperature reascend from the lowest depths and mingle with the upper beds.

Fogs are frequently formed over sand-banks, because the cold water which covers them produces a local precipitation of atmospheric vapour. The contour of these fogs are perfectly defined when seen from a distance: they reproduce the form and accidents due to the submarine soil. Moreover, we often see clouds arrested over these points, which look from afar like the peaks of mountains.

CHAPTER II.

CURRENTS OF THE OCEAN.

". . . . . seas that sweep
The three-decker's oaken mast." TENNYSON.

THE OCEAN is a scene of unceasing agitation; "its vast surface rises and falls," to use the image suggested by Schleiden, "as if it were gifted with a gentle power of respiration; its movements, gentle or powerful, slow or rapid, are all determined by differences of temperature."

Heat increases its volume and changes the specific gravity of the water, which is dilated or condensed in proportion to the change of temperature. In proportion as it cools, water increases in density, and descends into the depths until it reaches a constant temperature of four degrees twenty-five minutes below zero, which it preserves in all latitudes at the depth of a thousand yards, according to M. D'Urville.

If the water continues to cool, and reaches zero, it becomes lighter than it was at four degrees twenty-five minutes, and ascends in a state of congelation—a process which, by an admirable provision of nature, can only take place at the surface. So long as the temperature is above four degrees twenty-five minutes, water is light, and ascends to the surface, while colder water sinks to the bottom. Below four degrees twenty-five minutes the process is reversed; the first phenomenon is always in force under the Equator, the second near the Poles. The evaporation, which is in continual operation in warm seas, forming vast rain-clouds at the expense of the sea, is compensated by unceasing currents of colder water flowing from the Poles. This evaporation has a direct influence, moreover, on the density of sea water, and is pointed out by Dr. Maury as a remarkable instance of the compensations by which the oceanic waters are governed: "According to Rodgers' observations," he says, "the average specific gravity of sea water on the parallels of thirty-four degrees north and south, at a mean temperature of sixty-four degrees, is just what it ought to be, according to saline and thermal laws; but its specific gravity, when taken from the Equator at a mean temperature of eighty-one degrees, is much greater than, according to the same laws, it ought to be—the observed difference being ·0015, whereas it ought to be ·0025. Let us inquire," he adds, "what makes the equatorial waters so much heavier than they ought to be.

"The anomaly occurs in the trade-wind region, and is best developed between the parallel of forty degrees in the North Atlantic and the Equator, where the water grows warmer, but not proportionally lighter. The water sucked up by the trade-winds is fresh water, and the salt it contained, being left behind, is just sufficient to counteract by its weight the effect of thermal dilatation upon the specific gravity of water between the parallels of thirty-four degrees north and south. The thirsting of the trade-winds for vapour is so balanced as to produce perfect compensation, and a more beautiful instance than we have here stumbled upon is not, it appears to me, to be found in the mechanism of the universe."

The oceanic currents are due to a great number of causes: the duration and force of the winds, for instance; the rise and fall of tides all over the globe; the variations in the density of the waters; according to its temperature, and the evaporating powers of the atmosphere; the depth and degree of saltness to which we have already alluded; finally, to the variations of barometric pressure.

The currents which furrow the ocean present a striking contrast with the immobility of the neighbouring waters; they form rivers of a determinate breadth, whose banks are formed by the water in repose, and whose course is often made quite perceptible by the vrachs and other aquatic plants which follow in their train.

In order to comprehend the origin of these *pelagic rivers*, it is necessary to consider the laws which govern the atmospheric currents, in particular the *trade-winds*. "Hence," says Maury, "in studying the system of oceanic circulation, we set out with the very simple assumption, that from whatever part of the ocean a current is found to run, to that same part a current of equal volume is bound to return; for on this principle is based the whole system of currents and counter currents." The differences of temperature between equinoctial and polar countries generate two opposing currents, the upper one proceeding from the Equator to the Poles, the lower one directed from the Poles towards the Equator. On reaching the Equator, the cold current of air from the Poles is warmed and rarified, and ascends to the upper beds of the atmosphere, whence it is again led to its point of departure; there it is again cooled, and returns with the lower current towards the tropical regions. But the rotatory movement of the earth modifies the direction of these atmospheric currents. The movement by which it is carried from west to east being almost nothing at the Poles, but inconceivably rapid under the Equator, it follows that the cold air, in proportion as it advances towards the Tropics, ought to incline a little towards the west. This is just what takes place with these counter currents. The *north-east trade-winds*, which prevail in the northern hemisphere, move in a sort of spiral curve, turning to the west as they rush from the Poles to the Equator, and in the opposite direction as they move from the Equator towards the Poles; the immediate cause of this motion being the rotation of the earth on its axis. "The earth," says Dr. Maury, "moves from west to east. Now, if we imagine a particle of atmosphere at the North Pole, where it is *at rest*, to be put in motion in a straight line towards the Equator, we can easily see how this particle of air, coming from the very axis of diurnal rotation, where it did not partake of the diurnal motion, would, in consequence of its own *vis inertiæ*, find as it travelled south that the earth was slipping from under it, as it were, and it would appear to be coming from the north-east and going towards the south-west; in other words, it would be a north-east wind."

In the same manner, the upper currents of air, which proceed towards the Poles with equatorial rapidity, ought to outstrip the atmospheric beds, which are gifted with much smaller rapidity of motion towards the Poles, and turn them towards the east in consequence. These are the south-west and north-west counter trade-winds, which, passing above the *north* and *south-east trades*, often sweep the surface of the sea in the latitudes of the Temperate zone. The two *trades* are separated by a belt more or less broad, where the friction experienced at the surface of the sea neutralizes their impulse towards the west; in general, the current of air there is an ascending current. This belt, which does not exactly correspond with the Equator, is called the *Zone of Calms*, where atmospheric tempests frequently occur, and the winds make the entire tour of the compass, which has acquired for them the name of *tornadoes.*

The trade-winds, whose movement towards the west is retarded by the friction which the waves of the ocean oppose to them, communicate to these waves, by a sort of reaction, a tendency towards the west, or, to speak more exactly, towards the south-west in the northern hemisphere, and towards the north-west in the opposite hemisphere. The currents on the surface of the water which result from this reaction, reunite under the Equator, and form the *grand equinoctial* current which impels the waters of the east towards the west. This movement is stronger at the edges than in the middle of the current, because the force which produces it acts there with more energy: it results from this, that the currents bifurcate more readily when any obstacle presents itself to its movement. In the Atlantic Ocean, bifurcation takes place a little to the south of the Equator; the southern branch descends along the coast of Brazil, and probably returns by reascending along the west coast of Africa. The northern branch follows the coast of Brazil and Guiana, enters the Sea of the Antilles, and directs its course, reinforced by the current which reaches it from the north-east, into the Bay of Honduras, traverses the Yucatan Channel, and enters the Gulf of Mexico, whence it debouches by the Florida Channel, under the name of the *Gulf Stream*. Of this oceanic marvel Dr. Maury observes that "there is a river in the bosom of the ocean; in the several droughts it never fails, and in the mightiest floods it never overflows; its banks and its bottom are of cold water, while its current is of warm; it takes its rise in the Gulf of Mexico, and empties itself into the Arctic Seas. This mighty river is the Gulf Stream. In no other part of the world is there such a majestic flow of water; its current is more rapid than the Amazon, more impetuous than the Mississippi, and its volume is more than a thousand times greater. Its waters, as far as the Carolina coast, are of indigo blue; they are so distinctly indicated that their line of junction can be marked by the eye." Such is Dr. Maury's description of this powerful current of warm water, which traverses the Atlantic Ocean, and influences in no slight manner the climate of Northern Europe, and especially our own shores.

The Gulf Stream thus described by the American *savant* issues from the Florida Channel, with a breadth of thirty-four miles, and a depth of two thousand two hundred feet, moving at the rate of four and a half miles per hour. The temperature of the water in the vicinity is about thirty degrees Cent. From the American coast the current takes a north-east direction towards Spitzbergen, its velocity and volume diminishing as it expands in breadth. Towards the forty-third degree of latitude it forms two branches, one of which strikes the coast of Ireland and of Norway, whither it frequently transports seeds of tropical origin: it also warms the frozen waters of the glacial sea. The other branch, inclining towards the south, not far from the Azores, visits the coast of Africa, whence it returns to the Antilles. Throughout this vast circuit may be seen all sorts of plants and driftwood, with waifs and strays of every description borne on the bosom of the ocean. "Midway the Atlantic, in the triangular space between the Azores, Canaries, and Cape de Verd Islands, is the great Sargasso Sea, covering an area equal in extent to the Mississippi Valley: it is so thickly matted over with the Gulf Weed (*Fucus Natans*), that the speed of vessels passing through it is actually retarded, and to the companions of Columbus it seemed to mark the limits of navigation; they became alarmed. To the eye at a little distance it seemed sufficiently substantial to walk upon." These moving vegetable masses, always green, which tail off to a steady breeze, serving as an anemometer to the mariner, afford an asylum to multitudes of mollusks and crustaceans.

The Gulf Stream plays a grand part in the Atlantic system. It carries the tepid water of the equinoctial regions into the high latitudes; beyond the fortieth parallel the temperature is sixteen degrees Cent. Urged by the south-west winds which predominate in that zone, its tepid waters mix with those of the Northern Sea, softening the rigour of the climate in these regions. To the south of the great bank of Newfoundland, the warm current, in vast volume rushing from the Florida Straits, meets the cold currents descending from the Arctic Circle through Baffin's Bay and the Sea of Greenland, running with equal velocity towards the south. A portion of these waters reascend towards the Pole along the western coast of Greenland. It is to this conflict of the polar and equatorial waters, that the formation of the banks of Newfoundland is ascribed. Each of these great currents having unceasingly deposited the débris carried in its bosom, the bank has been thus formed bit by bit in the concourse of ages.

The difference of temperature between the Gulf Stream and the waters it traverses gives birth inevitably to tempests and *cyclones*. In 1780 a terrible storm ravaged the Antilles, in which twenty thousand persons perished. The ocean quitted its bed and inundated whole cities; the trunks of trees, mingled with other débris, were tossed into the air; numerous catastrophes of this kind have earned for the Gulf Stream the title of the King of the Tempests. In consequence of the numerous nautical documents which have been placed at the command of the National Observatory of Washington, and the admirable use made of them by the late Naval Secretary and his assistants, the directions and range of these cyclones engendered by the Gulf Stream may be foreseen, and their most dangerous ravages turned aside. As an example of the utility of Dr. Maury's labours in settling the direction of storms in the traject of the Gulf Stream, we quote a well-known instance: In the month of December, 1859, the American packet *San Francisco* was employed as a transport to convey a regiment to California. It was overtaken by one of these sudden storms, which placed the ship and its freight in a most dangerous position. A single wave, which swept the deck, tore out the masts, stopped the engines, and washed overboard a hundred and twenty-nine persons, officers and soldiers. From that moment the unfortunate steamer floated upon the waters, a waif abandoned to the fury of the wind. The day after the disaster the *San Francisco* was seen in this desperate situation by a ship which reached New York, although unable to assist her. Another ship met her some days after, but, like the other, could render no assistance. When the report reached New York, two steamers were despatched to her assistance; but in what direction were they to go? what part of the ocean were they to explore? The luminaries of Washington Observatory were appealed to! Having consulted his charts as to the direction and limits of the Gulf Stream at that period of the year, Dr. Maury traced on a chart the spot to which the disabled steamer was likely to be driven by the current, and the course to be taken by the vessels sent to her assistance. The crew and passengers of the *San Francisco* were saved before their arrival. Three ships, which had seen their distressing situation, had been able to reach them, and the steamers sent to their assistance only arrived to witness the safety of the passengers and crew. But the point where the steamer foundered shortly after they were transferred to the rescuing ships was precisely that indicated by Dr. Maury. If the ships sent to their assistance had reached in time, the triumph of SCIENCE would have been complete.

The equinoctial currents of the Pacific are very imperfectly known. It is believed, however, that they traverse the Great Ocean in its whole length, and bifurcate opposite the Asiatic coast, where the weakest branch bends northward until it encounters the polar current from Behring's Straits, when it returns along the Mexican coast. The larger branch inclines towards the south, passing round Australia, where it is met by one or many counter currents coming from the Indian Ocean—of the complicated and dangerous nature of which both Cook and La Peyrouse speak.

The cold waters from the Antarctic Pole are carried towards the Equator by three great oceanic rivers. The first bifurcates in forty-five degrees; one portion goes round Cape Horn; the other—Humboldt's current—ascends the Chilian and Peruvian coasts up to the Equator, ameliorating the rainless climate as it goes, and making it delightful. A second great current takes the direction of the African coast, and is divided at the Cape, ascending both the east and west coasts of Africa. On either side of the warm current which escapes from the intertropical parts of the Indian Ocean, but especially along the Australian coast, a polar current wends its way from the Antarctic regions, carrying supplies of cold water to modify the climate and restore the equilibrium in that part of the world. This cold current turns at first towards the west, then towards the south in the direction of Madagascar; more to the south still it is driven back by the polar current from Cape Horn. It is thus that the warm waters from the Bay of Bengal, pressed by the Indian polar current, circulate between Africa and Australia, one lateral branch of the current sweeping along the south coast of this vast continent.

The monsoons which reign in the Indian Ocean tend still more to complicate the currents, already sufficiently intricate and confused. But it is not intended at present to occupy the reader's attention further with these questions of intricate currents.

We have already spoken of a submarine current which appears to carry the waters of the Mediterranean into the Atlantic Ocean. Its existence is in some respects established by calculations, which prove that the quantity of salt water supplied by the upper current through the Straits of Gibraltar is equal to seventy-two cubic miles per annum, while the quantity of fresh water brought down by the rivers is equal to six, and the quantity lost by evaporation to twelve cubic miles per annum. This would leave an annual excess of sixty-six cubic miles, if the equilibrium was not re-established by an under current flowing into the Atlantic. This hypothesis would appear to have been confirmed by a very curious fact.

Towards the end of the seventeenth century, a Dutch brig, pursued by the French corsair *Phœnix*, was overhauled between Tangier and Tarifa, and seemed to be sunk by a single broadside; but, in place of foundering and going down, the brig, being freighted with a cargo of oil and alcohol, floated between the two currents, and, drifting towards the west, finally ran aground, after two or three days, in the neighbourhood of Tangier, more than twelve miles from the spot where she had disappeared under the waves. She had therefore traversed that distance, drawn by the action of the under current in a direction opposite to that of the surface current. This ascertained fact, added to some recent experiments, lend their support to the opinion which admits of the existence of an outward current through the Straits of Gibraltar. Dr. Maury quotes an extract from the "log" of Lieutenant Temple, of the United States Navy, bearing the same inference. At noon on the 8th of March, 1855, the ship *Levant* stood into Almeria Bay, where many ships were waiting for a chance to get westwards. Here he was told that at least a thousand sail were waiting between the bay and Gibraltar, "some of them having got as far as Malaga only to be swept back again; indeed," he adds, "no vessel had been able to get out into the Atlantic for three months past." Supposing this current to run no faster than two knots an hour, and assuming its depth to be four hundred feet only, and its width seven miles, and that it contained the average proportion of solid matter, estimated at one-thirtieth, it appears that salt enough to make eighty-eight cubic miles of solid matter were carried into the Mediterranean in those ninety days. "Now," continues Dr. Maury, "unless there were some escape for all this solid matter which has been running into the sea, not for ninety days, but for ages, it is very clear that the Mediterranean would long ere this have been a vat of strong brine, or a bed of cubic crystals."

For the same reason, Dr. Maury considers it certain that there is an under current to the south of Cape Horn, which carries into the Pacific Ocean the overflowings of the Atlantic. In fact, the Atlantic is fed unceasingly by the great American rivers, while the Pacific receives no important affluent, but ought to be, and is, subjected to enormous losses, in consequence of the evaporation continually taking place at the surface.

TIDES.

Tides are periodical movements produced by the attraction of the sun and moon. This action, which influences the whole mass of the earth, is made manifest by the swelling movement of the waters. The attractive force exercised by the moon is three times that of the sun, in consequence of its approximation to the earth, as compared to the greater luminary.

In order to comprehend the theory of tides, we shall first consider the *lunar* influences, putting aside for a moment the *solar* action.

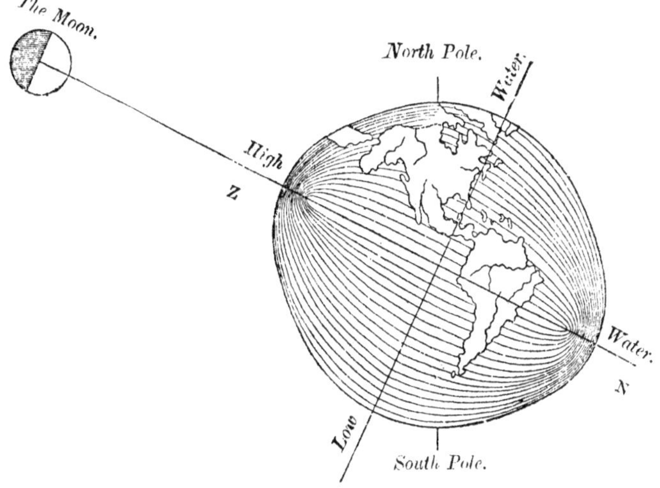

Fig. 5. Lunar Tides.

The attraction which the moon exercises upon any point on the earth's surface is in the inverse ratio of the square of its distance. If we draw a straight line from the moon passing through the centre of the earth, this line will meet the surface of the waters at two points, diametrically opposite to each other—namely, Z and N (Fig. 5); one of these points would be to the moon its *zenith*, the other its *nadir*. The point of the sea which has the moon in the zenith—namely, that above which the moon is perfectly perpendicular—will be nearest to the planet, and will consequently be more strongly attractive to the centre of the earth, while the points diametrically opposite to which the moon is the *nadir* will be more distant, and consequently less strongly attracted by that luminary. It follows that the waters situated directly under the moon will be attracted towards it, and form an accumulation or swelling at that point; the waters at the antipodes being less strongly attracted to the moon than to the centre of the earth, will form also a secondary swelling on the surface of the sea, thus forming a double tide, accumulating at the point nearest the moon and at its antipodes. At the intermediate points of the circumference of the globe, where the waters are not subjected to the direct attraction of the moon, the sea is at low water, as represented in Fig. 5.

The earth, in its movement of rotation, presents, in the course of twenty-four hours, every meridian on its surface to the lunar attraction; consequently, each point in its turn, and at intervals of six hours, is either under the moon, or ninety degrees removed from it: it follows, that in the space of a lunar day—that is to say, in the time which passes between two successive passages of the moon on the same meridian—the oceanic waters will be at high and low tide twice in the month on every point of the surface of the globe. But this result of attraction is not exercised instantaneously. The moon has passed from the meridian of the spot before the waters have attained their greatest height; the flux reaches its maximum about three hours after the moon has culminated; and the watery mountain follows the moon all round the globe, from east to west, about three hours in its rear.

It is obvious, however, that the great inequalities of the bottom of the sea; the existence of continents; the slopes of the coast, more or less steep; the different breadths of channels and straits; finally, the winds, the pelagic currents, and a crowd of local circumstances,—must materially modify the course of the tides. Nor is the moon the only celestial body which influences the rise and fall of the waters of the sea. We have already said that the sun asserts an influence on the waves.

It is true that, in consequence of its great distance, this only amounts to a thirty-eight-hundredth part of that of the earth's satellite. The inequality which exists between the solar and lunar days—the latter exceeding the first by fifty-four minutes—has also the effect of adding to or subtracting from this force alternately. When the sun and moon are in *conjunction* (Fig. 6), or in opposition, that is to say, placed upon the same right line, their attraction on the sea is combined, and a *spring* tide is produced. This happens at the period of the *syzygies*—the period of new and full moon. At the period of the *quadrature*, or the first and last quarters, the solar action, being

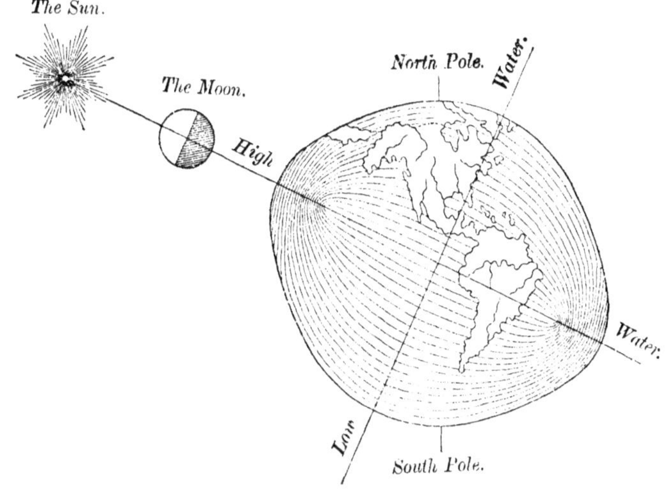

Fig. 6. Lunar-Solar Tides.

opposed to that of lunar attraction, tends to produce a sensibly weaker tide.

These effects are never produced instantaneously; but, the impulse once given, it will continue to influence the tides for two or three days, the highest and lowest tides being nearly in the proportion of 138 to 63, or of 7 to 3. The highest tides occur at the *equinoxes*, when the moon is in perigee; the lowest at the *solstices*, when it is in apogee. In our ports, and along the coast, the water rises twice in twenty-four hours, when it is said to be high water; when it retires, it is low water: they are respectively the *flux* and *reflux* of the waves.

The tide is retarded every day about fifty minutes, the lunar day being twenty-four hours fifty minutes of mean time. If, for instance, it is high water to-day at two o'clock in the morning, that of the next day will take place at fifty minutes past two. Low water does not occur, however, at the half of the intermediate time; the flux is more rapid than the reflux: thus at Havre, Boulogne, and at corresponding places on this side of the Channel, it takes two hours and eight minutes more in retiring; at Brest, the difference is only sixteen minutes more than the flux. The daily retardation of high water by the passage of the moon in the meridian, at the equinoxes, is a constant quantity for the same locality, which can be determined by direct observation.

The height of the tide varies in the different regions of the globe, according to local circumstances. The eastern coast of Asia and the western coast of Europe are exposed to extremely high tides; while in the South Sea Islands, where they are very regular, they scarcely reach the height of twenty inches. On the western coast of South America, the tides rarely reach three yards; on the western coast of India they reach the height of six or seven; and in the Gulf of Cambay it ranges from five to six fathoms. This great difference makes itself felt in our own and adjoining countries: thus, the tide, which at Cherbourg is seven and eight yards high, attains the height of fourteen yards at Saint Malo, while it reaches the height of ten yards at Swansea, at the mouth of the Bristol Channel, increasing to double that height at Chepstow, higher up the river. In general, the tide is higher at the bottom of a gulf than at its mouth.

The highest tide which is known occurs in the Bay of Fundy, which opens up to the south of the isthmus uniting Nova Scotia and New Brunswick. There the tide reaches forty, fifty, and even sixty feet, while it only attains the height of seven or eight in the bay to the north of the same isthmus. It is related that a ship was cast ashore upon a rock during the night, so high that at daybreak the crew found themselves and their ship suspended in mid-air far above the water!

In the Mediterranean, which only communicates with the ocean by a narrow channel, the phenomena of tides is scarcely felt, and from this cause—that the moon acts at the same time upon its whole surface, which are not sufficiently abundant to increase the swelling mass of waters formed by the moon's attraction; consequently, the swelling remains scarcely perceptible. This is the reason why neither the

Black Sea or White Sea present a tide, and the Mediterranean a very inconsiderable one. Nevertheless, at Alexandria the tide rises twenty inches, and at Venice this height is increased to about six feet and a half. Lake Michigan is slightly affected by the lunar attraction.

Professor Whewell has prepared maps, in which the course of the tidal wave is traced in every country of the globe. We see here that it traverses the Atlantic, from the fiftieth degree of south latitude up to the fiftieth parallel north, at the rate of five hundred and sixty miles an hour. But the rapidity with which it proceeds is least in shallow water. In the North Sea it travels at the rate of a hundred and eighty miles. The tidal wave which proceeds round the coast of Scotland traverses the German Ocean and meets in St. George's Channel, between England and Ireland, where the conflict between the two opposing waves presents some very complicated phenomena.

The winds, again, exercise a great influence on the height of the tides. When the impulse of the wind is added to that of the attracting planet, the normal height of the wave is considerably increased. If the wind is contrary, the flux of the tide is almost annihilated. This happens in the Gulf of Vera Cruz, where the tide is only perceptible once in three days, when the wind blows with violence. An analogous phenomenon is observable on the coast of Tasmania.

The rising tide sometimes strikes the shore with a continuous and incredible force. This violent shock is called the *surf*. The swell then forms a billow, which expands to half a mile. The surf increases as it approaches the coast, when it sometimes attains the height of six or seven yards, forming an overhanging mountain of water, which gradually sinks as it rolls over itself. But this motion is not in reality progressive—it transports no floating body. The surf is very strong at the Isle of Fogo, one of the Cape de Verd Islands in the Indian Ocean, and at Sumatra, where the surf renders it dangerous and sometimes impossible to land on the coast. Fig. 7 represents the effects of the surf at Point du Raz, on the coast of Brittany, near Cape Finisterre. The winds adding their influence to these causes, give birth on the surface of the sea to waves or billows, which increase rapidly, rising in foaming mountains, rolling, bounding, and breaking one against the other. "In one moment," says Malte Brun, "the waves seem to carry sea-goddesses on its breast, which seem to revel amid plays and dances; in the next instant, a tempest rising out of them, seems to be animated by its fury. They seem to swell with passion, and we think we see in them marine monsters which are prepared for war. A strong, constant, and equal wind produces long swelling billows, which, rising on the same line, advance with a uniform movement, one after the other, precipitating themselves upon the coast. Sometimes these billows are

Fig. 7. Effects of Hurricane at Point du Raz, Cape Finisterre.

suspended by the wind or arrested by some current, thus forming, as it were, a liquid wall. In this position, unhappy is the daring navigator who is subjected to its fury." The highest waves are those which prevail in the offing off the Cape of Good Hope at the period of high tide, under the influence of a strong north-west wind, which has traversed the South Atlantic, pressing its waters towards the Cape. "The billows there lift themselves up in long ridges," says Dr. Maury, "with deep hollows between them. They run high and fast, tossing their white caps aloft in the air, looking like the green hills of a rolling prairie capped with snow, and chasing each other in sport. Still, their march is stately, and their roll majestic. The scenery among them is grand. Many an Australian-bound trader, after doubling the Cape, finds herself followed for weeks at a time by these magnificent rolling swells, furiously driven and lashed by the "brave west winds." These billows are said to attain the height of thirty, and even forty feet; but no very exact measurement of the height of waves is recorded. One of these mountain waves placed between two ships conceals each

Fig. 8. Height of Waves off the Cape of Good Hope.

of them from the other—an effect which is partially represented in Fig. 8. In rounding Cape Horn, waves are encountered from twenty to thirty feet high, but in the Channel they rarely exceed the height of nine or ten feet, except when they come in contact with some powerful resisting obstacle. Thus, when billows are dashed violently against the Eddystone Lighthouse, the spray goes right over the building, which stands a hundred and thirty feet above the sea, and falls in torrents on the roof. After the storm of Barbadoes in 1780, some old guns were found on the shore, which had been thrown up from the bottom of the sea by the force of the tempests.

If the waves, in their reflux, meet with obstacles, whirlpools and whirlwinds are the result—the former the terror of navigators. Such are the whirlpools known in the Straits of Messina, between the rocks of Charybdis and Scylla, celebrated as the terror of ancient mariners, and which were sung by Homer, Ovid, and Virgil:

> "Scylla latus dextrum, lævum irrequieta Charybdis,
> Infestat; vorat hæc raptis revomitque carinas.
> . . . Incidit in Scyllam, cupiens vitare Charybdim."

These rocks are better understood, and less redoubted in our days. At Charybdis, there is a foaming whirlpool; at Scylla, the waves dash against the low wall of rock which forms the promontory, scarcely noticed by the navigator of our days.

Another celebrated whirlpool is that of Euripus, near the Island of Eubœa; another is known in the Gulf of Bothnia. But perhaps the best known rocky danger is the Maelström, whose waters have a gyratory movement, producing a whirlpool at certain states of the tide, the result of opposing currents, which change every six hours, and which, from its power and magnitude, is capable of attracting and engulfing ships to their destruction, although chiefly dangerous to smaller craft.

To the combined effects of tides and whirlpools may also be attributed the hurricanes, so dreaded by navigators, which so frequently visit the Mauritius and other parts of the Indian Ocean. In periods of the utmost calms, when there is scarcely a breath to ruffle the air, these shores are sometimes visited by immense waves, accompanied by whirlwinds, which seem capable of blowing the ships out of the water, seizing them by the keel, whirling them round on an axis, and finally capsizing them. "At the period of the changing monsoon, the winds, breaking loose from their controlling forces, seem to rage with a fury capable of breaking up the very fountains of the deep."

The hurricanes of the Atlantic occur in the months of August and September, while the south-west monsoon of Africa and the south-east monsoon of the West Indies are at their height; the agents of the one drawing the north-east trade-winds into the interior of Mexico and Texas, the other drawing them into the interior of Africa, greatly disturbing the equilibrium of the atmosphere.

The Polar Seas.

The extreme columns of the known world are Mount Parry, situated at eight degrees from the North Pole, and Mount Ross, twelve degrees from the South Pole. Beyond these limits our maps are mute; a blank space marks each extremity of the terrestrial axis. Will man ever succeed in passing these icy barriers? Will he ever justify the prediction of the poet Seneca, who tells us that "the time will come in the distant future when Ocean will relax her hold on the world, when the immense earth will be open, when Tethys will appear amid new orbs, and where Thule (Iceland) shall no longer be the extreme limit of the earth?"

"Venient annis
Sæcula seris quibus oceanus
Vincula rerum laxet et ingens
Pateat tellus, Tethysque novos
Detegat orbes, nec sit terris
Ultime Thule." *Medea.*

No one can say; every step we have taken in order to approach the Pole has been dearly purchased; and it is not without reason that navigators have named the south point of Greenland, Cape Farewell. Of the number of expeditions, for the most part English, which have been fitted out, at the cost of nearly a million sterling, to explore the Frozen Ocean, one-twentieth have had for their mission to ascertain the fate of the lamented Sir John Franklin.

The first navigator who penetrated to Arctic polar regions was Sebastian Cabot, who in 1498 sought a north-west passage from Europe to China and the Indies. Considering the date, and the state of navigation at that period, this was perhaps the boldest attempt on record. Scandinavian traditions attribute similar undertakings to the son of the King Rodian, who lived in the seventh century; to Osher, the Norwegian, in 873; and to the Princes Harold and Magnus, in 1150.

Sebastian Cabot reached as high as Hudson's Bay, but a mutiny of his sailors forced him to retrace his steps. In 1500, Gaspard de Cortereal discovered Labrador; in 1553, Sir Hugh Willoughby Nova Zembla; and Chancellor the White Sea, about the same time. Davis visited in 1585 the west coast of Greenland, and two years later he discovered the strait which bears his name. In 1596 Barentz discovered Spitzbergen, which was again seen by Hendrich Hudson, who sailed up to and beyond the eighty-second parallel. Three years later Hudson gave his name to the great Labrador Bay, but he could get no farther. His crew also revolted, and he was left in the ship's launch with his son, seven sailors, and the carpenter, who remained faithful. Thus perished one of our greatest navigators.

The Island of Jan Mayen was discovered in 1611; the channel which Baffin took for a bay, and which bears his name, was discovered in 1616. Behring discovered, in his first voyage in 1727, the strait which separates Siberia from America; he sailed through it in 1741, but his ship was stranded, and he himself died of scorbutic disease.

In the year 1771 the Polar Sea was discovered by Hearne, a fur merchant; it was explored long after by Mackenzie.

From the year 1810, when Sir John Ross, Franklin, and Parry turned their attention to the Arctic regions, these expeditions to the Polar Seas rapidly succeeded each other. In 1827 Parry reached the eighty-second degree of north latitude; and in 1845 Sir John Franklin, with the ships *Erebus* and *Terror*, and their crews, departed on their last voyage, from which neither he nor his companions ever returned. There is now no doubt that they perished miserably, after having discovered the north-west passage, which Captain M'Clure also discovered, coming from the opposite direction, in 1850. In 1855 the expedition of Dr. Elisha Kane found the sea open from the Pole.

The Antarctic Pole had in the meantime attracted the attention of navigators. In 1772 the Dutch captain, Kerguelen, discovered an island which he took for a continent. In 1774 Captain Cook explored these regions up to the seventy-first degree of latitude. James Weddell, in a small whaler, sailed past this parallel in 1823. Biscoe discovered Enderby's Land in 1831. The *Zelée* and *Astrolabe*, under the command of Captain Dumont D'Urville, of the French Marine, and the American expedition, under Captain Wilkes, reached the same region in 1838. The former discovered Adelia's Land. Finally, in 1841, Sir James Clarke Ross, nephew of Sir John Ross, with the *Erebus* and *Terror*, penetrated up to the seventy-eighth degree south latitude. Here he discovered the volcanic islands which he named after his ships, and, farther to the south, a new continent or land, which he called Victoria's Land.

While these efforts were being made to penetrate the ice which surrounds the Antarctic Pole, a region having little which could attract human enterprise, the interests of commerce seemed to call for obstinate and persevering attempts to penetrate to the Arctic Pole. In spite of these numerous expeditions, however, which extend over two centuries, the regions round the North Pole are far from being known to geographers. The fogs and snows which almost always cover them were the source of many errors made by the earlier navigators. In his first voyage, made in 1818, Sir John Ross was led to think that Lancaster Sound was closed by a chain of mountains, which he called the Croker Mountains; but in the following year Captain Parry, in command of two ships, the *Hecla* and *Griper*, discovered that this was an error. This celebrated navigator discovered Barrow's Straits, Wellington Channel, and Prince Regent inlet; Cornwallis, Sir Byam Martin, and Melville Islands, to which the name of Parry's Archipelago has been given. In this short voyage he gathered more new results than were obtained by his successors during the next forty years. He was the first to traverse these seas. Upon Sir Byam Martin Island he has described the ruins of some ancient habitations of the Esquimaux. He passed the winter on Melville Island. In order to attain his chosen anchorage in Winter's Bay, he was compelled to saw a passage in the ice of a league in length, which involved the labour of three days; but scarcely were they moored in their chosen harbour than the thermometer fell to eighteen degrees below zero. They carried ashore the ship's boats, the cables, the sails, and log-books. The masts were struck to the maintop; the rest of the rigging served to form a roof, sloping to the gunwale, with a thick covering of sail-cloth, which formed an admirable shelter from the wind and snow. Numberless precautions were taken against cold and wet under the decks. Stoves and other contrivances maintained a supportable degree of temperature. In each dormitory a false ceiling of impermeable cloth interposed to prevent the collection of moisture on the wooden walls of the ship. The crew were divided into companies, each company being under the charge of an officer, charged with the daily inspection of their clothes and cleanliness—an essential protection against scurvy. As a measure of precaution, Captain Parry reduced by one-third the ordinary ration of bread; beer and wine were substituted for spirits; and citron and lemon drinks were served out daily to the sailors. Game was sometimes substituted to vary a repast worthy of Spartans. As a remedy against *ennui*, a theatre was fitted up and comedies acted, for which occasions Parry himself composed a vaudeville, entitled "The North-west Passage; or, the End of the Voyage." During this long night of eighty-four days, the thermometer in the saloons marked 28°, and outside 35° below zero, and for a few minutes actually reached 47°. Some of the sailors had their members frozen, from which they never quite recovered. One day the hut which served as an observatory was discovered to be on fire. A sailor who saved one of the precious instruments lost his hands in the effort; they were completely frost-bitten in the attempt.

Nevertheless, the month of June arrived, and with it the opportunity of making excursions in the neighbourhood: it was found that, in Melville Island, the earth was carpeted with moss and herbage, with saxifrages and poppies. Hares, reindeer, the musk-ox, northern geese, plovers, white wolves and foxes, roamed around their haunts, disputing their booty with the crew. Captain Parry could not risk a second winter in this terrible region. He returned home as soon as the thaw left the passage open.

In 1821, Captain Parry undertook a second voyage with the *Fury* and *Hecla*. He visited Hudson's Bay and Fox's Channel. In his third voyage, undertaken in 1824, he was surprised by the frost in Prince Regent's Channel, and was constrained to pass the winter there. The *Fury* was dismantled, and, being found unfit for service, Captain Parry was obliged to abandon her and return to England.

Accompanied by Sir James Ross, Parry again put to sea in the *Hecla*, in April, 1826. On his third voyage, on leaving Table Island on the north of Spitzbergen, Parry placed his crew in the two training ships, *Enterprise* and *Endeavour;* the first under his own command, the second under orders of Sir James Ross. Sometimes they sailed, sometimes hauled through the crust of the ice; sometimes the ice, which pierced their shoes, showed itself bristling with points, intersected into valleys and little hills, which it was difficult to scale. In spite of the courage and energy of their crews, the two ships scarcely advanced four miles a day, while the drifting of the ice towards the south led them imperceptibly towards their point of departure. They reached latitude eighty-two degrees forty five minutes fifteen seconds, however, and this was the extreme point which they attained.

In the month of May, 1829, Sir John Ross, accompanied by his nephew, James Clark Ross, again turned towards the Polar Seas. He entered Prince Regent's Channel, and there he found the *Fury*, which had been dismantled and abandoned by Parry, in these regions, eight years before. The provisions, which the old ship still contained, were quite a providential resource to Ross's crews. The distinguished navigator explored the Boothian Peninsula, and passed four years consecutively in Port Felix, without being able to disengage his vessel, the *Victory*. This gave him ample leisure to become familiar with the Esquimaux. Sir John Ross, in his account of this long sojourn in polar countries, has recorded many conversations with the natives, which our space does not permit us to quote. From this terrible position he was extricated, and emerged with his crew from this icy prison, when all hope of his return had been abandoned. After being exposed to a thousand dangers, Ross and his crew were at last observed by a whaling ship, which received them on board, after many efforts to attract attention. On learning that the ship which had saved them was the *Isabella*, formerly commanded by Captain Ross, he made himself known. "But Captain Ross has been dead two years," was the reply.

We need not repeat here the enthusiastic reception Captain Ross and his companions met with on their arrival in London.

During an excursion made by the nephew of the Commander (afterwards Sir James Clark Ross), he very closely approached the North Magnetic Pole. This was at eight o'clock, on the morning of the 1st of June, 1831, on the west coast of Boothia. The dip of the magnetic needle was nearly vertical, being eighty-nine degrees fifty-nine seconds—one minute short of ninety degrees. The site was a low flat shore, rising into ridges from fifty to sixty feet high, and about a mile inland.

Contrary to the judgment of many officers of experience in polar explorations, the last and most fatal of all the expeditions was undertaken by Sir John Franklin, with one hundred and thirty-seven picked officers and men, in the ships *Erebus* and *Terror*. The adventurers left Sheerness on the 26th of May, 1846, the ships having been strengthened in every conceivable way, and found in everything calculated to secure the safety of the expedition. On the 22nd of July the ships were spoken by the whaler *Enterprise*, and, four days later, they were sighted by the *Prince of Wales*, of Hull, moored to an ice-berg, waiting an opening to enter Lancaster Sound. There the veil dropped over the ships and their unhappy crews. In 1848, their fate began to excite a lively interest in the public mind. Expedition in search of them succeeded expedition, at immense cost, sent both by the English and American authorities, and by Lady Franklin herself, some of which penetrated the Polar Seas through Behring's Straits, while the majority took Baffin's Bay. In 1850, Captains Ommaney and Penny discovered, at the entrance of Wellington Channel, some vestiges of Franklin, which led to another expedition in 1857, which was got up by private enterprise, of which Captain M'Clintock had the command. Guided by the indications collected in the previous expedition, and intelligence gathered from the Esquimaux by Dr. Rae in his land expedition, Captain M'Clintock in the yacht *Fox* discovered, on the 6th of May, 1859, upon the north point of King William's Land, a cairn or heap of stones. Several leaves of parchment, which were buried under the stones, bearing date the 28th of April, 1848, solved the fatal enigma. The first, dated the 24th of May, 1847, gave some details ending with "all well." The papers had been dug up twelve months later to record the death of Franklin, on the 11th of June, 1847. The survivors are supposed to have been on their way to the mouth of the River Back, but they must have sunk under the terrible hardships to which they were exposed, in addition to cold and hunger.

In September, 1859, Captain M'Clintock returned to England, bringing with him many relics of our lost countrymen, found in the theatre of their misfortunes.

It only remains to us to say a few words on the latest voyages undertaken in the Polar Seas. After the return of Captain M'Clintock, in 1850, Captain M'Clure, leaving Behring's Straits, discovered the north-west passage between Melville and Baring's Island, which passage had been sought for without success during so many ages. He saw the thermometer descend fifty degrees below zero. In the month of October, 1854, he returned to England, and at a subsequent period it was ascertained with certainty that, before his death, Franklin knew of the other passage which exists to the north of America, to the south of Victoria Land, and Wollaston.

The expedition of Dr. Kane entered Smith's Strait in 1853, and advanced towards the north upon sledges drawn by dogs; the mean temperature, which ranged between thirty degrees and forty degrees below zero, fell at last to fifty degrees. At eleven degrees from the Pole they found two Esquimaux villages, called Etah and Peterovik, then an immense glacier. A detachment, conducted by Lieutenant Morton, discovered, beyond the eightieth degree of latitude, an open channel inhabited by innumerable swarms of birds, consisting of swallows, ducks, and gulls, which delighted them by their shrill, piercing cries. Seals (*phoca*) enjoyed themselves on the floating ice. In ascending the banks, they met with flowering plants, such as *Lychnis*, *Hesperis*, &c. On the 24th of June, Morton hoisted the flag of the *Antarctic*, which had before this seen the ice of the South Pole on Cape Independence, situated beyond eighty-one degrees. To the north stretched the open sea. On the left was the western bank of the Kennedy Channel, which seemed to terminate in a chain of mountains, the principal peak rising from nine thousand to ten thousand feet, which was named Mount Parry. The expedition returned towards the south, and reached the port of Uppernavick exhausted with hunger, where it was received on board an American ship. Dr. Kane, weakened by his sufferings, from which he never quite recovered, died in 1857.

We cannot conclude this rapid sketch of events connected with the expeditions to the Arctic Pole without noting a geological fact of great and singular interest. When opportunities have presented themselves of examining the rocks in the regions adjoining the North Pole, it has been found that great numbers belong to the coal measures. Such is the case in Melville Island and Prince Patrick's Island. Under the ice which covers the soil in these islands coal exists, with all the fossil vegetable débris which invariably accompany it. This shows that in the coal period of geology, the North Pole was covered with the rich and abundant vegetation, whose remains constitute the coal-fields of the present day; and proves to demonstration that the temperature of these regions was, at one period of the earth's history, equal to that of equatorial countries of the present day. What a wonderful change in the temperature of these regions is thus indicated! It is, indeed, a strange contrast to find coal formations under the soil covered by the polar ice. Let us suppose that human industry should dream of establishing itself in these countries, and drawing from the earth the combustible so needed to make it habitable, thus furnishing the means of overcoming the rigorous climatic conditions of these inhospitable regions.

The Antarctic Pole is probably surrounded by an icy canopy, not less than two thousand five hundred miles in diameter, and numerous circumstances lead to the conclusion that the vast mass has diminished since 1774, when the region was visited by Captain Cook. The Antarctic region can only be approached during the summer, namely, in December, January, and February.

The first navigator who penetrated the Antarctic Circle was the Dutch captain, Theodoric de Gheritk, whose vessel formed part of the squadron commanded by Simon de Cordes, destined for the East Indies. In January, 1600, a tempest having dispersed the squadron, Captain Gheritk was driven as far south as the sixty-fourth parallel, where he observed a coast which reminded him of Norway. It was mountainous, covered with snow, stretching from the coast to the Isles of Solomon. The report of Simon de Cordes was received with great incredulity, and the doubts raised were only dissipated when the New South Shetland Islands were definitively recognised. The idea of an Antarctic continent is, however, one of the oldest conceptions of speculative geography, and one which mariners and philosophers alike have found it most difficult to relinquish. The existence of a southern continent seemed to them to be the necessary counterpoise to the Arctic land. The *Terra Australis incognita* is marked on all the maps of Mercator, round the South Pole, and when the Dutch officer, Kerguelen, discovered, in 1772, the island which bears his name, he quoted this idea of Mercator as the motive which suggested the voyage. In 1774, Captain Cook ventured up to and beyond the seventy-first degree of latitude under the one hundred and ninth degree west longitude. He traversed a hundred and eighty leagues, between the fiftieth degree and sixtieth degree of south latitude, without finding the land of which mariners had spoken: this led him to conclude that mountains of ice, or the great fog-banks of the region, had been mistaken for a continent. Nevertheless, Cook clung to the idea of the existence of a southern continent. "I firmly believe," he says, "that near the Pole there is land where most part of the ice is formed which is spread over the vast Southern Ocean. I cannot believe that the ice could extend itself so far if it had not land—and I venture to say land of considerable extent—to the south. I believe, nevertheless, that the greater part of this southern continent ought to lie within the Polar Circle, where the sea is so encumbered with ice as to be unapproachable. The danger run in surveying a coast in these unknown seas is so great, that I dare to say no one will venture to go farther than I have, and that the land that lies to the south will always remain unknown. The fogs are there too dense; the snow-storms and tempests too frequent; the cold too severe; all the dangers of navigation too numerous. The appearance of the coast is the most horrible that can be imagined. The country is condemned by nature to remain unvisited by the sun, and buried under eternal hoar frost. After this report, I believe that we shall hear no more of a southern continent." This description of these desolate regions, to which the great navigator might have applied the words of Pliny, "*Pars mundi a natura damnata et densa mersa caligine*," only excited the courage of his successors. In our days, several expeditions have been fitted out for the express survey of regions which may be characterised as the abode of cold, silence, and death. In 1833, a free passage opened itself into the Antarctic Sea. The Scottish whaling ship, commanded by James Weddell, entered the pack ice, and penetrated it in pursuit of seals; but having, by chance, found the sea open on his course, he forced his way up to seventy-four degrees south latitude, and under the thirty-fourth degree of longitude, but the season was too advanced, and he and his crew retraced their steps. The voyage of Captain Weddell caused a great sensation, and suggested the possibility of more serious expeditions. Twelve years later three great expeditions were fitted out: one, under Dumont D'Urville, of the French Marine; an American expedition, under Captain Wilkes, of the United States Navy; and an English expedition, under Sir James Clark Ross.

Dumont D'Urville, who perished so miserably in the railway catastrophe at Versailles in 1842, passed the Straits of Magellan on the 9th of January, 1838, having under his command the two corvettes *Astrolabe* and *Zelée*. He expected to find it as Weddell had described, and that, after passing the first icy barrier, he should find an open sea before him. But he was soon compelled to renounce this hope. The floating icebergs became more and more closely packed and dangerous.

The southern icebergs do not circulate in straits and channels already formed, like those of the North Pole, but in enormous detached blocks which hug the land. Sometimes in shallow water they form belts parallel to the base of the cliffs, intersected by a small number of sinuous narrow channels. These icy cliffs present a face more or less disintegrated as they approximate to the rocky shore. The blocks of ice form at first huge prisms, or tabular, regular masses of a whitish paste; but they get used up by degrees, and rounded off and separated under the action of the waves, which chafe them, and their colour becomes more and more limpid and bluish. They ascend freely towards the north, in spite of the winds and currents which carry them towards the Equator. One year with another these floating icebergs accumulate with very striking differences, and it is only by a rare chance that they open up a free passage such as Captain Weddell had discovered. These floating islands of ice have been met with in thirty-five degrees south latitude, and even as high as Cape Horn.

The two French ships frequently found themselves shut up in the icebergs, which continued to press upon them, and driven before the north winds, until the south wind again dispersed their vast masses, enabling them to issue from their prison in health and safety. In some cases D'Urville found it necessary to force his ship through fields of ice by which he was surrounded and imprisoned, and to cut his way by force through the accumulating blocks, using the corvette as a sort of battering-ram. In 1838 he recognised, about fifty leagues from the South Orkney Isles, a coast, to which he gave the name of *Louis Philippe's* and *Joinville's Land.* This coast is covered with enormous masses of ice, which seemed to rise to the height of two thousand six hundred feet. Ross discovered still more lofty peaks, such as Mount Penny and Mount Haddington, rising about seven thousand feet. The English navigator states that this land is only a great island. The crew of D'Urville's ship being sickly and overworked, he returned to the port of Chili, whence he again issued for the South Pole in the following January.

On this occasion his approach was made from a point diametrically opposite to the former. He very soon found himself in the middle of the ice. He discovered within the Antarctic Circle land, to which he gave the name of *Adelia's Land.* The long and lofty cliffs of this island or continent he describes as being surrounded by a belt of islands of ice at once numerous and threatening. D'Urville did not hesitate to navigate his corvettes through the middle of the band of enormous icebergs which seemed to guard the Pole and forbid his approach to it. For some moments his vessels were so surrounded that they had reason to fear, from moment to moment, some terrible shock, some irreparable disaster. In addition to this, the sea produces around these floating icebergs, eddies, which were not unlikely to draw on the ship to the destruction with which it was threatened at every instant. It was in passing at their base that D'Urville was able to judge of the height of these icy cliffs. "The walls of these blocks of ice," he says, "far exceed our masts and riggings in height; they overhang our ships, whose dimensions seem ridiculously curtailed. We seem to be traversing the narrow streets of some city of giants. At the foot of these gigantic monuments we perceive vast caverns hollowed by the waves, which are engulfed there with a crashing tumult. The sun darts his oblique rays upon the immense walls of ice as if it were crystal, presenting effects of light and shade truly magical and startling. From the summit of these mountains, numerous brooks, fed by the melting ice produced by the summer heat of a January sun in these regions, throw themselves in cascades into the icy sea.

"Occasionally these icebergs approach each other so as to conceal the land entirely, and we only perceive two walls of threatening ice, whose sonorous echoes send back the word of command of the officers. The corvette which followed the *Astrolabe* appeared so small, and its masts so slender, that the ship's crew were seized with terror. For nearly an hour we only saw vertical walls of ice." Ultimately they reached a vast basin, formed on one side by the chain of floating islands which they had traversed, and on the other by high land rising three and four thousand feet, rugged and undulating on the surface, but clothed over all with an icy mantle, which was rendered dazzlingly imposing in its whiteness by the rays of the sun. The officers could only advance by the ship's boats through a labyrinth of icebergs up to a little islet lying opposite to the coast. They touched the land at this islet; the French flag was planted, possession was taken of the new continent, and, in proof of possession, some portions of rock were torn from the scarped and denuded cliffs. These rocks are composed of quartzite and gneiss. The southern continent, therefore, belongs to the primitive formation, while the northern region belongs in great part to the transition, or coal formation. According to the map of Adelia's Land, traced by D'Urville over an extent of thirty leagues of country, the region is one of death and desolation, without any trace of vegetation.

A little more to the north, the French navigator had a vague vision on the white lines of the horizon of another land, which he named *Coast Clear* (Côte Clarie), the existence of which was soon confirmed by the American expedition under Commodore Wilkes. This officer has explored the southern land on a larger scale than any other navigator, but he suffered himself to be led into error by the dense fogs of the region, and has laid down coast lines on his map where Sir James Ross subsequently found only open sea—an error which has very unjustly thrown discredit on the whole expedition.

The English expedition entered this region on Christmas Day, 1840, which was passed by Ross in a strong gale, with constant snow or rain. Soon after, the first icebergs were seen, having flat tabular summits, in some instances two miles in circumference, bounded on all sides by perpendicular cliffs. On New Year's Day, 1841, the ships crossed the Antarctic Circle, and reached the edge of the pack ice, which they entered, after skirting it for several days. On the 5th, the pack was passed through, amid blinding snow and thick fog, which on clearing away revealed an open sea, and on the 11th of January land was seen directly ahead of the ships. A coast line rose in lofty snow-covered peaks at a great distance. On a nearer view, this coast is thus described: " It was a beautifully clear evening, and two magnificent ranges of mountains rose to elevations varying from seven thousand to ten thousand feet above the level of the sea. The glaciers which filled their intervening valleys, and which descended from near the mountain summits, projected in many places several miles into the sea, and terminated in lofty perpendicular cliffs. In a few places the rocks broke through their icy covering, by which alone we could be assured that lava formed the nucleus of this, to all appearance, enormous iceberg. This antarctic land was named Victoria Land, in honour of the Queen. It was coasted up to latitude seventy-eight degrees south, and near to this a magnificent volcanic mountain presented itself, rising twelve thousand feet above the level of the sea, which emitted flame and smoke in splendid profusion. The flanks of this gigantic mountain were clothed with snow almost to the mouth of the crater from which the flaming smoke issued. At a short distance,

Ross discovered the cone of an extinct or, at least, inactive volcano nearly as lofty. He gave to these two volcanoes the names of his vessels, *Erebus* and *Terror* (Fig. 9)—names perfectly in harmony with the surrounding desolation. The ice-covered cliffs rose about a hundred and ninety feet high, and appear to be about three hundred feet deep, soundings being found at about four hundred fathoms. In the distance, towards the south, a range of lofty mountains were observed, which Ross named *Mount Parry*, in honour of his old

Fig. 9. Mounts Erebus and Terror.

commander. When Ross retraced his steps, the expedition had advanced as far as the seventy-ninth degree of south latitude.

It may be said of polar countries, that they form a transition state between land and sea, for water is always present, although in a solid state; the surface is always at a very low temperature, snow does not melt as it falls, and the sea is thus sometimes covered with a continuous sheet of frozen snow; sometimes with enormous floating blocks of ice which are driven by the currents. Meeting with these floating masses of ice is one of the dangers of polar navigation. Captain Scoresby has given a very detailed description of the different kinds of ice met with in the Arctic Seas. The ice-fields of this writer form extensive masses of solid water, of which the eye cannot trace the limits, some of them being thirty-five leagues in length and ten broad, with a thickness of seven to eight fathoms; but generally these ice-fields rise only four to six feet above the water, and reach from three to four fathoms beneath the surface. Scoresby has seen these ice-fields forming in the open sea. When the first crystals appear, the surface of the ocean is cold enough to prevent snow from melting as it falls. On the approach of congelation the surface solidifies, and seems as if covered with oil; small circles are formed, which press against each other, and are finally soldered together until they form a vast field of ice, the thickness of which increases from the lower surface.

The water produced from melted ice is perfectly fresh—the result of a well-known physical cause. When a saline solution like sea water is congealed by cold, pure water alone passes into the solid state, the saline solution becomes more concentrated, increases in density, and, sinking to the bottom, remains liquid. Blocks of ice, therefore, in the Polar Seas, are always available for domestic use. There are, however, salt blocks of ice which are distinguished from fresh-water ice by their opaqueness and their dazzling white colour: this saltness is due to the sea water retained in its interstices. Scoresby amused himself sometimes by shaping lenses of ice, with which he is said to have set fire to gunpowder, much to the astonishment of his crew.

The ice-fields, which are formed in higher latitudes, are driven towards the south by winds and currents, but sooner or later the action of the waves breaks them up into fragments. The edges of the broken icebergs are thus often rising and continually changing: these asperities and protuberances are called *hummocks* by English navigators; they give to the polar ice an odd, irregular appearance. Hummocks form themselves of the stray, broken icebergs which come in contact with each other at their edges, and thus form vast rafts, the pieces of which may exceed a hundred yards in length.

When these icebergs are separated by open spaces, through which vessels can be navigated, the pack ice is said to be open. But it often happens that mountains of ice occur partly submerged, where one edge is retained under the principal mass, while the other is above the water. Scoresby once passed over a *calf*, as English mariners call these icy mountains, but he trembled while he did so, dreading lest it should throw his vessel, himself, and crew into the air before he could pass it. The aspect of the ice-fields vary in a thousand ways. Here it is an incoherent chaos resembling some volcanic rocks, with crevices in all directions, bristling with unshapely blocks piled up at random; there it is a strongly-marked plain, an immense mosaic formed of vast blocks of ice of every age and thickness, the divisions of which are marked by long ridges of the most irregular forms; sometimes resembling walls composed of great rectangular blocks, sometimes resembling chains of hills, with great rounded summits.

In the spring, when a thaw sets in, and the fields begin to break up, the pieces of light ice which unite the great blocks into unique masses are the first to melt; the several blocks then separate, and the motion of the water soon disperses them, and the imprisoned ships find a free passage. But a day of calm is still sufficient to unite the dispersed masses, which oscillate and grind against each other with a strange noise, which sailors compare to the yelping of young dogs.

When a ship is shut up in one of these floating ice-fields, inexplicable changes sometimes occur in the vast incoherent aggregations. Vessels, which think themselves immovable, are found in a few hours to have completely reversed their positions. Two ships shut in at a short distance from each other, were driven many leagues without being able to perceive any change in the surrounding ice. At other times ships are drawn with the floating ice-fields, like the white bears, who make long voyages at sea upon these monster vehicles. In 1777 the Dutch vessel, the *Wilhelmina*, was driven with some other whaling ships from eighty degrees north back to sixty-two degrees, in sight of the Iceland coast. During this terrible journey the ships were broken up one after the other. More than two hundred persons perished, and the remainder reached land with difficulty.

Lieutenant De Haven, navigating in search of Sir John Franklin, was caught in the ice in the middle of the channel in Wellington Strait. During the nine months which he remained in captivity, he drifted nearly thirteen hundred miles towards the south; and the ship *Resolute*, abandoned by Captain Kellet in an ice-field of immense extent, was drifted towards the south with this vast mass to a much greater distance.

Some curious speculations are hazarded by Dr. Maury, arising out of his investigations of winds and currents, facts being revealed which indicate the existence of a climate, mild by comparison, within the Antarctic Circle. These indications are a low barometer, a high degree of aerial rarefaction, and strong winds from the north. "The winds," he says, "were the first to whisper of this strange state of things, and to intimate to us that the Antarctic climates are in winter very unlike the Arctic for rigour and severity." The result of an immense mass of observation on the polar and equatorial winds reveals a marked difference in atmospherical movements north, as compared with the same movements south of the Equator; the equatorial winds of the northern hemisphere being only in excess between the tenth and thirteenth parallel, while those of the southern hemisphere are dominant over a zone of forty-five degrees, or from thirty-five degrees south to ten degrees north.

"The fact that the influence of the polar indraught upon the winds should extend from the Antarctic to the parallel of forty degrees south, while that from the Arctic is so feeble as scarcely to be felt in fifty degrees north, is indicative enough as to the difference in degree of aerial rarefaction over the two regions. The significance of the fact is enhanced by the consideration that the 'brave west winds,' which are bound to the place of greatest rarefaction, rush more violently and constantly along to their destination than do the counter-trades of the northern hemisphere. Why should these polar-bound winds differ so much in strength and prevalence, unless there be a much more abundant supply of caloric, and, consequently, a higher degree of rarefaction, at one pole than at the other?"

That this is the case is confirmed by all known barometrical observations, which are very much lower in the Antarctic than in the Arctic, and Dr. Maury thinks is doubtless due to the excess in Antarctic regions of aqueous vapour and this latent heat.

"There is rarefaction in the Arctic regions. The winds show it, the barometer attests it, and the fact is consistent with the Russian theory of a Polynia in polar waters. Within the Antarctic Circle, on the contrary, the winds bring air which has come over the water for the distance of hundreds of leagues all around; consequently, a large portion of atmospheric air is driven away from the austral regions by the force of vapour."

CHAPTER III.

LIFE IN THE OCEAN.

"See what a lovely shell, small and pure as a pearl,
Frail, but a work divine, made so fairly well,
With delicate spore and whorl, a miracle of design." TENNYSON.

"THE appearance of the open sea," says Frédol, from whose elegant work this chapter is chiefly compiled, "far from the shore—the boundless ocean—is to the man who loves to create a world of his own, in which he can freely exercise his thoughts, filled with sublime ideas of the Infinite. His searching eye rests upon the far-distant horizon. He sees there the ocean and the heavens meeting in a vapoury outline, where the stars ascend and descend, appear and disappear in their turn. Presently this everlasting change in nature awakens in him a vague feeling of that sadness 'which,' says Humboldt, 'lies at the root of all our heartfelt joys.'"

Emotions of another kind and equally serious are produced by the contemplation and study of the habits of the innumerable organised beings which inhabit the great deep. In fact, that immense expanse of water, which we call the sea, is no vast liquid desert; life dwells in its bosom as it does on dry land. Here this mystery reigns supreme in the midst of its expansions, luxuries, and agitations. It pleases the Creator. It is the most beautiful, the most brilliant, the noblest, and the most incomprehensible of His manifestations. Without life, the world would be as nothing. The beings endowed with it transmit it faithfully to other beings, their children, and their successors, which will be, like them, the depositaries of the same mysterious gift; the marvellous heritage thus traverses years and hundreds of years without losing its powers; the globe is redolent with the life which has been so bounteously distributed over it. In the words of Lamartine, "We know what produces life, but we know not what it is;" and this ignorance is perhaps the powerful attraction which provokes our curiosity and excites us to study.

Every living being is animated by two principles, between which a silent but incessant combat is being carried on—*life*, which assimilates, and *death*, which disintegrates. At first, life is all powerful—it lords it over matter; but its reign is limited. Beyond a certain point its vigour is gradually impaired; with old age it decays; and is finally extinguished with time, when the chemical and physical laws seize upon it, and its organization is destroyed. But the elements, though inert at first, are soon reanimated and occupied with a new life. Every plant, every animal is bound up with the past, and is part of the future, for every generation which starts into life is only the corollary upon that which expires, and the prelude of another which is about to be borne. Life is the school of death; death is the foster-mother of life.

Life, however, does not always exhibit itself at the moment of its formation. It is visible later, and only after other phenomena. In order to develope itself, a suitable soil or other medium must be prepared, and other determinate physical and chemical conditions provided. The presence and diffusion of living beings are no chance products; they follow rigorously an order of law. Speaking of the higher forms of animal life, the Duke of Argyll says, in his able and satisfactory work, "The Reign of Law,"—"In all these there is an observed order in the most rigid scientific sense, that is, phenomena in uniform connexion and mutual relations which can be made, and are made, the basis of systematic classification. These classifications are imperfect, not because they are founded on ideal connexions where none exist, but only because they fail in representing adequately the subtle and pervading order which binds together all living things."

The knowledge of fossils has thrown great light upon the regular and progressive development of organization. The evolution of living beings seems to have commenced with the more rudimentary forms; the more ancient rocks, until very recently, had revealed no traces of life, and what has been revealed tends to confirm this view. In the Cambrian rocks of Bray Head, county Wicklow, the *Oldhamia* is a zoophyte of the simplest organization, and the Rhizapods found near the bottom of the Azoic rocks of Canada are the lowest form of living types, and it is only in beds of comparatively recent formation that complex organization exists. Vegetables first show themselves, and even among these the simplest forms have priority. Animals afterwards appear, which, as we have seen, belong to the least perfect classes. The combinations of life, at first simple, have become more and more complex, until the creation of man, who may be considered the masterpiece of organization.

If we expose a certain quantity of pure water to the light and air in the spring, we should soon see it producing shades of a yellowish or greenish colour. These spots, examined through the microscope, reveal thousands of vegetable agglomerates. Presently thousands of animalcules appear, which swim about among the floating masses, nourishing themselves with its substance. Other animalcules then appear, which, in their turn, pursue and devour the first.

In short, life transforms inanimate into organized matter. Vegetables appear first, then come herbivorous animals, and then come the carnivorous. Life maintains life. The death of one gives food and development to others, for all are bound up together—all assist at the metamorphoses continually occurring in the organic as in the mineral world, the result being general and profound harmony—harmony always worthy of admiration. The Creator alone is unchangeable, omnipotent, and permanent; all else is transition.

The inhabitants of the water are much more numerous than those of the solid earth. "Upon a surface less varied than we find on continents," says Humboldt, "the sea contains in its bosom an exuberance of life of which no other portion of the globe could give us any idea." It expands in the north as in the south; in the east as in the west. The seas, above all, abound with it; in the bosom of the deep, creatures corresponding and harmonizing with each other sport and play. Among these especially the naturalist finds instruction, and the philosopher subjects for meditation. The changes they undergo only impress upon our minds more and more a sentiment of thankfulness to the Author of the universe."

Yes, the ocean in its profoundest depths—its plains and its mountains, its valleys, its precipices, even in its ruins—is animated and embellished by innumerable organized beings. These are at first plants, solitary or social, erect or drooping, spreading into prairies, grouped in patches, or forming vast forests in the oceanic valleys. These submarine forests protect and nourish millions of animals which creep, which run, which swim, which sink into the sands, attach themselves to rocks, lodge themselves in crevices, which construct dwellings for themselves, which seek for or fly from each other, which pursue or fight, caress each other lovingly, or devour each other without pity. Charles Darwin truly remarks somewhere that our terrestrial forests do not maintain nearly so many living beings as those which swarm in the bosom of the sea. The ocean, which for man is the region of asphyxia and death, is for millions of animals the region of life and health: there is enjoyment for myriads in its waves; there is happiness on its banks; there is the blue above all.

The sea influences its numerous inhabitants, animal or vegetable, by its temperature, by its density, by its saltness, by its bitterness, by the never-ceasing agitation of its waves, and by the rapidity of its currents.

We have seen in preceding chapters that the sea only freezes under intense cold, and then only at the surface, and that at the depth of five hundred fathoms the same permanent temperature exists in all latitudes. On the other hand, it is agreed that the agitations produced by the most violent storms are never felt beyond the depth of twelve or thirteen fathoms. From this it follows that animals and vegetables, by descending more or less, according to the cold or disturbing movements, can always reach a medium which agrees with their constitutions.

The hosts of the sea are distinguished by a peculiar softness. Certain pelagic plants present only a very weak, feeble consistence; a great number are transformed by ebullition into a sort of jelly. The flesh of marine animals is more or less flaccid; many seem to consist of a diaphanous mucilage. The skeleton of the more perfect species is more or less flexible and cartilaginous; and it rarely attains, as to weight and consistency, the strength of bone exhibited by terrestrial vertebrate animals. Nevertheless, both the shells and coral produced in the bosom of the ocean are remarkable for their stony solidity. Among marine bodies, in short, we find at once the softest and hardest of organized substances.

The separation of organized beings, nourished by the ocean, is subjected to certain fixed laws. We never find on the coast, except by evident accident, the same species that we meet with far from the shore; nor on the surface, creatures whose habits lead them to hide in the depths of ocean. What immense varieties of size, shape, form, and colour, from the nearly invisible vegetation which serves to nourish the small zoophytes and mollusks, to the long, slender algæ, of fifty, and even five hundred, yards in length! How vast the disparity between the microscopic infusoria and the gigantic whale!

"We find in the sea," says Lacepede, "unity and diversity, which constitute its beauty; grandeur and simplicity, which give it sublimity; puissance and immensity, which command our wonder."

In the following pages we shall figure and describe many inhabitants of the sea; but how many remain still to figure and describe! During more than two thousand years research has been multiplied, and succeeded by research without interruption. "But how vast the field," as Lamarck observes, "which Science has still to cultivate, in order to carry the knowledge already acquired to the degree of perfection of which it is susceptible!"

"When the tide retires from the shore, the sea leaves upon the coast some few of the numberless beings which it bears in its bosom. In the first moments of its retreat, the naturalist may collect a crowd of substances, vegetable and animal, with their various characteristic colours and properties. The inhabitants of the coast find there their food, their commerce, and their occupations. At low water the nearest villages and hamlets send their contingents, old and young, men, women, and children, to the harvest. Some apply themselves to gathering the ribboned seaweed (*Zostera*), the membranous *Ulva*, the sombre brown *Fucus vesiculosus*, formerly a source of great wealth to the dwellers by the sea, being then much used in making kelp; others gather the small shells left on the sands; boys mount upon the rocks in search of whelks (*Buccinum*), mussels (*Mytilus*), detach limpets (*Patella*), and other edible marine animals, from the rocks to which they have attached themselves. On some coasts, shells, as *Mactra*, *Cytheria*, and *Bucardia*, are sought, for their beauty. By turning the stones, or by sounding the crevices of the rocks with a hook at the end of a lath, polypes and calmars are sometimes surprised—sometimes even sea and conger eels, which have sought refuge there; while the pools, left here and there by the retiring tide, are dragged by nets of very small mesh, in which the smaller crustaceous mollusks and small fish are secured.

In the Mediterranean and other inland seas, where the tide is almost inappreciable, there exist a great number of animals and vegetables belonging to the deep sea, which the waves or currents very rarely leave upon the sea shore. There are others so fugitive, or which attach themselves so firmly to the rocks, that we can watch them only in their habitats. It is necessary to study them floating on the surface of the waves, or in their mysterious retirements. Hence the necessity that naturalists should study the living productions of the salt water even in the bosom of the ocean, and not on the sea shore.

The means generally employed for this purpose is a drag-net, sounding-line, and other engines suitable for scraping the bottom, and breaking the harder rocks. In a voyage which Milne Edwards made to the coast of Sicily, he formed the idea of employing an apparatus invented by Colonel Paulin, which consisted of a metallic casque provided with a visor of glass, and consequently transparent, which fixed itself round the neck by means of a copper collar made water-tight by stuffing—a diving-bell, in short, in miniature. It communicated with an air-pump by means of a flexible tube. Four men were employed in serving the pump, two exercising it while the other two rested themselves. Other men hold the extremity of a cord, which was passed over a pulley attached at a higher elevation, and enabled them to hoist up the diver with the necessary rapidity in emergencies. A vigilant observer held in his hand a small signal cord. The immersion of the diver was facilitated by heavy leaden shoes, which assist him at the same time to maintain his vertical position at the bottom. M. Edwards made the descent with this apparatus in three fathoms' water with perfect success. He was thus enabled to study, in their most hidden and most inaccessible retreats, the radiate animals, mollusks, crustaceans, and annelids, especially their larvæ and eggs, and by his descriptions to contribute most essentially to make known the functions, manners, and mode of development of certain inhabitants of the sea, whose sojourn and habits would seem to sequestrate them for ever from our observation.

Another and easier mode of studying the living creatures sheltered by the sea was first suggested by M. Charles des Moulins of Bordeaux, in 1830. The *aquarium*, which is charged with fresh or salt water, according to the beings it is intended to contain, serves the same purpose for the inhabitants of the deep which the aviary does for the birds of the air—cages of glass being used in place of iron wire or wicker-work, and water in place of atmospheric air.

When a globe is filled with fresh water, and with mollusks, crustaceans, or fishes, it is observed, after a few days, that the water loses its transparency and purity, and becomes slightly corrupt. It necessarily follows that the water must be changed from time to time. Changing the water, however, causes much suffering, and even death to the animals. Besides, the new water does not always present the same composition, the same aeration, or the same temperature with that which is replaced. To obviate this defect, and taking a leaf out of Nature's book, M. Moulins proposed to put into the vase a certain number of aquatic plants floating or submerged — duckweed, for example—which would act upon the water in a direction inverse to that of the animals inhabiting it. It is known that vegetables assimilate carbon, while decomposing the carbonic acid produced by the respiration of animals, thus disengaging the oxygen indispensable to animal life. In this simple manner was the necessary change of water obviated. The same happy idea has been successfully applied to salt water, and aquariums for salt water plants and animals have been proposed on a great scale. That of the Zoological Gardens of Paris, in the Bois de Boulogne, inaugurated in 1861, is perhaps the largest in the world. It is a solid stone building of fifty yards in length by about twelve broad, presenting a range of forty reservoirs of Angers slate, running north and south. The reservoirs are nearly cubical, presenting in front the strong glass of Saint Gobain, which permits of the interior being seen. They are lighted from above; but the light is weak, greenish, uniform, and consequently mysterious and gloomy, giving a pretty exact imitation of the submarine light some fathoms down. Each reservoir contains about two hundred gallons of water. It is furnished with rocks disposed a little in the form of an amphitheatre, and in a picturesque manner. Upon the rocks, various species of marine vegetables are planted. The bottom is of shingle, gravel, and sand, in order to give certain animals a sufficiently natural retreat.

Ten of these reservoirs are intended for marine animals. The water employed is never changed, but it is kept in continual agitation by circulation, produced by a current of water led from the great pipe which feeds the Bois de Boulogne. This water, being subjected to a strong pressure, compresses a certain portion of air, which, being permitted to act on a portion of the sea water contained in a closed cylinder placed below the level of the aquarium, makes it ascend, and enter with great force into a reservoir, into which it is thrown from a small jet. The sea water thus pressed absorbs a portion of the air, which is drawn with it into the reservoir. A tube placed in a corner of the reservoir receives the overflow, and conducts it into a closed carbon filter, whence it passes into a gravelly underground reservoir, returning again to the closed cylinder. The water is once more subjected to the pressure of air, and again ascends to the aquarium. The cylinder being underground, a temperature equal to about sixteen degrees Cent., which is nearly the uniform temperature of the ocean, is easily maintained. During winter, the aquarium is heated artificially.

CHAPTER IV.

ZOOPHYTES.

"Nature is nowhere more perfect than in her smaller works."
"Natura nusquam magis quàm in minimis tota est." PLINY.

In these early pages it will not be out of place to offer a few considerations on animals in general, including the whole kingdom as well as the great divisions which form the subject of this particular volume. But nothing is less promising as a subject of study than the whole animal series, nothing more difficult than to seize upon any real analogy between beings of types so varied, of organization so dissimilar. The arrangements which naturalists have established in order to study and describe animals—the divisions, classes, orders, families, genera, and species—are admirable contrivances for facilitating the study of creatures numerous as the sands of the sea shore. Without this precious means of logical distribution, the individual mind would recoil before the task of describing the innumerable phalanxes of contemporary animal life. But the reader must never forget that these methodical divisions are pure fictions, due to human invention: they form no part of nature; for has not Linnæus told us that nature makes no leaps, *natura non facit saltus?*—by which he means to tell us that nature passes in a manner almost insensibly from one stage of organization to another, altogether irrespective of human systems.

It is, however, when we come to watch the confines of the animal and vegetable kingdom that we realise how difficult it is to seize the precise line of demarcation which separates the great kingdoms of Nature. We have seen in the "Vegetable World" germs of the simplest organization, as in the Cryptogamia, spores, as in the Algæ, and fruitful corpuscles, as in the Mosses, which seem to be invested with some of the characteristics of animal life, for they appear to be gifted with organs of locomotion, namely, vibratile cilia, by means of which they execute movements which are to all appearance quite voluntary. Alongside these, vegetable germs and fecundating corpuscles, known as *antherozoides* among the Algæ, Mosses, and Ferns, which, when floating in water, go and come like the inferior animals, seeking to penetrate into cavities, withdrawing themselves, returning again, and again introducing themselves, and exhibiting all the signs of an apparent effort. Let us compare the Infusoria, or even the Polypi, Coral insects, and Gorgons, with these shifting vegetable organisms, and say if it is easy to determine, without considerable study, which is the plant and which the animal. The precise line of demarcation which it is so desirable to establish between the two kingdoms of Nature is indeed difficult to trace.

The word *zoophyte*, to which this comparison introduces us, seems very happily applied: it is derived from the Greek word ζῶον, *animal*, and φυτὸν, *plant;* and is, as it seems to us, quite worthy of being retained in Science, because it consecrates and materialises, so to speak, a sort of fusion between the two kingdoms of Nature at their confines. Let us guard ourselves, however, from carrying this idea too far, and, upon the faith of a happy word, altering altogether the true relations of created beings. In adopting the name *zoophyte*, to indicate a great division of the animal kingdom, the reader must not imagine that there is any ambiguity about the creatures designated, or that they belong at once to both kingdoms, or that they might be ranged indifferently in the one or the other. Zoophytes are animals, and nothing but animals; the justification for using a designation which signifies animal plant is, that many of them have an exterior resemblance to plants; that they divide themselves by offshoots, as some plants do, and are sometimes crowned with organs tinted with lively colours, like some flowers.

This analogy between plants and zoophytes is nowhere more apparent than in the coral. Rooted in the soil and upon rocks, the form of its branches many times subdivided, above all, the coloured appendages which at certain periods so closely resemble the corolla of a flower, have all the form and appearance of plants. Until the eighteenth century most naturalists classed the coral as Linnæus did, without the least hesitation, with analogous creations in the vegetable world. Réaumur long contended for the contrary opinion; but it is only in our day that the animal nature of the coral is satisfactorily established. The *sea anemone* may be cited as another striking example of the resemblance borne by certain inferior organisms to vegetables. We hold, then, that we are justified in using the word *zoophyte* to designate the beings which now occupy our attention.

We shall not surprise our readers by telling them that the structure of the zoophyte, especially in its inferior orders, is excessively simple. They are the first steps in the scale of animal life, and in them a purely rudimentary organization was to be expected. In these beings—true types of animal life—the several parts of the body, in place of being disposed in pairs on each side of its longitudinal plane, as occurs in animals of a higher organization, is found to radiate habitually round an axis or central point, and this whether in its adult or juvenile state. Zoophytes have not generally an articulate skeleton, either exterior or interior, and their nervous system, where it exists, is very slightly developed. The organs of the senses, other than those of touch, are altogether absent in the greater part of beings which belong to this, the lowest class of the last division of the animal kingdom.

Several questions arise here: Has the zoophyte sentiment, feeling, perception? Has it consciousness, sense, sensibility? The question is insoluble; it is an abyss of obscurity. The coral, or rather the aggregation of living beings which bear the name, are attached to the rock which has seen their birth, and which will witness their death: the infusoria, of microscopic dimensions, which revolve perpetually in a circle infinitesimally small. The Amibæ, the marvellous Proteus, which in the space of a minute changes its form a hundred times under the surprised eyes of the observer, is, in truth, a mere atom charged with life. Yet all these beings have an existence to appearance purely vegetative. In their obscure and blind impulse, have they consciousness or instinct? Do they know what takes place at the three thousandth part of an inch from their microscopic bodies? To the Creator alone does the knowledge of this mystery belong.

In consequence of the numerous differences of structure which exist among zoophytes, some recent authors divide them into four classes: namely, *Sponges*, *Infusoria*, *Acalephes*, and *Echinoderms*. But, following the best authorities which have recently treated of these animals, we shall divide them into

I. Protozoa, including the *Infusoria*, *Foraminifera*, and *Spongiadæ*.

II. Polypifera, including the *Hydræ*, *Sertularia*, and *Pennatulariæ*.

III. Echinodermata, or Sea-urchins and Star-fishes.

Our space will prevent our doing more than presenting to the reader in succession the most characteristic types of each of these groups.

I. THE PROTOZOA.

The Protozoares represent animal life reduced to its most simple expression. They are organized atoms, mere animated and moving points, living sparks. As they are the simplest forms of animal life as regards their structure, so also they are the smallest. Their microscopic dimensions hide them from our view. The discovery of the microscope was a necessary step to our becoming acquainted with these beings, whose existence was ignored by the ancient world, and only revealed in the seventeenth century by the discovery of the microscope. When armed with this marvellous instrument, applied to examine the various liquid mediums—as when Leuwenhoek, for example, applied the magnifying glass to the inspection of stagnant water, with its infusions of macerated vegetable and animal substances—when he scrutinized a drop of water borrowed from the ocean, from rivers, or from lakes, he discovered there a new world—a world which will be unveiled in these pages.

Some modern writers believe that the Protozoa is a mere *cellular organism*, that being the principal and end of organization, such as we find it in the cellular vegetable. According to this hypothesis, the Protozoares would be the cellulars of the animal kingdom, as the Algæ and Mushrooms are of the vegetable world. This idea is so far wrong, that it has been founded upon the empire of pure theory. "In reality," says Paul Gervais and Van Beneden, "the animals to which we extend it very rarely resemble elementary cellulars." The tissue of which the bodies of the Protozoa are composed is habitually destitute of cellular structure. They are formed of a sort of animated jelly, amorphous and diaphanous, and have received from Dujardin the name of *Sarcoda*, or soft-fleshed animals.

Infinitely varied in their form, the Protozoares are furnished with *vibratile cilia*, which are organs of locomotion belonging to the lower animals inhabiting the liquid element. Their bodies are sometimes naked, sometimes covered with a siliceous, chalky, or membranous cuirass. They are divided into two great classes, the *Rhizopoda* and *Infusoria*.

CLASS RHIZOPODA.

Gervais and Van Beneden include under the name of *Rhizopods*, or *foot-rooted* animals (so called from ριζα, *root;* πους, ποδος, *footed animals*), those of the simplest organization, which may be characterised by the absence of distinct digestive cavities, and the presence of vibratile cilia, as well as by the soft parts of their tissues. This tissue emits prolongations or filaments which admit of easy extension, sometimes simple, sometimes branching. Occasionally we see these branching filaments withdraw themselves towards the mass of the body, disappear, and gradually melt into its substance in such a manner that the individual seems to absorb and devour itself. If, in exceptional cases, some of the superior animals, as the wolf, devour each other, the rhizopods go much farther: they devour themselves, so to speak!

The rhizopods are found both in fresh and salt water. They live, as parasites, on the body of worms and other articulated animals. The class is divided into many orders. We shall speak here only of three; namely, the *Amibæ*, *Foraminifera*, and *Noctiluca*.

THE AMIBÆ.

In nearly all ancient animal and vegetable infusions, not quite putrid—upon all oozy beds covering bodies which have remained for some time in fresh or sea water—we find the singular beings which belong to this order. They are the simplest organisms in creation, being reduced to a mere drop of living matter. Their bodies are formed of a gelatinous substance, without appreciable organization. The quantity of matter which forms them is so infinitesimal, that it becomes incredibly diaphanous, and so transparent that the eye, armed with the microscope, traverses it in all directions, so that it is necessary to modify the nature of the liquid in which it is held in suspension, and introduce the phenomenon of refraction in order to observe them.

It would be difficult to say exactly what is the form these creatures assume. They frequently have the appearance of small rounded masses, like drops of water; but, whatever their form may be, it is always so unstable, that it changes, so to speak, every moment, so that it is found impossible to make a drawing from the model under the microscope—the design must be finished by an appeal to memory. This instability is the characteristic manifestation of life in the *Amiba*, which are naked beings, without apparent organization; in fact, it occupies the first step in the scale of creation.

The transparent immovable drop under consideration emits an expansion, and a lobe of a vitreous appearance upon its circumference, which, gliding like a drop of oil upon the object-glass of the microscope, begins by fixing itself to it as a supporting point, afterwards slowly attracting to itself the whole mass, and thus gradually increasing its bulk under the observer's eye.

The *Amiba*, according to their dimensions and degree of development, successively emit a greater or smaller number of lobes, none of which are precisely alike, but, after having appeared for an instant, each successively re-enters into the common mass, with which it becomes completely incorporated. Variable in their respective forms, these lobes present appearances quite different in the several genera. They are more or less lengthy, more or less fringed, and often branching; sometimes they are filiform, sprouting in all directions over the animal mass, which rolls in the liquid like the husk of a small chestnut.

If we ask how these animals are nourished, in which no digestive apparatus can be distinguished, the question is difficult to answer. It is thought that they are nourished by simple absorption, and by absorption only. In the interior of the gelatinous mass which constitute the animals, however, granules and microscopic portions of vegetables are frequently discovered. "We can conceive," says Dujardin, "how these objects have penetrated to the interior, if we remark, on the one hand, that in creeping on the surface of the glass, to which they adhere very exactly, the *Amiba* can be made to receive, by pressure, foreign substances into their own bodies, by means of the alternate contraction and extension of the various parts natural to them, and, on the other hand, that the gelatinous mass is susceptible of spontaneous depressions—here and there near to or even at the surface of the spherical cavities, which successively contract themselves and disappear in connection with the strange body which they have absorbed."

The *Amiba* are often observed to be tinted red or green; this arises from the special colouring-matter which has been absorbed into its mass.

The question arises, How do these creatures, so simple in their organization, propagate their species?

We believe that they are chiefly multiplied by parting with a lobe, which, in certain conditions, is enabled to live an independent existence, and develope itself, thus forming a new individual. This is what naturalists term generation by division—*fissiparism* or *fission*. The absence of a nutritive and reproductive apparatus in the *Amiba*, and the want of stability in their forms, explain how nearly impossible it is to characterise as species the numerous individuals daily met with in infusions of organic matter in stagnant water. In order to distinguish some of the groups, Dujardin bases his descriptions upon their size and the general form into which they expand.

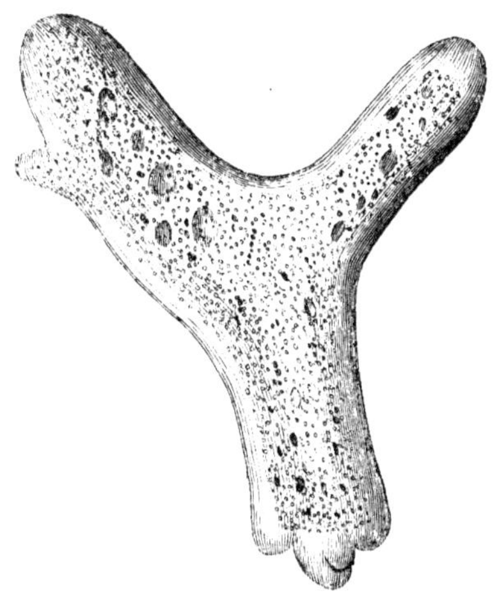

Fig. 10. Amiba princeps (Ehrenberg), magnified 100 times.

We shall be able to form some idea of the appearance of these beings, rendered mysterious by their very simplicity, by throwing a glance upon the two accompanying figures (Figs. 10 and 11), borrowed from the Atlas of Dujardin's great work, "Les Zoophytes Infusoires," which we shall have occasion to quote more than once.

We have said that the *Amiba* change their form every few moments under the eyes of the observer. Fig. 11 represents the changes of form through which they pass, according to Dujardin, when examined under the microscope.

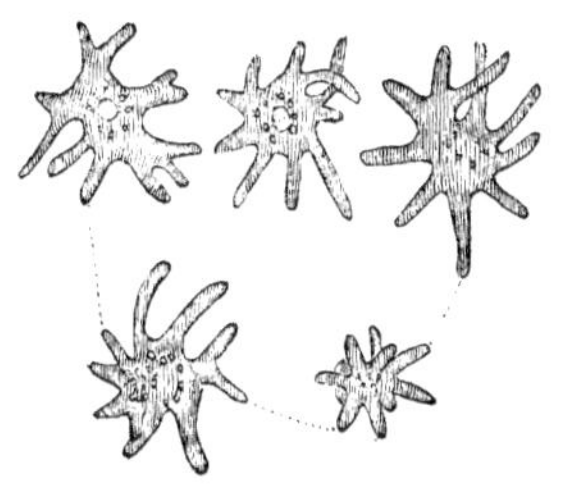

Fig. 11. Various forms of Amiba diffluens (Müller), magnified 400 times.

Dujardin points out very clearly the identity of structure between organisms like *Amiba* and such forms as *Difflugia* and *Arcella*. All these creatures are without trace of mouth or digestive cavity, and the entire body is a single cell, or aggregation of cells, which receive their nutriment by absorption; for, although the creatures have neither mouth nor stomach, yet, according to Professor Kölliker, it takes in solid nutriment, and rejects what is indigestible. When in its progress through the water one of these minute organisms approaches one of the equally minute Algæ, from which it draws nourishment, it seizes the plant with its tentacular filaments, which it gradually encloses on all sides; the filaments, to all appearance, becoming more or less shortened in the process. In this way the captive is brought close to the surface of the body; a cavity is thus formed, in which the prey is lodged, which closes round it on all sides. In this situation it is gradually drawn towards the centre, and passes at last entirely into the mass. The engulfed morsel is gradually dissolved and digested.

THE FORAMINIFERA.

There is nothing small in Nature. The idea of littleness or greatness is a human conception—a comparison which is suggested by the dimensions of his own organs. Nature, on the other hand, compensates smallness by numbers. The result produced by the bones of some large animals is also accomplished by the accumulated spoils of millions of animalcules. The history of the Foraminifera is a striking example of this great truth.

What, then, is a Foraminifer? It is a very small zoophyte, a shell nearly invisible to the naked eye; for, in general, its dimensions rarely exceed the two hundredth part of an inch; in short, it is strictly microscopic. Examine under a microscope the sand of the ocean, and it will be found that one-half of it consists of the débris of shells, of various but well-defined forms, each habitually pierced with a number of holes. To this they are indebted for their name Foraminifera, from *foramen*, a hole. With these microscopic animalcules Nature has worked wonders in geological times; nor have the wonders ceased in our days.

Many beds of the terrestrial crust consist entirely of the remains of Foraminifera. In the most remote ages in the history of our planet, these zoophytes must have lived in innumerable swarms in the seas of the period; they buried themselves in the bottoms of the seas, and their shells, heaped up during many ages, have finished by forming hills of great thickness and extent. We may say, to give an example, that during the Carboniferous period, a single species of these zoophytes has formed, in Russia alone, enormous beds of calcareous rock. Many beds of cretaceous formation are, in great part, composed of Foraminifera, and they exist in immense numbers in the white chalk which cover and form the vast mountains ranging from Champagne, in France, nearly to the centre of England.

But it is to the Tertiary formation that these zoophytes have contributed the most enormous deposits. The greater part of the Egyptian pyramids is only an aggregation of *Nummulites*. A prodigious number of Foraminifera present themselves in the tertiary deposits of the Gironde, of Italy, and of Austria. The chalk so abundant in the basin of Paris is almost entirely composed of Foraminifera. The remains of these creatures are so abundant in the Paris chalk, that M. d'Orbigny found upwards of fifty-eight thousand in a small block, scarcely exceeding a cubic inch of chalk, from the quarries of Chantilly. This fact, according to this author, implies the existence of three thousand millions of these zoophytes in the cubic metre (thirty-nine inches and a small fraction) of rock! As the chalk from these quarries has served to build Paris, as well as the towns and villages of the neighbouring departments, it may be said that Paris, and other great centres of population which surround it, are built with the shells of these microscopic animals.

The sand of the littoral of all existing seas is so full of these minute but elegant shells, that it is often half composed of them. M. d'Orbigny found in three grammes (forty-six grains troy) of sand from the Antilles, four hundred and forty thousand shells of Foraminifera. Bianchi found in thirty grammes (four hundred and sixty-seven grains) from the Adriatic, six thousand of these shells. If we calculate the proportion of these beings contained in a cubic metre alone of sea-sand, we reach a figure which passes all conception. What would this be if we could extend the calculation to the immensity of surface covered by the waves which surround the globe?

M. d'Orbigny has satisfied himself, by microscopic examination of sands from all parts of the globe, that it is the débris of Foraminifera which form, in all existing seas, those enormous deposits which raise banks, obstruct the navigation in gulfs and straits, and fill up ports, as may be seen in the port of Alexandria. In common with the corals and madrepores, the Foraminifera are the great agents in forming the isles which surge up under our eyes from the bosom of the ocean in the warmer regions of the globe. Thus shells, scarcely appreciable to the sight, suffice by their accumulations to fill up seas, while performing a very considerable part in the great operations of Nature, although it may not be apparent to us.

Our exact knowledge of the Foraminifera is of very recent date. Great numbers of minute particles, of regular and symmetrical form, were long distinguished on the sands of the sea shore. These corpuscular atoms early attracted the attention of observers. But with the discovery of the microscope, these small elegant shells, which were among the curiosities revealed by the instrument, assumed immense importance. We have stated that these corpuscles are nothing but the shell or solid framework of a crowd of marine animalculæ: we may then consider them as living species analogous to the Ammonites and Nautilus of geological times. Linnæus has placed them in this last genus, which would include, according to that author, all the multilocular shells. In 1804, Lamarck classed them among the molluscous cephalopods. But Alcide d'Orbigny, who has devoted long years study and observation, and may be considered the great historian of the Foraminifera, makes it appear that this mode of classification was inexact. Dujardin separated them altogether from the class of mollusks, and showed that they ought to be consigned to an inferior class of animals. These minute creatures, in short, are deficient in the true appendages analogous to feet, which exist in the higher mollusks. They simply possess filamentous expansions, very variable in their form.

We have stated that the Foraminifera are of microscopic dimensions. With some trifling exceptions, this is generally true; but there exist a number of species which are visible to the naked eye. Such are the *Nummulites*, spoken of above as entering into the composition of the stony masses of the Pyramids of Egypt. The *Nummulites pyramidas* is circular in form, and about an inch in diameter. The Foraminifers found in the nummulite formation of Tremsted, in Bavaria, between Munich and Saltzberg, are still larger, being nearly double the size of the nummulite of the Pyramids; in short, they are the giants of this tribe of animals.

After these remarks, we may venture to give some idea of the structure and classification of these beings, whose part in the work of creation have, in former times, been so considerable.

The bodies of the Foraminifera are formed of a gelatinous substance, sometimes entire and round, sometimes divided into segments, which can be placed upon a line, simple or alternate, wound up into a spiral form or rolled round its axis, like a ball. A testaceous envelope, modelled upon the segments, follows the various modifications of form, and protects the body in all its parts. From the extremity of the last segment of one or many openings of the shell, or of the numerous pores, issue certain long and slender filaments, more or less numerous, which are divided and subdivided over their whole length, like the spreading branches of a tree. They can attach themselves to external bodies with force enough to determine the progression of the animal. Being formed of transparent non-colouring matter, they may be said to be mere expansions, which vary in form and length according to the conditions of the ambient medium. The filaments have also very variable positions: sometimes they form an unique and retractile band, issuing from a single opening; sometimes they project themselves across from numerous little pores in the shell, which covers the last segment of the animal. These pores, or openings, give the name to the creatures under consideration.

In conclusion, the filaments, contractile and variable in their form, which constitute the feet and arms of these little creatures, appear to have something poisonous in them; it is stated that the Infusoria are at once paralysed in their motions when brought in contact with the minute arms of the Foraminifera. "It is probably by this means," says M. Frédol, "that these creatures succeed in catching their prey. Is it not worthy of remark that these beings, however small their size and slight their form, are unpitying flesh-eaters? The smallest, the weakest, and the most microscopic animal in existence thus becomes, by means of a homœopathic dose of poison, a most formidable destroyer."

Another singular observation on these little filaments or arms we owe to Dujardin. This naturalist observed that, when a *miliola* attempted to climb up the walls or sides of a vase, it could improvise, as it were, on the instant, and, at the expense of its own substance, a provisional foot, which stretched itself out rapidly and performed all the functions of a permanent member. The occasion served, this temporary foot seemed once more to return to the common mass, and was absorbed into the body. It would thus appear that with these minute creatures the presence of a necessity gives the power to create an organ by the mere will of the creature, while man, with all his genius, cannot manufacture a hair. To the present day, however, we have not been able to discover any organ of nutrition in the Foraminifera; they have no stomach, properly so called, but Nature has gifted them with a peculiar tissue, at once gelatinous and contractile, and essentially simulative, which probably serves the same purpose.

We have already said that the shells of these minute zoophytes vary much in form. They are generally many-chambered, each chamber communicating by pores in the walls; the different gelatinous parts of the animalcules are, in this manner, placed in continual communication with each other. Alcide d'Orbigny, to whom we owe almost all that is known of the class, has distributed them into six families, making the form of the shell the basis of their arrangement. These six families include sixty genera, and more than sixteen hundred species, the families being as follows:—

I. Monostega.—Animals consisting of a single segment. Shell of a single chamber.

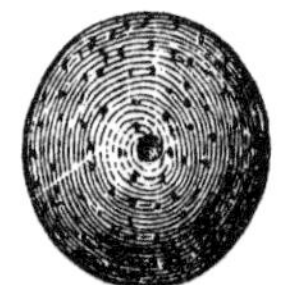

Fig. 12. Orbulina universa.

II. Stichostega.—Animal in segments, arranged in a single line.

Fig. 13. Dentalina communis.

Shell in chambers, superimposed linearly on a straight or curved axis.

III. Helicostega.—Animal in segments, spirally arranged. Chambers piled or superimposed on one axis, forming a spiral erection. In Fig. 19 we have a horizontal section of *Faujasina*, in which the spiral convolutions are visible on the truncated half of the shell.

Fig. 14. Operculina.

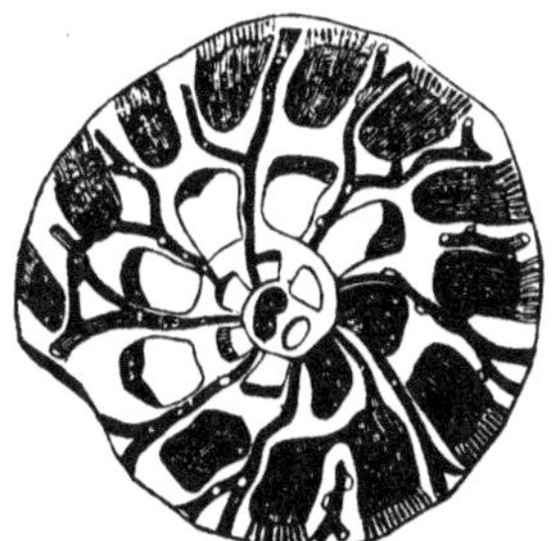
Fig. 19. Faujasina.

IV. Entomostega.—Animal composed of alternating segments forming a spiral. Chambers superimposed on two alternating axes, also forming a spiral.

Fig. 15. Nummulitis lenticularis.

Fig. 16. Cassidulina.

V. Enallostega.—Animal formed of alternate segments. Non-spiral

Fig. 17. Textilaria.

chambers disposed alternately along two or three axes, also non-spiral.

VI. Agathistega.—Animal formed of segments wound round an axis. Chambers formed round a common axis, each investing half the circumference.

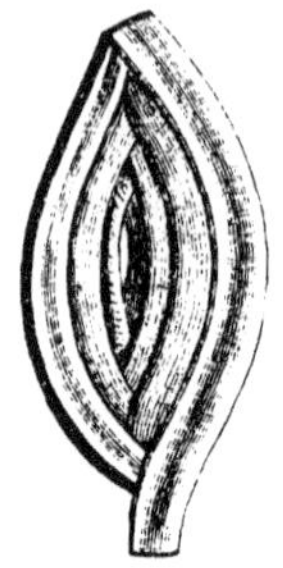

Fig. 18. Spiroloculina.

The simplest form of Foraminifera is illustrated by Fig. 12 (*Orbulina universa*), which is a small spherical shell, having a lateral aperture, the interior of which has been occupied by the living jelly, to which the shell owes its existence. In the second order, the shell (Fig. 13), *Dentalina communis*, advances beyond this simple type by a process of linear budding, the first cell being spherical, with an opening through which a second segment is formed, generally a little larger than the first. This new growth is successively followed by others developed in the same way, until the organism attains its maturity, when it exhibits a series of cells arranged end on end, in a slightly curved line.

In the next group the gemmation takes a spiral bias, producing the nautilus shape which misled the earlier naturalists. In some cases all the convolutions are visible, as in *Operculina* (Fig. 14). In others, the external convolute conceals those previously formed, as in *Nummulitis lenticularis* (Fig. 15), *Cassidulina* (Fig. 16), *Textilaria* (Fig. 17), and *Alveolina oblonga*, d'Orbigny (Fig. 23), the latter forming part of the eocene formation in the quartz and greystone rocks of the neighbourhood of Paris; one figure representing the shell entire, and the other a vertical section, while the small figure between represents it in its natural size.

In the fourth group the shell is spiral, with the chamber equilateral, with a larger and smaller side, the position being alternately reversed as the segments are multiplied, as in *Cassidulina* (Fig. 16). In the succeeding group the new segments are arranged alternately on opposite sides of the central line, as in *Textilaria* (Fig. 17), thus forming two alternating non-spiral parallel segments, each connected by a single orifice.

The sixth family differ entirely in appearance and structure from the other Foraminifera. They are more opaque than the other orders, having a resemblance to white porcelain, which presents a rich amber-brown hue when viewed by transmitted light. They are more or less oblong, each new segment being nearly equal to the entire length of the shell, so that the terminal orifice presents itself alternately at its opposite extremities, sometimes in one uniform plane, as in *Spiroloculina* (Fig. 18), and *Faujasina* (Fig. 19). At other times each new segment, instead of being exactly opposite each other, is a little on one side.

Professor Williamson has shown that the shell enclosing each new segment is at first very thin; but as additional calcareous chambers

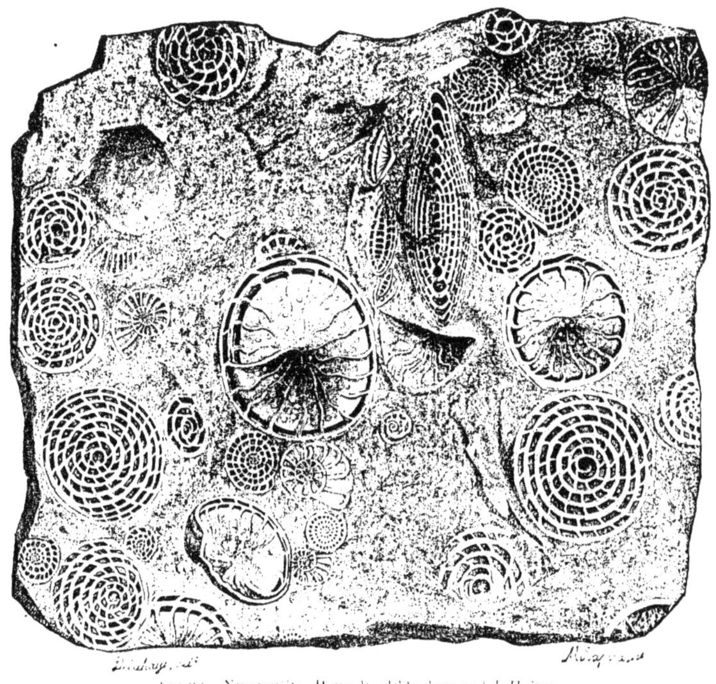

Fig. 20. Nummulites Ramondi (D'Archiac and J. Haime).

are formed, each addition not only encases the new gemmation of the soft animal, but extends over all the exterior of the previously formed shell. The exact manner in which this is accomplished is doubtful; but the Professor thinks it probable that the soft animal has the power of diffusing its substance over the shell, and thus depositing upon its surface additional layers of calcareous matter.

The fossil Foraminifera are chiefly distinguished from recent and existing species by the size of the former. While the living forms range from one-fourth to the one-hundredth part of an inch, the tertiary strata abound in examples of *Nummulites*, varying from the eighth of an inch to the size of half-a-crown. The engraving is a drawing from Nature, by MM. d'Archaic and Haime, of a piece of nummulitic rock, of Nousse, in the Landes, in which a great variety of sizes and forms are exhibited.

The Nummulina belong to the third family, or Helicostega, in which the outer convolutions completely embrace the earlier formed ones. Hence it is only by making microscopic sections, or thin slices, that their structure can be fully seen. When such a section is carried horizontally through the centre of the shell, the segments present a spiral arrangement, which, like the convolutions, are remarkable for their small size, and consequent great number.

With respect to the distribution of the Foraminifera according to geological periods, we may briefly state that they have been found in every formation from the Silurian to the Tertiary. The species, at first

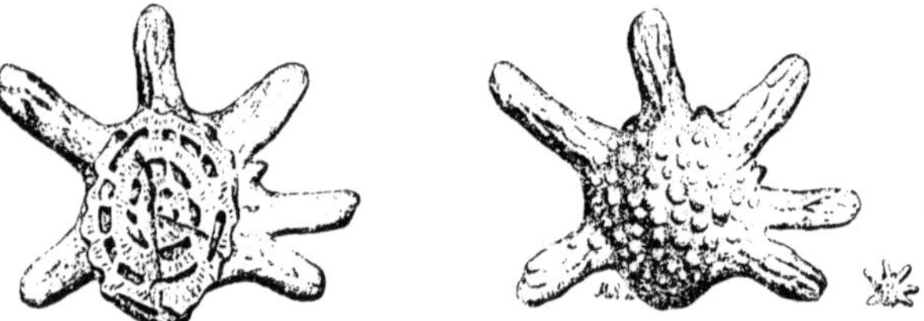

Fig. 21. Siderolites calcitrapoides (Lamarck).

very simple in their forms, begin to appear in increasing numbers in the carboniferous formations. They become more numerous, and, at the same time, more complex in their forms, in the Cretaceous period; they are still more diversified and appear to have multiplied much more rapidly in the Tertiary period, where they attain the maximum of their numerical development. In the celebrated quarries of St. Peter, at Maestrecht, the *Siderolites calcitrapoides* of Lamarck are found in the upper chalk (Fig. 21). In the calcareous formation of Chaussy, in the Seine and Oise district, and other parts of the Paris basin, the *Fabularia discolithes* (Fig. 22) of Defrance is found. Finally, the *Dactylopora cylindracea* of Lamarck (Fig. 24) is found in the eocene formation of Valmondois and in the chalk of Grignon. At first, this little creature was thought to be a polype; but d'Orbigny, in his "Prodrome de Paleontologie," has placed it among the Foraminifera, thinking that it appeared to occupy a place between the two classes.

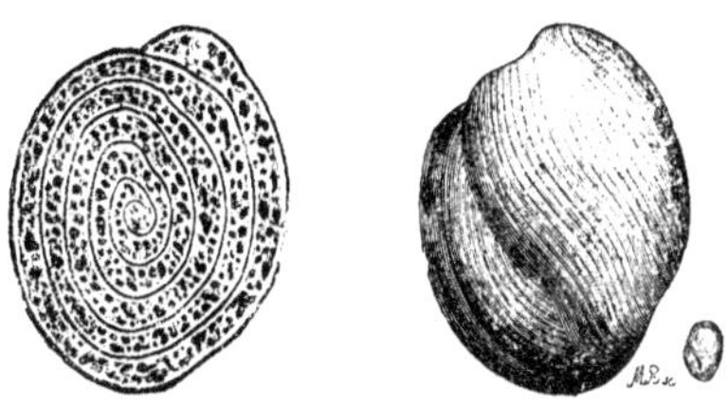

Fig. 22. Fabularia discolithes (Defrance).

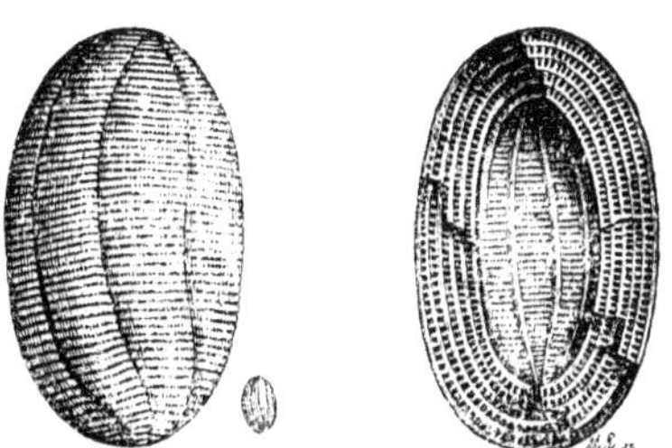

Fig. 23. Alveolina oblonga (d'Orbigny).

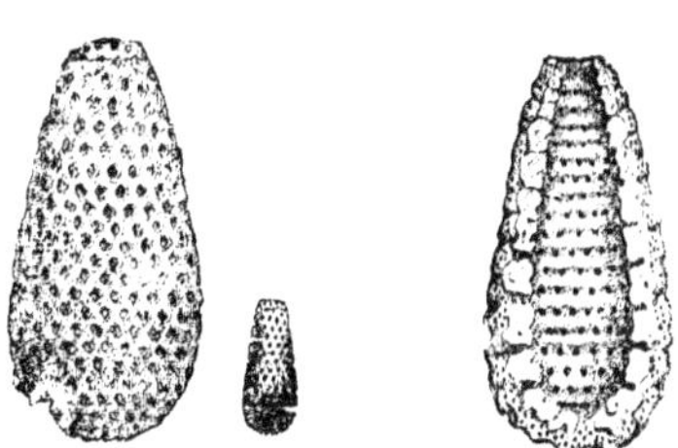

Fig. 24. Dactylopora cylindracea (Lamarck).

The existing Foraminifera are by no means equally distributed in every ocean. Some genera belong to warm countries, others to temperate and cold climates. They are much more numerous, however, and much more varied in their forms, in warm than in cold climates, and, we may add, larger also, for Sir E. Belcher brought a recent species from Borneo which measured two inches in diameter.

Before passing on to the study of the Infusoria, a few words may be offered on the *Noctiluca*, a genus of animals usually referred to the class Acalephæ. One species only of this genus has been described, which occurs occasionally on the English coast in prodigious numbers. It is a small creature, scarcely the hundredth part of an inch in diameter, according to Mr. Huxley (Fig. 25, *Noctiluca miliaris*). It was discovered by M. Surriray, in 1810, who describes it as a spherical gelatinous mass, scarcely bigger than a pin's head, with a long filiform tentacular appendage, a mouth, an œsophagus, one or many stomachs, and branching ovaries—thus exhibiting a certain complexity of organization. De Blainville took the same view, and placed it among the *Diphydæ*. Van Beneden and Doyère, on the other hand, deny its relation to the *Acalephæ*, conceiving its organization to be much more simple: they place it with the *Rhizopoda*. Quatrefages adopts the same view, denying the existence of a true mouth or intestinal canal: he considers the so-called stomachs as simple "vacuoles," similar to those observed in the Rhizopoda and Infusoria. Mr. Huxley, describing it in the "Journal of Microscopical Science" (vol. iii.), says it has nearly the form of a peach, a filiform tentacle, equal in length to the diameter of the body, occupying the place where the stalk of the peach might be, which depends

Fig. 25. Noctiluca miliaris.

from it, and exhibits slow wavy motions when the creature is in full activity. "I have even seen a *noctiluca*," he adds, "appear to push against obstacles with this tentacle."

"The body," he continues, "is composed of a structureless and somewhat dense external membrane, which is continued on to the tentacle. Beneath this is a layer of granules, or rather of gelatinous membrane, through whose substance minute granules are scattered without any very definite arrangement; from hence arises a net-work of very delicate fibrils, whose meshes are not more than one three-hundredth part of an inch in diameter, which gradually pass internally—the reticulation becoming more and more open—into coarser fibres, taking a convergent direction towards the stomach and nucleus. All these fibres and fibrils are covered with minute granules, which are usually larger towards the centre."

Mr. Huxley is inclined to think, from all he has observed, that the animal has a definite alimentary cavity, and that this cavity has an excretory aperture distinct from the mouth.

Surriray discovered the *noctiluca* while investigating the cause of phosphorescence of sea water at Havre, where it was abundant in the basins; sometimes in such abundance as to form a crust on the surface of the water of considerable thickness. "This singular little creature," says M. Frédol, "offers here and there in its interior certain granules, probably germs, and also luminous points, which appear and disappear with great rapidity—the least agitation determining their lustre." The *noctiluca* are so abundant in the Mediterranean and in some parts of the channel, that in a cubic foot of sea water, which has been rendered phosphorescent by their presence, it is calculated that there exist about twenty-five thousand.

Class Infusoria.

With the Infusoria we return to the domain of the infinitely little.

The waters, both fresh and salt, are inhabited by legions of active, ever-moving beings, of dimensions so small as to be inappreciable to the naked eye; these minute creatures are disseminated by millions and thousands of millions in the great deep, and all knowledge of them would have escaped us, as they escaped the knowledge of the ancients, but for the discovery of the microscope, the sixth sense of man, as it has been happily expressed by the historian and poet Michelet. Another writer of equally poetical mind, M. Frédol, tells us that "the infusorial animalcules are so small that a drop of water may contain them in many millions. They exist in all waters, the fresh as well as the salt, the cold as well as the hot. The great rivers are continually discharging them in vast quantities into the sea."

"The Ganges transports them in the course of one year in masses equal to six or eight times the size of the great pyramid of Egypt. Among these animalcules, according to Ehrenberg, we may reckon seventy-one different species.

"The water collected in vases between the Philippine and the Marianne Isles at the depth of twenty-two thousand feet (making some allowance for erroneous soundings), have yielded a hundred and sixteen species. Near the Poles, where beings of higher organization could not exist, the Infusoria are still met with in myriads; those which were observed in the Antarctic Seas, during the voyages of Captain Sir James Ross, offer a richness of organization, often accompanied by elegance of form, quite unknown in more northern regions. In the residuum of the blocks of ice floating about in latitude seventy-eight degrees ten minutes, nearly fifty different species were found. Many of them had ovaries, according to Ehrenberg, still green, which proved that they had struggled successfully with the rigours of the climate in searching for food.

At a depth in the sea which exceeds the height of the loftiest mountain, Humboldt asserts that each bed of water is animated by an innumerable phalanx of inhabitants imperceptible to the human eye. These microscopic creatures are, in short, the smallest and the most numerous creations in Nature. They constitute with human beings one of the wheels of that very complicated machine, the globe. They are in the rank and at the station willed for them, as determined in the great First Thought. Suppress these microscopic beings, and the world would be incomplete. It was said, and wisely said, long, long ago, "there is nothing so small to the view but that it may become great by reflection."

The Infusoria, in short, abound everywhere. We find their remains on the loftiest mountain ridges, and in the profoundest depths of the sea. They increase and multiply alike under the Equator, and towards the polar regions. The seas, rivers, ponds—the flower vase which rests upon the casement—even our tissues, and the fluids of our bodies—all contain infusorial animalcules. Whole beds of strata, often many feet thick, and covering a surface of considerable extent, are almost exclusively formed of their accumulated débris. It is to the Infusoria that the mud of the Nile and other fluviatile and lacustrine deposits owe its prodigious fertility. To them also is due the red or green layer of colouring matter found in ponds and tanks at certain seasons. When exposed to great solar heat, in order to extract the salt, as it is in the vast artificial basins, hollowed out for the purpose in the salt marshes near the sea shore in the south of France, the salt water, when it reaches a certain degree of concentration, acquires a fine rose colour, which is due to the presence of innumerable masses of small Infusoria having a reddish shell. Finally, let us add that the solid débris of certain fossil Infusoria, of surprising minuteness, have formed the stone so much used by workers in metal, which is known as *tripoli*.

The study of these creatures is intensely interesting to the naturalist, the philosopher, the physician, and the general reader. They have had a great part assigned to them in Nature, as is evident in the formation of certain beds of rock of immense extent, in which the geologist traces their action.

Our earliest knowledge of the Infusoria is traceable to the seventeenth century; to the celebrated naturalist, Leuwenhoek, we are indebted for their discovery. On the 24th of April, 1676, this observer saw for the first time some infusorial animalcules. Fifty years later, Baker and Trembley studied them anew. In 1752, Hill essayed the first attempt at their classification. In 1764, Wiesberg gave them the name of Infusoria, because he found them in such great abundance in animal and vegetable *infusions*. Müller published a special book upon them.

From that time the Infusoria have been considered as forming a special group among the radiate animals; afterwards, in the pages of Baer and of De Blainville, we see in these creatures, so imperfect in appearance, only the indeterminate prototype of other classes. But ideas changed altogether respecting them when microscopes of great power, and armed with achromatic lens, were employed in their study. Thanks to the labours of Ehrenberg and Dujardin, we have arrived at a better comprehension of the organization of these infinitely small beings. Naturalists have established, with more exactness, the limits of the zoological group to which they belong.

Some stagnant waters are so filled with Infusoria that it is only necessary to dip at random into the liquid medium to procure them in abundance. In other waters they form a bed, occupying the whole basin. In general, it is necessary to search for them where the water is calm, and occupied by vegetation of some kind, such as the *confervæ*, or *lemna*, &c., in the marshes, and *ceramium* if in the sea. Certain Infusoria live not only in water, but also in places habitually moist, as among tufts of mosses; in beds of *oscillaria*, on moist soil, or on air-damp walls. Others live as parasites on the exterior or in the interior of animals, such as *hydra*, *lombrics*, and *naïads*. Quantities of them are found in the liquid excrements and other products of certain organisms, and they have been noted even in women's milk.

But, as their name indicates, it is in aqueous infusions, vegetable or animal, that these animalcules abound. Armed with a microscope, the reader may, with very little trouble, afford himself the pleasure of studying these animals. It is only necessary to place some organic débris—the white of an egg, or some grass, for example—in a vase with a large mouth, filled with water, and expose it to the light and air. Certain reagents, as phosphate of soda, the phosphates, nitrates, or oxalates of ammonia, or carbonate of soda added to these infusions, will singularly favour the development of Infusoria.

There are also some accidental infusions which seem to furnish these microscopic beings in great abundance. Water which stagnates in garden soil or in vegetable mould, in the watering-cart or in flower vases, is filled with myriads of these beings.

So much for the medium in which they live, move, and have their being. Let us pass on to their organization. We have already dwelt on their extreme minuteness; their mean size is the mere fraction, a fifth of the twelfth part of an inch; the largest species scarcely reveal themselves to the naked eye. They are generally colourless; some of them are, nevertheless, green, blue, red, brown, and even blackish. Seen on the object-glass of the microscope, they appear to be gelatinous, transparent, and naked, or invested with an envelope more or less resistant, which we shall designate after Dujardin by the term *Sarcoda*, a substance which is homogeneous, diaphanous, elastic, contractile, and, above all, destitute of every kind of organization. They are usually ovoid or globular. Those most frequently met with, and which attract the most attention from observers, are furnished with *vibratile cilia*, which cover the whole body, acting as paddles. These organs are evidently intended to propel the animal from one place to another. At other times they appear to be employed in conveying food to the mouth, if we may use the expression. Some Infusoria are without these cells, having only one or many very slender filaments, the undulating movement of which suffices to determine their progression through the liquid which surrounds them.

Authors who have written on the Infusoria have sometimes, like Leuwenhoek, Ehrenberg, and Pouchet, attributed to them a very complex structure. Others, like Müller, Cuvier, and Lamarck, have considered them to be gifted with an organization extremely simple. We shall probably find that the truth lies between these two extremes.

In the superior Infusoria, besides the granules, the interior globules, vesicles full of liquid, vibratile cils, and a tegumentary system, more or less complex, we find the substance which is called *Sarcoda.*

The digestive apparatus of the Infusoria has been the subject of numerous observations, and has been provocative of very animated discussions. In the inferior order of the class, which comprehends the very smallest animalcules, it has not been found possible to observe the organization of the digestive apparatus in a satisfactory manner. Some writers think they have no mouth, what has been taken for that organ being only hollow dimples on the surface of the body; others recognise the existence of a buccal orifice, sometimes furnished with a solid armature. As to the arrangements of the interior cavities in which digestion takes place, we know nothing certain.

The digestive apparatus is better understood in the superior Infusoria, called *ciliate,* namely, those provided with *vibratile cils.* These cils seem to determine the currents of the liquid, leading the nutritive corpuscles suspended in the water towards the entrance of the digestive apparatus. They form, in some sort, the prehensile organs which seize the aliment. The cils are, at the same time, the organs intended to facilitate respiration; in short, these little whips playing upon the water unceasingly round the Infusoria, is just the action required for the absorption of the oxygen contained in the water. These cils, then, serve at once for the propulsion of the animal, for its nutrition, and for its respiration, presenting a remarkable example of cumulative functions in physiology.

The corpuscles of nutritive substances directed towards the buccal orifice by the vibratile cils soon disappear in the interior of the animal. Availing himself of this fact and the transparency of the animal, Herr Gleichen, a German physiologist of the last century, conceived the happy idea of colouring the water which contained these animalcules with a finely-powdered carmine; he traced the colouring matter in the bodies of some of them. But it was reserved for Ehrenberg to avail himself of the same artifice in order to study the internal structure and mode of absorbing nutritive matter in these minute creatures. This physiologist fed many groups of Infusoria, some of them with water coloured with carmine, others with indigo and other colouring matters. He saw, besides, some coloured globules, nearly uniform in size, in different individuals of the same species. From this he arrived at the conclusion that the colouring matter was deposited in many of the surrounding dimples. Ehrenberg thought that each of these dimples was a stomach, and that the introduction of the food into the interior of these reservoirs, as well as the evacuations, were produced by means of an intestine around which these stomachs are arranged. In some cases he even thought he could distinguish the outlines of this intestinal canal, and its connection with numbers of ampula or bladders. Generalizing the conclusions drawn from his observations, in short, we find that his class, Infusoria, embraced two very different forms of animal life, which he divided into *Infusoria*, *Polygastrica*, and *Rotifera*, the latter division including those known as Wheel animalcules; the *Polygastrica* being so called from his idea that the typical forms possessed a number of stomachs. In some, Ehrenberg counted four stomachs, an organization which brings these microscopic beings into a strange kind of comparison with the ox and the goat. In others he counted two stomachs.

Other observers were not slow in raising objections to these views. Dujardin, especially, was much opposed to the batch of stomachs attributed to these creatures by the German physiologist. He attempted to establish the fact that the coloured globules which appeared in the bodies of the Infusoria, while subjected to a regimen of carmine and indigo, are not confined by a membrane; that is to say, they are not contained in intestinal sacs. According to Milne Edwards, " they are a species of basins, constituted," he says, " by the alimentary matter with which each is gorged, united into a rounded pasty mass, where it could no longer be dispersed, but would continue to advance, still preserving its form. We have, in short, seen these spherules changing their places, and passing one another in their progress from the mouth to the intestinal canal. That they could not do this is evident, if many stomachs were attached to the intestinal canal!"

This opinion, due to the patient and precise studies of Dujardin, has been adopted by most naturalists of eminence. Besides, this learned microscopist does not admit that there was in the sarcodic mass of Infusoria any pre-existent cavity destined to receive the food. In a word, he does not recognise any stomach whatever. This view of the extreme simplicity of structure in the Infusoria has, however, met with much opposition. To accord them neither four nor two stomachs, it is not necessary to deprive them of the organ altogether.

Meyen represents them as having one great hollow stomach occupied by a pulpy matter, into which the alimentary masses are successively absorbed. "All recent observations," says Milne Edwards, "tend to establish the fact that the digestive apparatus of the ciliate Infusoria consists of—first, a mouth; second, of a pharyngeal canal, in which the food often assumes the form of a *bolus;* third, of one great stomach with distinct walls, and more or less distant from the common tegumentary membrane; fourth, of an excretory orifice."

This mouth presents sensible differences both as to its position and conformation, often occupying the bottom of a hollow, the edges of which are furnished with well-developed *cilia*, the action of which attracts the aliment; in short, the mouth is a sort of decoy at the bottom of a simple pit, being at once contractile and prehensile, the interior part being sometimes capable, according to Milne Edwards, of being turned inside out in the form of a trumpet, while in a great many species it is provided with a peculiar armature, consisting of a band of rigid bristles disposed in the form of a bow-net, and susceptible of dilation and contraction, according to the wants of the animal. The œsophagus, which is connected by means of the canal with the mouth, has generally an oblique direction backwards, often terminating in a great undivided stomach.

The reproduction of the Infusoria exhibits some very surprising phenomena, while it offers another proof of the wonderful means Nature employs for perpetuating the races of animals. They can be reproduced by three different processes: 1. By *gemmæ*, or budding, somewhat after the manner of plants. 2. By sexual reproduction; for in these little creatures it has recently been discovered that sexual differences exist. 3. By the spontaneous division of the animal into two individuals—a process known to zoologists as *fissiparism* or *fission.*

Among these three processes, that which appears best understood is the last. The singular phenomenon of spontaneous division may be witnessed by any one having patience to examine the creature long enough, isolated from its innumerable companions, under the microscope. The oblong body of the animal will soon be observed to contract at the middle, the compression becoming more and more marked. The lower segment soon begins to show a few vibratile cils, thus indicating the place which will soon be a new mouth; the organ soon becomes more and more distinct, and now the Infusoria literally cuts itself into two parts. We see, at first, the fragment of glutinous substance fluttering on the edge of the plate; the two halves then separate from each other very quickly, each moiety having finally a perfect resemblance to the primitive animal. This process is represented in Fig. 26, A and B being the adult, C the same in course of separation, D after its completion. Assuredly this is one of the most remarkable phenomena which the study of living beings can present. "By this mode of propagation," says Dujardin, "an infusoria is the half of the one which preceded it, the fourth of the parent of that, the eighth of its grand-parent, and so on, if we can apply the terms father or mother to animals which must see in its two halves, the grandfather

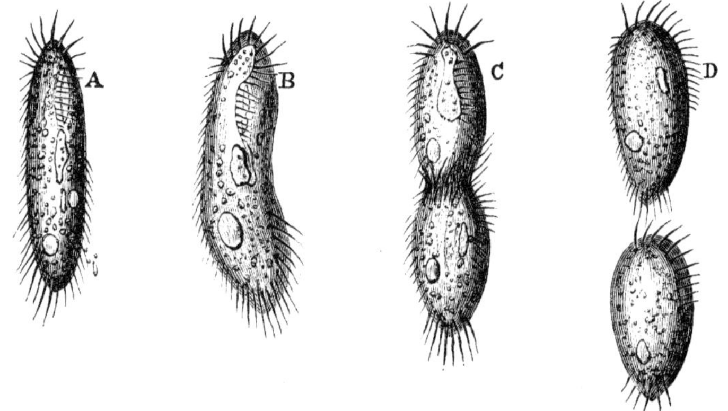

Fig. 26. Propagation of an Infusoria by spontaneous division.

himself by a new division again living in his four parts. We might imagine such an infusoria to be an aliquot part of one like it, which had lived years, and even ages before, and which by continued subdivision into pairs might continue to live for ever by its successive development."

This mode of generation, however, enables us to comprehend the miraculous fecundity of these beings. The process defies calculation, if we wished to be precise. We may, however, arrive at a proximate estimate of the number which may be derived from a single individual by this process of fission. It has been found that at the end of a month two *stylonichiæ* had a progeny of more than one million and forty-eight thousand individuals, and that in a lapse of forty-two days a single paramecium had produced more than one million three hundred and sixty-four thousand forms like itself.

Life is spread over Nature in such abundance that the smallest infusoria has its parasite a little smaller; these in their turn serving as "a dwelling and pasture ground," to use Humboldt's words, for still smaller animalcules, as represented in Fig. 27—*a* being parasites in various stages; *b*, the larger animalcule on which they have established themselves.

The prodigious number to which the calculation would reach, if we were to add the other modes of propagation, viz. by germs and by budding, we dare not mention: it would only be necessary to place a

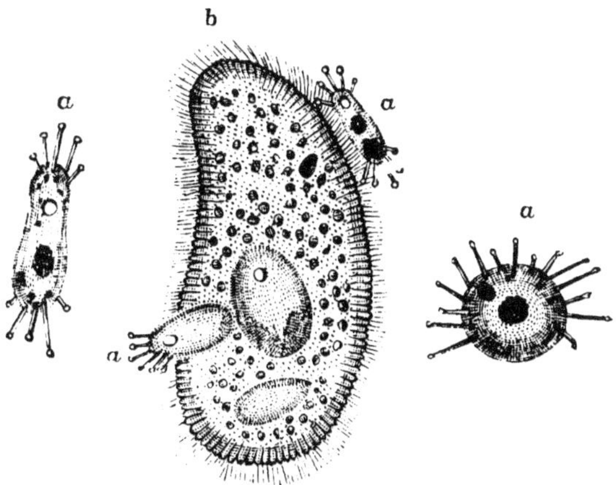

Fig. 27. Paramecium aurelia and its Parasites.

single germ in a favourable condition for its development, in order to produce myriads of these microscopic animalcules in a very few days.

We have seen three modes of reproduction in the Infusoria; it is possible that a fourth mode exists, to which its partisans give the name of *spontaneous generation*. According to their views, an infusoria can be produced without egg-germ or pre-existent parent. It would be sufficient to expose organic matter, animal or vegetable, to the action of the air and water at a suitable temperature, in order to see this matter organize itself, and form itself into living infusorial animals.

Such is the general enumeration of the question of spontaneous or *heterogeneous* generation, on which so much has been written in the last ten years. The great expounders of the doctrine have been the two French naturalists, MM. Pouchet and Joly. Their views have, however, made little progress; they have, on the contrary, met with vigorous opposition from the generality of French naturalists, and from most of the members of the Académie des Sciences of Paris, who have raised their voices against a doctrine which is contrary to the ordinary course of nature. In short, the direct observations made upon the theory of "primitive generation" are as yet wanting in necessary exactness; those observers who profess to have witnessed the sudden origin of the minutest of the infusoria from elementary substances have in all probability overlooked the organic structure of these elementary bodies. The wonderful changes of form undergone by many infusoria have their limits, and the laws governing them have still to be defined. With the poet we may say:

"Grammatici certant et adhuc sub judice lis est."

Many of the Infusoria are subject to metamorphoses, and it has already been ascertained that certain species which have been considered as distinct are only transition forms of the same species depending on age.

We know that it is common for insects to enclose themselves in protecting envelopes, and to remain for whole months shut up in this their retreat, to all appearance dead. Similar facts have been observed in the Infusoria. We have even seen some of these beings surrounding strange bodies as if in a mass of jelly, forming a sort of living envelope around them.

The average duration of life with them is only a few hours; but certain species present, in relation to the duration of life, phenomena which are only imperfectly known, but which never fail to excite the surprise and admiration of the naturalist. By drying certain infusoria with care, it is possible to suspend and indefinitely prolong its life. Thus dried, and covered with a powder, which shelters it from every breath of wind, it may be carried to any given distance, through any indefinite period of time—abandoned on some ledge of rock, on a housetop, in the cleft of a wall, or under the capital of a column; but let a drop of water approach it, and the dormant being awakes immediately—the microscopic Lazarus springs again into existence: feeds and multiplies as before: and its life, suspended possibly for years, resumes its interrupted course!

Into what a world of reflection does not a revelation of this mysterious property of a living creature plunge us!

The physiologist Müller has noted another peculiarity in infusorial life. These animalcules can lose a part of their bodies without being destroyed; the dead part disappears, and the individual, diminished by one-half, or reduced to a fourth of its former size, continues to live as if nothing had happened. Müller has observed a kalpode (*Kolpoda meleagris*) thus melt before his eyes until scarcely a sixteenth part of its body remained. After its loss, this sixteenth part of an animal continued to swim about without troubling itself as to its diminished proportions. "The infusoria," says Frédol in "La Monde de la Mer," "present yet another kind of decomposition. If we approach the drop of water in which it swims with the barb of a feather dipped in ammonia, the animalcule is arrested in its movement, but its cils continue to move rapidly. All at once, upon some point of its circumference, a notch is formed, which increases bit by bit until the whole animal is dissolved. If a drop of pure water is added, the decomposition is suddenly stopped, and what remains of the animalcule recommences its swimming movements." (Dujardin.)

We may divide the Infusoria into two orders—the *Ciliate Infusoria*, namely, those provided with vibratile cilia, and the *Flagelliferous Infusoria*, those, namely, which have arms or branches. The greater part of Infusoria belong to the first order, which comprehends many families; our space limits us to the mention here of a few typical forms only in each group, selecting those which appear the most interesting, from their size, structure, rarity, or abundance.

Flagelliferous Infusoria.

The family of *Vibrionidæ*, so named from their darting or quivering motion, includes the eel-like microscopic animalcules, which occur in stale paste, vinegar, &c., with some others, which are parasitic on living vegetables, such as *Vibrio tritici*, which infest the grains of wheat, producing the destructive disease called corn-cockle or purples. They are filiform animals, extremely slender, without appreciable organization, internal stomach, or apparent organs of locomotion. They are the first animalcules which show themselves in any infusion of organic matter. By using microscopes of the highest magnifying power, traces of very thin, short lines can be perceived, either straight or sinuous, the thickest of them not exceeding the thousandth part of the fraction of an inch. They are contractile, and propagated by spontaneous division, or *fission.* Among them some resemble right lines, more or less distinctly articulated, and endowed with a very slow movement; these are *Bacteridæ.* Others are flexuous and undulating, and more or less lively; these are true *Vibrions.* Others have the body fashioned in the form of a corkscrew, turning unceasingly upon themselves with great rapidity; these are the *Spirillidæ,* having an oblong fusiform or filiform body, which undulates or turns spirally upon itself.

The *Bacterium termo* (Fig. 28) is the smallest of the Infusoria. It is found, at the end of a short time, in all vegetable or animal infusions exposed to the air. It shows itself in infinite numbers, forming swarms of animalcules, which disappear as other species multiply in the liquid, to which animals it serves for nourishment. When the infusion becomes too fœtid for these new species to live in it, in consequence of fermentation or putrefaction, the *Bacterium termo* reappears. This species was one of the first observed; Leuwenhoek found it in the white matter in the teeth and gums, which is called teeth tartar. It is also found in the fluids of various animals which have been affected by disease.

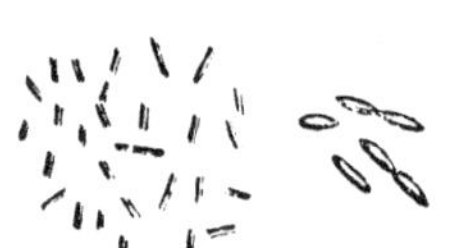

Fig. 28. Bacterium Termo (Müller), magnified 600 times. The same, magnified 1600 times.

The *Wand-like Vibrion* (Fig. 29) has the body transparent, filiform, with long articulations, often appearing as if broken at each connection. It moves very slowly in the water. Leuwenhoek observed this second species joined to the first in the teeth tartar, and also in a great number of organic infusions. "There is no microscopic object," says Dujardin, "which excites the admiration of the observer more vividly than the twisting spirillum (Fig. 30). He is struck with surprise when he first contemplates this little creature, which, under the greatest magnifying power, only presents the appearance of a thin black line, fashioned like a corkscrew, which

Fig. 29. Vibrion Baguette (Müller), magnified 300 times.

Fig. 30. Spirillum Tournoyant (Ehr.), magnified 300 times.

every instant turns upon itself with marvellous velocity, such as the eye can scarcely follow, or the mind divine the cause which produces this startling phenomenon.

The *Monads* are other infusorial animalcules which make an early appearance in vegetable infusions. They constitute a family that are destitute of any covering. The substance of their bodies can swallow itself, or draw itself out more or less; many of the flagelliform whip-like filaments serve as organs of locomotion. They are sometimes provided with lateral appendages disposed as a kind of tail. Their organization is extremely simple; their whip-like filaments are so fine as to be scarcely perceptible, their length being sometimes double and even quadruple the length of the animal itself.

The *Lentille Monad* (Fig. 31) is a species which is frequently met with in vegetable and animal infusions. The older microscopists had it indicated under the form of a globule, moving in a slow and vacillating manner. The globule is formed of a homogeneous transparent substance, swollen into tubercles on its surface, and throws out obliquely a whip-like filament, three, four, or even five times the length of the body of the Monad.

The *Cercomonad* of Davaine was discovered by this gentleman in the still warm dejections of cholera patients. Its body is pyriform, having, in front, a vibratile filament, very long, very flexible, and easily agitated. Behind the body there is a thicker straight filament attaching itself sometimes to neighbouring corpuscles, round which, in this case, the *Cercomonad* oscillates like the ball of a pendulum round its stem.

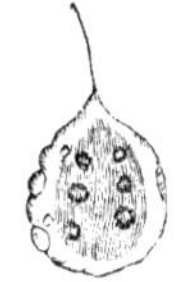

Fig. 31. Monade Lentille (Dujardin), magnified 1000 times.

The *Volvoxeæ* are inhabitants of fresh limpid water, full of confervæ and other aquatic plants. The *Volvoxeæ* are, according to Dujardin, animalcules of a green or yellowish brown colour, regularly disseminated in the thickness and near the surface of a gelatinous and transparent globe, which would become hollow and be filled with water in its perfect state. In this state, from five to eight smaller globules, with the same organization, appear destined to undergo the same changes when they are released by the rupture of the globule. These animalcules are each furnished with one or two flagelliform filaments, which, by their agitation, determine the movement by rotation of the mass.

The Revolving Volvox, *V. globator* (Figs. 32 and 33) is found in great abundance, during summer, in tanks and ponds of stagnant water. It consists of green or brownish-yellow globules about the eighth part of an inch, formed of animalcules scattered round a gelatinous and diaphanous spherical membrane, each furnished with a flagelliform filament and with a reddish interior point, which Ehrenberg took for an eye. Leuwenhoek first observed this Volvox in marshy waters. This eminent naturalist has left a very interesting account of his observations on these microscopic inhabitants of the waters, displaying an amount of patience and address which cannot be too much admired; his observations were made with a simple lens, which he constructed himself. In one hand he held his instrument, which was very coarse if we compare it to the more perfect and infinitely more powerful instruments now in use; whilst, in the other hand, he carried to his eye the glass tube full of water which contained the object under observation. "The microscopes of Leuwenhoek," says Dujardin, "were the very smallest bi-convex lens, mounted in a silver frame. He made a collection of twenty-six, which he bequeathed to the Royal Society of London. These instruments, subject to all the inconveniences of a maximum of spherical aberration and a total want of stability, were only fit for use in the hands of Leuwenhoek himself, who had acquired, in his labour of twenty years, habits of observation which compensated, in great part, for the want of perfection in his instruments."

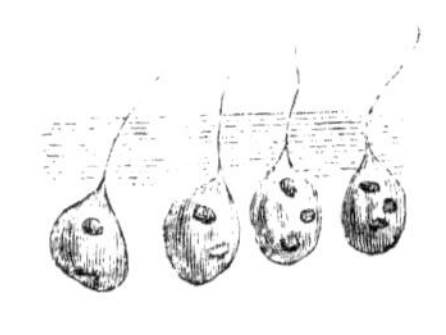

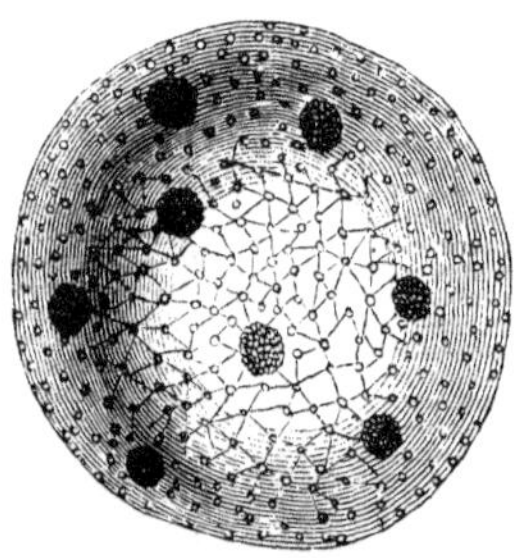

Figs. 32 and 33. Volvox Globator (Müller), magnified 700 times.

The *Euglenia* are infusoria usually coloured green or red. Their form is very variable. They are oblong or fusiform in shape, swelling at the middle during action, and contracted or bowl-shaped in repose, or after death. They are furnished with the usual whip-shaped filament, which issues from an opening in front, and from one or many reddish points irregularly placed anteriorly.

Euglenia viridis (Fig. 34) is the most common species, and, perhaps, the most widely diffused of all the Infusoria. It is this animalcule which habitually covers stagnant pools with its floating surface of green, and which forms, on the surface of marshy waters, the shining pellicle so strongly coloured, which, collected upon paper, so long preserves its brilliant tint.

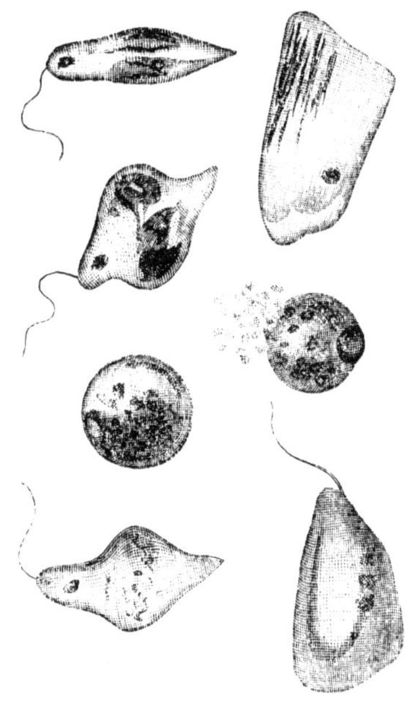

Fig. 34. Euglenia viridis (Ehr.), magnified 350 times.

The *Euglenia sanguinea*, at first green, becomes subsequently of a blood colour. It has often been met with by microscopists. Ehrenberg, who first described it, attributes to its great abundance the red colour of some stagnant waters. Its presence explains the pretended miracle of water changing into blood, which was frequently invoked by the Egyptian priests.

Ciliate Infusoria.

Let us now take a glance at some of the more remarkable species of Ciliate Infusoria. The bodies of these creatures are all more or less translucent. They have not substance enough, in fact, to reach a state of opacity. Their bodies are more or less globular or ovoid, sometimes fashioned like a shuttle, or curved while growing, sometimes swollen in the middle like an ampulla, or bell-shaped, and flattened into a discoid shape; some slightly resemble a tadpole, a thimble, a shoe, a rose-bud, a flower, even a seed.

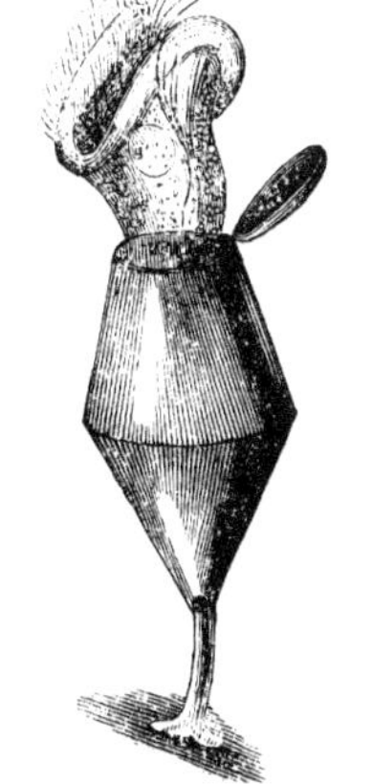

Fig. 35. Cothurnia pyxidiformis (Udekem).

The Paramecians have a soft flexible body, usually of oblong form, and more or less depressed. They are provided with a loose reticulated covering, through which issue numerous vibratile cils, arranged in a regular series.

They were known to the older naturalists, and it is in this group that organization is carried to the highest perfection it attains among the Infusoria. The Paramecium possess, besides their reticulated and contractile tegument, cilia disposed in such a manner as to serve at once for locomotion, for prehension, that is, for seizing its food, and as a means of respiration. They are furnished with a mouth, at the bottom of which the whorl excited by the cils, determines, according to Dujardin, the hollowing out of a cavity, formed after the manner of a cul-de-sac, and also the formation of *vacuoles* with permanent partitions, in which are enclosed the substances which the animalcules have swallowed along with the water.

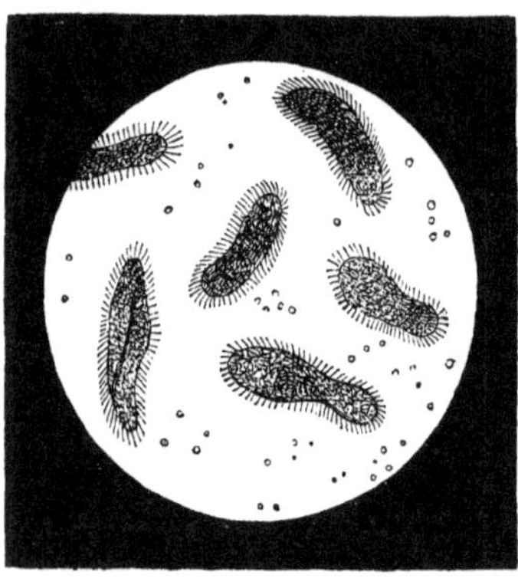

Fig. 36. Paramecium bursaria (Pritchard).

The Paramecium are propagated by spontaneous division, as already described. They abound, as we have said, in stagnant water, or in pure water which is occupied by aquatic plants, sometimes in such prodigious quantities that they become troublesome. They occur also in flower vases where the water is not frequently renewed.

The species of this genus have an oblong compressed body, with an oblique longitudinal fold, directed towards the mouth, which is lateral. They are sufficiently large to be observed by the common lens, or eye-glass. *Paramecium aurelia* appears chiefly in vegetable infusions. It is common in ditches and moats with aquatic plants.

Humboldt's assertion is fully verified in the case of the Infusoria under consideration, which is often found with its parasites. These are small creatures, cylindrical in form, and provided with suckers. Swimming vigorously in the water, they devote themselves to chasing the Paramecium. When they have overtaken the fugitive, they throw themselves upon it, and establish themselves there. They soon multiply in the interior of its body, and their starving progeny suck and devour the unfortunate animalcule, which serves them at once for dwelling-house and larder.

Another of the parasites which prey upon the Paramecium, in

place of pursuing it, remains perfectly quiet until one of these approach, when it throws itself upon its victim, and is carried along with it. It buries itself in the body of the Paramecium, and, in a short time, multiplies to such a degree, that sometimes fifty of them are found on a single individual. Poor victim!

The *Nassula* have the body entirely covered with cilia; they are ovoid or oblong in form, contractile, the mouth placed laterally and dentate, or surrounded with a band of horny bristles, the band dilating and contracting according to the size of the prey which it would swallow. It either advances to seize the prey, which the movement of vibratile cils have failed to draw within the vortex of its mouth, or, as in the case of the Paramecium, it is sometimes obliged to seek for its prey. These curious infusoria live in stagnant waters, feeding on the débris of aquatic plants, from which they draw their chief nourishment as well as their colour.

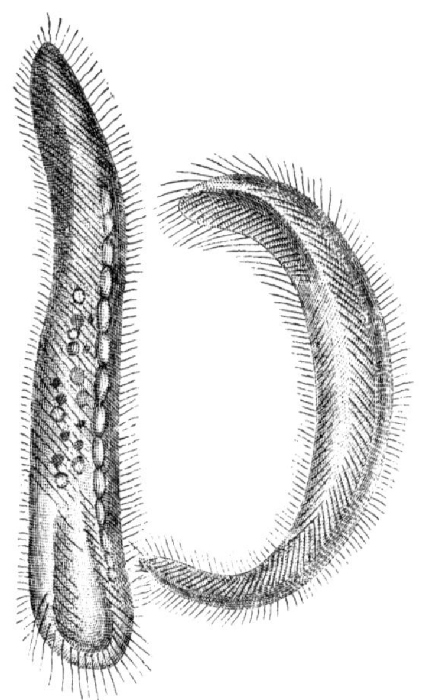

Fig. 37. Condylostoma patens (Duj.), magnified 350 times.

The *Bussarians* are animals with an oval or oblong contractile body, provided also with vibratile cils, especially on the surface, having also a large mouth, surrounded with cilia, forming a sort of moustache, spirally arranged.

Among the species belonging to this group may be noted the *Condylostoma patens* (Fig. 37), remarkable for its size and voracity. It sometimes attains the twelfth of an inch, and abounds on every shore from the Mediterranean to the Baltic. Another Bussarian, the *Plagiostoma* of the *Lombric*, lives between the intestines and the external muscular bed of the annelid, which bears the name of *Lombric*. To the group of *Urceolarians* belong the *Stentors*, which are in number the most numerous of the Infusoria; they are, for the most part, visible to the naked eye.

The *Stentors* are inhabitants of fresh, tranquil water, not subject to agitation, and covered with water plants. They are nearly all coloured green, blackish, or blue; their bodies covered with cilia. They are eminently contractile, and very variable in form. They can attach themselves temporarily, by means of the cils, at their posterior extremities, when they assume a trumpet-like form, the bell of which is closed by a convex membrane, the edge being furnished with a row of very strong obliquely-placed cils, ranged in a spiral, meeting at the mouth, which is placed near this edge. When they swim freely, they alternately resemble a club, a spindle, or a sphere. The *Stentor Mülleri* is seen in ponds in the neighbourhood of Paris and elsewhere; it has been found even in the basins of the Jardin des Plantes (Fig. 38).

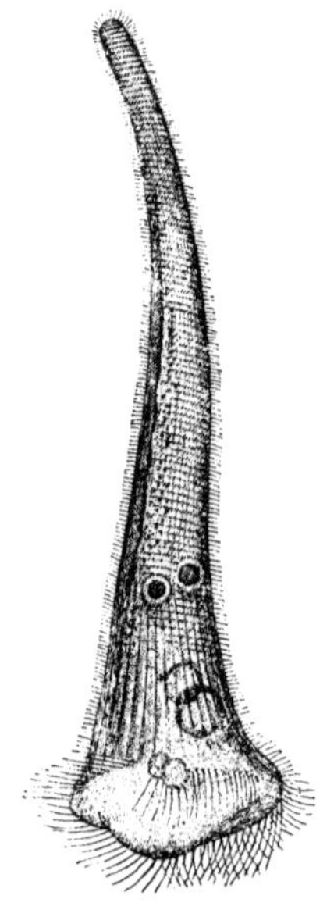

Fig. 38. Stentor Mülleri (Enr.), magnified 75 times.

The animals which constitute this genus are fixed in the first part of their existence, but free in the second. So long as they are fixed, they resemble, in their expanding state, a bell or funnel, with the edges reversed and ciliate. When they become free, they lose their crown of cils, take a cylindrical form, more or less ovoid and elongated, and move themselves by means of a new organ. "There is no animal," says Dujardin, "which excites our admiration in a higher degree than the Vorticellate Infusoria, by their crown of cils, and by the vortex which it produces; by their ever-varying forms; above all, by their *pedicle*, susceptible of rapid spiral contraction, by drawing the body backward and again extending it. This *pedicle* is a flat membranous band, thicker upon one of its edges than the other, and containing on the thicker side a continuous channel, occupied, at least in part, by a fleshy substance, analogous to that of the interior of the body. During contraction, this thick edge is shortened more than the thin side, and hence results the precise form of the spiral of the corkscrew.

CHAPTER V.

POLYPIFERA.

"Happy is he who, satisfied with his humble fortune, lives contentedly in the obscure state where God has placed him."—RACINE.

ENTERING on the class Polypifera, we leave the domain of the infinitely small to enter the world of the visible. Beside the Infusoria, the Polypifera, which are sometimes several inches in length, are very powerful beings. Science has made great advances in giving us an exact knowledge of these singular beings. Many scientific prejudices have been dissipated, many errors have been corrected. The Polypi, as they are defined in the actual state of Science, correspond not only with the *Polypes, properly so called*, of Cuvier and De Blainville, but also with the *acalephous zoophytes* of the same authors. We now know that certain Polypes engender *medusæ*, or acalephous zoophytes, and that there exist some medusæ scarcely differing in their structure and habits of life from the ordinary Polypes.

Thus regarded, the type of the Polypes comprehend a great variety of animals, the bodies of which are generally soft or gelatinous substances. The principal and smaller divisions, to the number of more than two, are arranged round an imaginary axis, represented by the central part of the body. These divisions of the body have in their ensemble the appearance of a regular cylinder, of a truncated cone, or of a disk. They are invested with a skin or envelope of calcareous or siliceous corpuscles, and even a portion of the deepest-lying tissues may be invaded by a calcareous deposit, the mass of which belongs sometimes to an individual; sometimes it is common to many, constituting what is called a Polypier; of which Professor Grant says, "there is but one life and one plan of development in the whole mass, and this depends, not on the Polypi, which are but secondary, and often deciduous parts, but on the general fleshy substance of the body;"* "the ramifications," says Dr. Johnston, "being disposed in a variety of elegant plant-like forms. The stem and branches are alike in texture: slender, horny, fistular, and almost always jointed at short and regular intervals, the joint being a mere break in the continuity of the sheath, without any character of a proper hinge, and formed by regular periodical interruptions in the growth of the polypidoms. Along the sides of these, or at their extremities, we find the denticles or cup-like cells of the polypes arranged in a determinate order, either sessile or elevated on a stalk." Near the base of each of these there is a partition or diaphragm, on which the body of the polype rests, with a plain or tubulous perforation in the centre, through which the connection between the individual polype and the common medullary pulp is retained. Besides the cells, there are found at certain seasons a larger sort of vesicle, readily distinguished from the others by their size, and the irregularity of their distribution, which are destined to contain and maturate the ovules.

With these animals the digestive tube is very simple, and presents only one distinct orifice; the same opening serving at once for receiving the food and the expulsion of the residuum of digestion. This is one of Dame Nature's economies, which it is not for us to dispute: we must record it without further remark.

In nearly all the Polypes the sexes are separate; the generation is sometimes sexual; but these beings multiply also by what the zoologists call gemmation, or buds. They are provided with organs of the senses; nearly all of them have eyes—an immense progress in organization as compared with the animals which have hitherto engaged our attention. Their respiration is effected by the skin—another instance of the economy of Nature. The apparatus of their circulation is indistinct, but they have a nourishing fluid analogous to the blood in vertebrated animals. Vibratile cells and stinging hairs often cover the entire surface of the Polypi.

These general remarks may appear obscure and insufficient to the larger number of our readers. They are necessarily so; they are generalities upon animals very little known, even to naturalists. We

* "Outlines of Comparative Anatomy."

quit this difficult ground, trusting to make the special study of the several types we shall have to describe more interesting. The group of Polypes divide themselves into many classes, namely, the *Sponges*, the *Alcyonidæ*, the *Zoantharia*, the *Discophora*, and *Ctenophora*. It will be our task to describe in succession the habits and characters of each of these classes, dwelling on such species as appear to us to offer to the reader most real interest.

SPONGIA.

The Sponge is a natural production, which has been known from times of the highest antiquity. Aristotle, Pliny, and all other writers who occupied themselves with natural history in ancient times, are agreed in according to it a sensitive life. They recognise the curious fact that the sponge evades the hand which tries to seize it, and clings to the rocks on which it is rooted, as if it would resist the efforts made to detach it. Pliny, Dioscorides, and their commentators, even formed the idea that sponges were capable of feeling, that they adhered to their native rock by special force, and that they shrunk from the hand which tried to seize them. They even distinguished males from females. Erasmus, however, criticising Pliny, concludes that he may pass over all he has written upon the sponge. The sponge, in short, was to the ancients something between a plant and an animal.

Rondelet, the friend of the celebrated Rabelais, whom the merry curate of Meudon designated under the name of *Rondibilis*, who was himself a physician and naturalist of Montpellier, denied at first the existence of sensibility in sponges. He originated the idea that these productions belonged to the vegetable world—an idea which Tournefort, Gaspard Bauhin, Rey, and even Linnæus, in the first editions of his "Systema Naturæ," supported by the great authority of their names. Afterwards, influenced by the convincing labours of Trembley and some other observers, Linnæus withdrew the sponges from the vegetable world. He satisfied himself, in short, that certain polypiers much resembled sponges in the nature of their parenchyma, and that, on the other hand, the assimilation of sponges with plants was not such as could be maintained. Neuremberg, Peyssonnel, and Trembley maintain the animal nature of sponges, and their views are adopted by Linnæus, Guettard, Donati, Lamouroux, and Ehrenberg, on the Continent, and by Ellis, Fleming, and Grant in England. They live at the bottom of the seas in five to twenty-five fathoms of water, among the clefts and crevices of the rocks, always adhering and attaching themselves, not only to inorganic bodies, but even growing on vegetables and animals, spreading, erect, or pendent, according to the body which supports them and their natural habit.

The power of fixing themselves to other objects, which certain animals possess, is very singular. Nevertheless, it is certain that whole tribes exist consisting of innumerable strictly adherent species, which live and die attached to some rock or other object; and among these are all polypiers, such as the sponges and corallines. It follows that they are wholly dependent on external agencies for their means of existence. "The poor little creatures," says Alfred Frédol, "receive their nourishment from the wave which washes past them; they inhale and respire the bitter water all their lives; they are insensible to that which is only the hundredth part of an inch from their mouth."

In the months of April and May, these animalcules engender germs, round, yellow, or white, whence proceed certain ovoid granular embryos furnished towards their largest extremity with small vibratile cils. They are thrown off by the currents, which serve as a stomach, and form swarms of larvæ round the polypier. They swim about with a gliding wavy motion, and when they have been some time in the water they usually come to the surface; but they are also often carried off by the current. During two or three days they seem to seek a convenient place to fix themselves. Once fixed, the larvæ loses the cilia, spreads itself out, and takes the form of a flattened gelatinous disk.

Its interior organization consists of contractile cellules and numerous spiculæ—"a tribe," says Gosse, "of the most debateable forms of life, long denied a right to stand in the animal ranks at all, and even still admitted there doubtingly and grudgingly by some excellent naturalists. Yet such they certainly are, established beyond reasonable controversy as true and proper examples of animal life."

It may, then, be safely asserted that all naturalists are now satisfied of the animal nature of sponges, although they represent the lowest and most obscure grade of animal existence, and that so close to the confines of the vegetable world, that it is difficult in some species to determine whether they are on the one side or the other. "Several of them, however," says Mr. Gosse, "if viewed with a lens under water while in a living state, display vigorous currents constantly pouring forth from certain orifices; and we necessarily infer that the water thus ejected must be constantly taken in through some other channel. On tearing the mass open, we see that the whole substance is perforated in all directions by irregular canals, leading into each other, of which some are slender, and communicate with the surface by minute but numerous pores, and others are wide, and open by ample orifices; through the former the water is admitted, through the latter it is ejected." It is not to be denied, however, that these beings constitute, in spite of investigations of modern naturalists, a group still somewhat problematical, and still very imperfectly known as regards their internal organization.

Sponges are masses of a light elastic tissue, which is, at the same time, resistant, full of air cils, and with much varied exterior arrangements. Nearly three hundred species are known, the different appearances of which have been characterised by names more or less singular. There is, for instance, the Feather Sponge, the Fan Sponge, the Bell, the Lyre, the Trumpet, the Distaff, the Peacock Tail, and Neptune's Glove.

There are river sponges and sea sponges.

The first are irregular and arenaceous masses, which pile themselves upon plants and solid bodies immerged in fresh water. Such are the *spongilles*, upon which anatomic and embryonic observations have very frequently been made in relation to the group more immediately under consideration.

The second is found in almost every sea; especially are they found in the Mediterranean, the Red Sea, and the Mexican Gulf. Affecting warm and quiet waters, they attach themselves to bold and rugged rocks at depths ranging from five to twenty-five fathoms. They are erect, pendent, or spreading, according to their form or position. Fig. 39, drawn from Nature, represents a very remarkable form of sponge, which was fished up in sixty fathoms.

The sponge is very common in the Mediterranean and round the Grecian Archipelago, and is known vulgarly under the name of the Marine Mushroom, the Sailor's Nest, and the fine soft sponge of Syria. It is a mass more or less rounded, covered with a mucous bed, glutinous above, formed of a light elastic but resisting tissue full of gaps, and riddled with air-cells. This tissue is formed of delicate flexible fibres, uniting in all directions by anastomose, but presenting numerous pores, which are formed by what is termed osculation, having irregular *conduits*

Fig. 39. Spongia, half the natural size, attached to its rocky bed.

which connect them. In this tissue certain very small solid bodies are discovered, named *spiculæ*. The *spiculæ* are siliceous or calcareous in their nature, varying according to the species, and sometimes varying even in the same species. Some of these resemble needles, others are pin-like, and others again resemble very small stars.

The physiological function of those tubes and orifices which present themselves on all parts of the sponge, has been interpreted in various ways. Ellis, writing in 1765, supposes that they were the orifices of the cells occupied by the polypi. In 1816, Lamarck still advocated this opinion; and even now we find the observer, whose notes M. Frédol has edited with so much judgment, asserting that "the inhabitants of the sponge are a species of fleeting, transparent, gelatinous tube, susceptible of extension and contraction; young polypes, as we may call them, without consistence, without gills; incipient polypes, in short, of very simple but sufficient organization. The animalcule of the sponge is a stomach, without arms, very simple, very elementary—in short, an animal all stomach!"

This mode of considering the sponge is not conformable to the views of the leaders of modern science, however. Mr. Milne Edwards, for instance, in place of seeing in the sponge a collection of united beings, forming as it were a colony, considers each to be an isolated being, an unique individual. The innumerable canals by which the sponge is traversed, according to that author, are at once the digestive organs and breathing pores of the zoophyte. The vibratile cils are necessary to the renewed aeration of the water required as a respiratory fluid in the interior canals of the sponge. The currents in these channels have one constant direction. The water penetrates the sponge by numerous orifices of minute dimensions and irregular disposition; it traverses channels in the body of the zoophyte, which reunite somewhat like the root of a plant, in order to constitute the trunk and increase its substance; finally, the water makes its escape by special openings. According to this view, the channels of the sponge have a kind of cumulative physiology, performing the two functions of digestion and respiration. The rapid currents of aerated water which traverse them lead into them the substances necessary to the nourishment of these strange creatures, rejecting all excrementory matter. At the same time, the walls of these canals present a large absorbing surface which separates the oxygen with which the water is charged, and disengages the carbonic acid which results from respiration.

Sponges contain true eggs, from which embryo animalcules are produced; these are non-ciliate at first. In the interior of these eggs the contractile cellules have their birth; then the spiculæ; and when they are finally covered with the vibratile cils, aided by them these larvæ of ovoid form swim, or rather glide, through the water. The species of infusoria born of the sponge resemble the larvæ of various polypes at the moment they issue from the egg. "They soon attach themselves to some foreign body," says Mr. Milne Edwards, "and become henceforth immovable; no longer giving signs either of sensibility or of contractability, while in their enlargement they are completely transformed. The gelatinous substance of their bodies is channeled and riddled with holes—the fibrous framework is completed—the sponge is formed."

We may add, however, that other zoologists, and among them MM. Paul Gervais and Van Beneden, take a different view of the development of the sponges, and Dr. Johnston omits them altogether from his great work on "British Zoophytes." "If they are not the production of polypi," he says, "the zoologist who retains them in his province must contend that they are individually animals, an opinion to which I cannot assent, seeing that they have no animal structure or individual organs, and exhibit not one function usually supposed to be characteristic of the animal kingdom." Gervais and Van Beneden consider, as Milne Edwards does, that the embryos are at first movable, then fixed, many of them uniting together, and melting, as it were, into one common colony, which become a sponge, such as we see it. An isolated embryo might also, by throwing out germs, produce a similar colony, which would thus become a product of agamous generation. Thus it appears that Science is far from being settled in its views as to the organization and development of these obscure and complex formations; nor is it more advanced in its knowledge of the duration of life and the quickness of growth in sponges. It is agreed, however, on one point—namely, that the sponge-fisher may return to the same fishing-ground after three years from the last fishing. At the present time sponge-fishing takes place principally in the Grecian Archipelago and the Syrian littoral. The Greeks and Syrians sell the product of their fishing to the Western nations, and the trade has been immensely extended in recent times, when the sponge has become an almost necessary adjunct of the toilet as well as the stable, and in other cleansing operations.

Fishing usually commences towards the beginning of June on the coast of Syria, and finishes at the end of October. But the months

Plate II.—Sponge Fishing on the Coast of Syria.

of July and August are peculiarly favourable to the sponge harvest, if we may use the term. Latakia furnishes about ten boats to the fishery, Batroun twenty, Tripoli twenty-five to thirty, Kalki fifty, Simi about a hundred and seventy to a hundred and eighty, and Kalminos more than two hundred. The operations of one of these boats fishing for sponges on the Syrian coast is represented in Pl. I.

The boat's crew consists of four or five men, who scatter themselves along the coast for two or three miles in search of sponges under the cliffs and ledges of rock. Sponges of inferior quality are gathered in shallow waters. The finer kinds are found only at a depth of from twelve to twenty fathoms. The first are fished for with three-tined toothed harpoons, by the aid of which they are torn from their native rock; but not without deteriorating them more or less. The finer kinds of sponges, on the other hand, are collected by divers aided by a knife; they are carefully detached. Thus the price of a sponge, brought up by diving, is much more considerable than that of a harpooned sponge. Among divers, those of Kalminos and of Psara are particularly renowned. They will descend to the depth of twenty-five fathoms, remain down a shorter time than the Syrian divers, and yet bring up a more abundant harvest. The fishing of the Archipelago furnishes few fine sponges to commerce, but a great quantity of very common ones. The Syrian fisheries furnish many of the finer kinds, which find a ready market in France; they are of medium size. On the other hand, those which are furnished from the Barbary coast are of great dimensions, of a very fine tissue, and much sought for in England. On the Bahama banks, and in the Gulf of Mexico, the sponges grow in water of small depth. The fishermen, Spanish, American, and English, sink a long mast or perch into the water moored near the boat, down which they drop upon the sponges; by this means they are easily gathered.

In the Red Sea, the Arabs fish for sponges by diving, their produce being either sold to the English at Aden or sent to Egypt. Sponge-fishing is carried on at various other stations in the Mediterranean, but without any intelligent direction, and in consequence it is effected without any conservative foresight. At the same time, however, the trade in this product goes on increasing. But it is only a question of time when the trade shall cease; the demand which every year clears the submarine fields of these zoophytes cause

I 2

such destruction that their reproduction will soon cease to be equal to the demand.

In order to prevent this troublesome result, it is very desirable that the several species of sponges should be naturalized on the French and Algerian coast, and the cultivation and reproduction of the zoophyte protected. For this purpose, the rocky coasts of the Mediterranean, from Cape Cruz to Nice, and round the islands of Corsica and Hyères, in the Algerian waters, and even in some of the salt lakes of the departments near the Mediterranean, might be utilized. The whole of the Italian littoral would also be available under the new régime for this purpose.

M. Lamiral considered that the composition of the water of the Mediterranean being thought the same on the coasts of France, of Algeria, and on the Syrian coast, that the difference of temperature between the two latitudes—especially at the depth where the sponges flourish most—would not interfere with the existence of these robust zoophytes, and that their acclimatization on the coasts of France and Algeria would be a certain success. He remarked, moreover, that the more the sponges advanced towards the north, the finer and compacter their tissues became; and he argued from this fact, that a considerable improvement in the quality would result from the experiment.

The only difficulty, then, would consist in the transplanting sponges from Syrian waters to the coasts of France and Algeria. A submarine boat, such as M. Lamiral makes use of for operations conducted in deep water, would, according to this naturalist, give every facility for collecting sponges for the purpose. This boat can descend to great depths, and its crew can dwell there a considerable time, for it is continually fed with fresh air from above, which is conveyed by an air-pump and tube into the interior of the boat, so that the men could readily select such individuals as were suited for acclimatizing; removing the blocks of rock along with them, either by placing them in cases pierced with holes, or by towing them to their new abode. Everything seems to promise that in the following year the zoophytes would begin to multiply in their new country.

The larvæ might also be collected in the months of April and May, as they separate from the parent sponge, and be transplanted to favourable localities. At the end of three years, when these true submarine fields would be ripe for harvesting, they could be put in train for methodical collection by means of diving boats.

The toilet sponge is an article which produces a high price, often as much as forty shillings the pound for very choice specimens, a price which few commercial products attain, which prohibits its use, in short, to all but the wealthy. It is, therefore, very desirable to carry out the submarine enterprise of M. Lamiral. With the assistance of the Acclimatization Society of Paris, some experiments have already been made in this direction—so far without any satisfactory results, it is true, but everything indicates that by perseverance we shall see the enterprise crowned by the success it merits.

Such specimens as now reach our ports are chiefly distinguished by their appearance, quality, and origin.

The fine soft Syrian sponge is distinguished by its lightness, its fine flaxen colour, its form, which is that of a cup, its surface convex, voluted, pierced with innumerable small orifices, the concave part of which presents canals of much greater diameter, which are prolonged to the exterior surface in such a manner that the summit is nearly always pierced throughout in many places. This sponge is sometimes blanched by the aid of caustic substances, acids, or alkalies; but this preparation shortens its duration and changes its colour. This sponge is specially employed for the toilet, and its price is high. Those which are round-shaped, large, and soft, sometimes produce as much as five or six pounds.

The *Fine Sponge of the Archipelago* is scarcely distinguishable from that of Syria, either before or after being cleansed; nevertheless, it is weightier, its texture is not so fine, and the holes with which it is pierced are at once larger and less in number. It is nearly of the same country as the former, in fact, the fishing extending along the Syrian coast as well as the littoral of Barbary and the Archipelago.

The *Fine Hard Sponge*, called Greek, is less sought for than either of the preceding; it is useful for domestic and for certain industrial purposes. Its mass is irregular, its colour fauve; it is hard and compact, and pierced with small holes.

The *White Sponge of Syria*, called Venetian, is esteemed for its lightness, the regularity of its form, and its solidity. In its rough state it is brown in colour, of a fine texture, compact and firm. Purified, it becomes flaxen and of a looser texture. The orifice of the great channels which traverse it are edged with rough and bristly hairs.

The *Brown Barbary Sponge*, called the Marseileise, when first taken out of the water, presents itself as an elongated flattened body, gelatinous, round in shape, and charged with blackish mud. It is then hard, heavy, coarse, but compact, and of a reddish colour. By a simple washing in water it becomes round, still remaining heavy and reddish. It presents many gaps, the intervals of which are occupied by a sinuous and tenacious net-work. It is valuable for domestic use, because of the facility with which it absorbs water, and its great strength.

Other sorts of sponges are very abundant: The *Blonde Sponge* of

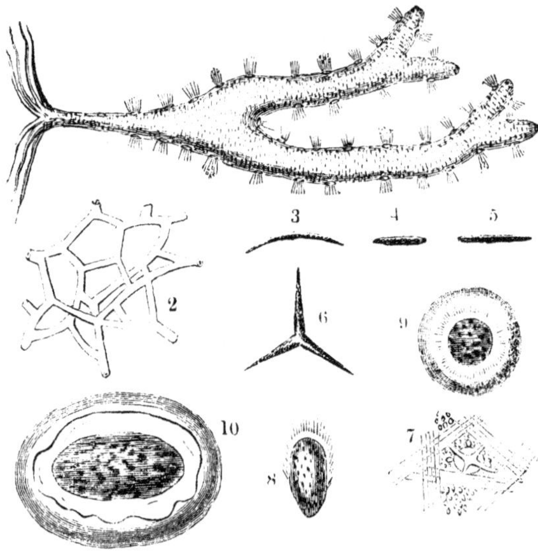

(From Dr. Grant.)

Fig. 40. *Spongia oculata*, showing the orifices and currents outwards. 2. Anastomosing horny substance of *Spongia communis*. 3. Siliceous spiculum of *S. papillaris*. 4. Of *S. cineria*. 5. *S. panicea*. 6. Calcareous spiculum of *S. compressa*. 7. Transverse section of a canal of *S. papillaris*, showing the structure of the ova passing along the canal. 8. Ovum of *S. panicea* seen laterally—the ciliæ anterior. 9. The same seen on the end, with a circle produced by the ciliary action. 10. Young *Spongia papillaris*.

the Archipelago, often confounded with the Venetian; the *Hard Barbary Sponge*, called Gelina, which only comes by accident into France; the *Salonica Sponge* is of middling quality; finally, the *Bahama Sponge*, from the Antilles, is wanting in flexibility and a little hard, and is sold at a low price, having few useful properties to recommend it.

Many species of *Spongia* are described as inhabiting British seas, but none of any commercial value. Regarding them as apolypiferous zoophytes, Dr. Grant has pointed out certain principles of analysis on which they may be grouped, according to the arrangement of the horny fibres, the calcareous and siliceous spiculæ, and the distribution and formation of their pores and orifices.

I. Groups of which the Constituent Structure is known.

Spongia.—Mass soft, elastic, more or less irregular in shape, very porous, traversed by many tortuous canals, which terminate at the surface in distinct orifices. Substance of the skeleton cartilaginous, fibres anastomosed in all directions, without any earthy spicula.—Example, *S. communis* (Fig. 40 [2]).

Calcispongia (Blainville).—Mass rigid or slightly elastic, of irregular form, porous, traversed by irregular canals, which terminate on the surface in distinct orifices; skeleton cartilaginous, fibres strengthened by calcareous spicula, often tri-radiate.—Example, *S. compressa* (Fig. 40 [6]).

Halispongia (Blainville).—Mass more or less rigid or friable, irregular, porous, traversed by tortuous irregular canals, which terminate at the surface in distinct orifices; substance cartilaginous, fibres strengthened by siliceous spicula, generally fusiform or cylindrical.—Example, *S. papillaris* (Grant) (Fig. 40 [3]).

Spongilla (Lamarck).—Mass more or less rigid or friable, irregular, porous, but not furnished with regular orifices or internal canals.—Example, *S. fluviatalis* (Linn.).

II. Groups depending on Characters of Surface or General Figure.

Geodia (Lamarck).—Fleshy mass, tuberous, irregular, hollow within, externally incrusted by a porous envelope, which bears a series of orifices in a small tubercular space.—Example, *G. gibberosa* (Schmeiger).

Cœloptychium (Goldfuss).—Mass fixed, pedicled, the upper part expanded, agariciform, concave, and radiato-porose above, flat and radiato-sulcate below; substance fibrous.—Example, *C. agarisidioideum* (Goldfuss). Fossils from the chalk of Westphalia.

Siphonia (Parkinson).—Mass polymorphous, free or fixed, ramose or simple, concave or fistulous above, porous at the surface, and penetrated by anastomosing canals, which terminate in sub-radiating orifices within the cup.

Myrmecium (Goldfuss).—Mass sub-globular, sessile, of a close fibrous texture, forming ramified canals which radiate from the base to the circumference. Summit with a central pit.

Scyphia (Oken).—Mass cylindrical, simple, or branched, fistulous, ending in a large rounded pit, and composed entirely of a reticulated tissue.

Eudea (Lamouroux).—Mass filiform, attenuated, sub-pedicellate at one end, enlarged and rounded at the other, with a large terminal pit; surface reticulated by irregular lacunæ, minutely porous.

Halirrhoa (Lamouroux).—Mass turbinated, nearly regular, circular, or lobate; surface porous; a large central pit on the upper face.

Happalimus (Lamouroux).—Mass fungiform, pedicellate below, expanding conically, with a central pit above; surface porous and irregularly excavated.

Cnemidium (Goldfuss).—Mass turbinate, sessile, composed of close fibres and horizontal canals, diverging from the centre to the circumference; a central pit on the upper surface, cariose in the exterior and radiate at the margin.

Ierea (Lamouroux).—Mass ovoid, sub-pedicellate, finely porous; pierced on the upper part by many orifices, the terminations of the internal tubes.

Tethium (Lamarck).—Mass sub-globose, tuberose, composed of a cariose firm substance, strengthened by abundance of siliciary spicula, fasciculated, and diverging from the centre to the circumference.

CHAPTER VI.

CORALLINES.

"As for your pretty little seed-cups or vases, they are a sweet confirmation of the pleasure Nature seems to take in superadding elegance of form to most of her works. How poor and bungling are all the imitations of art! When I have the pleasure of seeing you next, we shall sit down—nay, kneel down—and admire these things."—HOGARTH TO ELLIS.

THE Alcyonaria are so designated from their principal type, that of the Alcyons. The fresh-water species are composed of a fleshy, sponge-like mass, consisting of vertical, aggregated, membranaceous tubes, which are open on the surface. In these tubes the polypes, which are Isidians, are located. The mouth is encircled with a single series of filiform tentacula, which, like those of the whole family, are depressed or incomplete on one side. The eggs are contained in the tubes, and are coriaceous and smooth. The tentacula of these polypes are generally eight, disposed somewhat like the barbs of a feather, and toothed on their edges like a saw, which has procured them the name of *Ctenoceros*, from the Greek word χτεις, a comb. Their bodies present eight perigastric lamellæ; their polypier is often formed of spiculæ. We shall see, farther on, that among the Gorgonidæ the polypier ceases to be parenchymous—that is, spongy and cellular; that its axis assumes a horny and resistant consistence, which becomes stony in the corallines. In this last group, the external bed, which is the special lodging of the polypi, always remains soft on the surface. We shall have a general idea of the organization, manners, and mode of multiplication among the Alcyonaria when we come to treat of corals and their strange history. The class Alcyonaria is divided into many orders. We shall consider—I. The *Tubiporinæ*. II. The *Gorgonidæ*. III. The *Pennatulidæ*. IV. The *Alcyonaria*, properly so called.

I. THE TUBIPORINÆ.

form a group consisting of several species, which live in the bosom of tropical seas, in which the Coral Islands form so prominent a feature. The group is exclusively formed of the curious genus *Tubipora*.

The *Tubipora* is a calcareous polypier, formed by a combination of distinct, regularly-arranged tubes, connected together at regulated distances by lamellar expansion of the same material. The aggregate formation resulting from this combination of tubes constitutes a rounded mass, which often attains a very considerable size. In Fig. 41 we have a representation of the zoophyte *Tubipora musica* and its product, which is sometimes designated by the vulgar name of Sea-Organ. In the engraving, 1 is the calcareous product, reduced to half its size; 2, is a portion in its natural size; 3, the tubes magnified, and containing the polype which occupies the summit of the tube, the

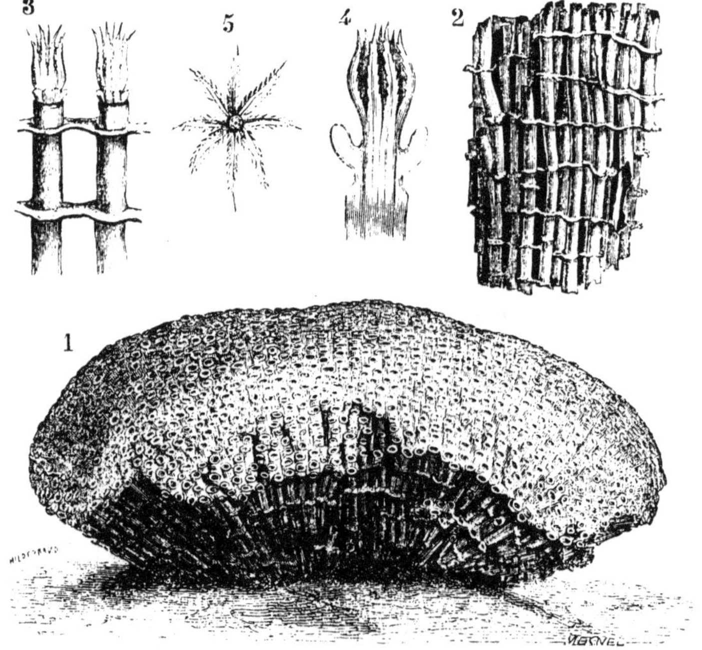

Fig. 41. Tubipora musica (Linn.), half the natural size.

whole of which constitutes this curious polypier; 4, is the polype magnified: 5, the head or collection of tentacula of the individual polype.

Zoologists of the last century confounded all the species of this genera inhabiting the tropical seas, making only one species, to which they gave the name of *Tubipora musica*. But it is now known that there are many species of *Tubiporæ*, readily distinguishable in a fresh condition by a difference in the colour of the polypes. The tissue of these singular beings is an intensely red colour. The disposition of their tubes in the style of organ pipes has always attracted the attention of the curious inquirer into the secrets of Nature.

II. GORGONIDÆ.

Milne Edwards divides this order into three natural groups:—I. The *Gorgonidæ*. II. The *Isidians*. III. The *Corallines*.

The *Gorgonians* are composed of two substances: the one external,

Fig. 42. Fan Gorgon, Gorgonia flabellum (Linn.).

sometimes gelatinous and fugitive; sometimes, on the contrary, cretaceous, fleshy, and more or less tenacious. Animated with life, this membrane is irritable and encloses the polype; it becomes friable or arenaceous in drying. The second substance, internal and central, sustains the first, and is called the *axis*. This axis presents a horny appearance, and was formerly believed to possess chemical characters analogous to the horns and hoofs of some of the vertebrated animals. It has recently been asserted that the tissues of these polypiers consist essentially of a particular substance which resembles horn, but which is called *Corneine*. A little carbonate of lime is sometimes found united with this substance, but never in a sufficient quantity to give it a stony consistence. This outer covering developes itself in concentric beds, between the portion of the axis previously formed and the internal surface of the sclerotic covering.

Fig. 43. Fan Gorgon, magnified.

The mode of growth in this axis presents great variations. Sometimes it remains simple and rises like a slender rod, sometimes it has numerous branches. It is *arborescent* when the branches and their accompaniments take different directions so as to constitute tufts. It is *panicled* when they arrange themselves on both sides of the stem or principal branches, after the manner of the barbs of a feather. It is *flabelliform* when the branches rise irregularly under the same plane; *reticulated* when branches are so disposed as to be attached to each other by net-work in place of remaining free.

The *Gorgonidæ* are found in every sea, and always at considerable depths. They are larger and more numerous between the Tropics than in cold or even temperate climates. Some of these polypiers scarcely attain the twelfth of an inch in height, while others rise to the height of several feet.

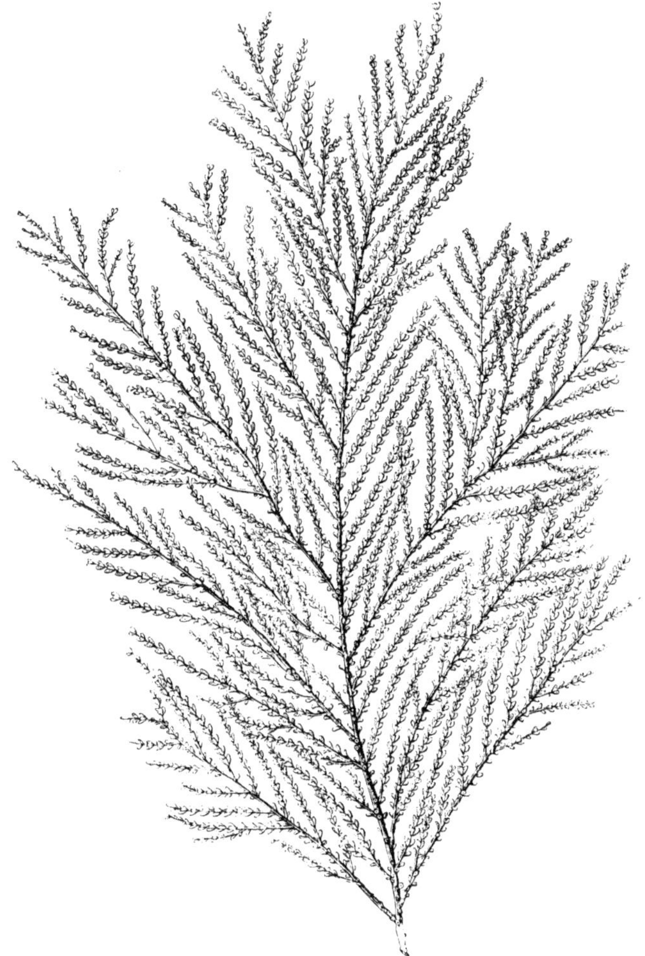

Fig. 44. Gorgonia verticellata (Pallas).

Formed in the bosom of the ocean, it is only necessary to behold these singular creations in order to admire the brilliant colours which decorate their semi-membranaceous branches. The brilliancy of their robes are singularly diminished, have almost entirely disappeared, indeed, when they make their appearance in the cases of our natural history collections.

The *Fan Gorgon*, from the Antilles (Fig. 42), is a species which often attains the height of eighteen or twenty inches, and nearly as much in breadth. The net-work of its interstices with its unequal and serried meshes, resembling fine lace, have led to its designation of *Sea Fan*. Its colour is yellow or reddish. In Fig. 43 we have the *Fan Gorgon* magnified to twice its natural size, showing the curious details of its organization.

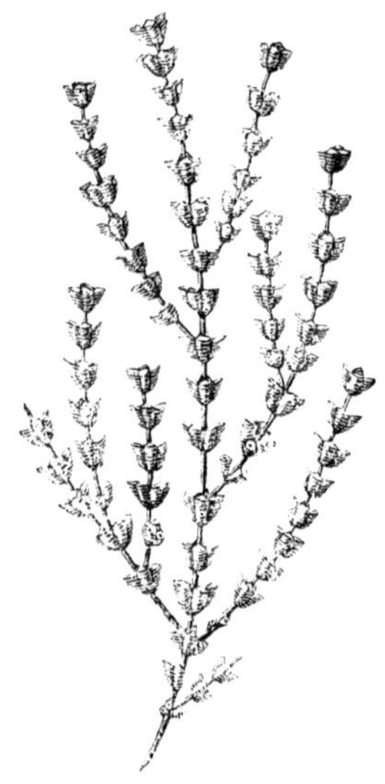

Fig. 45. Gorgonia verticellata (Pallas), magnified four times.

The Whorled Gorgon (*G. verticellata*), which is found in the Mediterranean, is yellowish in colour, and also of elegant form. It is sometimes called the Sea Pen. This species is represented in Fig. 44, while Fig. 45 represents a small branch magnified four times, in order to give an exact idea of its form.

The Gorgons are not known to be useful either in the arts or in medicine. They are ornamental in cabinets, and interesting both as objects of study and of zoological curiosity.

Isidians.

The *Isidæ* constitute an intermediate group between the *Gorgons* and *Corallines*. Their polypier is arborescent, but its axis is formed of articulations alternately calcareous and horny. The principal genus is that of the *Isis*, which is met with in the Indian Ocean, on the American coast, and in Oceania. The inhabitants of the Molucca Islands use these animals medicinally as a remedy in certain diseases; but as they use them for the most opposite maladies, it may be doubted if they are really efficacious in any medicinal point of view.

The *Isis corolloïdis* of Oceania has a polypier with numerous slender branches, furnished with cylindrical knots at intervals, contracted towards the middle, finely striated, and rose-coloured. *Isis hippuris*, represented in Fig. 46, has a singular resemblance to the Common Marsh Plant (*Hippuris vulgaris*).

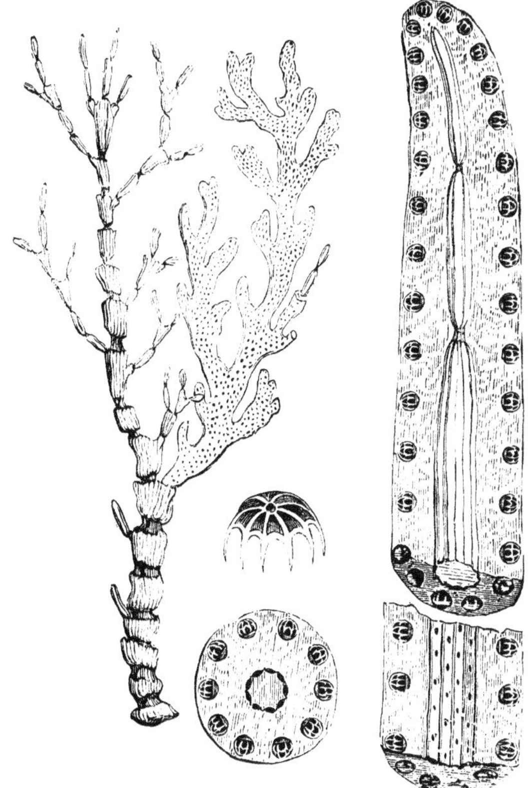

Fig. 46. Isis hippuris.

Four other species of Isidians are known. The same family includes the genera of *Melitæa* and *Mopsea*, which, however, our limits forbid us to describe.

Corallinæ.

The group of Corallines consist of a single genus, *Corallium*, having a common axis, inarticulate, solid, and calcareous, the typical species of which furnishes matter hard, brilliant, and richly coloured, and much sought after as an object of adornment. This interesting zoophyte and its product requires to be described with some detail.

From very early times, the coral has been adopted as an object of finery. From the highest antiquity also, efforts were made to ascertain its true origin, and the place assignable to it in the works of Nature. Theophrastus, Dioscorides, and Pliny considered that the coral was a plant. Tournefort, in 1700, reproduced the same idea. Réaumur slightly modified this opinion of the ancients, and declared his opinion that the coral was the stony product of certain marine plants. Science was in this state when a naturalist, who has acquired a great name, the Count de Marsigli, made a discovery which threw quite a new light on the true origin of this natural product. He announced that he had discovered the flowers of the coral. He represented these flowers in his fine work, "La Physique de la Mer," which includes many interesting details respecting this curious product of the ocean. How could it be longer doubted that the coral was a plant, since he had seen its expanded flowers?

No one doubted it, and Réaumur proclaimed everywhere the discovery of the happy Academician.

Unhappily, a discordant note soon mingled in this concert. It even emanated from a pupil of Marsigli!

Jean André de Peyssonnel was born at Marseilles in 1694. He was a student of medicine and natural history at Paris when the Académie des Sciences charged him with the task of studying the coral on the sea shore. Peyssonnel began his observations in the neighbourhood of Marseilles in 1723. He pursued it on the North African coast, where he had been sent on a mission by the Government. Aided by a long series of observations as exact as they were delicate, Peyssonnel demonstrated that the pretended flowers which the Count de Marsigli thought he had discovered in the coral, were true animals, and showed that the coral was neither plant nor the product of a plant, but a being with life, which he placed in the first 'round' of the zoological ladder. "I put the flower of the coral," says Peyssonnel, "in vases full of sea water, and I saw that what had been taken for a flower of this pretended plant, was, in truth, only an insect, like a little sea-nettle, or polype. I had the pleasure of seeing removed the claws or feet of the creature, and having put the vase full of water, which contained the coral, in a gentle heat over the fire, all the small insects seemed to expand. The polype extended his feet, and formed what M. de Marsigli and I had taken for the petals of a flower. The calyx of this pretended flower, in short, was the animal which advanced and issued out of its cell."

The observations of Peyssonnel were calculated to put aside altogether theories which had lately attracted universal admiration, but they were coldly received by the naturalists, his contemporaries. Réaumur distinguished himself greatly in his opposition to the young innovator. He wrote to Peyssonnel in an ironical tone: "I think (he says) as you do, that no one has hitherto been disposed to regard the coral as the work of insects. We cannot deny that this idea is both new and singular; but the coral, as it appears to me, never could have been constructed by sea-nettles or polypes, if we may judge from the manner in which you make them labour."

What appeared impossible to Réaumur was, however, a fact which Peyssonnel had demonstrated to hundreds by his experiments at Marseilles. Nevertheless, Bernard de Jussieu did not find the reasons he urged strong enough to induce him to abandon the opinions he had formed as to their vegetable origin. Afflicted and disgusted at the indifferent success with which his labours were received, Peyssonnel abandoned his investigations. He even abandoned science and society, and sought an obscure retirement in the Antilles as a naval surgeon, and his manuscripts, which he left in France, have never been printed. These manuscripts, written in 1744, were preserved in the library of the Museum of Natural History at Paris. The title is comprehensive and sufficiently descriptive. It should be added, in order to complete the recital, that Réaumur and Bernard de Jussieu finally recognised the value of the discoveries and the validity of the reasoning of the naturalist of Marseilles. When these illustrious *savants* became acquainted with the experiments of Trembley upon the fresh-water hydræ; when they had themselves repeated them; when they had made similar observations on the sea anemone and alcyonidæ; when they finally discovered that on other so-called marine plants animalcules were found, similar to the hydra, so admirably described by Trembley;—they no longer hesitated to render full justice to the views of their former adversary.

While Peyssonnel still lived forgotten at the Antilles, his scientific labours were crowned with triumph at Paris; but it was a sterile triumph for him. Réaumur gave to the animalcules which construct the coral the name of *Polypes*, and *Polypier* to the product itself, for such he considered the architectural product of the polypes. In other words, Réaumur introduced into Science the views which he had keenly contested with their author. But from that time the animal nature of the coralline has never been doubted.

Without pausing to note the various authors who have given their attention to this fine natural production, we shall at once direct our attention to the organization of the animalcules, and the construction of the coral.

M. Lacaze-Duthiers, professor at the Jardin des Plantes of Paris, published in 1864 a remarkable monograph, entitled "L'Histoire Naturelle du Corail." This learned naturalist was charged by the French Government, in 1860, with a mission, having for its object the study of the coral from the natural history point of view. His observations upon the zoophytes are numerous and precise, and worthy of the successor of Peyssonnel; but for close observation, practical conclusions, and popular exposition, the world is more indebted to Charles Darwin than to any other naturalist.

A branch of *living* coral, if we may use the term, is an aggregation of animals derived from a first being by budding. They are united among themselves by a common tissue, each seeming to enjoy a life of its own, though participating in a common object. The branch seems to originate in an egg, which produces a young animal, which attaches itself soon after its birth, as already described. From this is derived the new beings which, by their united labours, produce the branch of coral or polypier.

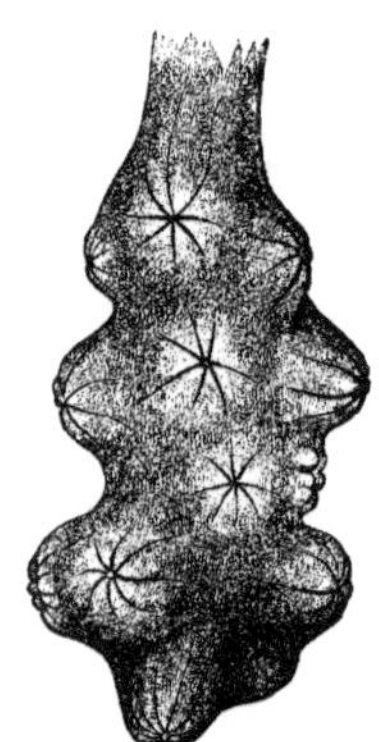

Fig. 47. Living Bed of Coral after the entrance of the Polypes. (Lacaze-Duthiers.)

This branch is composed of two distinct parts: the one central, of a hard brittle and stony nature, the well-known coral of commerce; the other altogether external, like the bark of a tree, soft and fleshy, and easily impressed with the nail. This is essentially the bed of the living colony. The first is called the polypier, the second is the colony of polypes. This bed (Fig. 47) is much contracted when the water is withdrawn from the colony. It is covered with salient mammals or protuberances, much wrinkled and furrowed.

Each mammal encloses a polype, and presents on its summit eight folds, radiating round a central pore, which presents a star-like appearance. This pore as it opens gives to the polypes the opportunity of coming out. Its edge presents a reddish calyx, like the rest of the bark, the festooned throat of which presents eight dentations.

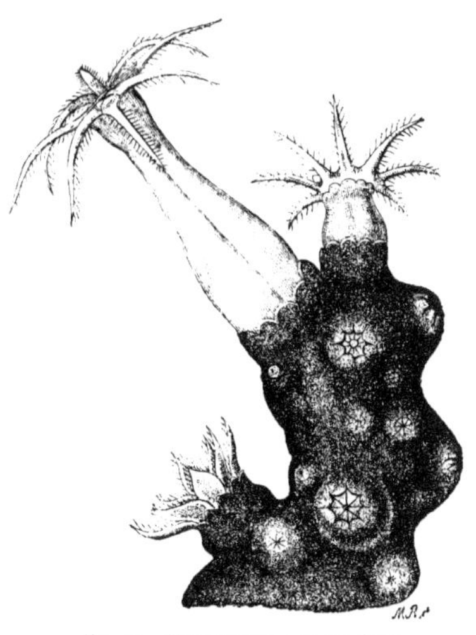

Fig. 48. Three Polypes of the Coral. (Lacaze-Duthiers.)

The polype itself (Fig. 48) is formed of a whitish membranous tube nearly cylindrical, having an upper disk, surrounded by its eight tentacula, bearing many delicate fibres spreading out laterally. This assemblage of tentacula resembles the corolla of some flowers; its form is very variable, but always truly elegant. Fig. 49 (which is borrowed from M. Lacaze-Duthiers' great work) represents one of these forms of the polypier.

The arms of the polype are at times subject to violent agitation: the tentacula become much excited. If this excitement continues, the tentacula can be seen to fold and roll themselves up as shown in Fig. 50. If we look at the expanded disk, we see that the eight tentacula attach themselves to the body, describing a space perfectly circular, in the middle of which rises a small mammal, the summit of which is occupied by a small slit like two rounded lips. This is the mouth of the polypes, the form being very variable, but well represented in Fig. 50, where the organ under consideration is displayed.

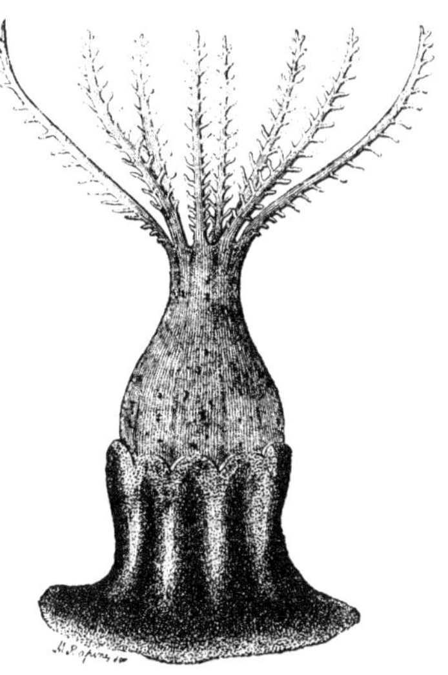

Fig. 49. Coral Polype. (Lacaze-Duthiers.)

A cylindrical tube connected with the mouth represents the œsophagus or gullet; but all other portions of the digestive tube are very rudimentary. The œsophagus connects the general cavity of the body with the exterior, and looks as if it were suspended in the middle of the body by certain folds, which issue with perfect symmetry from eight points of its circumference. The folds which thus fix the œsophagus form a series of cells, above each of which it attaches itself, and supports an arm or tentaculum.

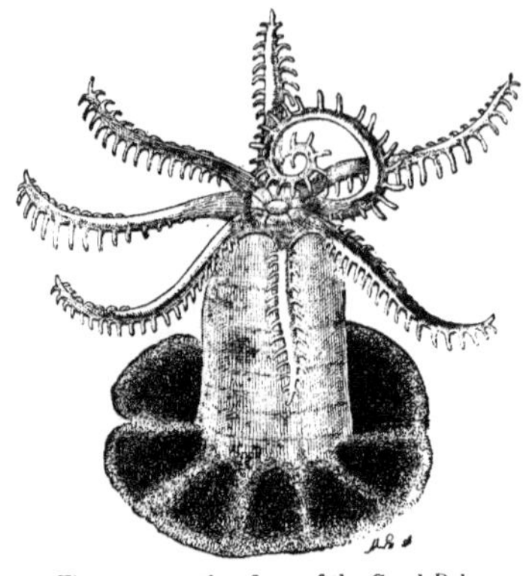

Fig. 50. Another form of the Coral Polype. (Lacaze-Duthiers.)

Let us pause an instant over the soft and fleshy bark in which the polypes are engaged. Let us see also what are the mutual relations which exist between the several inhabitants of one of these colonies, how they are attached to one another, and what their connection with the polypier.

The thick fleshy body, soft, and easily impressed with the finger, is the living part which produces the coral; it extends itself so as exactly to cover the whole polypier. If it perishes at any one point, that part of the axis which corresponds with the point no longer shows any increase. An intimate relation, therefore, exists between the bark and the polypier. If the bark is examined more closely, three principal elements are recognised—a common general *tissue*, some *spicula*, and certain *vessels*. The general tissue is transparent, glossy, cellular, and contractile.

The *spiculæ* are very small calcareous concretions, more or less elongated, covered with knotted joints bristling with spines, and of regular determinate form (Fig. 51). They refract the light very vividly, and their colour is that of the coral, but much weaker in consequence of their want of thickness. They are uniformly distributed throughout the bark, and give to the coral the fine colour which generally characterises it.

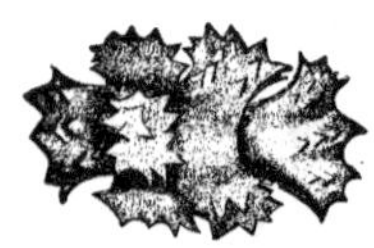

Fig. 51. Coralline Spicula. (Lacaze-Duthiers.)

The vessels constitute a net-work, which extends and repeats itself in the thickness of the crust. These vessels are of two kinds (Fig. 52); the one, comparatively very large, is imbedded in the axis, and disposed in parallel layers; the others are regular and much smaller. They form a net-work of unequal meshes, which occupies the whole thickness of the external crust. This net-work has direct and important connection with the polypes on the one hand, and with the central substance which forms the axis on the other. It communicates directly with the general cavity

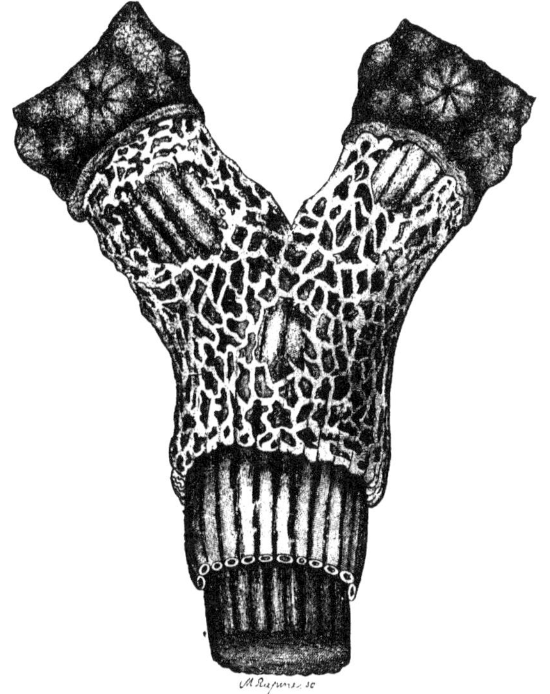

Fig. 52. Circulating Apparatus for the nutritive fluids in the Coral. (Lacaze-Duthiers.)

of the body of the animal by every channel which approaches it, while the two ranges of net-work approach each other by a great number of anastomosing processes. Such is the vascular arrangement of the coral.

The circulation of alimentary fluids in the coral is accomplished by means of vessels near to the axis, without, however, directly anastomosing with the cavities containing the animalcules which live in the polypier; they only communicate with those cavities by very delicate intermediary canals. The alimentary fluids they receive from the secondary system of net-work, which brings them into direct communication with the polypes. The alimentary fluids elaborated by the polypes pass into the branches of the secondary and irregular net-work system, in order to reach the great parallel tubes which extend from one extremity of the organism to the other, serving the same purpose to the whole community.

When the extremity of a branch of living coral is torn or broken, a white liquid immediately flows from the wound, which mingles with water, and presents all the appearance of milk. This is the fluid aliment which has escaped from the vessel containing it, charged with the débris of the organism.

What occurs when the bud produces new polypes? It is only round well-developed animals, and particularly those with branching extremities, in which this phenomenon is produced. The new beings resemble little white points pierced with a central orifice. Aided by the microscope, we discover that this white point is starred with radiating white lines, the edge of the orifice bearing eight distinctly traced indentations. All these organs are enlarged step by step until the young animal has attained the shrub-like or branched aspect which belongs to the compound polype. The tube is branching, and the orifices from which the polypes expand become dilated into cup-like cells.

The coral of commerce, so beautiful and so appreciated by lovers of bijouterie, is the polypier. It is cylindrical, much channeled on the surface, the lines usually parallel to the axis of the cylinder, the depressions sometimes corresponding to the body of the animal. If the transverse section of a polypier be examined, it is found to be regularly festooned on its circumference. Towards its centre certain sinuosities appear, sometimes crossing, sometimes trigonal, sometimes in irregular lines, and in the remaining mass are reddish folds alternating with brighter spaces which radiate from the centre towards the circumference (Fig. 53). In the section of a very red coral, it will be observed that the colour

Fig. 53. Section of a Branch of Coral. (Lacaze-Duthiers.)

is not equally distributed, but separated into zones more or less deep in colour, containing very thin preparations which crack, not irregularly, but parallel to the edge of the plate, and in such a manner as to reproduce the festoons on the circumference. From this it may be deduced that the stem increases by concentric layers being deposited, which mould themselves one upon the other. In the mass of coral certain small corpuscles occur, charged with irregular asperities, much redder than the tissue into which they are plunged. These are

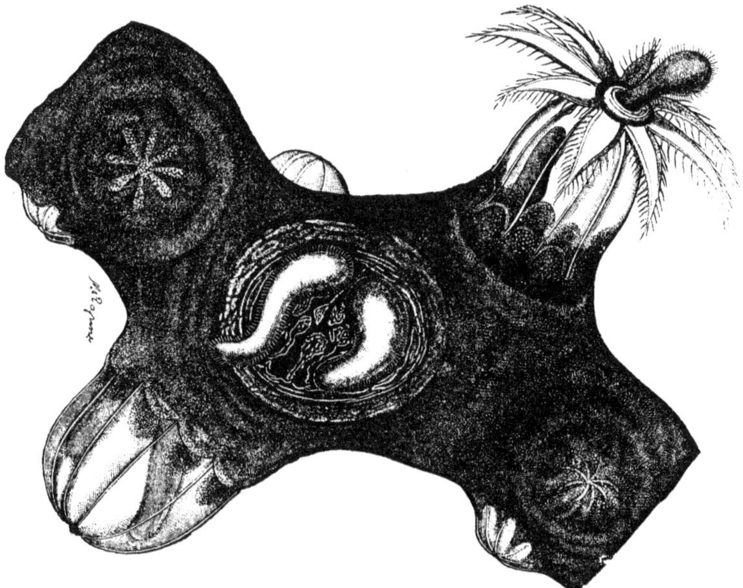

Fig. 54. Birth of the Coralline Larvæ. (Lacaze-Duthiers.)

much more numerous in the red than in the light band, and they necessarily give more strength to the general tint.

To the mode of reproduction in the coral polypes, so well described by Lacaze-Duthiers, we can only devote a few lines. Sometimes, according to this able observer, the polypes of the same colony are all either male or female, and the branch is *unisexual;* in others there are both male and female, when the branch is *bisexual.* Finally, but very rarely, polypes are found uniting both sexes.

The polype is viviparous; that is to say, its eggs become embryos inside the polypes. The larvæ remain a certain time in the general cavity of the polypes, where they can be seen through its transparency, as exhibited in Fig. 54. Aided by the magnifying powers of the microscope, coral larvæ may here be perceived through the transparent membranous envelope. From this position they escape from the mouth of the mother in the manner represented in the upper branch. The animal then resembles a little white grub or worm, more or less elongated. The larva is, however, still egg-shaped or ovoid; moreover, it is sunk in a hollow cavity, and covered with cilia, by the aid of which it can swim. Sometimes one of its extremities becomes enlarged, the other remaining slender and pointed. Upon this an opening is formed communicating with the interior cavity: this is the mouth. The larvæ swim backwards; that is to say, with the mouth behind.

It is only at a certain period after birth that the coral polype fixes itself and commences its metamorphoses, which consist essentially in a change of form and proportions. The buccal extremity is diminished and tapers off, whilst the base swells, and is enlarged—it becomes discoid; the posterior surface of this sort of disk is a plane, the front representing the mouth, at the bottom of a depression edged with a great cushion. Eight mammals or swellings now appear, corresponding to the chambers which divide the interior of the disk: the worm has taken its radiate form. Finally, the mammals are elongated and transformed into tentacula. In Fig. 55 a young coral polype is represented fixed upon a bryozoare, a name employed by Ehrenberg for zoophytes having a mouth and anus. It forms a small disk, the fortieth part of an inch in diameter, and having its spicula already coloured red. Fig. 56 shows the successive forms of the young polypes in the progressive phases of their development—being a young coralline polype fixed upon a rock still contracted. Fig. 57 is a similar coralline attached to a rock and expanding its tentacula. It also represents a small pointed rock covered with polypes and polypiers of the natural size and of different shapes, but

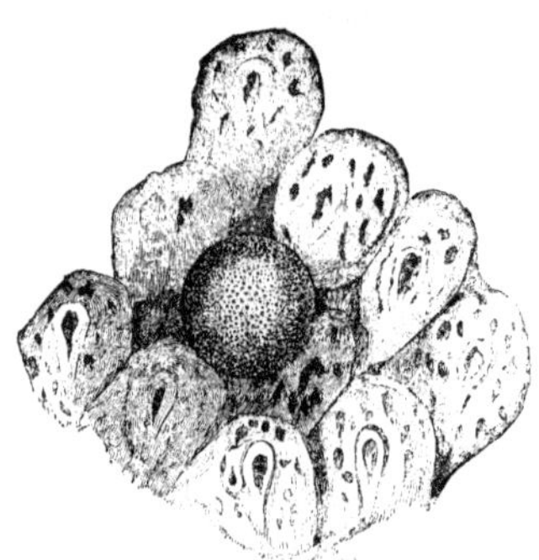

Fig. 55. Very young Polypes, attached to a Bryozoare.

all young, and indicating the definite form of development which the collective beings are to assume.

The simple isolated state of the animal, whose phases of development we have indicated, does not last long. It possesses the property of producing new beings, as we have already said, by budding. But how is the polypier formed? If we take a very young branch, we find in the centre of the thickness of the crust a nucleus or stony substance resembling an agglomeration of spicula. When they are sufficient in number and size, these nuclei form a kind of stony plate, which is imbedded in the thickness of the tissues of the animal. These *laminæ*, at first quite flat, assume in the course of their development a horse-shoe shape. Figs. 59 and 60 will give the reader some idea of the form in which the young polypiers present themselves. Fig. 59 represents the corpuscles in which the polypiers have their origin; Fig. 60, the rudimentary form of the coralline polypier.

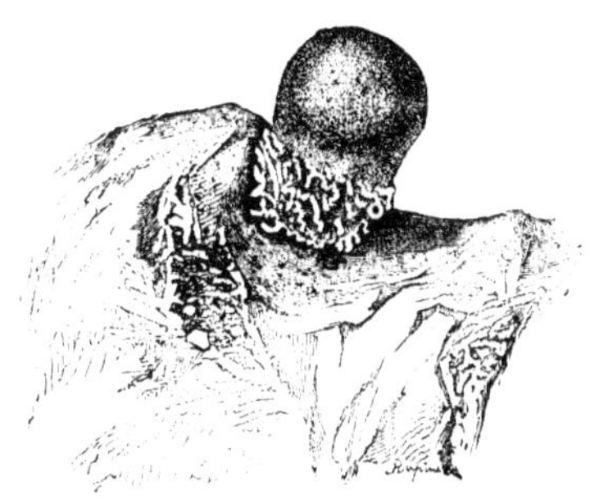

Fig. 56. A young Coral Polype fixed upon a Rock. (Lacaze-Duthiers.)

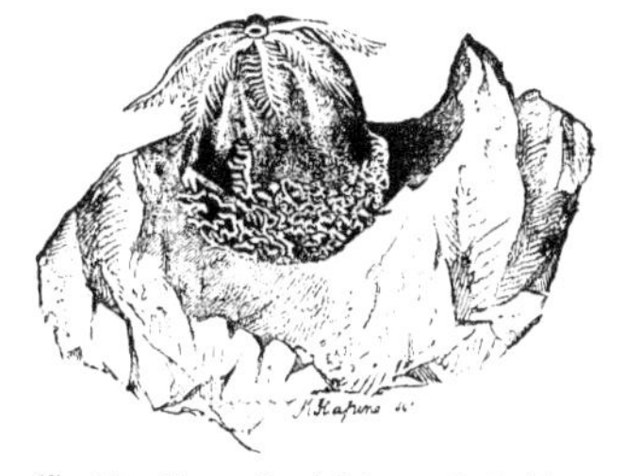

Fig. 57. Young Coral Polype attached to a Rock and expanded. (Lacaze-Duthiers.)

Our information fails to convey any precise notion of the time necessary for the coral to acquire the various proportions in which it presents itself.

Darwin, who examined some of these creatures very minutely, tells us that "several genera (Flustra, Eschara, Cellaria, Cresia, and others) agree in having singular movable organs attached to their cells. The organs in the greater number of cases very closely resemble the head of a vulture; but the lower mandible can be opened much wider than a

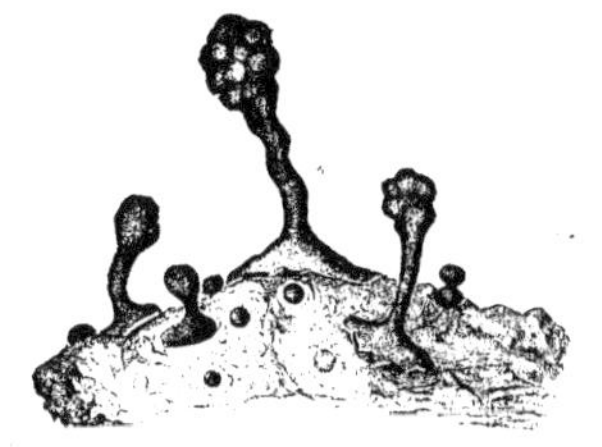

Fig. 58. A Rock covered with young Coral Polypes and Polypiers. (Lacaze-Duthiers.)

real bird's beak. The head itself possesses considerable powers of movement, by means of a short neck. In one zoophyte the head itself was fixed, but the lower jaw free; in another it was replaced by a triangular hood, with a beautifully-fitted trap-door, which evidently answered to the lower mandible. In the greater number of species each cell was provided with one head, but in others each cell had two.

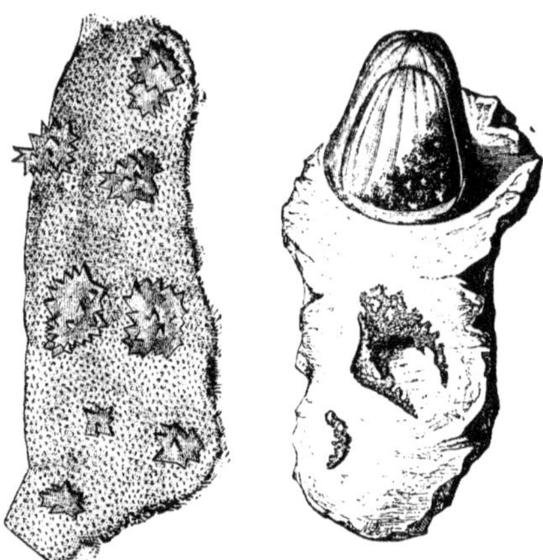

Fig. 59. Corpuscles from which originate the Polypier. Fig. 60. First form of the Polypier. (Lacaze-Duthiers.)

"The young cells at the end of the branches of these corallines contain quite immature polypi, yet the vulture heads attached to them, though small, are in every respect perfect. When the polypus was removed by a needle from any of the cells, these organs did not appear to be in the least affected. When one of the vulture-like heads was cut off from a cell, the lower mandible retained its power of opening and closing. Perhaps the most singular part of their structure is, that when there are more than two rows of cells on a branch, the central cells were furnished with these appendages of only one-fourth the size of the outside ones. Their movements varied according to the species; but in some I never saw the least motion, while others, with the lower mandible generally wide open, oscillated backwards and forwards at the rate of about five seconds each turn; others moved rapidly and by starts. When touched with a needle, the beak generally seized the point so firmly that the whole branch might be shaken."

In the *Cresia*, Darwin observed that each cell was furnished with a long-toothed bristle, which had the power of moving very quickly: each bristle and each vulture-like head moving quite independently of each other; sometimes all on one side, sometimes those on one branch only moving simultaneously, sometimes one after the other. In these actions we apparently behold as perfect a transmission of will in the zoophyte, though composed of thousands of distinct polypi, as in any distinct animal. "What can be more remarkable," he adds, "than to see a plant-like body producing an egg, capable of swimming about and choosing a proper place to adhere to, where it sprouts out into branches, each crowded with innumerable distinct animals, often of complicated organization!—the branches, moreover, sometimes possessing organs capable of movement independent of the polypi."

Passing to the coral fishing, it may be said to be quite special, presenting no analogy with any other fishing in the European seas, if we except the sponge fisheries. The fishing stations which occur are found on the Italian coast and the coast of Barbary; in short, in most parts of the Mediterranean basin. In all these regions, on abrupt rocky beds, certain aquatic forests occur, composed entirely of the red coral, the most brilliant and the most celebrated of all the polypiers, *Coralium decus liquidi!* During many ages, as we have seen, the coral was supposed to be a plant. The ancient Greeks called it the *daughter of the sea* (Κοράλλιον κόρη ἁλός), which the Latins translated into *corralium* or *coralium*. It is now agreed among naturalists that the coral is constructed by a family of polypi living together, and composing a polypier. It abounds in the Mediterranean and the Red Sea, where it is found at various depths, but rarely less than five fathoms, or more than a hundred and fifty. Each polypier resembles a pretty red leafless under-shrub bearing delicate little star-like radiating white flowers. The axes of this little tree are the parts common to the association; the flowrets are the polypes. These axes present a soft reticulated crust, full of little cavities, which are the cells of the polypi, and are permeated by a milky juice. Beneath the crust is the coral, properly so called, which equals marble in hardness, and is remarkable for its striped surface, its bright red colour, and the fine polish of which it is susceptible. The ancients believed that it was soft in the water, and only took its consistence when exposed to the air:

"Sic et coralium, quo primum contigit auras
Tempore, durescit." OVID.

The fishing is chiefly conducted by sailors from Genoa, Leghorn, and Naples, and it is so fatiguing, that it is a common saying in Italy that a sailor obliged to go to the coral fishery should be a thief or an assassin. The saying is a gratuitous insult to the sailor, but conveys a good idea enough of the occupation.

The barks sent to the fishing range from six to fifteen tons; they are solid, and well adapted for the labour; their rig is a great lateen sail, and a jib or staysail. The stern is reserved for the capstan, the fishers, and the crew. The fore part of the vessel is reserved for the requirements of the patron or master.

The lines, wood, and irons employed in the coral fisheries are called the engine: it consists of a cross of wood formed of two bars, strongly lashed or bolted together at their centre; below this a great stone is attached, which bears the lines, arranged in the form of a sac. These lines have great meshes, loosely knotted together, resembling the well-known swab.

The apparatus carries thirty of these sacs, which are intended to grapple all they come in contact with at the bottom of the sea. They are spread out in all directions by the movement of the boat. The coral is known to attach itself to the summit of a rock and to develope itself, forming banks there, and it is to these rocks that the swab attaches itself so as to tear up the precious harvest. Experience, which in time becomes almost intuitive, guides the Italian fisher in discovering the coral banks. The craft employed in the great fishery have a patron or captain, the bark having a poop with a crew of eight or ten sailors, and in the season it is continued night and day. The whole apparatus, and mode of using it, is shown in Pl. II.

When the patron thinks that he has reached a coral bank, he throws his engine overboard. As soon as the apparatus is engaged, the speed of the vessel is retarded, the capstan is manned by six or eight men, while the others guide the helm and trim the sails. Two forces are thus brought to act upon the lines, the horizontal action of the vessel and the vertical action of the capstan. In consequence of the many inequalities of the rocky bottom, the engine advances by jerks, the vessel yielding more or less according to the concussion caused by the action of the capstan or sail. The engine seizes upon the rugged rocks at the bottom, and raises them to let them fall again. In this manner the swab, floating about, penetrates beneath the rocks where the coral is found, and is hooked on to it. To fix the lines upon the coral and bring them home, is a work of unheard-of labour. The engine long resists the most energetic and repeated efforts of the crew, who, exposed almost naked to the burning sun of the Mediterranean, work the capstan to which the cable and engine are attached, while the patron urges and excites them to increased exertion, and

Plate III.—Coral Fishing on the Coast of Sicily.

the sailors trim the sail and sing with a slow and monotonous tone a song, the words of which improvise in a sort of psalmody the names of the saints most revered among the seafaring Italian population.

The lines are finally brought home, tearing or breaking blocks of rock, sometimes of enormous size, which are brought on board. The cross is now placed on the side of the vessel, the lines are arranged on the deck, and the crew occupy themselves in gathering the results of their labour. The coral is gathered together, the branches of the precious zoophyte are cleansed, and divested of the shells and other parasitic products which accompany them; finally, the produce is carried to and sold in the ports of Messina, Naples, Genoa, or Leghorn, where the workers in jewelry purchase them. Behold, fair reader, with what hard labour, fatigue, and peril, the elegant bijouterie with which you are decked is torn from the deepest bed of the ocean!

III. THE PENNATULIDÆ, OR SEA-PEN.

This curious family received from Cuvier the name of *Swimming polypi*, and from Lamarck that of *Floating polypi*. The name of *Pennatulæ*, by which they are generally known, is taken from their resemblance to a quill, *penna*. In the words of Lamarck, "it seems as if Nature, in forming this composite animal, had wished to copy the external form of a bird's feather." Our fishermen call it the *cock's comb*, which is not inapt, but less expressive of its peculiarities. This polypier is "from two to four inches in length, of a uniform purplish-red colour, except at the hip or base of the stalk, where it is pale orange-yellow; the skin is thickish, very tough, and of a curious structure, being composed of minute crystalline cylinders, densely arranged in straight lines, and held together by a tenacious glutinous matter, the cylinders being about six inches in diameter, in length straight and even, or sometimes slightly curved, and of a red colour, which communicates itself to the zoophyte." (Johnston.) The animals by which it is formed constitute colonies, which, however, are only attached to the rocks by an enlarged basis; it appears to live generally at the bottom of the sea; its root, if we can use the term, buried in the sands or mud; its polypiferous portion sallying out into the water. The agitation of the waves and the fishermen's nets often displace these aggregates of creation, and then they float at various depths in the bosom of the ocean.

The stalk of the polypier is hollow in the centre, having a long slender bone-like substance, which is white, smooth, and square, but tapering at each extremity to a fine point. The polypi, which are fleshy and white, are provided with eight long retractile tentacula, beautifully ciliated on their inner edge with two series of short processes strengthened with crystalline spicula. The mouth in the centre of the tentacula is somewhat angular, bounded by a white ligament, a process from which encircles the base of each tentaculum, which thus seems to issue from an aperture. The ova lie between the membranes of the pinnæ; they are globular, of a yellowish colour, and by a little pressure can be made to pass through the mouth. The polypi are distributed with more or less regularity in such a manner that one of the extremities of the common axis is always naked: this part has been compared to the tubulous part of a feather. The stem, common to the colony, is a solid central axis, more or less developed, which is covered with a fleshy fibrous substance, susceptible of dilation and contraction.

The *Pennatulidæ* comprehend three genera; namely, those with polypes on bipinnate wings, having—according to Dr. Johnston—

Polypidoms plumose, in	Pennatula.
Polypidoms virgate, or wand-shaped	Virgularia.
Polypes, unilateral and sessile . . . . . . Polypidom, linear-elongate	Pavonaria.

In the genus *Pennatula*, the polypes are disposed in transverse rows upon the outer and inner edge, in a series of prolongations in the form of a feather. These winged species of polypiers are somewhat scythe-shaped, well developed, and furnished with a great quantity of pointed spiculæ, which are constituted of bundles at the base of the calyx. The space between the two rows of appendages is sometimes a tissue, sometimes scaly, sometimes granulous. Of the *Pennatula* five species are known, and all of them appear to be gifted with phosphorescent properties. We may note among these species *Pennatula spinosa* (Fig. 61), which inhabits the Mediterranean, and takes its name from its colour; *Pennatula phosphorea*, which abound in most European seas, being found in great plenty, clinging to the fishermen's lines round our own northern shores, more especially when they are baited with mussels.

P. phosphorea is of a reddish purple, the base of the smooth stalk pale; the raches roughened with close-set papillæ, and furrowed down the middle; pinnæ close; polype cils uniserial, tubular, with spinous apertures. (Sibbald.)

Bohadsch says the *Pennatulæ* swim by means of their pinnæ, which they use as fishes do their fins. Ellis says, "it is an animal that swims about in the sea, many of them having a muscular motion as they swim along;" these motions being effected, as he tells us in another place, by means of the pinnules or feather-like fins, "evidently designed by Nature to move the animal backward or forward in the sea." Cuvier tells us they have the power of moving by the contraction of the fleshy part of the polypidom, and also by the combined action of its polypes. Dr. Grant says, "a more singular and beautiful spectacle could scarcely be conceived than that of a deep purple *P. phosphorea* with all its delicate transparent polypi expanded, and emitting their usual brilliant phosphorescent light, sailing through the still and dark abyss, by the regular and synchronous pulsations of the minute fringed arms of the whole polypi;" while Linnæus tells us that "the phosphorescent sea-pens which cover the bottom of the ocean cast so strong a light, that it is easy to count the fishes and worms of various kinds which sport among them."

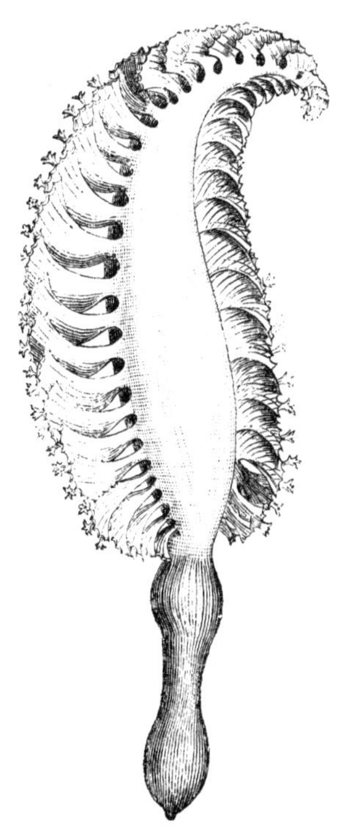

Fig. 61. Sea-pen, *Pennatula spinosa*. (Edes.)

Lamarck, Schweigger, and other naturalists, however, reasoning from what is known of other compound animals, deny the existence of this locomotive power in these zoophytes; "and there is little doubt," says Dr. Johnston, "that these authors are right, for, when placed in a basin of sea water, the *Pennatulæ* are never observed to change their position; they remain in the same spot, and lie with the same side up or down, just as they have been placed. They inflate the body until it becomes to a considerable degree transparent, and only streaked with intercepted lines of red, which distend at one place and contract at another; they spread out the pinnæ, and the polypes expand their tentacula, but they never attempt to swim, or perform any process of locomotion."

P. mirabilis is common in the east and north coasts of Scotland.

The *virgularias* differ from the *pennatula* chiefly in their development, relative to the axis of the colony and the shortness of the pinnæ, which carry the polypes; and in this, that no spiculæ enter into the composition of its softer parts. *V. mirabilis* is found in the North Sea, on the coast of Scotland, and as far north as Norway. In Zetland it is known as the sea-rush. It is abundant in Belfast Lough, but, from its brittle nature, perfect specimens are difficult to obtain.

"It seems," says Sowerby, "to represent a quill stripped of its feathers. The base looks like a pen in this as in other species, swelling a little way from the end, and then tapering. The upper part is thicker, with alternate semicircular pectinated swellings, larger towards the middle, tapering upwards, and terminating in a thin bony substance, which passes through the whole extent, and is from six to ten inches in length."

In a communication to Dr. Johnston, from Mr. R. Patterson of Belfast, commenting on Müller's figure of *Virgularia*, he tells us that in the longest specimen he had, no two plumes were precisely alike—so unlike, indeed, that the artist copying one, could not for a moment hesitate, after raising her eyes from her paper, to look at the animal, as to which she was copying.

Its short waving and deeply dentated wings are of a brilliant yellow. The polypes, which appear upon their lobes, are whitish, transparent, and form a fringe of small diaphanous white stars (Figs. 62 and 63). We may figure to ourselves a slender wand-like and much-elongated polypier, carrying only a non-contractile polype on one side, which would give us an idea of the Pavonaria, of which we know only one species, which is from the Mediterranean.

Virgularia mirabilis is undoubtedly one of the finest polypiers found in the ocean. Two series of half-moon shaped wings, obliquely horizontal, are placed symmetrically round an upright axis. They embrace the stem somewhat in the manner termed *petiolate* by botanists, clasping it alternately; or, shall we say, like two broad ribbons rolled round a stem in an inverse direction, in such a manner as to

Fig. 62. Loose-winged Virgularia, Virgularia mirabilis (Lamarck).

produce the effect of two opposing flights of stairs. These wings are waving, vandyked, and fringed on their outer edge, and of a brilliant yellow; the dentature of the fringe being the lodging of their pretty little polypes, which display occasionally their gaping mouths and expanded gills. The polypes are white and semi-transparent. When they display their rays, the margin of

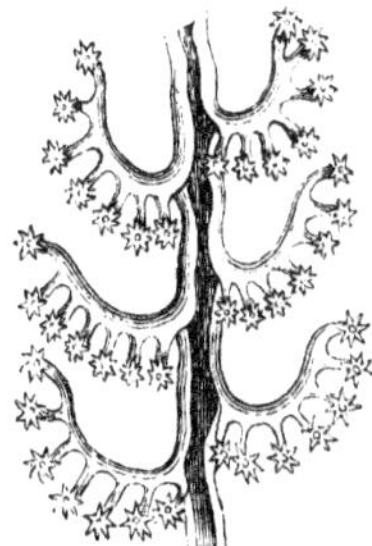

Fig. 63. Branch of Virgularia, enlarged.

each wing presents an edging of silvery stars.

The *Umbellularia* have a very long stem, supported by a bone (Fig. 64) of the same length, and terminated at the summit only by a cluster of polypes. They have been found in the Greenland and other northern seas.

The *Veretillum*, which inhabit the Mediterranean (Fig. 65), have a simple cylindrical body, without branchiæ, and

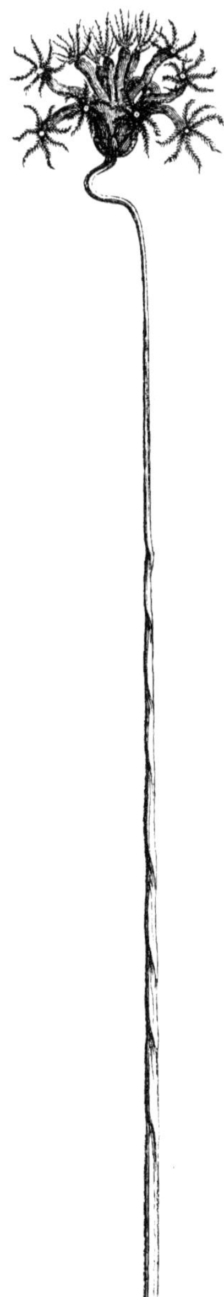

Fig. 64. Umbellularia Greculandica (Lamarck).

a rudimentary polypier, furnished with very large polypes of a whitish colour.

IV. THE ALCYONARIA PROPER.

The beings which compose this group have the fleshy polypier always adherent, without axis or solid interior stem. They are divided into four families or tribes. One of these, the *Cornularia*, are zoophytes, and live in isolation, or gathered together in small numbers on the surface of a common membraniform expansion. The *Cornularia cornucopia* live on the coast of Naples, *C. crassa* on the Algerian coast. Other genera make their appearance on the coast of Scotland, of Norway, in the Red Sea, and in the Indian Ocean they appear in great numbers.

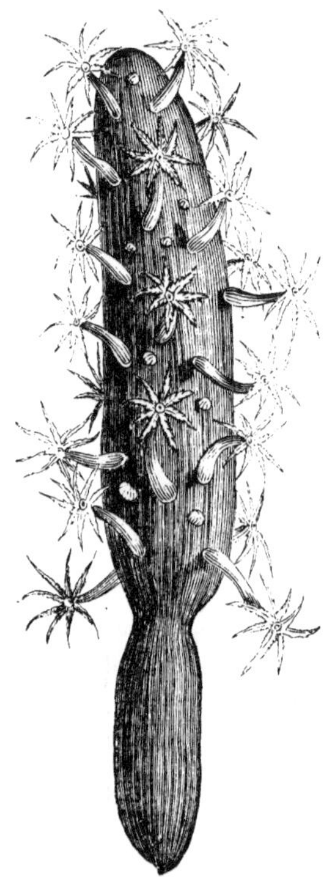

Fig. 65. Veretillum cynomorium (Lamarck).

In the *Alcyonaria*, properly so called, the polypier is very thick, of a semi-cartilaginous consistence, granular, and rough to the touch.

The genus *Alcyonium* is numerous in species and widely dispersed. *A. digitatum* is very common on our coasts, and on many parts of the coast scarcely a stone or shell is dredged up from deep water which does not serve as a support to some one or more species of *Alcyonium*. It is known by various popular names by our sea-side population, such as *cow's paps*, from its resemblance to the teats of the cow—*dead man's fingers*, from the occasional resemblance of its finger-like lobes to a man's fingers.

The polypidom is a simple obtuse process, the outer skin of which is tough and coriaceous, studded all over with star-like figures, which on examination are found to be divided into eight rays, indicating the number of the polypi enclosed in its transparent vesicular membrane. It is dotted with minute calcareous grains, and marked with eight longitudinal lines or septa, stretching between the membrane and the central stomach, which divide the intermediate space into an equal number of compartments. These lines not only extend to the base of the tentacula, but run across the anal disk, and terminate in a central mouth. The tentacula are short, obtuse, ciliate on the margins, and strengthened at their roots by numerous crystalline spiculæ. The polype cells are oval, placed just under the skin, and are the terminating points of certain long canals which traverse the whole polypier. The polypes, which are distributed over the whole surface, can withdraw into the cavities; they are, besides, of an extremely vital sensibility: the least shock impresses itself on the tentacula, the impulse of a wave even producing contraction; in response, the animal, which is well developed, sallies out perceptibly, but immediately retires again to hide itself in the cell.

We find on the coast, in the Channel, and in the North Sea, *Alcyonium digitatum*, the mass of which is of a reddish white, ferruginous, or orange; *A. stellatum*, found on the shores of the Mediterranean, is expanded in its upper part, narrow towards its base, very rough on the surface, and rose-coloured; *A. palmatum* is cylindrical, branching at the summit, of a deep red, except at the base, where it is yellow: this is met with in the Mediterranean.

We may note as a type, altogether different from any yet touched upon, the *Nephtys*, in which the polypier is a coriaceous tissue bristling with spiculæ over its whole surface. In *N. Chabroli*, the polypier is squat, with thick spreading arms covered with lobiliform branches, the tubercular polypier of which are columnar and obtuse, the sicula green, and the tentacula of the polypes yellow.

"On a cursory view," says Dr. Johnston, "the polypodium of the three families embraced appear very dissimilar, and accordingly, by many recent authors, they have been scattered over the class, and placed widely asunder. The affinity between them, however, is generally acknowledged, and had been distinctly perceived by some of the earliest zoophytologists. Thus Bohadsch found so much in common in the typical pennatulæ and a species of *Alcyonium*, that he has not hesitated to describe them as members of the same genus; and, although the more systematic character of Pallas prevented him from falling into this error, if error it can be called, he did not the less recognise the relationship between the genera or families. Pallas also tells us that his *Pennatula cynomorium* differs from the *Alcyonium* only in this, that the former is a movable and the latter a fixed polypidom; and he saw with equal clearness the connection which exists between these genera and the shrub-like *Gorgonia*. Of the *Pennatula mirabilis* he had doubts whether it was not rather a species of *Gorgonia*, until he perceived that the stem was attenuated at each end and free; and of the Sea-pens generally, Ellis remarks that they are 'a genus of zoophytes not far removed from the *Gorgonias*, on account of their polype mouths, as well as having a bone in the inside and flesh without.' 'On the other hand, the *Gorgoniæ* seem,' says Pallas, 'with the exception of their horny skeleton, to be nearly similar in structure to the *Alcyonia;* but as there are species of *Gorgonia* which are suberose internally, and almost of a uniform medullary consistence, even this mark of distinction fails to separate the tribes, and we have little left to guide us in arranging these esculent species excepting their external habits.' "

"With most polypiers," says Frédol, "the elementary individual, in spite of the adhesion established among them, possesses a vital energy all its own; it is in some respects quite independent. They have each its own particular will, which it is difficult to mistake for a common will; but it is not thus with the *Pennatula*. Their association consists of a non-adherent polypier, which moves—obscurely, it is true—but still it moves. To what does this lead? To this: that the parts which they possess in common, in place of being horny or calcareous—that is, completely inert—are fleshy, with contractile powers; that is to say, animated. Consequently, the polypes of the *Pennatula* are less independent of each other than the coral polypes, which have a central, perhaps a sensible organ, common to all, which binds them to each other, giving a certain unity to their acts. The Coralline polypiers have no will; the *Pennatula* have.

CHAPTER VII.

ZOANTHARIA, OR ANIMAL FLOWERS.

> "I saw the living pile ascend
> The mausoleum of its architects,
> Still dying upwards as their labour closed:
> Slime the material, but the slime was turned
> To adamant by their petrific touch."
>
> MONTGOMERY'S *Pelican Island.*

THE zoophytes which constitute the class *Zoantharia* are quite great personages. Some of them are eighteen or twenty inches long; at the same time, others scarcely exceed the eighth part of an inch in length. They live in all seas, and seem to have existed through many ages of the earth's history; they appear at an early geological period, and they have performed an important part in its formation; we shall see that, with great numbers of them, parts cut off from their bodies continue to live and become new individuals.

The name of *Zoantharia* was first given to the class by Gray; but here we give it a somewhat wider signification, embracing under it the madrepores and starred stones of Lasueur, who is reminded of a field enamelled with small flowers when he sees the little polypes of *Porites Astroïdes* in full blow. "But it is only," says Johnston, "when they lie with their upper disk expanded, and their tentacula displayed, that they solicit comparison with the boasts of Flora; for, when contracted, the polypes of the madrepores conceal themselves in their calcareous cups, and the actiniæ hide their beauty, assuming the shape of an obtuse cone or hemisphere of a fleshy consistence, or elongating themselves into a sort of flabby cylinder that indicates a state of relaxation and indolent repose."

These zoophytes are flesh-eaters, and consume quantities truly prodigious, of animals such as the crustaceans, worms, and small fishes. They are all marine, nearly all attached to the same spot for life, and they live in colonies. Some few are isolated and live by themselves, either free or attached to the soil. They differ altogether from the animals belonging to the *Alcyonaria* by their disposal of, and mode of multiplying, tentacula. These appendages in the *Zoantharia* never present the *bipinnate* arrangement which is observable in the *Alcyonaria.* They are habitually simple, and, if they present ramifications, these are only exceptional. In nearly every instance, the tentacles exist to the number of twelve, eighteen, twenty-four, and even larger numbers, which form a sort of concentric crown to the animal.

Zoantha thalassanthos (Lesson), which has given its name to the group, consists of large turf-like tufts of coral attached to a rock. Its animalcules are packed closely together, and their expanded flower-like heads have a curious resemblance to a mass of flowers in full bloom. They are borne on bending root-like stems of pure white, interlacing one with the other, surmounted by a fusiform or spindle-shaped body, pediculate and swelling towards the middle, but truncate at the summit, of a reddish-brown colour, marked with longitudinal stripes more highly coloured; its consistence is firm and parchment-like. From the body issues a tube, narrow, muscular, contractile, and red in colour, terminating at the summit in eight elongated arms or tentacula, of a pure yellow, traversed by a nervure of the same colour. The edges of these arms are fringed with fine pinnæ, parallel to each other, of a bright maroon colour, and resembling the barbs of a feather. According to Lesson, the arms of this *Zoantha* are kept unceasingly in motion, which produces in the water small oscillating currents, in the course of which the animalcules on which the polypi feed are precipitated into the stream leading to their mouths.

The tendency to produce a calcareous polypier is a property almost universal with animals of this class. Zoologists are agreed in dividing them into three very distinct orders—namely, the Antipathidæ, consisting of the genera *Antipathes, Cirripathes,* and *Seipathes,* in which the polypier is of a horny consistence; the Madreporidæ, in which the polypier is calcareous and stony; finally, the Actinidæ, which produce no polypiers.

ANTIPATHIDÆ.

We need not dwell upon this group, which is comparatively uninteresting. They correspond with the family of *Gorgonidæ* among the *Alcyonaria*, which they resemble in having the central axes branching after the manner of a shrub; but the polypi have the mouth surrounded with a crown of six simple tentacula. The axis is of a harder and denser tissue than that of the Gorgons, and presents on its surface small spiniform projections. The polypiferous crust, with which they are covered, is in general very arenaceous, and is so easily detached, that it is rare to see in collections anything but the denuded skeleton of the colony. In *A. arborea*, the polypier is fragile and brittle; when dry, the branches, always slender and delicate, resemble the barbs of a feather. The colour is of a deep black, or rather bistre and *terra de sienna* tint. Under a powerful lens, the extremities of the branches appear to be covered with small spines, and the trunk is formed of oval and irregular concentric beds, which are the zones of growth. Its consistence is firm, so that it can be worked up and converted into chaplets for pearls and other bijouterie: it is known in commerce as *black coral.*

MADREPORIDÆ.

The *Madrepora* are better known than their congeners. They are sometimes, but erroneously, designated corals, since the coral forms no part of this group.

The Madrepores are remarkable for the calcareous crust which always surrounds their tissue, and determines the formation of their polypier. They are in other respects easily recognised by the star-like structure of their polypier, in which may always be distinguished a visceral chamber, the circumference of which is furnished with perpendicular laminæ or partitions, which are always directed towards the axis of the body. When sufficiently developed they constitute, by their assemblage, a star-like body formed of a great number of rays. The polypier is always calcareous. The consolidation of the envelope of each polype produces at first a kind of sheath, to which Milne Edwards has given the name of the wall. The partitions which proceed from the interior towards the axis of the visceral chamber occupy the subtentacular cells; the terminal and open portion designated the calyx is in organic continuity with the polype, which has retired thither more or less completely as into a cell.

Milne Edwards remarks that the polypiers of the *Madrepora* present in their structure five principal modifications, due in part to the fundamental number of which the chambered cells are the multiple, and in part to the mode of division in the visceral chamber, and finally to the manner in which its tissue is constituted. M. Edwards avails himself of this peculiarity of structure in order to divide the Madrepores into fixed sections; namely, *Madrépores apores*, *Madrépores perforés*, *Madrépores tabulés*, *Madrépores tuberleux*, and *Madrépores rugueux*. In the group of Aporous Madrepores, the polypier is perhaps the most highly organized. We find there a well-developed and very perfect wall, and a well-developed visceral apparatus. The calyx is neatly starred; the number of rays in the earlier stages being six, which soon afterwards reach from twelve to twenty-four. The cells between the chambers are sometimes open in all their depth, sometimes more or less shut up by transverse plates; these, being independent of each other, are never reunited in the breadth of the visceral cavity, so that they constitute discoid plates such as we find in *tabular* and *rugose* Madrepores.

The animals belonging to this group, which may be characterised as *stelliform* or star-like, are very abundant in every sea, and in several geological formations. They constitute many families, among which may be noted the MILLEPORINA of Ehrenberg, the polypier of which Dr. Johnston describes as "calcareous, fixed, plant-like, branching or lobed, with cells scattered over the whole surface, distinct, sunk in little fosses, obscurely stellate, the lamellæ narrow and almost obsolete." (JOHNSTON'S *Zoophytes*, vol. i. p. 194.) In *Turbinolia*, the animal is simple, conical, striped, furrowed externally with larger and smaller ribs, the mouth surrounded by numerous tentacula, and solidified by a calcareous polypier, which is free, conical, and also furrowed externally; attenuated at the base, but enlarged at the summit, and terminating in a shallow radiated lamellar cup or cell. Several species have been dredged off the coast of Cornwall, and the west coast of Scotland and Ireland.

T. melletiana is described as coral-white, wedge shaped, somewhat compressed, with interspaces or ribs equidistant, smooth, and glossy. Above, the ribs turn over the edge, and are continued into the centre of the enlarged cup, forming its lamellæ. "That the zoophyte must have lived for some time after having become a movable thing, is proved," says Dr. Johnston, "by the ribs being continued beyond or round the point of attachment." The specimen here described was dredged alive, and Professor Forbes says of it that "it is a most interesting and beautiful species, the more so as it is certainly identical with Defrance's *Turbinolia melletiana*, found in both the crag formations."

The *Caryophilliæ* (Lamarck), from καρύα, a nut, and φύλλον, a leaf, have the polypier permanently fixed, simple, striated longitudinally, and the summit hollowed into a lamellated star-like cup; the animal, actinia-like, is provided with a simple, or double crown of tentacula, projecting from the surface of star-like, cylindrical, cone-shaped cells. In *C.*

Fig. 66. Caryophillia cyathus (Lamarck).

cyathus (Lamarck) (Fig. 66), which inhabits the Mediterranean, the polypes are of a greyish colour, the tentacula streaked with black. The polypier is erect and upright, sometimes cylindrical, and generally so firmly attached to the rock as to seem a part of it. The lamellæ are of three kinds: one large and prominent, between every pair of which there are three, sometimes five, smaller ones, the centre one being divided into two portions forming an inner series. The lamellæ are arched entire and striated on the sides, whence the margin appears somewhat crenelated. "It is found," says Mr. Couch, "of all sizes, from a mere speck to an inch in height. In a very young state, it is sometimes found parasitical on *Alcyonium digitatum*, on shells, and on the stalks of seaweeds; but as these substances are very perishable, and offer no solid foundation, large specimens are never found on them. In its young state the animal is naked, and measures about the fifteenth of an inch in diameter, and about the thirty-second of an inch in height. In the earliest state in which I have seen the calcareous polypidom, there were four small rays, which were free or unconnected down to the base; in others I have noticed six primary rays, but in every case they were unconnected with each other. Other rays soon make their appearance between those first formed; they are mere calcareous specks at first, but afterwards increase in size. The first union of rays is observed as a small calcareous rim at the base of the polype, which afterwards increases in height and diameter with the age of the animal."

The animals of this interesting polypier are vividly described by Dr. Coldstream, in a communication to Dr. Johnston, as he observed them at Torquay:—

"When the soft parts are fully expanded," he says, "the appearance of the whole animal closely resembles an actinia. When shrunk, they are almost entirely hid amongst the radiating plates. They are found pendent," he adds, "from large boulders of sandstone, just at low-water mark. Sometimes they are dredged from the middle of the bay. Their colour varies considerably. I have seen the soft parts white, yellowish, orange-brown, reddish, and of a fine apple-green. The tentacula are usually paler."

The *Caryophylliæ* are sometimes dredged from great depths; Professor Travers dredged one in eighty fathoms, and Dr. Johnston remarks that the existence of an animal so vividly coloured at so great a depth is worthy of remark. "When taken," says the professor, "the animal was scarcely visible, being contracted; when expanded, the disk was conspicuously marked by two dentated circles of bright apple-green, the one marginal and outside the tentacula, the other at some distance from the transverse and linear mouth. In the dark, the animal gave out a few dull flashes of phosphorescent light."

In addition, we may mention the assertion of Mr. Swainson, that *C. ramea*, common in the Mediterranean, is occasionally found on the Cornish coast; but Dr. Johnston thinks it improbable that it could have escaped the attention of Mr. Couch and Mr. Peach, had it been so.

As belonging to this family, we present here illustrations of *Flabellum pavoninum*, Lesson (Fig. 67).

Of the *Occulinæ*, the animal is unknown, but is contained in

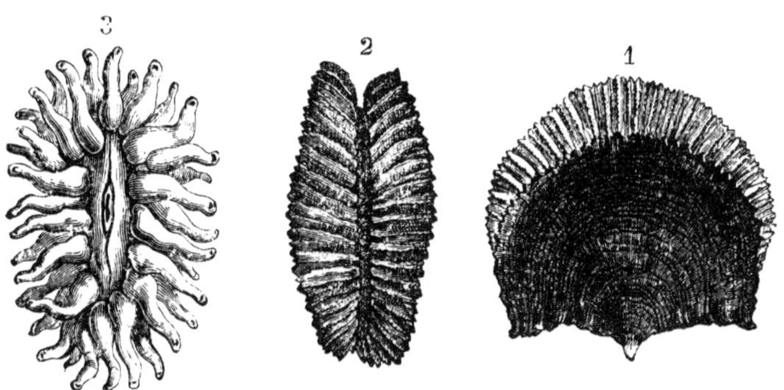

Fig. 67. Flabellum pavoninum (Lesson).
1. Vertical position. 2. Upper edge, with its plates and median thread. 3. Form of the animal.

regular round radiated cells, more or less prominent, and scattered on the surface of a solid, compact, fixed tree-like polypier. The individuals dispose themselves in ascending spiral lines, and appear to be regularly dispersed on the surface of the several branches. The typical species, *O. virginea*, formerly known as the White Coral, although it differs widely in reality from the true Coral, both in its structure and by its star-like polypiferous cells (Fig. 68), is found in the Mediterranean and also in the equatorial seas. Over the specimen we see (2) a portion of a branch magnified, in order that the reader may appreciate numerically the form of polype over its cells.

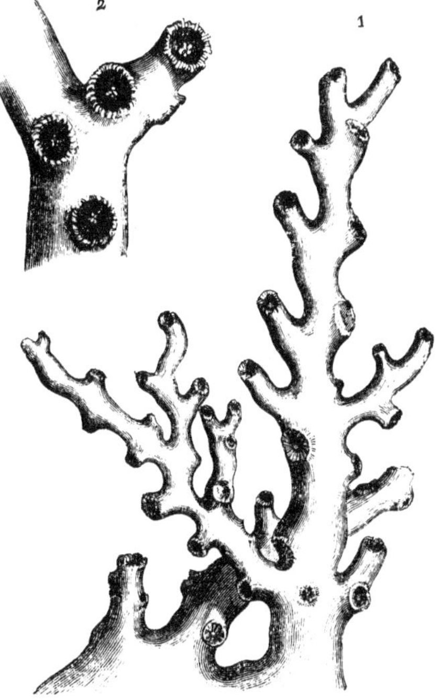

Fig. 68. Occulina virginea (Lamarck).

The species formerly named *Occulina flabelliformis*, and which now bears the name of *Stylaster flabelliformis*, which is represented in

Fig. 69. Stylaster flabelliformis (Lamarck).

Fig. 69, will give an excellent idea of these arborescent zoophytes.

It is a polypier in form of a fan, with many very unequal branches; the larger branches are smooth, the middle-sized are covered with small points. This fine zoophyte is found in the seas which surround the Isle of Bourbon and the Mauritius, a fine example of which is to be seen in the collection of the Museum of Natural History of Paris.

Astræacea.

How diversified are the forms of aquatic life! "Nature revels in these diversities," to paraphrase the saying of one of the ancient kings of France. Here are animals, the frame of which might have been

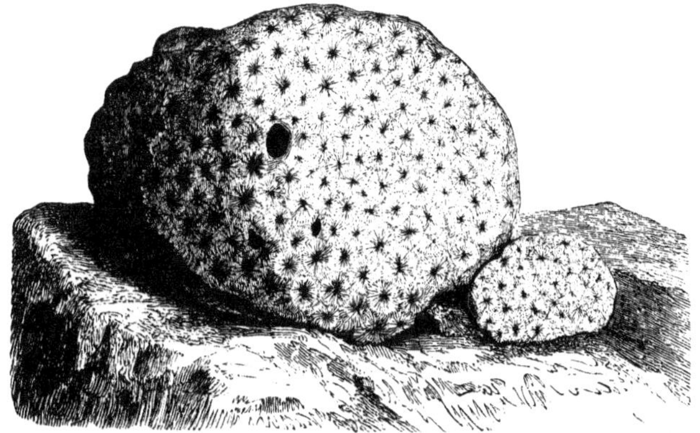

Fig. 70. Astrea punctifera (Lamarck).

designed by a geometrician. They are called Sea-stars (*Astrea*). Their resemblance to the well-known figure was too striking to escape the observation of naturalists; but the organization of these creatures of the ocean is far from being rigorously regular, for Nature rarely employs perfectly straight lines, giving an evident preference to circles and waving lines.

Sea-stars are animals without vertebræ, very frequently depressed or pentagonal, with arms nearly equal, and dispersed in rays, which are more or less triangular. The animal has habitually five arms. They live at an immense depth in the ocean. In the exploring survey in the Atlantic, preparatory to laying down the Atlantic Telegraph cable, several star-fishes were discovered at the depth of more than two hundred and fifty fathoms, belonging to species of which traces are found in some of the oldest geological strata. They are essentially marine animals, there being nothing found in fresh water at all resembling them.

The *Astrea* are inhabitants of the Indian Ocean, where they are found in a great variety of forms, which has led to their subdivision into many genera by Messrs. Milne Edwards and J. Haime. The animals are short, more or less cylindrical, with rounded mouth placed in the centre of a disk, covered with a few rather short tentacula; the cells are shallow, with radiating lamellæ in *Astrea punctifera* (Fig. 70), forming by their union a many-formed polypier, which often encrusts other bodies. In short, this polype may be described as a parasite, for it generally attaches to some other bodies, and it is by no means unusual to meet with shells attached to shells.

The *Meandrina* differ from the *Astreas* in having the surface

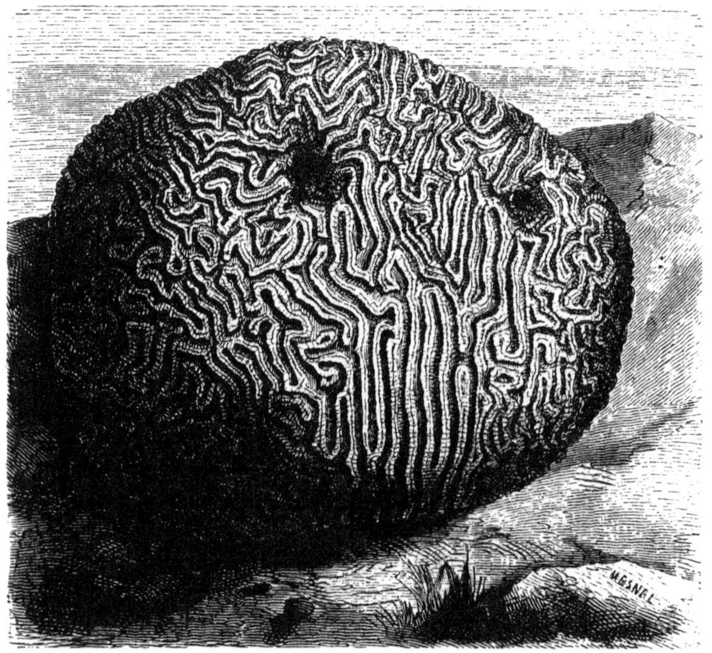

Fig. 71. Meandrina cerebriformis (Lamarck).

hollowed out into shallow sinuous elongated cells, furnished on each side of the mesial line with hooked lamellæ, ending against one or other of the ridges with separate valleys; the polypier, which is calcareous, being fixed, simple, and inversely conical when young, and globular when old. The animals have each a distinct mouth, and lateral series of short tentacula; they are contained in shallow cells, meeting at the base, and forming by their union long and tortuous hollows. *Meandrina cerebriformis* (Fig. 71), so called from its resemblance to the folds of the brain, is a native of the American Seas.

The *Fungia*, so called by Lamarck from their resemblance to the

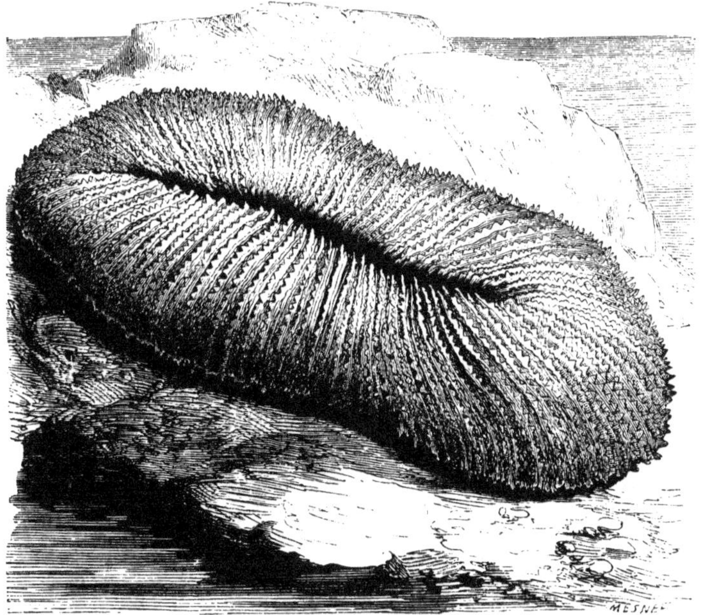

Fig. 72. Fungia echinata (Milne Edwards).

vegetable Fungi, are too remarkable in their appearance to be passed over in silence. The major part of the species only occur in recent geological strata. Nevertheless some of the species were very numerous in the Cretaceous period, and even find representatives in the Silurian period; it is this group in which Madrepores of great size are found.

The family, as we have already said, take their names from their supposed resemblance to the Mushroom. "But," says Peyssonnel, "there is this difference between terrestrial and marine mushrooms—

that the former have leaflets below, and those of the ocean have them above (Fig. 72). These leaflets are only expansions of the Madrepores. Now, although I have not actually examined these petrified Mushrooms of the sea, I have no reason to doubt but that they are true genera or species of Madrepores, containing, like others, the zoophytes which form them. In my travels in Egypt, in 1714 and 1715, I never heard it said that the Nile could produce them." In

Fig. 73. Fungia agariciformis (Lamarck).

this last remark, Peyssonnel makes allusion to the opinion entertained by many ancient authors, that the Fungia were productions of the Nile.

The animal is gelatinous or membranous, generally simple, depressed, and oval, with mouth superior and transverse, in a large disk, which is covered by many thick cirrhiform tentacula; the polypier is rendered solid internally by a calcareous solid deposit of a simple figure, having a star of radiating, acutely-pointed lamellæ above, and simple rays, full of wrinkles, beneath. There are nine species, mostly natives of the Indian Seas, which De Blainville arranges in three groups, according as they are simple and circular, simple and compressed, or complex and oblong. In *Fungia echinata*, represented in Fig. 72, we have a species which inhabits the Indian and Chinese Seas. It belongs to the last group, being oblong in form, convex above, and concave below. The hollow, from which the lamellæ or chamber-walls proceed, are of considerable length; the toothed partitions are very irregular, thin and prickly, resting upon their lower edge, in order to leave the concave portion of the field free to a host of excrescences, resembling the roof of a grotto studded with small stalactites.

The conformation of the softer parts of this polypier has been described by many travellers. The upper portion of the body of the animal, corresponding to the lamelliform part of the polypier, is furnished with scattered tentacula, very long in some species, and remarkably short in others. These tentacula appear to terminate in a small sucker. The animal seems to recover its position with difficulty, when overturned. In order to complete our description of these curious madrepores, we may refer to *Fungia agariciformis*, represented in Fig. 73. This remarkable species inhabits the Red Sea and the Indian Ocean, and is here represented with its polypes.

De Blainville gave the name of MADREPORÆA to the second group of his stony *Zoantharia*, placing them after the *Madrephylliæ*. The products of this section are generally arborescent, with small, partially lamelliform cells, which are constantly porous in the interstices of the walls of the cells, this being its most important characteristic. Thus the visceral apparatus constitutes the essential part of the polypier, presenting no side plates, the visceral chamber being open from the base to the summit, and neither filled with dissepiments, pulpy matter, nor with tabulæ.

The history of these inhabitants of the deep is extremely obscure, and will probably always remain so; the most beautiful of their productions are intertropical, and consequently beyond the reach of discriminating observers during the life of the animal. Solander proposed to divide the genus according to certain characteristics in the growth of the polypier, and De Blainville has rearranged the groups formed by Lamarck, Lamouroux, and Goldfuss, with special reference to the soft parts of the animals figured by Lesueur, Quoy, Gaimard, and others, who have observed them in their native state.

The perforated *Zoantharia* form three very natural families: the *Eupsammidæ*, the *Madreporidæ*, and the *Poritidæ*. The first have the solid parts of the polypes, simple or complex, with well-developed lamellar portions, the central column spongiose, walls granular, semi-ribbed, and perforated. The second are composite, increasing by gemmation; walls spongy and porous; septa lamellous, and well-

Fig. 74. Dendrophyllia ramea, half natural size (De Blainville).

developed. In the third the visceral chambers are divided into two equal parts by the principal septa, which are more developed than the others, meeting by their inner edge. The *Dendrophylliæ* (Fig. 74) are conspicuous among the *Eupsammidæ*.

We shall describe three genera, the two first of which belong to the MADREPORÆA, and the last to the family of the *Porides*.

Dendrophyllia ramea, represented in Figs. 75 and 76, is an elegant madrepore of the Mediterranean. Its polypier presents a very large trunk charged with short ascending branches; it usually attains to about a yard and a half in height. The polypes are provided with a great number of tentacula, in the centre of which the mouth is placed. They are deeply buried in the cells, which radiate from numerous unequally *saillant* plates. Peyssonnel, who had seen the polype of this colony, says: "I may observe that the extremities or summits of the branching madrepore, the species in question, which in the Provençal we call Sea-fennel, is soft and tender, filled with a glutinous and transparent mucous thread, similar to that which the snail leaves on its

Fig. 75. Dendrophyllia ramea (De Blainville). Natural size, with polypiers.

Fig. 76. A part magnified.

path. These extremities are of a fine yellow colour, five or six lines in diameter; soft, and more than a finger's breadth in length. I have seen the animal nestling in them; it seemed to be a species of cuttle-fish or sea-nettle. The body of this sea-nettle must have filled the centre; the head being in the middle, surrounded by many feet or claws, like those of the cuttle-fish. The flesh of this animal is very delicate, and is easily reduced to the form of a paste, melting almost under the touch."

The madrepores abound in all intertropical seas, taking a considerable part in the constitution of the reefs which form the coral and madreporic islands so conspicuous in the ocean. The tree-like *Dendrophyllia* (*D. ramea*, Figs. 75 and 76) have cells of considerable depth, radiating into numerous lamellæ, forming a widely-branching arborescent polypier, externally striated, internally furrowed, and truncate at the extremities. The animals are actiniform, furnished with numerous cleft tentacula, in the centre of which is the polygonal mouth. In the *Lobophyllia*, the tentacula are cylindrical, the cells conical, sometimes elongated and sinuous, with a sub-circular opening terminating the few branches of the polypier, which is fixed, turbinate, and striated. The Plantain Madrepore, *M. plantaginea* (Lamarck), is an interesting example; the polypier presenting itself, as in Fig. 77, in tufts, with slender and prolific branches.

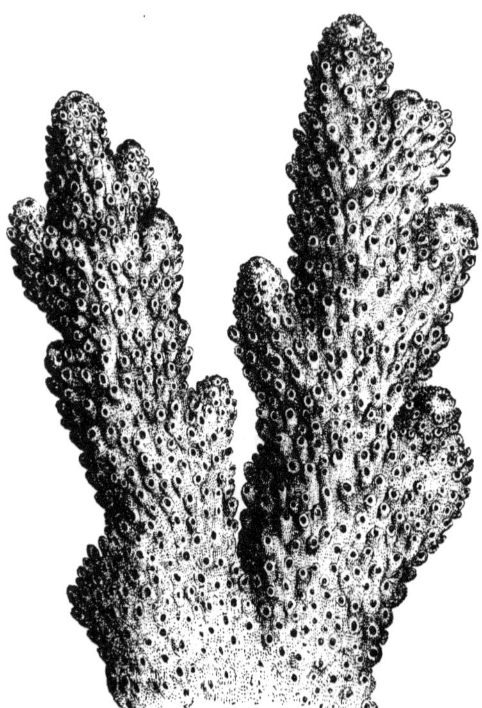

Fig. 77. Madrepora plantaginea (Lamarck).

In *Madrepora palmata*, vulgarly named Neptune's Car, we have a large and beautiful species, whose expanding branches are flat, round at the base, and forming in lobes, whose length is often as much as three feet high, with a breadth of twenty inches, and a thickness of two to two and a half: this fine madrepore is found in the Caribbean Sea and among the Antilles.

Porites.

The Porites are madrepores produced by a pitcher-shaped fleshy animal, with twelve short tentacula; the cells are unequally polygonal, imperfectly defined, slightly radiating by thread-like pointed rays, with prickles placed at intervals. The polypier is polymorphous or many-formed, composed of a reticulated and porous tissue, the individuals forming it being always completely united together. Externally it presents the figure of an irregular trellis-work, more or less loosely connected in its meshes. As a type of this organization, we give a figure of the Forked Porites (*P. furcata,* Fig. 78), of the natural size. The branches are generally dichotomous, that is, rising in pairs obtusely lobed. In some of the species the rays are more

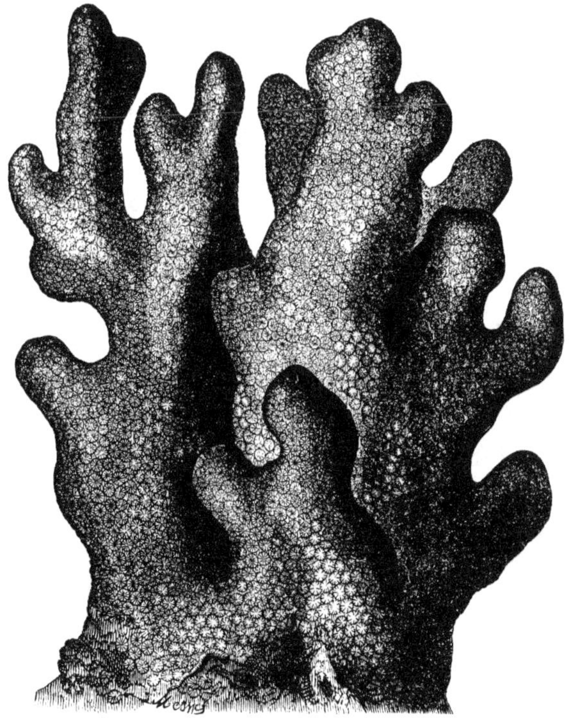

Fig. 78. Porites furcata (Lamarck), natural size.

fully marked, and resemble a bed of miniature anemones thickly crowded together, as in *Gonispora columna*, in which the polypes have a central mouth, round which the twelve short tentacula radiate; the polypier is stony, fixed, branched, or lobed, having a free surface covered with a great number of regular stars, which are highly characteristic, and cannot be confounded with those of an astrea or madrepore.

In the Tabulate Madreporides, the polypier is essentially composed of a highly-developed mural system. The visceral chambers are divided into a series of stages or stories, by perfect diaphragms or plates placed transversely, the plates depending from the walls and forming perfect horizontal divisions, extending from one wall of the general cavity to the other. In order that the reader may form some idea of the Tabulate Madrepores, one of the polypiers known as *millepores* is here represented. The millepores were first separated

Fig. 79. Millepora alcicornis (Linn.), one-fourth natural size.

from the madrepores by Linnæus, along with a great number of species distinguished by the minuteness of their pores or polypiferous cells (Fig. 79), represented above, as nearly allied, and, perhaps, identical, with Dr. Johnston's *Cellepora cervicornis*, a species found in deep water on the Devonshire and Cornwall coasts, and, indeed, all round our west coast. "A single specimen of this millepore is about three inches in height," says Dr. Johnston, "and somewhat more in breadth. It rises from a broad flattened base, and begins immediately to expand and divide into kneed branches or broad segments, many of which anastomose, so as to form arches and imperfect circles. The extreme segments are dilated and variously cut, sometimes truncate, both sides being perforated with numerous pores just visible to the naked eye, and arranged in rows; the pores circular, and level with the surface on the smooth and newly-formed parts; but in the older parts they form apertures of urceolate cells, which appear to be formed over the primary layer of cells, giving to the surface a roughish or angular appearance. The orifice is simple, contracted, with a very small denticle on one side; the thickness of the branches varies from one half to two lines; the interior is cellular; the new parts are formed of two layers of horizontal cells, but the older parts are thickened by cells superimposed on the primary layers."

Millepora moniliformis is a species which attaches itself to the branches of the gorgons, and forms there a series of little rounded or lateral lobes. The animal is unknown, the cells very small, unequal, completely immersed, obsoletely radiate and scattered; the polypier fixed, cellular within, finely porous and reticulated externally, extending into a palmated form.

Of tuberous or wrinkled madrepores, which consist almost entirely of fossil species chiefly belonging to the Silurian formation, we shall only note *Cyathophyllum* as one of the best known species.

There is no spectacle in Nature more extraordinary, or more worthy of our admiration, than that now under consideration. These zoophytes, whose history we are about to investigate—these wretched beings gifted with a half-latent life only—these animalcules so small and so fragile—labour silently and incessantly in the bosom of the ocean, and, as they exist in innumerable aggregated masses, their cells and solid axes finish by producing in the end enormous stony masses. These calcareous deposits increase and multiply with such incalculable rapidity, that they not only cover the submarine rocks as with a carpet, but they finish by forming reefs, and even entire islands, which rise above the surface of the ocean in a manner remarkable at once for their form and the regularity with which they repeat themselves.

In noting the Indian and Pacific Oceans, navigators had long been struck with the appearance of certain earthy bases, which presented a conformation altogether singular. In 1601, Pyrard de Laval, speaking of the Malouine (now the Falkland) Islands, said: "They are divided into thirteen provinces, named atollons, which is so far a natural division in that place, that each atollon is separated from the other, and contains a great number of smaller islands. It is a marvel to see each of these atollons surrounded on all sides by a great bank of stone—walls such as no human hands could build on the space of earth allotted to them. These atollons are almost round, or rather oval, being each about thirty leagues in circumference, some a little less, others a little more, and all ranging from north to south, without any one touching the other. There is between them sea channels, one broad, the other narrow. Being in the middle of an atollon, you see all around you this great stone bank, which surrounds and protects the island from the waves; but it is a formidable attempt, even for the boldest, to approach the bank and watch the waves as they roll in and break with fury upon the shore."

Since the publication of Laval's description, many circular isles, or groups of islands, analogous to these atollons, since called *atolls,* have been discovered in the Pacific Ocean and other seas. The naturalist Forster, who accompanied Cook in his voyage round the world, first made known the more remarkable characteristics of these gigantic formations. He perfectly comprehended their origin, which he was the first to attribute to the development of the calcareous zoophytic polypier.

After Forster, many other naturalists—Lamouroux, Chamisso, Quoy, Gaimard, Ehrenberg, Ellis, Darwin, Couthony, and Dana—have furnished Science with many precious lessons on the natural history of coral islands and madreporic reefs. We can only glance at a few of the more remarkable genera of these interesting creatures.

"Those occupying the same polypier," says Frédol, "live in perfect harmony; they constitute a family of brothers, physically united in the closest bonds of union. They occupy the same dwelling, each having its separate chamber; but the power of abandoning it is denied them. Attached each to its cell, they are driven to trust in Providence for the food which never fails them; moreover, what is eaten by each mouth profits the whole community. Urged on by a wonderful instinct, the polypes labour together at the same work; isolated, they would be weak and helpless; in combination, they are strong." M. Lacaze-Duthiers has even demonstrated that *Antipathes glaberrima*, *Gorgonia tuberculata* (Lamarck), *Leiopathes glaberrima*

Plate IV.—Coral Island of Clermont-Tonnerre, in the Pomotouan Archipelago.

(Gray), and *Leiopathes Lamarckii* (Haime), were present on the same polypier, the *Gerardia* of Lamarck. It is thus recognised that, under the general denomination of polypiers, very distinct species are found, some being of the *Hydra* type, others belonging to the *Plumularia*. The first are very common on our coast: they include the *Tubularia*, the *Campanularia*, and the *Sertularia*.

The Reed Tubularia (*T. indivisa*) produces a remarkably curious polypier: its numerous stems are horny, yellow, and marked at intervals with irregular knots, resembling the joints of a straw. Their lower extremity is tortuous, and apt to adhere to foreign bodies; the upper part is nearly upright, and slightly flexuous, the whole resembling some flowering plant, without leaves or lateral branches. The *Campanularias* are altogether different; the end of the branches whence the polypes issue are broad and bell-shaped, *C. dichotoma* presenting a stem of brownish colour, thin as a silken thread, but strong and elastic. The polypes are numerous, a branch eight inches in height being inhabited by as many as twelve hundred individuals.

The *Sertularias* have a horny stem, sometimes simple, sometimes branching, and may easily be mistaken for small plants. Their name is derived from the Latin *sertum*, a bouquet; and, indeed, they can only be described as trees in miniature, with branches yellow and semi-transparent, each tree having seven, eight, twelve, or twenty small panicles, each of which will contain about five hundred animalcules, the tree itself containing probably ten thousand associated polypes. Occasionally *Sertularia argentea* is said to afford shelter and employment for a hundred thousand of these creatures. *S. falcata*, having all the grace and elegance of the delicate and slender Mimosa, is now placed among the Bryozoares.

The minute cells in which the polypes are lodged are not always arranged in the same manner. Sometimes the cells occupy one side only; in other instances they occupy both; sometimes they are grouped like the pipes of an organ, at others they are ranged spirally round the stem, or arranged at intervals, forming horizontal rings round it.

The *Alcyonaria* are very common on some parts of our coast, where scarcely a stone or shell is dredged up that does not support one or more specimens known to the fishermen as "cow's paps," "dead men's fingers," and other popular names. This round and lobed fleshy mass is quite a colony in itself; placed in pure sea water, it very soon presents certain yellow or grass-like points, which gradually expand and display themselves in their native transparent and animated coralline. Each of these polypes have eight dentate petals, in the centre of which is the mouth; the body of the polype is tubular, varying externally in length, traversed internally throughout its entire mass by a tissue studded with reddish spiculæ, and furrowed with small reed-like ribbons, common to all the individuals of the association.

Among the *Tubiporidæ* may be noted *Tubipora musica* (Linnæus), from the Indian Ocean, characterised by its stony tubes, simple, numerous, straight or flexible, parallel, and slightly radiating, of a fine purple, and united together at intervals by transverse bands, so as to resemble the pipes of an organ. The polype is a brilliant grass green, according to Péron; the tentacula furnished on each side with two or three rows of granulous fleshy papillæ, to the number of sixty to eighty (Lesson).

The *Gorgonia* is studded with calcareous or siliceous spiculæ which form a crust in drying. This crust is friable, and frequently preserves the colours more or less brilliant which characterise it. Their cells are sometimes hollowed out of the plain surface; sometimes they occur in the projecting mammals; these are smooth, rough, or scaly—sometimes pendent the one from the other.

The polypiers attach themselves to solid bodies, sometimes even to each other, grafting themselves or interlacing each other in all directions. In colour they are whitish, pure white, yellow, and apple-green; their shades, passing from olive-brown to deep blue, from vermilion to violet, and from pale yellow to pearly-grey. Each tube or cell contains an individual. The cells are more or less deep, according to the species. The polypes are composed generally of a hidden portion more or less tubular, and of a star-like portion more or less displayed. This latter portion presents from eight to twelve soft and granulous wattles, susceptible of expansion, like the petals of a flower. When these appendages are displayed, they often attain twice the height of the body; in this state they are nearly transparent, except towards the extremity. They extend or compress these wattles, dilate or contract the mouth according to their wants; but their digestive tube is firmly soldered to the cell, while the axis which supports the cells is motionless. What a singular combination is here presented! Trees, one-half of which are animated, growing at the bottom of the sea; animalcules, one-half of which is imprisoned, and riveted to their person; their stomachs in the bark, their arms on a branch, their movements perfect repose!

These minute silent workers are active and indefatigable; their task is to separate the salt and other chemical particles from the waters of the ocean, and, while feeding themselves, secrete and organise the axis which bears their lodging. They love the warmer regions of the ocean; in colder regions, the results of their labours are extremely limited: the one forms a sward of submarine life, which carpets the rocks; the other produces animated stalactites, great shrubs, whole forests of small trees. The electric cable, which unites Sardinia to the Genoese fort, was so encrusted with polypiers and bryozoares, that certain portions taken from the water for repairs had attained the size of a small barrel.

The atolls present three unfailing and constant peculiarities. Sometimes they constitute a great circular chain, the centre of which is occupied by a deep basin, in direct communication with the exterior sea, through one or many breaches of great depth. These are the *atolls*, described more than two centuries ago by Pyrard de Laval; sometimes they surround, but at some distance, a small island, in such a manner as to constitute a sort of skeleton or girdle of reefs; finally, they may form the immediate edging or border of an island or continent. In this last case, they are called fringing littorals, or edging reefs. At the distance of a few hundred yards only from the edge of some of these reefs, the sea is of such a depth that the sounding-lead has failed to reach the bottom.

In order to give an idea of the general form of these atolls, although they are rarely so regular, the reader is referred to Pl. III., which represents one of these islands of the Pomotouan Archipelago, in the Indian Ocean. It represents the island of Clermont-Tonnerre, figured by Captain Wilkes in the American Exploring Expedition. The exterior girdle of rocks here surrounds a basin nearly circular. Such is the general form—the typical form, so to speak—of the coral isles, of which this is a fair representation.

The zoophytes which form these mineral accumulations belong to diverse groups, and nowhere have the results of observations made upon these atolls been more minutely described than in Mr. Darwin's remarks on the grand *Cocos Island* situated to the south of Sumatra, in the Indian Ocean.

No writer, it seems to us, has reasoned on these atolls more comprehensively than the author of the "Origin of Species." "The earlier voyagers," he says, "fancied that the coral-building animals instinctively built up their great corals to afford themselves protection in the inner parts; but so far is this from the truth, that those massive kinds, to whose growth on the exposed outer shores the very existence of the reef depends, cannot live within the lagoon, where other delicately-branching kinds flourish. Moreover, in this view, many species of distinct genera and families are supposed to combine for one end; and of such a combination not a single instance can be found in the whole of Nature. The theory that has been most generally received is, that atolls are based on submarine craters, but when the form and size of some of them are considered, this idea loses its plausible character. Thus, the Suadiva atoll is forty-four geographical miles in diameter in one line by thirty-four in another; Rimsky is fifty-four by twenty miles across; Bow atoll is thirty miles long, and, on an average, six miles broad. This theory, moreover, is totally inapplicable to the Northern Maldivian atolls in the Indian Ocean, one of which is eighty-eight miles in length, and between ten and twenty in breadth."

The various theories which had been propounded failing to explain the existence of the coral islands, Mr. Darwin was led to reconsider the whole subject. Numerous soundings taken all round the Cocos atoll showed that at ten fathoms the prepared tallow in the hollow of the sounding-rod came up perfectly clean, and marked with the impression of living polypes. As the depth increased, these impressions became less numerous, but adhering particles of sand succeed, until it was evident that the bottom consisted of smooth sand. From these observations, it was obvious to him that the utmost depth at which the coral polypes can construct reefs is between twenty and thirty fathoms Now, there are enormous areas in the Indian Ocean in which every island is a coral formation raised to the height to which the waves can throw up fragments and the winds pile up sand; and the only theory which seems to account for all the circumstances embraced, is that of the subsidence of vast regions in this ocean. "As mountain after mountain and island after island slowly sunk beneath the water," he says, "fresh bases would be successively afforded for the growth of the corals. I venture to defy anyone to explain in any other manner how it is possible that numerous islands should be distributed throughout vast areas, all the islands being low, all built of coral absolutely requiring a foundation within a limited depth below the surface."

The *Porites*, according to Mr. Darwin, form the most elevated deposits of those which are situated nearer the level of the water: *Millepora complanata* also enters into the formation of the upper banks. Various other branched polypiers present themselves in great numbers in the cavities left by the *Porites* and *Millepora* crossing each other. It is difficult to identify species occupying themselves in the deeper parts, but, according to Darwin, the lower parts of the reefs are occupied by polypes of the same species as in the upper parts; at the depth of eighteen fathoms and upwards, the bottom consists alternately of sand and polypiers. The total breadth of the circular reef or ring which constitute the atoll of the Keeling's or Cocos Island varies from two hundred to five hundred yards in breadth. Some little parasitic isles form themselves upon the reefs, at two or three hundred yards from their exterior edge, by the accumulation of the fragments thrown up here during great storms. They rise from two to three yards above the sea level, and consist of shells, polypiers, and sea urchins, the whole consolidated into hard and solid rock.

Mr. Darwin's description of a kind of Sea-pen, *Virgularia Patagonia*, throws some curious light on the habits of these creatures. "This zoophyte consists of a thin, straight, fleshy stem, with alternate rows of polypi on each side, and surrounding an elastic stony axis, varying in length from eight inches to two feet. The stem at one extremity is truncate, but at the other is terminated by a vermiform fleshy appendage. The stony axis, which gives strength to the stem, may be traced at the extremity into a mere vessel filled with granular matter. At low water, hundreds of these zoophytes might be seen projecting like stubble, with the truncate end upwards, a few inches above the surface of the muddy sand. When touched or pulled, they suddenly drew themselves in with force, so as nearly, or quite, to disappear. By this action, the highly elastic axis must be bent at the lower extremity, where it is naturally slightly curved; and I imagine it is by this elasticity alone that the zoophyte is enabled to rise again through the mud. Each polypus, though closely united to its brethren, has a distinct mouth, body, and tentacula. Of these polypi, in a large specimen there must be many thousands, yet we see that they act by one movement. They have also one central axis connected with a system of obscure circulation, and the ova are produced in an organ distinct from the separate individuals. For," adds Mr. Darwin, in a note, "the cavities leading from the fleshy compartments of the extremity were filled with a yellow pulpy matter which, under a microscope, consisted of rounded semi-transparent grains aggregated together into particles of various sizes. All such particles, as well as separate grains, possessed the power of rapid motion, generally revolving round different axes, but sometimes progressive."

The description of the Island of Cocos or Keeling is as follows:— "The ring-formed reef of the lagoon island is surmounted, in the greater part of its length, by linear islets. On the northern, or leeward side, there is an opening through which vessels can pass to the anchorage within. On entering, the scene was very curious, and rather pretty ; its beauty, however, entirely depended on the brilliancy of the surrounding colours. The shallow, clear, and still water of the lagoon, resting in its greater part on white sand, is, when illumined by a vertical sun, of the most vivid green. This brilliant expanse, several miles in width, is on all sides divided, either by a line of snow-white breakers from the dark heaving waters of the ocean, or from the blue vault of heaven by the strips of land crowned by the level tops of the cocoa-nut tree. As a white cloud here and there affords a pleasing contrast to the azure sky, so in the lagoon bands of living coral darken the emerald-green water.

"The next morning I went ashore on Direction Island. The strip of dry land is only a few hundred yards in width ; on the lagoon side there was a white calcareous beach, the radiation from which, under this sultry climate, was very oppressive. On the outer coast, a solid broad flat of coral rock served to break the violence of the open sea. Excepting near the lagoon, where there is some sand, the land is entirely composed of rounded fragments of coral. In such a loose, dry, stony soil, the climate of the intertropical regions alone could produce so vigorous a vegetation. On some of the smaller islets, nothing could be more elegant than the manner in which the young and full-grown cocoa-nut trees, without destroying each other's symmetry, were mingled into one wood. A beach of glittering white sand formed a border to those fairy spots.

"The natural history of these islands, from its very paucity, possesses peculiar interest. The cocoa-nut tree, at the first glance, seems to compose the whole wood; there are, however, five or six other trees. One of these grows to a very large size, but, from the extreme softness of its wood, it is useless; another sort affords excellent timber for shipbuilding. Besides the trees, the number of plants is exceedingly limited, and consist of insignificant weeds. In my collection, which includes, I believe, nearly the perfect Flora, there are twenty species, without reckoning a moss, lichen, and fungus. To this number two trees must be added, one of which was not in flower, and the other I only heard of. The latter is a solitary tree of its kind, and grows near the beach, where, without doubt, the one seed was thrown up by the waves.

"The next day I employed myself in examining the very interesting yet simple structure and origin of these islands. The water being unusually smooth, I waded over the flat of dead rock as far as the living mounds of coral, on which the swell of the open sea breaks. In some of the gulleys and hollows there were beautiful green and other coloured fishes, and the forms and tints of many of the zoophytes were admirable. It is excusable to grow enthusiastic over the infinite number of organic beings with which the sea of the Tropics, so prodigal of life, teems; yet I must confess, I think those naturalists who have described in well-known words the submarine grottoes, decked with a thousand beauties, have indulged in rather exuberant language.

"I accompanied Captain Fitzroy to an island at the head of the lagoon; the channel was exceedingly intricate, winding through fields of delicately-branched corals. At the head of the lagoon we crossed a narrow islet, and found a great surf breaking on the windward coast. I can hardly explain the reason, but there is, to my mind, much grandeur in the view of the outer shores of these lagoon islands. There is a simplicity in the barrier-like beach, the margin of green bushes and tall cocoa-nuts, the solid flat of dead coral-rock, strewed here and there with great loose fragments, and the line of furious breakers, all rounding away towards either hand. The ocean, throwing its waters over the broad reef, appears an invincible, all-powerful enemy; yet we see it resisted and even conquered by means which at first seem most weak and inefficient. It is not that the ocean spares the rock of coral; the great fragments scattered over the reef, and heaped on the beach whence the tall cocoa-nut springs, plainly bespeak the unrelenting power of the waves. Nor are any periods of repose granted; the long swell caused by the gentle but steady action of the trade-winds, always blowing in one direction over a wide area, causes breakers almost equalling in force those during a gale of wind in the temperate regions, and which never cease to rage. It is impossible to behold these waves without feeling a conviction that an island, though built of the hardest rocks—let it be porphyry, granite, or quartz—would ultimately yield and be demolished by such an irresistible power. Yet these low, insignificant coral islets stand, and are victorious; for here another power, as an antagonist, takes part in the contest. The organic forces separate the atoms of carbonate of lime, one by one, from the foaming breakers, and unite them into a symmetrical structure. Let the hurricane tear up its thousand huge fragments, yet what will that tell against the accumulated labour of myriads of architects at work night and day, month after month? Thus do we see the soft and gelatinous body of a polypus, through the agency of the vital laws, conquering the great mechanical power of the waves of an ocean which neither the art of man nor the inanimate works of Nature could successfully resist."

We have said that madreporic or coralline formations affect three forms, to which the names of *atolls*, *barrier reefs*, and *fringing reefs* have been applied. We have spoken of atolls; we shall now say a few words on barrier and fringing reefs.

Barrier reefs are formations which surround the ordinary islands, or stretch along their banks. They have the form and general structure of atolls. Like atolls, the barrier reefs appear placed on the edge of a marine precipice. They rise on the edge of a plateau which looks down on a bottomless sea. On the coast of New Caledonia, only two lengths of his ship from the reef, Captain Kent found no bottom in a hundred and fifty fathoms. This was verified at Gambier Island in the Pacific Ocean, in Qualem Island, and at many others.

According to Mr. Darwin, the barrier reef situated on the western coast of New Caledonia is four hundred miles long; that along the eastern coast of Australia extends almost without interruption for a thousand miles, ranging from twenty or thirty to fifty or sixty miles from the coast. As to the elevation of the islands thus surrounded with reefs, it varies considerably. The Isle of Tahiti rises six thousand eight hundred feet above the level of the sea; the Isle of Maurua to six hundred; Aituaki to three hundred; and Manonai to about fifty feet only.

Around the Isle of Gambier the reef has a thickness of a thousand and sixty feet, at Tahiti of two hundred and thirty. Round the Fiji Islands it is from two to three thousand.

The *fringing reefs* immediately surrounding the island, or a portion of it, might be confounded with the barrier reefs we have been describing, if they only differed in their smaller breadth; but the circumstance that they abut immediately on the coast in place of being separated by a channel or lagoon more or less deep and continuous, proves that they are in direct communication with the slope of the submarine soil, and permits of their being distinguished from the barrier reefs. The dangerous breakers which surround the Mauritius are a striking example of the fringing reef. This island is almost entirely surrounded by a barrier of these rocks, the breadth of which varies from a hundred and fifty to three hundred and thirty feet; their rugged and abrupt surface is worn almost smooth, and is rarely uncovered at low water. Analogous reefs surround the Isle of Bourbon; all round this island the polypiers construct on the volcanic bottom of the sea detached mammalons, which rise from a fathom to a fathom and a half above the water.

Madreporic coasting reefs present themselves also on the eastern coast of Africa and of Brazil. In the Red Sea, reefs of polypiers exist which may be ranked among the madreporic coasting reefs, in consequence of the limited breadth of the gulf. Ehrenberg and Hemprich examined a hundred and fifty stations in the Red Sea, all of which had outlying fringing reefs of this description.

It may be asked, With what rapidity are these coral and madreporic banks formed, so as to become *atolls* and *fringing reefs?* To answer this question even approximately is very difficult. On the coast of the Mauritius, according to M. d'Archaic,* the learned professor of the Jardin des Plantes, the edge of the reef is produced by *Madrepora corymbosa*, *M. pocillifera*, and two species of *Astrea*, which pursue their operations at the depth of from eight to fifteen fathoms. At the base is a bank of *Seriatopora*, from fifteen to twenty fathoms in

* "Cours de Paleontologie Stratigraphique."

height. At the bottom, the sand is covered with *Seriatopora*. At twenty fathoms we also meet with fragments of *Madrepora*. Between twenty and forty fathoms the bottom is sandy, and the sounding-rod brings up great fragments of *Caryophylla*. According to MM. Quoy and Gaimard, the *Astreas*, which, as these naturalists consider, constitute the greater part of the reefs, cannot live beyond four or five fathoms deep. *Millepora alcicornis* extends from the surface to the depth of twelve fathoms; the *Madrepores* and *Seriatopores* down to twenty fathoms. Considerable masses of *Meandrina* have been observed at sixteen fathoms; and a *Caryophylla* has been brought up from eighty fathoms in thirty-three degrees south latitude. Among the polypiers which do not form solid reefs, Mr. Darwin mentions *Cellaria*, found at a hundred and ninety fathoms deep, *Gorgonia* at a hundred and sixty, *Corallines* at a hundred, *Millepora* at from thirty to forty-five, *Sertularias* at forty, and *Tubulipora* at ninety-five fathoms.

According to Dana, none of the species which form reefs—namely, *Madrepora*, *Millepora*, *Porites*, *Astreas*, and *Meandrineas*—can live at a greater depth than eighteen fathoms. It is only near the surface of the water that the zoophytes which produce minerals and form madreporic banks put forth their powers; the points most exposed to the beating of the waves is that which is most favourable to their growth; it is there that the *Astreas*, *Porites*, and *Millepores* most abound.

The proportionate increase of the structures, according to Mr. Darwin, depends at once upon the species which construct the reefs and upon various accessary circumstances. The ordinary rate of increase of the madrepores, according to Dana, is about an inch and a half annually; and, as their branches are much scattered, this will not exceed half an inch in thickness of the whole surface covered by the madrepore. Again, in consequence of their porosity, this quantity will be reduced to three-eighths of an inch of compact matter. It is, besides, to be noted that great spaces are wanting; the sands filling up the destroyed part of the polypier are washed out by the currents in the great depths where there are no living polypiers, and the surface occupied by them is reduced to a sixth of the whole coralline region, which reduces the preceding three-eighths to one-sixth. The shells and other organic débris will probably represent a fourth of the total produce in relation to polypiers. In this manner, taking everything into account, the mean increase of a reef cannot exceed the eighth of an inch annually. According to this calculation, some reefs which are not less than two thousand feet thick would require for their formation a hundred and ninety-two thousand years.

It is necessary to add, however, that in favourable circumstances the increase of the masses of polypier may be much more rapid. Mr. Darwin speaks of a ship which, having been wrecked in the Persian Gulf, was found, after being submerged only twenty months, to be covered with a bed of polypiers two feet in thickness; he also mentions experiments made by Mr. Allen on the coast of Madagascar, which tend to prove that in the space of six months certain polypiers increased nearly three feet.

We proceed to the theoretic explanation of these curious mineral formations.

Naturalists and navigators have been much divided in opinion as to the true origin of these madreporic islands. Most of them have admitted that these enormous banks are composed of the mineral spoils and earthy detritus of the madrepores and corals, which, developing themselves in their midst, or upon the bed of the ocean, multiplying and superposing themselves, age after age, and generation after generation, have finally concluded by forming deposits of this immense extent. The growth of the vast madreporic column would be finally arrested by the want of water when its summit approached the level of the sea. It is thus that Forster, Péron, Flinders, and Chamisso have explained the formation of the *atolls* and *madreporic* reefs. This opinion has also found a supporter, in our times, in the French admiral, Du Petit Thouars. But he objects, with reason, that the polypiers cannot live at the prodigious depth of sea at which the base of these islets lie. It has therefore been found necessary to seek for another cause to satisfy the diverse conditions of the phenomena, and explain, at the same time, the strange circular arrangement of these islands, which is almost constant, and which it is essential to keep in view.

Sir Charles Lyell was of opinion that the base of an atoll was always the crater of an ancient submarine volcano, which, when crowned with corals and madrepores, would naturally reproduce this circular wall formed of heaped-up polypiers.

This theory supposes the existence of volcanic craters in the neighbourhood of all the coral islands. It is quite certain that these islands are often found not far from extinct volcanoes, and Sir Charles Lyell has published a very curious map in connection with the subject; nevertheless, the coincidence does not always exist. We have already remarked on the theory by which Mr. Darwin seeks to explain the complicated conditions of the phenomena. The explanation proposed accounts for the known facts, as well as the present appearance of the madreporic islands. The circular atolls and madreporic banks which are disposed as a sort of girdle, are principally formed of *porites*, *millepora*, and *astrea*, zoophytes which cannot exist at any great depth in the ocean, but which swarm on the rocks at some few fathoms only below the limits of the tide. These animals, by means of their accumulated débris, soon form a sort of coating round the island, which constitutes the littoral reefs: this marginal tongue or shoulder, according to Mr. Darwin, is the first stage in the existence of a madreporic island. At this point the author introduces a geological cause, namely, a great subsiding movement of the soil, in which the madreporic colony is sunk under the water. It is evident that after submersion the zoophyte will only continue to develope itself on the upper surface, and within the limits which its nature prescribes. The madrepores exhibiting their greatest vitality at the points most exposed to the fury of the waves, it will be near the outer edge of the reef that the development will be most rapid. If the subsidence of the island thus surrounded should still continue, as mountain after mountain and island after island slowly sink beneath the water, fresh bases would be successively afforded for the growth of the corals, and the outer edge elevated by their continual labour, thus transforming the space into a sort of circular lagune. The madreporic deposits would thus form an isolated girdle, and the lagune, which occupies the centre, would become deeper and deeper in proportion to the lowering of the soil. This is the second stage of the madreporic isle.

The existence of the atolls are thus subordinated to two principal conditions: the progressive subsidence of the shore washed by the sea, and the existence of coral formed of stony polypiers, the growth and multiplication of which are extremely rapid.

It follows from this that madreporic isles cannot exist in all seas; that they only have their birth in the Torrid zone, or at least near the Tropics, for it is only in these regions where the warmth exists, so necessary to their development, that the madrepores show themselves in greatest abundance.

The great field of madreporic formations, in short, are found in the warm parts of the Pacific Ocean. It is from this point, as from a common centre, round which are ranged the series of madreporic isles and islets, that it will be useful, in concluding this chapter, to trace their geographical distribution. We borrow the materials for this from Milne Edwards's tableaux of their distribution in the principal seas of the world.

It is, as we have said, only in the warm parts of the Pacific Ocean that the great mass of these islands are found. They give birth towards the south to the group of atolls known as the archipelago of the Bashee Islands, the extreme limit of the region being the Isle of Ducie. A multitude of other islands of the same nature are sparsely scattered over the sea, up to the east coast of Australia. There are enormous areas here, in which every single island is of coral formation, and is raised to the height at which the waves can throw up fragments. The Radack group is an angular square, four hundred miles long by two hundred and forty broad. Between this group and the Low Archipelago itself, eight hundred and forty miles by four hundred and twenty, there are groups and single islands covering a linear space of more than four thousand miles. To the north of the Equator, the archipelago of the Caroline Islands constitute a very considerable group of madreporic formation, comprehending upwards of a thousand, extending in a broad belt over nearly forty degrees of longitude. On the other hand, all along the coast of the American continent, round the Galapagos and the Isle of Paques, we find no trace of them. The reason assigned is, that in these regions a great current of cold water, flowing from the Antarctic Pole, so much lowers the temperature of the sea, that the zoophytes no longer possess the requisite vigour.

We still meet with atolls in the Chinese Seas, and madreporic barrier reefs are abundant round the Marianne and Philippine Islands. These marginal reefs form also an immense tract, from the Isle of Timor, along the south coast of Sumatra, up to the island of Nicobar, in the Bay of Bengal.

To the west of the Indian Peninsula, the Maldive and Laccadive

Islands form the extremity of another group of atolls, and important madreporic reefs, which extend towards the south, by the Maldives and the Chagos Islands; they consist of low coral formations, densely clothed with cocoa-nut trees. The Maldives, the most southerly cluster, include upwards of a thousand islands and reefs; the Laccadives, seventeen in number, are of similar origin. The Saya de Malha bank, towards the south-east, constitutes a further group of madreporic islets. Finally, the coast of the Mauritius, of Madagascar, of the Seychelles, and even the African continent, from the northern extremity of the Mozambique Channel to the bottom of the Red Sea, are studded with numerous reefs of the same nature. They fail, however, almost completely, along the coast of the Asiatic continent, where, among others, the waters of the Euphrates, the Indus, and the Ganges, enter the sea, and diversify its inhabitants. The western coast of Africa, and the east coast of the American continent, are almost entirely destitute of great madreporic reefs, but they abound in the Caribbean Seas. In the Gulf of Mexico, where the vast fresh-water current of the Mississippi debouches into the sea, they are unknown. It is principally on the north coast and upon the eastern flanks of the chain of West Indian Islands that the madreporic reefs show themselves in these regions.

The polypes which have produced these vast ranges of islands would be set down, at first sight, as the most incapable objects in creation for accomplishing it. In the case of the *Pennatulidæ*, the skin is coriaceous, strengthened with calcareous particles; the interior is a fibrous net-work containing a transparent jelly in the squares, and permeated by a certain number of longitudinal cartilaginous tubes; the soft part is uniformly gelatinous, but the skin is also coriaceous, with a great number of calcareous spicula placed parallel to one another, adding greatly to its strength and consistency.

The polypes are placed in this external fleshy crust; their position being marked by an orifice on the surface, distinguished by eight star-like rays, which open when the upper portion of the body is forced outwards, in which state it resembles a cylindrical bladder or nipple crowned with a fringe of tentacula, which surround the mouth. Under this orifice is the stomach, occupying the centre of the cylinder. The space between this stomach and the outer envelope is divided into eight equal compartments or cells by as many thin septa, originating in a labial rim or lip between the bases of the tentacula, which descend through the cylinder attached on the one side to the inner tunic of the body, and on the other to the stomach, which is thus retained in its position.

The protruding portion of the polype is very delicate, the internal viscera being, as it were, enclosed in a bladder formed of two very thin membranes in intimate union, so transparent as to permit a view of their arrangement. At the base of the body, where thickest, it coalesces with the base of the adjacent polype; thus constituting the common cortical portion into which each animalcule retreats at will, by a process in many respects resembling that by which a snail draws in its horns. In the greater number of *Asteroidæ* this common portion secretes carbonate of lime, which is deposited in the meshes of its tissues either in granules or in crystalline spiculæ, which imparts a solid consistency to the whole. The inner tissue meanwhile continues unaltered, being prolonged throughout the polypiferous mass, lining the cell, the abdominal cavity, and the longitudinal canals which permeate the whole polypier, as well as the tubular net-work with which the spaces between the canals is occupied. It is among these inner tissues that the buds or gemmæ are generated, by whose increase and evolution the polype mass is enlarged, the shape and size depending on the manner in which the buds are evolved; for in some, as in *Pennatulidæ*, determinate spots only have the appropriated organization, while in others, as in *Alcyonium*, the generative faculty appears to be undefined and more diffused.

The Actiniaria.

Here we leave the group of polypes which form united families. The Sea Anemones, of which the *Actinia* are the type, consist of *Zoanthaires*, which produce no polypiers, that is to say, of polypes whose covering remains always soft, and in whose interior nothing solid is produced. This order is usually divided into two families—the *Actiniadæ*, having the tentacles in uninterrupted circles, with no corallum, and the *Minyadinæ*, having globose bodies, and very short tentacula.

The modern aquarium exposes the spectator to many wonderful

surprises. Coiled up against the transparent crystal walls of the basin, he observes living creatures of the most brilliant shades of colour, and more resembling flowers than animals. Supported by a solid base and cylindrical stem, he sees them terminate like the corolla of a flower, as in the petals of the anemone: these are the animals we call *Sea Anemones*—curious zoophytes, which, as all persons familiar with the sea shore may have observed, are now seen suspended from the rocks, and presently buried at the bottom of the sea, or floating on its surface. These charming and timid creatures are also called *Actinia*, as indicating their disposition to form rays or stars, from the Greek ἀκτὶν, a ray.

The body of these animals is cylindrical in form, terminating beneath in a muscular disk, which is generally large and distinct, enabling them to cling vigorously to foreign bodies. It terminates above in an upper disk, bearing many rows of tentacles, which differ from each other only in their size. These tentacles are sometimes decorated with brilliant colours, forming a species of collarette, consisting of contractile and often retractile tubes, pierced at their points with an orifice, whence issue jets of water, which is ejected at the will of the animal. Arranged in multiples of circles, they distribute themselves with perfect regularity round the mouth. These are the arms of this species of zoophyte.

The mouth of the Actinia opens among the tentacles. Oval in form, it communicates by means of a tube with a stomach, broad and short, which descends vertically, and abuts by a large opening on the visceral cavity, the interior of which is divided into little cells or chambers. These cells and chambers are not all of the same dimensions; in parting from the cylindrical walls of the body, they advance, the one increasing, the others getting smaller, in the direction of the centre. Moreover, they have many kinds of cells, which dispose themselves in their different relations with great regularity—their tentacula, which correspond with them, being arranged in circles radiating more or less from the centre.

The stomach of the sea anemones fulfills a multitude of functions. At first, it is the digestive organ; it is also the seat of respiration; and is unceasingly moistened by the water, which it passes through, imbibes, and ejects. The visceral cavity absorbs the atmospheric air contained in the water; for the stomach is also a lung, and through the same organ it ejects its young! In short, the reproductive organs, the eggs, and the larvæ, are all connected with the tentacles or arms. In the month of September the eggs are fecundated, and the larvæ or embryos developed. As Frédol says in "La Monde de la Mer," "these animals bear their young, not upon their arms, but *in* their arms. The larvæ generally pass from the tentacula into the stomach, and are afterwards ejected from the mouth along with the rejecta of their food—a most singular formation, in which the stomach breathes, and the mouth serves the purposes of accouchement—facts which it would be difficult to believe on other than the most positive evidence."

"The Daisy-like Anemones (*Sagartia bellis*—Gosse), in the Zoological Gardens of Paris," says Frédol, "frequently throw up little embryos, which are dispersed, and attach themselves to various parts of the aquarium, and finally become miniature anemones exactly like the parent. An actinia which had taken a very copious repast ejected a portion of it about twenty-four hours later, and in the middle of the ejected food were found thirty-eight young individuals." According to Dalyell, an accouchement is here a fit of indigestion.

The lower class of animals have, in fact, as the general basis of their organization, a sac with a single opening, which is applied, as we have seen, to a great variety of uses. It receives and rejects; it swallows and it vomits. The vomiting becomes necessary and habitual—the normal condition, in short, of the animal—and is perhaps a source of pleasure to it, for it is not a malady, but a function, and even a function multiplied. In the sea anemone it expels the excrement, and lays its eggs; in others, as we have seen, it even serves the purposes of respiration; so that the animal flowers may probably be said to enjoy their regular and periodical vomit.

The sea anemones multiply their species in another manner. On the edge of their base certain bud-like excrescences may often be observed. These buds are by and by transformed into embryos, which detach themselves from the mother, and soon become individuals in all respects resembling her. This mode of reproduction greatly resembles some of the vegetative processes. Another and very singular mode of reproduction has been noted by Mr. Hogg in the case of *Actinia œillet*. Wishing to detach this anemone from the aquarium, this gentleman used every effort to effect his purpose; but only succeeded, after violent exertions, in tearing the lower part of the animal. Six portions remained attached to the glass walls of the aquarium. At the end of eight days, attempts were again made to detach these fragments; but it was observed, with much surprise, that they shrank from the touch and contracted themselves. Each of them soon became crowned with a little row of tentacula, and finally each fragment became a new anemone. Every part of these strange creatures thus becomes a separate being when detached, while the mutilated mother continues to live as if nothing had happened. In short, it has long been known that the sea anemones may be cut limb from limb, mutilated, divided, and subdivided. One part of the body cut off is quickly replaced. Cut off the tentacles of an actinia, and they are replaced in a short time, and the experiment may be repeated indefinitely. The experiments made by M. Trembley of Geneva upon the fresh-water polypi were repeated by the Abbé Dicquemare in the sea anemones. He mutilated and tormented them in a hundred ways. The parts cut off continued to live, and the mutilated creature had the power of reproducing the parts of which it had been deprived. To those who accused the Abbé of cruelty in thus torturing the poor creatures, he replied that, so far from being a cause of suffering to them, "he had increased their term of life, and renewed their youth."

The *Actiniadæ* vary in their habitat from pools near low-water mark to eighteen or twenty fathoms water, whence they have been dredged up. "They adhere," says Dr. Johnston, "to rocks, shells, and other extraneous bodies by means of a glutinous secretion from their enlarged base, but they can leave their hold and remove to another station whensoever it pleases them, either by gliding along with a slow and almost imperceptible movement (half an inch in five minutes), as is their usual method, or by reversing the body and using the tentacula for the purpose of feet, as Réaumur asserts, and as I have once witnessed; or, lastly, inflating the body with water, so as to render it more buoyant, they detach themselves, and are driven to a distance by the random motion of the waves. They feed on shrimps, small crabs, whelks, and similar shelled mollusca, and probably on all animals brought within their reach whose strength or agility is insufficient to extricate them from the grasp of their numerous tentacula; for as these organs can be inflected in any direction, and greatly lengthened, they are capable of being applied to every point, and adhere by suction with considerable tenacity, throwing out, according to Gaertner, of their whole surface a number of extremely minute suckers, which, sticking fast to the small protuberances of the skin, produce the sensation of roughness, which is so far from being painful that it even cannot be called disagreeable.

"The size of the prey is frequently in unseemly disproportion to the preyer, being often equal in bulk to itself. I had once brought me a specimen of *A. crassicornis*, that might have been originally two inches in diameter, which had somehow contrived to swallow a valve of *Pectin maximus* of the size of an ordinary saucer. The shell, fixed within the stomach, was so placed as to divide it completely into two halves, so that the body, stretched tensely over, had become thin and flattened like a pancake. All communication between the inferior portion of the stomach and the mouth was of course prevented; yet, instead of emaciating and dying of atrophy, the animal had availed itself of what undoubtedly had been a very untoward accident to increase its enjoyment and its chance of double fare. A new mouth, furnished with two rows of numerous tentacula, was opened up on what had been the base, and led to the under stomach; the individual had indeed become a sort of Siamese twin, but with greater intimacy and extent in its unions!"

The sea anemones pass nearly all their life fixed to some rock, to which they seem to have taken root. There they live a sort of unconscious and obtuse existence, gifted with an instinct so obscure that they are not even conscious of the prey in their vicinity until it is actually in contact, when it seizes it in its mouth and swallows it. Nevertheless, though habitually adherent, they can move, gliding and creeping slowly by successive contractile and relaxing movements of the body, extending one edge of their base and relaxing the opposite one.

At the approach of cold weather the *Actiniadæ* descend into the deepest water, where they find a more agreeable temperature.

We have said that the sea anemones are scarcely possessed of vital instinct; but they are capable of certain voluntary movements. Under the influence of light, they expand their tentacles as the daisy displays its florets. If the animal is touched, or the water is agitated in its neighbourhood, the tentacles close immediately. These tentacles appear occasionally to serve the purpose of offensive arms. The hand of the man who has touched them becomes red and inflamed.

M. Hollard has seen small mackerel, two to three inches long, perish when touched by the tentacles of the Green Actinia (*Comactis viridis*—Allman). This is a charming little animal; "the brilliancy of its colours and the great elegance of its tentacular crown when fully expanded," says Professor Allman, "render it eminently attractive; hundreds may often be seen in a single pool, and few sights will be retained with greater pleasure by the naturalist than that presented by these little zoophytes, as they expand their green and rosy crowns amid the algæ, millepores, and plumy corals, co-tenants of their rock-covered vase."

The toxological properties of the Actinia have been attributed to certain special cells full of liquid; but M. Hollard believes that these effects are neither constant enough nor sufficiently general to constitute the chief function of these organs, which are found in all the species and over their whole surface, external and internal. Though quite incapable of discerning their prey at a distance, the sea anemone seizes it with avidity when it comes to offer itself up a victim. If some adventurous little worm, or some young and sluggish crustacean, happens to ruffle the expanded involucrum of an actinia in its lazy progress through the water, the animal strikes it at once with its tentacles, and instinctively sweeps it into its open mouth. This habit may be observed in any aquarium, and is a favourite spectacle at the "Jardin d'Acclimitation" of Paris at noon on Sunday and Wednesday, when the aquatic animals are fed. Small morsels of food are thrown into the water. Prawns, shrimps, and other crustaceans and zoophytes inhabiting this medium, chase the morsels as they sink to the bottom of the basin; but it is otherwise with the Actinia; the morsels glide downwards within the twentieth part of an inch of their crown without its presence being suspected. It requires the aid of a propitious wand, directed by the hand of the keeper, to guide the food right down on the animal. Then its arms or tentacles seize upon the prey, and its repast commences forthwith.

The Actinia are at once gluttonous and voracious. They seize their food with the help of the tentacula, and engulf in their stomach, as we have seen, substances of a volume and consistence which contrast strangely with their dimensions and softness. In less than an hour, M. Hollard observed that one of these creatures voided the shell of a mussel, and disposed of a crab all to its hardest parts; nor

Plate V.—Sea Anemones.

1, 2, 3. A. sulcata. 4. Phymactis sanctæ Helenæ. 5. Actinia capensis. 6. A. Peruviana. 7. A. sanctæ Catherinæ. 8. A. amethystina. 9. Comactis viridis.

was it slow to reject these hard parts, by turning its stomach inside out, as one might turn out one's pocket, in order to empty it of its contents. We have seen in Dr. Johnston's account of *A. crassicornis* that when threatened with death by hunger, from having swallowed a shell which separated it into two halves, at the end of eleven days it had opened a new mouth, provided with separate rows of tentacula. The accident which, in ordinary animals, would have left it to perish of hunger, became, in the sea anemone, the source of redoubled gastronomical enjoyment.

"The anemones," Frédol tells us, "are voracious, and full of energy; nothing escapes their gluttony; every creature which approaches them is seized, engulfed, and devoured. Nevertheless, with all the power of their mouth, their insatiable stomachs cannot retain the prey they have swallowed. In certain circumstances it contrives to escape, in others it is adroitly snatched away by some neighbouring marauder more cunning and more active than the anemone.

In Pl. IV. are represented the principal species of Anemone usually observed in the aquarium. Figs. 1, 2, and 3, *A. sulcata*, is surmised by Johnston to be the young of *A. effœta* (Linn.) It is also quoted as a synonyme of *Anthea cereus*, from Drayton's stanza:

> "Anthea of the flowers, that hath a general charge,
> And Syrinx of the weeds, that grow upon the marge."

Fig. 4, *Phymactis Sanctæ Helenæ* (Edw.); Fig. 5, *A. capensis* (Lesson); Fig. 6, *A. Peruviana* (Lesson); Fig. 7, *A. Sanctæ Catherinæ;* Fig. 8, *A. amethystina* (Quoy); Fig. 9, *Comactis viridis* (Milne Edwards).

"It is sometimes observed in aquariums that a shrimp, which has seen the prey devoured from a distance, will throw itself upon the ravisher, and audaciously wrest the prey from him and devour it before his eyes, to his great disappointment. Even when the savoury morsel has been swallowed, the shrimp, by great exertions, succeeds in extracting it from the stomach. Seating itself upon the extended disk of the anemone, with its small feet it prevents the approach of the tentacles, at the same time that it inserts its claws into the digestive cavity and seizes the food. In vain the anemone tries to contract its gills and close its mouth. Sometimes the conflict between the sedentary zoophyte and the vagrant crustacean becomes serious.

When the former is strong and robust, the aggression is repelled, and the shrimp runs the risk of supplementing the repast of the anemone."

If the actinias are voracious, they can also support a prolonged period of fasting. They have been known to live two and even three years without having received any nourishment.*

Although the sea anemone is said to be delicate eating, man derives very little benefit from them in that respect. In Provence, Italy, and Greece, the Green Actinia is in great repute, and Dicquemare speaks of *A. crassicornis* as delicate food. "Of all the kinds of sea anemones, I would prefer this for the table; being boiled some time in sea water, they acquire a firm and palatable consistence, and may then be eaten with any kind of sauce. They are of an inviting appearance, of a light shivering texture, and of a soft white and reddish hue. Their smell is not unlike that of a warm crab or lobster." Dr. Johnston admits the tempting description, and does not doubt their being not less a luxury than the sea urchins of the Greeks, or the snails of the Roman epicures, but he was not induced to test its truth. Rondeletius tells us, having, as Dr. Johnston thinks, *A. crassicornis* in view, that it brings a good price at Bordeaux. *Actinia dianthus* also is good to eat, quoth Dicquemare, and Plaucus directs the cook to dress it after the manner of dressing oysters, with which it is frequently eaten. *Actinia coriacea* is found in the market at Rochefort during the months of January, February, and March. Its flesh is said to be both delicate and savoury.

With these general considerations, we proceed to note some of the more remarkable genera and species of these interesting creatures. Among these, the species represented in Pl. IV. are those usually seen collected in such aquariums as those of the Zoological Gardens of London and the Gardens of Acclimatization of Paris.

The first section of the *Actiniadæ*, according to Milne Edwards, includes the Common Actinia, the feet of which are broad and adherent, the lateral walls soft and imperforate. To this section belongs, among others, the genera *Anemonia*, *Actinia*, and *Metridium*.

The Green Actinia (*A viridis*) has very numerous tentacula, sometimes as many as two hundred, exceeding in length the breadth of the body, of a fine brownish or olive green, and rose-coloured at the extremity.

* "On en a vu vivre deux et même trois ans, sans recevoir de nourriture."—*Vie des Animaux*, p. 117.

Plate VI.—Sea Anemones.

1. Actinia dianthus. 2. Cereus gemmaceus. 3. Actinia bicolor. 4. Sagartia viduata. 5. Cereus papillossus. 6. Actinia picta 7. Actinia equina.

The trunk is of a greyish green or brown; the disk is brown with greenish rays. This species is plentiful in the Mediterranean and in the Channel. When attached to the vertical sides of a rock, a little below the surface of the water, in which position it is often seen on the shores of the Mediterranean, the tentacles hang suspended as if the animal had no power to display them in their radiate form; but when fixed horizontally in a calm sea, they are spread out in all directions, and are kept in a state of continual agitation; its long mane-like tentacula, fully expanded, float and balance themselves in the water in spite of the action of the waves, presenting a most interesting spectacle as it displays its beauties a few feet below the passing boat.

A. dianthus (Ellis), having a number of synonymes, is represented in Pl. V. Fig. 1; its body is smooth and cylindrical; the disk marked in the centre with clavate radiating bands; tentacula numerous, irregular, the outer small, and forming round the margin a thick filamentous fringe. This species attaches itself to rocks and shells in deep water, or within low-water mark, to which it permanently attaches itself, and cannot be removed without organic injury to the base. When contracted, the body presents a thick, short, sub-cylindrical form, about three inches long, and one and a half in diameter, and about five inches when fully expanded; the skin is smooth, of an uniform olive, whitish, cream, or flesh colour. The centre of the disk is ornamented with a circle of white bands, radiating from the mouth, the lamellæ running across, the circumference being perceptible through the transparent skin. From the narrow, colourless interspaces between the lamellæ the tentacula originate. "They are placed," says Dr. Johnston, "between the mouth and the margin, which is encircled by a dense fringe of incontestable beauty, composed of innumerable short tentacula or filaments, forming a thick, furry border." In Pl. V. Fig. 2 we have probably Gaertner's *Anthea cereus*, the body of which is a light chestnut colour, smooth, sulcated lengthwise, with tentacula rising from the disk to the number, in aged animals, of two hundred. *Sagartia viduata*—Gosse (Fig. 4) has the body adherent, cylindrical, without a skin, destitute of warts, emitting capsuliferous filaments from pores; nettling-threads short, densely armed with a brush of hairs; tentacles conical. *A. picta* (Pl. IV. Fig. 6), which Professor Edward Forbes changes to *Adamsia palliata*, is described by Mr. Adams, who first discovered it, "as longitudinally sulcated, having the edges of the base crenated; the lower part an obscure red, and the upper part transparent white, marked with fine purple spots; the outer circumference of the aperture has a narrow stripe of pink. When expanded, the superior division of the body seems formed of membrane. From perforated warts placed without order on the outer coat, issued white filamentous substances variously twisted together." "I have observed," he adds, "similar bodies ejected from the mouths of all the species of this genus which have fallen within my notice."

A. mesembryanthemum (Johnston).—The *A. equina* of Lesson (Pl. IV. Fig. 6), known in France as the *Cul d'ane*, is extremely common in the Channel on rocks between the tide marks. It attaches itself chiefly to rocks beaten by the waves and exposed to view at the moment of reflux. The body is from two to three inches in height, and from an inch to an inch and a half in diameter; hemispherical when contracted, it resembles a bell perforated at the summit, dilated into a cylinder. When fully extended the tentacula are nearly equal to the height of the body, of a uniform liver colour, or olive green, and sometimes streaked with blue, having a greenish line either continuous or in spots, the base generally of a greenish colour encircled with an azure blue line, often streaked with red. The tentacula are terminated by a small pore. Its colour is variable, but generally it is of a violet-red. Sometimes it presents round spots of a fine green; at other times it is only of a greenish hue; the edge of the feet have a narrow border of red, with green and blue beneath.

Metridium dianthus has a thick body with russet grey skin, the disk strongly lobed, thin and transparent round the mouth; the tentacula very numerous, very short, and occupying a broad, strong zone upon the disk. The mesial lines are whitish and wide apart; externally they are closer, papiliform, and brown. This species is found on stones and shells in the North Sea and in the Channel.

The verrucous, or warty section of the *Actiniadæ*, have the lateral walls of the body covered with agglutinated tubercles, and well-developed feet. To this section belongs the Coriaceous Cereus, *Actinia crassicornis* (Johnston), and *A. senilis* (Hollard and Dicquemare), which seems to vary in habit. Hollard describes them as frequently buried in the sands on the shore, while Cocks describes them "as attaching themselves to shells and stones in deep water, or attached on the littoral to the sides of rocks, in crevices, or on the face of clean stones in sheltered places." The body is variegated, green, and red; the tentacles thick, short, and greyish, with broad roseate bands.

The Anemones belonging to the fourth section, or tap-rooted actinia, have the base small, and terminating in a rounded point, and the body much elongated, as in *Edwardsia Calimorpha* (Fig. 80), in which the body is non-adherent, somewhat worm-like, having the mouth and tentacula seated on a retractile column, the lower extremity inflated, membranous, and retractile.

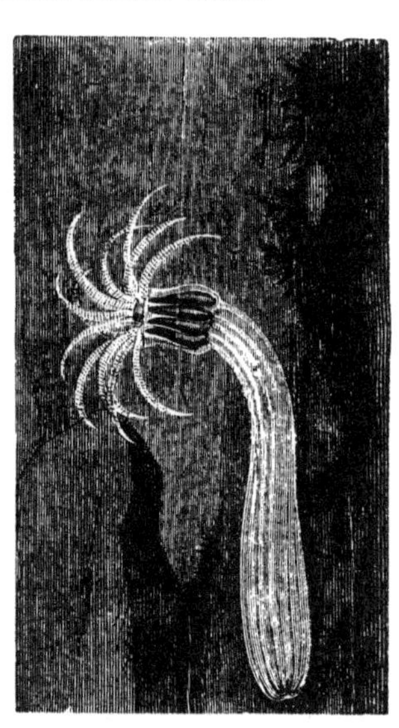

Fig. 80. Edwardsia Calimorpha (Gosse).

In the great family of the Actiniarians, Milne Edwards forms a special group of the Phyllactinæ. In this group the polypes are simple, fleshy, and present at once simple and composite tentacula. Such is *Phyllactis prætexta* (Fig. 81), which is found in the neighbourhood of Rio Janeiro. The zoophyte fixes itself upon the rocks on the sea shore, and covers itself with sand. Its trunk, of cylindrical form, is of a flesh-colour, with vertical lines, having red points. The interior tentacles form two simple elongated rows; the exterior tentacles are spatulate and lobed, not very unlike the leaves of the oak.

Another group, that of the Thalassianthidæ, is distinguished from the preceding by having all its tentacula short, pinnate, and branching, or papilliferous. One species only is known, *T. aster*, of a slate colour, which inhabits the Red Sea.

In the last group of Actiniadæ, as arranged by Milne Edwards, the polypes occur in clusters, and are multiplied by buds, rising from a common creeping, root-like, fleshy base; they thus present a sort of coriaceous polypier, as in *Zoanthus socialis* (Fig. 82). In the British Channel this species, which Dr. Johnston has named *Z. Couchii*, after Mr. Couch, jun., is found along the Cornish coast, on flat slates and rocks, in deep water, and from one to ten leagues from the shore. It is very small, resembling both in shape and size a split pea. When living, its surface is plain but glandular, becoming corrugated when preserved. When semi-expanded, which is its favourite state, it elevates itself to twice its ordinary height, becoming contracted about the middle, like an hour-glass. When the creature is fully expanded, the tentacula become distended and elongated to about the length of the transverse

Fig. 81. Phyllactis prætexta (Dana), natural size.

diameter of the body; and they are generally darker at their extremities than towards the base. Like all the Actiniadæ, the present species possess a power of considerably altering its shape; sometimes the mouth is depressed, and at others it is elevated into an obtuse cone. "This is one of the most inactive of its order," says Mr. A. Couch; "for, whether in a state of contraction or expansion, it will remain so for many days without apparent change. In its expanded state a touch will make it contract, and it will commonly remain so for many days." The trailing connecting-band is flat, thin, narrow, glandular, and of the same texture as the polype, sometimes enlarging into small papillary eminences, which, as they become enlarged, become developed into polypes.

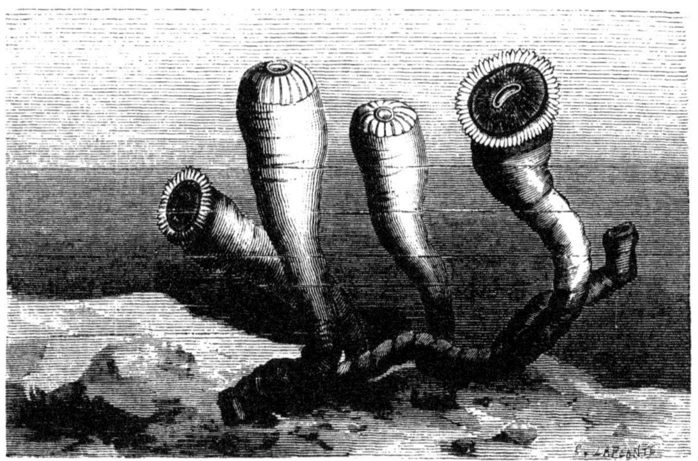

Fig. 82. Zoanthus socialis (Cuvier), natural size.

Minyadinians.

The Minyadinians seem to represent among the Zoanthairia the form peculiar to the Pennatula among the Alcyonians. In the case of

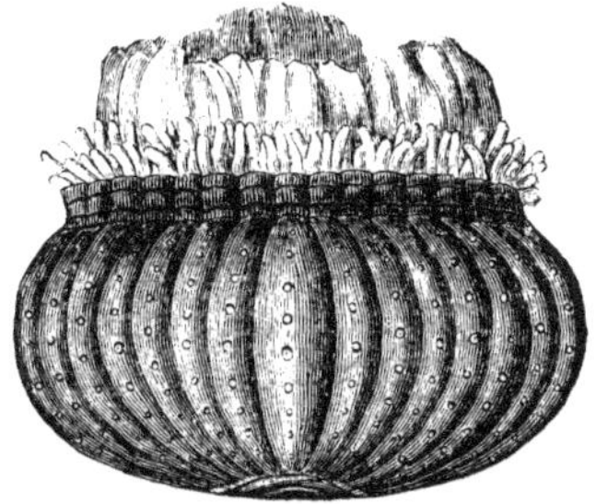

Fig. 83. Blue Minyade. Minyas cærulea (Cuvier), natural size.

these animals, the base of the body, in place of extending itself in a disk-like form, in order to grapple with the rock and other projections at the bottom of the sea, turns itself inwards, forming a sort of purse, which seems to imprison the air. From this results a sort of hydrostatic apparatus, aided by which the animals can float in the water and transport themselves from one place to another. The Blue Minyade (*Minyas cyanea*—Fig. 83) will serve as a type of this family; its globose, melon-like form is of azure blue, studded with white wart-like excrescences; it is flattened at its two extremities in its state of contraction, and it has three rows of tentacula, which are short, cylindrical, and white. The internal organs are of a delicate rose colour. Cuvier places this species among the Echinodermata, but the observations of Lesueur and Quoy, who were acquainted with the living animal, place it among the Actiniadæ. Many of the species, which are usually fixed, are still capable of swimming and of inflating their suctorial disks; therefore it is by no means certain that the free habit of *Minyas cyanea* is constant.

CHAPTER VIII.

ACALEPHÆ, OR SEA NETTLES.

"In nova fert animus mutatis dicere formas corpora."—OVID, MET.

THE class Acalephæ, from ἀκαλήφη, a nettle, so called from the stinging properties which many of them possess, include a great number of radiate animals of which the Medusæ are the type. They form the third class of Cuvier's zoophytes. The Acalephæ, forming the first order, are characterised as floating and swimming in the sea by means of the contraction and dilation of their bodies, their substance being gelatinous, without apparent fibres.

The great genus Medusæ is characterised by having a disk, more or less convex above, resembling a mushroom or expanded umbrella—the edges of the umbrella, as well as the mouth and suckers, being more or less prolonged into pedicles, which take their place in the middle of the lower surface; they are furnished with tentacula, varying in form and size, which have given rise to many subdivisions, with which we need not concern ourselves.

The substance of the disk presents an uniform cellular appearance internally, but, the cellular substance being very soft, no trace of fibre is observable. Taken from the sea and laid upon a stone, a Medusa weighing fifty ounces will rapidly diminish to five or six grains, sinking into a sort of deliquescence, from which Spalanzani concluded that the sea water penetrated the organic texture of its substance, and constituted the principal volume of the animal. Those which have cilia round their margins have also cellular bands running along their bases, and most of the projectile and extensile tentacula and filaments have sacs and canals containing fluids at their roots. Suckers are also found at the extremities, and along the sides of these tentacles in several genera are suckers, by which they are able more securely to catch their floating prey, or to anchor themselves when at rest. The indications of nerves or nervous system are too slight to be received as evidence, although Dr. Grant observed some structure which he thought could only belong to a nervous system, and Ehrenberg thought he observed eyes in *Medusa aurita*, as well as a nervous circle formed of four ganglion-like masses disposed round the mouth. But most naturalists seem to be of opinion that touch is the only sense of which any conclusive proof can be advanced.

Here we behold a class of bell-shaped semi-transparent organisms, which float gracefully in the sea—a great family of fragile, wandering animals, constituted in a most extraordinary manner. They look like floating umbrellas, breeches, or, better still, floating mushrooms, the footstalk replaced by an equally central body, but divided into divergent lobes at once sinuous, twisted, and fringed, so that one is at first tempted to take them for a species of root. The edges of the umbrella or mushroom are entire or dentate, sometimes elegantly figured, often ciliate, or provided with long filiform appendages which float vertically in the water.

Sometimes the animal is uncoloured, and limpid as crystal; sometimes it presents a slightly opaline appearance, now of a tender blue, or of a delicate rose colour; at other times it reflects the most brilliant and vivid tints.

In certain species the central parts only are coloured, showing brilliant reds and yellows, blues or violets, the rest being colourless. In others the central mass seems clothed in a thin iridescent or diaphanous veil, like the light evanescent soap-bubble, or the transparent glass shade which covers a group of artificial flowers.

The Acalephæ are animals without consistence, imbued with much water, so that we can scarcely comprehend how they resist the agitation of the waves and the force of the currents; the waves, however, float without hurting them, the tempest scatters without killing them. When the sea retires, or they are withdrawn from their native waters, their substance dissolves, the animal is decomposed, they are reduced to nothing; if the sun is ardent, this disorganisation occurs in the twinkling of an eye, so to speak.

When the Medusæ travel, their convex part is always kept in advance, and slightly oblique. If they are touched while swimming, even lightly, they contract their tentacula, fold up their umbrella, and sink into the sea. Like Ehrenberg, M. Kölliker thought he discovered visual and auditory organs in an *Oceania*, and Gegenbauer thought he detected them in other genera, such as *Rhizostoma* and *Pelagia*. The eyes are said to consist of certain small, hemispherical, cellulose, coloured masses, in which are sunk small crystalline globules, the free parts of which are perfectly naked. The supposed auditory apparatus is seated close to these organs; they are small vesicles filled with liquid; the eyes having neither pupil nor cornea, and the ears without opening or arch.

But it is in their reproduction that these evanescent beings present the most marvellous phenomena. At one period of the year the Medusæ are charged with numbers of very minute eggs, of the most lively colours, which are suspended in large festoons from their floating bodies. In some cases these eggs develop themselves grafted to their bodies, and are only detached at maturity. In other cases the larvæ produced bear no resemblance to the mother; they are elongated and vermiform, broad at their extremity; we speak of the microscopic *leeches*, which have vibratile cilia, scarcely perceptible, by which they execute the most lively motions. At the end of a certain time they are transformed into polypes, and furnished with eight tentacula. This preparatory sort of animal seems to possess the faculty of reproduction by means of certain buds or tubercles which develop themselves on the surface of the body, and also by filaments which start up here and there, so that a single individual originates a numerous colony. This polype is subjected to a transformation still more remarkable; its structure becomes complex, its body articulate, and it seems to be composed of a dozen disks piled one upon the other, like the jars of a voltaic pile; the upper disk is convex, and is separated from the colony after a convulsive effort; it becomes free, and an excessively small, star-like Medusa is the result; every disk, that is, every individual, is isolated one after the other in the same manner.

Thus of the sexual zoophytes which propagate their kind according to the usual laws; but others engender young which have no resemblance to the parent zoophyte at all: in this respect they are neuter, that is, non-sexual or *agamous.* These are produced by budding, or fissiparity, from individuals like themselves. They can also give sexual distinctions; but before this change takes place the creature, which was simple, is transformed into a composite animal, and it is from its disaggregation that individuals having sexual organs are produced, the process being that which has been called *alternate* generation. It goes on in a perfectly regular manner, although it is a fact that the young never resemble their mothers, but their grandmothers.

This great family of Zoophytes Gosse divides into:

Discophora, having the body in the form of a circular disk, more or less convex and umbrella-shaped, moving by alternate contractions and expansions of the disk.

Ctenophora, body cylindrical, moving by means of many parallel rims of cilia set in longitudinal lines on the surface.

Sophonophora, body irregular, without central digestive cavity like the others, having sucking organs, and moving by means of a contractile cavity, or by air-vessels.

The Discophora are again subdivided into *Gymnophthalmata*, having the eye-specks uncovered or wanting, a great central digestive

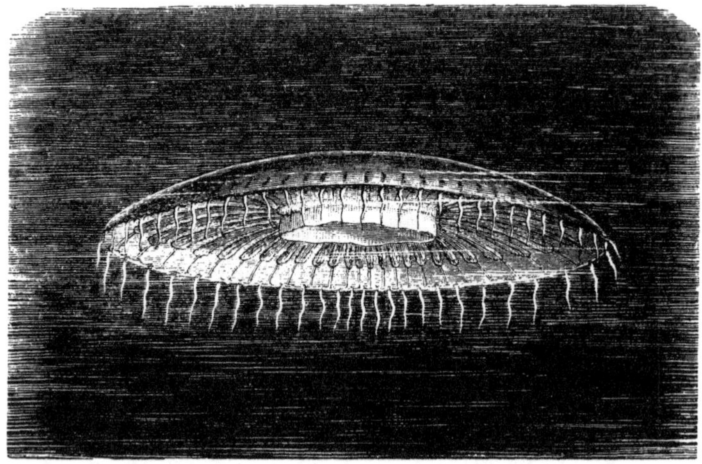

Fig. 84. Æquorea violacea, natural size (Milne Edwards).

cavity, circulating vessels proceeding to the margin quite simple or branched; and *Steganophthalmata*, having the eye specks protected by membranous hoods, or lobed coverings, circulating vessels much ramified, and united with a network. Of the Gymnophthalmata we have an example in *Æquerea violacea* (Fig. 84), in which the disk is slightly convex, glass-like in appearance, and furnished all round with very short, slender, thread-like, violet coloured tentacula; with circulating vessels, eight in number, quite simple, and ovaries placed on them; peduncle wide, expanding into many broad and long fringed lobes.

Fig. 85. Auriculated aurelius, one-third natural size. Aurelia aurita (Lamk.) Cyanea aurita (Cuvier).

The Steganophthalmata include the *Medusadæ* proper, in which the umbel is hemispherical, with numerous marginal tentacles, eight eyes covered by lobes, four ovaries, four chambers, four fringed arms, with a central and four lateral openings. *Aurelia aurita* (Fig. 85) is here represented as a type of the group; it is plentiful in the Baltic, and has been carefully studied by the Swedish naturalists. Rosenthal has made its anatomy his special study. Sars has also made it the subject of observations. In the same group we find the *Pelagia cyanella* of Péron, whose body is globose, scolloped with eight marginal tentacles, peduncles ending in four leaf-like, furbelowed arms, united at the base, having four ovaries, and appendages to the stomach, without orifices.

The *Pelagia*, as the name implies, belong to the deep sea. *P. noctiluca* has a transparent, glass-like disk, of a reddish-brown colour and warty appearance. It is found in the Mediterranean, about the coast near Nice, and is still more plentiful on the coast of Sicily, and on the African coast. Another species, *P. panopyra*, is very common in the Atlantic and Pacific, between the Tropics. The naturalist Lesson met whole banks of them in the equatorial ocean, about the twenty-seventh degree north latitude and the twenty-second degree west longitude. During the night, this species emits a brilliant phosphoric light, and living individuals, which Lesson succeeded in preserving, exhibited great luminosity in the dark. This medusa is remarkable for its semi-spherical disk, slightly depressed, umbilicate at the summit, a little compressed at the edges, and densely bristling on the surface with small elongated warts, but regularly festooned along the edges. In colour it is a delicate rose.

The animals which constitute this class of Zoophytes, and, in former times, so curious and so imperfectly known, were designated *Polypomedusæ*, in order to remind us that at one time they were called Medusæ, and at others ranged among the Polypes. It has, however, been recently discovered that, shortly after they issue from the egg, these zoophytes show themselves in the form of polypes, and that, at a later period, they assume the animal form, to which we give the name of *medusæ*. These animals are, then, true proteans: hence the very considerable difficulty of studying them—difficulties which have long reduced naturalists to despair. Even now their history is too obscure and too complicated to justify us in presenting it, except in its general features. We shall, therefore, content ourselves here with a description of the best known species of the class only—those, namely, which have particularly attracted the attention of naturalists, and which are, at the same time, of a nature to interest our readers.

The class of Discophoræ may be divided into four orders or families, namely:

I. THE HYDRAIDÆ, having single, naked, gelatinous, sub-cylindrical, but very contractile stems, mutable in form, mouth encircled with a single series of granulous filiform tentacula.

II. SERTULARIADÆ, plant-like, horny polypiers, rooted and variously branched, filled with semi-fluid organic pulp, the polypes contained within sessile cells disposed along the sides of the main stem or branchlets, but never terminal.

III. MEDUSADÆ. Umbel hemispherical, with marginal tentacula; having eight eyes covered by lobes, four ovaries, four cells, four fringed arms, a central opening, and four lateral openings.

IV. SIPHONOPHORA, having the animals double, and bell-shaped, one fitting into the cavity of the other; in *Dyphyes* the animal has a large air-vessel with numerous tentacula; in *Physalia*, the animal stretches over a cartilaginous plane.

The true form of the Medusa does not appear in the two first orders.

HYDRAIDÆ.

The Hydraidæ are, according to modern naturalists, Discophoræ arrested in their development. They comprehend the single genus Hydra, of which many species are known, whose habits and metamorphoses it will be our object to particularise.

Hydra vulgaris inhabits stagnant ponds and slowly-running waters. It is of an orange-brown or red colour, the intensity of the colour depending on the nature of its food, becoming almost blood-red when fed on the small crimson worms and larvæ to be found in such places. M. Laurent even succeeded in colouring them blue, red, and white, by means of indigo, carmine, and chalk, without any real penetration of the tissue, the buds from them acquiring the same colour as the mother, while the colour of the ova retains its natural tint, even when the Hydra mother has been fed with coloured substances during the progress of this mode of reproduction. The tentacula, usually seven or eight in number, never exceed the length of the body, tapering insensibly to a point.

Hydra viridis, the fresh-water polype, being more immediately within the sphere of our observation, naturally presents itself to our notice. It is common in ponds and still waters. It was noticed by Pallas, who was of opinion that offspring was produced from every part of the body. De Blainville, on the contrary, was of opinion that offspring was always produced from the same place; namely, at the junction of that part which is hollow and that which is not. Van der Höven, the Leyden professor, agrees with Pallas, and Dr. Johnston's opinions accord with Pallas. The green Hydra is common all over Europe, inhabiting brooks filled with herbage—attaching itself particularly to the duckweed of stagnant ponds, and more especially to the under surface of the leaf. The animal is reduced to a small greenish tubular sac, closed at one of its extremities, open at the other, and bearing round this opening from six to ten appendages, very slender, and not exceeding a line in breadth. The tubulous sac is the body of the animal (Fig. 87).

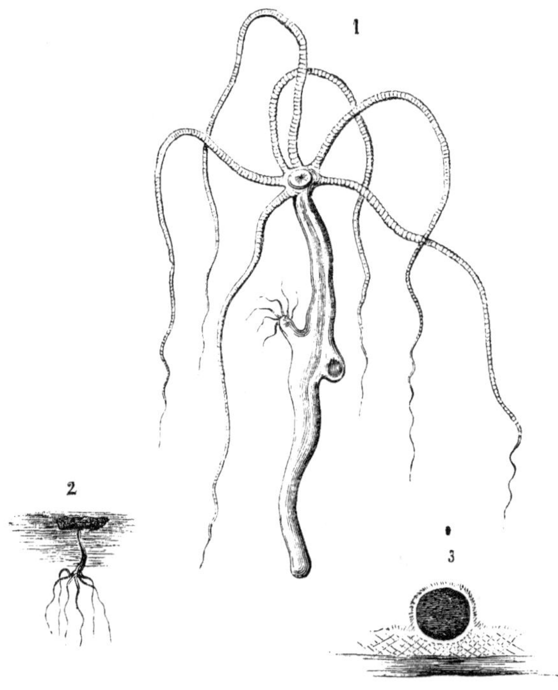

Fig. 86. Hydra vulgaris. 1. Hydra with ova and young, unhatched. 2. Egg ready to burst its shell. 3. Hydra of natural size attached to a piece of floating wood.

The opening is at once its mouth and the entrance to the digestive canal; the appendages, the tentacula or arms.

The Hydras have no lungs, no liver, no intestines, no nervous system, no heart. They have no organ of the senses, except those which exist in the mouth and the skin. The arms or branches are hollow internally, and communicate with the stomach. They are provided with vibratile cells, furnished with a great number of tuberosities disposed spirally, and containing in their interior a number of capsules provided each with a sort of fillet. These threads, which are of extreme tenacity, are thrown out when the animal is irritated by contact with any strange body. We may see these filaments wrapping themselves round their prey, sometimes even penetrating its substance, and effectually subduing the enemy. The green Hydra has thus a very simple organisation. Nevertheless, it would be a mistake to say the animal

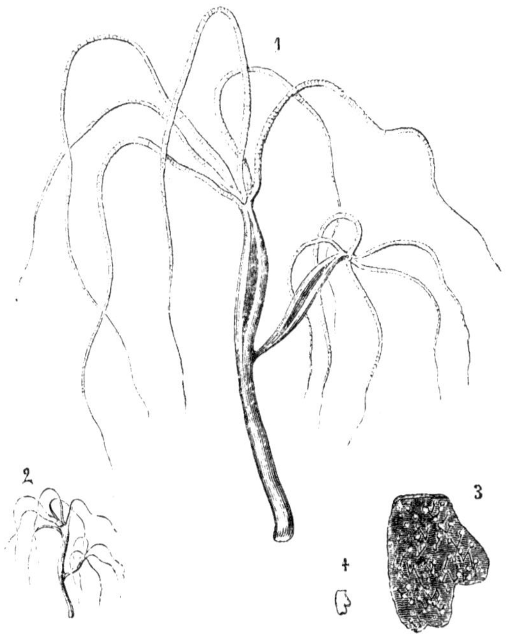

Fig. 87. Hydra viridis (Trembley). 1. Hydra magnified, bearing an embryo ready to detach itself. 2. Animal, natural size. 3. Bud much magnified. 4. Bud, natural size.

was imperfect, for it possesses everything necessary for its nourishment and for the propagation of its species.

There are learned men who have composed hundreds of volumes, who have published whole libraries—naturalists and physicists who have written more than Voltaire ever penned, but whose names are utterly forgotten. On the other hand, there are some who have left only two or three monograms, and yet their names will live for ever. Of this number is the Genevois, A. Trembley. This writer published in 1744 a "Memoir on the Fresh-water Polypes." In this little work he recorded his observations on some of these animals of smallest dimensions. He limited himself even to two sets of experiments: he turned the fresh-water polypes outside in, and he multiplied it by cutting it up. These experiments upon this little creature, which few persons had seen, have sufficed to secure immortality to his name. Trembley was tutor to the two sons of Count de Bentinck. He made his observations at the country-house of the Dutch nobleman, and he had, as he assures us, "frequent occasion to satisfy himself, in the case of his two pupils, that we can even in infancy taste the pleasures derivable from the studies of Nature!" Let us hope that this thought, uttered by a celebrated naturalist, who spoke only from what he knew himself, may remain engraved on the minds of our younger readers.

Trembley established by his observations, a thousand times repeated, that *Hydra viridis* can be turned outside in, as a glove may be, and so completely that what was the external skin of the zoophyte becomes its internal skin, and this without injury to the animal, which a day or two after this revolution resumes its ordinary functions. Such is the vitality of these little beings that the external skin soon fulfills all the functions of a stomach, digesting its food, while the intestinal tube expanding its exterior performs all the functions of an external skin; it absorbs and respires. But we shall leave Trembley to relate his very remarkable experiments. "I attempted," he says, "for the first time to turn these polypes inside out in the month of July, 1741, but unsuccessfully. I was more successful the following year, having found an expedient which was of easy execution. I began by giving a worm to the polype, and put it, when the stomach was well filled, into a little water which filled the hollow of my left hand. I pressed it afterwards with a gentle pinch towards the posterior extremities. In this manner I pressed the worm which was in the stomach against the mouth of the polype, forcing it to open—continuing the pinching-pressure until the worm was partly pressed out of the mouth. When the polype was in this state I conducted it gently out of the water, without damaging it, and placed it upon the edge of my hand, which was simply moistened, in order that the polype should not stick to it. I forced it to contract itself more and more, and, in doing so, assisted in enlarging the mouth and stomach. I now took in my right hand a thick and pointless boar's bristle, which I held as a lancet is held in bleeding. I approached its thicker end to the posterior extremity of the polype, which I pressed until it entered the stomach, which it does the more easily since it is empty at this place and much enlarged. I continued to advance the bristle, and, in proportion as it advanced, the polype became more and more inverted. When it came to the worm, by which the mouth is kept open on one side, and the posterior part of the polype is passed through the mouth, the creature is thus turned completely inside out; the exterior superficies of the polype has become the interior."

The poor animal would be justified in feeling some surprise at its new situation—disagreeably surprised we may add, for it makes every imaginable effort to recover its natural position, and it always succeeds in the end. The glove is restored to its proper form. "I have seen polypes," says Trembley, "which have recovered their natural exterior in less than an hour." But this would not have served the purpose of our experimenter. He wished to know if the polypes thus turned outside in could live in this state; he had consequently to prevent it from rectifying itself, for which purpose a needle was run through the body near the mouth—in other words, he impaled the creature by the neck.

"It is nothing for a polype only to be spitted," says Trembley. It is in fact a very small thing, as we shall see, for thus reversed and spitted they live and multiply as if nothing had happened.

"I have seen a polype," says this ingenious experimenter, "turned inside out, which has eaten a small worm two days after the operation. I have fed one in that state for more than two years, and it has multiplied in that condition.

"Having experimented successfully myself, I was desirous of having the testimony of others capable of forming opinions on the subject. M. Allamand was persuaded to put his hand to the work, which he did with the same success I had met with. He has done more, having succeeded in permanently turning specimens which had been previously turned, and which continue to live in their re-inverted state; he has seen them eat soon after both operations; finally, he has turned one for the third time, which lived some days, but perished without having eaten anything, although it did not appear that its death was the result of the operation."

We have said that the *Hydra viridis* has neither brain, nervous system, heart, muscular rings, lungs, nor liver; the organs of the senses—namely, those of sight, hearing, and of smell—have also been denied them. Nevertheless, they act as if they possessed all these senses. Oh Nature! how hidden are thy secrets, and how the pride of man is humbled by the mysteries which surround thee—by the spectacles which strike his eyes, and which he attempts in vain to explain!

Trembley states that the fresh-water polypes, having no muscular ring, can neither extend or contract themselves, nor can they walk. If touched, or if the water in which they are immersed is suddenly agitated, they are certainly observed to contract more or less forcibly, and even to inflect themselves in all directions; and by this power of extension, of contraction and inflection, they contrive to move from place to place; but these movements are singularly slow, the utmost space they have been observed to traverse being about eight inches in the twenty-four hours.

Painfully conscious of his powers of progression, however, he has found means of remedying it, and the aquatic snail is his steed; he creeps upon the shell of this mollusc, and by means of this improvised mount he will make more way in a few minutes than he would in a day by his own unassisted efforts.

The *Hydra viridis*, although destitute of organs of sight, are nevertheless sensible of light; if the vase containing them is placed partly in shade and partly in the sun, they direct themselves immediately towards the light; they appreciate sounds; they attach themselves to aquatic plants and other floating bodies. Without eyes, without brain, and without nerves, these animals lie in wait for their prey, recognise, seize, and devour it. They make no blunder, and only attack where they are sure of success. They know how to flee from danger; they evade obstacles, and fight with or fly before their enemies. There are, then, some powers of reflection, deliberation, and premeditated action in these insignificant creatures; their history, in short, is calculated to fill the mind with astonishment.

Trembley insists much upon the address which the Hydra employs to secure its prey: by the aid of its long arms, small animals, which serve to nourish it, are seized, for it is carnivorous, and even passably voracious. Worms, small insects, and larvæ of dipterous insects are its habitual prey. When a worm or woodlouse in passing its portals happens to touch them, the polype, taking the hint, seizes upon the wanderer, twining its flexible arms round it, and, directing it rapidly towards its mouth, swallows it. Trembley amused himself by feeding the Hydra, while he observed the manner in which it devoured its prey. "When its arms were extended, I have put into the water a woodlouse or a small worm. As soon as the woodlouse feels itself a prisoner it struggles violently, swimming about, and drawing the arm which holds it from side to side; but, however delicate it may appear, the arm of the polype is capable of considerable resistance; it is now gradually drawn in, and other arms come to its assistance, while the polype itself approaches its prey; presently the woodlouse finds itself engaged with all the arms, which, by curving and contracting, gradually but inevitably approach the mouth, in which it is soon engulfed." Frédol also notices a singular fact. "The small worms. even when swallowed by the polype," he says, "frequently try to escape; but the ravisher retains them by plunging one of its arms into the digestive cavity! What an admirable contrivance, by which the worms are digested while the arm is respected!"

The food of the fresh-water Hydra influences the colour of their bodies in consequence of the thinness and transparency of their tissues; so that the reddish matter of the woodlouse renders them red, while other food renders them black or green, according to its prevailing colour!

The multiplication of these creatures takes place in three different ways: 1. By eggs. 2. By buds, after the manner of vegetables. 3. By separation, in which an individual may be cut into two or many segments, each reproducing an individual.

We shall only say a few words on the first mode of reproduction. The eggs, according to Ehrenberg, come to maturity in the *H. viridis* at the base of the feet, where the visceral cavity terminates. They are carried during seven or eight days, and determine by their fall the death of the animal. When the Hydra has laid its eggs, according to M. Laurent, it gradually lowers itself until it covers them with half its body, which, spreading out and getting proportionably thin, passes into the condition of a horny substance, that glues the eggs disposed in a circle round the body to plants and other foreign substances. She ends her career by dying in the midst of her ova.

Trembley has studied with great care the mode of reproduction by budding—a process which seems to prevail in the summer months.

The buds which are to form the young polype appear on the surface of the body as little spherical excrescences terminating in a point. A few steps further towards maturity, and it assumes a conical and finally a cylindrical form. The arms now begin to push out at the anterior extremity of the young animal; the posterior extremity by which it is attached to the mother contracting by degrees, until it appears only to touch her at one point. Finally, the separation is effected, the mother and the young acting in concert to produce the entrance of this interesting polypule into the world. Each of them take with their head and arms a strong point of support upon some neighbouring body; and a small effort suffices to procure the separation: sometimes the mother charges herself with the effort, sometimes the young, and often both.

When the young polype is separated from the mother, it swims about, and executes all the movements peculiar to adult animals. The entrance into life and the virile age takes place with these beings at one and the same moment. Infancy and youth are suppressed in this little world.

So long as the young polype remains attached to the mother, she is the nurse; by a touching change, the young polype nurses her in his turn. In short, the stomach of the mother and her young have communication; so that the prey swallowed by the parent passes partially into the stomach of her progeny. On the other hand, while still attached to the mother, the little ones seize the prey, which they share in their turn with their parent by means of the communication Nature has arranged between the two organisms.

In the course of his experiments Trembley states another fact still more remarkable.

Upon a young polype still attached to its mother he observed a new polype or polypule, and upon this unborn creature was another individual. Thus three generations were appended to the mother, who carried at once her son, her grandson, and great-grandson.

"In observing the young polypes still attached to their mother," says Trembley, "I have seen one which had itself a little one which was just issuing from its body; that is to say, it was a mother while yet attached to its own mother. I had in a short time many young polypes attached to their mothers which had already had three or four little ones, of which some were even perfectly formed. They fished for woodlice like others, and they ate them. Nor is this all. I have seen a mother-polype which had carried its *third generation.* From the little one which she had produced issued another little one, and from this a third."

Charles Bennet, the naturalist of Geneva, says wittily, that a polype thus charged with all its descendants constitutes a living genealogical tree.

We have just spoken of turning polypes inside out! If one of these creatures is thus operated upon while it bears its young on the surface of its body, such of them as are sufficiently advanced continue to increase; although they find themselves in this sudden manner imprisoned in an internal cavity, they re-issue subsequently by the mouth. Those less advanced at the moment of reversal issue by little and little from the maternal sac, and complete their career of development on the newly-made exterior.

The third and most extraordinary mode of reproduction in the polypes has been discovered by Trembley in the case of the green Hydra. So surprised was this naturalist at the strange anomalies which surrounded these creatures, that he began to have doubts, and gravely to ask the question, Was this polype an animal? Is it a plant?

In order to escape from this state of indecision, it occurred to him to cut a Hydra into pieces. Concluding that plants alone could reproduce themselves by slips, he waited the result of the experiment for the conclusion he sought. On the 25th of November, 1740, he cut a polype into sections. "I put," he tells us, "the two parts into a flat glass, which contained water four or five lines in depth, and in such a manner that each portion of the polype could be easily observed through a strong magnifying glass. It will suffice to say that I had cut the polype transversely, and a little nearer to the anterior. On the morning of the day after having cut the polype, it seemed to me that on the edges of the second part, which had neither head nor arms, three small points were issuing from these edges. This surprised me extremely, and I waited with impatience for the moment when I could clearly ascertain what they were. Next day they were sufficiently developed to leave no doubt on my mind that they were true arms. The following day two new arms made their appearance, and, some days after, a third appeared, and I could now trace no difference between the first and second half of the polype which I had cut."

This is assuredly one of the most startling facts belonging to natural history. Divide a fresh-water polype into five or six parts, and at the end of a few days all the separate parts will be organised, developed, and form so many new beings, resembling the primitive individual. Let us add, that the polype which should thus have lost five-sixths of its body, the mutilated father of all this generation, remains complete in itself; in the interval, it has recuperated itself and recovered all its primitive substance.

After this, if a *Hydra vulgaris* wishes to procure for itself the blessings of a family, it has only one thing to do: cut off an arm; if it desire two descendants, let it cut the arm in two parts; if three, let it divide itself into three; and so on *ad infinitum*. "Divide one of the animals," says Trembley, "and each section will soon form a new individual in all respects like the creature divided." "A whole host of polypes hewn into pieces," says Frédol, "will be far from being annihilated." "On the contrary," we may say, in our turn, "its youth will be renewed, and multiplied in proportion to the number of pieces into which it has been divided." "The same polype," says Trembley, "may be successively inverted, cut into sections, and turned back again, without being seriously injured."

If a green Hydra is cut into two pieces, and the stomach is cut off in the operation, the voracious creature will, nevertheless, continue to eat the prey which presents itself. It gorges itself with the food, without troubling itself with the loss which it has sustained; but the food no longer nourishes it, for it merely enters by one opening, passes through the intestinal canal, and escapes by the other. It realises Harleville's pleasantry of M. de Crac's horse, in the piece of that name, which eats unceasingly, but never gets any fatter.

All these instances of mutilation, resulting in an increase of life, are very strange. The naturalists to whom they were first revealed could scarcely believe their own eyes. Réaumur, who repeated many of Trembley's experiments, writes as follows: "I confess that when I saw for the first time two polypes forming by little and little from that which I had cut in two, I could scarcely believe my eyes; and it is a fact that, after hundreds of experiments, I never could quite reconcile myself to the sight."

In short, we know nothing analogous to it in the animal kingdom. About the same period Charles Bennet writes: "We can only judge of things by comparison, and have taken our ideas of animal life from the larger animals; and an animal which we cut and turn inside out, which we cut again, and it still bears itself well, gives one a singular shock. How many facts are ignored, which will come one day to derange our ideas of subjects which we think we understand! At present we just know enough to be aware that we should be surprised at nothing."

Notwithstanding the philosophic serenity which Bennet recommends, the fact of new individuals resulting from dividing these fresh-water polypes was always a subject of profound astonishment, and of never-ending meditation.

Sertulariadæ.

All Hydraidæ, with the exception of the Hydra and a few other genera, are marine productions, varying from a few lines to upwards of a foot in height, attaching themselves to rocks, shells, seaweeds, and corallines, and to various species of shell-fish. Many of them attach themselves indiscriminately to the nearest object, but others show a decided preference. *Thuiaria thrya* attaches itself to old bivalves; *Thoa halecuia* prefers the larger univalves; *Antennularia antennina* attaches itself to coarse sand on rocks; *Laomedea geniculata* delights in the broad frond of the tangle; *Plumularia catherina* attaches itself in deep water to old shells, corallines, and ascidians, growing in a manner calculated to puzzle the naturalist, as it did Crabbe, the poet, who writes of it:

> "Involved in sea-wrack, here you find a race
> Which science, doubting, knows not where to place;
> On shell or stone is dropp'd the embryo seed,
> And quickly vegetates a vital breed."

Sertularia pumila, on the other hand, loves the commoner and coarser wracks. "The choice," says Dr. Johnston, "may in part be dependent on their habits, for such as are destined to live in shallow water, or on a shore exposed by the reflux of every tide, are, in general, vegetable parasites; while the species which spring up in deep seas must select between rocks, corallines, or shells." There seems to be a selection even as to the position on the rocks. According to Lamouroux, some polypiers always occupy the southern slopes, and never that towards the east, west, or north; others, on the contrary, grow only on these exposures, and never on the south, altering their position, however, according to the latitude, and its relation to the Equator.

The *Sertulariadæ* have a horny stem, sometimes simple, sometimes so branching that they might readily enough be mistaken for small plants, their branches being flexible, semi-transparent, and yellow. Their name is derived from *Sertum*, a bouquet. Each Sertularia has seven, eight, twelve, or twenty small panicles, each containing as many as five hundred animalcules; thus forming, sometimes, an association of ten thousand polypes. "Each plume," says Mr. Lister, in reference to a specimen of *Plumularia cristata*, "might comprise from four to five hundred polypi;" "and a specimen of no unusual size now before me," says Dr. Johnston, "with certainly not fewer cells on each than the larger number mentioned, thus giving six thousand as the tenantry of a single polypidom, and this on a small species." On *Sertularia argentea*, it is asserted, polypiers are found on which there exist not less than eighty to a hundred thousand.

Each colony is composed of a right axis, on the whole length of which the curved branches are implanted, these being longest in the middle. Along each of these branches the cells, each containing a polype, are grouped alternately. The head of the animal is conical, the mouth being at the top surrounded by twenty to twenty-four tentacles. These curious beings have no digestive cavity belonging to themselves; the stomach is common to the whole colony—a most singular combination, a single stomach to a whole group of animals! Never have the principles of association been pushed to this length by the warmest advocates of communism.

Certain species belonging to the colony, which seem destined to perpetuate the race, have not the same regular form. Destitute of mouth and tentacles, they occupy special cells, which are larger than the others. The entire colony is composed exclusively of individuals, male or female. "We have traced *Sertularia cupressina* through every stage of its development," say Messrs. Paul Gervais and Van Beneden. "At the end of several days, the embryos are covered with very short vibratile cells; their movement is excessively slow; then, from the spheroid form which they take at first, they get elongated, and take a cylindrical form, all the body inclining lightly sometimes to the right, sometimes to the left. The vibratile cells fading afterwards, the embryo attaches itself to some solid body, a tubercle is formed, and the base extends itself as a disk. At the same time that the first rudiments of the polype appear, the disk-like tubercle throws out on its flanks a sort of bud, and a second polype soon shows itself; its surface is hardened; the polypier appears in its turn, and the same process of generation is repeated; a colony of *Sertulariadæ* is thus established at the summit of a discoid projection. At the end of fifteen days the colony, which has been forming under our eyes, consists of two polypes and a bud, which already indicates a third polype. The sea-cypress, as this species is called, is robust, with longish branches decidedly fan-shaped, the pinnæ being closer and nearly parallel to each other. The cells form two rows, nearly opposite, smooth and pellucid. The branches in some specimens are gracefully arched, bending as it were under the load of pregnant ovaries which they carry, arranged in close-set rows along the upper side of the pinnæ. They are found in deep water on the coast of Scotland, and as far south as the Yorkshire coast and the north of Ireland. The cells, which are the abode of the polypes, are not always alike in their distribution. Sometimes they are ranged on two sides, sometimes on one only. Sometimes they are grouped like the small tubes of an organ, at other times they assume a spiral form round the stem, or they form here and there horizontal rings round it."

Medusadæ.

The Medusæ comprehend, not only the animals so designated in the days of Cuvier under that name, but also the polypes known as *Tubulariadæ* and *Campanulariadæ*.

If we walk along the sea shore, after the reflux of the tide, we may often see, lying immovable upon the sands, disk-like, gelatinous masses of a greenish colour and repulsive appearance, from which the eye and the steps instinctively turn aside. These beings, whose blubber-like appearance inspire only feelings of disgust when seen lying grey and dead on the shore, are, however, when seen floating on the bosom of the ocean, one of its most graceful ornaments. These are Medusæ. When seen suspended like a piece of gauze or an azure bell in the middle of the waves, terminating in delicate silvery garlands, we cannot but admire their iridescent colours, or deny that these objects, so forbidding in some of their aspects, rank, in their natural localities, among the most elegant productions of Nature. We could not better commence our studies of these children of the sea than by quoting a passage from the poet and historian Michelet: "Among the rugged rocks and lagunes, where the retiring sea has left many little animals which were too sluggish or too weak to follow, some shells will be there left to themselves and suffered to become quite dry. In the midst of them, without shell and without shelter, extended at our feet, lies the animal which we call by the very inappropriate name of the *Medusa.* Why was this name, of terrible associations, given to a creature so charming? Often have I had my attention arrested by these castaways which we see so often on the shore. They are small, about the size of my hand, but singularly pretty, of soft light shades, of an opal white; where it lost itself as in a cloud of tentacles—a crown of tender lilies—the wind had overturned it; its crown of lilac hair floated above, and the delicate umbel, that is, its proper body, was beneath; it had touched the rock—dashed against it; it was wounded, torn in its fine locks, which are also its organs of respiration, absorption, and even of love. . . . . The delicious creature, with its visible innocence and the iridescence of its soft colours, was left like a gliding, trembling jelly. I paused beside it, nevertheless: I glided my hand under it, raised the motionless body cautiously, and restored it to its natural position for swimming. Putting it into the neighbouring water, it sank to the bottom, giving no sign of life. I pursued my walk along the shore, but at the end of ten minutes I returned to my medusa. It was undulating under the wind; really it had moved itself, and was swimming about with singular grace, its hair flying round it as it swam; gently it retired from the rock, not quickly, but still it went, and I soon saw it a long way off."

Of all the zoophytes which live in the ocean there is none more numerous in species or more singular in their matter, more odd in their form or more remarkable in their mode of reproduction, than those to which Linnæus gave the name of Medusa, from the mythical chief of the Gorgons.

The seas of every latitude of the globe furnish various tribes of these singular beings. They live in the icy waters which bathe Spitzbergen, Greenland, and Iceland; they multiply under the fires of the Equator, and the frozen regions of the south nourish numerous species. They are, of all animals, those which present the least solid substance. Their bodies are little else than water, which is scarcely retained by an imperceptible organic network; it is a transparent jelly, almost without consistence. "It is a true sea-water jelly," says Réaumur, writing in 1710, "having little colour or consistence. If we take a morsel in our hands, the natural heat is sufficient to dissolve it into water."

Spallanzani could only withdraw five or six grains of the pellicle of a medusa weighing fifty ounces. From certain specimens weighing from ten to twelve pounds, only six to seven pennyweights could be obtained of solid matter, according to Frédol. "Mr. Telfair saw an enormous medusa which had been abandoned on the beach at Bombay; three days after, the animal began to putrefy. To satisfy his curiosity he got the neighbouring boatmen to keep an eye upon it, in order to gather the bones and cartilages belonging to the great creature, if by chance it had any; but its decomposition was so rapid and complete that it left no remains, although it required nine months to dissipate it entirely."

"Floating on the bosom of the waters," says Frédol, "the medusa resembles a bell, a pair of breeches, an umbrella, or, better still, a floating mushroom, the stool of which has here been separated into lobes more or less divergent, sinuous, twisted, shrivelled, fringed, the edges of the cap being delicately cut, and provided with long thread-like appendages, which descend vertically into the water like the drooping branches of the weeping willow."

The gelatinous substance of which the body of the Medusa is formed is sometimes colourless and limpid as crystal; sometimes it is opaline, and occasionally of a bright blue or pale rose colour. In certain species the central parts are of a lively red, blue, or violet colour, while the rest of the body is of a diaphanous hue. This diaphanous tissue, often decked in the finest tints, is so fragile, that when abandoned by the wave on the beach, it melts and disappears without leaving a trace of its having existed, so to speak.

Nevertheless, these fragile creatures, these living soap-bubbles, make long voyages on the surface of the sea. Whilst the sun's rays suffice to dissipate and even annihilate its vaporous substance on some inhospitable beach, they abandon themselves without fear during their entire life to the agitated waves. The whales which haunt round the

Hebrides are chiefly nourished by Medusæ which have been transported by the waves in innumerable swarms from the coast of the Atlantic to the region of whales. "The locomotion of the medusæ, which is very slow," says De Blainville, "and denotes a very feeble muscular energy, appears, on the other hand, to be unceasing. Since their specific gravity considerably exceeds the water in which they are immerged, these creatures, which are so soft that they probably could not repose on solid ground, require to agitate constantly in order to sustain themselves in the fluid which they inhabit. They require also to maintain a continual state of expansion and contraction, of systole and diastole. Spallanzani, who observed their movements with great care, says that those of translation are executed by the edges of the disk approaching so near to each other that the diameter is diminished in a very sensible degree; by this movement a certain quantity of water contained in the body is ejected with more or less force, by which the body is projected in the inverse direction. Renovated by the cessation of force in its first state of development, it contracts itself again, and makes another step in advance. If the body is perpendicular to the horizon, these successive movements of contraction and dilatation cause it to ascend; if it is more or less oblique, it advances more or less horizontally. In order to descend, it is only necessary for the animal to cease its movements; its specific gravity secures its descent."

It is, then, by a series of contractions and dilatations of their bodies that the Medusæ make their long voyages on the surface of the waters. This double movement of their light skeleton had already been remarked by the ancients, who compared it to the action of respiration in the human chest. From this notion the ancients called them *Sea Lungs.*

The Medusæ usually inhabit the deep seas. They are rarely solitary, but seem to wander about in considerable battalions in the latitudes to which they belong. During their journey they proceed forward, with a course slightly oblique to the convex part of their body. If an obstacle arrests them, if an enemy touches them, the umbrella contracts, and is diminished in volume, the tentacles are folded up, and the timid animal descends into the depths of the ocean.

We have said that the Medusæ constitute in the Arctic seas one of the principal supports of the whale. Their innumerable masses sometimes cover many square leagues in extent. They show themselves and disappear by turns in the same region, at determinate epochs—alternations which depend, no doubt, on the ruling of the winds and currents which carry or lead them. "The barks which navigate Lake Thau meet," says Frédol, "at certain periods of the year with numerous colonies of a species about the size of a small melon, nearly transparent—whitish, like water when it is mixed with a shade of aniseed. One would be tempted to take these animals at first for a collection of floating muslin bonnets."

The Medusæ are furnished with a mouth placed habitually in the middle of the neck. This mouth is rarely unoccupied. Small molluscs, young crustaceans, and worms, form their ordinary food. In spite of their shape, they are most voracious, and snap up their prey all at one mouthful, without dividing it. If their prey resists and disputes with it, the Medusa which has seized it holds fast, and remains motionless, and, without a single movement, waits till fatigue has exhausted and killed its victim, when it can swallow it in all security.

In respect to size, the Medusæ vary immensely. Some are very small, while others attain more than a yard in diameter. Many species are phosphorescent during the night.

Most Medusadæ produce an acute pain when they touch the human body. The painful sensation produced by this contact is so general in this group of animals, that it has determined their designation. Until very recently all the animals of the group have been, after Cuvier, designated under the name of Acalephæ, or sea nettles, in order to remind us that the sensation produced is analogous to that occasioned by contact with the stinging leaves of the nettle.

According to Dicquemare, who made experiments on himself in this matter, the sensation produced is very like that occasioned by a nettle, but it is more violent, and endures for half an hour. "In the last moments," says the abbé, "the sensation is such as would be produced by reiterated but very weak prickings. A considerable pain pervaded all the parts which had been touched, accompanied by pustules of the same colour, with a whitish point." "The sea-bladder," says Father Feuillée, "occasions me, on touching it, a sudden and severe pain, accompanied with convulsions."

"During the first voyage of the Princess Louise round the world," to quote Frédol, "Meyen remarked a magnificent physalia, which passed near the ship. A young sailor leapt naked into the sea, to seize the animal. Swimming towards it, he seized it; the creature surrounded the person of its assailant with its numerous thread-like filaments, which were nearly a yard in length; the young man, overwhelmed by a feeling of burning pain, cried out for assistance. He had scarcely strength to reach the vessel and get aboard again, before the pain and inflammation were so violent that brain fever declared itself, and great fears were entertained for his life."

Fig. 88. Chrysaora Gaudichaudi.

The organization is much more complicated than early observers were disposed to think it. During many ages naturalists were inclined to imagine, with Réaumur, that the Medusæ were mere masses of organized jelly, of gelatinized water. But when Courtant Dumeril tried the experiment of injecting milk into their cavities, and saw the liquid penetrating into true vessels, he began to comprehend that these very enigmatical beings were worthy of serious study—the study of subsequent naturalists, such as Cuvier, De Blainville, Ehrenberg, Brandt, Makel-Eschscholtz, Sars, Milne Edwards, Forbes, Gosse, and other modern naturalists, who have demonstrated what richness of structure is concealed under this gelatiniform and simple structure in the Medusæ; at the same time they have revealed to us most mysterious and incredible facts as connected with their metamorphoses.

Among the Medusæ proper, the most common are Aurelia, Pelagia, and Chrysaora. In the latter, *C. Gaudichaudi* (Fig. 88), the disk is hemispherical, festooned with numerous tentacles, attached to a sac-like stomach, opening by a single orifice in the centre of the peduncle, with four long, furbelowed, unfringed arms. Gaudichaudi's Chrysaora is found round the Falkland Islands. The disk forms a regular half-sphere, very smooth, and perfectly concave, forming a sort of canopy in the shape of a vault. The circle which surrounds it is divided into sections by means of vertical lines, regularly divided, of a reddish brown colour, which forms an edging to the umbrella-like disk. Twelve broad regular festoons form this edging. From the summit of these lobes issue twelve bundles of very long, simple, capillary tentacles, of a bright red. The peduncle is broad and flat, perforated in the middle, to which are attached four broad foliaceous arms.

Rhizostoma.

The Medusæ which bear the name of *Rhizostoma* have the disk hemispherically festooned, depressed, without marginal tentacles, peduncle divided into four pairs of arms, forked, and dentated almost to infinity, each having at their base two toothed auricles. Such is *Rhizostoma Cuvieri* of Péron (Fig. 89), the disk of which is of a bluish-white, like the arms, and of a rich violet over its circumference. This beautiful zoophyte is found plentifully in the Atlantic, living in flocks, which attain a great size. It is common in the month of June on the shores of the Saint Onge; in August on the English coast; and along the strand of every port in the Channel they are seen in the month of October in thousands, where they lie high and dry upon the shore on which they have been thrown by the force of the winds.

Such also is *R. Aldrovandi* (Fig. 90), which appears all the year round in calm weather. It is an animal much dreaded by bathers. It possesses an urticaceous apparatus, which produces an effect similar to the stinging-nettle when applied to the skin. If the animal touches the fisherman at the moment of being drawn from the water, it is apt to inflame the part and raise it into pustules.

Fig. 89. Rhizostoma Cuvieri.

Cassiopea and *Cephea* are two other types belonging to the same group. In *Cassiopea Andromeda* (Fig. 91), belonging to the first, the disk is hemispherical, but much depressed, without marginal tentacles or peduncle, but with a central disk, with four to eight half-moon-shaped orifices at the side, and throwing off eight to ten branching arms, fringed with retractile sucking disks. *Cephea Cyclophora*,

Péron (Fig. 92), is another very remarkable form of these strangely constituted organisms.

Having presented to the reader certain characteristic types of Medusadæ, we proceed to offer some general remarks upon the organization and functions of these strange creatures. We have, in short,

Fig. 90. Rhizostoma Aldrovandi.

selected these types because they have been special objects of anatomical and physiological study to some of our best naturalists.

The Medusæ have no other means of breathing but through the skin. We remark all over the body of these zoophytes certain cutaneous elongations, disposed so as to favour the exercise of the breathing function. Certain marginal fringes of extended surface, as well as the tentacle, are the special seats of the apparatus. The organs of digestion also present arrangements peculiar to themselves; the mouth is placed on the lower part of the body, and is pierced at the extremity of a trumpet-like tube, hanging sometimes like the tongue of a bell. The walls of the stomach, again, are furnished with a multitude of appendages, which have their origin in the cavity of the organ, and which are very elastic. The stomach, furnished with these vibratile cells, appears to secrete a juice whose function is to attack the food and render it digestible.

Fig. 91. Cassiopea Andromeda (Tilesius).

In some of the Medusadæ the central mouth is absent altogether. With the Rhizostoma, for instance, the stomachal reservoir has no inferior orifice; it communicates latterly with the canals which descend through the thickness of the arms, and open at their extremities through a multitude of small mouths. These are the root-like openings from which the animals derive their name of Rhizostoma, from the Greek words ῥίζα, root, and στόμα, mouth.

The arms of the Rhizostoma are usually eight in number, the free extremities of each being slightly enlarged; in these arms many small openings or mouths occur, which are the entrances to so many ascend-

Fig. 92. Cephea Cyclophora.

ing canals communicating with larger ones, as the veins do in the higher animals: the common trunk canal is thus formed, which directs itself to the stomach, receiving in its way thither all the lateral branches.

A very distinct circulation exists in the Medusæ. The peripheric part of the stomach suffers the nourishing liquid which has been elaborated in the digestive cavity to pass: this fluid then circulates through numerous canals, the existence of which have been clearly traced.

It is also a singular fact, that organs of sense seem to have been discovered in these Medusæ, which early observers believed to be altogether destitute of organization. "During my sojourn on the banks of the Red Sea," says Ehrenberg, in his work on the *Medusa aurita*, "although I had many times examined the brownish bodies upon the edge of the disk of the Medusæ, it is only in the month past that I have recognised their true nature and function. Each of these bodies consists of a little yellow button, oval or cylindrical, fixed upon a thin peduncle. The peduncle is attached to a vesicle, in which the microscope reveals a glandular body, yellow when the light traverses it, but white when the light is only reflected on it. From this body issue two branches, which proceed towards the peduncle or base of the brown body up to the button or head. I have found that each of these small brown bodies presents a very distinct red point placed on the dorsal face of the yellow head, and when I compare this with my other observations of similar red points in other animals, I find that they greatly resemble the eyes of the Rotifera and Entomostraca. The bifurcating body placed at the base of the brown spot appears to be a nervous ganglion, and its branches may be regarded as optic nerves. Each pedunculated eye presents upon its lower face a small yellow sac, in which are found, in greater or smaller numbers, small crystalline bodies clear as water." The presence of a red pigment in very fine grains is an argument in favour of the existence of visual organs in these zoophytes, for the small crystals disseminated in the interior of the organ would no doubt perform the part of refracting light which is produced by crystalline in the eyes of vertebrated animals. Moreover, it is found that there are marginal corpuscles analogous to these brown spots in other species of Medusæ. They are of a palish yellow, or quite colourless, and enclose sometimes a single, sometimes many calcareous corpuscles. When they are colourless, some naturalists have rather taken them for ears reduced to their most simple expression.

The Medusæ are not absolutely destitute of nervous system. We have seen that they have ganglions and probably optic nerves. Ehrenberg also states that they have ganglions at their base, which furnish them with nervous filaments.

Without entering further into the details of their delicate and complicated structure, we shall pause briefly on their mode of reproduction. We shall find here physiological phenomena so remarkable as to appear incredible, had not the researches of modern naturalists placed the facts beyond all doubt. "Which of us," says M. de Quatrefages, "would not proclaim the prodigy, if he saw a reptile issue from an egg laid in his court-yard which afterwards gave birth to an indefinite number of fishes and birds? Well, the generation of the Medusæ is at least as marvellous as the fact which we have imagined." Let us note, for example, what takes place with the Rose Aurelia, a beautiful medusa, of a pale rose colour, with nearly hemispherical disk, from four to five inches in diameter, whose edge is furnished with short russet-brown tentacles; taking for our guide the eloquent and learned author of the "Metamorphose in Men and Animals," M. de Quatrefages.

The Medusa, designated under the name of Rose Aurelia, lays eggs which are characterised by the existence of three concentric spheres. These eggs are transformed into oval larvæ, covered with vibratile cells, having a slight depression in front. They swim about for a short time with great activity, much like the infusoria, which they strikingly resemble in other respects.

At the end of forty-eight hours the movements decrease. Aided by the depression already noted, the larvæ attaches itself to some solid body, fixing itself to it at this point by the assistance of a thick mucous matter. A change of form soon takes place: it becomes elongated; its pedicle is contracted, and its free extremity swells into a club-like shape. An opening soon presents itself in the centre of this extremity, through which an internal cavity appears. Four little mammals have now appeared on the edge, which are elongated in the manner of arms. Others soon follow: these are the tentacles of a polype: the young infusoria has become a polype!

The polype increases by buds and shoots, just like a strawberry plant, which throws out its slender stems in all directions, covering all the neighbouring ground.

The young Medusa lives some time under this form. Then one of the polypes becomes enlarged and its form cylindrical. This cylinder is divided into from ten to fourteen superposed rings. These rings, at first smooth, form themselves into festoons, and separate into bifurcated thongs; the intermediate lines become channeled. The animal now resembles a pile of plates, cut round the edges. In a short time each ring is stirred at the free edge of its fringe: this becomes contractile. The rings are individualised. Finally, these annular creatures, obscure in their lives, isolate themselves. When detached, they begin to swim: from that time they have only to perfect and modify their form. From being flat, they become concave on the one side and convex on the other. The digestive cavity—the gastro-vascular canals—become more decided; the mouth opens, the tentacles are elongated, the floating marginal cirri become more and more numerous; and now, after all these metamorphoses, the Medusa appears: it perfectly resembles the mother.

Tubularidæ.

We have already said that recent researches have led to a separation of a class of animals from the Sertularia, and to their being united with the Medusæ. Of these creatures we formerly only knew one of the forms, namely, the polype form; or, rather, the first stage of it. During their earliest days they possess a polypier, furnished with tentacles, and a bell-shaped body. During their medusoid age, they present a central stomach, with four canals in the form of a cross, and four to eight tentacles with cirri. The animals constitute the Tubularidæ, comprehending many genera; among others the Tubularia and Campanularia, in studying which Van Beneden of Louvain discovered most interesting facts connected with the subject of alternate generation.

The class of zoophytes ranged among the Tubularia have the power of secreting an inverting tube of a horny nature, in which the fleshy body can move up and down, expanding its tentacles over the top. Others of them give forth buds, each of which takes the form of a polype, and these, being permanent, give it a shrub-like or branched appearance; it is now a compound polypier. The tube is branched, and the orifices from which the polypes expand usually dilate into cups or cells. This is the condition of the *Tubulari-campanulariadæ* groups, which are numerous round our own coast and in the Channel. The Tubularia are plant-like and horny, rooted by fibres, tubular, and filled with a semi-fluid organic pulp; polypes naked and fleshy, protruding from the extremity of every branchlet of the tube, and armed with one or two circles of smooth filiform tentacles; bulbules soft and naked, germinating from the base of the tentacles; embryo medusiform. "Some modern authors," says Frédol, "assure us that the tree-like form of these polypiers is a degraded and transitory form of the Medusæ. The Medusa originates the polypier, the polypier becomes a medusa." *Tubularia ramea* so perfectly resembles an old tree in miniature, deprived of its leaves, that it is difficult to believe it is not of a vegetable origin; it is now a vigorous tree in miniature, in full flower, rising from the summit of a brown-spotted stem, with many branches and tufted shoots, terminating in so many hydras of a beautiful yellow or brilliant red. *T. ramosa*, of a brownish colour and horny substance, rising six inches, is rooted by tortuous, wrinkled fibres, with flexible, smooth, and thread-like shoots, branching into a doubly permeate form. In *T. indivisa* the tubes are clustering; its numerous stems are horny, yellow, and from six to twelve inches in height, about a line in diameter, and marked with unequal knots from space to space, like the stalk of the oat-straw with the joints cut off. Their lower extremity is tortuous, attaching itself readily to shells and stones in deep water, flourishing in deep muddy bottoms, and upright as a flower, fixed by the tapering root-like terminations of its horny tube: a flowering animal, having, however, neither flower nor branch. At the summit of each stem, a double scarlet corolla is developed of from five to thirty-five petals, in rows, the external one spreading, those in the interior rising in a tuft; a little below, the ovarium appears, drooping when ripe like a bunch of orange-coloured grapes. After a time the petals of the corolla fade, fall, and die, and a bud replaces them, which produces a new polype; and so on. This succession determines the length of the stem. Each apparent flower throws out a small tube, which terminates it, and each addition adds one joint more to the axis, which it increases in length.

The Campanulariæ differ considerably from the above, the ends of their branches, whence the polypes issue, being enlarged into a bell-like shape, whence their name. *C. dichotoma* is at once the most delicate and most elegant of the species. It presents a brownish stem, thin as a thread of silk, but strong and elastic. The polypes are numerous: upon a tree eight or nine inches high there may be as many hundreds. *C. volubilis* is a minute microscopic species, living parasitically on corallines, sea-weed, and shelled animals. The stem is a capillary corneous tube, which creeps and twists itself upon its support, throwing out at alternate intervals a long slender stalk, twisted throughout or only partially, which supports a bell-shaped cup of perfect transparency, and prettily serrated round the brim. Dr. Johnston found the antennæ of a crab so profusely infested with them as to resemble hairy brushes. It is furnished, according to Hassall, with a delicate joint or hinge at the base of each little cup—a contrivance designed, it is imagined, to enable the frail zoophyte the better to elude the rude contact of the element in which it lives, by allowing it to bend to a force which it cannot resist.

The Campanulariæ increase by budding; the buds being found in much the same manner as in the Hydræ. It is a simple excrescence, which, in due time, takes the form of the branch from which it proceeds. These buds have their birth at certain distances, and form a polypier.

Siphonophora.

Alongside the Medusæ naturalists place certain marine zoophytes which are equally remarkable for their beauty and for their curious structure, the latter being so complicated that their true organization long remained unknown. They were known, until very recently, under the designation of Hydrostatic Acalephæ, or Hydra-medusæ. They are known in our days as Siphonophoræ. These inhabitants of the deep are graceful in form, and are distinguished by their delicate tissues and brilliant colours. Essentially swimmers, supported by one or many vessels filled with air—true swimming-bladders, more or less numerous, and of variable form—they float upon the waves, remaining always on the surface, whatever may be the state of the sea. They are natural skiffs, and quite incapable of immersion. The Siphonophoræ form four orders or families; namely, the *Diphydæ*, double-bell shaped animals, one fitting into the cavity of the other; *Physaliadæ*, having large oblong air-vessels and numerous tentacles of several forms, long, and pendant from one end of the shell, with a wrinkled crest; *Vilelladæ*, animals stretching over a cartilaginous plate with a flat body, an oblique, vertical, cartilaginous crest above, a tubular mouth below, and surrounded by numerous short tentacles; *Physophora*, consisting of a slender and vertical axis, terminating in an air-bladder, carrying laterally swimming-bladders, which lose themselves amongst a bundle of slender white filaments.

VILELLADÆ.

The Vilellæ assemble together in great shoals; in tropical seas and even in the Mediterranean they may be seen in fine weather floating

Fig. 93. Vilella limbosa (Lamarck).

on the surface of the waves. As described by De Blainville, the body is oval or circular, and gelatinous, sustained in the interior of the dorsal disk by a solid sub-cartilaginous frame, provided on the lower surface of the disk with extensible tentacular cirri. The family includes four genera; namely, *Vilella*, the Holothuria of the Chinese, which the reader will most readily comprehend from the brief description we shall give of the Mediterranean Vilella (*V. limbosa*—Fig. 93), which has been very minutely examined by M. Charles Vogt, of Geneva, from whose work on the "Inferior Animals of the Mediterranean" our details are borrowed. *V. spirans,* sometimes called *V. limbosa,* was discovered in the Mediterranean, between Monaco and Mentone, by Forskahl, who most erroneously took it for a holothuria. On the upper surface of the animal is a hydrostatic apparatus, the object of which is to maintain its equilibrium in the ambient element. This apparatus consists of a shield and a crest, organs of which M. Vogt gives a very detailed description; but it is on the under surface that the principal organs of the Vilella are exhibited. These are not seen when the animal swims, because under such circumstances the vertical, oblique crest only is visible. The lower surface is concave, with a sort of mesial nucleus, presenting at the extremity of a trumpet-like prolongation, whitish and contractile, a sort of central mouth, surrounded by tentacular cirri, the external row being much longer than the internal ones. This was formerly thought to be the stomach of the Vilella. In the present day, this appendage is known to be the central polype around which are grouped other whitish and much smaller appendages, the base being surrounded by little yellow bunches. These are supposed to be the reproductive organs. Between the crest and the shield numerous free tentacles present themselves, vermiform in appearance, cylindrical, and of a sky-blue colour, which are kept in continual motion.

The Vilella is therefore not an isolated individual, but a group or colony, in which the individuals intended to be reproductive are the most numerous, and occupy the inferior parts.

The central polype, by its size and structure, is distinguishable at the first glance from all the other appendages of the lower surface of the body. It is a cylindrical tube, very contractile and pear-shaped, swollen into a round ball, or considerably elongated. Its mouth is round and much dilated; it opens in the cylindrical or trumpet part, which is contained in a sac in the form of elongated fusci, clothed in the whitish integuments which formed the body of the polype when perfect. At the bottom of the sac two rows of openings are observed, which lead to a vascular network extending over the whole body; the membranous parts, while affecting various conditions in their arrangement, are nevertheless in direct communication with all the reproductive individuals.

It is a general characteristic of all colonies of polypi that the digestive cavities of the individuals composing them meet and inosculate in a common vascular system. The Vilellæ present the same conformation. Only in their case the vascular system is extended horizontally, this being the essential character of the union of all the individuals constituting the colony, with the canals common to all, in which the nourishing fluids circulate, elaborated for all and by all. It is a true picture of social communism realised by Nature.

The central polype is alone destined to absorb the food. M. Vogt has always found in its interior cavity fragments of the shells of crustaceans, the remains of small fishes; and he has often seen the hard parts which resist digestion discharged through the trumpet-like opening. This central polype nourishes itself and also all the others, but is itself sterile.

The tentacles are hollow cylinders, completely closed at the extremity. These are strong muscular tubes of considerable thickness, the interior of which is filled with a transparent liquid. They are enveloped in a strong membrane of a deep blue colour. The epidermis is furnished with small stinging capsules, formed of a sac with comparatively thick walls. If this sac is compressed under the microscope it explodes, opening at a determinate part, and throwing out an apparatus forming a long stiff filament, which is implanted on a conical channel and surrounded with points. "I know not," says M. Vogt, "if all this machinery can re-enter the capsule after it has exploded; but I presume that the animal can extend itself and withdraw at pleasure. A tentacule of Vilella sufficiently compressed presents a surface bristling with these cirri, so as to resemble a brush. The tentacles themselves are in continual motion, and I have no reason to doubt that the observation of Lesson, who saw them cover small crustaceans and fishes, may be perfectly true. These stinging organs doubtless serve the same purpose as with other animals of the same class; namely, to kill the prey which the tentacles have enabled them to secure." Thus the Vilellæ have their javelins, as the Greek and Roman warriors had, and a lasso, as the cavaliers of Mexico and Texas have.

The reproducing individuals form the great mass of the appendages attached to the under surface of the Vilella. The form of the individuals is much more varied, inasmuch as they are extremely contractile. Nevertheless, they have considerable resemblance to the corolla of a hyacinth.

These reproductive individuals are, then, at the same time nurses. The Medusæ originating by budding in the case of those reproductive individuals, constitute the sexual state of the Vilellæ. They exist, in short, in two alternate states: the one sexual, producing eggs; in this state they are isolated individuals of the Medusadæ, which never group themselves or form colonies: the other aggregate state is non-sexual, and in it they form swimming colonies, under the special designation of *Vilellæ*.

The Vilellæ, so called by Lamarck, are found widely diffused in the seas of Europe, Asia, America, and Australia. One species, *V. limbosa*, is often taken on the southern coasts of England. The animals are also met with far at sea, and often huddled together in considerable masses, old and young together.

Such is a brief account of the strange facts to which the careful study of the lower class of marine animals initiates us. Naturalists range along with them the *Rataria* and *Porpita*.

The Rataria have the body oval or circular, sustained by a compressed sub-cartilaginous framework, much elevated, having a muscular, movable, longitudinal crest below, and provided in the middle with a free proboscidiform stomach and a single row of marginal tentacular suckers. De Blainville was inclined to consider the very small animals which Eschscholtz termed Ratariæ as young and undeveloped *Vilellæ*. M. Vogt doubts not that the Ratariæ are young Vilellæ which have acquired, by little and little, the elliptical form, but that the limb is only furnished at a later period to the reproductive individuals. These Ratariæ are engendered, according to Vogt, by the naked-eyed Medusæ born of the Vilellæ, and owe their existence to the eggs produced by these Medusæ.

The Porpitæ constitute, like the Vilellæ, colonies of floating animals furnished with a cartilaginous, horizontal, and rounded skeleton, but they are destitute of crest or veil. The body is circular and depressed, slightly convex above, with an internal circular cartilaginous support, having the surface marked by concentric striæ crossing other radiating striæ; the upper surface being covered by a delicate membrane only. The body is concave below; the under surface is furnished with a great number of tentacles, the exterior ones being longest, and also with small cilia, each terminating in a globule, which sometimes contains air; the interior tentacles are shorter, simple, and fleshy. In the centre of these tentacula is the mouth, in form of a small proboscis, leading to a simple stomach surrounded by a somewhat glandular substance. The editors of the last edition of the "Règne Animal" only mention one species—*P. gigantea*, a native of the Mediterranean and other warm seas, of a beautiful blue colour. Lamarck gives four species. De Blainville and others consider with Cuvier that they are only varieties, which Eschscholtz re-unites under one species. In Fig. 94 we have represented *P. pacifica* (Lesson), the disk of which is twelve lines in diameter, without comprehending the tentacles. This disk is finely radiated on the under surface with a brilliant argentine nacre. The membranous fold which surrounds it is cut into, leaving light and perfectly straight festoons. It is of a clear celestial blue colour, and very transparent. The tentacles are much compressed, very thin and cylindrical, of a light blue, and the glands are of an indigo blue colour. All the reproductive individuals, which are placed in the lower part of the body, are of a perfect hyaline white.

Fig. 94. Porpita pacifica (Lesson).

This beautiful Porpita was discovered by Lesson on the Peruvian coast, where it occurs in swarms closely packed on the surface of the sea. "Its manner of life," says Lesson, "is perfectly analogous to that of the Vilella. Their locomotion on the sea is purely passive, at least in appearance. Their disk laid flat on the surface upon the water-line, leaves them to float freely and in a horizontal direction, the irritable arms hanging all round them."

Physophora.

This family includes the *Physophora*, properly so called, the *Aga-*

Fig. 95. Physophora hydrostatica (Forskahl).

lina, and the *Stephanomia*, for the history of which we are indebted to the curious observations of M. Vogt. Fig. 95 is a representation of *Physophora hydrostatica*, after M. Vogt's memoir. We see that the animal is composed of a slender vertical axis, terminating in an aerial bladder, carrying laterally certain vesicles, known as swimming-balls, which terminate in a bundle of whitish slender threads.

The aerial bladder is brilliant and silvery, punctured with red spots. The swimming-bladders are encased in a transparent and somewhat cartilaginous capsule, which is continued into the common median trunk, the latter being rose-coloured, hollow, and very contractile; in short, it presents very delicate muscular fibres, which expand themselves on the external fan of the capsule, and is closed on all sides.

The swimming-bladders are of a glass-like transparency, and of a firm, compact tissue. They are attached obliquely and alternately upon a common axis, presenting an exterior curvature, a round opening, furnished with a fine, muscular, and very contractile limb, and arranged like the iris of the eye. Their power of resistance is increased by certain horny hollow threads, which are in direct communication with the cavity of the vertical trunk, and have their origin in a common circular canal.

"The animal," says Vogt, "is enabled to guide itself in any direction by means of the swimming apparatus or air-bags. These, on opening, are filled with water, which is again ejected in the contractile movement, for their movements may be compared to that of the umbrella of the Medusæ. It is the violent expulsion of this liquid which enables the animal to advance diagonally through the water, a kind of motion which is the consequence of its organization; for where both rows of air-bags are working in the direction of the axis of the trunk, the organism will incline to the side which works most, but always in such a manner that the aerial vesicle will be borne forward."

In its lower parts the trunk expands, becomes flat, and winds itself in a spiral. It is hollow, and encloses a transparent viscous liquid, in which very small granules are observed, which appear to be the result of digestion. This disk is attached to three different sorts of appendages; we shall first address ourselves to the tentacles.

These form a crown or bundle of vermiform appendages, of a reddish colour, over an inch in length, and which are kept continually in motion: these are formed of a glass-like cartilaginous substance;

they are conical tubes, closed on all parts except at the point where the tentacle is attached to the disk. Their cavity is filled with the granulous liquid already mentioned. On the under surface of the disk, and to the inside of these tentacles, the polypes and fishing-lines are attached.

The anterior part of the polype is formed of a glass-like substance, which changes its form in the most varied and surprising manner. It bears a roundish mouth at its summit. In its posterior part the polype presents a straight hollow stem, of reddish colour; but near to

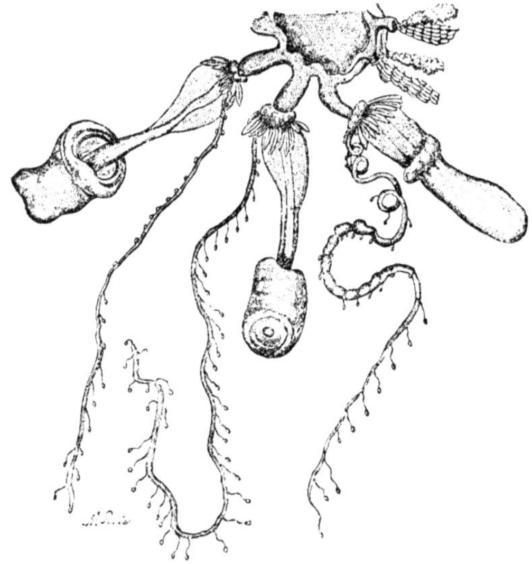

Fig. 96. P. hydrostatica, with a portion of the disk, three polypes, and reproductive clusters attached.

this red stem we find a thick tuft of cylindrical appendages, from the middle of which springs the extensible and contractile filaments which Vogt calls the *fishing-lines* (fil pêcheur), and of which he has given the following very strange account:

"Each of these appendages consists of an assemblage of cylindrical tubes somewhat resembling and analogous to a filament of confervæ. All these tubes are traversed by a continuous canal, which originates in the internal cavity of the stem of the polype. Each fragment of the line is capable of a prodigious extent of elongation and contraction, but where completely drawn back the pieces fold themselves up somewhat in the manner of a pocket foot-rule. It is to the combined effect of contraction and the unfolding of the pieces that these lines owe the marvellous changes of length which they present." In Fig. 96 are represented the polypes and fishing-lines of *P. hydrostatica,* with a portion of the disk and two pairs of reproductive clusters.

In this figure it will be observed that each fragment or joint has implanted, near the articulation, a secondary line, which bears the stinging organ. Each of these filaments consists of three parts: a straight stem, muscular, contractile, and hollow, the cavity of which communicates with that of the trunk which carries it; a middle part, a sort of tube containing, in a considerable internal cavity, a transparent liquid; finally, an inflated stinging organ, which terminates the apparatus. This last is egg-shaped, and consists internally of a hyaline substance of cartilaginous consistence, in the interior of which we find a great cavity, which opens from within, near the base of the capsule; to the inside of this cavity a second muscular sac is attached all round the opening of the capsule, in such a manner that the opening leads directly into the cavity of the sac. This cavity conceals in its interior a long filament usually rolled up in a spiral, as illustrated in Fig. 97, where the two urticant capsules of the stinging apparatus of *Physophora hydrostatica* are represented, one of them being a section, magnified by twelve diameters. This spirally rolled-up filament consists of a large quantity of very small, hard, sabre-shaped, corpuscular bodies, supported the one against the other, and having their points turned inwards. These objects Vogt terms "urticant sabres:" the extremity of the filament consists of curved corpuscles, larger, of a brownish yellow, very strong, and with a double point. M. Vogt had also opportunities of observing the action of these stinging capsules. He has seen them burst naturally, and he has also obtained artificially the same result. In the former case the filament issues from the opening left at the base of the capsule with a sort of explosion. "The use," he says, "of the fishing-lines becomes evident when we see a Physophora in repose in a vase large enough for its full development; then it takes a vertical position; the lines elongate themselves more and more, by unfolding one by one the secondary lines with stinging capsules, and the Physophora now resembles a flower posed upon a tuft of roots, with extremely long and delicate rootlets reaching the bottom of the vase. But in the case of the Physophora the living roots are in continual motion. Each line is elongated, foreshortened, and contracted in a thousand ways. The least movement of the water causes the stinging capsules to be suddenly drawn up, the lines hauled in most rapidly being those near the crown of tentacles. This continuous play of the lines has no other object than to attract the prey destined

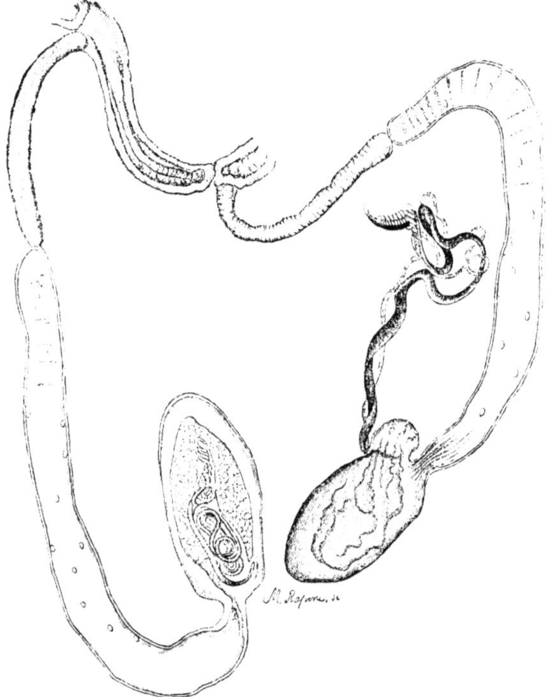

Fig. 97. Offensive apparatus of Physophora hydrostatica.

to feed the polype, and we cannot find any better comparison for them than the fishing-lines to which they have been compared. The moment that some small microscopic medusæ, larvæ, or crustaceans come within the sphere of those redoubted lines, it is at once surrounded, seized, and led with irresistible force towards the mouth of this polype by a gentle and gradual contraction of the line; the stinging organs, complicated as we have seen them to be in the Phy-

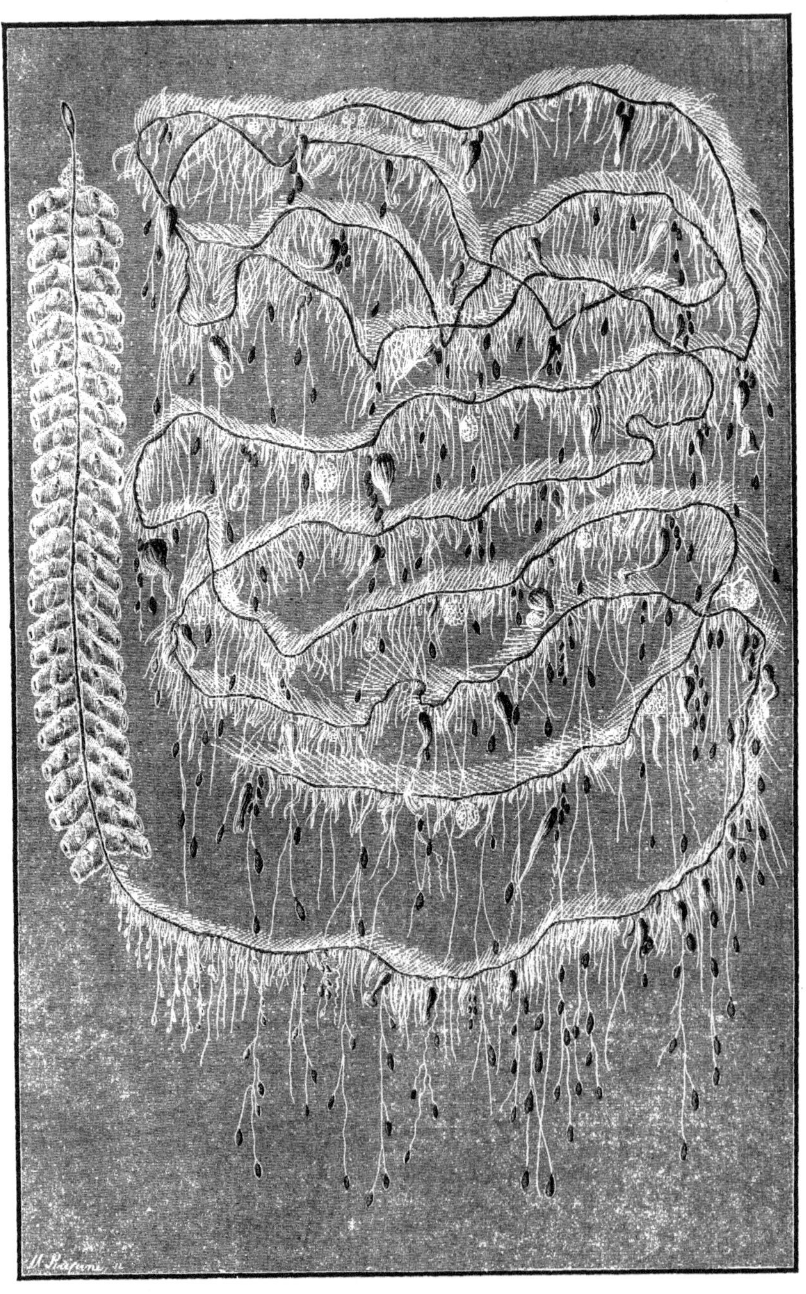

Plate VII.—Agalma rubra, three-fifths natural size

sophora, thus serve the same purpose as the stinging organs disposed on the arms of the Hydræ, or on the external surface of the tentacles and prolific polypes of the Vilellæ.

Can there be any animal form more graceful than *Agalma rubra*, which is reproduced in Plate VII. from Vogt's Memoir? This beautiful creature is common in the Mediterranean, on the coast near Nice, from November till the month of May. Towards the middle of December Vogt found nearly fifty individuals in the space of an hour, opposite to the Port of Nice, all following the same current; a prodigious quantity of Salpæ, Medusæ, and small Pteropodean Mollusks accompanying them.

"I know nothing more graceful," says Vogt, "than this Agalma as it floats along near the surface of the waters, its long, transparent, garland-like lines extended, and their limits distinctly indicated by bundles of a brilliant vermilion red, while the rest of the body is concealed by its very transparency; the entire organism always swims in a slightly oblique position near the surface, but is capable of steering itself in any direction with great rapidity. I have had in my possession some of these garlands more than three feet in length, in which the series of air-bags measured more than four inches, so that in the great vase in which I kept them the column of swimming bags touched the bottom, while the aërial vesicle floated on the surface. Immediately after its capture the columns contracted themselves to such a point that they were scarcely perceptible, but when left to repose in a spacious vase, all its shrunken appendages deployed themselves round the vase in the most graceful manner imaginable, the column of swimming-bladders remaining immovable in their vertical position, the air-bags at the surface, while the different appendages soon began to play. The polypes, planted at intervals along the common trunk of rose-colour, began to agitate themselves in all directions, taking a thousand odd forms; the reproductive individuals, like the tentacles, were contracting and twisting themselves about like so many worms; the tentacles were stirred, the ovarian clusters began to dilate and contract, the spermatic air-bells agitated the waters with their umbrellas, like the Medusæ; but what most excited my curiosity, was the continuous action of the fishing-lines, which continued to unroll and contract in a most surprising manner, retiring altogether sometimes with the utmost precipitation. All who have witnessed these living colonies detach themselves reluctantly from the strange spectacle, where each polype seems to play the part of the fisherman who throws his line, furnished with baited hooks, withdrawing it when he feels a nibble, and throwing again when he discovers his disappointment. These efforts continue in full vigour for two or three days, and I have succeeded sometimes in feeding them with the small crustaceans which swarm on our coasts."

Of the "personelle" of these colonies a few words will not be misplaced. The common axis of the *Agalma* is a hollow muscular tube, the length of which may be three feet, and its breadth an eighth or tenth of an inch; it is traversed by a double current of granulous liquid; at its summit is the aërial vesicle; beneath are the swimming vessels. These are disposed along the trunk in a double series, attaining sometimes the number of sixty; their structure is analogous to the same organs in the Physophora.

In examining the posterior portion of the trunk, traversing polypes are observed at intervals, whose base is surrounded by a cluster of reddish grains, each of which is armed with a *line*, and with its surrounding filament, terminating in a tendril of a red vermilion colour, which is a perfect arsenal of offensive and defensive arms. There we find "sabres" of divers sizes, and poniards of various forms, the whole constituting a truly formidable stinging apparatus.

These warlike engines, these arms of attack and defence with which man surrounds himself, Nature has freely bestowed on these little creatures with which the ocean swarms in some places. It might be said that, after having created these graceful creatures to ornament and decorate the depths of the ocean, the Creator was so pleased with His work that He furnished them with arms for their protection and defence against all attacks from without.

Among these creatures we may note the pretty *Apolemia contorta* of Milne Edwards (Fig. 98), which also inhabits the Mediterranean, and particularly the coast of Nice, and is no less admirable in its structure than *Agalma rubra*. This elegant species is often met with in the Gulf of Villafranca near Nice, and has been figured and described by Milne Edwards, Charles Vogt, and also by M. de Quatrefages, who asks the reader "to figure to himself an axis of flexible crystal, sometimes more than a mètre (forty inches), all round which are attached, by means of long peduncles or footstalks equally transparent, some hundreds of bodies, sometimes elongated, sometimes flat and formed like the bud of a flower. If we add to this garland of pearls of a vivid red colour, an infinity of fine filaments, varying in thickness, and give life and motion to all these parts, we have even now only a very slight and imperfect idea of the marvellous organism." The

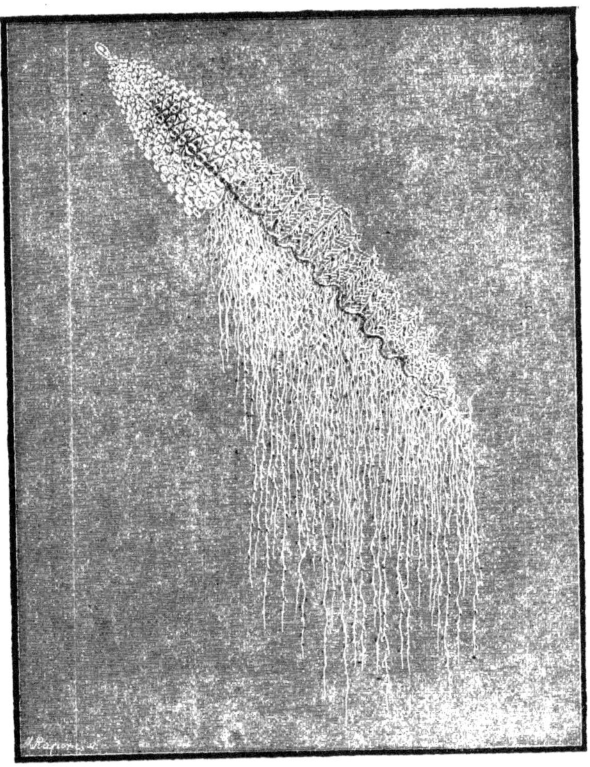

Fig. 98. Apolemia contorta, one-third natural size (Milne Edwards).

air-bells in *Apolemia contorta* consist of a mass having the form of an elongated egg cut in the middle. They are arranged in a vertical series of twelves, and the axis which supports them is terminated by the aërial vesicle. This axis is always arranged in a spiral form, even in its greatest expansion, is of a fine rose tint, and flattened into the form of a ribbon; it is marked in all its length with asperities or hollow dimples, in which the filamental appendages originate.

The nursing polypes have been called *poboscidiferous* organs by Mr. Milne Edwards, who has studied them carefully. They are rendered conspicuous at a glance by the bright red colour of their digestive cavity and their extreme dilatability. At the base of their stems the very delicate filaments called fishing-lines are attached, which are furnished with a multitude of stinging tendrils of a reddish colour. These tendrils slightly resemble those of the Agalmæ, and the sabre-like weapons are not wanting.

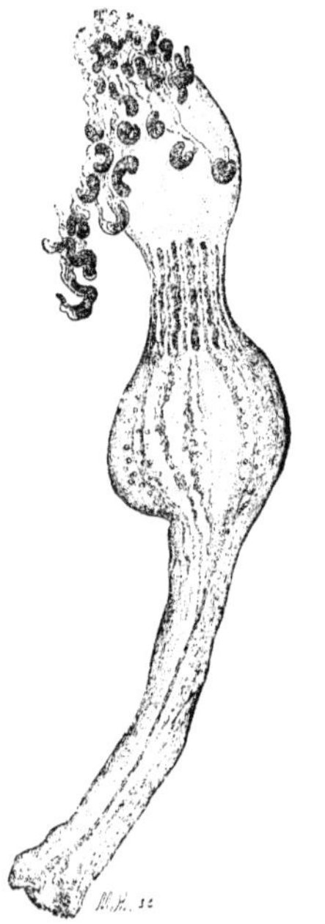

Fig. 99. Apolemia contorta, magnified 12 times.

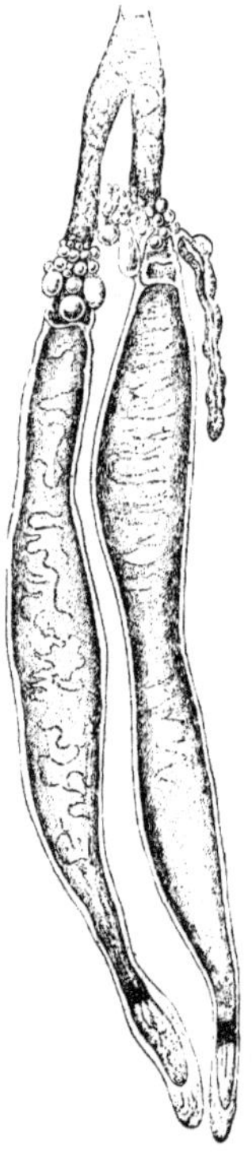

Fig. 100. Apolemia contorta, reproductive pair, magnified 12 times.

Between the nursing polypes are placed in pairs the reproductive individuals, having the form of an elongated tube very dilatable, and closed at the free end. They have, then, no mouth! Milne Edwards calls these "vesicular appendages," and M. Kœlliker, tentacles. The buds arranged at the base of each prolific individual vary; but, according to M. Vogt, they are always there in pairs—a male and female at the base of each stem. Figs. 99 and 100 represent the colony we have endeavoured to describe, 99 being the nursing individual of *Apolemia contorta* magnified twelve times, 100 representing the reproductive pair under the same magnifying power.

THE DIPHYDÆ.

We have seen that the *Physophora*, the *Agalma*, and the *Apolemia* have for the use of the colony a vast number of swimming vesicules and a terminal aërial vesicule. It is much the same in the *Prayæ* or Diphydæ. In this family a great number of natatory vesicles are connected with the terminal aërial vesicle, as in Fig. 101, *Praya diphys.* This species is widely diffused in the sea which bathes the Nicean coast, but it is very difficult to procure perfect specimens. M. Vogt

Fig. 101. Praya diphys (Blainville).

found fragments more than three feet long which swam on the surface, and was in its state of contraction not more than a finger's length. This species has been met with at Porta della Praya and at San Yago, one of the Cape de Verde islands.

The colony of the Praya presents two great locomotive bell-shaped masses, between which the common trunk is suspended, and to which it can retire. This cylindrical trunk, which is thin and transparent, carries from space to space certain groups very exactly circumscribed and individualised. Each of these groups consists of a nursing polype, having its fishing-line with a special floating air-bladder, a reproductive bud male or female, and a protecting casque enveloping the whole.

Another species having a great resemblance to the *Praya* is *Galeolaria aurantiaca* (Plate VIII.) or Orange Galeolaria, which is represented on the opposite page, borrowed from the fine " Memoir of the Inferior Animals of the Mediterranean," by Charles Vogt. Here we find only two great floating bladders placed at each extremity of a common trunk, and serving the purpose of a locomotive apparatus to the whole colony. This trunk carries in like manner polypes placed at regular intervals forming isolated groups, provided each with its protecting plates. But there is no special swimming apparatus for each of these groups. Moreover, each colony is either male or female.

PHYSALIA.

Let us finally note among the Siphonophoræ a zoophyte which has attracted great attention, and has been described under many names. Sailors call it the sea-bladder, from its resemblance to that organ; it is also known as the Portuguese man-of-war, from its fancied resemblance to a small ship as it floats along under its tiny sail. Naturalists after Eschscholtz call it *Physalia utriculus*, from the Greek word φυσαλὶς, a bubble, and utriculus from its stinging powers. It was long thought that the Physalia was an isolated individual. But, according to recent researches, they form, like the species already desciibed, an animal republic.

Let us imagine a great cylindrical bladder dilated in the middle, attenuated and rounded at its two extremities, of eleven or twelve inches in length, and from one to three broad. Its appearance is glassy and transparent, its colour an imperfect purple, passing to a violet, then to an azure above. It is surmounted by a crest, limpid and pure as crystal, veined with purple and violet in decreasing tints. Under the vesicle float the fleshy filaments, waving and contorted into a spiral form, which sometimes descend perpendicularly like so many threads of celestial blue. Sailors believe that the crest which

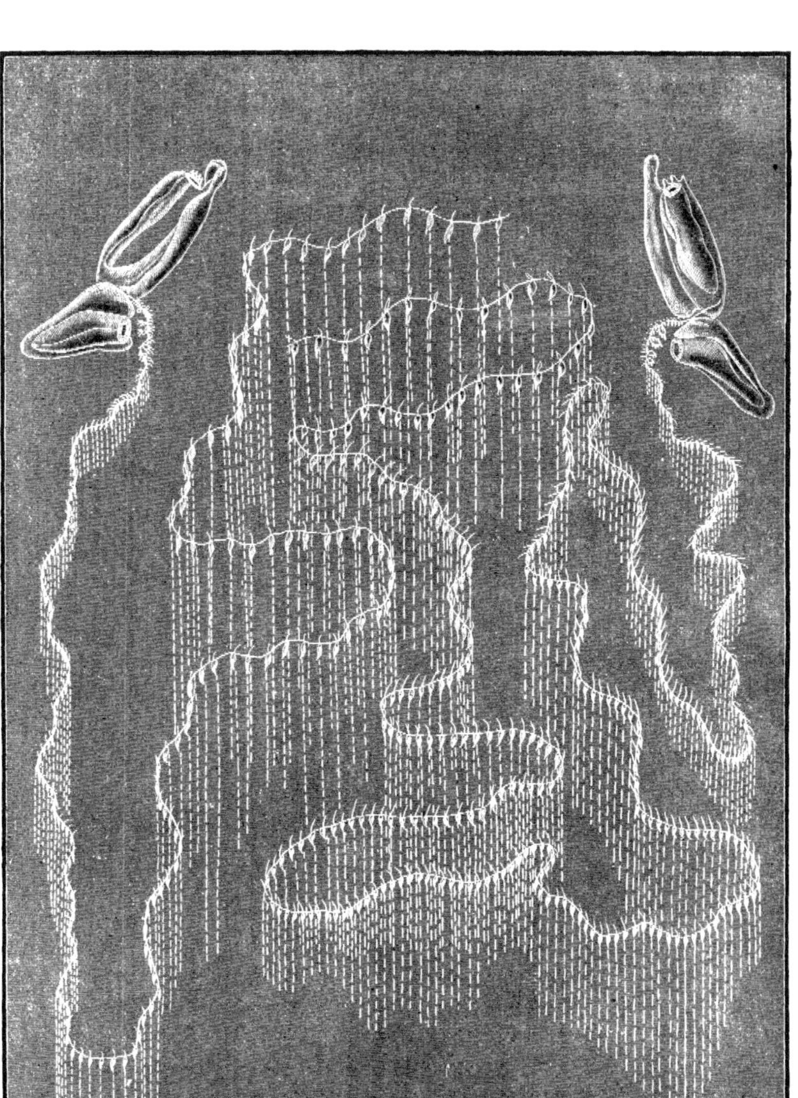

Plate VIII.—Galeolaria aurantiaca. (Vogt.)

surmounts the vesicle performs the office of a sail, and that they tell the navigator "how the wind blows," as they say. With all respect to the sailors, the bladder-like form, with its aërial crest, is only a hydrostatic apparatus, whose office is to lighten the animal, and modify its specific gravity. Mr. Gosse thinks otherwise however.

"This bladder," says Gosse, in his "Year by the Sea-side," "is filled with air, and therefore floats almost wholly on the surface. Along the upper side, nearly from end to end, runs a thin edge of membrane, which is capable of being erected at will to a considerable height, fully equal at times to the entire width of the bladder, when it represents an arched fore-and-aft sail, the bladder being the hull. From the bottom of the bladder, near the thickest extremity, where there is a denser portion of the membrane, depends a crowded mass of organs, most of which take the form of very slender, highly contractile movable threads, which hang down into the deep to a depth of many feet, or occasionally of several yards.

"The colours of this curious creature are very vivid; the bladder, though in some parts transparent and colourless, and in some specimens almost entirely so, is in general painted with richest blues and purple, mingled with green and crimson to a smaller extent, these all being, not as sometimes described, iridescent or changeable, but positive colours independent of the incidence of light, and, for the most part, possessing great depth and fulness. The sail-like, erectile membrane is transparent, tinted towards the edge with a lovely rose-pink hue, the colours arranged in a peculiar fringe-like manner. When examined anatomically, the bladder is found to be composed of two walls of membrane, which are lined with cilia, and have between them the nutritive food which supplies the place of the blood. Besides this, the double membrane is turned in or inverted like a stocking prepared for putting on; and thus there is a bladder within a bladder, both having double walls; the inner (*pneumatocyst*) much smaller than the outer (*pneumatophone*), and contracted at the point where it is turned in to the almost imperceptible orifice. The inner sends up closed tubular folds into the crest, which, being arrested by the membranous walls of the outer sac, give to the sail that appearance of verticle wrinkles which is so conspicuous."

When it is filled with air the body is almost projected out of the water. In order to descend it is necessary to compress itself or dispel the air, in part, for the centre of gravity in the animal is displaced, according as the air is in the vesicle or in the crest. When the last is distended it rises out of the water, and becomes nearly vertical; in short, it then becomes a sort of sail. The floating appendages beneath the body are of divers kinds. Some of these are reproductive individuals; some are nurses; some are tentacles; finally, there are organs designated under the name of *Sondes* by French naturalists; probes or suckers, we may call them, forming offensive and defensive arms truly formidable; for these elegant creatures are terrible antagonists. Dutertre, the veracious historian of the Antilles, relates the following: "This 'galley' (our Physalia), however agreeable to the sight, is most dangerous to the body, for I can assert that it is freighted with the worst merchandise which floats on the sea. I speak as a naturalist, and as having made experiments at my own personal cost. One day, when sailing at sea in a small boat, I perceived one of these little 'galleys,' and was curious to see the form of the animal; but I had scarcely seized it, when all its fibres seemed to clasp my hand, covering it as with birdlime, and scarcely had I felt it in all its freshness (for it is very cold to the touch) when it seemed as if I had plunged my arm up to the shoulder in a cauldron of boiling water. This was accompanied with a pain so strange that it was only with a violent effort I could restrain myself from crying aloud."

Another voyager, Leblond, in his "Voyage aux Antilles," relates as follows: "One day I was bathing with some friends in a bay in front of the house where I dwelt. While my friends fished for sardines for breakfast, I amused myself by diving, in the manner of the native Carribeans, under the wave about to break; having reached the other side of one great wave, I had gained the open sea, and was returning on the top of the next wave towards the shore. My rashness nearly cost me my life: a Physalia, many of which were stranded upon the beach, fixed itself upon my left shoulder at the moment the wave landed me on the beach. I promptly detached it, but many of its filaments remained glued to my skin, and the pain I experienced immediately was so intense that I nearly fainted. I seized an oil flask which was at hand, and swallowed one half, while I rubbed my arm with the other: this restored me to myself, and I returned to the house, where two hours of repose relieved the pain, which disappeared altogether during the night."

Mr. Bennett, who accompanied the exploring expedition under Admiral Fitzroy as naturalist, ventured to test the powers of the Physalia. "On one occasion," he says, "I tried the experiment of its stinging powers upon myself, intentionally. When I seized it by the bladder portion, it raised the long cables by muscular contraction of the bands situated at the base of the feelers, and, entwining the slender appendages about my hand and finger, inflicting severe and peculiarly pungent pain, it adhered most tenaciously at the same time, so as to be extremely difficult of removal. The stinging continued during the whole time that the minutest portion of the tentacula remained adherent to the skin. I soon found that the effects were not confined to the acute pungency inflicted, but produced a great degree of constitutional irritation: the pain extended upwards along the arm, increasing not only in extent but in severity, apparently acting along the course of the absorbents, and could only be compared to a severe rheumatic attack. The pulse was accelerated, and a feverish state of the whole system produced: the muscles of the chest, even, were affected; the same distressing pain being felt on taking a full respiration as obtains in a case of acute rheumatism. The secondary effects were very severe, continuing for nearly three-quarters of an hour; the duration being probably longer in consequence of the time and delay occasioned by removing the tentacula from the skin, to which they adhered, by the aid of the stinging capsules, with an annoying degree of tenacity. On the whole being removed, the pain began to abate; but during the day a peculiar numbness was felt, accompanied by an increased temperature in the limb on which the sting had been inflicted. For some hours afterwards the skin displayed white elevations or weals on the parts stung similar to those resulting from the poison of the stinging nettle. The intensity of the pain depends in some degree upon the size and consequent power of the creature. After it has been removed from the water for some time, the stinging property, although still continuing to act, is found to have perceptibly diminished. I have observed also, that this irritative power is retained for some weeks after the death of the animal in the vesicles of the cables, and even linen cloth which has been used for wiping off the adhering tentacles, when touched, still retained the pungency, although it had not the power of producing such violent constitutional irritation."

The question has been much agitated, without being positively resolved, whether the Physalia are venomous or not: if they can kill or make sick the man or animal which swallows them. Listen to the opinions of M. Ricord-Madiana, a physician of Guadaloupe, who made direct experiments with a view to settling the question. "Many inhabitants of the Antilles," he says, "say that the 'galleys' are poisonous, and that the negroes make use of them, after being dried and powdered, to poison both men and animals. The fishermen of the islands also believe that fish which have swallowed them become deleterious and poison those who eat them, a prejudice which has been adopted by many travellers, and has even found its way into scientific books. We can state, as the result of direct experiment, that though the 'galley' will burn the ignorant hand which is touched by its tentacles, when dried in the sun and pulverized, it becomes mere grains of dead matter, producing no effect whatever upon the animal economy."

On the other hand, we read in P. Labat's Voyage, vol. ii., p. 31, "that the bécune should not be eaten without some precaution, for this fish being extremely voracious, greedily devours all that comes within its reach in and out of the water, and it often happens that it meets and swallows 'galleys,' which are very caustic, and a violent poison. The fish does not die, but its flesh absorbs the venom and poisons those who eat it." "There is every reason to believe," says M. Leblond, in the work already quoted, "that the sardine, as well as many other species of fish, after having ate the tentacles of the 'galley,' acquires a poisonous quality. Supping at an auberge on one occasion, with other persons, a bécune was served up, of which gastronomers are very fond, and which is usually perfectly harmless: five persons partook of it, and immediately afterwards exhibited every symptom of being poisoned. This was manifested by a burning heat in the region of the stomach. I bled two of them: one was cured by vomiting; one other would take nothing but tea and some culinary oil. The colic continued during the night, and had disappeared in the morning, but he entertained so great a horror of water, that during the remainder of the voyage a glass of it presented to him made him turn pale." M. Leblond concludes, from this and other facts, that the fishes which eat the Physalia become a poison for those who eat them, although it does not appear that he had any evidence of the fish having ate the "galley," or any other poison.

"Let us report our own experiments," continues M. Ricord-Madiana.

"I. I had placed a 'galley' in the sun, in order to dry and pulverize it. A nest of ants were there who devoured the whole of it. Now, many persons in the islands think that these insects will not touch venomous fishes.

"II. Another 'galley,' which I had left on the table in my laboratory, was attacked by a number of great flies, who deposited their eggs there; these were duly hatched, and the larvæ fed on the decomposed zoophyte.

"III. On the 12th of July, 1823, I saw on the sands in the Bay between Saint Mary and La Goyave, at Guadaloupe, many Physalia recently cast ashore. Having a dog with me, with the assistance of my servant, I made him swallow the freshest of them, with all its filiform tentacles, pushing it down his throat, while my servant held his mouth open; five minutes after, the dog exhibited symptoms of great pain on the edges of its lips, it foamed at the mouth and rubbed it in the sand, or upon the grass, leaping about, passing its paws over its jaws, and exhibiting every symptom of excessive pain. I mounted my horse, and, in spite of its sufferings, the poor animal followed me as it was wont. After twenty minutes, when its sufferings seemed over, I had a piece of bread which I gave it, and it ate it with appetite, swallowing it without any difficulty; it only seemed to feel the pain on the edges of its mouth: it was well enough all day, and had evacuations which gave no indication that the Physalia had any influence over the digestive organs. Next day, and the day following, it was as well as usual, exhibiting no signs of inflammation either in the mouth or throat.

"IV. On the 20th of the same month, I took two 'galleys' on the sea-shore and cut them in pieces; then, with a spoon, I had them forced down the throat of a puppy, which still sucked its mother; this strong dose of Physalia had no effect upon it, the tentacles having probably been surrounded, by the fleshy parts of the animal in dividing it, so as not to touch the mouth: it seems probable, therefore, that the internal mucous is capable of subduing the irritation, which is so distressing when applied to membranes exposed to the external air. We swallow some things with impunity, which we could not support in the mouth if the burning substance remained there.

"V. I have also procured many 'galleys' since these experiments, and having placed them in a glass-tube, left them to dry and had them pulverized; twenty-five grains of this powder administered to a very young dog produced no deleterious effects. Twice this quantity administered to a young cat produced no more, nor has this surprised me, for, if the fresh animal has no poisonous properties, how can it be supposed that drying the zoophyte can have increased its poisonous properties, if it really possesses them? On the contrary, it is more reasonable to suppose that, by desiccation, the deleterious principle from any animal, whether *Physalia* or *Holothuria*, should lose infinitely in its principle by evaporation, and other changes that heat and air produce in the process of drying.

"VI. I have had a 'galley' cut into pieces, and got a fat young chicken to swallow them. It caused no inconvenience. Three hours after, I had the chicken killed and roasted; then I ate it, and made my servant eat it too. Neither of us experienced any inconvenience from it, a certain proof that it is not from eating Physalia that the fish becomes poisonous.

"VII. I put twenty-five grains of powdered *Physalia* in a little 'bouillon;' I swallowed the dose without the least fear, and I felt no inconvenience from it."

After these experiments, which are certainly quite conclusive, what are we to think of the story related of a certain M. Tébé, the managing partner of a house in Guadaloupe, who fell a victim to his cook, who is said, after having sought in vain to poison him with the rasping of his nails, which he had spread carefully over the roasted fish daily served up for dinner, determined, seeing that he had signally failed by other means, to put into his soup a pulverized Physalia. An hour after his repast, this gentleman appeared in the burgh of Lamantin, at a little distance from his habitation, and, while entering the city with some friends, he was seized with violent pains in the stomach and intestines, racking him as if by the most corrosive poison. His illness increased until the next day, when he died, under the most excruciating pains. On examination, the stomach and intestines were found to be violently inflamed and corroded, as if he had been poisoned with arsenic, and I have no doubt that it was with this poison, or some other corrosive substance, that M. Tébé really was poisoned. The negroes never make known the substance with which they commit a poisoning; they confess all but the truth, which they are sworn never to reveal—the means they employ, so far as the

Fig. 102. *Physalia utriculus* (Eschscholtz).

poisoning material is concerned are never communicated by confession.

The habits of the Physalia are still imperfectly known, but among the many strange forms of brilliant colour and elegant contour, which swarm in the warmer parts of the ocean, "none," says Gosse, "take a stronger hold on the fancy of the beholder, certainly none is more familiar than the little thing he daily marks floating in the sun-lit waves, as the ship glides swiftly by, which the sailors tell him is the Portuguese man-of-war. Perhaps a dead calm has settled over the sea, and he leans over the bulwarks of the ship scrutinizing the ocean-rover at leisure, as it hastily rises and falls on the long, sluggish heavings of the glassy surface. Then he sees that the comparison of the stranger to a ship is a felicitous one, for at a little (Fig. 102) distance it might well be mistaken for a child's mimic boat, shining in all the gaudy painting in which it left the toy-shop.

"Not unfrequently, one of these tiny vessels comes so close alongside, that, by means of the ship's bucket, with the assistance of a smart fellow, who has jumped into the 'chains' with a boat-hook, it is captured, and brought on deck for examination. A dozen voices are, however, lifted, warning you by no means to touch it, for well the experienced sailor knows its terrible powers of defence. It does not now appear so like a ship as when it was at a distance. It is an oblong bladder of tough membrane, varying considerably in shape, for no two agree in this respect; varying also in size, from less than an inch to the size of a man's hat. Once, on a voyage to Mobile, when rounding the Florida reef, I was nearly a whole day passing through a fleet of these little Portuguese men-of-war, which studded the smooth sea as far as the eye could reach, and must have extended for many miles. They were of all sizes within the limits I have mentioned."

Generally, there is a conspicuous difference between the two extremities of the bladder, one end being rounded, the other more pointed, or terminating in a small knob-like swelling or beak-shaped excrescence, where there is a minute orifice; sometimes, however, no such excrescence is visible, and the orifice cannot be detected.

"That wonderful river," continues Mr. Gosse, in his nervous, eloquent style, "with a well-defined course through the midst of the Atlantic—that Gulf stream—brings on its warm waters many of the denizens of tropical seas, and wafts them to the shores on which its waves impinge. Hence it is that so many of the proper pelagic creatures are from time to time observed on the coasts of Cornwall and Devon. The Portuguese man-of-war is among them, sometimes paying its visit in fleets, more commonly in single stranded hulks. Scarcely a season passes without one or more of these lovely strangers occurring in the vicinity of Torquay. Usually," he adds in a note, "in these stranded examples the tentacles and suckers are much mutilated by washing on the shore. The fishermen, who pick them up, always endeavour to make a harvest of their capture, not by selling, but by making an exhibition of them."

The Physalia seem to be gregarious in their habits, herding together in shoals. Floating on the sea between the tropics in both oceans, they may be seen now carried along by currents, now driven by the trade-winds, dragging behind them their long tentacular appendages, and conspicuous by their rich and varied colouring, from pale crimson to ultramarine blue. "Certainly," says Lesson, "we can readily conceive that a poetical imagination might well compare the graceful form of the Physalia to the most elegant of sailing-vessels, even if it careened to the wind under a sail of satin, and dragged behind it deceitful garlands which struck with death every creature which suffered itself to be attracted by its seductive appearance."

If fishes have the misfortune to come in contact with one of these creatures, each tentacule, by a movement as rapid as a flash of light, or sudden as an electric shock, seizes and benumbs them, winding round their bodies as a serpent winds itself round its victim. A Physalia of the size of a walnut will kill a fish much stronger than a herring. The flying fish and the polypes are the habitual prey of the Physalia. Mr. Bennett describes them as seizing and benumbing them by means of the tentacles, which are alternately contracted to half an inch, and then shot out with amazing velocity to the length of several feet, dragging the helpless and entangled prey to the sucker-like mouths and stomach-like cavities concealed among the tentacles, which he saw filled while he looked on. Dr. Wallach thinks Mr. Bennett must have been mistaken in what he saw; "because he has observed that in a great number of instances the Physalia is accompanied by small fishes which play around and among the depending tentacles without molestation. He has in so many cases seen this, and even witnessed the actual contact of the fishes with the tentacles, with no inconvenience to the former, that he too hastily concludes that the urticating organs are innocuous." "Surely," says Gosse, "the premises by no means warrant such an inference. There is no antagonism between the two series of facts witnessed by such excellent observers; the venomous virulence of these organs has been abundantly proved by many naturalists, myself among the number, and Mr. Bennett to his cost, as already narrated. We can only suppose that the injection of the poison is under the control of the Physalia's will, and the impunity of the bold little fishes is sufficiently accounted for."

Among the Physalia captured on our coast, one was obtained at Tenby, by Mr. Hughes, who has given a report of the capture, in which he mentions a circumstance as "normal," which excited Mr. Gosse's curiosity; it was said to be accompanied by "its attendant satellites, two *Vilellæ*. In reply to his inquiries, Mr. Hughes says, "My authority for the association of the Vilella with Physalia is Jenkins, the collector of Tenby, who was attending me when it was found. The Physalia was taken by me first; and, while I was admiring it, I noticed that Jenkins continued his search for something. Immediately afterwards, he came up with the Vilella in his hand, at the same time stating they were generally found with the Portuguese man-of-war. As I had found him very honest and truthful in his dealings with me, I accepted his information as correct."

Ctenophora.

We have now reached the last class of polypes; those, namely, which Cuvier designates *Hydrostatic Acalepha*, and which De Blainville calls the *Ciliobranchiá*. The body of these polypes present marginal fringes furnished with vibratile cilia, which are swimming organs. Moreover, as these vibratile fringes are inserted directly over the principal canal, in which the nourishing fluid circulates, they ought necessarily to concur in the act of respiration, by determining the renewal of the water in contact with the corresponding portion of the tegumentary membrane.

The class may be divided into three orders or families, namely, *Beröe*, *Callianirea*, and *Cestea*.

The creatures belonging to these three orders swarm in the deep sea; they often appear quite suddenly, and in vast numbers, in certain localities.

The *Beröes* of Forskahl have been studied with great care

by Mr. Milne Edwards. They inhabit the Gulf of Naples, and other parts of the Mediterranean; the sailors of Provence call them Sea-cucumbers. The body (Fig. 103), cylindrical in form, is of a pale rose colour, thickly studded with small reddish spots, so numerous as to appear entirely punctured with them. It presents eight blue sides, with very fine vibratile cils, which by their reflection produce all the colours of the rainbow. The substance of the body is gelatinous, its appearance glass-like; its form varies according as the animal is in motion or repose. Sometimes it swells up like a ball; sometimes it reverses itself, so as to resemble a bell; at others it is elongated and cylindrical; at its lower extremity it presents a large mouth; at its upper extremity is found a small nipple, having at its base a spherical point of a reddish colour, enclosing many crystalloid corpuscles, which rest upon a sort of nervous ganglion, whose physiological function is not very well determined. A vast stomach, considering its size, occupies the whole interior of the body of the Beröe: the circulation is also much developed in this zoophyte. The circulating apparatus contains a moving fluid charged with a multitude of circular, colourless globules, which flows from a vascular ring round the mouth towards the summit of the body; in the interior are eight superficial canals, which flow under the ciliated sides, and re-descend by two much deeper canals; but the Beröes have no heart. *Beröe ovata* is a beautiful

Fig. 103. Beroë Forskahli (Edwards).

species, seldom exceeding three inches and a half in length, and two and a half in its larger transverse diameter; is described by Browne, in his "Jamaica," as "of an oval form, obtusely octangular, hollow, open at the larger extremity, transparent, and of a firm gelatinous consistence; it contracts and widens with great facility, but is always open and expanded when it swims or moves. The longitudinal radii are strongest in the crown or smallest extremity where they rise from a very beautiful oblong star, and diminish gradually from thence to the margin, each being furnished with a single series of short, slender, delicate appendages, or limbs (cilia), that move with great celerity in all directions, as the creature pleases to direct its flexions, and in a regular accelerated succession from the top to the margin. It is impossible to express the liveliness of the motions of those delicate organs, or the beautiful variety of colour which rise from them to play to and fro in the rays of the sun; nor is it easy to express the speed and regularity with which the motions succeed each other from one end of the rays to the other." "The grace and beauty which the entire apparatus presents in the living animal," says Gosse, "or the marvellous ease and rapidity with which it can be alternately contracted, extended, and bent at an infinite variety of angles, no verbal description can sufficiently treat. Fortunately the creature is so common in summer and autumn on all our coasts, that few who use the surface can possibly miss its capture. It is worthy of a poet's description, which it has received:

'When first extracted from her native brine,
Behold a round, small mass of gelatine,
Or frozen dewdrop, void of life and limb;
But round the crystal goblet let her swim
'Midst her own elements; and lo! a sphere
Banded from pole to pole; as diamond clear,
Shaped as bard's fancy shapes the small balloon,
To bear some sylph or fay beyond the moon.
From all her bands see lurid fringes play,
That glance and sparkle in the solar ray
With iridescent hues. Now round and round
She whirls and twirls; now mounts, then sinks profound.'"

DRUMMOND.

Beside the Beröe, naturalists place the Cydippa, which is frequently confounded with the former. The Cydippæ are globulous or egg-shaped, furnished with eight rows of cils, corresponding with as many sections more or less distinct, and terminated by two long filiform tentacles issuing from the base of the zoophyte and fringed on the sides. "It is," says Gosse, "a globe of pure colourless jelly, about as big as a small marble, often with a wart-like swelling at one of its poles, where the mouth is placed. At the other end there are minute orifices, and between the two passes the stomach, which is flat or wider in one diameter than the other." *Cydippa pilens*, found abundantly in the spring on the Belgian coast, is so transparent that it is scarcely visible in the water, where it seems to be a living, moving crystal. *C. densa*, which abounds in the Mediterranean, is of a crystalline white, with rows of reddish cirrhi, terminating in two tentacles, much longer and coloured red; it is about the size of a hazel-nut, and phosphorescent. Within the clear substance of the *Cydippa*, on each side of the stomach, there is a capacious cavity, which communicates with the surface, and within each cavity is fixed the tentacle, of great length and very slender, which the animal can at pleasure shoot out of the orifice and suffer to trail through the water, shortening, lengthening, twisting, twining, or contracting it into a tiny ball at will, or withdrawing it into its cavity, short filaments being given off at intervals over the whole length of this attenuated white thread-like apparatus, each of which can also be lengthened or shortened, and coiled individually. These proceed only from one side of the thread-like tentacle, although, at a casual glance, they seem to proceed now from one side, now from the other.

Callianira.

The Callianira form a sort of connecting-link between the *Beröes* and the *Cestidæ*. Their bodies are smooth and regular, vertically-elongated, compressed on one side and as if lobated on the other; in substance they are gelatinous, hyalin, and tubular, obtuse at both extremities, with buccal openings between the prolongations of the side, and two pair of conical appendages resembling wings, capable of expansion, on the edges of which two rows of vibratory cilia are ranged. A great transversal opening presents itself at one of the extremities, a small one at the other. The animal is furnished with two branching tentacles, but without cilia.

CESTIDÆ.

In *Cestum*, or Venus's Girdle, as it is vulgarly called, we have a long, gelatinous, ribbon-like body, fine, regular, and very short, but much extended on each side, while the edges are furnished with a double row of cilia; the lower surface is also furnished with cils, but much smaller in size and number. On the middle of the lower edge is the mouth, opening into a large stomach. This alimentary canal runs across the middle of its length, and from it extends, as in the Medusæ, a series of gastric canals, which carry the nutriment into all

Fig. 104. Cestum veneris (Lesueur).

parts of the body. There are many species of Cestum; among them the best known is *C. veneris* (Fig. 104), which is found in the Mediterranean, particularly in the sea which bathes the coasts of Naples and Nice, where the fishermen call it the sea-sabre—*sabre de mer*. This curious zoophyte unwinds itself on the bosom of the waters, like a scarf of iridescent shades. It is the scarf of Venus traversing the waves, under the fiery rays of the sun, which has coloured it with a thousand reflections of silver and azure blue.

CHAPTER IX.

ECHINODERMATA.

"Ultra magis pisces et Echinos æquora celent."—*Hor. Ep.*

In their "Natural History of the Echinodermata," Messrs. Hupé and Dujardin divide this vast natural group into five orders or families, namely: 1, *Asteroïdæ*, which includes the true star-fishes; 2, *Crinoïdæ*, stone lilies, calcareous, stem composed of movable pieces; 3, *Ophiuræ*, having the disk much depressed, the rays simple, and furnished with short stems; 4, *Echinidæ*, comprehending the animals known as sea-eggs, or sea-urchins, distinguished by their rounded form and absence of arms; 5, *Holothuroïdæ*, with soft lengthened cylindrical body, covered with scattered suckers.

The Echinodermata, from the Greek words ἐχῖνος, rough, and δέρμα, skin; indicating an animal bristling with spines like the hedgehog's. They are animals sometimes free, sometimes attached by a stem, flexible or otherwise, and radiating, that is, presenting an appearance more or less regular in all its parts, after the manner of a circle or star, its form being globular, egg-shaped, cylindrical, or like a pentagonal plate; or, lastly, like a star, with more or less elongated branches, which secrete either in all their tissues or only in the integument very numerous symmetrical calcareous plates of solid matter, sometimes forming an internal skeleton or regular shell covered with a more or less consistent skin, often pierced with holes, from which the feet or tentacula issue; they are frequently furnished with appendices of various kinds, such as prickles, scales, &c.

The organisation of the Echinodermata is the most perfect of all the zoophytes, serving as a transition between them and animals of more complicated frame. They have a digestive and vascular system, and a muscular system is almost always present; in short, they have internal or external respiratory organs, and a rudimentary nervous system has been detected in many of the species. The nutritive system is very simple, presenting in most of the family a single orifice in the centre of the lower surface of the body, destitute of teeth, performing the functions both of mouth and anus. De Blainville says that "the liver is apparent and rather considerable in the star-fishes, forming bunches occupying the whole circumference of the stomach, and extending to the cavities of the appendages where these exist." The mouth and gullet is admirably adapted for securing the testaceous mollusks, and other substances on which they feed.

Reproduction in the Echinodermata appears to be monœcious. Ovaries are, as far as is known, the only organs of generation. They vary in number in different species. The sexes are usually separate: the young are produced by eggs, the embryo of which undergo important metamorphoses. Immediately after birth, the young asteriæ have a depressed and rounded body, with four club-shaped appendages or arms at their anterior extremity. When they are a little more developed, papillæ may be observed on the upper surface, in fine radiating rows: after twelve days the fine rays begin to increase, and after eight days more two rows of feet, or tentacula, are developed under each ray, which assist in the locomotion of the animal by alternate elongation and contraction, performing also the office of suckers. Like most other zoophytes, they have the power of reproducing parts of their bodies which may have been accidentally destroyed.

Asterias, or Star-fishes.

As to the animal which commonly and sometimes scientifically bears the name of Star-fish, in walking on the sea-shore at low tide, your eyes have often seen this strange creature half buried in the sand. It is so regular and geometrical in its form that it has more the appearance of being the production of man's hand than of a creation which breathes and moves. The divine geometrician who created it never realised a creature more regularly finished in shape, or more perfectly harmonious in symmetry.

The *star-fish* has five perfectly equal arms. They resemble a cross of honour, which has five branches. The *star of the brave*, the *star of honour*—these somewhat trivial words recall, nevertheless, the resemblance which exists between the two objects; doubtless, man has here taken Nature for his copy. It must, however, be remarked that, though five is the general number of lines in the star-fish, this number is not constant; it varies with different genera, species, and even with

Fig. 105. Asterias rubens (Lamarck).

individuals. The connection of the arms with the disk presents equally remarkable differences. In the genus *Culcita*, the disk is so much developed that it constitutes, so to speak, the entire animal, whilst the arms form only a slight protuberance upon its circumference. In the genera *Luidia*, on the contrary, the disk is reduced to minimum, whilst the arms are of great length and very slender.

The colours of the *star-fish* vary greatly; they vary from a yellowish-grey, a yellow-orange, a garnet-red, to a dark violet, as their name indicates.

Star-fishes are exclusively and essentially beings of the sea; they are never seen in fresh water; they dwell amongst the submarine herbage, seeking for sandy coasts; they generally are found at moderate depths, but there are some species which are found at the great depth of a hundred and fifty fathoms.

Asterias are met with in almost every sea and under all latitudes, but they are most numerous and their forms are more richly varied in the seas of tropical regions. There are about a hundred and forty species described.

The body of the Asteria is supported by a calcareous envelope composed of juxta-posed pieces at once various and numerous. The number of these pieces is estimated at more than eleven thousand in the Red Sea Starfish (*Asterias rubens,* Fig. 105), a species very

Fig. 106. Asterias aurantiaca (Lamarck).

common in Europe. The body of the *Asterias rubens* is likewise furnished with spines, granules, and tubercules, the shape, number, and disposition of which serve to characterise the genera and the species.

Another species, *Asterias aurantiaca*, will give an exact idea of the general type of animals of this order. This zoophyte, which is represented in Fig. 106, is common in the northern seas; it has five rather long arms, furnished with spines which are of an orange colour—hence its name. When we see one of these animals stranded upon the shore, it appears to be entirely destitute of all power of progression. But the *star-fish* is not always immovable; it is provided with an apparatus for locomotion, which appears to serve at the same time the purposes of respiration; for Nature is very economical in her gifts to the least-organised beings; she bestows upon them feet, with respiratory organs, or lungs, which have the power of locomotion.

The muscular system, as already stated, is almost always present in the Echinodermata, but the organs of locomotion are very various, the principal being the membranous tubes usually termed feet, or ambulacra, which issue from the ambulacral apertures; but besides these, the rays themselves are movable, and in animals which are free to move from place to place these are used for the purpose. Thus in the common star-fish the rays may be bent towards the upper or lower surface of the disk, so as to facilitate its advance either in water over small spaces or up the vertical face of rocks. These ambulacra are very numerous, disposed in rows along the under surface of the rays; thus in *A. aurantiaca* there are two simple rows of feet attached to each ray, and the vesicular part is deeply cleft into two lobes; while in *A. rubens* (Fig. 105) there are two double rows on each ray, and each foot has one undivided vesicle.

Each of these ambulacra consists of two parts, an internal and generally vesicular portion placed within the body, and a tubular portion outside, projecting from the surface through an aperture in the skin or shell, the tube being closed at the extremity, and terminating in a sucker, usually in the form of a disk slightly depressed in the centre. The feet are thus muscular fleshy cylinders, hollow in the centre, and very extensible; by means of them the animal draws itself forward. The foot is extended by the contraction of its internal vesicle, which forces the fluid into the hollow tube, or, where the vesicle is wanting, by projecting the fluid into the tube by a communicating vessel. The tubular part is thus distended and elongated, and again retracts itself by means of its muscular fibres, by which action the fluid is forced back into the interior. In progression the animal extends a few of its feet, attaches its suckers to the rocks or stones, then, by shortening its feet, it draws its body forward. The progression of the Asterias is thus very slow, and so regular that only the closest observation enables the spectator to discover the movement which produces it. Like the movements of the hands of a watch, the eye cannot quite follow it. When an obstacle presents itself—if, for example, a stone comes in its way—it raises one of the rays in order to obtain a point of support, then a second ray, and, if necessary, a third,—and thus the animal creeps over the stone with as much ease as if it walked over the smooth sands. In the same way the animal creeps up perpendicular rocks, which is accomplished by means of these ambulacra and suckers. Frédol says: "If an Asteria is turned upon its back it will at first remain immovable, with its feet shut up. Soon, however, out come the feet, like so many little feelers; it moves them backward and forward, as if feeling for the ground; it soon inclines them towards the bottom of the vase, and fixes them one after the other. When it has a sufficient number attached the animal turns itself round. It is not impossible, whilst walking on the sea-shore, to have the pleasure of seeing one of these star-fishes walking upon the sand. A day rarely passes without one of them being thrown upon the strand by the tide, and then abandoned by the retreating waters. Generally they are left dead, this is not always the case, however; they are sometimes only benumbed. Place them in a vase full of sea-water, or simply in a pool on the shore, and you will sometimes see them recover from this death-like condition, and execute the curious movements of progression which we have described. The motions of an Asterias thus saved form a very curious spectacle.

The mouth of this animal is situated on the lower surface of the disk. At this point the constitutive pieces of the carapace leave a circular space, covered by a fibrous resistant membrane, pierced at the centre by a rounded opening. This opening is sometimes armed with hard papillæ, which play the part of teeth. The mouth almost directly abuts on the stomach, which is merely a globular sac, filling nearly all the central portion of the visceral cavity.

"Thus," says Mr. Milne Edwards, "in *Asteracanthion glacialis* the stomach is globulous, but imperfectly divided into two parts by a fold of its internal membrane; the first chamber, thus limited, appears to be more especially devoted to the transformation of the elementary matter into a liquid paste, which passes, in small portions, into the upper chamber. This is continued upwards through a small intestine, and communicates laterally with five cylindrical prolongations, which each divide themselves again into two much elongated tubes, furnished with a double series of hollow branches, each terminating in a cul-de-sac." These organs advance into the interior of the rays or arms of the Asterias.

Imagine, then, an animal bearing digestive tubes in its arms—the same organ serving for digestion and progression. What lessons in economy does not the study of Nature teach us! The products of digestion find an absorbent surface of great extent in the rays of the Asterias. They ought necessarily to pass rapidly from it into the circumjacent nourishing fluid.

The star-fishes are very voracious; they even attack mollusks which are covered with shells. M. Pouchet mentions having taken eighteen species of *Venus* intact, each being six lines in length, from the stomach of one large Asterias which he dissected upon the shores of the Mediterranean. It is now even said that the star-fishes eat many oysters.

Ancient naturalists were not ignorant that the star-fish was capable of eating oysters; but they believed that they waited for the moment when the bivalve would open its valves to introduce one of their rays into the opening. They imagined that having thus put one foot into the other's domicile, they soon put four, and finished by reaching and devouring the savoury inhabitant of the shell. Modern observations have modified the ideas of former naturalists upon this point. In order to obtain possession of and swallow an oyster, it appears that the star-fish begins its approaches by bringing its mouth to the closed edges of the oyster-shell; this done, with the assistance of a particular liquid which its mouth secretes, it injects a few drops of an acrid or venomous liquid into the interior of the oyster-shell, which forces it to open its valves. An entrance once obtained, it is not long before it is invaded and ravaged. Professor Rymer Jones gives another explanation of the transaction. According to this naturalist the oyster is seized between the rays of his ravisher, and held under his mouth by the aid of his suckers; the Asteria then inverts its stomach, according to the professor, and envelopes the entire oyster in its inmost recesses, while, doubtless, distilling a poisonous liquid. The victim is thus forced to open its shell, and becomes the prey of the enemy which envelopes it.

Whatever may be the modes of procedure employed by the star-fish, it is now clearly ascertained, however incredible the fact may at first appear, that it swallows oysters in the same manner as is practised at the oyster shop.

This little being, formed of five arms, and without any other apparent member, accomplishes a work which man is quite unable to execute—it opens an oyster without an oyster-knife.

If reasoning man had no other means of nourishment than oysters, and was without a knife to open them, it is very certain that with all his genius he would be puzzled how to get at the inaccessible and savoury bivalve so obstinately closed against him. The star-fish devours dead flesh of all kinds; their sole occupation is to feed themselves, and they keep up an incessant and active chase after all sorts of corrupt animal matter. The Asterias thus performs in the bosom of the sea the same part that certain birds and insects play on shore; they are its scavengers, and feed their bodies upon the carcases of animals which, if abandoned to the action of the elements, would become a cause of infection.

In the same manner that certain animals render the air healthy, the Asterias help, on a considerable scale, to keep the sea which shelters them in a pure and healthy state. Zoologists are not agreed upon the manner in which respiration operates on the star-fishes. Nevertheless they think that the principal part in this phenomenon devolves upon the sub-cutaneous branchiæ which in each ray constitute two double series of bladders. The function of circulation is equally unknown. The vascular apparatus is sufficiently developed in this zoophyte, and appears to have for its centre an elongated canal with muscular walls, which may with justice be honoured with the name of heart. A little ring surrounding the œsophagus, and from which issue certain delicate white chords, which are prolonged into the furrows of the arms, present us with all that can be designated a nervous system in the star-fishes. Among organs of sense we may mention, as the apparatus of touch, the *tentacular ambulacraira*, as well as those which are disseminated upon the dorsal surface of the disk. The eyes are considered to be certain bright red points which are situated at the extremity of the arms and on the under surface—a most singular position for the organs of sight. The eyes must, besides, be very imperfect, for they possess no crystalline. Ehrenberg insists upon the existence of eyes in some species, attributing the function to those red spots however; while Rymer Jones attributes the indications in which this originates to an extremely delicate sense of touch in the star-fishes. Professor Edward Forbes, while he admits the existence of ganglions in the nervous system to be extremely doubtful, seems, by the frequent use of the terms eye and eyelids, to admit that the specks in question were visual organs; the weight of authority inclines therefore to Ehrenberg's view, that if not eyes in the strict sense of the term, they serve the purposes of vision, modified and adapted to the wants of the animal.

The star-fishes have distinct sexes, with individual differences; their eggs, which are round and reddish, undergo curious phases of development. They produce little worm-like creatures, covered with vibratile hairs, like the infusoria, which swim about with great vivacity; these little creatures are subject to considerable changes. In the year 1835 M. Sars described, under the name of *Bipinnaria asterigera*, an enigmatical animal resembling a polype from the arms at one extremity of the body, while the other terminated in a tail, furnished with two fins; but it was chiefly remarkable as having an Asterias attached to the extremity which carried the arm; he expressed an opinion, which was soon placed beyond any doubt, that this *bipinnaria* was an Asterias in its course of development. The egg becomes a sort of infusoria, the infusoria becomes a *bipinnaria*, and this produces the Asterias. In short, the bipinnaria does not become an Asterias by any metamorphoses analogous to that so well known amongst insects—the butterfly, for example—but becomes, so to speak, the foster-mother or nurse to the bipinnaria. The larva is large, and it is at the cost of a very small internal rudiment of this larva that the Asterias is developed: the Asterias robs the larva of its stomach and intestines, and turns it into a visceral apparatus for its own use. But the Asterias makes itself a mouth of any of the pieces most remote from the primitive mouth of the larva. Thus the bipinnaria divides itself; it gives its stomach and intestines, and keeps its œsophagus and mouth, and it can live several days after the Asterias is detached from it.

Can anyone imagine the existence of a being with only a mouth and œsophagus, which has neither stomach nor intestines, because another animal has possessed itself of them for its own use? The study of the lower animals abounds in surprises of this kind. It is a chain of unforeseen facts; of natural impossibilities; of realised points necessarily reversing all notions obtained in the study of beings which have a higher place in the animal scale. The history of the star-fishes would be incomplete were we to omit mentioning the most remarkable traits of their organisation with which naturalists are acquainted. The animals exhibit in the highest degree the vital phenomena of dismemberment and restoration, that is to say, of the faculty of reconstructing organs which they have lost. These arms, the structure of which is so complicated, and which protect such important organs, may be destroyed by accident. The animal troubles itself little at this mutilation: if he loses an arm it disquiets him but little; another is immediately procured. We often see in our collections of Asterias specimens wanting in symmetry because they have been taken before the new members which are in process of development have attained their definite length. Professor Rymer Jones mentions an instance of redintegration very complete and most curious. This naturalist had an isolated ray of Asterias which he had picked up; at the end of five days he observed that four little rays and a mouth had been produced; at the end of a month the old ray was completely destroyed, and this apparently useless fragment had been replaced by a new being, quite perfect, with four little symmetrical branches. This faculty of reproducing organs, which we have noted in describing the fresh water polypes, the sea anemone, &c., exists also in many other zoophytes, but in none more strikingly than in the Asterias. But a still more startling fact remains to be mentioned: one more strange and more mysterious, for it does not belong to the physical or organic order, but appears to belong to the moral world. The star-fishes commit suicide! Certain of these animals appear to escape from dangers which menace them by self-destruction. This power of putting an end to existence we only find on the highest and lowest steps of the animal scale. Man and the star-fishes have a common moral platform, and it is that of self-destruction! This power of dismemberment, however, seems to be confined to the *Ophrocoma* and *Luidia*—at least, it is only carried out to its full extent in these generæ.

Mysteries of Nature, who can sound your depths? Secrets of the moral world, what being but God has the privilege of comprehending you? A large species of Star-fish (*Luidia fragillissima*), which inhabits the English seas, has this instinct of suicide to a great extent. The following account by Professor Edward Forbes of an attempt to capture a Luidia gives a good illustration of its powers:—"The first time that I took one of these creatures," the professor says, "I succeeded in placing it entire in my boat. Not having seen one before, and being ignorant of its suicidal powers, I spread it out on a rowing bench, the better to admire its form and colours. On attempting to remove it for preservation, to my horror and disappointment I found only an assemblage of detached members. My conservative endeavours were all neutralised by its destructive exertions; and the animal is now badly represented in my cabinet by a diskless arm and an armless disk. Next time I went to dredge at the same spot I determined not to be cheated out of my specimen a second time. I carried with me a bucket of fresh water, for which the star-fishes evince a great antipathy. As I hoped, a Luidia soon came up in the dredge—a most gorgeous specimen. As the animal does not generally break up until it is raised to the surface of the sea, I carefully and anxiously plunged my bucket to a level with the dredge's mouth, and softly introduced the Luidia into the fresh water. Whether the cold was too much for it, or the sight of the bucket was too terrific, I do not know; but in a moment it began to dissolve its corporation, and I saw its limbs escaping through every mesh of the dredge. In my despair I seized the largest piece, and brought up the extremity of an arm with its terminal eye, the spinous eyelid of which opened and closed with something exceedingly like a wink of derision."

The mind remains confounded before such spectacles, and we can only say, with Mallebranche, "It is well to comprehend clearly that there are some things which are absolutely incomprehensible."

This is doubtless the reason that in collections of natural history we rarely find star-fishes, and especially the Luidia, entire; the moment the animal is seized by fisherman or amateur, in its terror or despair it breaks itself up into small fragments. To preserve them whole they must be killed suddenly, before they have time to be aware of their danger. For this purpose, the moment they are drawn from the sea they must be plunged into a vase of cold fresh water; this saltless liquid is instant death to these creatures, which in this condition perish suddenly before they have time to mutilate themselves. The star-fish is a curious ornament in our natural history collections, but in this state they represent very imperfectly the elegance and particular grace of this curious type. To understand the star-fishes, they must be seen in an aquarium, where we can admire the form, figure, movements, and manners of these marvellous beings.

The Asterias is the constellation of the sea. It is said that heaven, reflected during the night on the silvery surface of the ocean, let one of the stars which decorate the resplendent vaults fall into its depths.

Crinoïdea.

We quoted the maxim of Linnæus in the earlier pages of this volume, that Nature makes no leaps. Nature proceeds by means of insensible transitions, rising by degrees from one organic form to another. Most of the animals hitherto described are immovably fixed to some solid object; at least, such is their condition in the adult state. We are about to describe zoophytes, free of all fetters; animals "which walk in their strength and liberty."

Between zoophytes fixed to the soil, like the corals, gorgons, and aggrègate zoophytes, such as sea-urchins and holothurias, Nature has placed an intermediate race, namely, the Crinoïdea, a class of zoophytes which are attached to a rock by a sort of root armed with claws, having a long flexible stem, which enables them to execute movements in the circle limited only by the length of this stem, just as the ox or goat in our paddocks is confined by its tether to the space circumscribed by the length of its rope.

Let the reader picture to himself a star-fish borne upon the summit of a flexible stem firmly rooted in the soil, and he has a general idea of the zoophytes which compose the order of the Crinoïdea. Naturalists of the seventeenth century bestowed the name of stone lilies on these curious products. This rather poetical image proves that the conformation of these creatures had at an early period attracted observation, presenting the naturalist with the most curious of his lessons. The encrinites raise, as from the dead, a whole world buried in the abyss of the past. At the present time only two genera of these zoophytes exist, whilst in the early ages of the world the ocean must have swarmed with them. Encrinites abounded in the seas during the transition and secondary epoch. It was one of the most numerous of the animal tribes which inhabited the salt waters of the ancient world. In traversing some parts of France, we tread under our feet myriads of these beings, whose calcareous remains form vast beds of rock. The encrinites gradually disappeared from the ancient seas; their species were diminished as the globe became older or modified in its conditions, so that at the present time only a few types remain in our seas—such as the *Comatula* of the Mediterranean; *Pentacrina*, the Medusa's-head of the Antilles; and the European *Pentacrinus*—all of them very rare, and probably destined soon to disappear, carrying with them the last reminiscence of the zoological races of the ancient world: and here lies the real interest which the Crinoïdea presents to the thinking man. The encrinites most common in the fossil state are *Pentacrinus fasciculosus*, belonging to the lias; *Apiocrinus Roissyanus*, which is found in the oolite or jurassic rocks; and *Encrinus liliformis*, which appertains to the Triassic period. These three fixed zoophytes seem to have existed in great numbers during the first ages of the world—namely, the Silurian period. They attained their maximum of development during the Devonian age, when their numbers began to decrease. According to M. D'Orbigny, there are thirty-nine genera found in the palæozoic rocks, two in the triassic, seven in the jurassic, five in the cretaceous, and only one in the tertiary strata. Of all these genera only one, namely, *Pentacrinus*, is found in the modern epoch to represent the varied forms of these the first inhabitants of the seas.

The free Crinoïdæ, that is, those not rooted to the soil by a stem, of which the *Comatula* may be considered the type, only appeared at a later period. They are absent in the palæozoic and triassic rocks, but appear to have attained their maximum of development in the jurassic period.

The numerous fossilized remains of these curious creations, which abound in different rocks, attracted the attention of learned men at an early period. The encrinites were among the earliest objects of scientific description. As early as the sixteenth century, the celebrated mineralogist, George Agricola, mentions them under the names of *Entrochites*, *Trochites*, and *Astroïtes*. At the same time, and since that epoch, the Crinoïdæ, which we know by the name of stone-lilies and which characterises the *Muschelkalk* rocks, have been known under the name of Enchrinus, from κρίνον, a lily.

During the eighteenth century the works upon the Crinoïdæ were very numerous, though not very correct. They sometimes reported these organic remains to be vegetable; sometimes they were beings allied to the star-fishes; at others they were the vertebral column of fishes. Towards the year 1761, however, Guettard, one of the most learned naturalists of his time, understood the real nature of these productions. He had occasion to examine a recent Enchrinus sent from Martinique under the name of *Sea-Palm*, which was in reality *Pentacrinus caput Medusæ*. The comparison of the living individual with the fossil fragment described by his predecessors, and of which he had specimens in his collections, enabled him to ascertain the real origin of the fossil Enchrinoidæ. The beautiful fragment which still exists in the Museum of Natural History at Paris has long been considered unique, but it is now known that others exist in different museums. Since that date the Crinoïdæ have been examined and described by observers such as Miller, Forbes, D'Orbigny, and Pictet, of whose discoveries the following is a brief résumé:

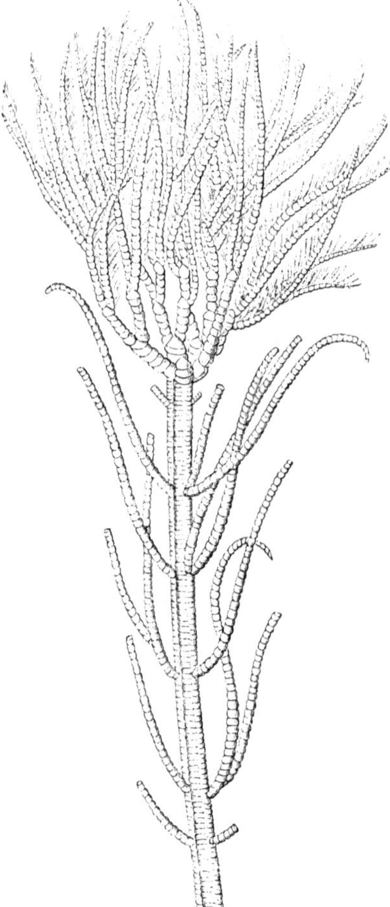
Fig. 107. Pentacrinus caput Medusæ (Müller).

"The species of fixed Crinoïdæ actually living are *Pentacrinus caput*

Medusæ (Fig. 107), and *Pentacrinus Europæus* (Fig. 108). These curious zoophytes resemble a flower borne upon a stem, which terminates in an organ called the calyx, but which is, properly speaking, the head of the animal. Arms, more or less branching, spring from

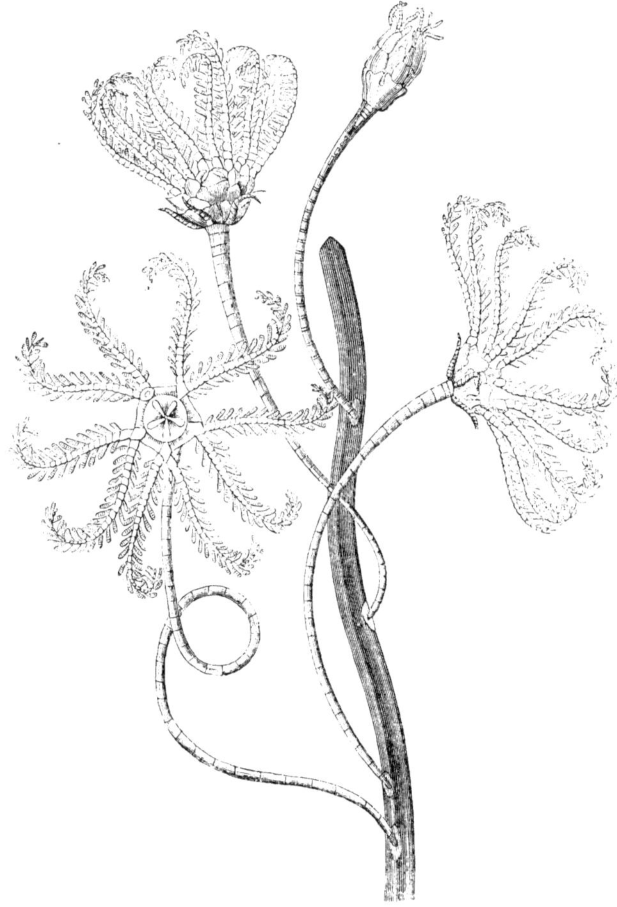

Fig. 108. Pentacrinus Europæus (Thompson).

this calyx, their ramifications, so formed, consisting of many pieces articulated to each other. The calyx is supported by a stem, varying in height, formed of pieces secreted by the living tissues which surround them. The articulations of this stem are usually very numerous, cylindrical, and present a series of rays striated upon their articulated faces. In *Pentacrinus* they are prismatic and pentagonal; that is, they present five projecting angles, and on their articulated face a star with five branches, or, better still, a rose with five petals. At the base of the stem of this animal-plant, in many of the Crinoïdæ we find a sort of spreading root, which is implanted in the rocks, and is capable of growing by itself, of nourishing the stem, and of producing new ones.

The root and stem of the fixed encrinites seem to indicate that the animal can only live with the head erect. Their normal condition is thus quite different from that of any other of the Echinoderms, almost all of which keep their mouths invariably directed downwards.

The Medusæ heads are chiefly found on rocky beds, or in the midst of banks of corals, at great depths. There, firmly fixed by their roots, their long stems raise themselves vertically; then, with expanded calyx and long-spreading arms, they wait for the prey which passes within their reach in order to seize it.

The *Pentacrinus caput Medusæ* have, as we have said, been fished up from great depths in the Antilles. Its very small calyx is borne upon a stem of from eighteen to twenty inches in height, terminating in long movable arms, the internal surface of which bear its tentacles in a groove. In the middle of the arms is a mouth, and at the side the orifice for the expulsion of the digested residuum.

In the Medusæ head and European Pentacrine (*P. Europæus*, Fig. 108), the presence of a digestive apparatus has been distinctly traced. It is a sort of irregular sac, with a central mouth on the upper surface, and another orifice situated at a little distance from the mouth, and evidently intended as an outlet for the products of digestion. The arms of these creatures, which are spreading or folded up according to their wants, are provided with fleshy tentacula, which, serving at once as organs of absorption and as vibratile cils, are at the same time organs of respiration. Such are these curious beings: they occupy a sort of middle or transition state between animals permanently fixed to some spot and those capable of motion, representing in our own times the last remains of extinct generations. Every type of the Crinoïdæ furnished with arms present incontestable examples in their mode of reproduction or redintegration—that is, of the power of restoring those parts of the body broken or destroyed by accident; but as we have already drawn the attention of the reader to this strange faculty of renewing organs which many of the zoophytes possess, we will not here enlarge further upon the subject.

The Crinoïdæ are not all like the two species which have been described. There is an entire family of animals belonging to this class; namely, the *Comatula*, which are fixed in their early days, but separate themselves from the rooted stem in their adult age, and, throwing off the bonds imposed on their youth, live side by side with the asterias, with whose company they seem much pleased. The encrinites and the star-fishes thus live in company, and that at prodigious depths, and under a body of water which no light can reach. Imagine the existence of animals which pass their lives in such eternal funereal darkness. The family of Comatula are found in the seas of both hemispheres. Their bodies are flat—a large calcareous plate formed like a cuirass upon their backs—presenting, besides, cirri composed of numerous curling articulations, the last of which terminates in a hook. The ventral surface presents two orifices: the one in the centre corresponding to a mouth, the other evidently intended for the discharge of the products of digestion. This animal is provided with five arms, which diverge directly from the centre plate or cuirass. The branches of these arms have *ambulacral grooves*, comprehending a double row of fleshy tentacles, in the centre of which is the ambulacral groove, properly so called, clothed with vibratile cils over their whole surface. These cils or hairs guide the current which drives the various substances on which it feeds; such as the organic corpuscles of sea-weeds, and microscopic animalcules floating in the sea, towards its mouth. They are also powerful aids to respiration.

The movements of these curious creatures are very slow, their only object being to catch the bodies of animals and marine plants, or, by extending or contracting their arms, to feel their way through the water to some new locality. Sometimes, also, in order to change their feeding-ground, the Comatula abandon the submarine forests, herbage, and sea wracks; and float through the water, moving their arms with considerable rapidity in search of a new station.

The Mediterranean Comatula (Fig. 109) is largely diffused on the European shores of the Mediterranean. Its spreading arms extend to three or four inches; its colour purple, shaded, and spotted with white upon the ventral surface.

Were a traveller to tell us that he had seen animals drop their eggs upon forests of stone; that these eggs, after executing their progressive evolutions, finally become individuals in all respects like their parents, which attach themselves to the soil by a root like any flower of the fields, or to the mother-stem like the branch of a tree, until in due course they attained the adult state, when the flexible band which holds them fixed either to the soil or parent-stem breaks, and the

Fig. 109. Comatula Mediterranea (Lamarck), natural size.

animal, now free, launches itself into the liquid medium, and goes to live a proper and independent existence;—in listening to a recital so opposed in appearance to the ordinary laws of Nature, we should be inclined to tax the narrator of such incredible facts with error or folly. Nevertheless all these facts are now perfectly established. The being which presents these marvels has nothing of the fabulous about it. It is the *Comatula Mediterranea*: it lives at the bottom of the sea, the surface of which is incessantly tracked by our vessels.

OPHIURADÆ.

The Ophiuras are thus named from two Greek words (ὄφις, a serpent, and οὐρὰ, a tail), from their fancied resemblance to the tail of a serpent. These zoophytes are met with in almost every sea, but chiefly in those of temperate regions; they are very common on every shore, and have been remarked by fishermen from the earliest times on account of their singular form, the disposition of their arms, which resemble the tail of a lizard, and by the singularity of their movements. The general characteristics of this remarkable group of Echinodermata, as described by Dujardin and Hupé, are as follows: They are radiary marine animals creeping at the bottom of the sea, or upon marine plants. In form they present a sort of coriaceous disk, which is either bare or covered with scales, which contains all the viscera, and of five very flexible simple or branching arms, each sustained by a series of vertebral internal pieces, naked or covered with granules, scales, or bristles. Certain fleshy tentacula thrown out laterally are organs of respiration. The mouth is situated in the middle of the lower surface of the disk, and opens directly into a stomach in the shape of a sac; it is circumscribed by five re-entering angles corresponding with the intervals of the arms, having a series of calcareous pieces, which perform the function of jaw-bones. This mouth is prolonged by five longitudinal clefts, garnished with papillæ or calcareous pieces, which correspond to one of the arms. A series of calcareous pieces in the shape of vertebræ spring from the extremity of each of these clefts, which occupy all the interior of the arms, having a furrow in the middle of the ventral surface for the reception of a nursing vessel, and laterally between their expansions are certain cavities, from whence issue certain fleshy retractile tentacula; the visceral cavity opens by one or two clefts on the ventral surface of each side of the base of the arms.

The Ophiuradæ move themselves by briskly contracting their arms so as to produce a succession of undulations analogous to those by which a serpent creeps along. Some of these zoophytes are rather active; but others attach themselves by their arms to the branches of certain other polypes, like the Gorgons, and remain immovable for a considerable time, waiting their prey somewhat like a spider in the midst of his web.

The family of Ophiuradæ is divided into two great sections: that of the Ophiura, which comprehends several genera, amongst others that which gives its name to the family, and that of the Euryalina or Asterophytes.

The family of Ophiuradæ constitute a group distinguished by their five simple, articulated, very mobile, and non-ramified arms, which

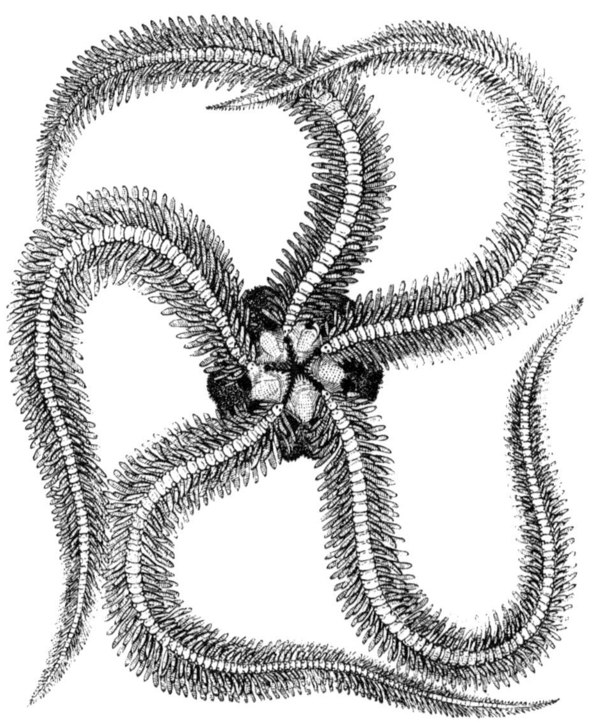

Fig. 110. Ophiocoma Russei (Lutken), natural size.

are attached to a small disk or shield plate, with flexible thread-like cirri between the rays. *Ophiura natta* is very common, and has been known from very early times in European seas. It is of a greenish colour, with transverse bands, which become more obscure upon the arms as the distance from the disk increases. This disk is from six to seven-eighths of an inch in size, the upper part covered with unequal plates, in shape like tiles; the arms are four times the length of the diameter of the disk, very slender and tapering. The zoophyte to which Lamarck gave the name of *Ophiura fragile* has now its place among the Ophisthrix, the specific name, indicating a particularity of structure in all these small creatures derived from their fragile formation. In short, these beings have so little consistency that they crumble, as it were, under the touch, and become reduced to pulp under the slightest pressure. In Fig. 110 we give the representation of an Ophiura of the natural size, which Lutken has since called *Ophiocoma*

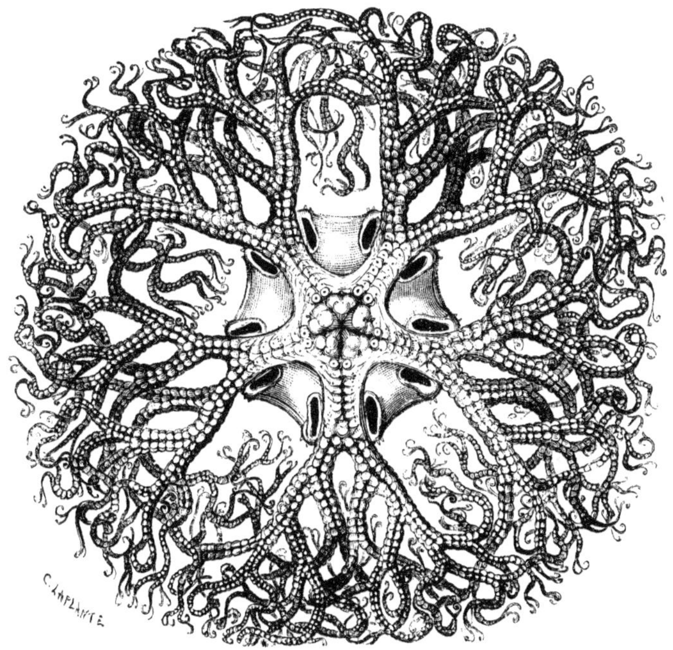

Fig. 111. Asterophyton verrucosum (Lamarck).

Russei. This Echinoderm, which lives in the seas of the Antilles, is furnished with five very flexible rays, which are armed with from three to four rows of spines, those on the upper part of the body being very hard ones; the body and arms of this creature are of reddish brown, streaked with a great number of little white lines.

The principal type of the Euryalina is the curious and complex *Asterophyton verrucosum* of Lamarck. They include animals remarkable for the extremely complicated development of their arms—the very multiplied ramifications of these, towards the extremities, being divided into many thousand very slender appendages, the principal use of which is doubtless locomotion, but at the same time they constitute a series of living thread-like fillet which seem intended to seize and close upon the animals which serve as prey to this little flesh-eater. The *Asterophyton verrucosum*, which is represented in Fig. 111, is yellowish; its disk about four inches, its arms sixteen to eighteen. It inhabits the Indian Ocean. Another species, *Euryala arborescens*, is met with on the coasts of Sicily and other parts of the Mediterranean. Nothing can be more elegant than these animated disks, which resemble nothing so much as a delicate piece of lace—a piece of living lace moving in delicate festoons in the bosom of the ocean.

Echinidæ.

The singular shape of the Echinidæ, or Sea-urchins, and the spiny prolongations with which their bodies are covered, has in all ages attracted the attention of naturalists. Aristotle applied to them the name ἐχῖνος, which signifies urchin. When, however, one sees the body of one of these animals thrown on the sea shore, it is difficult, at first, to find a reason for this designation. The body of the sea-urchin is furnished with a species of spine. It is a sort of shell, nearly spherical, empty in the interior, its surface presenting reliefs admirable for their regularity—an egg-shell sculptured by Divine hands. In order to see the urchin with its spines, it is necessary to seize it in the water at the bottom of the sea, where it rolls and moves its little prickly mass: it is then only that the real urchin, the prickly sea-urchin, is to be seen, bristling with prickles, and strongly resembling, to compare the physical with the mental, those amiable mortals whose character is so well depicted in the saying, "Whom they rub they prick."

In his book on "The Sea," Michelet puts the following conversation into the mouth of a sea-urchin:

"I am born without ambition," says the modest Ichinoderm. "I ask for none of the brilliant gifts possessed by those gentlemen the molluscs. I would neither make mother-of-pearl nor pearls; I have no wish for brilliant colours, a luxury which would point me out; still less do I desire the grace of your giddy Medusas, the waving charm of whose flaming locks attracts observation and exposes one to shipwreck.

Oh mother! I wish for one thing only: *to be*—to be without these exterior and compromising appendages; to be thick-set, strong, and round, for that is the shape in which I should be the least exposed; in short, to be a centralised being. I have very little instinct for travel. To roll sometimes from the surface to the bottom of the sea is enough of travel for me. Glued firmly to my rock, I could there solve the problem, the solution of which your future favourite, man, seeks for in vain—that of safety. To strictly exclude enemies and admit all friends, especially water, air, and light, would, I know, cost me some labour and constant effort. Covered with movable spines,

Fig. 112. Echinus mamillatus (Lamarck), natural size.

enemies will avoid me. Now, bristling like a bear, they call me an urchin."

Let us now look a little more closely at the general structure of the sea-urchins—in zoological language, Echinidæ.

The body of the sea-urchin is globular in form, slightly egg-shaped, or of a disk slightly swollen. It consists essentially of an exterior shell or solid carapace, clothed in a slight membrane furnished with vibratile cils. This carapace is formed of an assemblage of contiguous polygonal plates, adhering together by their edges. Their arrangement is such that the test or shell may be divided into vertical zones, each springing from a central point on the summit; terminating at a point of the spheroid, diametrically opposite—namely, the circumference of the buccal orifice. These vertical zones are of two kinds, some larger and others straighter, each zone consisting of a double row of plates, the first charged with movable spines, the second pierced with holes disposed in regular longitudinal series, from which emerge certain fleshy tentacula which, as we shall see presently, serve as feet to the animal. When armed with these bristling spines, the sea-urchins resemble the hedgehogs; but when the spines are down, they look very much like a melon or an egg, to which their shape and calcareous nature have sometimes led to their being compared by the vulgar as well as by the learned. We shall give a tolerably exact idea of the two different aspects which the carapace of the urchin presents, when the spines are erect and lowered, by reference to Fig. 112 (*Echinus mamillatus*), which represents the animal bristling with spines, and Fig. 113, in which the same species

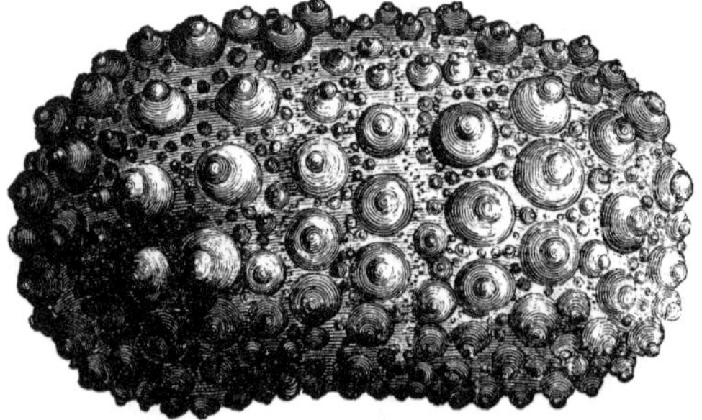

Fig. 113. Echinus mamillatus. Sea Lichen without spines, natural size.

is represented after death, when deprived of these weapons of defence: and how complicated these defences must be! It has been calculated that more than ten thousand pieces, each admirably arranged and united, enter into the composition of the shell of the sea-urchin, to which no other can be compared. To abbreviate slightly Gosse's description of that wonderful piece of mechanism, the sea-urchin: "A globular hollow box has to be made, of some three inches in diameter, the walls of which shall be scarcely thicker than a wafer, formed of unyielding limestone, yet fitted to hold the soft tender parts of an animal which quite fills the cavity at all ages. But in infancy the animal is not so big as a pea, and it has to attain its adult dimensions.

The box is never to be cast off or renewed; the same box must hold the infant and veteran urchin. The limestone can only increase in size by being deposited. Now the vascular tissues are within, and the particles they deposit must be on the interior walls. To thicken the walls from within, leaves less room in the cavity; but what is wanted is *more* room, ever more and more. The growing animal feels its tissues swelling day by day, by the assimilation of food: its cry is, 'Give me space! a larger house, or I die!' How is this problem solved? Ah! there is no difficulty. The inexhaustible wisdom of the Creator has a beautiful contrivance for the emergency. The box is not made in one piece, nor in ten, nor a hundred. Six hundred distinct pieces go to make up the hollow case; all accurately fitted together, so that the perfect symmetry of the outline remains unbroken; and yet, thin as their substance is, they retain their relative positions with unchanging exactness, and the slight brittle box retains all requisite strength and firmness, for each of these pieces is enveloped by a layer of living flesh; a vascular tissue passes up between the joints, where one meets another, and spreads itself over the whole exterior surface."

This being so, the glands of the investing tissue secrete lime from the sea water, and deposits it after a determinate and orderly pattern on every part of the surface. Thus the inner face, the outer face, and each side and angle of polyhedron, grow together, and the form characteristic of the individual is maintained with immutable mathematical precision. The dimensions and shape of these prickles are very variable. In certain Echinidæ they are three or four times the diameter of the body. In the urchin, properly so called, they are only three-fourths or four-fifths that diameter. They sometimes resemble short bristles. These defensive weapons have tubercles for supports, which are arranged on the surface of the animal with perfect regularity. At the base they present a small head separated by compression. This head is hollow on its lower face, presenting a cavity adapted to a tubercle of the shell. Each of the prickles, notwithstanding its extreme minuteness, is put in action by a muscular apparatus.

In the prickles, or spines and tentacula (ambulacra, *feet suckers*) we see the external organs of the Echinodermata. The former are instruments of defence and progression; the latter, strange as it may appear, serve them to walk with. When it is considered that each of these prickles is put in motion by several muscles, it is impossible to repress our wonder and surprise at the prodigious number of organs brought into action in the sea-urchin. More than twelve hundred prickles have been counted upon the shell of *Echinus esculentus*, a representation of which is given in Fig. 114. If we add to this first supply of spines other smaller and in some sort accessary spines, we shall arrive at a total of three thousand prickles. Each sea-urchin thus bears as many weapons as ten squadrons of lancers. When it is considered, further, that in each sucker or ambulacra there

Fig. 114. Echinus esculentus (Lamarck), natural size.

exist not less than a hundred tubes, each having an orifice, you will have a total of four thousand visible appendages upon the body of an animal of very small dimensions. If it is considered, finally, that no shell exists more admirably symmetrical, elegant, or more highly ornamental than the carapace of the urchin, it will readily be admitted that Nature has been most prodigal in her gifts to one of the humblest beings in creation—a creature which passes its existence in crawling in obscurity at the bottom of the sea. What elegance of form, eternally hidden from the eyes of man, sleeps under the heavy mass of water; and yet man imagines that everything in Nature has been created for his use and for his glory.

M. Hupé records a somewhat curious observation in connection with the spines, which serve as a means of defence to our Echinodermata. He found a small mollusc, of the genus *Stelifera*, which had sought shelter in *Leixidaris imperialis*, an urchin, native of Australia; in a word, the interior of one of these prickles had been hollowed and enlarged so as to serve as a retreat for this improvised guest.

What unexpected facts does the study of animals present! Nature has bestowed a protecting armour upon one little being; another still smaller animal discovers this and places itself for shelter under the protection of these levelled bayonets! Numerous anecdotes are told of them. Thus: A man ignorantly put into his mouth one of these creatures, with all its prickles, and, being detected, thought himself, in his pride, compelled to swallow it because he was being looked at; immediately his mouth was full of blood. The next day he was in such a state of suffering that he could neither eat nor drink, and for a long time his life could only be preserved by nourishing injections of soup, cream, and rice.

Now let us see by what organic mechanism the urchin contrives to transport itself and walk. The tentacula, or suckers, are hollow internally, and, as we have said, are provided with small muscles. By the influx of liquid which they inclose they become inflated throughout all their prickles, in such a manner that they can attach themselves to any solid body, at the will of the animal, by means of their terminal suckers. Frédol, in "Le Monde de les Mers," thus explains the urchin's mode of progression: "Let us imagine," he says, "one of these creatures to be at rest; all its spines are immovable, and all its filaments repose within the shell; some of these involuntarily escape; they extend themselves and feel the ground all round them; others follow, but the animal is firmly fixed. If it wishes for change of place, the anterior filaments contract themselves, whilst the hinder ones loosen their hold, and the shell is carried forward. The sea-urchin can thus advance with ease, and even rapidity. During his progression the suckers are only slightly aided by the spines. It can travel either on the back or stomach; whatever their posture, they have always a certain number of prickles, which carry them, and suckers, with which they attach themselves. In certain circumstances the animal walks by turning upon itself, like a wheel in motion."

Nothing is more curious than to see a sea-urchin walk upon smooth sand. But for the colour, it might be mistaken for a chestnut with its bristling envelopes, the spines serving as feet to put the little round prickly mass in motion. They have even been observed to form themselves into a ball, and roll along like a globular fagot of prickles.

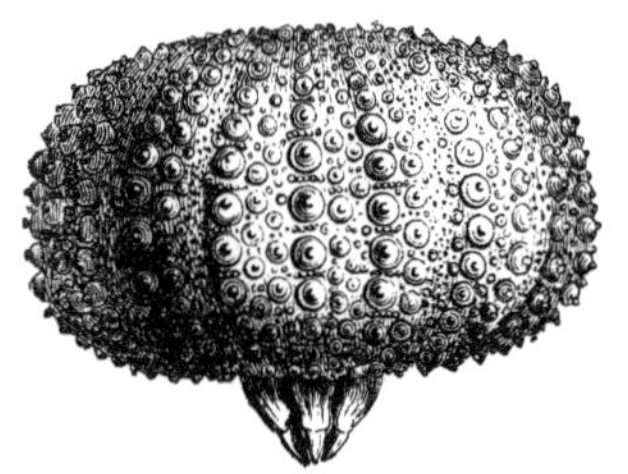

Fig. 115. Buccal armature of Echinus lividus.

One of the most singular organs of the sea-urchin is its mouth. It is monstrous. Placed underneath the body, it occupies the centre of a soft space invested with a thick resisting membrane: it opens and shuts incessantly, showing five sharp teeth (Fig. 115), projecting from the surface, the edges meeting at a point, as represented here, supported and protected by a very complicated framework, which has received the name of Aristotle's Lantern (Fig. 116). Fig. 115 represents *Echinus lividus* in its normal state; the other shows the masticatory organs, that is to say, Aristotle's Lantern. To give the reader a more complete idea of the buccal organ in the sea-urchin, let him glance at one from the southern seas, *Clypeaster rosaceus*, represented in Fig. 117, an outline of the entire animal, the buccal apparatus being placed under the shell, which has been broken in Fig. 116, so as to lay this organ bare.

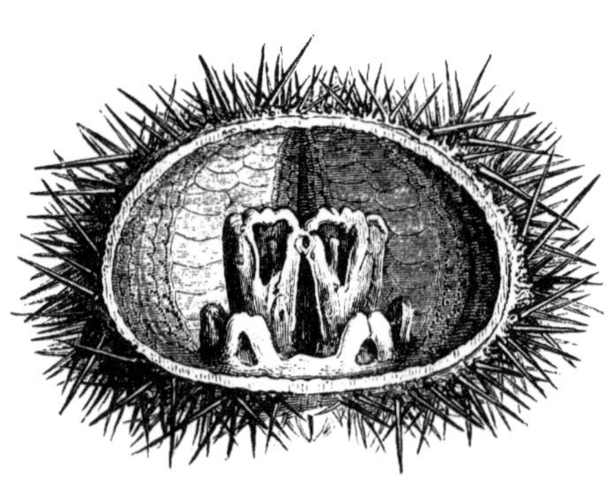

Fig. 116. Masticating apparatus of Echinus lividus.

The shape of the *Clypeaster rosaceus* is oval, straighter in front, and thick and rounded at the edges. It is more common and more largely distributed than any other living species, and it is supplied with four or six ambulacra, or feet.

I never could understand why the dental framework of the sea-urchin has been called Aristotle's Lantern, for this formidable apparatus resembles the front view of a battery of cannon more than a lantern. It consists of a series of pieces designated by the names of compass, scythe, pyramid, and plumula, which it would serve no useful purpose to describe.

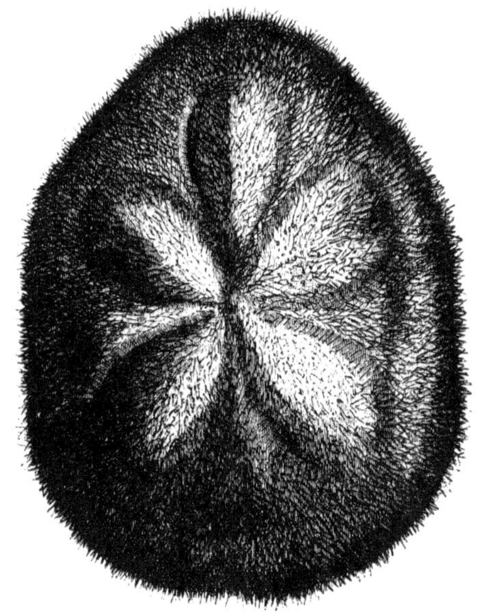
Fig. 117. Clypeaster rosaceus (Lamarck).

We have said that the mouth of the urchin is monstrous in proportion to its size, and the teeth of proportionate dimensions. As these project from a very formidable mouth, one can easily be assured of the sharpness of their extremities by intruding his fingers on them. In fact, it is necessary that these organs should be singularly powerful, because, as we shall see farther on, the sea-urchin makes incisions in the solid rock with them, and hollows out shelter for himself. The strong and sharp teeth grow at the base in proportion as they are used at the points, as is the case with some of the rodent mammalia. By this means they are always sharp and in good condition. Five groups of powerful muscles are used to work these terrible grinders.

To this formidable mouth is attached an œsophagus or gullet, and an intestine which extends along the interior walls of the carapace, describing the circumference of its principal contour.

The regimen of the Echinidæ is still imperfectly known; nevertheless, from the presence of shells, fragments of polypiers, crustaceans, and even other Echinodermata in their intestinal tube, it is to be inferred that a certain number of them at least are carnassiers or flesh-eaters, while others are supposed on the same evidence to be vegetarians. The organs of respiration of the Echinidæ appear to be certain flattened vesicles in the form of very delicate laminæ, which adhere to the internal surface of the walls of the body, and float freely in the liquid with which the visceral cavity is filled. These organs, known as the internal *branchiæ*, are in communication with the central canal and ambulacral tubes. The heart is spindle-shaped, tapering above, swelling below. There are two distinct vascular systems, one intestinal, the other cutaneous.

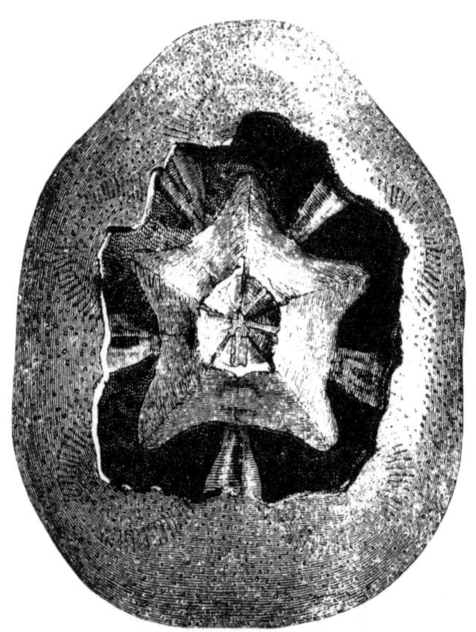

Fig. 148. Skeleton and Masticating Apparatus.

Their nervous system consists of a ring, which surrounds the gullet, and is placed at a short distance from the mouth. In this ring the nervous trunks have their origin. In relation to the senses, that of touch is highly developed. Certain branching tentacula, which surround the mouth, fashioned like nippers, and the ambulacral tentacles, are its principal organs. They appear to be altogether destitute of organs of sight. It has sometimes been argued that four or five red points at the summit of the dorsal face are eyes; but this opinion has not been maintained, nor has any "crystalline" been found in these spots to justify it. Captain de Condé states that he examined a sea-urchin with long spears in a pool of water, which he tried to catch, when he saw it direct its flight towards his hand, all its defences being erect. Surprised at this manœuvre, he tried to seize it from another quarter; its spines were instantly directed to the other side. "I have thought from that time that the urchin saw me, and prepared to resist my attack. In order, however, to satisfy myself whether or not the movement in the water caused by my approach might have produced the effect described, I repeated the experiment with greater caution.

But the creature always directed its spines in the direction of the object which threatened it, whether it was in the water or out of it." He satisfied himself that these animals certainly could see, and that their spines served them as a means of defence.

These wonderful spines, this calcareous envelope, this armour so marvellously studded, with which Nature has so bountifully provided the Echinidæ, appear to have been insufficient, inasmuch as these very spines, in order to secure the safety of the animal, are gifted with the power of hollowing a dwelling for themselves out of solid rocks of the hardest material, such as granite and sandstone. They fix themselves to its surface by means of their tentacles; they make an incision by means of their strong teeth, removing the débris with their spines as fast as it is produced. When the hole is large enough, they entrench themselves in it, with their spines and their threatening pikes levelled to protect them from all external assaults. To M. Cailaud, the conservator of the museum of Nantes, we are indebted for an excellent account of the manner in which this buccal apparatus is made to operate. "The Lantern of Aristotle," says this author, "forms the mandibullary apparatus; the teeth are five in number, and they may as well receive the denomination of a series of saws and picks as of teeth, for they are surprisingly adapted to the excavation of holes in the hardest rock. These five picks are about the eighth of an inch long, and they serve the sea-urchin at once as masticators and excavating implements. In opening the jaws, these five teeth strike the stone forcibly rather than scrape it." This property of hollowing their dwelling out of the solid rock appears, however, to belong to only a small number of the Echinidæ; most of them are content to hide themselves under the stones, while the species having the spines slender and the shell very thin bury themselves in the sand, with which they cover themselves entirely, leaving only a small hole to breathe through. The *Spatangus*, which is furnished with short thick spines on the under part of its body, which spread out at the extremity like the channel of a spoon, proceeds with its mining operations as follows:—According to Mr. Jonathan Franklin, "Figure to yourselves, reader, the animal on the sea-shore. He commences his operations by turning the lower spines in such a manner as to form a hollow on the sand bank, in which he sinks by his own weight, but as he sinks, a great number of the spines are brought into action, throwing up the sand with increased activity, while the sand thrown up, returning again, soon covers the body of the worker, and he has soon buried himself beneath the surface. In this situation the long hair-like spines situated upon the back begin to play their part; they prevent the sand from entirely covering the animal by forming a little round hole, through which water is introduced to the mouth and respiratory organs." The hiding-place of the sea-urchin is, however, easily detected in the sand by the hole thus arranged for the respiration of the animal, and the fishermen think they can predict storms according to the depth of the hole.

The Echinidæ are reproduced by eggs, which are red and nearly microscopic. As it issues from the egg the larvæ has the appearance of a very minute fish. It is not at once converted into the perfect animal, but undergoes a certain metamorphose analogous to that of the caterpillar into the butterfly. But, as we have already stated in treating of the Asteriæ, it produces, at a certain stage, by some sort of internal process of generation, a sea-urchin, which, being at first only an organ of the larvæ, begins to live an independent life when the nursing larvæ has destroyed itself. The manner in which the urchin unfolds itself at the expense of the larvæ is quite analogous to that which the asterias present: it is another case of alternate generation, of which our space does not permit us to give even a general outline.

Sea-urchins are found in every sea: they dwell in sandy bottoms, and sometimes upon rocky ground. They are caught with wooden pincers when in shallow water; when found at the water's edge, they may be taken by a gloved hand.

The urchin, like the crab, which it also resembles in taste, becomes red when boiled; only certain species are comestible, however. In Corsica and Algeria the Melon-shaped Urchin (*Echinus melo*) is much esteemed. In Naples and in the French ports of the Channel the *Echinus lividus* is eaten. In Provence the Common Sea-urchin (*Echinus esculentus* and *Echinus granulosus*) are the favourites.

Sea-urchins are eaten raw like oysters. They are cut in four parts, and the flesh taken out with a spoon; they are sometimes, but more rarely, dressed by boiling, and eaten from the shell like an egg, using long sippets of bread: hence the name of sea-eggs, which they bear in many countries.

Plate IX.—Sea Urchins lodged in the rocks they have excavated.

Sea-eggs were a choice dish upon the tables of the Greeks and Romans; they were then served up with vinegar or hydromel, with the addition of mint or parsley. When Lentulus feasted the priest of Mars—the Flamen Martialis—this formed the first dish at supper. Sea-eggs also appeared at the marriage feast of the goddess Hebe. "Afterwards," says the poet, "came crabs and sea-urchins, which do not swim in the sea, but content themselves by travelling on the sandy shore." For my own part, I have only once partaken of sea-urchin, and they appeared to me to be food fit for the gods; but perhaps the circumstances sufficiently explain this dash of culinary enthusiasm. The Reserve restaurant at Marseilles has not always been the vast stone edifice we now behold, backed majestically by the mountain, and fronting the sea on the promenade of the Corniche du Prado. In 1845 it rose quite at the entrance of the port, a small glass cage, suspended as it were by a magic thread between the heavens and the sea. From this aerial dwelling, overhanging with unheard-of audacity the waters which surrounded it on all sides, we gazed on the most wonderful prospect in the world, and reposed ourselves while enjoying this intoxicating scene, during which the ships were continually entering the port, passing under our very feet. It was in this enchanted palace that sea-urchins were served up, supported by the traditional bouillabaise.

As I have said, it appeared to me delicious. Was it the Provençal dish, the savoury bouillabaise, which contributed to my appreciation of the humble sea-urchin of the Mediterranean? Was not the marvellous view which I enjoyed from the heights of my empyreum of glass the indirect cause of it? This is a tender and charming problem which I love to leave floating in the clouds, half evanescent, of my youthful recollections.

Holothuria.

The ignorant, like you and I, call the Holothuria the Cornechon, or Sea-cucumber, and perhaps, for two reasons, they are not far wrong. The term sea-cucumber expresses with wonderful exactness the shape of the animal, and its habitation, the sea; and, again, it would puzzle the most learned to explain the word *Holothuria*. The body of this strange creature presents the form of an elongated and worm-like cylinder; its dimensions are so variable that, while some species are only an inch or two in length, others attain thirty and even forty. In general, the skin of the Holothuria is thick and leathery; it includes muscles, and is armed occasionally with small projecting hooks or fangs, which enable the creature to hang for a few seconds on to foreign bodies. From this coriaceous envelope issue tentacular feet analogous to those described in the sea-urchin and sea-star.

When we open a Holothuria we find nearly the whole internal cavity occupied with little white tubes. We know that the fabulous cucumber spoken of in the Arabian Nights was stuffed with pearls by the talking-bird. With our poor animal this, alas! is not so. These are no pearls, but simple prosaical tubes containing the ova. The mouth opens at the extremity of the body; it forms a sort of funnel, and is surrounded, as by a glory, with an elegant circle of tentacula. In the living animal, when it feels itself in security, these tentacles expand themselves like the corolla of a flower. When the fisherman seizes a Holothuria in the water this crown of tentacles ceases to appear, for the animal has the power of withdrawing it quite suddenly, and now it resembles nothing so much as a common leech. If, however, it is preserved in fresh sea-water and left in peace—if we treat it, in short, with the regard due to its elegant crown of tentacula—this elegant ornament will be expanded in all its glory. Immediately below the mouth is a muscular pharynx, which is contained in a long intestine, with many convolutions, which terminate in the posterior part of the body in an orifice whence is thrown from time to time a little jet of water. The terminal portion of the intestinal canal in these animals is enlarged, introducing us to a system of numerous tubes which branch off into the visceral cavity, receiving the water from without while breathing by its posterior extremity; the animal can at will fill this reservoir or eject the water, and it is by these alternate movements of aspiration and its reverse that it renews the oxygen necessary for respiration. The circulation appears to form a complete circle, there being no heart or central agent; but a ring round the gullet from which issue five principal nervous chords, which represent the nervous system.

The Holothurias are of separate sexes, and they differ from the sea-urchins and asterias in this: that their larvæ are converted bodily into a young holothuria without losing their organs. The bodies of certain species are lubricated by an acrid and corrosive liquid: thus *H. oceania*, described by Lesson, which is about forty inches in length, secretes at the surface of its body an irritating fluid, which produces an intolerable itching in the finger which touches it. Nor can the inhabitants of the South Sea Islands look at it without loathing. Fig. 119 represents the

Fig. 119. Holothuria lutea (Quoy and Gaimard).

Stychopus luteus of Brandt, who gives it as a distinctive character three rows of tentacular feet on the ventral surface.

We have spoken of the strange suicidal tendency of the sea-stars: the Holothuria exhibits the same phenomenon, but, having no brittle envelope like the asterias, it cannot break itself into bits in the presence of its disconcerted enemy; but kills itself in this manner. Having some cause of grief and trouble—such, for instance, as the attack of an enemy or the pursuit of some fisherman—by a sudden and unexpected movement it ejects its teeth, its stomach, its digestive apparatus, and reduces itself to a simple empty membranous sac, with an unfurnished mouth; and, as a singular fact, this empty sac still shrinks and contracts in the hand which grasps it. It must be admitted that this is a strange mode of evading its enemies: the soldier rarely throws his arms away in the moment of danger! But the Holothurias possess a wonderful recuperative power also; and it is probably quite conscious, when it thus empties itself to disappoint its pursuer, that it can promptly replace the organs which it has voluntarily parted with.

Dr. Johnston relates that he had forgotten for some days to supply a Holothuria with fresh water. The creature, in consequence, ejected its tentacles, its buccal apparatus, digestive tubes, and a portion of its ovaries. Still it was not dead, but was sensible to the least movement, and lived to reproduce all its organs anew.

Not only do the Holothuria eject their organs and afterwards renew them, but they divide themselves spontaneously into two portions. Their two extremities are first enlarged; then their middle parts gradually become straight, like a thread; finally, this thread breaks, and each separate part of the animal becomes a perfect Holothuria. It has been cut into two pieces, and each of these pieces becomes a new being.

The habits of these animals are but little known. They inhabit the seas, and are spread over every latitude. Their very limited movements consist in a kind of reptation or crawling motion, produced by the undulations of their bodies or by the contractions of their feet. Holothurias are generally found in the act of creeping upon stones or on portions of submarine rock, but always in sheltered places, for they appear to dread the action of light. They sometimes find themselves caught by fishermen in their nets. If held in the hand they contract, their bodies become hard and rigid, and the sea water with which they are filled is ejected with force. We need not add that fishermen reject with disdain the Holothurias taken in their nets; the sea-cucumber has never been thought worthy of a place on our tables. Truth is on this side, error on that, is a maxim as true in morals as in the cookery. The sea-cucumber, which Europeans disdain, is a favourite dish among the Chinese. The fishery, prepara-

Plate X.—Fishing for and Curing the Holothuria in the Indian Ocean.

tion of, and transport of these animals to market plays an important part in the commerce and industry of the East. One rather large species, the *Holothuria tubulosa*, in which, by-the-bye, a singular parasite fish (*Fierasfer fontanesii*) lives, is common in the Mediterranean. This species is eatable, and much relished at Naples. In the Ladrone Islands *Holothuria guamensis* is preferred. But nowhere is it esteemed of such importance as in the Malayan and Chinese seas. In these countries, and on most of the shores of the Indian Ocean, the *Holothuria edulis*, vulgarly called *Trepang*, is eaten with delight. Thousands of junks are annually equipped for the Trepang fisheries. The Malay fishermen carry to this fishery a degree of patience and dexterity truly remarkable. Lying down in the fore part of their vessels, and holding in their hands a long bamboo, terminating by a sharp hook, their eyes, accustomed to this fishing, frequently discover the animal at a distance of not less than thirty yards, as it creeps along the surface of the submarine rocks or corals. The fisher darts his harpoon at this distance, and seldom misses his prey. When the water is shallow, that is to say, not more than four or five fathoms deep, divers are sent down to obtain these culinary monsters, who seize them in their hands, and in this manner can take five or six at a time. To prepare the fish and preserve them for transport to the markets, the Malay and Chinese fishermen boil them in water, and flatten them with stones. They are then spread out on bamboo mats to dry; first in the sun, and then by smoking them. Thus prepared, they are enclosed in sacks, and shipped to the Chinese ports, where they are particularly esteemed. This fishery takes place in the months of April and May.

In his voyage to the South Pole Captain Dumont d'Urville, in traversing the Chinese seas, had an opportunity of assisting at this fishery, which he has described very graphically. We quote the passage in which the French navigator relates what he witnessed at this curious scene. While the ships were lying quietly at anchor, "we saw," he says, "entering the bay, four Malay proas, bearing Dutch colours, which dropped their anchors about a cable's length from Observatory Islet. The padrones or captains of these vessels soon presented their salutations, and informed me that they had started from Macassar at the end of October with the western monsoon, and that they came to fish for Holothuria (trepang) along the coasts of New Holland from

Melville Island to the Gulf of Carpentaria, where the east wind met them and assisted their return, when they revisited all the points of the coast, anchoring in every bay where they hoped to find fish. We were in the first days of April; the east monsoon was definitively established; the Malay fishermen were returning in their circuit, and, in passing, they came to exercise their industry in Raffle's Bay. An hour after their arrival they were all at work, and the laboratory for the preparation of their fish was established within our view. The roadstead had no longer the aspect of a vast solitude: wreaths of smoke crowned the summit of Observatory Island, where, as if by enchantment, several large sheds had sprung up, while numerous vessels, supplied with divers, were proceeding to fish for Holothurias, which were passed immediately to the furnaces erected for curing them. In the course of my voyage I have often remarked little walls constructed of dry stones, consisting of several half-circles joined one to the other. I had often, but vainly, tried to discover the use of these little structures: I was now enlightened. The Malays arrived. Their boats were scarcely anchored when several large boilers, in the shape of a half-sphere, the diameter of which might be about forty inches, were placed upon the stone walls of which I have spoken, and now served as improvised furnaces. Near to them are sheds, composed of four strong posts driven into the earth, supporting roofing covered with hurdles, on which it is probably intended to dry the fish. During their sojourn in this bay, the fishermen, having fine weather, made no use of these sheds, having probably only prepared them as a precaution.

"A crowd of men actively employed in establishing their laboratories gave an unaccustomed appearance to the bay, which could not fail to attract the savage inhabitants of the main land. Very soon, indeed, we could see them hastening from all sides, and nearly all reached the little island, either by swimming or wading through the sheet of shallow water which separates it from the main land. I only saw one pirogue, made of the bark of a tree badly put together, which gave a passage to three of these visitors. When night arrived, the Malays had finished all their preparations; some of them remained to guard what they had left on shore, all the others returned to their boats.

"In the interval, a boat from the Astrolabe being wanted to carry some visitors from the island, I profited by the occasion to visit one of the proas, accompanied by M. Roquemauel. We were received with much politeness, and even cordiality, by the captain or padrone of the boats. He showed us over his little ship. The keel appeared to us sufficiently solid; even the lines did not want elegance; but great disorder seemed to reign in the stowage department. From a kind of bridge, formed by hurdles of bamboos and junk, we saw the cabin, which looked like a poultry-house; bags of rice, packets, and boxes were huddled together. Below was the store of water, of cured trepang, and the sailors' berths. Each boat was furnished with two rudders, one at each end, which lifted itself when the boat touched the bottom. The craft was furnished with two masts, without shrouds, which could be lowered on to the bridge at will by means of a hinge; they carry the ordinary sail; the anchors are of wood, for iron is rarely used by the Malays; their cables are made of ratan fibre; the crew of each bark consists of about thirty-seven, each shore-boat having a crew of six men. At the moment of our visit they were all occupied in fishing operations, some of them being anchored very near to us. Seven or eight of their number, nearly naked, were diving for trepang; the padrone alone was unoccupied. An ardent sun darted his rays upon their heads without appearing to incommode them, an exposure which no European could hold up under. It was near mid-day, and the moment, as our Malay captain assured us, most favourable for the fishing. In fact, we saw that each diver returned to the surface with at least one fish and sometimes two in his hands. It appears that the higher the sun is above the horizon, the more easily is the creature distinguished at the bottom. The divers were so rapid in their movements that they scarcely touched the boat into which they threw the fish before they dived again. When the boat was filled with fish, it proceeded to the shore, and its place was supplied by an empty one. I followed one of these, to witness the process of curing which they adopted.

"The Holothuria of Raffle's Bay is from five to six inches long and about two in diameter; it is a gross fleshy mass, somewhat cylindrical in form, but no external organ is visible. The mollusc glues itself to the rocks at the bottom of the sea, and, as it can only move very slowly, the Malay divers seize it readily. The greatest merit of a fisherman is to have a practised eye, to distinguish the animal at the bottom, and to dive directly to the spot where it lies. To preserve the fish, the fishermen throw them, while still living, into a cauldron of boiling sea water, where they are stirred about by means of a long pole, which is supported upon another pole fixed in the earth, but having a forked end, which acts as a lever. In this process the trepang gives up all the water it contains, and is withdrawn at the end of two minutes. A man armed with a large knife now extracts the entrails, and it is thrown into a second cauldron, having only a small quantity of water, seasoned with *mimosa* bark. The object of this second operation is to smoke the animal in order to preserve it the better, for the bark is consumed in the process. The trepang is now placed upon hurdles and dried in the sun. When sufficiently dried, it is stowed away in the hold of the proa.

"It was about two o'clock in the afternoon when the divers ceased their labours and came ashore. My tent was soon surrounded. I recognised the captain of the proa among them who had previously visited me. He approached and examined all the instruments used in the Observatory with great attention, seeking to discover their use. I showed him a gun with percussion cap, which astonished him greatly, especially when I pointed out to him its great superiority over the flint-lock. He assured me that these arms were still unknown in the Celebes, his country; but he failed to convince me of that. He questioned me as to the places we had visited, and where we were going. I endeavoured to sketch a map of New Holland, New Zealand, and New Guinea upon a leaf. He then took my pencil, and added to it the Indian Archipelago, the coasts of China and Japan, and the Philippine Islands. Surprised, in my turn, I asked him if he had visited all these places. He replied in the negative; but added that he knew their position perfectly, and could easily take his vessel to any of them. Finally, the interview terminated by his asking for a glass of arrack. I do not know if this intelligent Malay professed the Mahometan religion, but I do know that he drank half a bottle of wine and a quarter of a pint of arrack without being at all the worse for it. He then offered me some prepared trepang, inviting me to taste it, which I did; to me it appeared to resemble the lobster in taste. My men liked it, and thankfully accepted the captain's offer; for my part, I felt an utter repugnance even to taste it.

"According to the account I had from the Malay captain, the price of trepang in the Chinese markets was fifteen rupees, about thirty shil-

Plate XI.—Synapta Duvernæa. (Quatrefages.)

lings, the pekoul, or a hundred and twenty-five pounds. He estimated his cargo to be worth about a hundred and twenty pounds. The fishing had occupied he and his crew three months. From the earliest times this commerce has belonged exclusively to the Malay fishermen, and it will always be difficult for Europeans to compete with them. The Malay vessels are equipped on the most economical principle, and the men are wanting neither in sobriety, intelligence, or activity.

"It was nearly four o'clock when the Malays finished their operations. In less than half an hour they had embarked their cargo; the tents were struck, and, together with the boilers, carried back to the boats, which were already preparing to set sail. At eight o'clock in the evening they hoisted sail and left the bay."

Some idea may be formed of the extent and importance of the Holothuria fishing by the number of ships which it attracts in this part of the East. Captain King assures us that two hundred vessels annually leave Madagascar to fish for the *sea slug*, as it is sometimes called. Captain Flinders, being on the coast of Australia, learnt that a fleet of sixty vessels, having a hundred men on board, had left Madagascar two months previously in the same pursuit.

Among the Holothurias, one particular genus, the *Synapta*, is distinguished from others of the family by the absence of the ambulacral feet, and by the fact of its uniting both sexes in one individual. This remarkable Echinoderm, *Synapta duvernea*, is represented in Pl. XI. M. Quatrefages, who discovered it in the Channel, gives the following description of it in his great work, "Le Souvenirs d'un Naturaliste." "Imagine," he says, "a cylinder of rose-coloured crystal as much as eighteen inches long and more than an inch in diameter, traversed in all its length by five narrow ribbons of white silk, and its head surmounted by a living flower, whose twelve tentacles of purest white fall behind in a graceful curve. In the centre of these tissues, which rival in their delicacy the most refined products of the loom, imagine an intestine of the thinnest gauze gorged from one end to the other with coarse grains of granite; the rugged points and sharp edge of which are perfectly perceptible to the naked eye.

"But what most struck me at first in this animal was, that it seemed literally to have no other nourishment than the coarse sand by which it was surrounded. And then when, armed with scalpel and microscope, I ascertained something of its organisation, what unheard-of marvels were revealed! In this body, the walls of which scarcely reach the sixteenth part of an inch in thickness, I could distinguish seven distinct layers of tissue, with a skin, muscles, and membranes. Upon the petaloid tentacles, I could trace terminal suckers, which enabled the Synapta to crawl up the side of a most highly polished vase. In short, this creature, denuded to all appearance of every means of attack or defence, showed itself to be protected by a species of mosaic, formed of small calcareous shield-like defences, bristling with double hooks. the points of which, dentated like the arrows of the Caribbeans, had taken hold of my hands."

If one of these Synapta is preserved alive in sea-water for a short time, and subjected to a forced fast, a very strange phenomenon will be observed. The animal, being unable to feed itself, successively detaches various parts of its own body, which it amputates spontaneously. A great compression or ring is first formed, and then the separation of the condemned part takes place quite suddenly. "It would appear," says M. Quatrefages, "that the animal. feeling that it had not sufficient food to support its whole body, was able successively to abridge its dimensions, by suppressing the parts which it would be most difficult to support. just as we should dismiss the most useless mouths from a besieged city."

This singular mode of meeting a famine is employed by the Synapta up to the last moment. After a few days, in fact, all that remains of the animal is a round ball, surmounted by its tentacles. In order to preserve life in the head, the animal has sacrificed all the other parts of its body.

In order to find natural novelties—to find unforeseen subjects of study and reflection, it is not necessary to run over the world or travel great distances. It is only necessary to visit the banks of the nearest river, or descend to the sea shore, and leave the sea to reveal a fragment of the marvels which it conceals in its bosom.

MOLLUSCA.

The class Mollusca constitute one of the four great divisions of the animal kingdom. In its typical figure, "the mollusc, as represented in Fig. 120, presents the following parts, and is supposed to be bilaterally symmetrical: H, is the hæmal parts, in which the heart is situated, commonly called the dorsal part, although the word is used in a different sense in different divisions of the animal

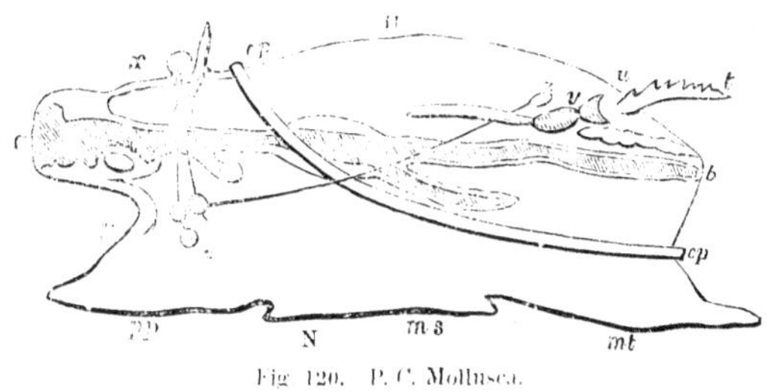

Fig. 120. P. C. Mollusca.

kingdom. In the same manner the opposite region (N) is not termed the ventral, but the neural part, in philosophical anatomy. It is the region in which the great centres of the nervous system are placed. The termination (*a*) is the anterior or oval part; the other end (*b*), the posterior or anal part: between these extremities the intestines take a straight course. The neural surface is that upon which the majority of molluscs move, and by which they are supported, and it is commonly modified to subserve these purposes by the formation of a muscular expansion or disk, called the foot. Three regions, in many genera very distinctly divided from one another, may be distinguished in this foot: an anterior, the *Propodium* (*p p*); a middle, the *Mesopodium* (*m s*); and a posterior, the *Metapodium* (*m t*). In addition to these, the upper part of the foot, or middle portion of the body, may be prolonged into a muscular enlargement on each side, just below the junction of the hæmal with the neural region, the *Epipodium* (*e p*). The mass of the body between the foot proper and the part of the abdomen which bears the epipodium may be termed the mid-body, or *Mesosoma*. On the upper part of the sides of the head are two pairs of organs, namely, the eyes and tentacles. In the hæmal region the integument may be modified and raised up into a fold at the edges, either in front or behind the anus. When so modified, it is called a mantle, *Pallium*. In front of the anus again, the *branchiæ* (*t*) project as processes of the hæmal region. Among the internal organs, the heart (*u v*) lies in front of the branchiæ in the hæmal regions, the nervous ganglia (*x y z*), of which there are three principal pairs, being arranged around the elementary canal which they encircle."

Such is the general type of the class Mollusca, of which, however, the variations are innumerable. They are all soft-skinned animals, without either articulated exterior or annular external skeleton. Their nervous system, being without cerebro-spinal axis, is entirely composed of ganglions, which are all reunited in the œsophagus without constituting in any case a lengthened median chain. Their digestive organs are complete—that is, they are provided with two apertures; their principal organs are symmetrical and according to a plan, usually curving, by which their bodies are divided into two parts.

Our limits forbid us to dwell upon the organization, manners, and distribution of these soft flimsy creatures: our object will be to make known, as they come before us, the more curious and important species, following a scientific order conformable to the divisions established by the best modern naturalists.

Molluscs vary so singularly among themselves, that it is difficult to establish unity in their little world. We propose dividing them into two principal series, the first of which establishes in some sort the passage between the zoophytes, whose history we have just concluded, and the mollusc, properly so called. This first series or subdivision, to which Milne Edwards has given the name of *Molluscoïda*, includes under that term the Bryozoaires, Ascidians, and Tunicata.

The Molluscs, properly so called, are grouped into four classes: I. Acephalous Molluscs. II. Gasteropodous Molluscs. III. Pteropodous Molluscs. IV. Cephalopodous Molluscs.

CHAPTER X.

MOLLUSCOÏDA.

"Nature geometriseth and observeth order in all things."
SIR THOMAS BROWNE.

THE Bryozoaires, or Polyzoa, as British naturalists prefer to call them, form the boundary-line which divides the humble mollusc from the humbler zoophytes. In consequence of this intermediate organization, these creatures were long considered as polypes; but De Blainville, Milne Edwards, and Ehrenberg almost simultaneously began to separate them from the molluscs, and form them into a separate group. Subsequent naturalists, while considering the Molluscoïda as truly and wholly molluscous, admit that the distinction proposed by the French naturalists are most important, and should be retained as a primary subdivision, confining it to those molluscs which have the neural region comparatively little developed, and the nervous system reduced to a single or at most a pair of ganglia, and the mouth surrounded by a more or less perfect circlet of tentacles: an arrangement which would include the *Brachiopoda* with the *Polyzoa.*

Marine plants are sometimes observed to be quite covered with a velvety parasitic matter, which may at a first glance be mistaken for a moss. This apparent moss, however, is simply an aggregation of animalcules, each of which has its separate cell, which is placed quite contiguous to its neighbour.

These little creatures thus form an entire community. Each cell is formed by the skin which has been encrusted by calcareous salts, or other organic matter, hardened after the manner of a horn. This kind of shell protects the animal from the attacks of its enemies. This mode of retreat at the bottom of a protecting shelter is very frequently adopted in the whole series of molluscs. The oyster shuts itself up by closing its valves, and the snail retires into its shell. This assemblage of small cells presented by the Bryozoaires has long been known as a polypier. "We propose," says our author, "with very good reasons, to call it a *Testier*, or shell-builder."

This testier, in which each cell has its opening, is furnished with a naked cushion, dentate, spinous, or protected by an operculum or lid, and presents itself under every variety of form. It is sometimes an assemblage of branching tubes, occasionally a rounded mass of spongy appearance, and now it presents itself as a flat lamelliform inarticulated expansion. In some of the marine species the shell of the mussel is covered as with a fine lace.

It is a remarkable fact that these cells are not always inert. They seem to enjoy the power of motion. It is well known that the leaves and branches of the sensitive plant (*Mimosa*) contracts and expands under the touch of the finger; the same phenomenon, according to Mr. Rymer Jones, takes place on touching the cells of certain species of Bryozoaires. The moment they are touched they quickly incline themselves, and the movement is immediately communicated from one to the other, until all the cells of the community are in motion.

Returning to the organization of the little creature which occupies the cell, it is found that the upper and retractile portion, which is of extreme delicacy, terminates anteriorly in a circle of long tentacles, in the centre of which is the mouth. These tentacles are fringed laterally by a series of vibratile cilia. "When the animal displays itself," says Frédol, "this circle of microscopic threads of extreme tenuity first show themselves rising from the summit of the cell; this is followed by the upper part of its body, which is more or less flexible; the tentacles follow between the threads, pushing them on one side."

These tentacles are furnished on the back with a dozen appendages like very fine hairs, attached to them nearly at right angles, in addition to the lateral cils already spoken of, which play a very important part in the arrangements of most microscopic animals. At the moment when the tentacles appear outside the cell, the tunic of the animalcule, which has the power of expanding or contracting itself, is gradually unrolled. It soon spreads out its pretty little arms, the appendages and cils beginning their rapid vibrations, until the eye, deceived by the rapidity and regularity of their movements, is dazzled, and the beholder begins to think that he sees rosy drops of dew waving to and fro, twisting and untwisting themselves. The corpuscles which float round the animal are violently agitated, as if they were under the influence of some strong breeze. Unhappy, indeed, is the fate of the unfortunate infusoria which chance leads at this moment into the fatal circle.

In many species, observers have discovered a special organ called the *vibracule*, which deserves our attention for a moment. It is a hollow filament, situated at the upper and outer angle of each cell, filled with a substance which is at once fibrous and contractile, admitting of some very remarkable movements, which occur regularly, and generally at very short intervals. At first the filament inclines itself towards the base, trembles, oscillates, and seems to sink; presently it recovers itself, and inclines in the opposite direction, where it repeats the same operation with the same order and in the same time. "What are the functions thus performed?" asks Frédol. "Are they, we would ask, independent up to a certain point of the will of the Bryozoaire? What is their purpose?" We think he answers, "That this organ serves the purpose of cleansing, and especially that of strengthening, the entrance to the cell. It even continues its movement after the animal has been mutilated or killed. The poor sickly or dead creature continues to be defended by its protecting vibracule."

The prey which is drawn into the vortex by the tentacles and their appendages enters into the mouth, to which is attached a pharynx, œsophagus, stomach, and intestines. In the back or hæmal region, not far from the mouth, there is a special opening for this intestine.

Respiration is provided for in the Bryozoaires by the ciliate appendages which surround the mouth; they are at once tentacula and branchiæ. The animal presents no other trace of organs of the senses. A small ganglion and a few fillets constitute all of the nervous system which can be traced; neither heart nor blood-vessels have been found.

The egg, in the case of the Bryozoaires, gives birth to a young animal covered with hairs on its surface; it swims about freely until it has chosen a convenient place in which it can establish the new colony which it is to originate. But this choice is not made for itself alone; the young animal encloses under its hairy envelope two new individuals, which, young as they are, have already the appearance of adult Bryozoaires. At first, these only increase the *personnelle* of the colony by budding, but in a short time they produce eggs.

From these remarks it will be seen that the animalculæ of the Bryozoaires is more complex in its form and functions than that of the polypier, and the study of their anatomy confirms this conclusion. In their case the digestive organs are no longer a simple sac with a single orifice; there is a mouth, a pharynx, a gullet, a gizzard, a membranous stomach and intestines, with a special opening. We have descriptions of some species in which the gizzard seems to be provided with a certain number of interior teeth forming a wonderful pavement—a living mill for the purpose of grinding the food before it enters into the second stomach. The organization of this small creature reveals to our eyes a wonderful amount of combination—of admirable art immeasurably surpassing all that the most perfect human industry and human genius can accomplish.

After this general view of the organization of the group, we shall proceed to introduce the reader to some of their more characteristic species.

Under the leaves of water-lilies (*Nymphea*), pond-weed (*Potamogeton*), or upon floating fragments of submerged wood, are generally to be found certain Bryozoaires, animals described by Trembley under the name of *plumed polypes*. These are *Plumatellæ* (Fig. 121). These little diaphanous creatures constitute colonies which under the microscope resemble small branching shrubs; they consist of small slender tubes grafted one to the other, and having from forty to sixty retractile tentacula, which expand like the petals of a flower; they are furnished with vibratile cils, the movements of which serve the purpose of leading food into the mouth.

Fig. 121. Plumatella cristallina (after Roesel).

Another genus which is found in ponds in France, and which is also found in fresh water in Britain, is the *Cristatella* of Cuvier. "Perfect specimens of *C. mucella* occur from six lines to twenty-four in length by two or three in breadth," says Sir J. G. Dalyel, "of a flattened figure, fine translucent green colour, and fleshy consistence. Some of the shorter tend to an elliptical form, but those of larger dimensions are linear, with parallel sides and curved extremities. The middle of the upper and the whole of the under surface are smooth, the former somewhat convex, occasioned by a border of seventy or eighty, even up to three hundred and fifty, individual polypi, dispersed in a triple row, their number depending entirely on the size of the specimen. Each of these numerous polypi, though an integral portion of the common mass, is a distinct animal, endowed with separate action and sensation. The body rising about a line above a tubular fleshy stem, is crowned by a head, which may be circumscribed by a circle as much in diameter, of a horse-shoe shape, and bordered by a hundred tentacula. Towards one side, the mouth, of singular mechanism, seems to have projecting lips and to open as a valve, which folds up within, conveying the particles which are absorbed to the wide orifice of an intestinal organ, which descends, perhaps, in a convolution below; and returns again, terminating in an excretory canal under the site of the tentacula."

The inhabitants of the colony are then united in great numbers under one common envelope; these are longish filaments of the size of a swan's feather, reminding one of the appearance of the silk thread known by embroiderers as chenille. The downy appearance is produced by the collection of tentacula belonging to this curious swarm. The filamentous mass is the translucent row of cells in which these animalcules are lodged, and to which they retreat when disturbed. These cells are sometimes free in part, sometimes completely rooted to the stems of aquatic plants. The tentacles are of a fine transparent glass colour, the body being of a brown colour. Fig. 122 represents *Cristatella mucedo*, which is common both in this country and in France.

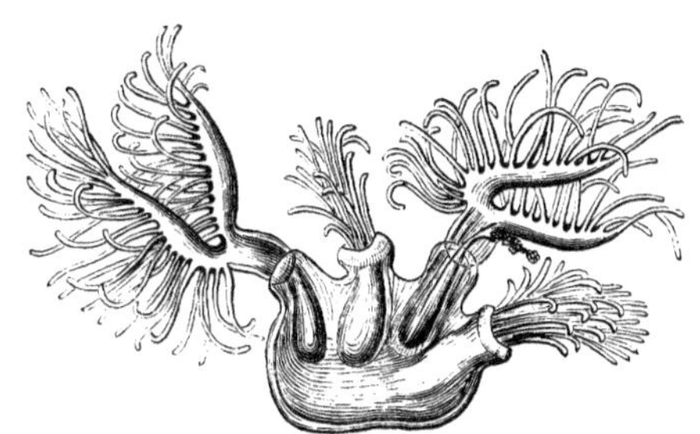

Fig. 122. Cristatella mucedo (Cuvier).

Most naturalists have now agreed to place among the Bryozoa certain species of animalcules which long remained imperfectly known. Amongst these are the *Flustra*, the *Eschara*, and other ascidians.

The Flustra are marine Bryozoa, whose skin in hardening forms a thin shell of horny or cellular appearance; their little cells, more or less horny, are grouped symmetrically, somewhat like the cells in a bee-hive. Sometimes they form a crust which covers the algæ and other submarine bodies; sometimes they form ribbon-like stems. In some species the cells are only found on one side; in others it occupies both. Their orifices are extremely small, and defended by spines quite microscopic (Fig. 123).

Fig. 123. Flustra foliacea (Linnæus).

Their tentacles are covered with cils, always vibratile, disposed in a straight line, which in their movements produce the effect which a row of animated pearls might be supposed to produce if rolled upwards from the base to the summit of the organ.

The Eschara form leaf-like expansions, the entrance to their cells having also their protecting spines.

The expansions still represent microscopic bee-hives, the inhabitants of which enjoy at once a common and an independent existence. As it is with the polypiers, so it is here; each eats for the benefit of itself and for the community. Labour and nutrition for the community, labour and food for itself.

Probably there reign among the inhabitants of one of these groups sentiments of brotherhood of which we have no idea. Since that which is digested by one of the family is beneficial, up to a certain point, to all, ought there not to be between the diverse individuals, especially between those nearest to each other, a physiological bond, more or less direct, to draw them together—a moral bond, more or less strong? What strange vitalities, organic combination, to find under the brilliant blue of the ocean!

Tunicata.

On seeing one of the *Tunicata* for the first time, a stranger to zoology would scarcely take them for animals at all. Almost always attached to submarine rocks, these beings have the form of a simple sac. Their skin, gelatinous, horny, or rock-like, is at times covered with marine plants and polypiers. They have neither arms, nor feet, nor head. But then they have a mouth, placed at the entrance of a digestive tube, and, in connection with the latter, a special opening intended for evacuations. The mouth is preceded by a great cavity, the walls of which are covered with vessels; for this cavity is the seat of respiration, and is covered with vibratile cilia. Thus the same canal serves first for respiration, and then, farther on, for digestion: another instance of the economy of Nature. Another remarkable instance of circulation is found: they have a heart, but no head.

This heart is the centre of a well-developed vascular system, but very unlike what usually obtains. The blood which traverses it takes such a course, that, in the space of a very few minutes, the heart changes its aurical into ventrical and its ventrical into aurical blood. At the same time the arteries are changed into veins and the veins into arteries. The consequence is, that the current which traverses these canals changes its direction with each contraction of the heart.

Simple as is their organization, the Tunicata have a nervous system. It is an unique ganglion, connected with divers small fillets. The organs of sensation present themselves in a very rudimentary fashion. We find eyes, and, after very minute search, a single ear has been found. They are propagated by budding, and also from eggs. The young are subject to some very curious metamorphoses, some particulars of which will be given farther on.

The Tunicata are divided into *Ascidia* and *Salpa*, to which some naturalists add the *Brachiopoda*.

Ascidians.

The *Ascidia*, from the Greek word ἀσχιδίον, leather bottle, have, as the name indicates, the shape of a bottle or purse. The analogy becomes

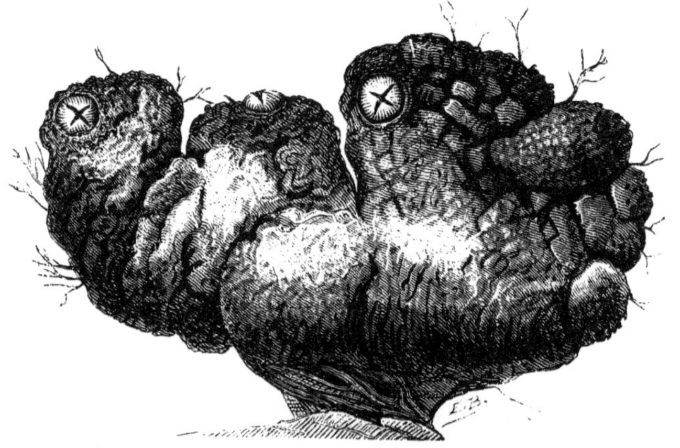

Fig. 124. Ascidia microcosmus (Cuvier).

more evident when it is considered that these creatures are habitually filled with water, which can be expelled by very slight pressure.

The Ascidians are sometimes free, sometimes united to others in a manner more or less intimate. Hence their division into the three groups of *simple*, *social*, and *composite* Ascidians.

Simple Ascidians attach themselves, each individual singly, to rocks and other submarine bodies, and generally at a fixed depth. *Ascidia microcosmus*, a Mediterranean species, represented in Fig. 124, may be quoted as a type of this division of Ascidians. The vulgar name of Cynthia, or the little world, is probably given from its being inhabited by quite an animated colony of algæ and polypiers, which dwell upon its surface, and give it a very peculiar, but not very attractive, appearance. The flavour of these molluscoids is very strong, which does not, however, hinder the poorer dwellers on the sea shore from eating them. The genus *Phallusia* is another type of the group. *Phallusia grossularia* is of a reddish colour, and about the size of a currant-berry: it usually lodges itself in the oysters of certain localities. At Ostend another species, *Phallusia ampulloïdes*, is found in prodigious quantities in the oyster parks, and is parasitic on living lobsters.

Social Ascidians comprehend living *Tunicata*, connected together on a common prolongation by the roots, but free and unconnected in all other respects. *Ascidia pedunculata* (Fig. 125) may be quoted as an example.

The Composite Ascidians are still more intimately associated together; a great number of these little beings live together in a single mass. Such are the Botrylla and the Pyrosoma.

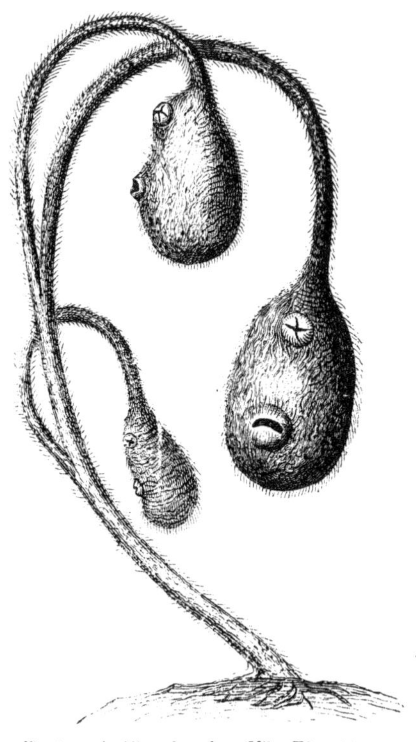
Fig. 125. Ascidia pedunculata (Milne Edwards).

The Botrylla is a genera the most interesting of all the groups under consideration. Only imagine from ten to twenty individuals, oval in form, more or less flattened, adhering by their dorsal surface to some submarine body, and holding on by their sides, so as to form a sort of wheel. "When we excite one of the branches," says Frédol, "a single mollusc contracts itself; when we touch the centre, they all seem to contract themselves (Cuvier). The buccal orifice is at the outer extremity of the radius; but the intestinal terminations abut on the common cavity, which occupies the centre of the wheel. Here we behold certain animals which eat separately, but which fulfill together as a community very singular functions—a kind of union and communism of which the moral world presents no prototype. With our molluscs, in place of two individuals united, we have a score. We may consider the entire star as one single animal with many mouths. But then, we have with it a luxury of organs for the function of intelligence which seeks and chooses, and parsimony of the organ of stupidity, which neither seeks nor chooses."

While the Botrylla is fixed and adherent, the Pyrosoma, on the contrary, is perfectly free. The animal colony which constitutes it floats and balances itself upon the waters, like the sea-pen or the physalia, of which we have spoken in treating of the zoophytes.

The name Pyrosoma has been given to these animals in consequence of their brilliant phosphorescent properties. According to the observations of Péron and Lesueur, nothing can exceed the brilliant and dazzling light emitted in the bosom of the ocean by these animals. From the manner in which the colonists dispose themselves, they form occasionally long trains of fire; but it is a singular fact that this phosphorescence presents the same curious characteristics that distinguish the cils of the Beroë; namely, that the colours vary instantaneously, passing with wonderful rapidity from the most intense red to yellow, from golden colour to orange, to green, or to azure blue. De Humboldt saw a flock of these brilliant living colonies floating by the side of his ship, and projecting circles of light having a radius of not less than twenty inches in diameter. He could see by this light the fishes which followed the ship's track, during many days, at the depth of from two to three fathoms.

Bibra, a Brazilian navigator, having caught six Pyrosoma, employed them to light up his cabin. The light produced by these little creatures was so bright, that he could read to one of his friends the description he had written of these his living torches.

Three species of Pyrosoma are known; namely, *P. elegans*, two or three inches in length, which inhabits the Mediterranean; *P. gigantea*, which is found in the same sea. It is a long bluish cylinder, bristling with tubercles, each of which is the abode of an animal, a citizen of this moving republic, and is attached to its colleagues by means of its gelatinous envelope: an alliance imposed by inexorable Nature—a forced species of socialism.

The third species, *P. atlanticus,* was discovered by Péron and Lesueur in the Equatorial seas.

These curious Ascidians are so created in rings as to constitute a long fine cylindrical tube, closed at one end and open at the other. By the contraction and dilation of the mass of beings, this great cylinder swims slowly through the open sea, lighting up the ocean with its phosphorescent light, shining through the water like a glowing fire. Mr. Bennett thus describes one of these pelagic appearances: "On the 8th of June, being then in lat. 30° S. and 27° 5′ W. long., having fine weather and a fresh south-easterly trade-wind, and the thermometer ranging from 78° to 84°, late at night the mate of the watch called me to witness a very unusual appearance in the water. This was a broad and extensive sheet of phosphorescence extending from east to west as far as the eye could reach. I immediately cast the towing-net over the stern of the ship, which soon cleaved through the brilliant mass, the disturbance causing strong flashes of light to be emitted, and the shoal, judging from the time the vessel took in passing through the mass, may have been a mile in breadth. On taking in the towing-net, it was found half filled with *Pyrosoma atlanticus,* which shone with a beautiful pale greenish light. After the mass had been passed through by the ship, the light was still seen astern, until it became invisible in the distance, and the ocean became hidden in the darkness as before this took place.

"The second occasion of my meeting these creatures was in a high latitude, and during the winter season. It was on the 19th of August, the weather dark and gloomy, with light breezes from north-north-east, in lat. 40° 30′ S., and 138° 3′ E. long., at the western entrance to Bass's Straits, and about 8 o'clock P.M., when the ship's wake was perceived to be luminous, while scintillations of the same light were abundant all round. To ascertain the cause, I threw the towing-net overboard, and in twenty minutes succeeded in capturing several Pyrosoma, which gave out their usual pale green light; and it was, no doubt, detached groups of these animals which were the occasion of the light in question. The beautiful light given out by these molluscans soon ceased to be seen; but by moving them about it could be reproduced for some length of time after. The luminosity of the water gradually decreased during the night, and toward morning was no longer seen."

The genus *Salpa* forms another interesting group of Tunicata.

The Biphora or Salpa (Fig. 126) are long transparent threads of the most delicate tissues, composed of rows of individuals placed side by side, and grafted, as it were, transversely: ribbons, in which each animal is grafted end on end to its sister: double parallel chains of social creatures, sometimes alternate, sometimes opposite: living chaplets, of which each pearl is an individual. Each individual presents an oblong diaphanous or prismatic body, more or less symmetrical, and often furnished in front, rarely behind, with tentaculiform appendages. So great is the transparency, that the various organs may be observed through the skin as they perform their several functions.

An ancient philosopher thought it a subject of regret that Nature had not thought of piercing the body with an opening sufficiently

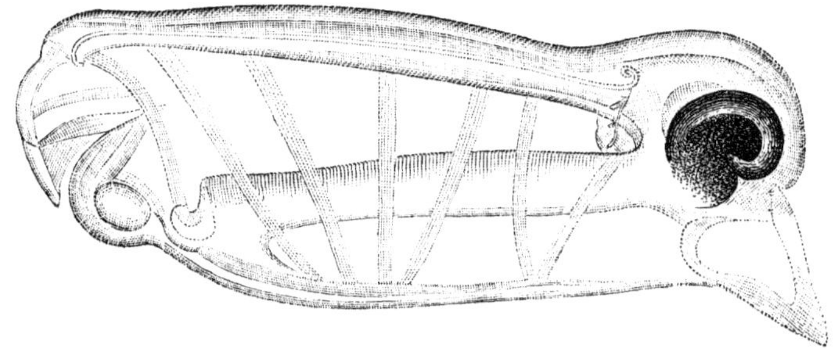

Fig. 126. Salpa maxima (Forsk).

large for each one to see what was passing in the interior. The creature which now occupies our attention would surely have satisfied the demands of our critic: its body is, metaphorically speaking, a house of glass.

In order to move itself, the Salpa has recourse to a singular artifice. It introduces water into its body through a posterior opening, furnished with a valve, which it expels by an anterior outlet situated near the mouth. It is thus pushed backwards, and swims, as it were, by recoil. Moreover, it swims with its belly upwards. All the elements of a chain of Salpas act in concert; they contract and dilate simultaneously; they advance as a single individual. One of them floats on the surface with the undulations of a serpent, so that, among sailors, they have gained the appellation of sea-serpents. These long, living trains abound in the Mediterranean, principally towards the African coast, and in the Equatorial seas. They are inhabitants of the open sea, and live immerged at considerable depths; but when the nights are calm they show themselves on the surface. As they spread themselves abroad with a strong phosphorescent light, they resemble long ribbons of fire, unrolling their long waving lines in spite of the waves, as in Fig. 127. What wonders they see who go down into the great deep! What sights are reserved for the navigator who traverses the Tropical seas during the silence of night!

When a chain of Salpas is drawn from the water, the rings separate,

Fig. 127. Phosphorescent chain of Salpas on the surface of the sea.

and they can no longer be made to adhere. The social bond has been dissolved by superior order.

Salpas are sometimes met with, isolated and solitary, whose exterior conformation differs much from that which is proper to the connected Salpa; so different, indeed, that it might belong to another type. But the observations of Chamisso, of Krohn, and of Milne Edwards, have revealed some very remarkable facts. By dint of time, patience, and sagacity, these observers have ascertained that the Biphora is viviparous, and that each species is propagated by alternate generation, the young creature being unlike its immediate parent. One of these generations is represented by the solitary individuals, the other by an aggregation of individuals. Each solitary Biphora engenders a new group—a chain; each constituted member of the chain engenders a solitary Salpa.

Thus a Salpa is not organized like its mother or daughter, but rather like its sister, its grandmother, or granddaughter—another example of alternate generation, which has already been discussed in treating of zoophytes.

Those marine creatures which pass their lives in a forced community—animals which eat, sleep, or rest always in company—who abandon themselves together to the soft caresses of the waves,—these colonies, or, rather, republics of animals, leading constantly the same monotonous existence,—reveal to us very strange things: an identical community of sentiments in a crowd of beings riveted by the same chain—a chain at once physical, intellectual, and moral!

He who has never brought his attention to bear upon the history of the inferior animals is a stranger to many surprising mysteries; in short, the study of natural history is the best means of adding to and extending the knowledge and ideas of the young.

CHAPTER XI.

ACEPHALOUS MOLLUSCA.

"Sigillatim mortales, cunctum perpetui."
APULEIUS.

We reach here the true Mollusca. The transition condition of the *Molluscoïda* has prepared us the better to comprehend the nature and habits of the molluscs, properly so called.

The name Mollusca indicates the characters which most struck the ancients: they are soft—in Latin, *molles;* their flesh is cold, humid, and viscous. In consequence of their very softness, they are generally furnished with an apparatus of defence or protection, in the shape of a calcareous cuirass, called a *shell* or *test*. According to the species this test is a coat of mail, a buckler, or a tower. The mollusc is thus armed and defended against all attacks from without, nearly after the manner of a knight of the middle ages; only the knight was not quite shut up in his armour, while the mollusc is attached to it by indissoluble organic bonds. "Such a life and such a habitation!" says Michelet. "In no other creature is there the same identity between the inhabitant and the nest. Drawn from its own substance, the edifice is the continuation of its fleshy mantle. It follows its form and tints. The architect has communicated its own substance to the edifice.

The shell of the Mollusca has been variously appreciated by naturalists. "We might regard the shell as the bone of the animal which occupies it," says a celebrated French naturalist; and then gives expression to a very different view. "We may say as a general thesis that testaceous molluscs are animals with whom ossification is thrown out on the external surface in place of the interior, as in the Mammifera, birds, reptiles, and fishes. In the case of the superior animals the bones lie in the depths of the body; in the shelled Mollusca the bones are placed on the superficies. It is the same system reversed."

Other zoologists reject as altogether untenable this assimilative theory. "The shell which serves as a dwelling and a shelter cannot," say these authors, "be considered as a skeleton, because it does not assume the external form of the animal; because it does not attach itself to the organs of locomotion; and, finally, because it is the product of secretion, which increases in proportion to the development of the body itself." This last opinion appears to us to be the most acceptable.

However that may be, from the immense variety of form and size, from the beauty and brilliancy of their colours, the shells of the molluscs are among the most attractive objects of natural history. Nor is it from their beauty alone that a fine collection of shells becomes interesting: a living creature has inhabited the shell, a creature which in its organization and its life, above all, by its habits, excites in a high degree our interest, curiosity, and admiration. It has been said that the shell "is like a medal struck by the hand of Nature to commemorate climates." In short, the waters of different regions of the globe, whether fresh or salt, are characterised by the presence of particular shells; moreover, the comparison of living shells with those which lie in a fossilized state buried in the depths of the soil, is a most important element of our knowledge touching the origin of the different beds out of which our globe is constituted.

Thus, we must not shut our eyes to these beings, in appearance so miserable and obscure, if we would possess a general knowledge of the animal kingdom. The Creator has endowed them with many wonderful gifts to embellish their lives, and who would dare to disregard them? Who could examine and compare their structure without being charmed with the study? Man, who descends into the depths of the earth in search of the precious metals—who dives into the deep in pursuit of the treasures it conceals—who stoops his head over works of art—would surely not refuse to bend himself for a moment to the sand of the sea, to gather in his hand, to bring nearer to his eyes, these marvellous works of the Divine Creator!

The true molluscs are divisible into two great classes: the Acephalous, or Headless, and those having a head of structure more or less perfect, which are called Cephalous Molluscs.

The Acephalous or Headless Molluscs are so called from the Greek ἀ, privative, and κεφαλή, head. They have no head; the body is surrounded by the folds of the skin; the shell consists of two valves. Such is a summary description of all the Acephalous Molluscs. They are sometimes naked, and sometimes enclosed in a shell or *test*, whence they are known as Testaceous Molluscs. They are called *bivalves*, because their shell consists of two halves, or valves united by a hinge. They are sheltered in this double carapace as a book is in its cover.

Although they have no head, they can feed themselves; they have feeling of some sort, and they reproduce their kind. They have friendships and enmities, perhaps even passions; probably these are not very lively, for most of them scarcely ever change their place, even to make the least movement. Many of them remain fixed to the rock on which they were hatched, and tumultuous sensations are not quite compatible with immobility.

The bivalves are found in every sea. The shell of the bivalve is ovoid, globulous, trigonal, heart-shaped, elongated like a pea-pod, or flat like the leaves of a tree, having an opening down the ventral side. In some one leaf is flat, the other round and swelling in the centre. The shell is thus an outer envelope, consisting of two pieces, more or less corresponding to each other in size and shape (of which the oyster is an example), formed of carbonate of lime deposited in membranous cells in its outer layers, the inner layers being composed of thin coatings of lime deposited in the outer surface of the tissue, called the mantle-leaves. The valves are united to the animal by the insertion of certain muscles, and by the horny epidermis of the mantle, which stretches over the edge of the valves. The hinge and ligament which unite the two valves consist of a dense elastic substance, somewhat resembling india-rubber; the hinge is formed of teeth, and cavities into which the teeth fit. The ligament acts in opposition to certain contractile muscles within, which draw them together, and is placed either within or without the hinge, or partly both. On separating the valves, the two leaves of the mantle present themselves. These are thin delicate leaves, furnished at the margin with sensitive tentacles and other organs of sense, and with glands sometimes highly coloured. The use of these organs is thus described by Mr. Rymer Jones:—

"When the animal is engaged in increasing the dimensions of its abode, the margin of the mantle is protruded and firmly adherent all round to the circumference of the valve with which it corresponds. Thus circumstanced, it secretes calcareous matter and deposits it upon the extreme edge of the shell, when the secretion hardens and becomes converted into a layer of solid testaceous substance. At intervals this process is repeated, and every newly-formed layer enlarges the diameter of the valve. The concentric strata thus deposited remain distinguishable externally, and thus the lines of growth marking the progressive increase of size may easily be traced."

"While the margin of the mantle is thus the sole agent in enlarging the circumference of the shell," the professor continues farther on, "its growth in thickness is accomplished by a secretion of a kind of calcareous varnish derived from the external surface of the mantle generally, which, being deposited layer by layer over the whole interior of the previously existing shell, progressively adds to its weight and solidity. There is, however, a remarkable difference in character between the material secreted by the marginal fringe and that furnished by the general surface of the mantle membrane. The former we have found more or less covered by glands appointed for the purpose, situated in the circumference of the mantle; but as these glands do not exist elsewhere, no colouring matter is ever mixed with the layers that increase the thickness of the shell, so that the latter always remain of a delicate whitish hue, and form the well known iridescent material usually distinguished by the name of nacre or mother-of-pearl." (*General Outline*, p. 385.)

The process by which shells attain their beautiful markings is thus described by Mr. Jones:—"The external surface is exclusively deposited by the margin of the mantle, which contains in its substance certain coloured spots, which are found to be of a glandular character, and to owe their peculiar character to a pigment they secrete, which is mixed with the calcareous matter; coloured lines are therefore found on the exterior of the shell wherever these glandular organs exist. Where the deposition of colour is kept up throughout the process of enlargement, the lines are unbroken and perfect; but where the coloured matter is furnished only at intervals, spots and patches of irregular form and increasing in size with the enlargement of the mantle are the consequence."

Bivalves move about and change from place to place by means of an extensible fleshy organ called, from some of its functions, a foot; in fact, it has less resemblance to a foot than to a large tongue. It is a muscular mass, capable of being pushed out from between the mantle and the valves, and varies much in form; it is in turn a hatchet, a ventilator, a pole, an awl, a finger, and a sort of whip. This foot is simple, forked, or fringed. In some species the tissues are spongy, and capable of receiving considerable quantities of water. When the organ swells, it is elongated and stiff; on the other hand, by suddenly expelling all the water, it gets small and pliable, and can now return to its shell. This organ is represented in Fig. 128 (*Donax trunculus*, Linn.), in which it is singularly developed. This bivalve is found on the sea shore in shallow water; it buries itself almost perpendicularly in the sands. They are so abundant on the French side of the Channel and on the shores of the Mediterranean, that they form a considerable portion of the people's food. These bivalves have the

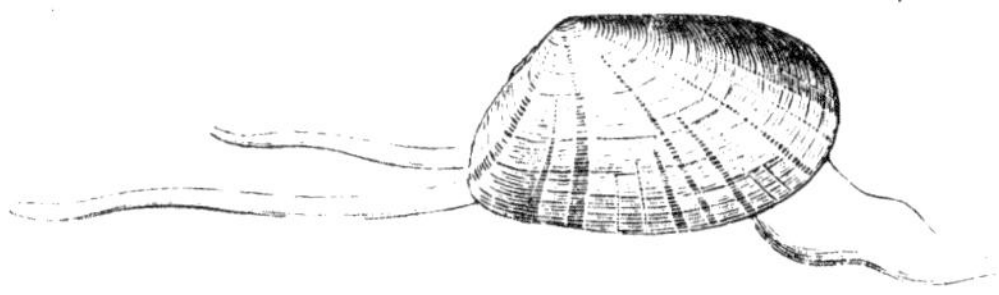

Fig. 128. Donax trunculus (Linnæus).

singular power of leaping to a considerable height and then throwing themselves to a distance of ten or twelve inches—a spectacle which may be witnessed any day at low water. When abandoned by the retreating tide, they try to regain the sea. If seized by the hand in order to drag them out of the sand, aided by their compressed, branched, and angular feet, they give to their shell the sudden and energetic movement under which the bounding action takes place.

The shell of the Donax is slightly triangular and compressed; its length exceeds its height; it is regular, univalve, unequally lateral, and its hinge bears three or four teeth on each valve. The action of these feet is very simple, and is compared by Réaumur to that of a man placed on his belly who, stretching out one hand, seizes upon some fixed object, and draws himself towards it. There is just this difference, that the movement of the member in the mollusc is altogether contractile.

The molluscs exist in such numbers that our space only permits us to describe a few families, or rather types of families, such as the Oyster, *Ostrea*; the Mussel, *Mytilus*; the Tridacna; the Cockle, *Cardium*; and the Ship Worm, *Teredo*.

1. The OSTREADÆ form a small group of Acephalous Mollusca, which includes the Oyster, *Ostrea spondylus*, the *Pectens*, the Hammerheads, *Malleus*, and the Pintadines, *Meleagrina*.

2. The MYTILIDÆ or Mussels are the type of another family, among which the ham-shaped *Pinna*, the *Anodonta*, and *Unio*, are the most remarkable members.

3. The TRIDACNA stand alone and unrivalled in respect to size, being much used in Roman Catholic churches to hold the holy water; hence their French name *Bénitier*.

4. The VENEREDÆ (Cockles) constitute with *Donax*, *Tellina*, and *Venus* one important family.

5. The PHOLADÆ (Borers) are a redoubtable family of destroyers, of which the *Teredo*, *Solen*, and *Pholas* are distinguished members.

OSTREADÆ.

The shell of the oyster we need not dwell upon; it is the one bivalve universally known. It is unequally valved, modified in shape by the form of the submarine body to which it happens to be attached. The lower or adherent valve is concave, always the largest; the upper one thin, usually flat; the shell is lamellar, rough externally, and seems to be composed of broken leaves, adhering slightly to each other, as if the successive leaves had been built up from within, and each succeeding layer was an enlargement upon its predecessor. The hinge which unites the valves is an elastic toothless ligament placed behind the centre, which opens the valves.

The interior surface of the valves is smooth and white, diaphanous or pearly towards the centre, but near the back an oval or rounded impression may be observed, to which a thick and whitish fleshy body is attached. This is the central muscle which draws the valves together, hermetically closing them upon the animal. This muscle is cut through in the process of opening the oyster.

The animal has no power of locomotion; its foot is very small and often wanting, no syphon, but lies with its mouth open, and slightly attached to the shell. The shell itself is always adherent, as if soldered to the rock or other submarine body, the point of adherence being near the summit of the lower valve, at the part called the *heel.*

Let us suppose the oyster opened by the double dissection of the ligament of the central muscle and of the adductor valves. When displayed before our eyes, we see in the bottom of the shell a flattened shapeless animal, semi-transparent, greyish, and somewhat oval-shaped. The gastronomist, who seldom sees beyond his nose, thinks that in spite of its culinary merits the oyster belongs to the lowest rank of animal existence; but he deceives himself, and does not know how complex and delicate is the organization of the humble bivalve. The animal is enveloped in a sort of smooth, thin, contractile tissue called the *mantle*, which folds round it, presenting two lobes, separated on the greatest part of its circumference, and forming a sort of hood, the summit of which abuts upon the hinge of the bivalve. The edges of this mantle are fringed with very small cilia, which the creature can extend and draw back at pleasure, and which seem to be gifted with a certain amount of sensibility. It is this mantle which secretes and deposits the calcareous matter which forms the shell, each plate of which is an enlargement on the preceding one, until it constitutes a pyramid of thin convex lamellæ.

At the point where the lobes of the mantle meet, near the summit of the valve, is the mouth of the animal, with its thin membranous lips. This organ is large and dilatable, and is accompanied by four flat triangular pieces, by means of which the animal introduces its food into the stomachal cavity.

A very short gullet is attached to the mouth, which leads to a pear-shaped stomach. After this stomach comes a slender sinuous intestine, which, leading obliquely towards the anterior, descends a little, then reascends, passes behind the stomachal cavity, nearly on a level with the mouth, crossing its first path in order to reach the posterior face of the adductor muscle, in the centre of which it terminates with a free opening. The stomach and intestines are surrounded on all sides by the liver, which alone constitutes a notable portion of the mass of organs. This liver is of a blackish colour, pervaded with a deep yellow liquid, which is the bile. Thus the stomach and intestines of the oyster are surrounded by the *liver;* the mouth is connected with the stomach, and the intestines open in the back.

The heart of the oyster is placed under the liver, and is surrounded closely by the terminal part of the intestines. It is composed, like the same organ in the superior animal, by two distinct cavities, an auricle and ventricle. From the ventricle issues a vessel, which is divided into three distinct canals. One of these carries the blood towards the mouth and tentacles; another carries it towards the liver; the last distributes the nourishing fluid to the rest of the body. The blood of the oyster is limpid and colourless; it passes successively from the auricle of the heart, where it is vivified, into the ventricle, and from this last cavity into the great vessel of which we spoke, which distributes it into the interior of the animal.

The oyster thus possesses a true circulation; not that double system which characterises the mammals, and which includes arterial and pulmonary action, but a simple circulation, as it exists in fishes and many other animals. It breathes also in the bottom of the water, after the manner of fishes, being, like the fish, provided with organs called gills or *branchiæ*, whose function is to separate the oxygen dissolved in the water from its other ingredients; these branchiæ, which are placed under the mantle, consist of a double series of very delicate canals, placed close together, not unlike the teeth of a fine comb.

Having no head, the oyster can have no brain; the nerves originate near the mouth, where a great ganglion is visible, whence issues a pair of nerves which distribute themselves in the regions of the stomach and liver, terminating in a second ganglion, situated behind the liver. The first nervous branch distributes its sensibility to the mouth and tentacles; the second, to the respiratory branchiæ.

With organs of the senses oysters are unprovided. Condemned to a sedentary life, riveted to a rock where they have been rooted, as it were, in their infancy, they neither see nor hear; touch appears to be their only sense, and that is placed in the tentacles of the mouth.

The mode of reproduction in these creatures is very peculiar. The oyster unites in itself the functions of both sexes. In the same organ are found the eggs—called *spat*—and the mobile corpuscles intended to fertilize them. The oyster is hermaphrodite.

The eggs are yellowish in colour, and exist in prodigious numbers in each individual. We are assured that an oyster may carry as many as two millions of eggs! Nature always makes ample provision for the preservation of species; but in spite of the most ample provision here displayed, man, in his reckless and wasteful gluttony, has all but defeated Nature. A tyro can compute how many individuals a bank of oysters reckoned at twenty thousand would produce, at the rate of two millions, or eight hundred thousand as other authorities assert, from each one annually, and it will amount to an incredible number—in fact, each would multiply itself by millions in three years; and yet, thanks to our improvident management, they get scarcer every year.

The spawning season is usually from the month of June to the end of September: during this season the oysters deposit their eggs in the folds of the mantle. During the period of incubation the eggs remain surrounded by mucous matter, which is necessary to their development, the whole having the appearance of a thick cream—this milky appearance being due to the accumulated mass of ova surrounded by the mucus: this mass undergoes various changes of colour while losing its fluidity, becoming successively yellowish, greyish, brown, and violet, a condition which indicates the near termination of the embryo state, for the oysters do not, like many other inhabitants of the sea, leave their ova; they incubate them in the folds of their mantle, and only discharge them when they can live without the maternal protection. Nothing is more curious to witness than a bank of oysters at the spawning season. Every adult individual of which it is composed throws out its phalanx of progeny. A living dust is seen to exhale from the oyster bank, troubling the water and giving it a thick cloudy appearance, which disseminates itself little by little in the liquid, until it dissipates and loses itself far from its focus of production. The *spat* is soon scattered far and wide by the waves; and unless the young oyster finds some solid body to which it can attach itself, it falls an inevitable victim to the larger animals which prey upon them. In this its infant state, when it has just left the protection of the parent shell, the microscope reveals the young bivalve, with its shell perfect, having an apparatus which is also a swimming *pad*, ready to adhere to the first solid body which the current drives it against. This pad or cushion (which is represented in Fig. 129) is furnished with vibratile ciliæ, disposed round the young shell. Aided by the powerful adductor muscles, with which it is also provided, this cushion is projected through the water at the will of the young inhabitant, which has every facility for the purpose: it is even said to swim about near the mother, before final dismissal from the maternal protection, seeking shelter at the least alarm between the valves of the parent shell. The pad disappears after the young oyster has finally attached itself to a permanent bed of its own.

Before this period of its life arrives, however, many are the dangers to which it is exposed: its enemies are numerous; they lie in ambush for it in every cranny! It has to guard itself against eddies and currents which would drive it out to sea, and mud banks in which it would be smothered. Crustaceans, worms, and polypes, with other equally voracious marine inhabitants, prey upon it. Last, but not least, come the terrible and multiplied engines of the eager fisherman—and we readily comprehend why the oyster is provided with such accumulated masses of ova.

If the young bivalve is fortunate enough to escape all the snares and dangers we have enumerated, it grows rapidly. It is quite microscopic at the period of its discharge from the parent shell; at one month it is of the size of a large pea, at the end of six months it is about three-quarters of an inch, a year after its birth an inch and a half to two inches, and finally, at the end of three years it has become merchandise; that is to say, it is in a state to be sent to the parks for preservation and feeding. In Fig. 130 we see a group of oysters,* of various ages, attached to a piece of wood: A being oysters of twelve to fifteen months, B five or six months, C three to four months, D one to two months, and E oysters twenty days after birth.

Fig. 129. Young Oysters furnished with locomotive organs.

The species of oysters usually eaten are the common oyster (*Ostrea edulis*, Linn.) of our own coasts and the opposite shore, and the horsefoot oyster (*O. hippopus*, Linn.). On the Mediterranean coast are the rose-coloured oyster (*O. rosacea*, Favanue), and the milky

* We give this illustration as representing the comparative size of the oysters at different ages; but it is necessary to state that the specimens were artificially attached to the block by means of glue for exhibition. Oysters always attach themselves by the back of the rounded shell near to the hinge, as stated at p. 324.

oyster (*O. lacteola*, Moquin), besides the small and little-known crested oyster (*O. cristata*, Born), and the folded oyster (*O. plicata*, Chemnitz). On the Corsican coast is the oyster called foliate (*O. lamellosa*, Brocchi).

There are two principal varieties of the common oyster dredged for on the French coast, which differ in size and delicacy of flavour. These are the Cancale and Ostend oyster. When the first has been fed for some time in the oyster park, and has assumed its greenish hue, it is designated the Marenna oyster, from the park so named in the Bay of Seudre. Of this green colour we shall speak elsewhere.

Fig. 130. Groups of Oysters of different ages attached to a block of wood.

The geographical distribution of oysters is universal; wherever there is a sea-board they abound. Who believed Uncle Jack when he told us in our youth of oysters growing on trees, and oysters so large that they required to be carved like a round of beef—of oysters on the Coromandel coast as large as soup-plates? Nevertheless Uncle

Jack's stories were true: there are oysters which require carving, and oysters have been plucked off trees. In some parts of America they grow very large. Virginia possesses nearly two million acres of oyster-beds. The sea-board of Georgia is famed for its immense supplies; the whole coast of Long Island, extending to a hundred and fifteen miles, is occupied with them, and all over the States evidence is to be seen of the estimate in which the favoured bivalve is held by the American people.

Natural oyster-beds are found in bays, estuaries, and other sheltered sinuosities of the coast, with shelving and not too rocky bottoms, such places being, according to the natural law of production, favourable for the increase of the colony. Such banks abound in every sea. In France the oyster-beds of Rochelle, of Rochefort, the Isles of Ré and Oleron, the Bay of St. Brieuc, of Cancale, and Granville, are famous for the quality of their produce.

On the Danish coast there are from forty to fifty oyster-banks, situated on the west coast of Schleswig; the best bed lying between the small Isles of Sylt, Amron, Fohr, Pelworm, and Nordstrand. At the point of Jutland, and opposite Shagen, beds less productive are found.

The great oyster-beds of England extend from Gravesend, in the estuary of the Thames and Medway, along the Kentish coast on the one hand, and the estuary of the Colne and other rivers on the Essex coast. The Frith of Forth is also famous for its oyster-beds, extending from Preston Pans, famous for its "Bearded Pandores," far up the estuary of the river; but, curiously enough, all these great banks, without exception, have been impoverished, and all but exhausted, by improvident dredging, in spite of the "close season" which has always existed.*

"He was a bold man who first ate an oyster," has been said before. The name of the courageous individual has not been recorded, but Mr. Bertram, in his "Harvest of the Sea," tells us a legend concerning him: "Once upon a time,"—it must have been a long time ago,—"a man of melancholy mood was walking by the shores of a picturesque estuary, listening to the monotonous murmur of the sad sea-waves,

* A friend, thoroughly conversant with the subject, protests against this charge against dredging. "The real reason of the diminution of their productiveness," he says, "is that from various causes (of which unsuitable temperature is believed to be the chief) there has, for some years, been no spat."

when he espied a very old and ugly oyster-shell all coated over with parasites and sea-weeds. It was so unprepossessing that he kicked it with his foot, and the animal, astonished at receiving such rude treatment on its own domain, gaped wide with indignation, preparatory to closing its bivalve still more tightly. Seeing the beautiful cream-coloured layers that shone within the shelly covering, and fancying that the interior of the shell itself must be beautiful, he lifted up the aged 'native' for further examination, inserting his finger and thumb within the valves. The irate mollusc, thinking, no doubt, that this was meant as a further insult, snapped its pearly door down upon his finger, causing him considerable pain. After releasing his wounded digit, our inquisitive gentleman very naturally put it in his mouth. 'Delightful!' exclaimed he, opening wide his eyes; 'what is this?' and again he sucked his finger. Then the great truth flashed upon him that he had found out a new delight—had, in fact, achieved the most important discovery ever made. He proceeded at once to realise the thought. With a stone he opened the oyster's stronghold, and gingerly tried a piece of the mollusc itself. 'Delicious!' he exclaimed, and there and then, with no other condiment than its own juice, with no accompaniment of foaming brown stout or pale Chablis to wash it down, no newly-cut, well-buttered brown bread, did that solitary anonymous man inaugurate the first oyster banquet."

Another story makes the act of eating the first oyster a punishment. The poetaster also had his views on the subject:

"The man had sure a palate covered o'er
With brass, or steel, that on the rocky shore
First broke the oozy oyster's pearly coat,
And risked the living morsel down his throat."

And ever since men have gone on eating oysters. Emperors and poets, princes and priests, pontiffs and statesmen, orators and painters, have feasted on the favoured bivalve.

Man has made use of the oyster from the most remote antiquity. Among the débris of festivals which precede by ages the epoch of written history, oyster-shells are found. On the "midden heaps" of northern Europe they are often discovered, mingling with other rubbish and with stone implements, evidently the refuse of very ancient feasts. We have all read of the classic feasts of the Romans, which began with oysters brought from fabulous distances. Vitellius ate oysters all day long, and the idea prevailed that he could eat a thousand. Calisthenes, the philosopher, was a passionate oyster eater, so was Caligula; Seneca the wise could eat his hundred, and the great Cicero did not despise the savoury bivalve. Lucullus had sea-water brought to his villa from the shores of the Campania, in which he bred them in great abundance for the use of his guests. To another Roman, Sergius Orata, we owe the original idea of the oyster-park. He invented the oyster-pond, in which he bred oysters, not for his own table, but for profit.

Among modern celebrities whose love of oysters is recorded, we may mention Louis XI., who feasted the learned doctors of the Sorbonne once a year on oysters. Another Louis invested his cook with an order of nobility, in reward for his skill in cooking them. Cervantes loved oysters, although he satirized oyster dealers. Marshal Turgot used to eat a hundred or two just to whet his appetite. Rousseau, Helvetius, Diderot, the Abbé Raynal, and Voltaire, are recorded lovers of oysters. Danton, Robespierre, and other of the revolutionists, frequented the oyster *salons* of Paris. Cambaceres was famous for his oyster feasts, and it is recorded of the great Napoleon that he always partook of the bivalve on the eve of his great battles, when they could be procured.

In short, it has been demonstrated as a gastronomic truth that there is no feast worthy of a connoisseur where oysters do not come to the front. It is their office to open the way by that gentle excitement which prepares the stomach for its sublime function, digestion; in a word, the oyster is the key of that paradise called appetite. "There is no alimentary substance, not even excepting bread, which does not produce indigestion under given circumstances," says Reveille-Parise, but oysters never. This is an homage which is due to them: "We may eat them to-day, to-morrow, eat them always, and in profusion, without fear of indigestion." Dr. Gastaldi could swallow, we are assured, his forty dozen with impunity—quite a bank must he have eaten. He was unfortunately struck with apoplexy at table before a *paté de foie gras*.

Montaigne quaintly says, to be subject to colic, or deny oneself oysters, presents two evils to choose from, since one must choose between the two, and hazard something for his pleasure.

England has always been famous for its oysters, and its pearls are said to have been the chief incentive to Cæsar's invasion. It is not, therefore, to be supposed that British magnates could be indifferent to the "native." But the bivalve has perhaps been more celebrated, in prose and verse, north of the Tweed than south, where silent enjoyment is more relished than noisy demonstration. Dugald Stewart, Hume, Cullen, and other Scotch philosophers of the last centuries, had their "oyster ploys" as an accompaniment to their "high jinks," in the quaint and dingy taverns of the old town of Edinburgh; and what the bivalve has been to modern celebrities let the *Noctes Ambrosianæ* tell.

The oyster may thus be said to be the palm and glory of the table. It is considered the very perfection of digestive aliment. From Stockholm to Naples, from London to St. Petersburg, it is always in request. At St. Petersburg they cost a rouble (nearly one shilling), and at Stockholm fivepence each. For the last year or two the English amphitryon must pay from two shillings to half a crown a dozen for choice natives.

For his daily nourishment a man of middle size requires a quantity of food equal to twelve ounces of dry azotic substance. According to this calculation, it would be necessary to swallow sixteen dozen of oysters to make up the necessary quantity. The small proportion of nutritive matter explains the extreme digestibility of the oyster. It also explains the immense consumption of them attributed to the Emperor Vitellius. The oyster is nothing more than water slightly gelatinized. Without this Vitellius, all emperor and master of the world as he was, never could have absorbed twelve hundred oysters by way of whetting his appetite.

The gourmets were long of opinion that the quadrangular pad or cushion in the bivalve was the most savoury and exciting part. Certain distinguished amateur performers adopted and proclaimed the principle of dividing transversely the body of the mollusc, and eating the cushion only. Natural history explains this gastronomical discovery. It recognises the fact that the bile secreted by the liver is contained in this substance, that it accelerates while it exhausts the qualitative surface of the tongue and palate, aiding also the functions of the stomach.

We have described the organization of the oyster, and we have said something of the enjoyment it confers. Did it ever occur to the various Societies for the Prevention of Cruelty to Animals to consider whether the oyster might not be a very proper object of their care? Let us see if we can bridge over the gulf.

We commence operations upon them by dragging them violently from their own element. We place them out afterwards in water-parks, more or less briny and unsuitable, filled with villanous green matter, which presently pervades their breathing apparatus, impregnating, obstructing, and colouring it; the oyster swells, fattens, and soon attains that state of obesity which verges on sickness.

When the poor creature has attained its livid green colour, it is fished up a second time. Alas! it is now doomed neither to return to the sea, to the park, nor to its native rock. It has water at its disposal only in the very small quantity which it can retain between its two valves, a quantity scarcely sufficient to keep away asphyxia. It is shut up in an obscure narrow basket—an ignoble prison-house, without door or window. It seems to be forgotten that they are animals: they are piled upon the pavement like inert merchandise. The basket is carried by railway; the animal, shaken out of existence almost, is at last landed at the door of some oyster-shop; and this is the critical moment for the poor bivalve! It is thrown into a tub with clean water enough to remind it of its former luxurious life, when it is again seized by the pitiless being who is now its fate. With a great knife he brutally opens the shell, cuts through the muscle by which it adheres to the valve, and violently detaches it, after breaking the hinges. It is now laid out on a plate, exposed to every current of air, and in this state of suffering it is carried to the table. There the pitiless gourmet powders it over with the most pungent pepper, squeezes over the wounded and still bleeding body the abomination of its race in the shape of citric or malic acid or vinegar, and then, alas! with a silver knife which cannot cut, he wounds and bruises it a second time; or, worse still, he saws and tears and rends it from its remaining shell; he seizes it with a three-pronged fork, which is driven through liver and stomach, and throws it into his mouth, where the teeth cut, crush, and grind it, and, while still living and palpitating, reduced to an inanimate mass, these organs first triturate it, while our gourmet is drinking its blood, its fat, and its bile.

We have said that oysters have no head, no arms—that they are

Plate XII.—Dredging for Oysters.

without eyes (although that is disputed), without ears, and without nose; that they do not stir—that they never cry!

Agreed, perfectly agreed; but all these negatives do not prevent its being sensible to pain. Two eminent Germans, Herren Brandt and Ratzeburg, have proved that they possess a well-developed nervous system, and if they possess sensation they must suffer. "Can an animal with nerves be impassible?" asks Voltaire. "Can we suppose any such impossible contradiction in Nature?"

There is consolation, however, for all concerned. Let the humanitarian fishermen, oyster-dredgers, merchants, and consumers, console themselves with the vast difference between the helpless imperfect mollusc and the higher classes of animals. In the case of the former we swallow the animal, scarcely thinking of its animal nature. It is the denizen of another element, lives in a medium in which we cannot exist, presents itself in a form, so to speak, degraded—an obscure vitality, motions undecided, and habits scarcely discernible. We may therefore see the oyster mutilated, mutilate them oneself, grind them, and swallow them, without emotion or remorse.

A learned naturalist dwelling on the sea shore possessed himself one day of a dozen oysters. He wished to study their organization; he turned them, and turned them again, examined their several parts inside and out. He made drawings of and described them, and, having satisfied himself that he had exhausted Science in observing, he swallowed them; the interesting bivalves had lost nothing of their excellence, and the examination did not prejudice the consummation.

Oyster fishing is pursued in a very different manner in different countries. Round Minorca, divers, with hammers attached to the right hand, descend to the depth of a dozen fathoms, and bring up in their left hand as many of the bivalves as they can carry, two fishermen, usually associating for the purpose, diving alternately until the boat is filled. On the English and French coasts the dredging machine is employed, as represented in Pl. XII. This operation is necessary to keep down vegetation, which would stifle the oysters; the engine is of iron, and is very heavy. It is thrown overboard, and descends to the bottom of the sea, which it ploughs and scrapes up, detaching the oysters, and throwing them into a net attached to the dredger. In this process oysters, large and small, are torn from their native bed, some going into the net, but a larger number, old and young, are torn from their native bed, and buried in the mud. It would be difficult to imagine a more destructive process; and when the habits of the oyster are considered, it is evidently one admirably contrived to destroy the race.

In France oyster dredging is conducted by fleets of thirty or forty boats, each carrying four or five men. At a fixed hour, and under the surveillance of a coastguard in a pinnace bearing the national flag, the flotilla commences the fishing. In the estuary of the Thames the practice is much the same, although no official surveillance is observed. Each bark is provided with four or five dredges, resembling in shape

Fig. 131. Drag-net employed in Oyster fisheries.

a common clasp purse. It is formed of network, with a strong iron frame, as represented in Fig. 131, the iron frame serving the double purpose of acting as a sucker, and keeping the mouth open, while giving it a proper pressure as it travels over the oyster-beds. When the boat is over the oyster scarp, the dredge is let down, and no more attractive sight exists than that presented by the well-appointed Whitstable boats on one side of the estuary, or the Colne boats on the other, as they wear and tack over the oyster-beds, bearing up from time to time to haul in the dredge, and empty its contents into the hold. The tension of the rope is the signal for hauling in, and very heterogeneous are the contents—sea-weeds, star-fishes, lobsters, crabs,

Plate XIII.

actinia, and stones. In this manner the common oyster fields on both sides of the Channel were ploughed up by the oyster dredger pretty much as the ploughman on shore turns up a field. The consequence was that, twenty years ago, the French beds were totally exhausted, and France had to look to foreign countries for its oyster. Oyster farms which had employed fourteen hundred men and two hundred boats were reduced to two hundred men and twenty boats. Similar results from over-dredging would have followed, no doubt, on this side the Channel had the mollusc not been protected by the company and private proprietors who held the oyster-beds in the large estuaries. This state of things in France led to some important discoveries in the science of oyster culture, which have produced important changes there.

The name of Sergius Orata has already been mentioned as a cultivator of oysters. He lived in the fifth century before our era, and according to Pliny he first attempted parking oysters at Baia in the times of the orator Lucius Crassus. He was the first to recognise the superior flavour of the oysters of the Lucrin Lake, the Avernus of the poets, probably for trade reasons of his own, for then, as now, Reveille-Parise remarks, writing on the subject, "tradesmen speculated on the weaknesses of human gourmandism." But Sergius really created a new industry, which is still practised in thousands of places much as he left it. As a proof of the perfection to which Sergius had brought oyster culture, his contemporaries said of him, in allusion to the hanging banks which he invented, that if he had been prevented from raising oysters in the Lucrin Lake, "he would have made them grow on the house-tops." The traveller who visits this celebrated lake finds only a miry puddle. The precious oysters placed there by Catiline's grandfather are metamorphosed into miserable eels, which leap in the mud, a vile mountain of ashes, coal, and pumice-stone, which was thrown up in a night like the mushroom, having reduced the once celebrated lake into the state described.

Rondeletius also speaks of a fisherman who understood the art of oyster culture.

The Neapolitan Lake Fusaro—the terrible Acheron of the poets—is a great oyster-park, in which Art is made effectually to aid Nature in the multiplication of its products. This famous oyster-bank, which is represented in Pl. XIII., lies in the neighbourhood of Baia and

Cumæ. It forms one of the most interesting spots in that beautiful bay. In the month of February, 1865, M. Figuier tells us he traversed its celebrated coast, seated himself on the banks of the historical lake, and tasted the produce of this curious manufacture of living beings, whose origin dates from the Roman period.

Lake Fusaro was in ancient times a place of evil report: Virgil immortalized it as the mythological Acheron, but its landscape had nothing of the sadness and desolation which accords with the sojourn of the dead. It is a salt pond, shaded with a girdle of magnificent trees. It is about a league in circumference, and about a fathom in

Fig. 132. Artificial Oyster-bank in Lake Fusaro.

depth at its deepest part; its bottom is muddy and black, like the rest of this volcanic region.

It will be understood, from what has been said, that the chief obstacle to the reproduction of oysters is the absence of any solid body to which the young spawn can attach itself, and the means of shelter from animals which prey upon them. The fishermen living on the shores of Lake Fusaro have long realised this, and provided against it by warehousing, as it were, in the lake near the sea, the oysters ready to discharge their spawn, while retaining the young generations captive in the protected basins, where they are sheltered from various causes of destruction to which oysters are exposed in the open sea.

Upon the bottom of the lake, and on its circumference, the proprietors of Fusaro have constructed hillocks here and there, with stones heaped up, artificial rocks, raised sufficiently to shelter the depôts from mud and slime. Upon these rocks they deposit the young oysters gathered in the Gulf of Tarentum. Each of these rock-works is surrounded by a girdle of piles, driven close to each other, and raised a little above the surface of the water, as represented in Fig. 132. Other piles are distributed in long lines, and bound to each other by a cord, from which is suspended fagots of young wood. In the spawning season the oysters which have been deposited on the

Fig. 133. Pillars with cords attached in Lake Fusaro.

artificial rocks discharge the myriads of young fry which have been nurtured in the folds of their mantles. The fagots suspended from the piles arrest the germ before it is driven away by the waves, much as a swan attaches itself to the first shrub which comes in the way. By these precautions the riverains of Fusaro have provided for the preservation of the young fry, besides removing many of the natural enemies of the young oyster.

In other places the piles are distributed in long lines and bound together by strong cords, from which fagots of brushwood are suspended, on which the young spawn lay hold, as in Fig. 133.

By means of these arrangements the pregnant oyster deposits its spawny progeny in quiet repose; the young germs are intercepted by the fagots and hurdles suspended between the piles, where the young oysters develop themselves under the favourable conditions of repose, temperature, and light. When the fishing season arrives, the piles and fagots which surround the beds are removed, and the oysters are gathered suitable for market. The oysters thus selected for sale are packed loosely in osier baskets and sunk, while waiting for purchasers, into a reserve or park. This park is established on the shores of the lake. It is constructed of piles which support a gangway provided with hooks, from which the baskets filled with living oysters are suspended, ready for sale.

Some twenty years ago the oyster-beds of France had become totally exhausted under the open system of dredging; and circumstances having brought the protective system pursued at Fusaro under the notice of M. Coste, a learned academician, to whom France is indebted for the restoration of the bivalve, M. Coste reported to the Emperor in 1858 that at Rochelle, Marennes, Rochefort, at the Isles of Ré and Oleron, where there had formerly been twenty-three oyster-beds, there were now only five, and these in danger of being destroyed by the increase of mussels; that at the Bay of St. Brieuc, so naturally suited for oyster culture, the beds were reduced to three; that even on the classic oyster grounds of Cancale and Granville, it was only by the most careful administration that decay was prevented, while the increasing numbers of consumers threatened altogether to destroy an industry essentially necessary for the support of a maritime population.

The impulse given by this report has been productive of the most satisfactory results in France. All along the coast the maritime populations are actively engaged in oyster culture. Oyster parks, in imitation of those of Fusaro, have sprung up. In his appeal to the Emperor, M. Coste suggested that the State, through the Administration of Marine, and by means of the vessels at its command, should take steps for sowing the whole French coast in such a manner as to re-establish the oyster-banks now in ruins, extend those which were prosperous, and create others anew wherever the nature of the bottom would permit. The first serious attempt to carry out the views of the distinguished academician was made in the Bay of St. Brieuc. In the month of April in the same year in which his report was received, operations commenced by planting three millions of mother-oysters which had been dredged in the common ground; brood from the oyster grounds of Cancale and Tréquiers were distributed in ten longitudinal lines on tiles, fragments of pottery, and valves of shells. At the end of eight months the progress of the beds was tested, and the dredge in a few minutes brought up two thousand oysters fit for the table, while two fascines drawn up at random contained nearly twenty thousand, from one to two inches in diameter. Two of these fascines exposed to public view at Béni and Patrieux excited the astonishment of the maritime population.

This result encouraged M. Coste to pursue his experiments upon a greater scale, and he now proposed to bring the whole littoral under a regulated system of oyster culture. In the roads of Toulon and in Lake Thau, which touches this port, the same system was put in force by the Administration of Marine as had already been done in the Bay of Arcachon and in the Isle of Ré. In these localities oyster culture assumed gigantic proportions. Associations were formed for the purpose of prosecuting them and forming oyster-parks.

These exertions roused the curiosity of foreign nations. Van Beneden, a distinguished naturalist of Louvain, and M. Eschrecht of Copenhagen, visited France to study the arrangements for oyster culture. M. Coste demonstrated that parks could be established on all places visited by the tide, and under his advice the Bay of Arcachon is now transformed into a vast field of production, which increases every day, giving the happiest presages of an abundant harvest. Already twelve hundred capitalists, associated with a similar number of fishermen, occupy a surface of nine hundred and eighty-eight acres, which emerge at low water. In this bay the State has organized two model farms for experimental purposes, in which tiles, fascines, and valves of shells are laid down with other appliances, to which the young oysters may attach themselves. These expedients have been so successful that the park, which has cost about £114, is now estimated to be worth about £8000 in money, with a total of five million oysters, large and small. The Isle of Ré, which was originally surrounded by a muddy bottom ill adapted for oyster culture, has been totally changed, so that in two years four leagues of foreshore have been turned into a rich and profitable oyster-bed; twelve hundred parks are in full activity, and two thousand others are in course of construction, the whole forming a complete girdle round the island.

Everyone has heard of the green oysters of Marennes, the preservation, amelioration, and ripening of these oysters, so to speak, representing a very considerable branch of industry in France. In order to give the reader some idea of its importance, we shall give here a brief summary of M. Coste's voyage of exploration on the French littoral.

The parks at Marennes, in which the oysters are placed in order to acquire the green colour which characterises them, are basins stretching along both banks of the Seudre for many leagues. They are locally known as *claires*, and differ from the oyster-parks of other countries in this particular—that, while the ordinary parks are so arranged as to be submerged at every return of the tide, the basins of Marennes are so arranged that they can only be submerged at spring tides; that is, at the new and full moon, when the waters rise beyond the ordinary level.

The basins or *claires* occupy from two hundred and fifty to three hundred square yards of superficies; two sluices permit of the entrance and withdrawal of water at will, so as to maintain it at the level most convenient to the industrial wants of the place, or to empty it altogether when it is necessary to cleanse the basin, pave the bottom, and furnish it with a fresh supply of oysters.

When these necessary works are completed, advantage is taken of the first spring tide to fill the basin. When the tide begins to ebb, the sluices are closed, so as to retain sufficient water in the basins; and while thus shut up, salt held in solution is deposited, and qualities analogous to those of marine bottoms are produced, purged by cleansing processes of all products offensive to the bivalves.

When the basin has been filled with sea-water for the necessary time, and the bottom is sufficiently impregnated, it is emptied and left to dry; and now, the soil being prepared, it only remains to furnish it with oysters of a mellow and ripe age, in order to give them their green hue. Towards the month of September, at low water, the whole sea-side population of Marennes go to gather oysters on the pavement left uncovered by the ebbing tide, or by using a dredger in the deeper parts of the *claires* where the water still remains. A temporary magazine for the reception of the oysters thus gathered is erected on the banks, which the water revisits twice a day. The young are reserved for cultivation on the parks or *claires;* the fullest are sold for consumption in the neighbourhood; but the quantity of oysters raised at Marennes is insufficient to supply the demand. About a third of the provision intended for the *claires* come from the coasts of Brittany, of Normandy, and La Vendée. "These foreign oysters," says M. Coste, "never attain the fine flavour of those bred in the locality. It is necessary to keep them for a long time in the *claires* before they are sufficiently ameliorated, and, even when they become green, they retain traces of their primitive nature, remaining hard, in spite of the new qualities imparted to them by cultivation; a certain bitterness remains, which is easily distinguished by the true amateur; it is the same with indigenous adult oysters. When they are taken at this stage of their existence the colouring does not succeed with them;—it is only, so to speak, the false brand used to give a speculative value to the merchandise. It is not enough that the mollusc should have a fine flavour; it must have the peculiar taste. It is not enough that it has the green hue; it is necessary that these qualities should pervade it from the earliest age, and that the culture of the *claires* should continue to the end." It is thus necessary that the oysters for the *claires* of Marennes should be selected when from twelve to eighteen months old, that the shells should be well-formed, and free from all foreign bodies adhering to the surface. Being thus carefully picked out, the oysters are distributed over the bottom of the *claires* with a shovel, and afterwards so arranged by the hand that they may not touch each other when they increase in size; that they do not embarrass each other by the movements of their valves; and that nothing should interfere with the regularity of their forms. The young colony reposes under a sheet of water from twelve to eighteen inches deep, which is, as we have said, only renewed at spring tides, which reach the level. Nor are the oysters abandoned to themselves in these privileged beds while they are growing and ripening. They are objects of continual care and of special manipulation. The spring tides visit the *claires* charged with mud, which, if deposited in the motionless basins, would act as a mortal poison to the young mollusc; hence the necessity of transporting them from one *claire* charged with mud into others free from such accumulations: and this is a process in constant operation until the animals are finally gathered for consumption. Oysters deposited in the *claires* aged eighteen months should remain two years before they are ready for use; but three and even four years are required to give them the full degree of perfection which characterises the best products of the Marennes oyster-parks.

Oysters placed in the reservoirs in an adult state become green, it is true, in a very few days, but they never attain the exquisite flavour of those which have been bred in the parks, and have undergone the costly manipulation described, from their earliest years.

The question arises, What is the colouring principle which is here in operation? The green colour is not general; it is shown principally on the branchiæ, upon the labial feelers and intestinal canal; it is rather undecided; and the colouring matter appears to differ chemically from all other known pigments of green colour. Must it be attributed to the soil of the *claire?* This is its most probable origin. But many naturalists insist that the colouring matter proceeds from an infusorial animalculæ, the green-coloured Vibrion. Others have hazarded the opinion that it is a disease of the liver in our unfortunate bivalve which produces the colour. Bile secreted in excess by a diseased liver would give a green hue to the parenchyma of the respiratory organs of an animal rendered sick by the exceptional treatment to which it has been subjected. Of these three opinions, says M. Figuier, the first, as we have said, presents the greatest appearance of probability.

The system of oyster farms, which has worked admirably for the companies themselves, has proved of doubtful utility, so far as the oyster-eating public is concerned, as the following sketch of the Whitstable oyster farms will show. The oyster farm at Whitstable is co-operative in the best sense of the term, and has been in operation for many years. The Company possesses large oyster grounds, and a fine fleet of boats kept for the purpose of dredging and planting the beds; it is established under the Joint Stock Companies Act, but there is no other way of entrance into it but by birth, as none of the free dredgermen of the town can hold shares. When a man dies his interest in the Company dies with him, but his widow, if he leaves one, obtains a pension. The affairs of the Company are managed by twelve directors, who are called "the jury."

"The layings at Whitstable," to summarise Mr. Bertram, "occupy about a mile and a half square; and the oyster-beds have been so prosperous as to have obtained the name of the 'happy fishing grounds.' Whitstable lies in a sandy bay, formed by a small branch of the Medway, which separates the Isle of Sheppey from the mainland. Throughout this bay, from the town of Whitstable at its eastern extremity to the old town of Faversham, which lies several miles inland, the whole of the estuary is occupied by oyster farms, on which the maritime population, to the extent of three thousand people and upwards, is occupied; the sum paid for labour by the various companies being set down at £160,000 per annum, besides the employment given at Whitstable in building and repairing boats, dredges, and other requisites for the oyster-fishing. The business of the various companies is to feed oysters for the London and other markets, to protect the spawn or floatsome, as the dredgers call it, which is emitted on their own beds, and to furnish, by purchase or otherwise, the new brood necessary to supply the beds which have been taken up for consumption."

We have hinted above that in oyster, as in other fisheries, a wasteful spirit of extravagance has hitherto prevailed. It appears, however, that no rule can be laid down even as to the particular year in which the oysters will spawn, much less where it will be carried to; for, although the artificial contrivances adopted by Sergius Orata for saving the spawn are perfectly well known to the parties interested here, they have not hitherto been imitated; the practice of the companies and private owners of oyster-layers being to purchase their young brood from the dredgers and others who fish along the public foreshore and open grounds on the Kent and Essex coasts, and even as far north as the Frith of Forth. The little bay of Pont, for instance, on the Essex coast, which is an open piece of water sixteen miles long and three broad, free to all, and which formerly yielded considerable supplies to Billingsgate, now gives employment to a hundred and fifty boats, each with crews of three or four men, who are wholly employed in obtaining young brood—that is, oysters from eighteen months to two years old, which they sell to the oyster farmers. The result is, that the oyster farms have become a vast monopoly. By tacit consent they agree to feed the market at some eight pounds sterling per bushel; they pay the dredger one-fourth of that sum; and as the common fishing grounds are thus rendered mere nurseries of young brood, the lover of the bivalve must reconcile himself to pay a monopoly price for the precious morsel.

The system pursued at Whitstable, and other oyster-parks in the estuary of the Thames and Medway, is most efficient. The oysters reared in them, called "natives," in contradistinction to those called "commons," which are bred in their natural beds, are justly considered to be very superior in flavour, although they are a mixed breed, being brought from every quarter to augment the stock.

The Thames, or "native" system, is as follows: Every year each layer is gone over and examined by means of a dredge, successive portions being done day by day, till it may be said that each individual oyster has been examined; the young brood is detached from its bed, the double oysters are separated, and all kinds of enemies killed. During three days in each week dredging is pursued for "planting;" that is, for transference from one bed to another more suitable for their growth or fattening, and for the removal of the dead or sickly oysters and mussels. On the other three days dredging for market takes place, when the more mature beds are dredged, and as many are lifted as are required. Not only is this constant dredging of the beds themselves necessary, but the public beds immediately outside require the same care to keep them in a fit state, and free from enemies.

The same story of over-fishing and improvidence extends round our whole coast. The far-famed Pandores obtained at Preston Pans, near Edinburgh, once so cheap, are becoming scarce and dear. The brood is caught and barreled for export to Holland and other places, especially the Thames oyster farms. English buyers pick the grown oysters for Manchester and other large provincial markets, and the Corporation of Edinburgh, the Duke of Buccleuch, and other proprietors of the foreshore, have just interfered in time to prevent the total destruction of the trade, when the wild song of the Cockenzie dredgerman might have been left to charm some future antiquary, as it is now said to charm the oyster into the dredge with its refrain:

"The herring it loves the merry moonlight,
The mackerel it loves the wind;
But the oyster it loves the dredger's song,
For it comes of a gentle kind."

The Scallop-shell (*Pecten*) is round, nearly equal-sided, resting on the right valve, which is more convex, and marked with radiating ribs. Linnæus made the mistake of confounding with the *Ostrea* a great number of shells, which, by their channeled edges and surfaces,

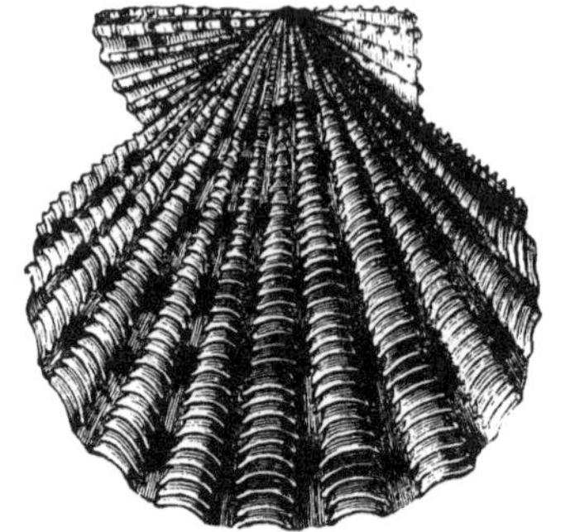

I. Pecten pallium. (Linn.)

II. Pecten purpuratus. (Lamarck.)

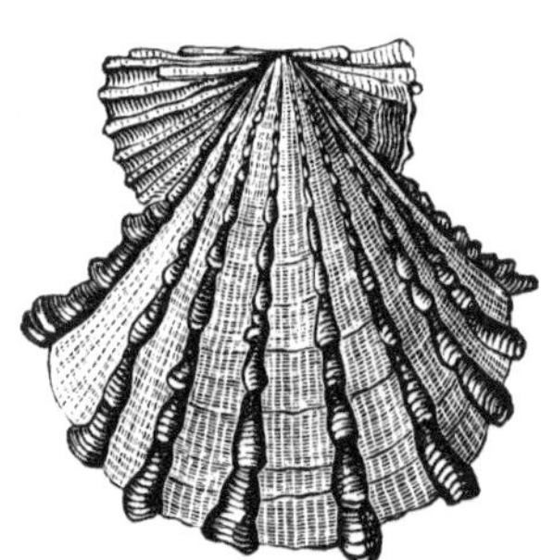

III. Pecten foliaceus.

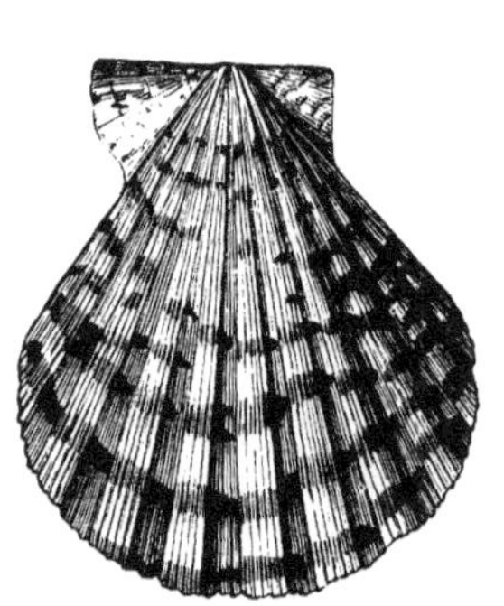

IV. Pecten tigris. (Lamarck.)

V. Pecten nodasus. (Linn.)

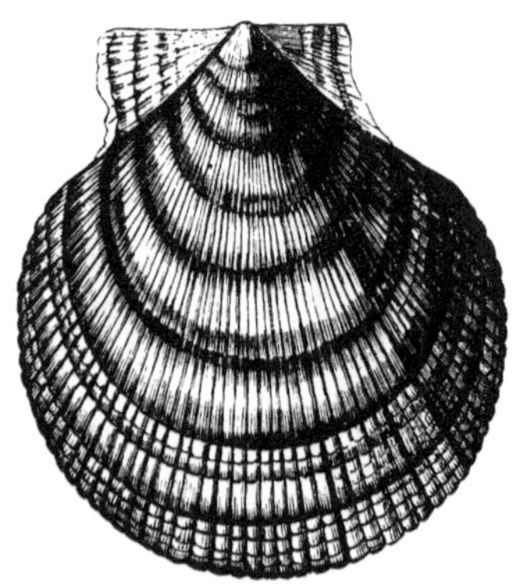

VI. Pecten islandicus. (Chemnitz.)

PLATE XIV.—Pectinidæ.

strongly reminded one of the arrangements of the teeth of a comb, whence their name of *Pecten.* They were well known to naturalists long before the time of Linnæus, under the name of *Pilgrims'* shells, a name which came into use from the practice which prevailed among pilgrims in the middle ages—we know not why—of ornamenting habits and hats with the valves of some of the species.

The shell of the *Pecten* is in general nearly circular, more or less elongated, and terminated towards the summit in a straight line, forming a sort of triangular appendage called the ear, to which the hinges are attached. The valves are very regular, but with no resemblance to each other. In some species, the shell of which is closely shut, the lower valve is more or less convex than the upper one. In others, both valves are convex. The hinge is without teeth, and the ligament, which is intended to close the shell, is inserted into a triangular depression or dimple. The retractile muscle is unequal, and nearly central. The valves are not nacred inside, and are formed on their exterior surface of numerous fluted channels, which spring from a lobe more or less pointed at the summit, diverging towards the circumference. The edges are sometimes smooth, as in the Watered Pecten (*P. pseudamussium*, Fig. 134), but more frequently they are formed in strips or scales, as in the Smooth-shelled Pecten (*P. glaber*, Fig. 135). Upon the whole, however, the Pectens are very variable, but always elegant in form; the colours are frequently lively and brilliant. In Pl. XIV., some of the most striking forms are represented, as in Fig. I., the Ducal Mantle (*Pecten pallium*), an inhabitant of the Indian Ocean, remarkable for its elegant form, its twelve radiating stripes, diverging towards the circumference, the horizontal furrows of its salient scales, and the striking distribution

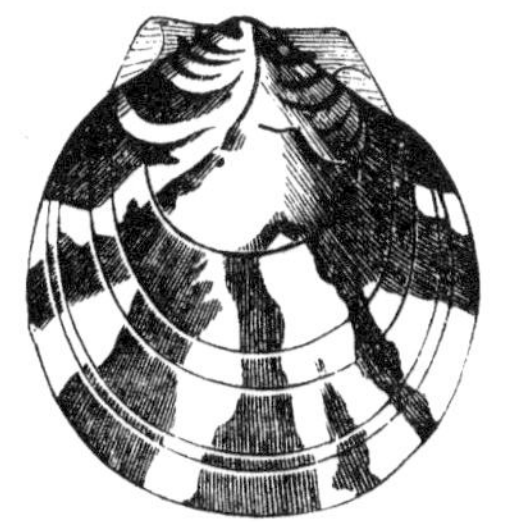

Fig. 134. Pecten pseudamussium (Chenu).

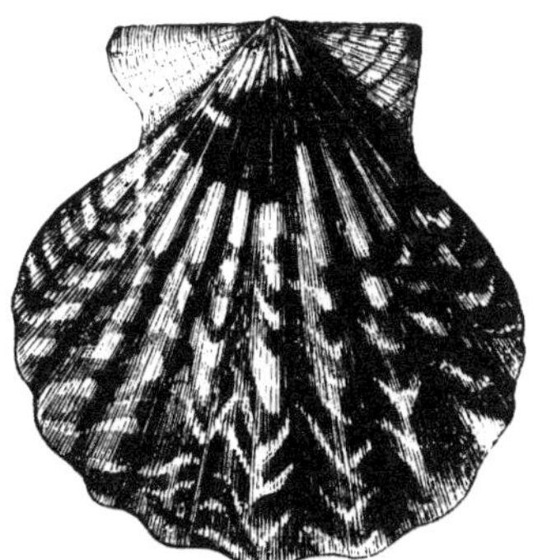

Fig. 135. Pecten glaber (Linnæus).

of its white spots upon a bed of red and brown marble; Fig. II., the Purple Pecten; Fig. III., the Coral Pecten; Fig. IV., the Tiger Pecten; Fig. V., the Foliaceous Pecten; and Fig. VI., the Northern Pecten.

The animal which inhabits the Pecten shell has the general form of the oyster, differing however from it in a remarkable manner. The edges of the mantle are furnished with multiplied fringes of simple tentacles, between which we find other tentacular appendages a little thicker, each terminating in a sort of small pearl, vividly coloured, to which is attached a nervous thread, which has been taken for an eye. Another difference: the branchiæ, in place of being connected by a striated lamina, as is the case in the oyster, are cut into parallel capillary filaments, forming a free and floating fringe, and the mouth is surrounded by salient many-cleft lips.

While the oyster shell is completely fixed to its bed, the Pecten is, on the contrary, perfectly free, and shifts from place to place, moving in the water even with a certain amount of agility; by smartly closing its half-opened valves and forcibly expelling the water, it moves backward by a sort of reaction; this action, repeated many times, compels the animal to move almost in spite of itself, and enables it to avoid danger, or directs its steps towards the spot it wishes to reach. Some naturalists even assert that, when raised to the surface, the Pecten half opens its shell in such a manner that the upper valve serves the purpose of a sail.

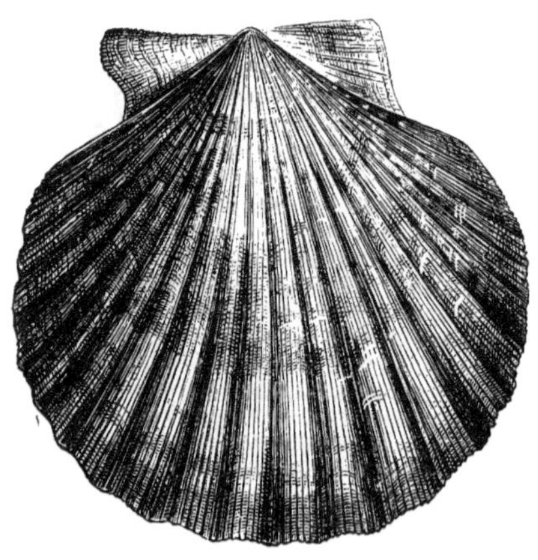

Fig. 136. Pecten opercularis (Linnæus).

The Pectens, of which a hundred species are described, are inhabitants of every known sea. Twenty species belong to Europe, among which we may mention *P. opercularis*, represented in Fig. 136; it inhabits European seas. Fig. 137 represents the White-mantled Pecten (*P. plica*, Linn.) of the Indian Ocean, and Fig. 138, the Concentric Pecten (*P. Japonica*) of the Japan seas.

The genus *Pectunculus* are abundant on the shores of the Mediterranean and along the Atlantic coast. If we take up at hazard a

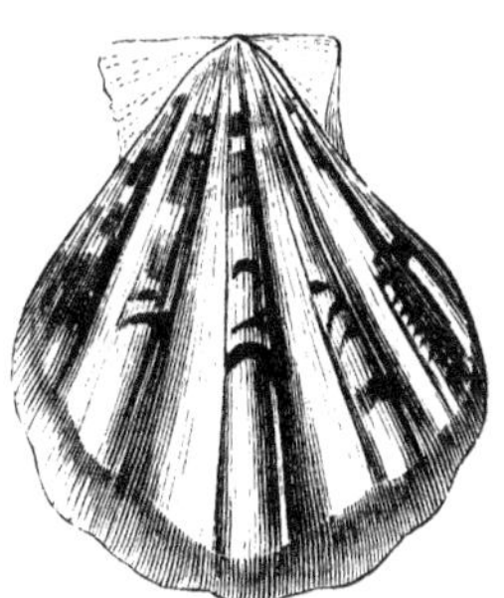

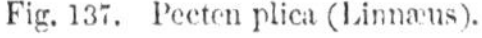
Fig. 137. Pecten plica (Linnæus).

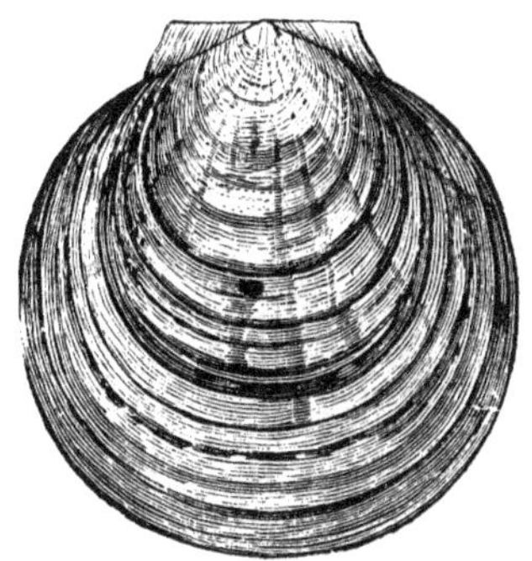
Fig. 138. Pecten Japonica (Gmellin).

handful of shells on any part of the French coast, one-third will consist of *Pectuncula*. They are found mixed with Cardium, Venus, Razor-fish, and Pectens. Their round and robust frame attracts much attention. They form the first of those charming infantile collection which are gathered at the mother's feet.

The animal which inhabits this pretty shell is moulded on its curva-

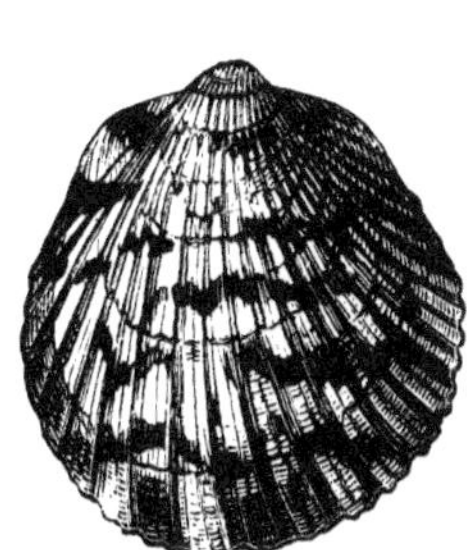
Fig. 139. Pectunculus aureflua (Reeve).

Fig. 140. Pectunculus delessertii (Reeve).

ture; like the shell, it is round and squat; it is furnished with a mouth, large, and thick for its size, and with double branchiæ. When the animal is taken alive, it sometimes exudes a thick mucous liquid over the shell, which has disgusted many a young collector with his conquest.

Among numerous species of *Pectunculus* we note as worthy of representation: *P. aureflua*, Reeve (Fig. 139); *P. delessertii*, Reeve

(Fig. 140); *P. pectiniformis*, Lamarck (Fig. 141); and *P. scriptus*, Born (Fig. 142).

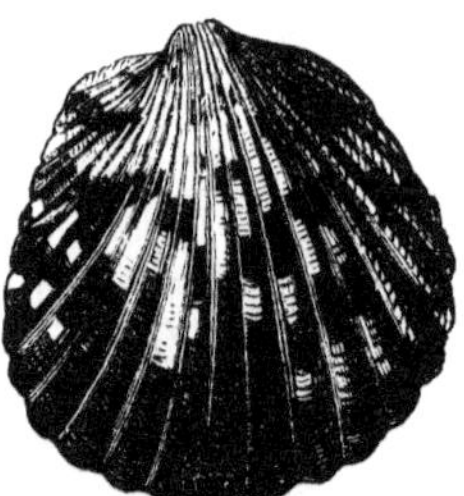

Fig. 141. Pectunculus pectiniformis (Lamarck).

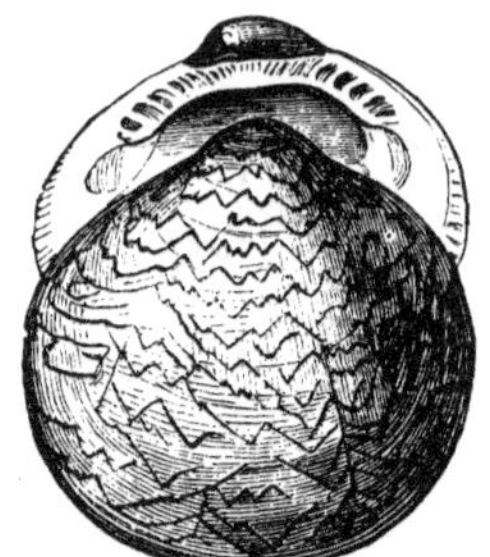

Fig. 142. Pectunculus scriptus (Born).

Among the Ostreadæ the shells of *Spondylus* are distinguished for their variety of form and the brilliant colours with which they are decorated. This makes them much sought after by amateur collectors, and procures for them a high price. The shell of *Spondylus* is solid and thick, with unequal adherent valves, nearly always bristling with spines, forming a very peculiar kind of ornamentation to the valves; the hinges have two very strong teeth. The animals which inhabit this shell resemble the oyster in many respects, but they still more closely resemble the Pectens. The edges of the mantle are provided with two rows of tentacles, the exterior row being, many of them, furnished at their extremities with coloured tubercles. As examples, we note several species of these bivalves for representation. *Spondylus regius* (Pl. XV. Fig. I.) is, perhaps, the most remarkable for its immense spines. *Spondylus radians*, Lamarck (Fig. III.), is noted for its elegant form. *Spondylus avicularis* (Fig. IV.) shows remarkable inequality in the valves. *Spondylus imperialis*, Chenu (Fig. II.), has long projecting spines, like feet, and the Scaly Spondylus (*S. crassisquama*, Fig. V.), is covered with scales arranged like so many roofing-tiles.

Like oysters, the genus Spondylus is frequently found firmly rooted to rocks and other submarine bodies, and, oftener still, heaped one upon the other, like herrings in their barrel.

These animals belong essentially to the seas of warm countries. We find them, however, occupying considerable space in the Mediterranean, where (Fig. VI.) the Ass-footed Spondylus (*S. gæderopus*) abounds.

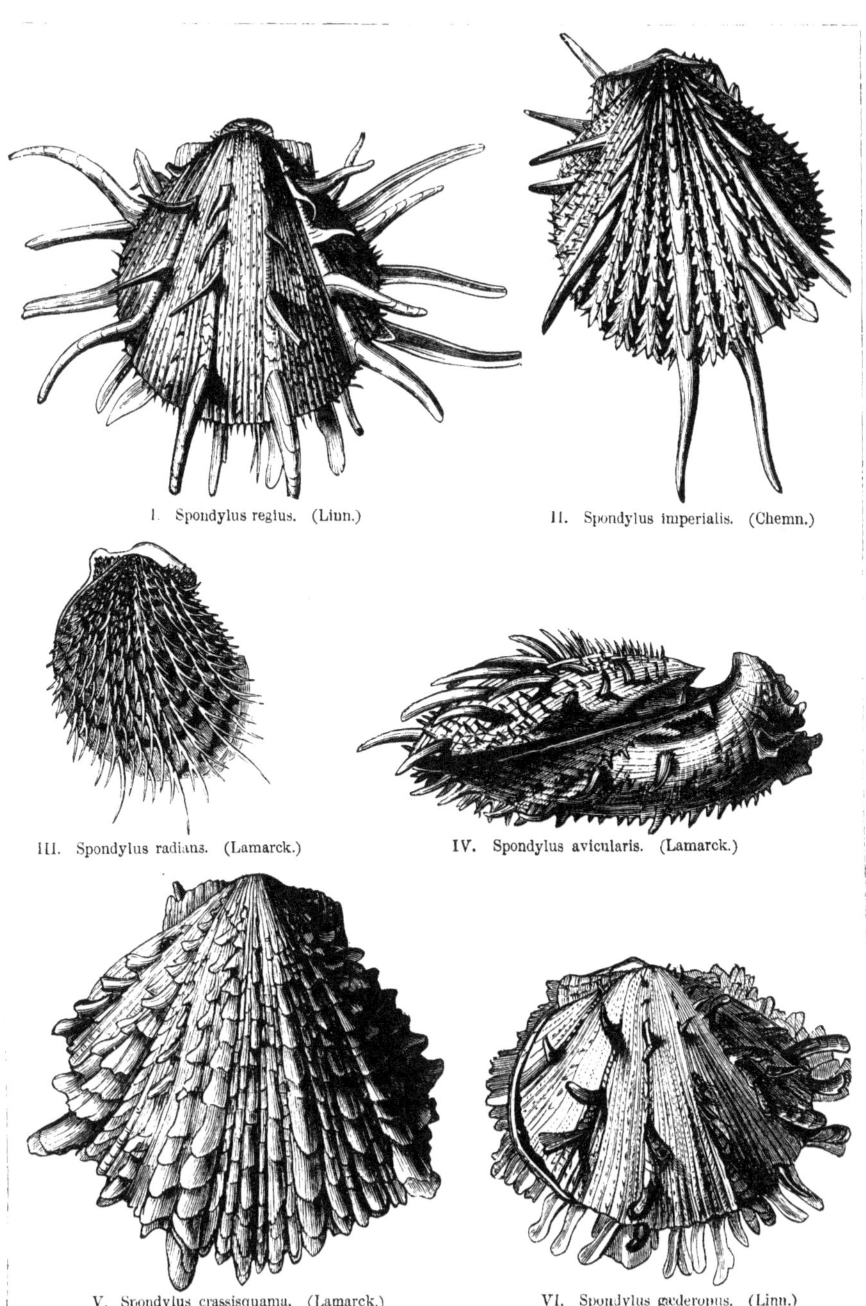

I. Spondylus regius. (Linn.)

II. Spondylus imperialis. (Chemn.)

III. Spondylus radians. (Lamarck.)

IV. Spondylus avicularis. (Lamarck.)

V. Spondylus crassisquama. (Lamarck.)

VI. Spondylus gæderopus. (Linn.)

Plate XV.—Spondylus.

But the most remarkable species of all is assuredly *Spondylus regius* (Pl. XV. Fig. I.). This species is a native of the Indian Ocean, and there scarcely exist three fragments of this rare shell in the museums of Europe. M. Chenu relates in one of his books an anecdote which would prove—if any proof were necessary—how far the desire of a collector to obtain possession of some rare and costly specimen will carry him in order to attain his object. "M. R——," says M. Chenu, "was Professor of Botany to the Faculty of Paris, and was, as sometimes happens, more learned than rich; he wished, on the invitation of a stranger, to purchase one of these shells at a very high price, which might be from 3000 to 6000 francs; the bargain was made, and the price agreed upon; it was only necessary to pay. The money in the professor's hands made only a small part of the sum the merchant was to receive for his shell, and he would not part with it without payment. M. R——, now consulting his desire to possess the shell more than his weak resources, made up secretly a parcel of his modest plate, and went out to sell it. Without consulting his wife, he replaced his silver plate by coverings of tin, and ran to the merchant to secure his coveted Spondylus, which he believed to be *S. regius*.

"The hour of dinner arrived, and we may imagine the astonishment of Madame R——, who could not comprehend the strange metamorphosis of her plate. She delivered herself of a thousand painful conjectures on the subject. M. R——, on his part, returned home happy with his shell, which he had committed to the safe custody of a box placed in his coat pocket. But, as he approached the house, he paused, and began for the first time to think of the reception he might meet with. The reproaches which awaited him, however, were compensated when he thought of the treasure he carried home. Finally, he reached home, and Madame R—— in her wrath was worthy of the occasion; the poor man was overwhelmed with the grief he had caused his wife; his courage altogether forsook him. He forgot his shell, and, in his trepidation, seated himself on a chair without the necessary adjustment of his garment. He was only reminded of his treasure by hearing the crushing sound of the broken box which contained it. Fortunately, the evil was not very great—two spines only of the shell were broken; but the good man's grief made so great an impression on Madame R——, that she no longer thought of her own loss, but directed all her efforts to console the simple-minded philosopher."

The tendency to throw out spines in Spondylus is one of its striking features. When the whole lower surface adheres to branches of coral, a very frequent occurrence, they are confined to the upper valve, but when a part only of the valve, the whole surface becomes covered.

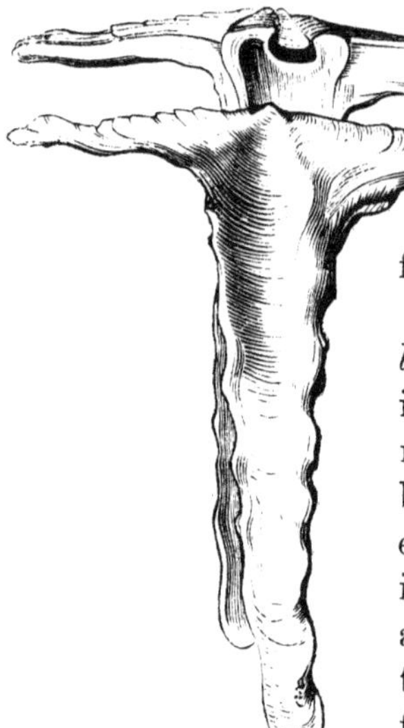

Fig. 143. Malleus alba (Lamarck).

The shells of the Hammerheads (*Malleus*) have a rough resemblance to the implement from which they derive their name. The valves are nearly equal, blackish, and somewhat wrinkled on the exterior, often brilliantly nacred in the interior. They are enlarged to the right and left of the hinge, forming prolongations on each side, which give them the fancied resemblance to the Hammerhead. At the same time they grow in a direction opposite to the hinge, which gives something approaching the handle of the implement.

This is the first feature which a glance at *Malleus alba* (Fig. 143) conveys. The hinge is without teeth, having instead a deep conical fossette or dimple, for the reception of a very strong ligament which acts upon the valves. The animal is contained in the interior of the shell, its mantle fringed by very small tentacular appendages. Only twelve actually living species of the genera are known, which are inhabitants of the Indian Ocean, of the Australian seas, and the Pacific Ocean.

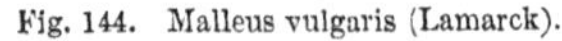

Fig. 144. Malleus vulgaris (Lamarck).

Another remarkable species, *Malleus vulgaris* (Fig. 144) is a rare shell, much valued and much sought after by amateurs and dealers.

The beautiful diaphanous nacre which embellishes the interior of so many ornamental cabinets are principally produced by the animal inhabiting the *Meleagrina*, a bivalve, sometimes designated the *pintadine*, or mother-of-pearl shell. This bivalve moors itself to the bottom of the sea by a strong byssus of a brownish colour. The door-posts of the shells are irregularly rounded in their young days; they are externally lightly foliated, and ornamented with bands of green and white, which spring from the summit in rays, and afterwards break off into two or three slightly scattered branches. In old age they become rugged and blackish. The shell is in its perfection when about eight or ten years old, their size being then about six inches in diameter, with a thickness of about an inch and a quarter.

Nacre is the hard and brilliant substance with which the valves of certain shells are lined in the interior. This substance is white, silky, slightly azure, and more or less iridescent. Most of the bivalves are supplied with nacre; some of them even yield a blue, or blue and violet pigment. The iridescent *Haliotis iris*, for instance, is an emerald-greenish blue of changing colour, with reflections of a purple violet. *Turbo argorastymus* (Linnæus) presents a mouth of bright silvery hue, while *Turbo chrysostomus* appears in all the glory of gold; but the Pintadine yields the purest white nacre, as well as the most uniform, and especially the thickest. This product owes its brilliant and delicate appearance to the play of light on it in its highly-polished state. For practical purposes the nacre is separated from the shell with an instrument; sometimes all the exterior part of the shell being dissolved away from the precious substance, leaving only the naked bed of nacre.

But the most interesting of all the nacre-bearing shells is the pearl oyster (*Meleagrina margaritifera*), the exterior, as well as the interior, of which is represented in Fig. 145. In the interior of the shell pearls are sometimes found so fine and so beautiful that they are only surpassed by the diamond. This shell is nearly round, and greenish in colour on the outside; it furnishes at once the finest pearls, under favourable circumstances, and the nacre so useful in many industrial arts. Fine pearls and nacre have, in short, the same origin. The nacre invests the whole interior of the shell of *Meleagrina margariti-*

fera ; being the same secretion which in the pearl has assumed the globular form: in one state it is deposited as nacre on the walls of the bivalve, in the other as a pearl in the fleshy interior of the animal. This nacre is therefore at once a calcareous and horny matter, which the animal secretes, and which it attaches to the interior walls of the

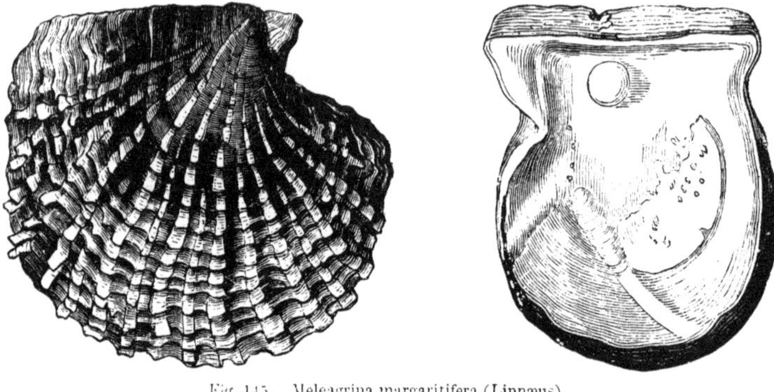

Fig. 145. Meleagrina margaritifera (Linnæus).
Outside of the shell. Inside of the shell.

shell during the several periods of its development. Pearls are formed of the same substance, only in place of being deposited upon the valves in beds, the material is condensed and agglomerated in small spheroids, which develop themselves either on the surface of the

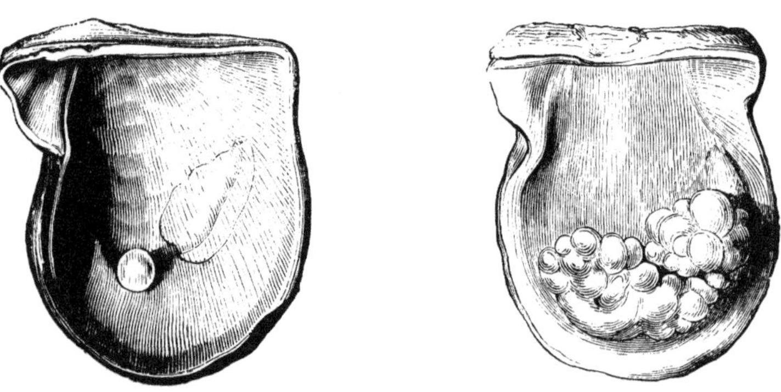

Fig. 146. Meleagrina margaritifera (Linnæus).

valves or in the fleshy part of the mollusc. Between nacre and pearls, therefore, there is only the difference of the form of deposition. Fig. 146 represents the pearl oyster with calcareous concretions in various states of progress.

The finest pearls, solidified drops of dew, as the Orientals term them in the language of poetry, are secretions supposed to be the result of disease in the animal. The matter, in place of being spread over the surface of the valves in their beds, is condensed either on the centre of the valves or in the interior of the organ, and forms a more or less rounded body. The pearls, when deposited on the valves, are generally adherent; those which originate in the body of the animal are always free. Generally we find some small foreign body in their centre which has served as a nucleus to the concretion, the body being perhaps a sterile egg of the mollusc, the egg of a fish, a rounded animalcule, a grain of sand even, round which has been deposited in concentric layers the beautiful and much-prized gem.

The Chinese, and other Eastern nations, are said to turn this fact in the natural history of bivalves to practical use in making pearls and cameos. By introducing into the mantle of the mollusc, or into the interior of a living valve, a round grain of sand, glass, or metal, they induce a deposit which in time yields a pearl, in the one case free, and in the other adhering to the shell. In some cases they are said to be produced in whole chaplets by the insertion of grains of quartz connected by a string into the mantle of a species of *Symphynota;* in other cases, a dozen Chinese figures seated have been produced by inserting small plates of figured tin in the valves of the same species.

The pearls are very small at first; they increase by annual beds deposited on the original nucleus, their brilliancy and shade of colour varying with that of the nacre from which they are produced. Sometimes they are diaphanous, silky, lustrous, and more or less iridescent; occasionally they turn out dull, obscure, and even smoky.

The pearl oyster is met with in very different latitudes; they are found in the Persian Gulf, on the Arabian coast, and in Japan, in the American seas, and on the shores of California, and in the islands of the South Sea; but the most important fisheries are found in the Bay of Bengal, Ceylon, and other parts of the Indian Ocean. The Ceylon fisheries are under Government inspection, and each year, before the fisheries commence, an official inspection of the coast takes place. Sometimes the fishing is undertaken on account of the State, at other times it is let to parties of undertakers. In 1804 the pearl fishery was granted to a capitalist for £120,000; but, to avoid impoverishing all the beds at once, the same part of the gulf is not fished every year.

The great fishery for mother-of-pearl Pintadines (*Meleagrina margaritifera*) takes place in the Gulf of Manaar, a large bay to the north-east of the island; it commences in the month of February or March, and continues thirty days, taken collectively, and occupies two hundred and fifty boats, which come from different parts of the coast; they reach the ground at daybreak, the time being indicated by a signal gun. Each boat's crew consists of twenty hands, and a negro. The rowers are ten in number. The divers divide themselves into two groups of five men each, who labour and rest alternately; they descend from forty to fifty feet, seventy being the very utmost they can accomplish, and eighty seconds the longest period the best divers can remain under water, the ordinary period being only thirty seconds. In order to accelerate their descent, a large stone is attached to a rope. According to travellers the oars are used to rig out a stage, across which planks are laid over both sides of the boat; to this stage the diving-stone is suspended. This stone is in the form of a pyramid, weighing about half-a-hundredweight; the cord which sustains it sometimes carries in its lower parts a sort of stirrup to receive the foot of the diver. At the moment of his descent he places his right foot in this stirrup, or, where there is no such provision, he rests it on the stone with the cord between his toes. In his left foot he holds the net which is to receive the bivalves; then, seizing with his right hand a signal-cord conveniently arranged for his purpose, and pressing his nostrils with the left hand, he dives, holding himself vertically, and balancing himself over his foot.

Each diver is naked, except the band of calico which surrounds the loins. Having reached the bottom, he withdraws his foot from the stone, which ascends immediately to the stage. The diver throws himself on his face, and begins to gather all the pintadines within his reach, placing them in his net. When he wishes to ascend he pulls the signal-cord, and is drawn up with all possible expedition.

A good diver, we have said, seldom remains more than thirty seconds under water at one time; but he repeats the operation three or four, and, in favourable circumstances, even fifteen or twenty times. The labour is extremely severe. On recovering the boat they sometimes discharge water tinged with blood by the mouth, nose, and ears.

They are also exposed to great danger from sharks, which lie in wait for and frequently devour the unhappy divers.

They continue to fish till mid-day, when a second gun gives the signal to cease. The proprietors wait on shore for their boats, in order to superintend their discharge, which must take place before night sets in, in order to prevent concealment and robbery.

In past times the Ceylon fisheries were very valuable. In 1797 they are said to have produced £144,000, and in 1798 as much as £192,000. In 1802 the fisheries were farmed for £120,000; but for many years the banks have been less productive, and are now said to yield the sum of £20,000 per annum.

The natives of the Bay of Bengal, those of the Chinese coast, of Japan, and the Indian Archipelago, all abandon themselves to the pearl fishery, the produce being estimated to realise at least £800,000. Fisheries analogous to those of Ceylon take place on the Persian coast, on the Arabian Gulf, along the coast of Muscat, and in the Red Sea.

In these countries the pearl fishing does not commence till the months of July and August, the sea being at that time calmer than in other months of the year. Arrived on their fishing-ground, the fishermen range their barques at a proper distance from each other, and cast anchor in water from eight to nine fathoms deep. The process is pursued here in a very simple manner. When about to descend the divers pass a cord, the extremity of which communicates with a bell placed in the barque, under the armpits; they put cotton in their ears, and press the nostrils together with a piece of wood or horn; they close their mouths hermetically, attach a heavy stone to their feet, and at once sink to the bottom of the sea, where they gather indiscriminately all shells within their reach, which they throw into a bag suspended round the haunches. When they require to breathe they sound the bell, and immediately they are assisted in their ascent.

On the oyster-banks off the Isle of Bahrein the pearl fishery produces about £240,000; and if we add to this the addition furnished by the other fisheries of the neighbourhood, the sum total yielded by the Arabian coast would probably not fall short of £350,000.

In South America similar fisheries exist. Before the Mexican conquest the pearl fisheries were located between Acapulco and the Gulf of Tehuantepec; subsequently they were established round the

Islands of Cubagua, Margarita, and Panama. The results became so full of promise that populous cities were not slow to raise themselves round these several places.

Under the reign of Charles V., America sent to Spain pearls valued at £160,000; in the present day they are estimated to be worth £60,000. In the places mentioned, the divers descend into the sea quite naked; they remain there from twenty-five to thirty seconds, during which space they can only secure two or three pintadines. They dive in this way a dozen times in succession, which gives an average of between thirty and forty bivalves to each diver.

The bivalve is carried on shore, and piled up on mats of Espartero grass. The mollusc dies, and soon becomes decomposed; it requires ten days to be thoroughly disorganized. When in a thoroughly corrupt state, they are thrown into reservoirs of sea-water, when they are opened, washed, and handed over to the dealers. The valves furnish *nacre*, and the parenchyma the *pearls*.

The valves are cleansed, and piled up in tons or casks; by raising their external surface plates of nacre are obtained more or less thick, according to the age of the mollusc.

Nacre of three kinds are distinguishable in commerce: silver-faced, bastard white, and bastard black. The first are sold in cases of two hundred and fifty to two hundred and eighty pounds; they are brought from the Indies, from China, and Peru. The ships of various nations import these shells as ballast. The second is delivered in casks of two hundred and fifty pounds weight; it is a yellowish white, and sometimes greenish; sometimes red, blue, and green.

Pearls form by far the most important branch of this material. When they are adherent to the valves they are detached with pincers; but, habitually, they are found in the parenchyma of the animal. In this case the substance is boiled, and afterwards sifted, in order to obtain the most minute of the pearls; for those of considerable size are sometimes overlooked in the first operation. Months after the mollusc is petrified, miserable Indians may be observed busying themselves with the corrupt mass, in search of small pearls which may have been overlooked by the workmen.

The pearls adherent to the valve are more or less irregular in their shape; they are sold by weight. Those found in the body of the animal, and isolated, are called *virgin pearls*, or *paragons*. They are globular, ovoid, or pyriform, and are sold by the individual pearl. In cleaning them, they are gathered together in a heap in a bag and worked with powdered nacre, in order to render them perfectly pure in colour and round in shape, and give them a polish; finally, they are passed through a series of copper sieves, in order to size them. These sieves, to the number of twelve, are made so as to be inserted one within the other, each being pierced with holes, which determine the size of the pearl and the commercial number which is to distinguish it. Thus, the sieve No. 20 is pierced with twenty holes, No. 50 with fifty holes, and so on up to No. 1000, which is pierced with that number of holes. The pearls which are retained in Nos. 20 to 80, said to be *mill*, are pearls of the first order. Those which pass and are retained between Nos. 100 to 800 are *vadivoe*, or pearls of the second order; and those which pass through all the others and are retained in No. 1000 belong to the class *tool*, or seed pearls, and are of the third order.

They are afterwards threaded; the small and medium-sized pearls on white or blue silk, arranged in rows, and tied with ribbon into a top-knot of blue or red silk, in which condition they are exposed for sale in rows, assorted according to their colours and quality. The small or seed pearls are sold by measure or weight.

In America the bivalve is opened with a knife, like the common edible oyster, and the pearl is obtained by breaking up the mollusc between the finger and thumb without waiting for its decomposition; nor is it boiled. This is a much longer and less certain process than that pursued in the East; but the Americans consider that the pearls are preserved in greater freshness by the process—that they get the true *orient* pearl, in short.

Some few pearls have become historical, from their size and beauty. A pearl from Panama, in the form of a pear, and about the size of a pigeon's egg, was presented in 1579 to Philip II., King of Spain: it was valued at £4000. A lady of Madrid possessed an American pearl in 1605 valued at 31,000 ducats.

The Pope Leo X. purchased a pearl of a Venetian jeweller for £14,000. Another was presented to the Sultan Soliman the Great by the Venetian Republic valued at £16,000. Julius Cæsar, who was a great admirer of pearls, presented one to Servilia which was valued at a million of sesterces, about £48,000 of our money.

There is no data for the volume or value of the two famous pearls of Cleopatra; one of these which the queen is said to have capriciously dissolved in vinegar and drank—Heavens preserve us from such a draught!—is said by some authors to have been worth £60,000; the other was divided into two parts, and suspended one half from each ear of the capitoline Venus. Another pearl was purchased at Califa by the traveller Tavernier, and is said to have been sold by him to the Shah of Persia for the enormous price of £180,000.

A prince of Muscat possessed a pearl so extremely valuable—not on account of its size, for it was only twelve carats, but because it was so clear and transparent that daylight was seen through it—he refused £4000 for it.

In the Zozema Museum at Moscow there is a pearl, called the "Pilgrim," which is quite diaphanous; it is globular in form, and weighs nearly twenty-four carats. It is said that the pearl in the crown of Rudolph II. weighed thirty carats, and was as large as a pear. This size, besides being indefinite, is more than doubtful.

The shahs of Persia actually possess a string of pearls, each individual of which is nearly the size of a hazel nut. The value of this string of jewels is inestimable.

At the Paris Exposition of 1855, Her Majesty the Queen exhibited some magnificent pearls; and on the same occasion the Emperor of the French exhibited a collection of 408 pearls, each weighing over nine pennyweights, all of perfect form and of the finest water. The Romans were passionately fond of pearls, and they have transmitted their taste to the Eastern nations, who attach notions of great grandeur and power to the possession of large and brilliant pearls.

The many interesting details connected with the oyster and its products have led us to write at greater length than we intended. With the *Meleagrina*, true proletarian of the ocean, we terminate the history of the first group of Acephalous Molluscs, whose mouths are largely opened, but which have neither tubes nor spiral openings.

CHAPTER XII.

THE MUSSEL—MYTILIDÆ.

> "Ecce inter virides jactatur mytilus algas."
>
> *Anthologia.*

This family of Acephalous Molluscs includes the Sea Mussel, *Mytilus;* the Pond Mussel, *Anodonta;* the Painter's Mussel, or Mulete, *Pina cardium*; and some others, in which the mantle is open before,

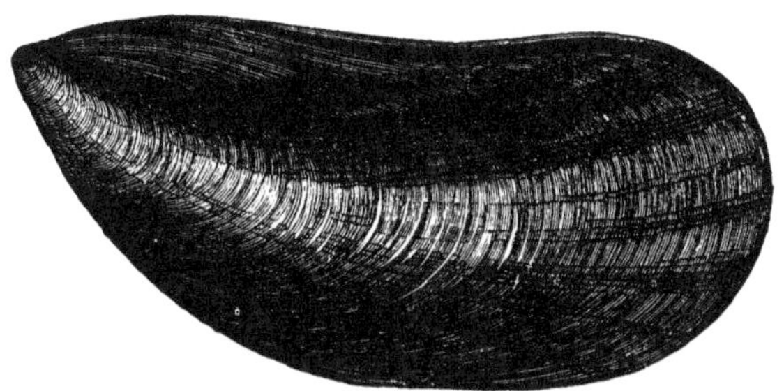

Fig. 147. Mytilus edulus (Linnæus).

with a distinct and separate opening for the issue of the residue of digestion; also a foot, which assists the animal to creep, or at least to draw itself forward, to guide it, and to attach itself by the byssus.

The well-known shell of the mussel (Fig. 147, *Mytilus edulus*) is longitudinal, equivalve, and regular, pointed at the base, with capacity to attach itself by a byssus; the hinge has no teeth, but a deep furrow, in which the ligament is located. In the genus *Mytilus* the byssus is divided to its base. In *Modiola* it has a common corneous centre. In *Pina* the anus is furnished with a long angular base. In all these genera the foot is small, its retractile muscles numerous, and the byssus large. In *Lythodemus* the byssus is rudimentary; the muscles are retractile, equal, and two pairs only. In *Anio, Cardium,* and *Hyria,* the foot is large and not byssiferous.

The animal, as described by M. Chenu, is elongate, oval, the lobes of the mantle simple or fringed, divided at the edge into two leaves, the interior being very short, bearing a fringe of small, cylindrical, and movable fillets; the exterior leaf is united to the shell very near the edge. The opening by which water and food are introduced supplies the branchiæ at the same time. The stomach consists of a white membrane, thin, like opaline, and presenting itself in longitudinal folds; the liver is granulous, composed of greenish grains more or less deep, contained in the meshes of a whitish tissue forming a thickish bed, which surrounds the stomach, the intestines taking the direction of the median and dorsal line, and beneath the heart are received and terminate in a small appendage, floating in the cavity of the mantle near to the hinge. The foot is, perhaps, the remarkable organ of the mussel: it is small, semi-lunar when not in motion, but capable of great elongation, resembling thus a sort of conical tongue, having a longitudinal furrow on its side. It is put in motion by several pairs of muscles, all of which penetrate and are interlaced with the tissue: behind it is the silky byssus. The mouth is large, and furnished with two pairs of soft palpi, which are pointed and fixed by their summit. Abdominal masses emanate, and on each side a pair of nearly equal branchiæ. Two additional muscles, one anterior and small, the other posterior, large, and rounded. At the base of the foot is a gland which furnishes a viscous secretion; this viscous liquid is organized and moulded in the groove of the foot, and forms a thread, and originates the byssus; it is a bundle of hairs, mane, or thread, which holds on to its shell.

The byssus plays an important part in the organization of the mussel. While the oyster remains eternally riveted to its rock, until torn from it by violence, the mussel moves about, and in this motion the byssus is an active agent. The mussel attaches its byssus to some fixed object, and drawing upon it, as upon a line, the shell is displaced. The house is drawn onwards; the animal is in motion. It takes great strides, but a fraction of an inch satisfies its desires; it is, however, an advance upon the oyster, and a lesson in mechanics. The mussel stretches out its foot, and, at the point chosen, it hooks on a hair of the byssus; then, withdrawing the foot suddenly, and hauling on the thread, the animal and shell are moved forward. Every time it repeats this motion it seems to attach an additional hair, so that at the end of the four and twenty hours it has used many inches in length of cordage. In the byssus of some mussels we find as many as a hundred and fifty of these small threads, with which the animal anchors itself most securely to the rock. Aided by this cordage, the mussel suspends itself to vertical rocks, holding on a little above the surface of the water, so that the shell is smooth and polished as compared with the coarse and rugged shell of the oyster.

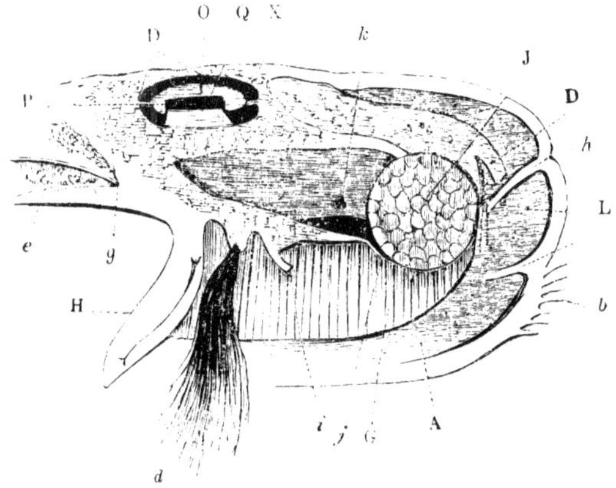

Fig. 148. Byssus, mantle, and oviduct.

A, right lobe of the mantle; D, rectum; G, branchiæ; H, foot; J, posterior muscle; L, superior tube; O, heart; P, ventricle; Q, auricle; X, pericardium; *b*, tentacles; *d*, byssus; *e*, gland of the byssus; *g*, retractile muscle of the foot; *h*, valves of the mantle; *i*, oviduct; *j*, orifice of the excretory organ; *k*, internal ditto.

The mussels, like the oysters, are gregarious, and widely diffused over all European seas. They abound on both sides the Channel, their lower price having procured for them the name of "the poor man's oyster;" but it is infinitely less digestible and savoury than its congener.

Many of our readers may think that mussels are found on the shore in a state of nature, of good size, well-flavoured, and fit for the table. Nothing of the kind! Detached from the rocks and cliffs of the sea, where it has been growing in a natural state, it is lean, small, acrid, and unwholesome food; and it is only when human industry intervenes to ameliorate this child of Nature that it becomes palatable and wholesome food. In order to trace the ameliorative process by which the coriaceous flesh of the mussel was rendered tender, fat, and even savoury, we must conduct the reader back into the middle ages.

Some time in 1236 a barque, freighted with sheep and manned by three Irishmen, came to grief upon the rocks in the creek of Aiguillon, a few miles from Rochelle. The neighbouring fishermen who came to the relief of the crew succeeded with great difficulty in saving the life of the master, a man named Walton. Exiled upon the lonely shore of the Aunis, with a few sheep saved from shipwreck, Walton at first supported himself by hunting sea-fowl, which frequented the shore and neighbouring marshes in vast flocks. He was a skilful fowler, and invented or adapted a peculiar kind of net, which he called the *night net.* This consisted of a net some three or four hundred yards in length by three in breadth, which he placed horizontally, like a screen, along the quiet waters of the bay, retaining it in its position by means of posts driven into the muddy bottom. In the obscurity of the night the wild-fowl, in floating along the surface of the waters, would come in contact with the net, and get themselves entangled in its meshes.

But the Bay of Aiguillon was only a vast lake of mud, in which boats moved with difficulty, and Walton, having arranged his bird-net, began to consider what kind of boat would enable him most conveniently to navigate this sea of mud. The flat-bottomed, square-sided boat, known in our rivers as a *punt,* and on the Norman coast as an *acon,* was the result. Walton's boat had a wooden frame some three yards long and one in breadth and depth, the fore part of which sloped down into the water, in the form of a prow, at a slight angle. In propelling the boat the rower, who occupied the stern of the punt, knelt on his right knee (as represented in Fig. 149), inclining forward, with one hand on each edge, and the left leg outside the boat. A vigorous push with the left foot gave the frail boat an impulse, under which it rapidly traversed the bay from one point to the other.

The mussels swarmed in the little bay; and Walton soon remarked that they attached themselves by preference to that part of his post a little above the mud, and that those so placed soon became fatter, as well as more agreeable to the taste, than those buried in the mud. He saw in this peculiarity the elements of a sort of mussel culture which might become a new branch of industry. "The practices he introduced," says M. Coste, "were so happily adapted to the requirements of the new industry that, after eight centuries, they are still the rules by which the rich patrimony he created for a numerous population is governed. He seems to have applied himself to the enterprise conscious not only of the service he was rendering to his contemporaries, but desirous that their descendants should remember him, for in every instance he has given to the apparatus which he invented the form of his initial letter W. After due consideration, Walton

Fig. 149. Punt or Pirogue of the Marsh.

began to carry out his design. He planted a long range of piles along the low marshy shore, each pair forming a letter V, the front of the letter being towards the sea, and each limb diverging at an angle of forty-five degrees. These posts were driven about a yard asunder; they were about twelve feet long, six feet being above water, and interlaced with branches wattled together, so as to form continuous hurdles, each about two hundred yards long, which are called *bouchots*. By the assistance of this apparatus, which intercepted spat which would otherwise have been swept away to sea by the tide, Walton formed a magnificent collection of mussels; but he did not abandon his isolated piles. These, being without fascines or branches, and always submerged, arrested the spat at the moment of emission."

The advantages of this system of culture adopted by the Irish exile were so obvious that his neighbours along the shore were not slow to imitate his example. In a short time the whole bay was covered with similar bouchots. At the present time these lines of hurdles form a perfect forest in the little creek. About two hundred and thirty thousand piles support a hundred and twenty-five thousand fascines, which, according to M. Coste, "bend all the year under a harvest

Fig. 150. Isolated piles covered with the spawn of mussels.

which a squadron of ships of the line would fail to float." There are about five hundred of these bouchots in the bay, each from two hundred to two hundred and fifty yards in length and six feet high.

The isolated piles are without palisadoes, and are uncovered only at spring tides. In the months of February and March the spat collected on them scarcely equals in size a grain of linseed; by the month of May it will be about the size of a split pea; in July, a small haricot bean: this is the moment for its transplantation. In this month the *bouchotiers*, as the men occupied in this culture are called, launch their punts and proceed to the part of the bay where these piles are driven. They detach with a hook the agglomerated masses of young mussels, which they gather in baskets, and carry them to their bouchots. These bouchots, that is to say, the piles covered with fascines and branches, are of four different heights, forming, so to speak, four stages, according to the age and growth of the mussel. Each stage receives the mollusc suitable to it. In the first stage of its existence the mussel cannot endure exposure to the air, and remains constantly under water, except at the period of spring tides. These are gathered in sacks made of old matting, or suspended in interstices of the basket-work. "These immense palisades," says M. Coste, "cover themselves with black clusters of mussels developed between the meshes of their tissues." At that time the second rows are cleared away to make

Fig. 151. Piles, with basket-work, covered with mussels in a fit state to be gathered in.

room for younger generations; the mussels, which no longer dread the air, are transported to the more advanced bouchots, which remain above water in all tides, where they stay till they are fit for market, which usually happens after ten or twelve months of culture on the more advanced bouchots.

But, in order to prepare for this consummation, they are subjected to a second and even a third remove. There is no longer any danger in subjecting them to the air for many hours. From this they pass to a fourth stage, termed *Amont* (Fig. 151). From this stage the full-grown mussel is removed. Under this system of culture the reproduction, nursing, collecting, and preparing for market, are made simultaneously. From July to January the mussel trade is in full operation, and the flesh in perfection. From February to April is the close season; their flesh is then poor and leathery. It is also remarked that those which inhabit the upper rows of the wicker-work are of a mellower flavour than those on the lower ranks, and that the intermediate rows are an improvement on those which are buried in the mud, although even these are preferable to mussels gathered on the sea shore in a state of nature.

M. Coste gives a graphic description of the manner in which this industry is carried on. "Having supplied the neighbouring villages," he says, "for the purpose of supplying the more distant cities, the bouchotiers land their punts, filled with mussels, which their wives carry into grottoes hollowed out of the cliffs; there they clean and pack them in hampers, baskets, and panniers, for conveyance by carts or pack-horses. They depart on their respective journeys at night, so as to reach their markets at La Rochelle, Rochefort, Surgéres, Saint-Jean-d'Angely, Angoulême, Niort, Poictiers. Tours, Angers, and Saumur, at an early hour. A hundred and forty horses and ninety carts make upwards of thirty-three thousand journeys annually to these cities. Besides this, forty or fifty boats come from Bordeaux, the isles of Ré and Oleron, and from the sands of Olonne, making an aggregate of seven hundred and fifty voyages per annum, distributing the harvest of the little bay at places where horses could not serve the purpose.

"A bouchot, well furnished, supplies annually, according to the length of its wings, from four to five hundred charges. The charge is a hundred and fifty kilogrammes (over three hundred pounds), and sells for five francs; a single bouchot thus carries a harvest equal in weight to a hundred and thirty to a hundred and forty thousand pounds, equal in value to £100; the whole bay probably yielding a gross revenue of £480,000. This figure, and the abundant harvest which produces it, gives only a slight idea of the alimentary resources of the sea shore; and every part of the coast, properly adapted for the purpose, could be turned to equal advantage. In the meantime, the Bay of Aiguillon remains a monument of what one man may accomplish."

While commending the mussel as an important article of food, we must not conceal the fact, that it has produced in certain persons very grave effects, showing that for them its flesh has the effects of poison. The symptoms, commonly observed two or three hours after the repast, are weakness or torpor, constriction of the throat and swelling of the head, accompanied by great thirst, nausea, frequent vomitings, and eruption of the skin and severe itching.

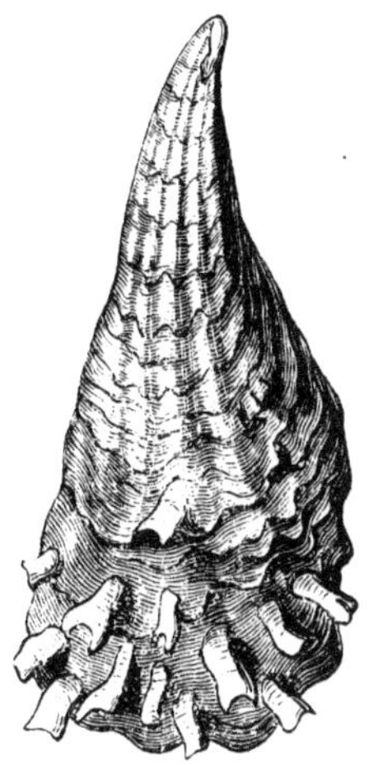

Fig. 152. Pina radis (Linnæus).

The cause of these attacks is not very well ascertained; they have in turn been ascribed to the presence of copper pyrites in the neighbourhood of the mussel; to certain small crabs which lodge themselves as parasites in the shell of the mussel; to the spawn of star-fishes or medusæ that the mussel may have swallowed. But, probably, the true cause of this kind of poisoning resides in the predisposition of individuals. The remedy is very simple: a vomit, accompanied by drinking plentifully of a light acidulated beverage.

The genus *Pina*, so called by Linnæus, from one of the species which was so designated from the resemblance of its byssus to the aigrette or plumelet which the Roman soldiers attached to the helmet. French naturalists name them *jambonneau*, from their singular resemblance to a dried ham (Figs. 152 and 153), their brown, smoky colour not a little aiding the resemblance. This shell is fibrous, horny, very thin and fragile, compressed, regular, and equivalve, triangularly pointed in front, round or truncated behind. The hinge is linear, straight, and without teeth; the ligament, in great part internal, occupies more than half the anterior half of the dorsal edge of the shell, forming a straight elongated fossette.

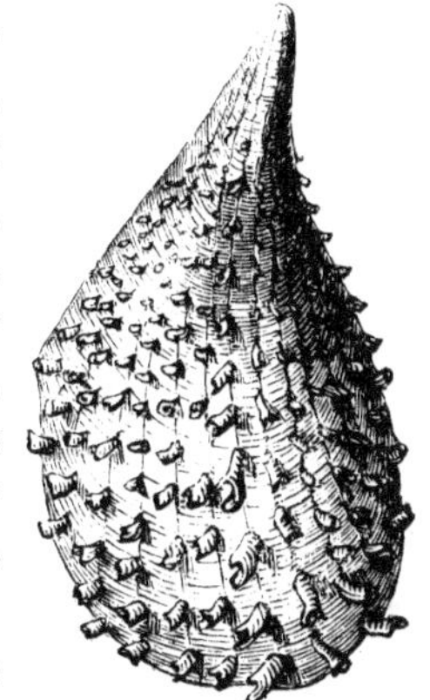

Fig. 153. Pina nigrina (Lamarck).

The animal is thick, elongated, with mantle open behind, presenting a conical furrowed foot, bearing a considerable byssus.

The *Pinæ* are found in almost every sea, and at various depths; they are constantly attached by their byssus, and in a vertical position, the larger side of their shell being uppermost. They assemble on sandy bottoms in considerable numbers. The byssus has in all ages fixed the attention of the Mediterranean fishermen upon these curious shells. With its tuft of fine silky hairs, six or seven inches in length, and its fine reddish-brown colour, articles of luxury are formed, which are often mentioned by the Latin writers. The threads of the byssus, which are remarkable for their unalterable colour, were formed by both Greeks and Romans into a fabric to which there is nothing analogous in the world. The Maltese and Neapolitans still fashion soft tissues from it, but the stuffs so manufactured are pure objects of curiosity.

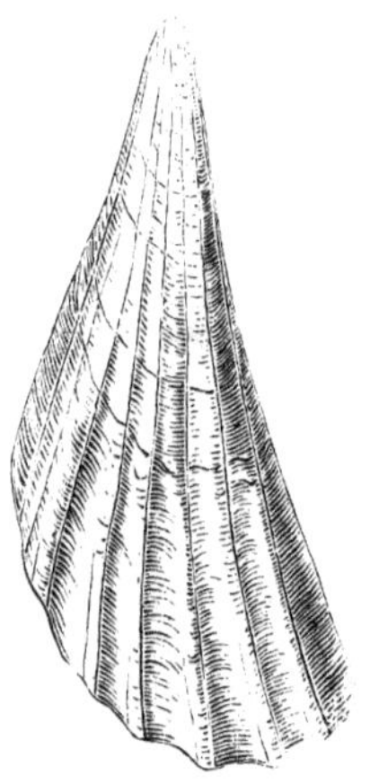

Fig. 154. Pina bullata (Swainson).

Twelve species are described as living in the several seas. *Pina nobilis* (Fig. 155), the byssus of which was employed in the ancient Neapolitan industry, inhabits the shores of the Mediterranean. *Pina bullata*, Swainson (Fig. 154), is also a well-known species.

The pond mussels, *Anodonta*, are found in lakes, rivers, and seas of almost every region of the globe. Their shells are rounded or oval, generally very thin, regular, and equivalve, not gaping, the hinges without teeth, whence their name from the Greek, ὀδόντος, without teeth. These shells are nacred inside, but very plain; their external epidermis being of a grave tint of greenish black.

Fig. 155. Pina nobilis, with its byssus (Linnæus).

The *Anodonta cygnea* (Fig. III., Pl. XVI.) is broad, deep, and light, and is sometimes employed for skimming the cream off milk. The genus is divided into many groups, the principal forms of which are represented in Pl. XVI.

The river mussels, *Unio*, are, like the Anodontas, found in the muddy bottoms of all countries. The animal resembles the Anodonta, but the shell pre-

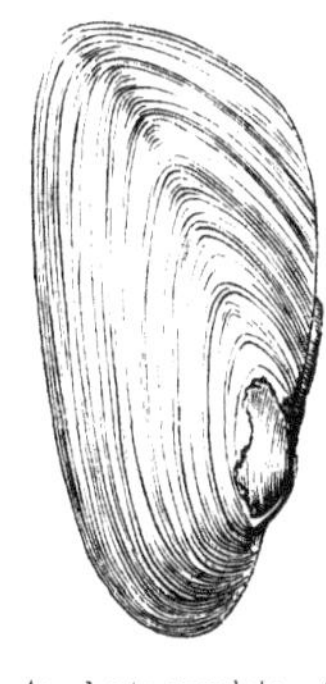

I. Anodonta angulata. (Lea.)

II. Anodonta ensiformis. (Spix.)

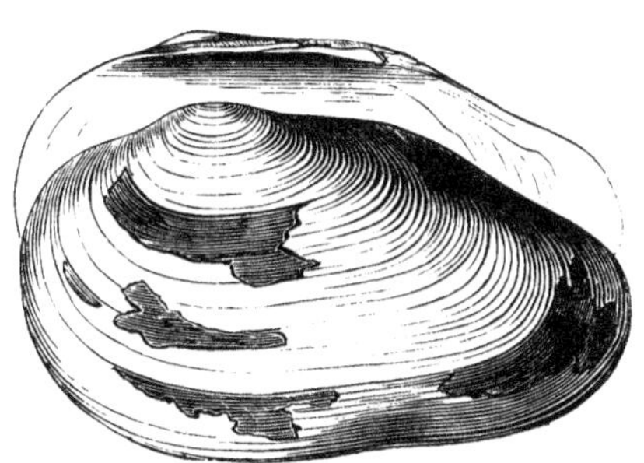

III. Anodonta cygnea. (Linn.)

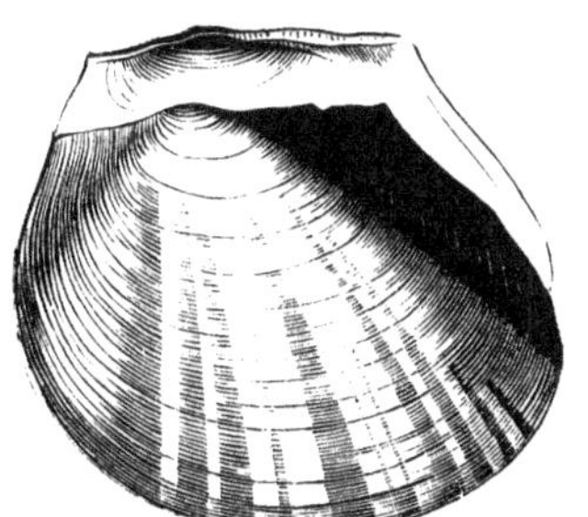

IV. Anodonta magnifica. (Lea.)

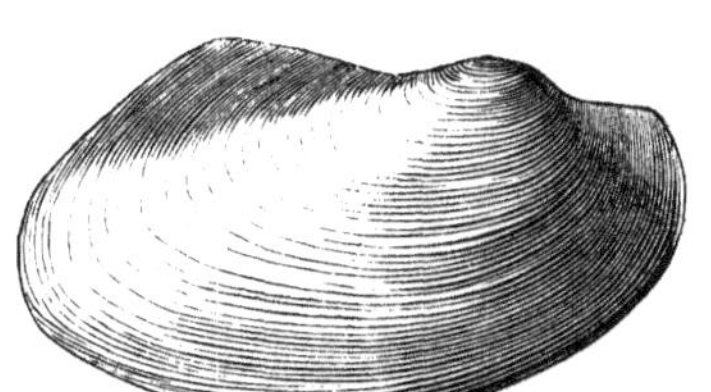

V. Anodonta anserina. (Spix.)

VI. Anodonta latomarginata. (Lea.)

PLATE XVI.—Anodonta.

sents a toothed hinge. The lower face of the valve is nacrous, but shaded with purplish violet, copreous, and iridescent; the anterior face is of a green colour, which varies from tender to blackish green.

Among the species found in European seas may be noted the Rhine mussel, a large species, the nacre of which is employed for ornamental purposes. *Unio littoralis* (Cuvier), represented in Fig. 156, and the painter's mussel, *Unio pictorum* (Fig. 157), employed in the arts to contain certain colours. Those known as the river mussels are leathery, of an insipid taste, and scarcely eatable: the finest species are found in the great American rivers.

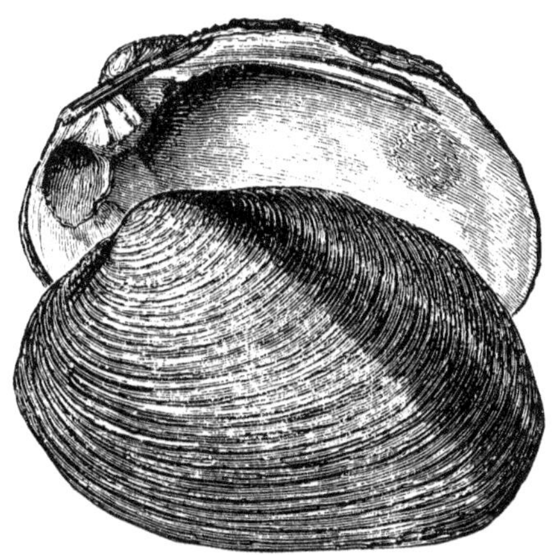

Fig. 156. Unio littoralis (Cuvier).

Mussels, as we have seen, produce pearls of moderate value Linnæus, who was aware of the origin of the Pintadine pearls, and of pearls in general, was also aware of the possibility of producing them artificially

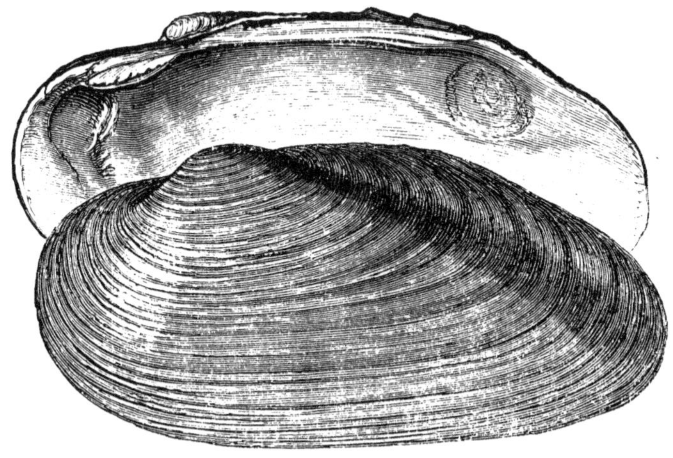

Fig. 157. Unio pictorum (Linnæus).

from various molluscs. He suggested bringing together a number of mussels, piercing holes in their shells with an auger in order to produce a wound, and afterwards pack them for five or six years to give the pearl time to form. The Swedish Government consented to try the experiment, and long did so in secret; pearls were produced, but they were of no value, and the enterprise was abandoned as unsuccessful.

Scottish pearls were much celebrated in the middle ages, and between the years 1761 and 1784 pearls to the value of £10,000 were sent to London from the rivers Tay and Isla; "and the trade carried on in the corresponding years in the present century," says Mr. Bertram, "is far more than double that amount." The pearl, according to Mr. Bertram, is found in a variety of the mussel, which is characterised by the valves being united by a broad hinge, and having a strong fibrous byssus, with which it attaches itself to other shells, to rocks, and other solid substances. "The pearl fisheries of Scotland," he adds, "may become a source of wealth to the people living on the large rivers, if prudently conducted." Mr. Unger, a dealer in gems in Edinburgh, having discerned the capabilities of the Scotch pearl as a gem of value, has established a scale of prices which he gives for them, according to their size and quality; and it is now a fact that the beautiful pink-hued pearls of our Scottish streams are admired beyond the orient pearl. Empresses and queens, and royal and noble ladies, have made large purchases of these gems; and Mr. Unger estimates the sum paid to pearl-finders in the summer of 1864 at £10,000. The localities successfully fished have been the classic Doon, the Forth, the Tay, the Don, the Spey, the Isla, and most of the Highland rivers of note.

Among molluscs, the genus *Tridacnæ* furnish the largest shells known among Acephalous Molluscs. The historian of the wars of Alexander the Great speaks of oysters inhabiting the Indian Ocean which were more than a foot long; these were probably *Tridacnæ*, the shells of which were most likely to be seen by the Macedonian conquerors. The valves of *Tridacna gigas* are sometimes found a yard and a half in length, and weighing five hundred pounds. Magnificent examples may be seen in the church of Saint Sulpice, Paris, where they hold the holy water. These beautiful shells were the gift of the Venetian Republic to Francis I. Under Louis XIV., the

Plate XVII.—Tridacna gigantea.—Holy Water Basin in the Church of Saint Sulpice at Paris.

curé Languet had them presented to the church of Saint Sulpice, where they are used as fonts for holy water. Another pair are exhibited in the church of Saint Eulala, at Montpelier, but much smaller in size. The shells of *Tridacnæ* are formed, as represented in Pl. XVII., of three acute angles, festooned on their edges by broad sides bristling with white scales. The hinges have two teeth; the ligament is elongated and external.

The animal of *Tridacnæ* is remarkable for its fine colours. *Tridacna safrana* is of a beautiful blue round the edges, rayed through a shade of very pale blue. More in the interior is a row of small moons of a yellowish green; the centre is a bright violet, with brownish longitudinal punctured lines. "We have at this moment before our eyes," say the travellers Quoy and Gaimard, "one of the most charming spectacles that can be seen, when at a little depth beneath the surface a number of these animals display the brilliant velvety colours and varying shades of their submarine parterres. As we can only perceive the gaping opening of the valves, we may imagine to ourselves what is its first aspect." The mantle of the animal is closed and ample; its edges are swollen, and reunited in nearly its whole circumference in such a manner as to leave only three very small openings—two in the upper part; the one serves the purpose of discharging the products of digestion, the other gives entrance and exit to the water necessary for respiratory purposes. The third opening is in the lower part of the body, and free; it leaves an opening for the passage of the foot, which is enormous, and is surrounded with an ample tuft of byssoidal fibres.

Aided by this silky tuft, the animal attaches itself to the rocks, and suspends its weighty shell from them. If it is intended to remove those attached to the sides of the rock, it is necessary to cut the cords of the tendonous byssus, by which it is held suspended, with a hatchet.

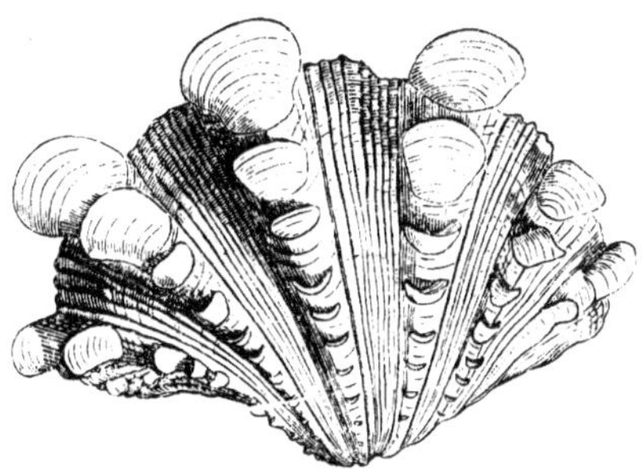

Fig 158. Tridacna squamosa (Lamarck).

All the Tridacnæ are inhabitants of Tropical seas. The *Tridacna gigas* is a native of the Indian Ocean. The flesh, though coriaceous and by no means of an agreeable flavour, is a great resource to the poor Indians. The accompanying representations of *Tridacna squamosa* (Figs. 158 and 159) will convey a general idea of the genus.

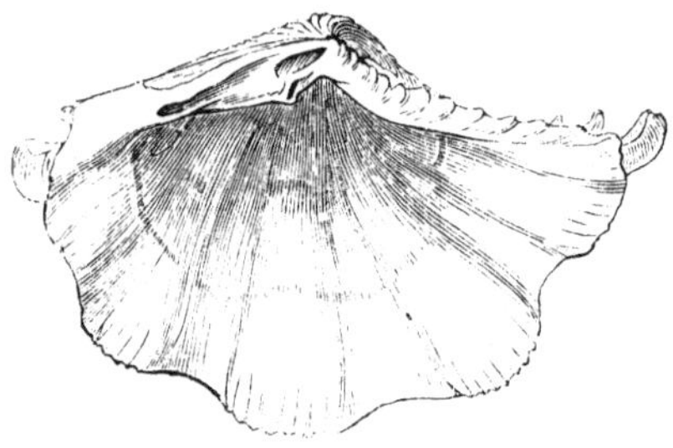

Fig. 159. Tridacna squamosa, on the inside (Lamarck).

In the small family of which we have made the Tridacna the representative, as well as in some preceding families, the mantle of the animal is more or less largely open, but never with such a prolongation as to form tubes. In the *Cardiums*, now under consideration, as well as *Donax*, *Tellina*, and *Venus*, the respiratory organs are somewhat modified, so as to adapt them to the habits of the animal. All these molluscs live buried in the mud or sand, and two great tubes issuing from the interior of their bodies bring the atmospheric air into communication with their respiratory organ—namely, the *branchial leaves*.

The Cardiums, so called from the fancied resemblance which most of the shells bear in shape to a heart (*καρδία*), are abundantly diffused in every sea. The shell is convex, as we see in *C. hians* (Fig. 160),

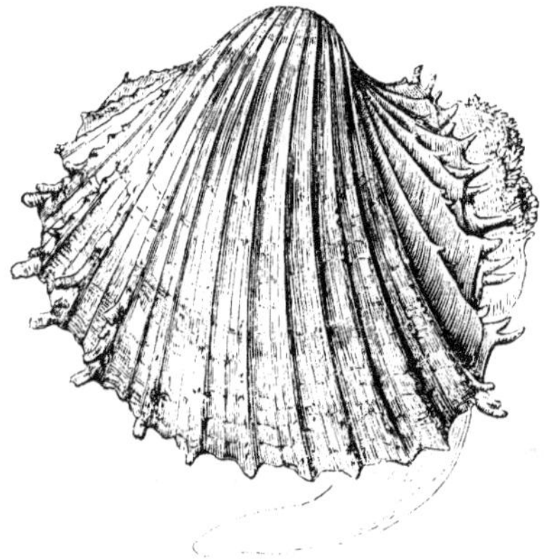

Fig. 160. Cardium hians (Brocchi).

Fig. 161. Cardium Greenlandicum (Chem nitz).

some what heart-shaped, equivalved, the edges dentate or corrugated, the hinge furnished with four teeth upon each valve. The accessary ornaments vary with the species, some being smooth, as in *Cardium*

Greenlandicum, Chemnitz (Fig. 161); others, and by far the greater number, are furnished with regular sides, generally obtuse, sometimes in ridges diverging from the point and armed with straight or curved spines, arranged in the oddest manner, as in *Cardium aculeatum* (Fig. 162).

In *C. hians* (Fig. 160), the mantle has a large opening in front, fringed anteriorly with papillæ in the form of tentacula; the inhabitant of the shell has a very large foot, with a bend or knee near the middle; its mouth is transverse and funnel-shaped, and furnished with a triangular appendage. One of the peculiarities in the organization of these molluscs is its direct connection with their mode of life. In short, these molluscs, which most commonly live on the sea shore, and bury themselves in the sand to the depth of four or five inches, are enabled to breathe, to draw water for their nourishment, and also

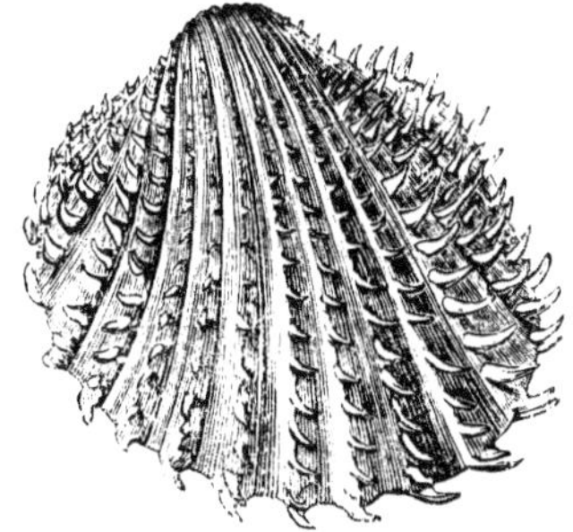

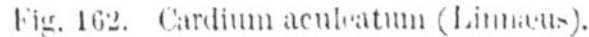

Fig. 162. Cardium aculeatum (Linnæus).

Fig. 163. Cardium edulus (Linnæus).

to throw off the products of digestion, by having the mantle prolonged into two tubes, the orifices of which reach to the surface of the soil. By means of these feet and an extremely curious organ of locomotion, the Cardiums can at will issue from their holes and re-enter them. The fishermen of the shore easily recognise the presence of these animals by the little jets of water which they throw up through the sands.

These molluscs are found in every sea on the globe, and under all latitudes. Many of them belong to our own and the French coasts, where they are eagerly sought for by collectors, as well as for food. The flesh of the animal, however, is coriaceous, and little esteemed. The species most common on the littoral of the Atlantic is *Cardium edulus* (Fig. 163), its white or fawn-coloured shell being hollowed out into six and twenty furrows, forming so many corrugated ripples on its side.

Cardium costatum (Fig. 164) is an exotic species which inhabits

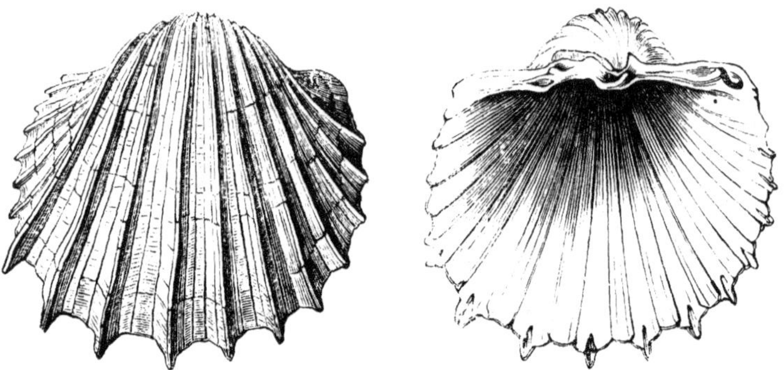

Fig. 164. Cardium costatum (Linnæus).

the coast of Guinea and the Senegal, the shell of which, white and fragile, is much sought after by collectors, and brings a high price when the two valves can be identified as belonging to the same individual.

Along the shores of the Channel and in the Mediterranean there are few bivalves more abundant than the several species of the genus *Donax*. They live near the shore in shallow water, burying themselves perpendicularly in the sand. They have the very singular habit, considering their apparent helplessness, of being able to leap to a certain height and then project themselves ten or twelve inches. This may often be witnessed in the case of individuals left by the retreating tide; if seized by the hand, and attempts are made to disengage them from the sand, they continue to impress on their shell a sudden and energetic movement, aided by the elasticity of their foot, which is at once decisive and angular.

The shell of the *Donax* is nearly triangular in shape, compressed, longer than it is high, regular, equivalve, not equilateral; the hinge with three or four teeth on each valve.

The animal is slightly compressed, and more or less triangular. Its mantle, which forms two symmetrical lobes enveloping the body, is open pretty nearly in all its extent, but is united posteriorly, and terminates in two syphons or nearly equal tubes, as in Fig. 128, p. 323. One of these tubes serves the purpose of respiration: it is the *bronchial syphon.* The other, serving the purpose of ejecting the products of digestion, is termed the *anal* tube. The tentacles of the bronchial tube seem to be possessed of exquisite sensibility. When

Fig. 165. Donax rugosus (Linnæus).

Fig. 166. Donax denticulatus.

touched, the animal draws in its syphon, and only puts it forth anew when the danger has passed. The species of *Donax* are very numerous, especially in the Asiatic and American seas. Among the European species we may mention *Donax rugosus* (Fig. 165) and *Donax denticulatus* (Fig. 166).

Fig. 167. Tellina radiata (Linnæus).

Next to *Donax* naturalists rank the genus *Tellina*, which includes many species of very minute shells, all remarkable for their beauty of form, and for their brilliant and varied colours. One of these, called the Rising Sun (*Tellina radiata*), is represented in Fig. 167. The Tellinas are found in every sea; the French coast furnishes many species: examples, *Tellina virgata* (Fig. 168) and *Tellina sulphurea* (Lamarck)

Fig. 168. Tellina virgata (Linnæus).

(Fig. 169). In Fig. 170 *Tellina donacina* is represented with its two vital tubes, or syphons.

Fig. 169. Tellina sulphurea (Lamarck). Fig. 170. Tellina donacina (Linnæus).

The respective genera of *Venus* and *Cytherea* owe their mythological names to the beauty of their shells, which are distinguished for the elegance of form and variety of colouring with which the shell is ornamented. These acephalæ of size so small, like their congeners, inhabit every sea; they are found in every region of the globe, more than a hundred and fifty species being known. The shell is elliptic in form, the valves smooth, striated, spiny, and lamellous, like those of Cardium and Donax. Like these, they bury themselves in the sand.

Among the vast number of species, many of them are extremely rare, and much sought after by collectors in consequence of their great beauty. In the principal ports of France, *Venus verrucosa* (Fig. 171), and another species known in the south of France under the name of Clovisse, are eaten there like oysters. Prepared with fine herbs, the clovisse, we have M. Figuier's authority for saying, is not to be despised. "We may be believed also," he adds, "if we add that nothing is more delicious than to eat the living clovisse torn from the rock of the Phara of Lake Thau, when the Mediterranean sun of a day in winter is shining down upon us, the heart rejoicing in its twentieth year." In Pl. XVIII. some of the principal species are represented, along with some of the more remark-

Fig. 171. Venus verrucosa (Linnæus).

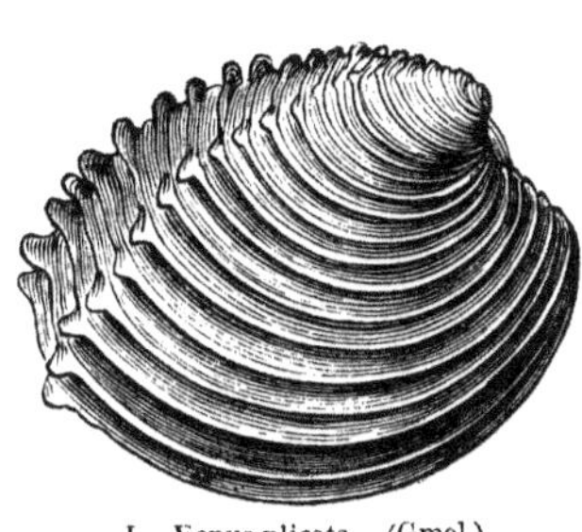

I. Venus plicata. (Gmel.)

II. Venus puerpera. (Linn.)

III. Venus reticulata. (Linn.)

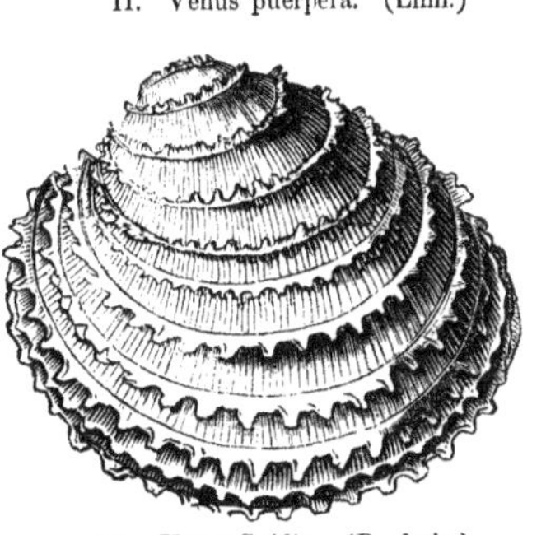

IV. Venus Gnidia. (Broderip.)

V. Cytherea zonaria. (Lamarck.)

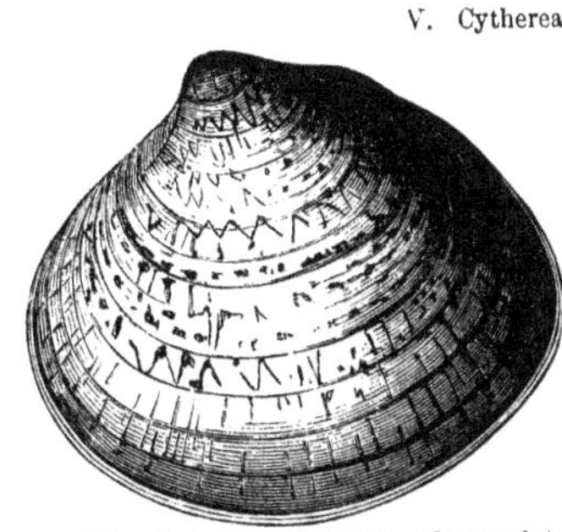

VI. Cytherea petechialis. (Lamarck.)

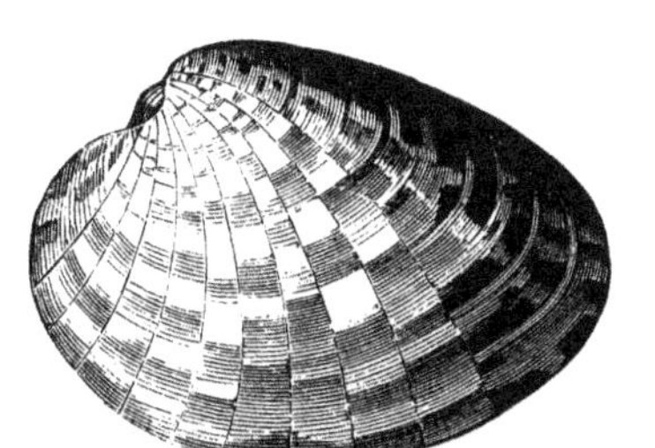

VII. Cytherea maculata. (Linn.)

PLATE XVIII.—Venus and Cytherea.

able species of *Cytherea*. In Fig. 172 we have the elegantly pencilled shell of *Cytherea geographica*, together with the animal in its natural connection.

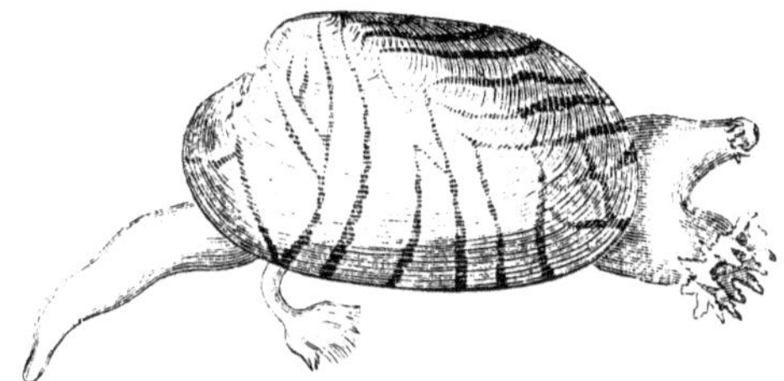

Fig. 172. Cytherea geographica (Chemnitz).

The last sections of Acephalous Molluscs which we shall notice are the Solens, Pholades, and Teredos, which have received from Cuvier the common designation of *Acephales renfermé*. The kind of life of these molluscs is most singular. Not only do they bury themselves in the sand, as those do of which we have been speaking — they even excavate a dwelling for themselves in the solid rock of hardest stone, and even in wood. They may be called mining or boring molluscs—their labour, incessant, obstinate, slow, silent, and hidden, often causing terrible ravages in the constructions of man.

The Solens, or Razor-fish, are easily recognised by their elongated shell gaping at both extremities. These molluscs live buried vertically in the sand, a short distance from the shore; the hole which they have hollowed, and which they never quit, sometimes attains as much as two yards in depth; by means of their foot, which is large, conical, swollen in the middle, and pointed at its extremity, they raise themselves with great agility to the entrance of their hole. They bury themselves rapidly, and disappear on the slightest approach of danger.

When the sea retires, the presence of the Solen is indicated by a small orifice in the sand, whence escape at intervals bubbles of air. In order to attract them to the surface, the fishermen throw into the hole a pinch of salt; immediately the sand becomes stirred, and the animal presents itself just above the point of its shell. It must be seized at once, for it disappears again very quickly, and no renewed efforts will bring it to the surface a second time.

This shell has by some been compared to a knife-handle; by others to a razor, which has become its popular name. It is a thin, transparent, long and slender equivalved bivalve, with parallel edges, gaping and truncated at both extremities. The tints are rose-coloured, bluish grey, and violet; the valves slightly covered with an epidermis of a greenish brown.

The animal which lives in this elegant dwelling has the form of an elongated cylinder. Its mantle is closed in its whole length, and only open at the ends at one side for the passage of the food, and at the other for the passage of a tube formed of two syphons united together. This curious shell, the various species of which are represented in Pl. XIX., are known as razor-fish, sabre-fish, and other names, which in some respects indicate the peculiar form of the shell.

In the *Pholadæ* we have a family which not only bury themselves

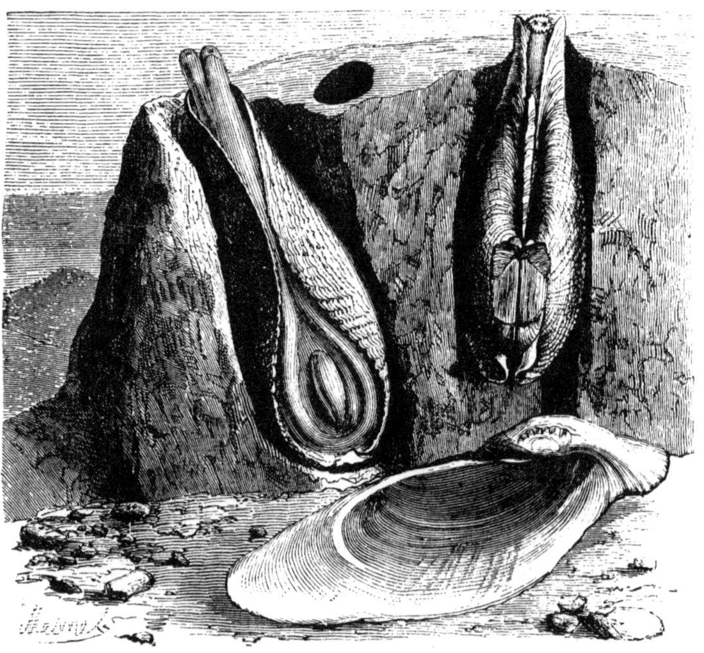

Fig. 173. Pholades dactylus, having hollowed out a shelter in a block of gneiss.

in the sand, like the Solens and their congeners, but they are able in some mysterious way to excavate for themselves a dwelling in argillaceous rocks, and even in harder stone. The engraving represents *P. dactylus*, which has hollowed itself a home out of a block of gneiss. This dwelling is a cell just deep enough to contain the animal and its shell, as represented in Fig. 173. To excavate its cell at the bottom of one of these gloomy retreats seems to be all that the animal lives for. To ascend to the summit or sink to the bottom of their narrow dormer window makes up all the accidents of existence to these strange creatures;

I. Solen siliqua. (Linn.)

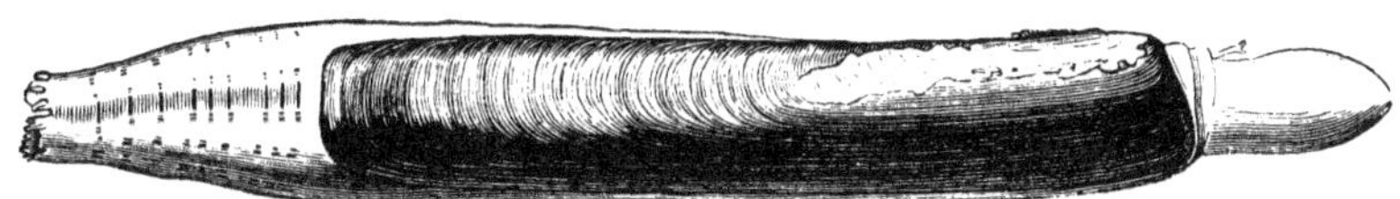

II. Solen vagina. (Linn.)

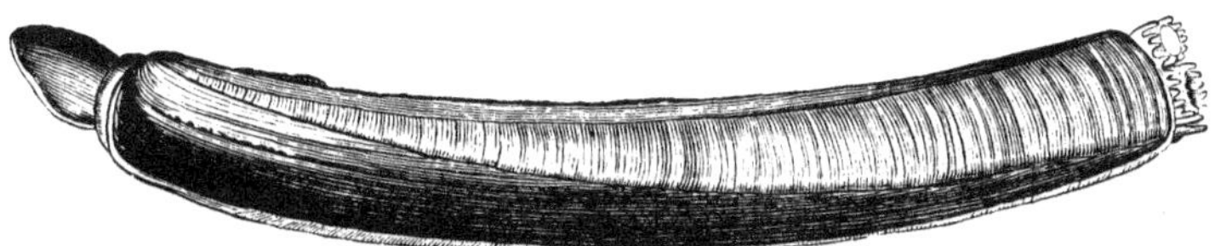

III. Solen ensis. (Linn.)

IV. Solen ensis major. (Lamarck.)

V. Solen ambiguus. (Lamarck.)

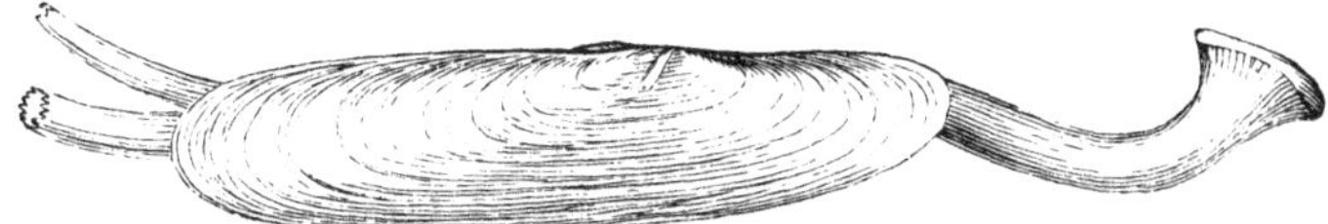

VI. Solen legumen.

PLATE XIX.—Razor-fish. Solenidæ.

they are born to dig their grave, and there they die in the groove of a rock. What a profound mystery does the organization of animal life present! What thoughts does not the life of these little beings suggest! Submerged at the bottom of the waters, penned up eternally in a gallery of stone not an inch in depth! For what were they created? Human intelligence recoils before such unfathomable mysteries!

How the Pholadæ contrive, with their inefficient tools, to bore into the heart of the stone which shelters them, is a point by no means settled. The organization of the mollusc is not even perfectly known. In its structure the shell differs notably from other Acephalous Molluscs, which led Linnæus to place it with the multivalve shells. Between the two ordinary valves, in short, this shell presents certain accessary pieces, smaller than the true valves, and placed near the hinge, as represented in *Pholas dactylus* (Fig. 174), pieces which would not be there without a purpose.

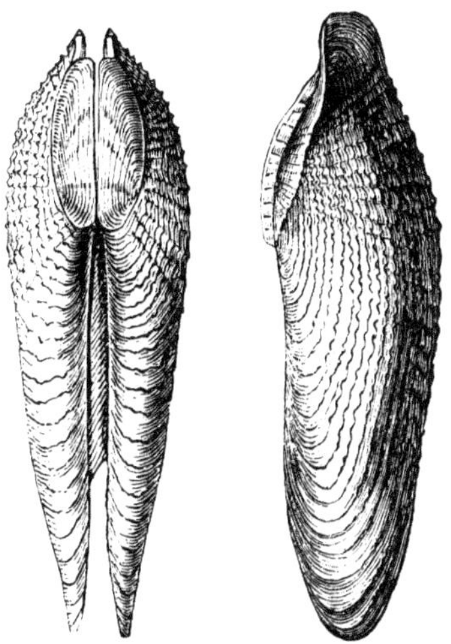

Fig. 174. Pholas dactylus (Linnæus).

The shell is equivalve, gaping on each side, swelling below, very thin, transparent, and white. The animal is a thick, white, elongated, fleshy body; its mouth opening anteriorly, throws out a long tube traversed by two canals or syphons, through one of which the water necessary for the respiration of the animal is absorbed, and ejected through the other. Through another opening in the mantle a very thick and short foot is protruded.

"We lift one from its cavity," says Gosse, "all helpless and unresisting, yet manifesting its indignation at the untimely disturbance by successive spasmodic contractions of these rough yellow syphons, each accompanied with a forcible *jet d'eau*, a polite squirt of sea-water into our face; while at each contraction in length the base swells out, till the compressed valves of the sharp shell threaten to pierce through its substance."

By what means do the Pholades contrive to hollow out their cell? What implement do they employ in their very limited space? This has long puzzled philosophers. The animal was supposed by some to secrete an acid which dissolved the stone and other substances. But how could this be done without dissolving the shell? De Blainville thought that a simple movement of the shell, incessantly repeated, would suffice to pierce the stone macerated by the water inhaled through the breathing apparatus. Experiment proves that this explanation is the correct one. Mr. Robertson, of Brighton, exhibited living Pholades in the act of boring through masses of chalk: "A living combination of three implements: a hydraulic apparatus, a rasp, and a syringe." "If you examine these living shells," says Gosse, "you will see that the fore part, where the foot protrudes, is set with stony points arranged in transverse and longitudinal rows, the former being the result of elevated ridges, radiating from the hinge, the latter that of the edges of successive growths of the shell. These points have the most accurate resemblance to those set on a steel rasp in a blacksmith's shop. It is interesting to know that the shell is preserved from being itself prematurely worn away by the fact that it is composed of aragonite, a substance much harder than those rocks in which the Pholas burrows. The animal," Gosse adds, "turns in its burrow from side to side when at work, adhering to the interior by the foot, and therefore only partially rotating to and fro. The substance is abraded in the form of a fine powder, which is gradually ejected from the mouth of the hole by contraction of the bronchial syphon."

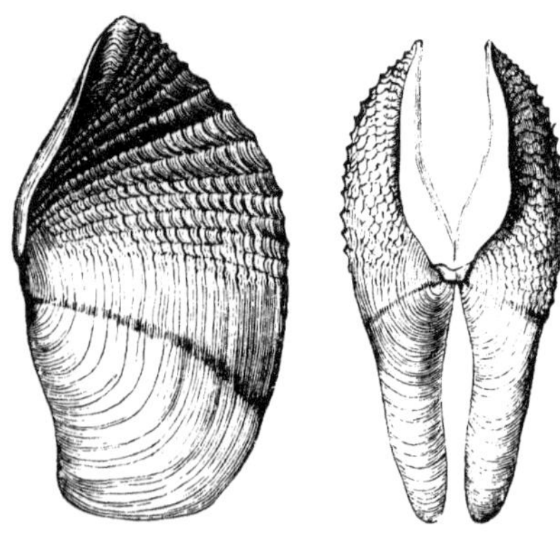

Fig. 175. Pholas crispata (Linnæus).

The Pholades are met with on every sea shore, and are plentiful in the Channel; on the French coast they are called *Dails*, and sought for their fine flavour. As examples of the genus, we may quote *Pholas dactylus* (Fig. 174); *Pholas candida*, found in the Channel, and in the Atlantic Ocean, which lives buried in the mud or in decayed wood; *Pholas crispata* (Fig. 175), also found in the Channel; *Pholas papyracea* (Fig. 176); and *Pholas melanoura* (Fig. 177).

Besides this curious property of boring and burrowing in the hollows of wood and stone, the Pholades possess another important character—that of phosphorescence. The bodies of many genera of Mollusca have the property of shining in the dark, but none emit a light more brilliant than that of the Pholades. Those who eat the Pholades in an uncooked state (which is by no means rare, for the flavour of the mollusc does not require the aid of cooking to render it palatable) would appear in the dark as if they had swallowed phosphorus; and the fisherman who, in a spirit of economy, supped on this mollusc in the dark, would give to his little ones the spectacle of a fire-eater on a small scale.

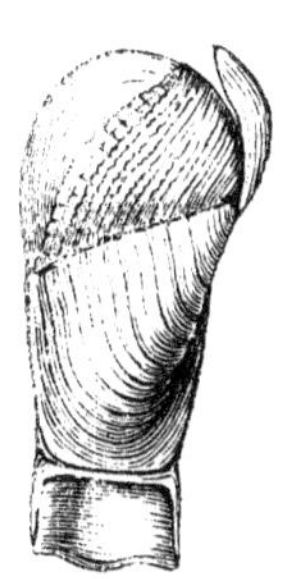
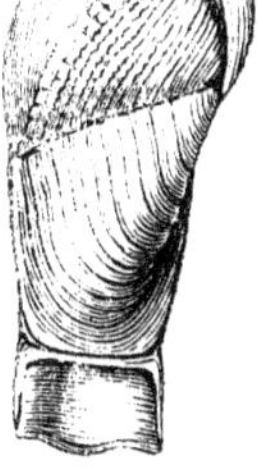

Fig. 176. Pholas papyracea (Solander).

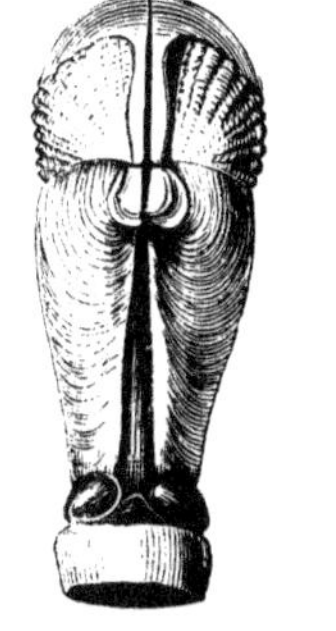
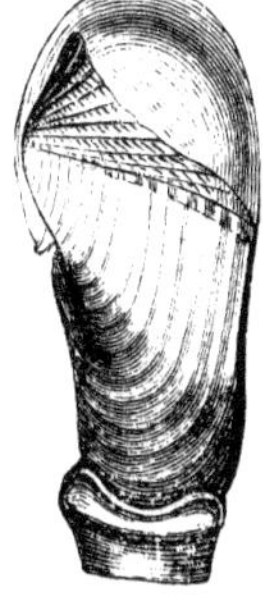

Fig. 177. Pholas melanoura (Sowerby).

The perforations produced in stone by the Pholades have become important evidence in a geological sense. In many countries there were evident signs of a considerable sinking of the earth. But in no place is the evidence of this so clear as in the monument of high antiquity on the Pozzuolan coast, known as the Temple of Serapis.

In speaking of the culture of oysters by the Romans, we had occasion to mention the disappearance of the Lucrin Lake, and its replacement by an enormous mountain, the Monte Nuovo. Now, Pozzuolo is situated at the foot of Monte Nuovo. We need not add that the whole neighbourhood is volcanic. Pozzuolo touches on the Solfaterra, on the Lake Avernus, and is not far from Vesuvius; and in the bay is the monument of other days, erroneously called the Temple of Serapis. In reality it was most probably a thermal establishment, established for its mineral waters, although the world has agreed to call it a temple.

However that may be, the building has been nearly levelled by the hand of time, aided by the hand of man; and the ruins now consist of three magnificent marble columns of about forty feet high. But the curious and important fact is, that these three columns, at about ten feet above the surface, are riddled with holes, and full of cavities bored deeply into the marble, and these borings occupy the space of three feet on each column. The cause of these perforations is no longer doubtful. In some of the cavities the shell of the operator is still found, and it seems settled among naturalists that it belongs to a species of Pholas, although M. Pouchet, a naturalist of Rouen, denies this: "As far," he says, "as I have been able to judge from the fragment which I extracted from this temple, which is destitute of the hinge, it is infinitely more probable that this mollusc is a species of the genus *Corallisphaga*." In spite, however, of M. Pouchet's scepticism, the mass of evidence is opposed to his theory.

There are two modes of explaining the fact to which we have called attention. To enable the stone-boring molluscs which live only in the sea to excavate this marble, the temple and columns must have been buried several fathoms deep in sea-water. It is only in these conditions that the borers could have made an incision, and laboured at their ease, in the marble column.

But since the same traces of perforation are now visible ten feet above the surface, it follows that, after being long immersed under water, the columns have been elevated to their present position. The temple has been restored to its primitive state, carrying with it, engraved in marble, ineffaceable proofs of its immersion. Sir Charles Lyell has consecrated a long chapter to the successive sinking and elevation of this temple, which proves the fact most conclusively.

Beside the Pholades naturalists usually place the *Teredos:* marine animals having a special and irresistible inclination for submerged wood; for while wood exposed to the air becomes a prey to terrestrial animals, so submerged wood is subject to invasion by aquatic animals, of which the Teredo is by far the most formidable. The Teredos in the bosom of the ocean perforate the hardest timbers, whatever be their essence. The galleries bored by these imperceptible miners riddle the whole interior of a piece of wood, destroying it entirely, without the slightest external indication of its ravages. The galleries

Plate XX.—Temple of Serapis at Pozzuolo.

sometimes follow the thread of the wood; sometimes they cut it at right angles; the miners, in fact, change their route the moment they meet in their way either the furrows hollowed out by one of their congeners, or some ancient and abandoned gallery. By a strange kind of instinct, however multiplied may be their furrows or tubes in the same piece of wood, they never mingle—there is never any communication between them. The wood is thus attacked on a thousand diverse points, until it is invaded and its entire substance destroyed. It is by secret ravages of this kind that the piles and other submarine constructions upon which bridges are built are often riddled and perforated. They appear to all outward examination as solid and perfect as at the moment they were first driven; but they yield to the least effort, bringing ruin and destruction on the edifices they support. Ships have been thus silently and secretly mined, until the planks crumbled into dust under the feet of the sailors. Others have gone down with their crews, entirely caused by the ravages of these relentless enemies, which are terrible from their very littleness.

M. Quatrefages, who has minutely studied the organization and habits of the Teredos in the Port of Saint Sebastian, reports the following fact, which will give the reader some idea of the rapidity with which these dangerous molluscs pursue their ravages:—

A boat, which served as a passage-boat between two villages on the coast, went down in consequence of an accident at the commencement of spring. Four months after some fishermen, hoping to turn her materials to advantage, raised the boat. But in that short space of time the Teredos had committed such ravages that the planks and timbers were riddled and worm-eaten so as to be totally useless.

At the beginning of the eighteenth century, half the coast of Holland was threatened with annihilation because the piles which support its dikes and sea-walls were attacked by the Teredo, and it proved no contemptible foe. Many hundreds of thousands of pounds were expended in order to avert the threatened danger. Fortunately, a closer attention to the habits of the mollusc has brought a remedy to a most formidable evil; the mollusc has an inveterate antipathy to rust, and timber impregnated by the oxide of iron is safe from its ravages. This taste of the Teredo being known, it is only necessary, in order to scatter this dangerous host, to sink the timber which is to be submerged in a tank of prepared oxide of iron—clothed, in short, in a thick cuirass of that antipathy of the Teredo, iron rust. Ships' timbers are also served with the same protecting coating; but the copper in which ships' bottoms are usually sheathed serves the same purpose.

The singular Acephalous Mollusc known to naturalists as the *Teredo navalis*, and popularly as the Ship Worm (Fig. 178), has the appearance of a long worm without articulations. Between the valves of a little shell, with which it is provided anteriorly, may be seen a sort of smooth truncature, which surrounds a swelling projecting pad or cushion. This cushion is the only part of the body of the animal which can be regarded as a foot. Starting from this point, all the body of the Teredo is enveloped by the shell and mantle, which form a sort of sheath communicating by two syphons with the exterior.

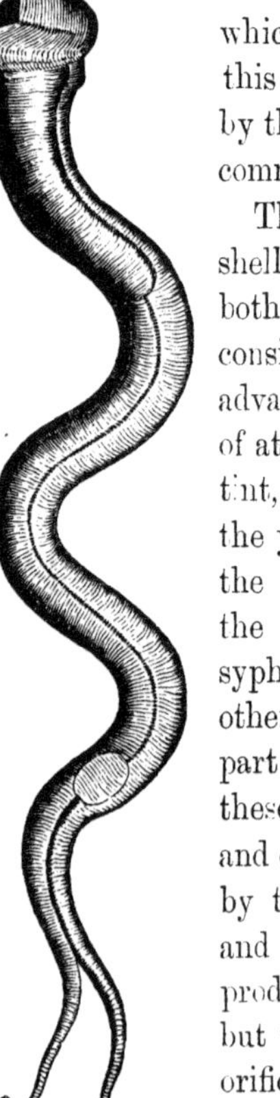
Fig. 178. Teredo navalis (Linnæus).

The mantle adheres to the circumference of the shell. Above, it forms two great folds, which may both be swollen by the afflux of the blood, and acquire considerable size. One of these folds placed in advance, which is called the *cephalic hood*, is worthy of attention. The tissue of the mantle is of a greyish tint, very light, and transparent enough, especially in the young, to permit of the mass of liver, the ovary, the branchiæ, and the heart being distinguished in the interior, even to counting its pulsations. The syphons are extensible, and attached the one to the other for about two-thirds of their length, the upper part being longer and thinner than the lower. It is by these tubes that the aerated water enters which feeds and enables the animal to breathe. It is discharged by the second tube, when deprived of its oxygen, and no longer respirable, carrying with it the useless products of digestion. This movement is continuous; but from time to time the animal shuts at once the orifices of both tubes, and slightly contracts itself.

The shell, seen on the side, presents an irregularly triangular form; it is nearly as broad as it is long; its two valves are solidly attached the one to the other above and below by the mantle in such a manner as only to permit of very slight movements. It is coloured in yellow and brown lines; sometimes it is quite plain. On the upper edge of the anterior truncature of the body of the animal is the mouth, a sort of funnel, flat and slightly bell-shaped, furnished with four labial palpi, a stomach without any peculiar feature, and a well-developed intestine.

The heart consists of two auricles and a ventricle, which beat at very irregular intervals, four or five in the minute. The blood is colourless, transparent, and charged with small irregular corpuscles. The art of breathing is accomplished in the branchiæ, or gills, and mantle. Nevertheless the one half of the blood returns to the heart without passing through these branchiæ.

The nervous system is well developed, and consists of a brain, nervous filaments, and of ganglions, which are distributed in the mantle, the branchiæ, and the syphon tubes.

The adult animal is surrounded by a sort of sheath, consisting of a solid mucus, which has sometimes been described erroneously as forming part of the animal. The Teredo, shut up in this tube, is limited in its movements; when observed in a vase, its motions are slow and deliberate—movements of extension and contraction, by the aid of which it contrives with difficulty to change its place; but nothing indicates a true creeping movement. In a state of nature, according to M. Quatrefages, the body of the animal is stretched out to three times its length without diminishing in any respect its proportional thickness; the afflux of water penetrating under the mantle, and of the blood which accumulates in the interior vessels, sufficiently accounting for a phenomenon which at the first glance is very singular.

The Teredo deposits a spherical greenish-yellow egg. Shortly after fecundation, these eggs are transformed into larvæ. At first naked and motionless, these larvæ are soon covered with vibratile cils, when they begin to move, at first by a revolving pirouette, afterwards swimming about freely in the water. When one of these larvæ has found a piece of submerged wood, without which it probably could not live, the curious spectacle is observed of a being which fabricates, step by step, and as it requires them, the organs necessary for the performance of its functions. It begins by creeping along the surface of the wood by means of the very long feet with which it is furnished. Then it is observed from time to time to open and shut the valves of the little embryo shell which partly envelopes it. As soon as it has found a part of the wood sufficiently soft and porous for its purpose, it pauses, attacks the ligneous substance, and soon produces a little pore, or cell, which will be the entrance to the future canal.

Once fairly lodged in this little cell, the young Teredo is rapidly developed; it covers itself with a coating of mucous matter, which, condensing by degrees, assumes a brownish tint, forming a solid covering, with two small holes for the passage of the syphon tubes. At the end of three days this covering has become quite solid; it is the commencement of the organized tube, in which the animal is to be developed. When secured beneath this opaque screen, the little miner is no longer exposed to observation; but if his cell is opened at the end of a few days, it is found that it has secreted a new shell, larger and more solid than the original one; it is the shell of the adult animal.

The young Teredo, which feeds on the raspings of the wood, increases rapidly; it passes from first a spheroid form to an elongated shape, and when its body can no longer be contained in the shell, it projects beyond the edge, and would find itself naked were it not protected by its membranous sheath, which adheres to the walls of the ligneous channel, now the dwelling-place of the animal.

The process by which a creature soft and naked like the Teredo should break into a solid piece of the hardest wood so quickly, and destroy it with so much facility, was long a mystery. Until very recently, the shell was looked on as the implement of perforation. But in that case the shell should preserve certain traces of its action upon surfaces so resistent as oak and fir; but the shell, on the contrary, is perfect, with no signs of friction. On the other hand, the muscular apparatus of the Teredo is not calculated to put the shell into rotatory action, were the process a boring one. It does not seem therefore possible to attribute these perforations to a simple physical action.

Some naturalists have suggested, in explanation of this phenomenon, that the animal is furnished with the means of secreting a liquid capable of dissolving the woody fibre. This has been met by the statement that, in whatever way the wood is attacked, whether the gallery is excavated with or across the fibre of the wood, the groove is as exactly and neatly cut as if it had been perforated by the sharpest tool, and that a corroding dissolvent could not act with this regularity, but would attack the harder and more tender parts unequally. This objection, which M. Quatrefages opposes to the idea of a chemical solvent, appears to us to admit of no reply. But, while opposing unassailable reasons against two theories, the learned author does not leave us without a very reasonable explanation of a very puzzling phenomenon. "Let us not forget," he says, "that the interior of the gallery is constantly saturated with water; consequently all the points of the walls which are not protected by the tube are subjected to constant maceration. In this state a mechanical action, even very inconsiderable, would suffice to clear away the bed of fibre thus softened, and, if this action is in any degree continuous, it suffices to explain the excavation of the galleries, however extensive their ramifications. Again, the upper cutaneous folds, especially the cephalic hood already mentioned, having the power of expanding at will by an afflux of blood, covered with a thick coriaceous epidermis, and moved by four strong muscles, seems to me very capable of performing the operation. It appears very probable that it is this hood which is charged with the removal of the woody fibre, rendering it incapable of resistance by previous maceration, which may also be assisted by some secretion from the animal." That the fleshy parts of the mollusc, acting upon the surface, softened by long maceration in water, is the true boring implement employed by the Teredo, is, probably, the only explanation the case admits of; at all events, in the present state of our knowledge, the explanation of the learned naturalist is the most reasonable which can be given.

As an appendage to the history of the Teredo, we shall here add a few words on a very curious animal, which has received the strange name of the Watering Pot (*Aspergillum*). This animal, which is represented in Fig. 179, inhabits a calcareous tube, thick, solid, of considerable length, and nearly cylindrical, presenting at one extremity an opening fringed with one or many foliaceous folds in the form of frills, and at the other extremity a convex disk, pierced with holes like a watering-pot: whence its name. The animal is attached by certain muscles to the interior of the tube. Chenu, to whom we are in-

Fig. 179. Aspergillum vaginiferum (Lamarck).

debted for our information respecting this curious mollusc, tells us "that the animal which inhabits this curious shell was first described by Russel, whose account of it is deficient in the anatomical details, which might explain the utility of the holes in the disk of the central fissure, and of the spiriform tubes found there." We suppose that this arrangement is necessary in order to facilitate respiration; and M. De Blainville thinks the small tubes are intended for the passage of the fillets which are necessary to fix the animal to the body on which it is to live, and in such a manner as to admit of its movements round a fixed point.

The animal which inhabits the *Aspergillum* is elongated, contractile, and only occupies the upper part of the tube, but it can stretch itself out sufficiently for all its wants. Shells of this genus are very rare, although a great number of species are known. They are found in the Red Sea, and in the seas of Australia and Java. The shells are generally of a white or yellowish tint; some have the tube covered with a glutinated sand, mixed with small fragments of shells of diverse colours. We know nothing of their habits, and their singular forms have left naturalists in doubt as to the place which should be assigned to them in the method of arrangement. It is only after having recognised the existence of two valves, which was detected with great difficulty just under the disk, and forming part of the sheath in which the animal is encased, that it has been decided to range them with the *Tubicola*, and with the shells, presenting an arrangement analogous or equally singular. These molluscs are, as M. Chenu says, little known, rare, and hence much sought for by collectors. They are exclusively exotic, the most common species being from Java. It is imported into Europe by the Dutch.

CEPHALOUS MOLLUSCA.

We take leave of our little decapitated friends of Headless Mollusca or *Acephalæ*, and direct our attention to those molluscs to which Nature has been more generous, and furnished with a head. This head, however, is still carried humbly; it is not yet *os sublime dedit;* it is drawn along an inch or so from the ground, and in no respect resembles the proud and magnificent organ which crowns and adorns the body of the greater and more perfectly organized animals.

The organization of the Cephalous Mollusca present three principal types, which has led to their being divided into three classes, after their more salient characteristics of form and locomotive apparatus; namely, *Gasteropodæ*, *Pteropodæ*, and *Cephalopodæ*.

In the class *Gasteropoda* (from γαστὴρ, belly, ποῦς, gen. ποδὸς, foot) the locomotive apparatus consists of a flattened muscular disk, placed under the belly of the animal, aided by which it creeps. The Snail (*Helix aspersa*), the Slug (*Limax rufus*), and the Porcelains (*Cyprea tigris*), are types of this class.

In the *Pteropoda*, from πτερὸν, wing, and ποῦς, foot, the locomotive apparatus assumes the form of wings, or membranous swimming-fins, placed on each side of the neck. The *Hyalea* and *Clio* are types of this class.

In the *Cephalopoda*, from κεφαλὴ, head, and ποῦς, foot, the locomotive apparatus consists of arms, or tentacles, which surround the mouth in numbers more or less considerable. The Cuttle-fish (*Sepia*), and the Poulpes (*Octopodæ*) are types of this last class.

The Molluscous Gasteropodæ have the organs of respiration arranged for aerial respiration, as well as for respiration under water.

This physiological arrangement involves important differences in internal organization in these molluscs, and renders it convenient to divide them into two secondary groups; namely, *Pulmonary Gasteropods*, which breathe in the air, and by a species of lung, and *Non-pulmonary Gasteropods*, which breathe in the water, by means of branchiæ, or gills.

CHAPTER XIII.

PULMONARY GASTEROPODS.

"Escargot, escargot,
Montre-moi tes cornes."

THE *Pulmonary Gasteropods* comprehend those molluscs which, as we have said, live in the air and breathe the natural atmosphere. The respiratory organ is a cavity in the walls of which the blood-vessels form a complicated network. The air enters this cavity through an orifice, which the animal opens and shuts at will—a species of lung, in short, which is placed upon the back of the animal. They are both terrestrial and aquatic animals. In the latter case, they must come to the surface of the water in order to breathe, like the phocas and dolphins among the Mammifera. The terrestrial species comprehend two families: the Snails (*Helix*) and the Slugs (*Limax*). The aquatic species comprehend the single family of *Limnea*.

It is only necessary to witness the snail as it creeps along the gravel walks of a garden, or in the damp alleys of a park, in order to see that it is a being of higher organization than the molluscs, for the most part stationary, with which we have hitherto occupied ourselves. The Edible Snail (*Helix aspersa*) goes and comes; it roams and saunters after its own peculiar manner, searching for its food or its pleasure; it has a head and two prominent tentacles, which feel and seem to express their sensations; it has nerves, a brain, a strong mouth, and a well-formed stomach. It is, in short, a complete being; it remains to us a sort of resting-place after the obscure existences—the obtuse creatures which we have just passed in review.

Without being a type of intelligence, the snail is by no means imbecile; it knows very well how to choose a tree the fruit of which is agreeable to it. A fine cluster of grapes, a succulent pear, which the horticulturist devours with his looks, and hopes to devour otherwise, is sure to be the identical fruit which will be chosen by our enlightened depredator, so that it is possessed of judgment, comparison, and intelligent appreciation.

The body of the snail is oval, elongated, convex above, flat below. The convex or upper surface of the body is rugged, in consequence of the existence of numerous tubercles projecting slightly, and separated by irregular furrows; its anterior is terminated by an obtuse head, its posterior more flat and less pointed. All the flat portion, thick, soft, and upon which the animal moves itself by a creeping motion, bears the name of the foot. The head is not really very distinct, especially in the upper part, but the organs with which it is provided are prominent. These organs are in reality tentacles, although they are more popularly known as *horns*, especially among children—those charming ignoramuses—who have been taught to repeat the well-known stanza—

"Snail, snail, come out of your hole,
Or else I'll beat you black as a coal"—

which finds its counterpart in all European languages. There are two pair of these tentacles or horns; one pair quite in front and above, and another smaller and less forward. The first are distinguished by their size, and also by a black spot or point at their extremity, which is sometimes erroneously said to be the eye of the snail.

These tentacles differ in many respects from the same organs in other molluscs; they are retractile, and can be drawn altogether within the animal into a sort of sheath, by the contraction of a muscle. At the anterior extremity of the head we find a sort of plaited opening, which is the mouth; it is of moderate extent, closed in front by two lips, and armed with two shear-like organs of horny consistence, one of them being a sort of rasp, which occupies the plate of the buccal cavity, and may be called a tongue; the other is a median jaw, placed transversely in the membranous walls of the palate, terminating in a free edge, armed with small teeth. This cutting blade, however, executes no movement; but the lingual organ, pressing all alimentary matter forcibly against its lower edge, effects their mastication, and enables it to dispose of fruit, tender leaves, mushrooms, and other substances easily divided.

At the bottom of the mouth is an œsophagus, or gullet, to which succeeds a stomach of moderate size. The intestine lies in folds round the liver, which is divided into four lobes, and terminates in a special orifice.

The little lung of the snail is placed in a cavity, vast for its size, just above the general mass of the viscera, and occupies all the last spiral turn of the cavity.

The mechanism of respiration is as follows: The animal inhales the air into its lung by forcibly dilating the pulmonary orifice, which lies in the largest spiral turn of the shell. In order to expel the air respired by the lung, it withdraws its body into the narrower part of the shell, where it gathers itself up completely, even to its head and feet, and by this compression of all its little being it expels the air which fills it. These respiratory movements, however, are not regular, but succeed each other only at certain intervals. Life would be too hard for the poor snail were it passed in such violent efforts as would be necessary if it respired as the larger animals do. In its case the breathing is intermittent and imperfect; it is merely a rough attempt, as it were, at respiration, which becomes perfect in some of the higher branches of the animal kingdom.

The snail has a heart, consisting of a ventricle and auricle, connected with a well-developed arterial vascular system, while the venous system is imperfect. In short, the blood only returns from the various parts of the body to the respiratory apparatus, after traversing *lacunæ*, or air-cells, existing between the several organs.

The blood of the snail is colourless, or rather of a pale rose colour, slightly tinted with blue. They have a rudimentary brain, composed of a pair of thick ganglions, situated above the œsophagus, which are in connection with another pair of ganglions placed below, which, together, form a sort of collar, or ring. From this ring springs a great number of nervous cords, which are distributed to the mouth, the tentacles, the lung, and the heart. The skin, in those parts covered by the shell, exhibits great sensibility; it receives a considerable quantity of nervous filament, so that the sense of touch ought to possess extreme delicacy.

The tentacles, the skin of which is so fine and so sensitive, are the organs of touch. Other functions are sometimes attributed to them; the anterior tentacles are sometimes considered to be the organs of smell. This, at all events, is certain, that the snail is very sensible of strong odours, and is easily attracted by many plants the odour of which pleases them.

The black point which terminates the first pair of tentacles have been considered as eyes; but the existence of a visual organ is not quite admissible in the snail. They are quite insensible to sudden changes of light; they always travel in the dark, and never recognise obstacles placed before them. We may add that the snail is destitute of all organs of hearing. No noise appears to affect it, at least till the noise is so near as to agitate the air which immediately surrounds it. Indeed. the snail has not been well treated by Nature; the poor creature is at once blind, deaf, and dumb.

The snails are male and female in the same individual, each being at once male and female, or hermaphrodite. Their eggs are roundish, heavy, and of a whitish colour. The animal deposits them on the soil in little irregular heaps; at other times it deposits them one after the other, like the grains of a chaplet, in holes which it digs in the soil, or in the natural excavations created by moisture. The eggs are even found in the hollows of old trees; in fissures of walls or rocks.

When the young *Helix* issues from the egg, they are already provided with an extremely thin membranous shell. The timid and tender youth is conscious of its weakness and full of humility. It rarely trusts itself out of the obscure hole in which it was hatched; when it does, it is only at night, dreading the desiccating air, and, above all, the sun's rays, even with the house it always carries with it for shelter.

This calcareous and velluted house is spiral, which the animal has the inappreciable advantage of transporting without fatigue—a true wanderer. It is light, and sometimes quite disproportionate to the body of the animal, which it covers only in that part which contains the viscera and respiratory organs. The form of the shell is generally much variegated. Some are flattened, others are orbicular or globose; in some the spiral is very pointed. The edges of the shell are sometimes simple, sharp, and pointed; others, on the contrary, thick and inverted, presenting an edging of great solidity.

The spire is generally rolled up from right to left. A helix shell, the spiral of which follows the inverse direction, that is, from left to right, is a rarity much sought after by amateurs.

The ancients held snails in especial esteem for the table. The Romans had many species served up at their feasts, which they distinguished in categories according to the delicacy of their flesh. Pliny tells us that the best were imported from Sicily, from the Balearic Isles, and from the Isle of Capri, the last dwelling-place of the aged Tiberius. The largest came from Illyria. Ships proceeded to the Ligurian coast to gather them for the tables of the Roman patricians. The great consumption led to the establishment of parks (*Cochlearia*, Varro; *Cochlearum vivariá*, Pliny), in order to fatten the animals, as is now done with oysters. They were fed for this end upon various plants mixed with soup; when it was desired to improve the flavour a little wine and sometimes laurel leaves were added. These parks were formed in humid shady places surrounded by a foss or a wall. Pliny has even transmitted to us the name of the inventor of the *Cochleariæ*, a certain Fulvius Hispinus. Addison describes with details one of these establishments kept up by the Capuchins at Friburg in Switzerland, in imitation of the ingenious Roman gourmet we have named.

Among the Romans, snails were served at the funeral repast. Certain heaps of their shells, which are found in the cemetery of Pompeii, are the remains of those funeral festivities with which the inhabitants of the buried city honoured the tombs of their friends and relations.

The practice of eating snails had fallen into disuse in Europe when, in the seventeenth century, John Howard, the philanthropist, began to collect them with the view of reintroducing them as human food. He chose *Helix Varronis*, which was probably the species cultivated by the Romans; it surpasses all those of Europe in size, and was found plentifully in the district of Bagnes, in the Valois. Howard, having procured the breed from Bagnes, found their increase so rapid that the crops were likely to be devoured by the swarms of molluscs thus brought together, and steps were at once taken to destroy them. In other parts of Europe the snail continues to be sought for as an article of luxury. They are consumed at Vienna in great numbers during Lent, supplies being brought from the Swiss canton of Appenzell. At Naples a soup made from *Helix nemoralis* is sold publicly to the strange population with which the streets of that city swarm, for the king's pavement is their bed-chamber, dining-saloon, and work-room. In France, snails are a valuable resource to the poor in the southern departments.

The flesh of all snails is not alike in a culinary point of view. Amateurs class as first in quality *Helix vermicula,* called at Montpelier the Little Hermit, because it buries itself so deeply in its

Fig. 180. Helix aspersa (Müller).

shell. *Helix aspersa* (Figs. 180, 181, 182) is thought to be more tender and delicate. In Provence it is called *tapada*, that is, "closed," from the cretaceous *covercle* which closes its shell.

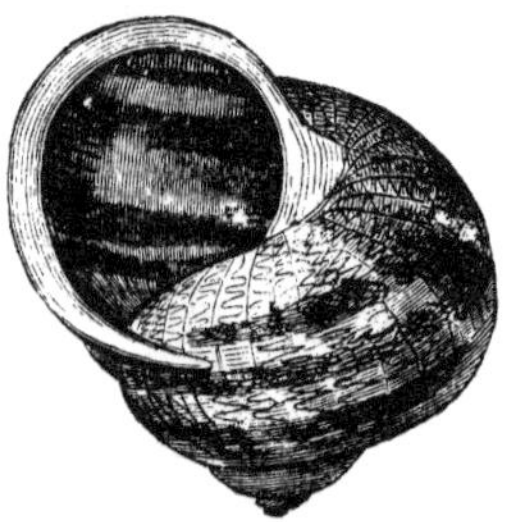

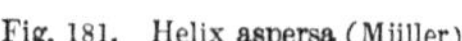

Fig. 181. Helix aspersa (Müller).

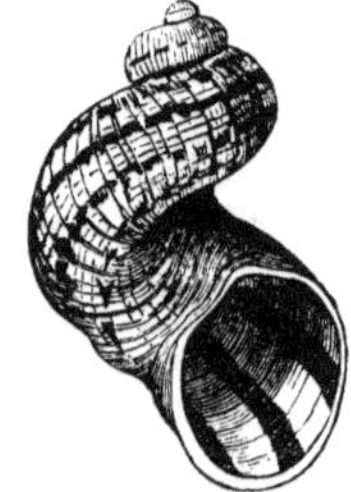

Fig. 182. Helix aspersa (Var. Scalaire).

In the north of France, and round Paris, *Helix pomatia* is the favourite culinary snail (Fig. 183). This is the species which is used as a speaking sign-board over the doors of the wine-shops and small restaurants in the neighbourhood of the Halles, at Paris. Its shell is globose and tun-shaped, very solid, marked with irregular transverse stripes of a brownish rust colour, with bands, often nearly effaced, of a deeper tint, and of the same colour. The animal is large, of a yellowish grey, and covered with elongated irregular tubercles.

Fig. 183. Helix pomatia (Linnæus).

Besides *Helix pomatia*, according to Moquin-Tandon, they eat in the north of France *Helix sylvatica* and *H. nemoralis;* at Montpelier, as we have already said, *H. aspersa* and *H. rhodostoma;* at Avignon, also, these, along with *H. vermicula*, are favourites. In Provence,

Fig. 184. Helix Mackenzii (Adams).

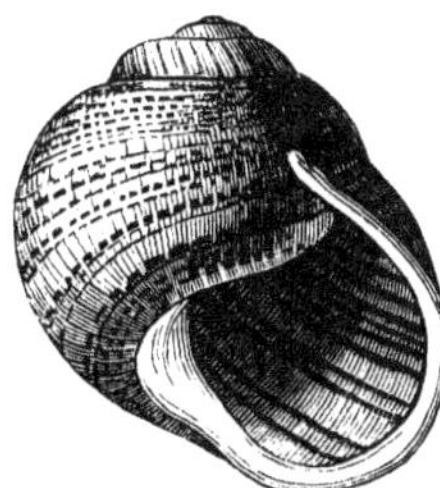

Fig. 185. Helix undulata (Ferussac).

Fig. 186. Helix translucida (Linnæus).

Helix Pisana, with *H. aspersa* and *melastoma*, are preferred. At Bonifacio, *Helix aspersa*, *H. vermicula*, and, more rarely, *H. rhodostoma;* and in other localities the smaller species and young individuals of the larger kinds are employed for feeding poultry.

Certain species are also employed for feeding ducks. Thus, in the neighbourhood of Montpelier, ducks are fed upon *Helix variabile* and

Figs. 187 and 188. Helix Waltoni (Reeve).

H. rhodostoma. Some fishes, especially the young salmon, are very partial to the flesh of snails.

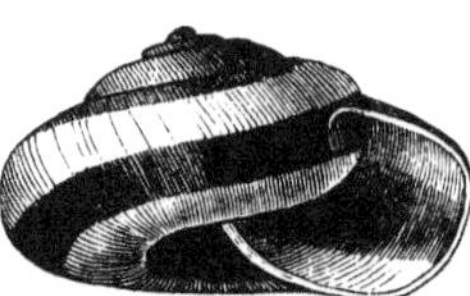

Fig. 189. Helix citrina (Linnæus).

Fig. 190. Helix Stuartia (Sowerby).

This very important genera is very numerous in species, which are distributed in groups according to the form of the shell; that is, whether

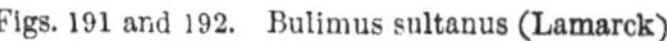

Figs. 191 and 192. Bulimus sultanus (Lamarck).

it be globulous, as in Fig. 184, tun-bottomed, as in Fig. 185, plain or biform, as in Fig. 186, or truncated, as in Figs. 187 and 188. These figures will give the reader some idea of the multiplied and elegant forms which the shells of *Helix* sometimes assume.

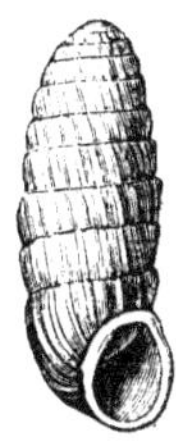

Figs. 193 and 194. Pupa uva (Linnæus).

In connection with the snails (*Helix*), we shall note some kindred genera which our space only permits us to name. Such is the genus *Bulimus*, the European species of which are numerous; some of them very small, others of medium size; of these *Bulimus sultanus* (Figs. 191 and 192). In Figs. 193 and 194, the Grey Pupa (*P. uva*), another congruous species, is represented.

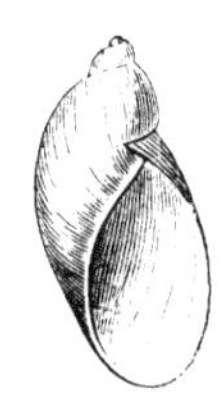

Fig. 195. Succinea putris (Linnæus).

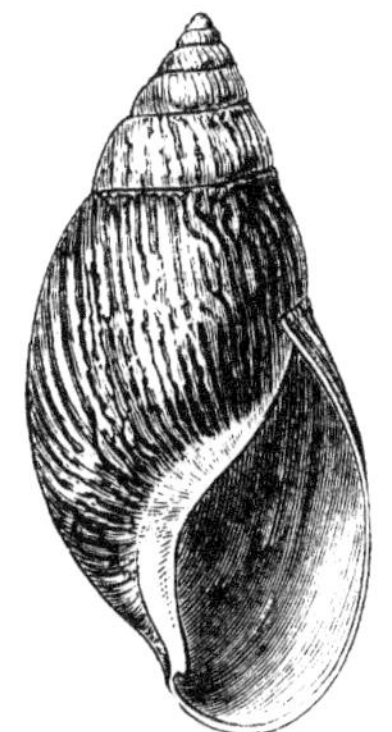

Fig. 196. Achatina zebra (Chemnitz).

Fig. 197. Vetrina fasciata (Ed. and Soul.)

Yet another typical species may be noted, which is found abundantly amid the grass and shrubs near brooks round Paris and elsewhere. It is *Succinea putris*, presenting a small, thin, diaphanous shell of a pale amber yellow, marked with close and very fine longitudinal stripes (Fig. 195). The *Zebra Agathina*, the *Achatina zebra* of Chemnitz, is a great snail, which devours shrubs and trees in warm countries (Fig. 196). Finally, *Vetrinas*, the shell of which is very small and very thin in some species—so small, indeed, in *Vetrina fasciata* (Fig. 197), that the animal cannot re-enter the shell—occupies a point of transition between *Helix* and *Limax*.

The Family of Limaceans (*Limax*) are terrestrial pulmonary molluscs, entirely naked, or having only a very small shell. The Limax varies very considerably in appearance, in consequence of its extreme contractibility. When seen creeping along on the surface of the soil, it has nearly the form of a very elongated ellipse, at one extremity of which is the head; the surface of the body in contact with the earth is flat, the other convex. Towards the anterior extremity, and upon the middle of the back, a portion of the skin projects as if it were detached from the body, and is ornamented with transverse stripes of various convolutions. This part is named the cuirass, or buckler, under which the animal can hide its head.

The mouth is a transverse opening in the front of the head; above are two pairs of tentacles, or horns, immensely retractile, cylindrical, and terminating in a small button; the lower tentacles are the shorter; the upper present at their summit a black point, as in *Helix*, which have sometimes been mistaken for the eyes.

Upon the right side of the cuirass, and hollowed in the thickness of its edge, which is large and contractile, whose function it is to give access to atmospheric air, it abuts on an internal cavity, also large, and is intended to promote respiration. The outer skin, or epidermis, is rayed in brownish furrows, its surface covered with a viscous glutinous substance, which permits of the animal creeping up the smoothest surfaces, locomotion being produced by the successive contraction and extension of the muscular fibres of the feet.

The internal organization of the Limax is analogous to that already described in the snails. The taste and smell in the Limaceans differ only very slightly from those organs in Helix. They are, like the snails, deaf, and nearly blind. They love fresh and humid places; they lodge themselves in the holes of old walls, under stones, or half-decomposed leaves, in the crevices of the bark of old trees, and even underground, coming forth only at night and in the morning. They show themselves especially after soft showers in spring and summer. In the garden, after one of these soft showers, many of these little creatures are sure to be met with in the more shaded alleys.

The Limax is essentially herbivorous. They seek, above all, for young plants, fruits, mushrooms, and half-decayed vegetables. They are very voracious, and cause great ravages in gardens and young plantations, and many are the devices of the artful gardener to destroy them. Lime and salt are their abomination; ashes and fine sand they avoid. They dislike the noonday sun, and the gardener knows it; he arranges little sheltering tiles, or planks of wood and stone, under which they retire, and then they are surprised to their destruction by the too knowing horticulturist, and slain in hecatombs.

There are thirty known species of Limax. Some are remarkable for their very striking colours. *Limax rufus* (Fig. 198) is common in

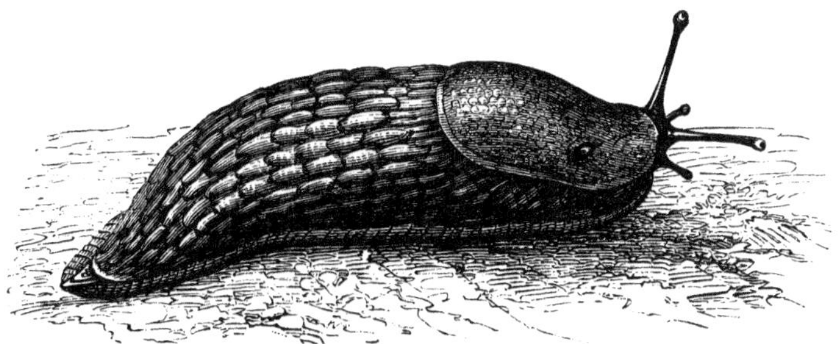

Fig. 198. Limax rufus (Linnæus).

woods, and well known for its large size and its colour of rich vermilion; it is known all over Europe, from Norway to Spain.

Among the Limaceans nearly destitute of shells we find *Testacella haliotidea* (Fig. 199), which is provided with a very small shell placed at its posterior extremity, just over the pulmonary cavity. This shell becomes more important in *Vetrina*, already spoken of as forming the point of transition between Limax and Helix. This passage from Limaceans entirely destitute of shells to those furnished with

Fig. 199. Testacella haliotidea (Draparnaud).

a very small shell, as in *Testacella*, is very exactly indicated by Nature. *Limax rufus*, spoken of above, presents, under the posterior part of the cuirass, calcareous, unequal, isolated granulations, which are, so to speak, the elements, as yet internal, of a shell which is on the point of being built. Other species in the same genus present under the cuirass a little rough, imperfect scale, which seems to be produced by a great number of these calcareous granulations, which show themselves in an isolated state in *Limax rufus*.

Limneans.

The Limneans, *Aquatic Pulmonary Gasteropods*, as we have already said, are the animals belonging to this group that have to come to the surface of the water to breathe, as the dolphins and phocas among the Mammifera do. The *Limnea*, *Planorbis*, and *Physa* are the principal members of this group.

The Limneans live in great numbers in the stagnant waters of all countries, particularly of temperate climates. They cannot remain long under water, being compelled frequently to rise to the surface in order to breathe atmospheric air. They are even observed, by a mechanism not very well understood, to turn themselves upside down, in such a manner as to present themselves feet uppermost, and to move slowly along in this position, creeping, as it were, through the water. It is difficult to comprehend how the movable liquid bed upon which the animal operates can offer resistance enough to permit of its creeping as if it were on a solid resisting body; it seems to produce the movement with the assistance of its foot, which is broad and thick, and shorter than the shell.

The Limneans have a large flat head, from each side of which issues a triangular contractile tentacle, carrying at its base and on the inner side an extremely small dot, or eye. The most considerable part of the body, comprehending the visceral mass, is spiral, and is contained in a thin diaphanous shell (Fig. 200), the turns in the spiral of which are generally elongated, the last turn being larger than all the others. The interior of this is occupied by the respiratory cavity, which communicates outwardly by an opening analogous to that which exists in the snails. This opening dilates and contracts in such a manner as to receive the air in the cavity, and exclude water when the animal feeds itself under the water. The mouth is a transverse slit between two rather thin lips, and is armed with small canine teeth. When the animal sallies from its shell, it has the appearance of a short trumpet. In its interior is a roundish, thick, and fleshy tubercle, not unlike the tongue of a paroquet. The true tongue, however, which lies at the bottom of the slit, is flat, oval-shaped, and supported by a cartilaginous or bony pedicle.

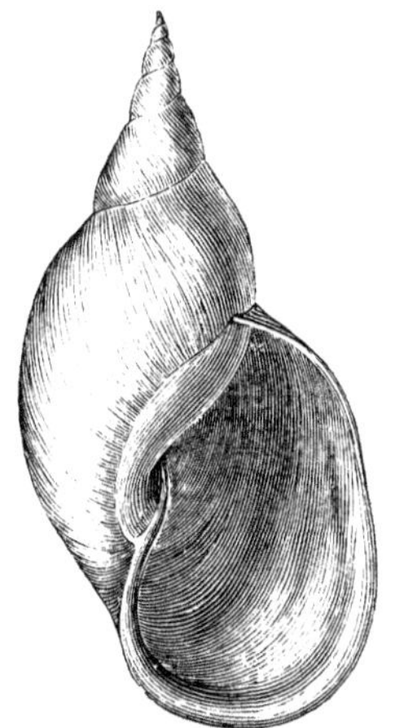

Fig. 200. Limnea stagnalis (Linnæus).

The Limneans, aided by this very complicated buccal apparatus, are enabled to feed themselves with vegetable substances, such as the leaves of aquatic plants, which they cut and bruise with their teeth. They are very active in the season, reproducing towards the end of spring. At this period little oval or semi-cylindrical masses are frequently found adhering to floating bodies, glittering and transparent as crystal. These are agglomerations of the eggs of Limneans. When winter sets in, the *Limnea* of our climate fall into a state of torpor, and sink more or less deeply into the mud of the lakes, marshes, rivers, or brooks, which they inhabit.

These molluscs are of no apparent utility, except to feed fishes and aquatic birds, which destroy them in great numbers.

Fig. 201. Planorbis corneus (Linnæus).

The Planorbis have an organization analogous to the Limneans, of which they are the faithful companions in stagnant waters. Their shells (Fig. 201) are thin, light, and disk-like in form, rolled round its plane in such a manner as to render all the turns of the spiral visible from above as well as below; it is concave on both sides, with an oval, oblong-shaped opening, and with an operculum or lid. The animal is conformable to the shell in shape. The visceral mass forms a very elongated cone, which unwinds itself absolutely, according to the spiral turns of the shell. The foot, or abdominal locomotive mass, is short, and very nearly round. The head is sufficiently distinct, and furnished with two very long filiform, contractile tentacles, having at their base, and on the inner side, a small organ, which looks like an egg. The mouth is armed in the upper part with cross-cutting teeth, and in the lower part with a tongue, bristling with a great number of hooked excrescences.

In habits the Planorbis resemble the Limneans: they creep like them on the surface of solid bodies, and swim in the water with the feet upwards and the shell down. They feed on similar substances, and their eggs are collected in gelatinous masses also. They pass the winter in a state of torpor, buried in the mud of the rivers they inhabit.

The principal species is *Planorbis corneus* (Fig. 201), which is common in the rivers of England and France.

Another group of molluscs, which occupy our fresh rivers and swim with the shell down and feet up, is represented by *Physa castanea* (Fig. 202). The genus *Physa* have an oval, oblong, or nearly globular shell, very thin, smooth, and fragile, opening longitudinally, narrow above, with the right edge sharp; the last turn of the spiral being largest of all.

Fig. 202. Physa castanea (Lamarck).

The animal appears to be intermediate in form between Planorbis and Limnea: it is oval in form, and unrolls itself like the Limneans, but its tentacles, in place of being triangular and thick like the latter, are elongated and narrow, like those of Planorbis. These little inhabitants of fresh water swim with facility, the feet upwards, the shell below, like the Limneans, and they feed on vegetables, like them.

CHAPTER XIV.

NON-PULMONARY GASTEROPODS.

"Ame tout aqueu poble éimable é banara."
REYBAUD.

In this family we reach a group of Gasteropods much more numerous, both in species and in special types, which respire by the aid of branchiæ, or gills. Cuvier divides them into many orders, based chiefly upon their respiratory organs. But we must limit ourselves to describing the curious shells belonging to the groups of *Tectibranchiæ*, *Pectinibranchiæ*, and *Cyclobranchiæ*.

The Tectibranchiæ have the gills attached either to the right side of the body or upon the back, arranged in the form of leaflets, more or less divided, but not symmetrical, and nearly covered by the mantle. *Bulla* and *Aplysia* are the two principal genera of the group, and may be considered as the type of two small families.

The *Aplysiæ* were known to the ancients under the name of sea-hares (*Lepus marinus*), from some fancied resemblance to the terrestrial hare. They were objects of profound horror, inspired either by their singular form, or from an acrid, caustic, and inodorous liquid which they secrete. A magic influence was attributed to them; they were supposed, for instance, to have influence over the female heart. It is not easy, however, to explain the evil renown acquired by an animal which is known to be gentle and even timid. They are naked and fat, somewhat resembling the Limneans in their oval, elongated form, their thickness in the dorsal region, and their posterior locomotion. Their head, which is very indistinct, is furnished with four tentacles, the anterior two of which are the largest, and somewhat resemble the ears of a hare. The eyes are found at the base of the posterior tentacles. These characters are observed in *Aplysia depilans*

(Fig. 203). *Aplysia inca* shows also the same arrangement (Fig. 204). In this family the mollusc is much more important from its volume than from its internal, rudimentary, and horny shell, which is contained in the branchial shield. In Fig. 205 we have the small and thin cartilaginous shell, which exists in the interior of the animal.

The Aplysiæ are found nearly in every region of the globe, not only upon the shores of the Continent, but on every island shore. They commonly inhabit sandy and muddy shores of small depths, or even the rocky recesses, or under shelter of the stones which have fallen from the cliffs. Their eggs consist of those long filaments which are discharged in immense numbers, and which fishermen call sea-worms. They feed upon certain algæ, with which the bottom of the sea is

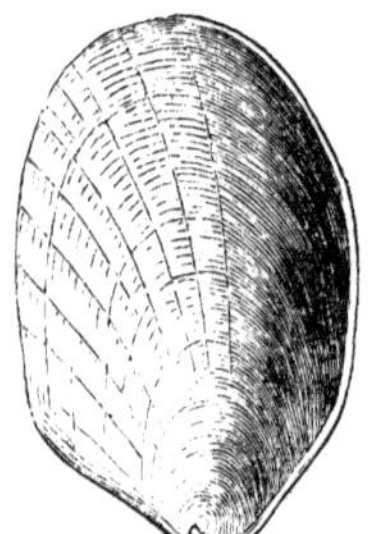

Fig. 203. Aplysia depilans (Linnæus).

Fig. 204. Aplysia inca (D'Orbigny)

Fig. 205. Shell of Aplysia inca.

covered; but they eat, also, small marine animals, such as the naked molluscs, annelids, and crustaceans.

We are the less astonished to see the Aplysiæ so gluttonous when we learn how liberally Nature has accorded to them organs of mastication, trituration, and digestion. Their mouth is formed of thick and muscular lips; a very long œsophagus or gullet succeeds, and this œsophagus does not communicate with a single stomach, but with four—one enormous membranous crop, an exceedingly muscular gizzard, with two accessary pockets, one of which terminates in the form of a sac. The gizzard has thick walls, and is furnished on the internal wall with cartilaginous quadrangular pyramids, the summits of which intertwine. This apparatus is intended to bruise the food when it reaches the third stomach. It is also armed with little hooks, the curvature of which is directed towards the entrance of the gizzard.

The genus *Bulla* differs materially from the Aplysiæ. They have a well-developed shell, the form of which is elegant; they are delicate in structure; their brilliant colours, consisting of red, black, or white bands, separated by many varied tints, cause these little molluscs to be much sought after for ornamental collections. The shell itself is oval or globulous, rolled up in a scroll, smooth, spotted, very thin and fragile, with a concave spiral, umbilicate, open in all its length, with a straight, wide, and cutting edge.

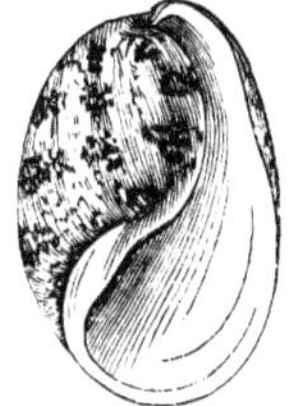

Figs. 206 and 207. Bulla ampulla (Linnæus).

Obtuse at its two extremities, neither the head of the animal nor the tentacles are very apparent. The gills are placed under the back, a little to the right and behind; its stomach, which alone fills a great

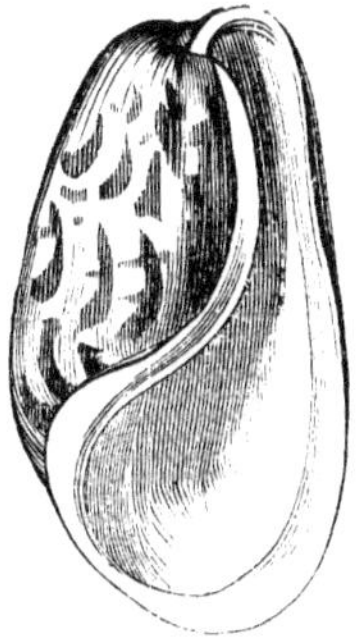

Fig. 208. Bulla oblonga (Adams).

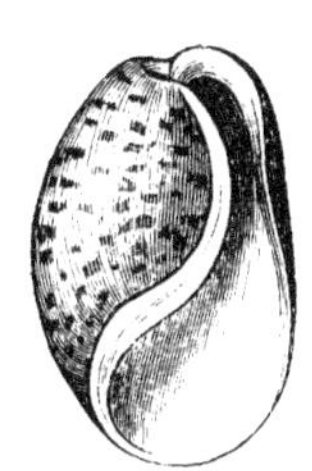

Fig. 209. Bulla aspersa (Adams).

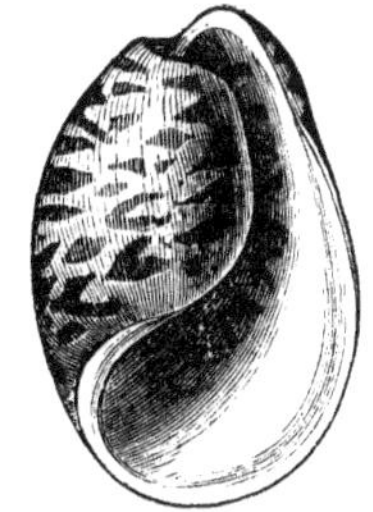

Fig. 210. Bulla nebulosa (Gould).

part of the cavity of the body, presents the peculiarity, already noted in the Aplysia, of being furnished with bony pieces, evidently intended to grind the food.

The Bullæ can swim with facility in deep water, but they evidently prefer the shallows and a sandy bottom, feeding upon smaller molluscs. They are found in every sea, but they abound chiefly in the

Indian Ocean and Oceania. Some species, however, such as *Bulla ampulla* (Figs. 206 and 207), the shell of which is shaded grey and brown, and the Water-drop (*Bulla hydatida*), inhabit European seas. *Bulla oblonga* and *Bulla aspersa* (Adams), and *Bulla nebulosa* (Gould), represented in Figs. 208, 209, and 210, are also well-known species.

In the Pectinibranchial Gasteropods the gills are composed of numerous leaflets cut like the teeth of a comb, and attached, on one or many lines, to the upper part of the respiratory cavity. They constitute the most numerous order of Cephalous Molluscs, comprehending nearly all the univalve spiral shells, and many others which are simply conical. They inhabit the sea, rivers, and lakes, and are of all sizes. The most remarkable genera to which we shall limit ourselves belong to the family of *Trochoïdæ* and *Buccinoïdæ*.

Trochoïdæ.

The genus *Trochus* are found in all seas, and near to the shore in the clefts of rocks, especially in places where seaweeds grow luxuriantly. Some of these thick, cone-shaped shells are extremely beautiful, being richly nacred inside, and remarkable for the beauty and diversity of colour exhibited. Generally smooth, the great spiral is, never-

Fig. 211. Trochus niloticus (Linnæus).

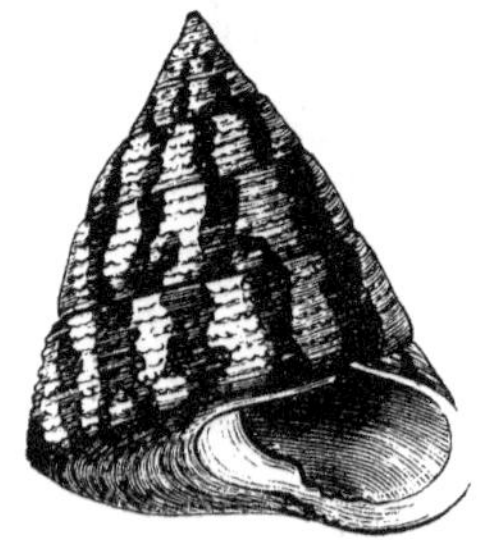

Fig. 212. Trochus virgatus (Gmel.).

theless, sometimes edged with a series of regular spines. The form is conical, the spiral more or less raised, broad and angular at the base; the opening entire, depressed transversely, and the edge disunited in the upper part.

The animal which inhabits this shell is also spiral; its head is furnished with two conical tentacles, having at their base eyes borne on a peduncle; its foot is short, round at its two extremities, edged or fringed in its circumference, and furnished with a horny operculum, circular and regularly spiral.

The family is divided into many sub-genera. Among the *Trochoïdæ*, properly so called, we may notice a typical species, *Trochus niloticus* (Fig. 211) and *Trochus virgatus* (Fig. 212). The *Zectaria* comprehend the false-sided *Trochoïdæ*, typical of which we may notice *Trochus inermis* (Fig. 213), whose greenish-yellow shell is found in

Fig. 213. Trochus inermis (Gmel.).

Fig. 214. Trochus Cookii (Chemnitz).

the American seas; *Trochus Cookii* (Fig. 214), whose rusty-brown shell is brought from the distant seas of Australia; and *Trochus imbricatus* (Fig. 215), whose white-coloured shell comes from the Antilles.

Fig. 215. Trochus imbricatus (Gmel.).

Fig. 216. Trochus agglutinans (Lamarck); Phorus conchyliophorus (Born).

Another remarkable species, the *Phorus conchyliophorus* (Born), *Trochus agglutinans* (Lamarck), is a native of the Antilles, popularly known as the Mason (Figs. 216 and 217), from the singular faculty it has of collecting on the back of its shell, in proportion as they increase in size, movable bodies, sometimes of considerable bulk, such as small flints, stems of plants, fragments of shells, all of which it carries: hence its name of Mason.

The Spurred Trochus, in the shell of which the turns of the spiral are studded with radiating spines, is represented by *Trochus stella*

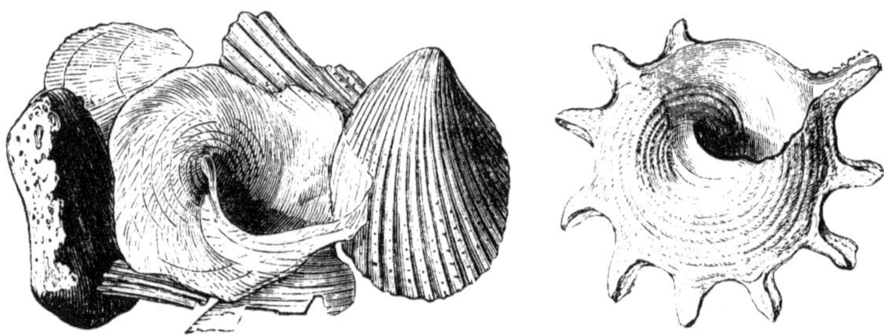

Fig. 217. Trochus agglutinans (Lamarck); Phorus conchyliophorus (Born).

Fig. 218. Trochus stella (Lamarck).

(Fig. 218) and *Trochus stellaris* (Fig. 220); they are natives of the Australian seas. *Trochus imperialis*, vulgarly called the Royal Spur, and *Trochus* or *Rotella Zealandica* (Fig. 219), the New Zealand Spur, the spiral turns of which are sculptured in descending furrows, and studded with imbricated scales, which form a projecting edging round

Fig. 219. Rotella Zealandica.

Fig. 220. Trochus stellaris (Gmel.).

the margin of the shell, and give it a radiating form. This species is of a violet brown above and white below, and is still rare in collections. *Rotella Zealandica*, from the Indian Ocean, whose shell, represented in Fig. 219, presents the most lively colours, forms one of a genus by no means numerous in species.

Beside the genus *Trochus* naturalists range a pretty marine shell, called the Sun-dial (*Solarium*), recognised by its profound umbilicus, wide and funnel-shaped, in the interior of which may be seen the little crenated teeth which follow the edge of every turn of the spiral up to the top. In most collections of these pretty shells we find the striped Sun-dial (*Solarium perspecticum* of Linnæus), from the Indian Ocean (Figs. 221, 222), the diameter of which is about two inches

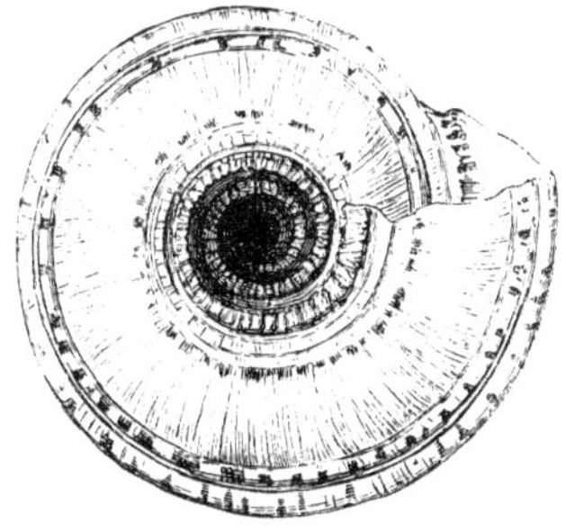

Fig. 221. Solarium perspecticum (Linnæus).

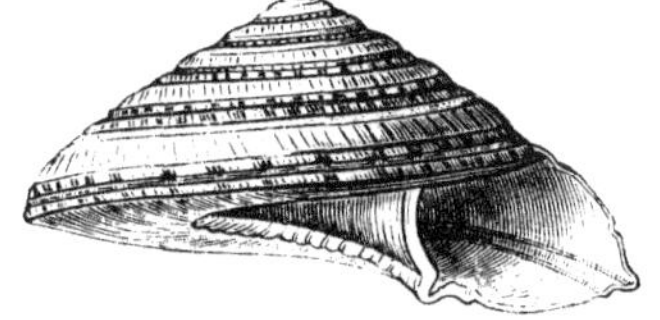

Fig. 222. Solarium perspecticum (Linnæus)

and a half. The Australian Sun-dial (*S. variegatum*, Linnæus, Fig. 223) is another species frequently seen in collections: it is as much variegated above as below, of a white and rusty brown. The minute trellised Sun-dial, which is only ten lines in diameter, comes from the coast of Tranquebar.

Fig. 223. Solarium variegatum (Linnæus).

The genus *Turbo* are very generally diffused, being found on every shore, where they cling to rocks beaten by the waves. About fifty

Fig. 224. Turbo margaritaceus (Linnæus).

Fig. 225. Turbo argyrostomus (Linnæus).

species are known, some of them large shells, others very small. *Turbo margaritaceus* (Fig. 224) is large, thick, and weighty, round-bellied, and deeply furrowed; in colour it is yellow, or rust-coloured, marked by square brown spots. *Turbo argyrostomus,* the Silver-mouthed Turbo (Fig. 225), is still larger, with projecting spines on the top of its larger spiral. *Turbo marmoratus* (Linnæus), the Marbled Turbo (Fig. 226), is the largest shell in the group. It is marbled,

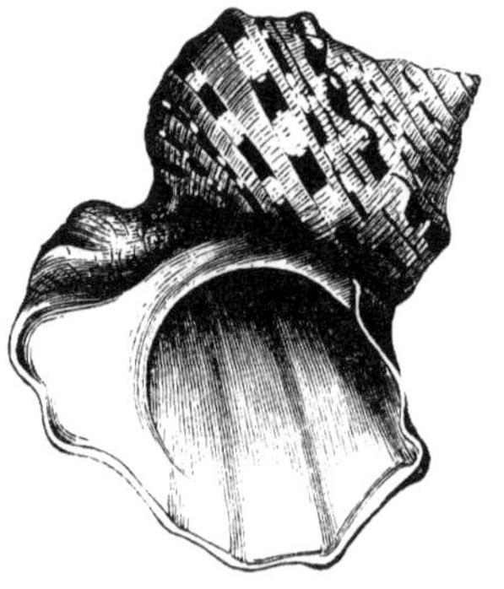

Fig. 226. Turbo marmoratus (Linnæus).

Fig. 227. Turbo undulatus (Chemnitz).

green, white, and brown outside, and superbly nacred within. The Gold-mouthed Turbo is so named from its nacre being of a rich golden yellow. The Wavy Turbo (*T. undulatus,* Fig. 227) is vulgarly known as the Australian Serpent's Skin. The shell is white, ornamented with longitudinal waving flexible lines of spots of green, or greenish-violet. *Turbo imperialis* (Fig. 228), from the Chinese seas, is green without, and brilliantly nacred within; it is vulgarly known as the paroquet.

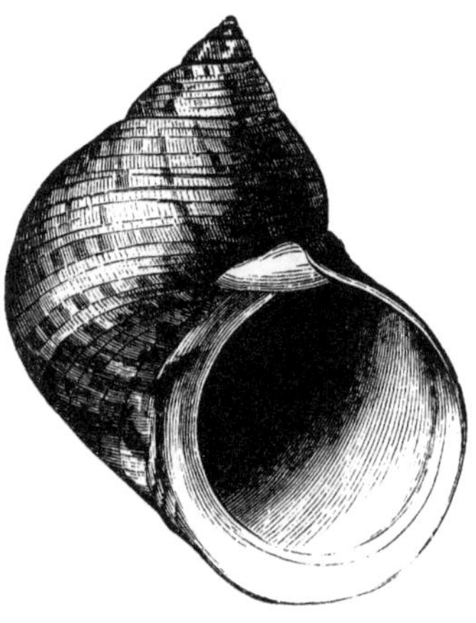

Fig. 228. Turbo imperialis (Gmel.).

The *Turbos* are found in the North seas, in the Channel, and on the Atlantic coast. The animal is eaten in nearly all the sea-ports of the Channel.

Near to the *Trochidæ* and *Turbos* in the system are the *Monodonta, Delphinula,* and *Turritella.*

The *Monodonta* are elegantly-marked shells, belonging to the seas of warm countries. *M. Australis* (Fig. 229) is a native of Australian seas. *M. labia* (Fig. 230) is a small brown shell, with white spots, which is very common on the shores of the Mediterranean.

Of the *Delphinula* only a small number of living species are known. They are natives of the Indian Ocean, and remarkable for the numerous spinous asperity of their shell (Fig. 231).

Fig. 229. Monodonta Australis (Lamarck).

Fig. 230. Monodonta labia (Lamarck).

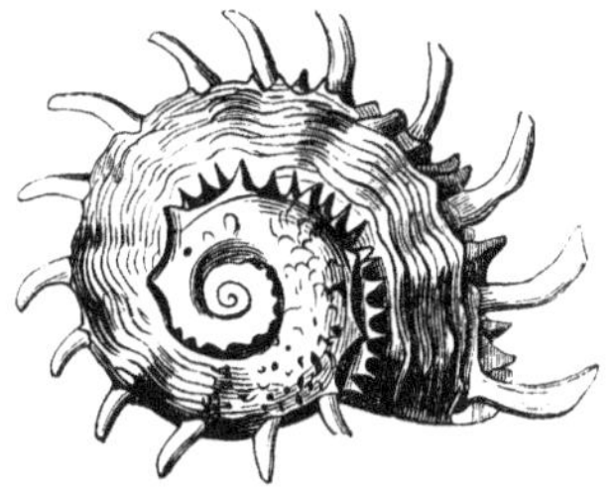

Fig. 231. Delphinula sphærula (Kiener).

The *Turritellidæ* are numerous, and found in every sea. All these shells, as their name indicates, represent a winding pyramid, terminating in a sharp point, some of them having fluted spirals, others

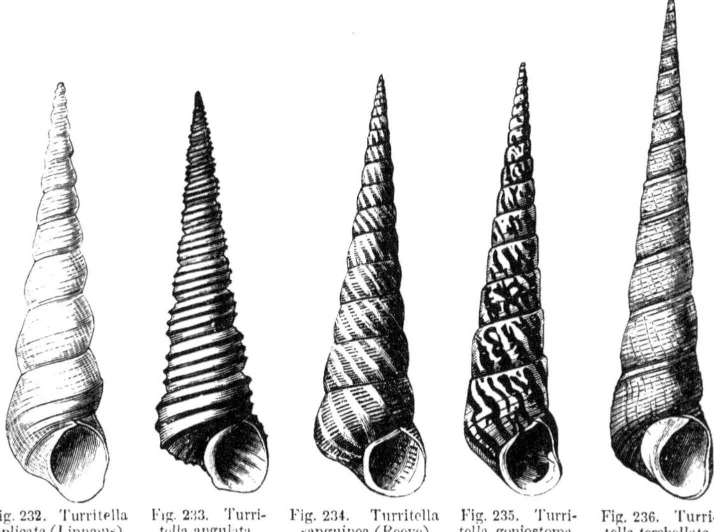

Fig. 232. Turritella replicata (Linnæus). Fig. 233. Turritella angulata (Sowerby). Fig. 234. Turritella sanguinea (Reeve). Fig. 235. Turritella goniostoma. Fig. 236. Turritella terebellata (Lamarck).

rounded, angular, or flat, and some of them elegantly pencilled. Figs. 232 to 236 represent some of the varied forms they assume.

The attention of naturalists has long been directed to a curious mollusc known under the name of *Janthina communis* (Fig. 237); its body is globular, and it presents an opening in front without contracting itself in order to form the head, which is long and trumpet-shaped, terminating in a large buccal opening, furnished with horny plates, and covered with little hooks; and two conical tentacles, slightly contracted, but very distinct, each bearing at their external base a long peduncle. The foot is short, oval, divided into two parts: the anterior, concave and cup-shaped; the posterior, flat and fleshy. It is this foot which bears a vesiculous mass like foam, which gives its peculiar character to the pretty mollusc. The mass consists of a great number of small bladders, which combine to keep the animal on the surface of the water. The shell is light, transparent, violet-coloured, and very much resembles the shell of the Helix. The *Janthinas* inhabit the deep sea, and often form banks of many leagues in extent. Messrs. Quoy and Gaimard have seen legions of Janthinas driven by the current. They have sailed during many days through these wandering tribes, which would be the sport of every gale if they could not, by drawing their heads within their shells and contracting their natatorial vesicles, diminish their volume and increase their weight at will, so as to sink quietly to the bottom of the water till the tempest was over. It is even pretended that at the approach of danger the *Janthina* discharges a liquid of a dark violet colour, which disturbs the water, and permits it to escape from its enemy.

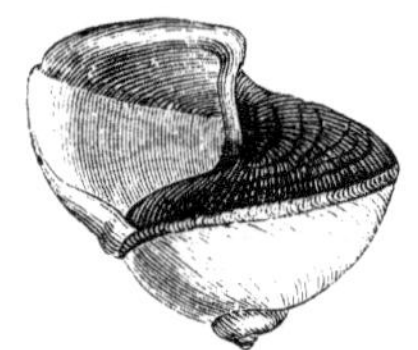

Fig. 237. Janthina communis (Lamarck).

BUCCINIDÆ.

This family includes a vast number of molluscs almost exclusively marine, among which are the beautiful genera *Conus*, *Porcelaina*, *Almea*, *Cassis*, and *Murex*, which we propose to pass in review.

The genus *Conus* is especially rich in species, as well as numerous in individuals. They are much sought after by collectors, being very rare, and command high prices. The shells belonging to this group present a very remarkable uniformity of shape, at the same time that the colours are very fine, and much varied in design. The shell is

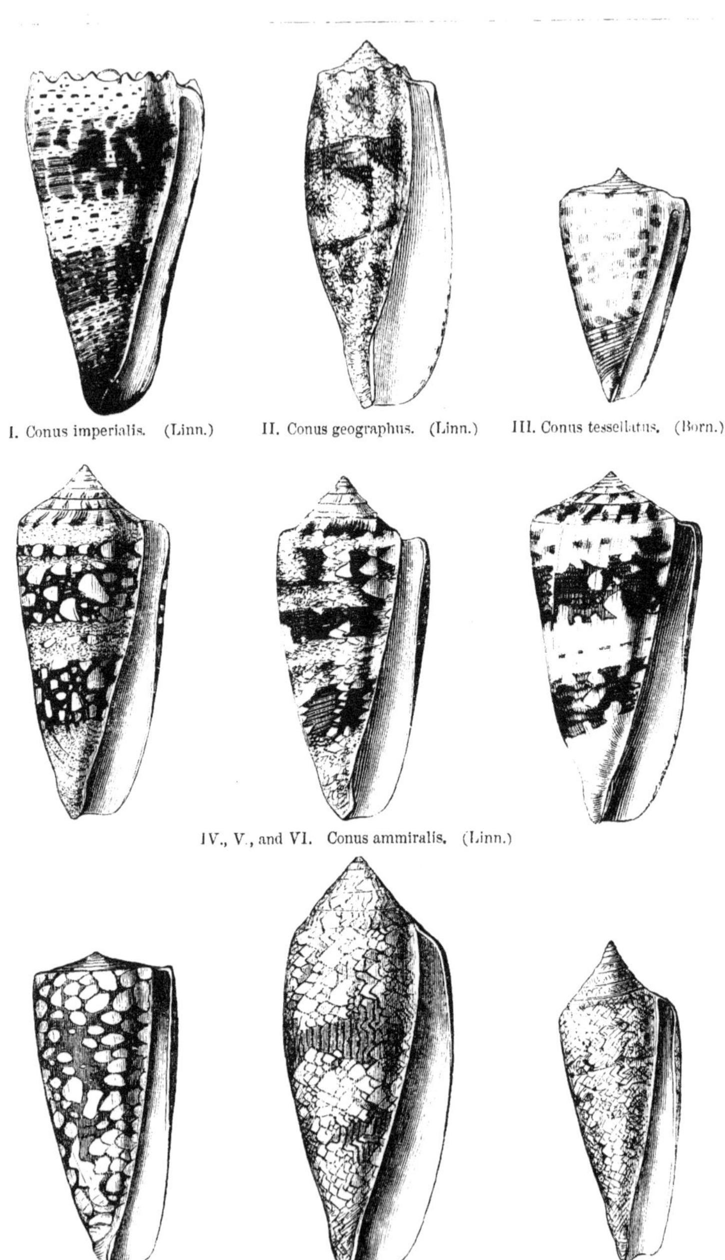

I. Conus imperialis. (Linn.) II. Conus geographus. (Linn.) III. Conus tessellatus. (Born.)

IV., V., and VI. Conus ammiralis. (Linn.)

VII. Conus nobilis. (Linn.) VIII. Conus textile. (Linn) IX. Conus gloria maris. (Chemn.)

Plate XXI.—Conus

thick, solid, inversely conical, wreathing spirally from the base to the apex, the spiral being generally short, the last turn constituting alone the greater part of the surface of the shell. The opening extends nearly along its whole length, occupying all the height of the last whirl. It is always narrow, its edges quite parallel; the columella presents neither fold nor curvature; the right edge is plain, sharp, and thin, detached from the front of the last spiral by a sloping hollow, more or less deep.

The animal which inhabits the Conus shell creeps upon a foot, elongated, narrow, truncate in front, furnished behind with a horny rudimentary operculum, altogether insufficient to cover the opening. The head, which is large, is elongated into a little snout, or muzzle, at the base of which rises on either side a conical tentacle, having an exterior eye upon its anterior extremity. At the extremity of the muzzle is the mouth, which is armed within with numerous horny hooks, inserted in the tongue. A cylindrical syphon, reversing itself in the shell, serves the purpose of carrying water to the branchiæ or gills. The shells inhabit the seas of warm countries, especially those lying between the Tropics, where they affect sandy coasts, with a depth of ten to twelve fathoms of water.

Among the species bearing a spiral crown, we may mention *Conus ædonulli*, of which many varieties are known, which come from the South American Seas and the Antilles. Of all species of the genus it is the rarest, and, consequently, most sought after for its rarity and beauty.

The commonest species is *Conus hebraica*, from the shores of Asia, Africa, and America. It is white with black spots, which are nearly square, arranged in transverse bands.

In Pl. XXI. we have represented some interesting species. *Conus imperialis* (Fig. I.) is a fine species, of white colour, with bands of a greenish yellow or tawny colour, ornamented with transverse, cord-like, articulated lines of white and brown. One of the largest species of the genus is *Conus geographus* (Fig. II.), which sometimes attains the length of six or seven inches; it is shaded white and brown.

Among the non-crowned species, we have represented in Fig. III. *Conus tessellatus*, common in the Indian Ocean. Its anterior part is violet in the interior. The spots with which it is surrounded are of a fine red or scarlet, or, in short, a red lead colour upon a white ground.

Conus ammiralis, of which three varieties, Figs. IV., V., and VI., are natives of the seas which bathe the Moluccas: they are beautifully marked varieties, of a brownish citron colour, marked with white spots nearly triangular, with tawny bands painted in very fine tracery. This species has been, and is still, much sought after by collectors, and presents many varieties besides those represented.

Among the shells, which seem almost ready to become cylindrical, may be noted *Conus nobilis* (Fig. VII.), a rare shell of yellowish colour approaching citron, ornamented with white spots. The golden drop, *Conus textile* (Fig. VIII.), is yellow in colour, ornamented with waving longitudinal lines of brown, and white corded spots edged with tawny colour. The glory of the sea, *Conus gloria maris* (Fig. IX.), is white in colour, banded with orange, and reticulated with numerous triangular white spots edged with brown. This is a native of the East Indies, and one of the most beautiful shells of the whole group.

The porcelain shells, or *Cypræa*, are brilliant, smooth, and polished, qualities which have procured for them the denomination under which they are best known. They are oval-shaped or oblong convex, with edges rolling inwards and longitudinal openings, narrow, arched, dentate on both edges, and notched at the extremities. The spiral, placed quite posteriorly, is very small, and often hidden by a calcareous bed of a vitreous appearance.

It is now known that the form and colouring of the shells vary very considerably, according to the age of the animal: so much so, indeed, that the same species examined at various stages of its growth would almost seem to species and even to genera essentially different.

In their youth Porcelains are thin, conical, elongated; with conspicuous, spiral, and large openings. The right edge soon becomes thicker, and folds itself inwardly; the opening is restricted; finally, the spiral is unfolded in successive folds from the right edge, and by successive deposits of the vitreous matter we have spoken of the opening is gradually contracted, its extremities hollowed out, its edges disconnected, and the shell, until now only shaded in pale tints, assumes its most brilliant colours, disposed in bands or spots, as exhibited in Pl. XXII., in which Figs. I. and II. are the adult shells, and Fig. III. the young shell, of *Cypræa Scottii*.

The animal which inhabits this shell is elongated, and is provided with a well-developed mantle, furnished on the inside with a band of tentacles; it is able to fold itself up in its shell in such a manner as

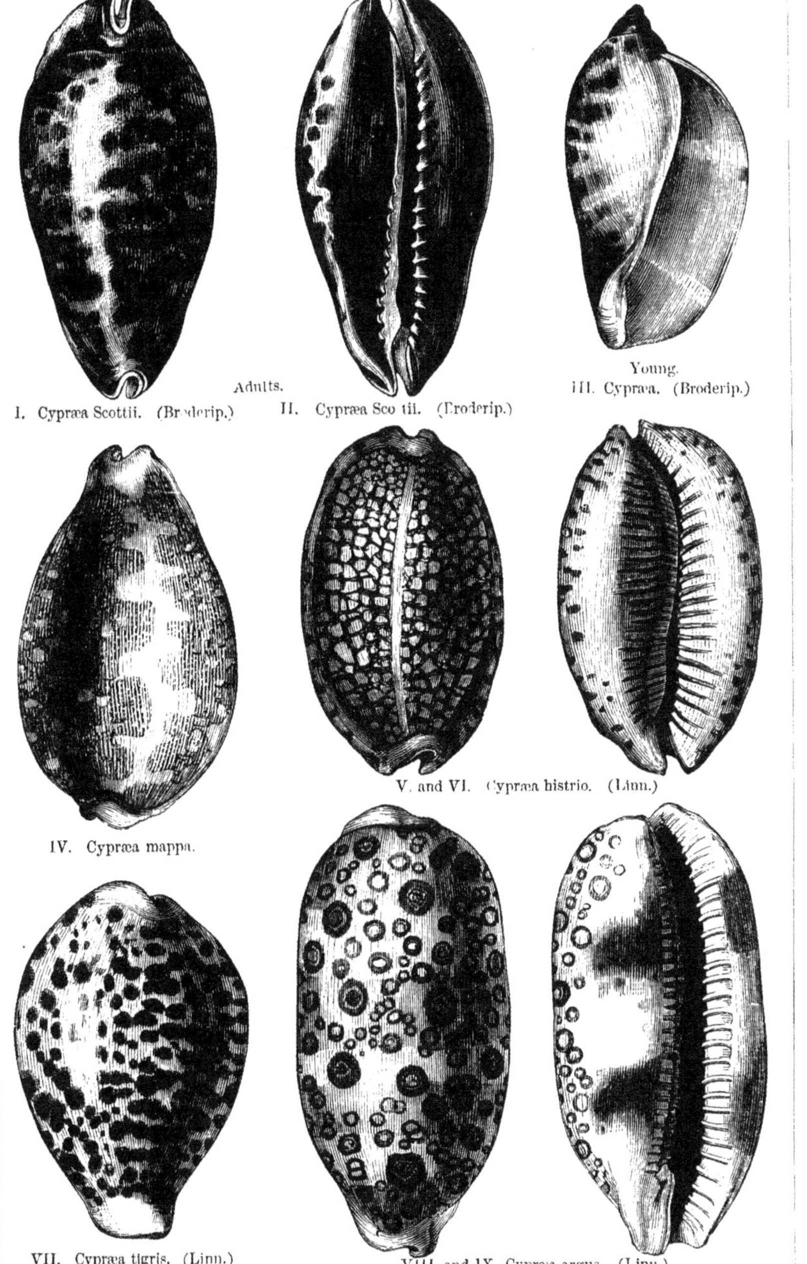

PLATE XXII.—Cypræadæ.

to be enveloped all round. The head is provided with two very long conical tentacles, each having a very large eye, in which a pupil and iris can be distinguished. The foot is oval, elongate, and without operculum, and is well represented in *Cypræa tigris* (Fig. 238). The Porcelains are found at a little distance from the shore, generally in clefts of the rocky bottoms; but sometimes they bury themselves in the sand. They are timid, shun the light, and only leave their retreats to creep about in search of food, which appears to be exclusively animal. These magnificent molluscs are natives of every sea. One small creature lives in the Channel; another and much larger species is found in the Adriatic; but the Indian Ocean is the home of the larger and finer species of porcelain shells.

As objects of curiosity and ornament these shells have been much in request in all ages. The inhabitants of the Asiatic coast make brace-

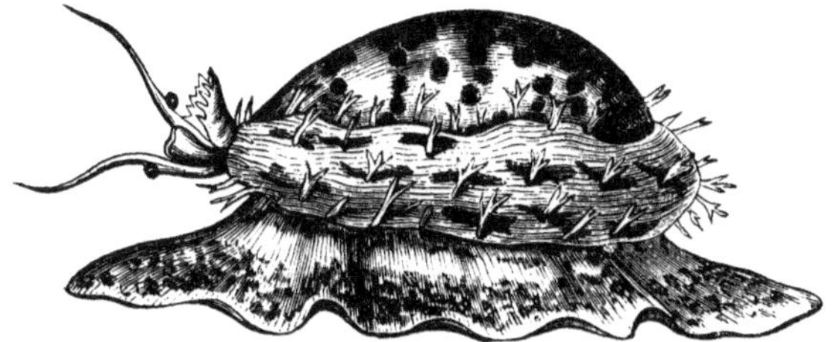

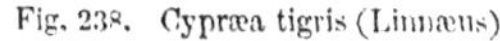
Fig. 238. Cypræa tigris (Linnæus).

Fig. 239. Cypræa coccinella (Lamarck).

lets, collars, amulets, and head-dresses of them, and use them to ornament boxes and harness. In New Zealand the chiefs carry a rare and choice species, suspended from the neck, as a badge of their rank or sign of distinction. This is *Cypræa coccinella* (Fig. 239). In some parts of India and Africa a very little species, the *Cowrie*, passes as current money. The species are, indeed, very numerous, and we can only find room for very brief descriptions of a few of the best known among them.

The Waving and Zigzag Porcelains, whose native country is unknown, are beautifully ornamented with waving and broken lines, as we see them in Figs. 240 to 243.

The Aurora Porcelain, of which we have spoken above, is nearly globular, of a uniform orange colour above, and white below; the teeth of the opening are of a bright orange. The shell is rare, and much sought after.

The Cowrie Porcelains, *Cypræa moneta* (Figs. 244 and 245), is a little oval shell, depressed, flat below, with very thick edges, and slightly waving. It is of a uniform yellowish white colour, sometimes

Figs. 240 and 241. Cypræa undata (Lamarck).

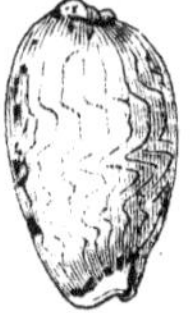

Figs. 242 and 243. Cypræa zigzag (Linnæus).

citron-yellow above and white below. There are usually twelve teeth in the opening. It comes from the Indian Ocean, the Maldivian Isles, and the Atlantic Ocean.

This shell, so common in collections, is gathered by the women on the shore of the Maldivian Isles, three days after the full moons and before the new moons; it is afterwards transported to Bengal, to India, and Africa, where, as we have already said, it is used by the negroes and other natives as money.

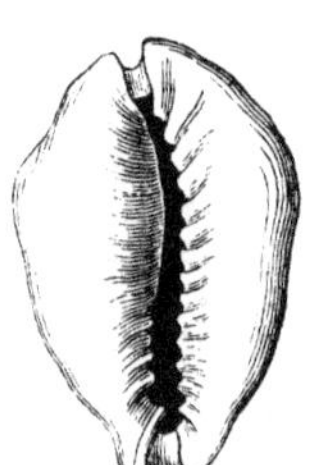
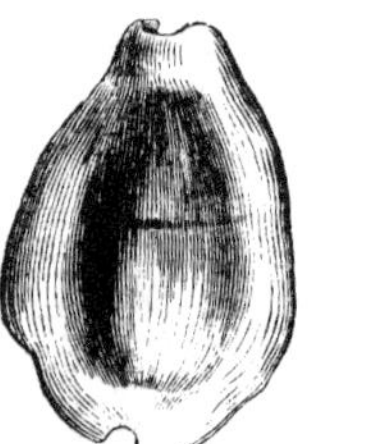
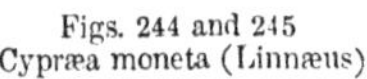

Figs. 244 and 245 Cypræa moneta (Linnæus).

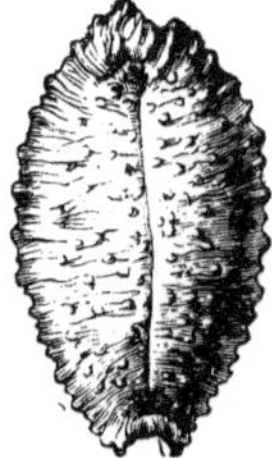
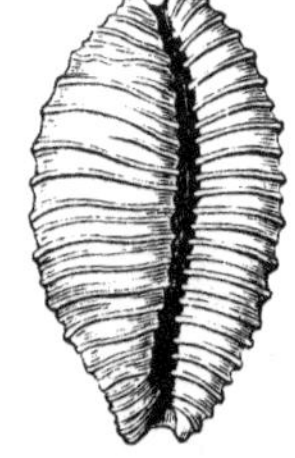

Fig. 246. Cypræa Madagascariensis (Gmel.). (1 and 2).

The Madagascar Porcelain, *Cypræa Madagascariensis* (Fig. 246), and the Granular Porcelain, *Cypræa nucleus* (Figs. 250 and 251), are beautifully marked species, having the general appearance of the Cowrie.

The species most abundant in the Channel is the little *Coccinelli* already mentioned; it is very small, oval, tun-bellied, the opening dilated in front with smooth transverse stripes of greyish, tawny, or rose colour, with or without spots.

Cypræa mappa (Pl. XXII., Fig. IV.) is oval-shaped, swelling below its sides, well-rounded, ornamented with small white spots below, with a dorsal branching line above; the interior is violet colour, with thirty-six teeth on one side and forty-two on the other. It belongs to the Indian Ocean.

The Harlequin Porcelain, *Cypræa histrio* (Figs. V. and VI.), from

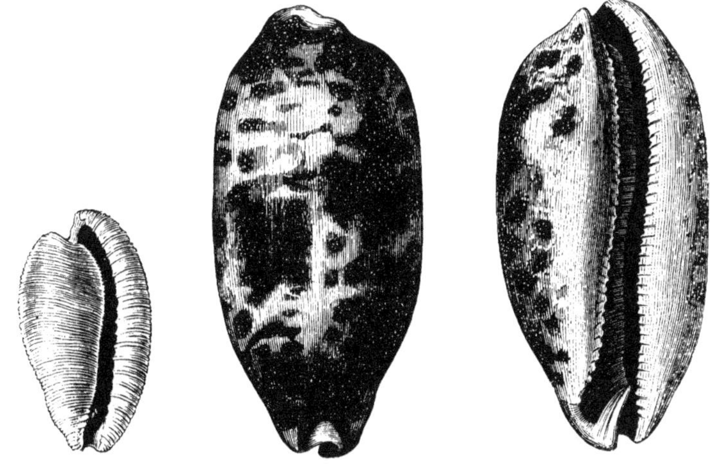

Fig. 247. Cypræa capensis (Gray). Figs. 248 and 249. Cypræa testudinaria (Linnæus).

the coast of Madagascar, is ornamented with white spots very closely arranged, and much circumscribed above, with black spots upon the sides. The under side is violet.

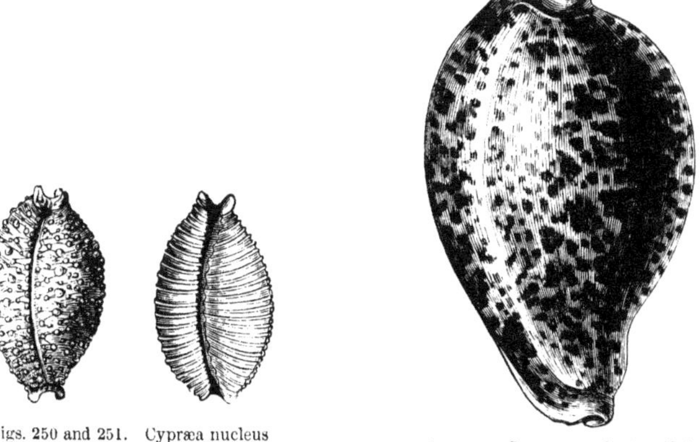

Figs. 250 and 251. Cypræa nucleus (Linnæus). Fig. 252. Cypræa pantherina (Sol.).

A very fine species, which is very common in collections, is found in the Indian Ocean, from Madagascar to the Moluccas—the Tiger

Porcelain, already figured with its inhabitant. This shell (Fig. VII.) is large, oval, tun-bellied, thick, and convex, of a bluish white, ornamented with numerous broad, black, round spots, much scattered, and a straight dorsal line, brown above and very white below. It has generally twenty-three teeth on each edge, quite white. Somewhat resembling the Tiger Porcelain is the *Cypræa pantherina* (Fig. 252), which is probably a variety of the same species. Another remarkable species is *Cypræa argus*, as represented in PL. XXII. (Figs. VIII. and IX.)

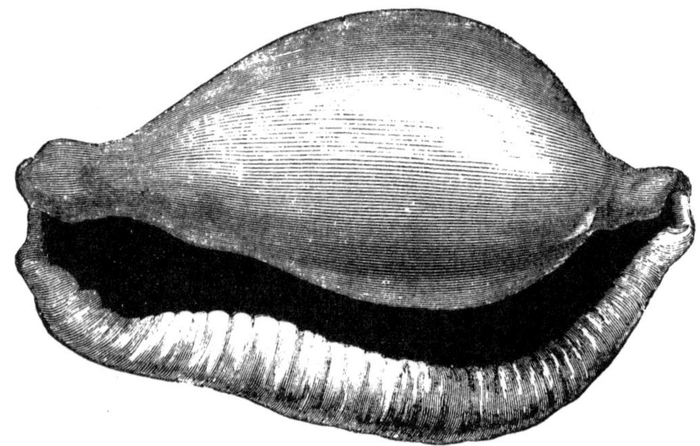

Fig. 253. Natural size of Ovula oviformis (Linnæus).

The genus *Ovula*, so called from their egg-shaped form, occupy a place near the cones in the system. The shell is highly polished, white or rose coloured, oblong or oval, convex, attenuate, and acuminate at the extremities without apparent spiral, the edges milled within the long, narrow, and curved opening, with teeth upon the left edge, and with a few ripples on the right edge. The Ovulæ are inhabitants of the Indian Ocean and Chinese seas. Some few species, however, belong to the Mediterranean and the Black Sea. The three species represented in Figs. 253, 254, and 255, present very singular contrasts of form and size.

Fig. 254. Natural size of Ovula cornea (Lamk).

In the genus *Voluta*, from *volvere*, to turn, the shell is oval, more or less tun-bellied. A spiral rising, slightly mammelate, the opening large, the edges notched, without channel; the columellar edge is lightly excavated and arranged in oblique folds. The right edge is arched, thick, or cutting, according to the species.

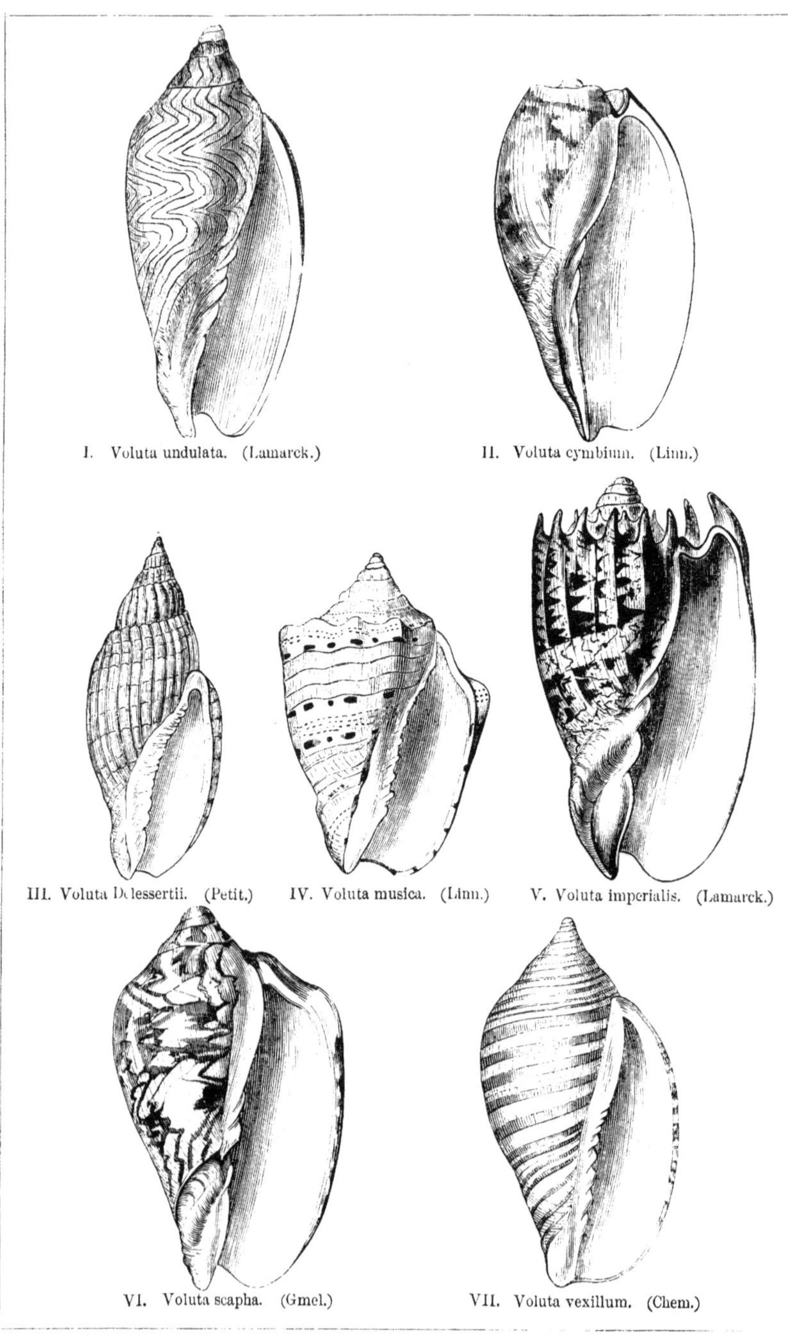
I. Voluta undulata. (Lamarck.)
II. Voluta cymbium. (Linn.)
III. Voluta Delessertii. (Petit.)
IV. Voluta musica. (Linn.)
V. Voluta imperialis. (Lamarck.)
VI. Voluta scapha. (Gmel.)
VII. Voluta vexillum. (Chem.)

PLATE XXIII.—Voluta.

The animal has a large head, provided with two tentacles. The mouth terminates in a thick trunk furnished with hooked teeth. The

Fig. 255. Ovula volva (Linnæus).

foot is very large, furrowed in front, and projecting from all parts of the shell, but without operculum. The Volutæ live on the sands near the shore; sometimes they are found high and dry, left by the retreating tide. Their shells, of various forms, are ornamented with the most lively colours, the surface covered with irregular lines, the tint of which is generally in strong contrast with that of the ground.

Among the more remarkable species illustrated in Pl. XXIII., we may note: Fig. I., *Voluta undulata;* Fig. II., *Voluta cymbium;* Fig. III., *Voluta delessertii;* Fig. IV., *Voluta musica;* Fig. V., *Voluta imperialis;* Fig. VI., *Voluta scapha;* and Fig. VII., *Voluta vexillum.*

Besides the genus Voluta, naturalists range the kindred genus *Oliva*, so named from their resemblance in form to the olive. Their nearly cylindrical shell is slightly spiral, polished, and brilliant as the Porcelains; its opening is still long and narrow, strongly notched

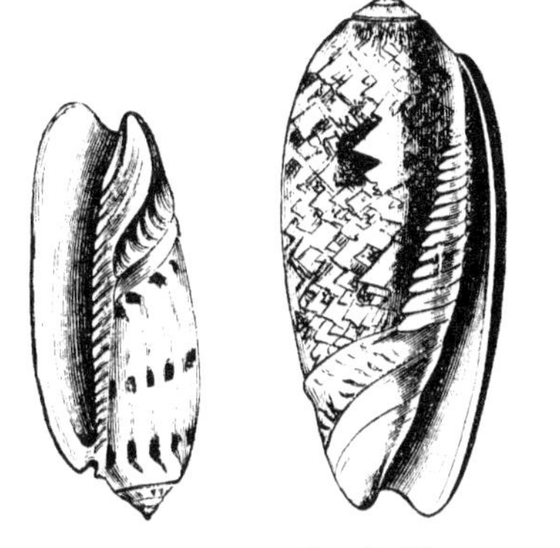

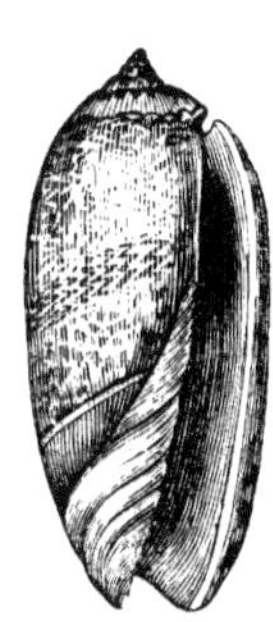

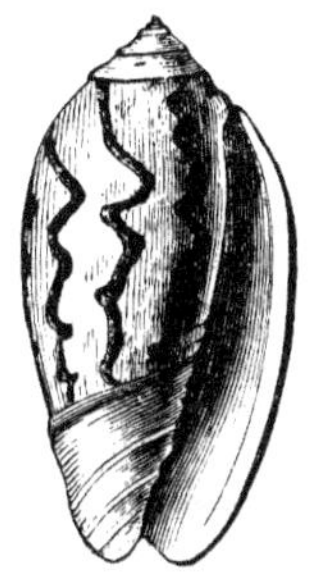

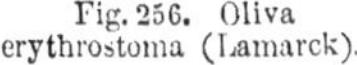

Fig. 256. Oliva erythrostoma (Lamarck).

Fig. 257. Oliva porphyria (Linnæus).

Fig. 258. Oliva irisans (Lamarck).

Fig. 259. Oliva Peruviana (Lamarck).

in front, its edge columellar, swollen anteriorly into a kind of cushion, and striped obliquely in all its length.

The Molluscs belong to the seas of warm countries, where they frequent the sandy bottoms and clear waters. They creep about with much agility, reversing themselves quickly when they have been overturned; they live upon other animals, and are flesh-eaters. They are, in fact, taken at the Isle of Tranu by using flesh as bait. The colours of the shell are very varied, and sometimes fantastically streaked. *Oliva erythrostoma* (Fig. 256) is ornamented externally with flexual lines of a yellowish-brown, with two brown bands, combined with the fine yellowish tint of gold colour within. *Oliva porphyria*, from the Brazil coast (Fig. 257), presents lines of a reddish-brown, regularly interlaced with spotted large brown marks, upon a flesh-coloured ground. *Oliva irisans* (Fig. 258) is painted in zigzag lines, close and brown, edged with orange-yellow, and with two zones of darker brown, and reticulated. *Oliva Peruviana* (Fig. 259) is furrowed with regularly spaced bands.

Mitra and Cassis.

Beside the Olives and Volutes in the system, and resembling them in many respects, we find the Mitres, so called from their resemblance to the bishop's mitre. They are natives of warm climates, such as the Indian Ocean, the Australian Seas, and the Moluccas. The shell of the Mitra is long, slender, and spiral, the spire ending in a point at the summit; the opening is small, narrow, and triangular, and notched in front. The inhabitant of the shell has the peculiarity of projecting from its mouth a sort of cylindrical trunk, which is long, very extensible as well as flexible, and probably prehensile, the use of which is only subject of surmise. *Mitra episcopalis* (Fig. 260), from the Indian Ocean, is white, ornamented with square spots of a fine red, and capable of high polish.

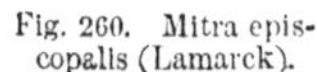

Fig. 260. Mitra episcopalis (Lamarck).

Fig. 261. Mitra papalis (Lamarck).

Mitra papalis (Fig. 261) has dentiform folds round the opening, which also crown each turn of the spiral; the spots are smaller, and much more numerous and varied in form than those of *M. episcopalis*.

In the casque *Cassis*, the shell is oval, convex, and the spiral of con-

Fig. 262. Cassis glauca (Linnæus). Fig. 263. Cassis rufa (Linnæus). Fig. 264. Cassis canaliculata (Brugières).

siderable height. The longitudinal opening narrow, terminating in front in a short channel, which becomes suddenly erect towards the back of the shell, as in *Cassis glauca* (Fig. 262), a glaring grey shell

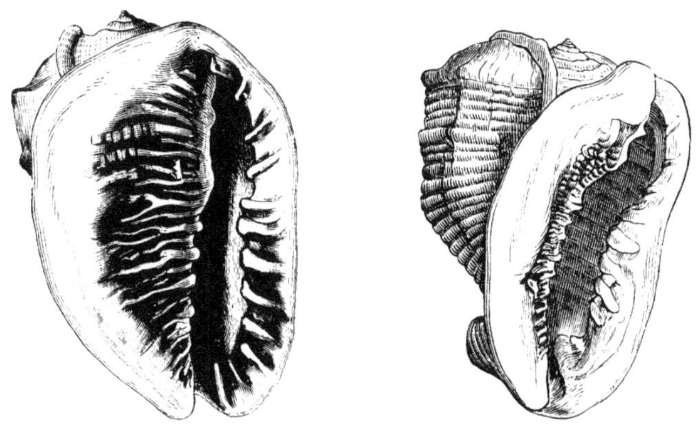

Figs. 265 and 266. Cassis Madagascariensis (Lamarck).

from the Moluccas. The columella is folded or toothed transversely, as in Fig. 263 (*Cassis rufa*); the right edge thick, furnished with a sort of pad externally, and dentate within. This shell is from the

Indian Ocean, and is of a fine purple colour, varied with black above; the edges of the opening being of a coral red colour, the teeth alone being white.

The head of the animal is large and thick, furnished with two conical elongated tentacles, at the base of which are the eyes. The mantle is ranged outside the shell, falling back upon the edges of the opening, and terminating at its anterior extremity in a long cylindrical channel, cloven in front, and passing by a hollow at the base into the bronchial cavity. The foot is large, and furnished with a horny operculum.

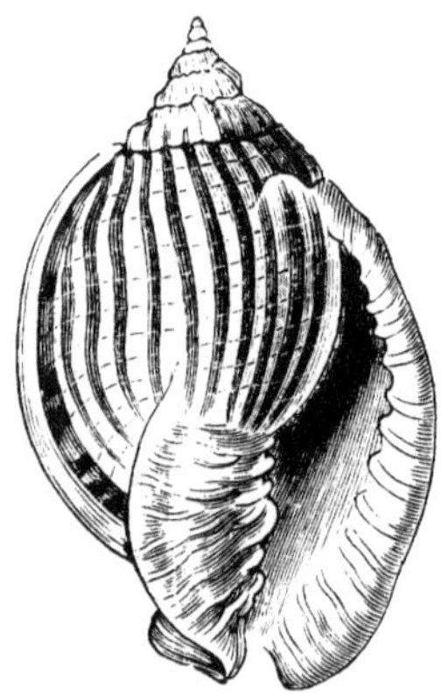

Fig. 267. Cassis zebra (Lamarck).

These animals keep near the shore, in shallow water. They walk slowly, and often sink themselves into the sand, where they prey upon small bivalves. They are not numerous in species; but specimens from the Indian Ocean are often large and beautifully marked. The shells of the less marked species are frequently used in India as lime, and employed as mortar.

Our space only permits us to mention, among the more curious specimens, *Cassis canaliculata* (Fig. 264), two varieties of *Cassis Madagascariensis* (Figs. 265 and 266), and the curious *Cassis undata* (Martini), *Zebra* (Lam.), or Zebra-marked Casque (Fig. 267).

Purpura.

The Purpuras have a classical name and history, having furnished the Greeks and Romans with the brilliant purple colouring matter which was reserved for the mantles of patricians and princes. The Purpura is an oval shell, thick-pointed, with short conical spiral, as in *Purpura capillus* (Fig. 268). In some it is tubercular or angular, the last turn of the spiral being larger than all the others put together. The opening is dilated, terminating at its lower extremity in an oblique notch. The columellar edge is smooth, often terminating in a point; the right edge often digitate, thick internally, and folded or rippled.

The animal presents a large head, furnished with two swollen conical tentacles, close together, and bearing an eye towards the middle of their external side. Its foot is large, bilobate in front, with a semicircular horny operculum.

The Purpuras inhabit the clefts of rocks in marine regions covered with algæ. On occasions they bury themselves in the sand. They creep about by the help of their foot in pursuit of bivalves, which they open by means of their short snout. They are found in all seas; but the larger species and greatest numbers come from warm regions, more especially from the Australian seas.

The Purpura of the ancients was not, as is generally thought, a vermilion red, but rather a very deep violet, which at a later period came to have various shades of red. The secret of its preparation was only known to the Phœnicians, that being most esteemed which came from Tyre. An English traveller, Mr. Wilde, has discovered on the eastern shores of the Mediterranean, near the ruins of Tyre, a certain number of circular excavations in the solid rock. In these excavations he found a great number of broken shells of *Murex trunculus*. It is probable that they had been bruised in great masses by the Tyrian workmen for the manufacture of the purple dye. Many shells of the same species are found actually living on the same coast at the present time.

Aristotle, in his writings, dwells upon the purple. He says that this dye is taken from two flesh-eating molluscs inhabiting the sea which washes the Phœnician coast. According to the description given by the celebrated Greek philosopher, one of these animals had a very large shell, consisting of seven turns of the spiral, studded with spines, and terminating in a strong beak; the other had a shell much smaller. Aristotle named the last animal *Buccinum*. It is thought that the last species is recognised in the *Purpura capillus* (Fig. 268), which abounds in the Channel. Réaumur and Duhamel obtained, in fact, a purple colour from this species, which they applied to some stuffs, and found that it resisted the strongest lye. The genus *Murex* is supposed to have been the first species indicated by Aristotle.

Up to the present time, the production of the purple remains a mystery. It was long thought this fine dye was furnished by the stomach, liver, and kidneys; but M. Lacaze-Duthiers has demonstrated that the organ which secretes it is found on the lower surface of the mantle, between the intestines and the respiratory organs, where it forms a sort of fascia, or small band. The colouring matter, as it is extracted from the animal, is yellowish; exposed to the light, it becomes golden yellow, then green, taking finally a fine violet tint. While these transformations are in progress a peculiarly pungent odour is disengaged, which strongly reminds one of that of assafœtida. That portion of the matter which has not passed into the violet tint is soluble in water; when it has taken that tint it becomes insoluble. The appearance of the colour seems provoked rather by the influence of the sun's rays than by the action of the air. The matter attains its final colour, in short, in proportion to the power of the sun's rays.

It is a question, how far the colour evolved under the solar rays remains indelible. It is known that the contrary is the case with the colouring matter of the cochineal insect, which changes very quickly when exposed to the sun. It is probably the remarkable resistance it opposes to the rays of the sun which recommended it to the ancients. The patricians of Rome, and the rich citizens of Greece and Asia Minor, loved to watch the magical reflections of the sun on the glorious colour which ornamented their mantles.

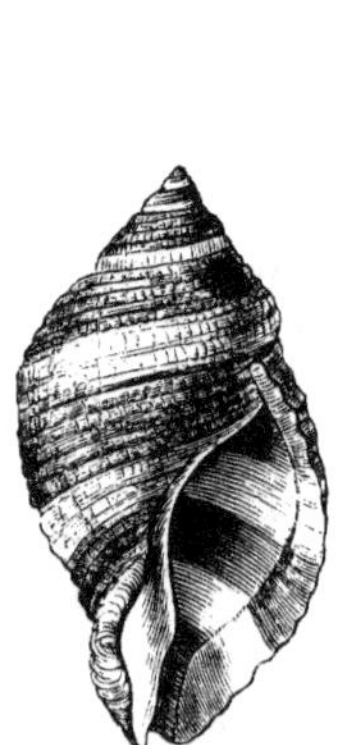

Fig. 268. Purpura lapillus (Linnæus).

Fig. 269. Purpura patula (Linnæus).

But to return to our humble shells. *Purpura lapillus* (Fig. 268) is a thick shell, oval acute, with conical spiral, generally of a faded or yellowish white, zoned with brown, and more or less spotted.

Purpura patula (Fig. 269) is a species so common in the Mediterranean that Columella thought it was from this species in particular that the Romans obtained their fine colour.

Purpura consul (Fig. 270) is one of the largest shells, and of a fine thick white colour.

The *Buccinums* resemble the Purpura in many respects. Their shell is oval or conical, much notched in front. They inhabit every

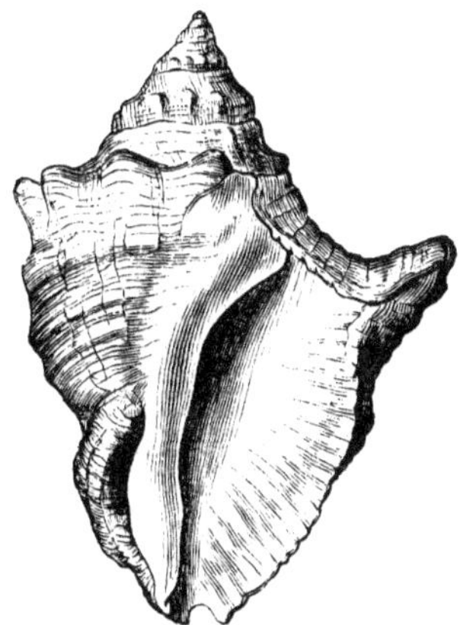

Fig. 270. Purpura consul (Linnæus).

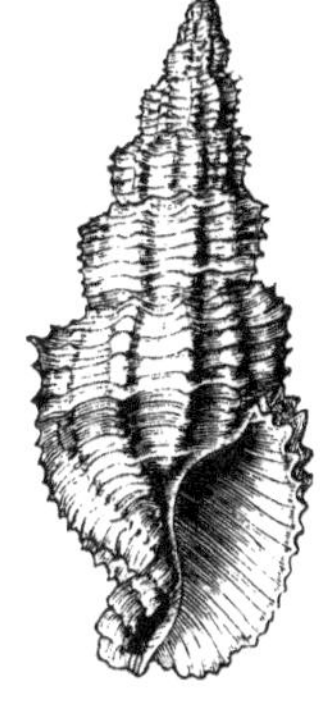

Fig. 271. Buccinum senticosum (Linnæus).

Fig. 272. Buccinum undatum (Linnæus).

sea, especially those of Europe. The animal has a small flat head, furnished with lateral tentacles or horns, bearing the eyes upon an external swelling, situated near their central length. We need only refer to Fig. 271, *Buccinum senticosum*, and *Buccinum undatum* (Fig. 272), for their general form, the well-known whelk of our markets.

Fig. 273. Harpa ventricosa (Lamarck).

The *Harpas* are shells of the Indian Ocean, richly enamelled within, and ornamented externally with slightly oblique longitudinal stripes in gay colours, with finely sculptured forms in the intervals; spiral very small, and opening large. Among the more attractive species are *Harpa ventricosa* (Fig. 273), *Harpa imperialis* (Fig. 274), and *Harpa articularis* (Fig. 275).

The *Murex*, or Rock Shells, include a large number of species, all remarkable for their bright colours and somewhat fantastical and varied forms. They are found in all seas, but become larger and more branching in the seas of warm regions. The shell is oval, or rather oblong, the spire more or less elevated, its surface generally covered with rows of spines, or tubercular ramifications. The opening, which

Fig. 274. Harpa imperialis (Lamarck).

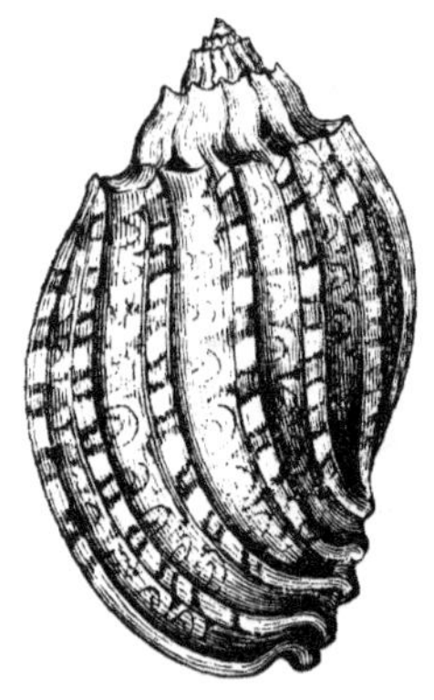

Fig. 275. Harpa articularis (Lamarck).

is oval, is prolonged in a straight canal often of very considerable length, as in Fig. 277 (*Murex haustellum*); the external edge is often smooth or rippled, the columellar edge sometimes callous.

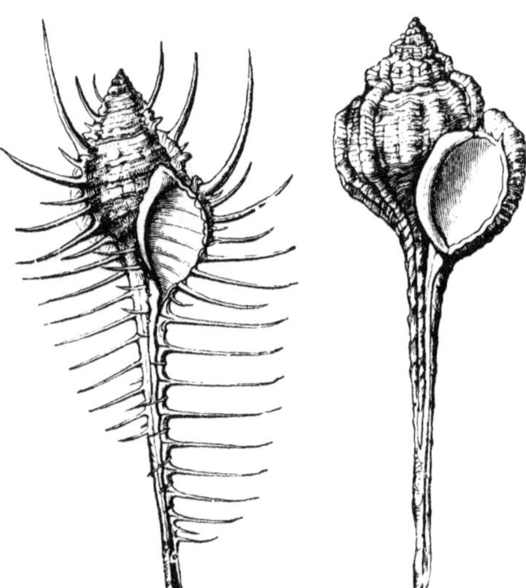

Fig. 276. Murex tenuispina (Lamarck). Fig. 277. Murex haustellum (Linnæus).

The head of the animal is furnished with two horns or tentacles, ocular upon their external side, the mouth elongated in the form of a trunk. The foot is large and round, and furnished with a horny operculum.

Among the species with long slender tube, covered with spines, one of the most notable is *Murex tenuispina* (Fig. 276), which is a native of the Indian Ocean and the Moluccas.

Among the strong-tubed species with long canal and no spines, from the same regions, is *Murex haustellum* (Fig. 277).

Among the short-tubed species, furnished with foliaceous and jagged fringes, is *Murex scorpio* (Fig. 278).

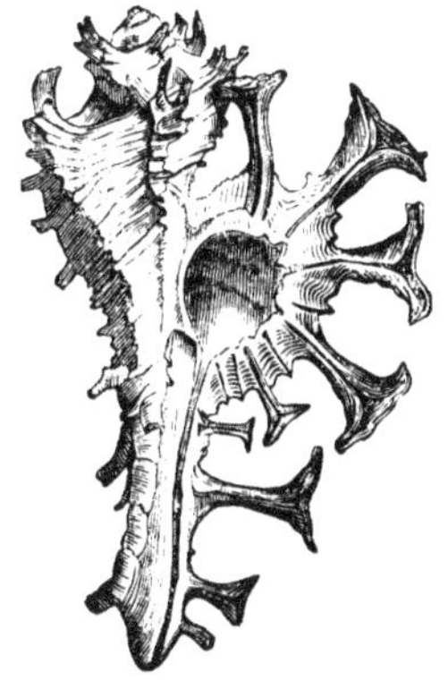

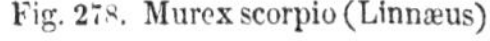

Fig. 278. Murex scorpio (Linnæus)

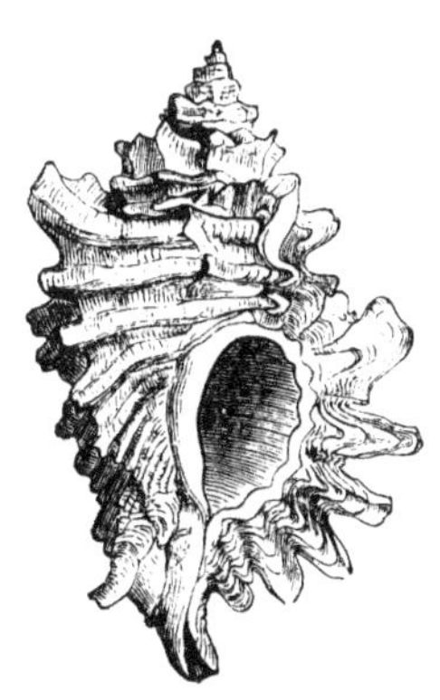

Fig. 279. Murex erinaceus (Linnæus).

One more typical species may be noted, namely, *Murex erinaceus* (Fig. 279), which is found on all the coasts of Europe, and especially

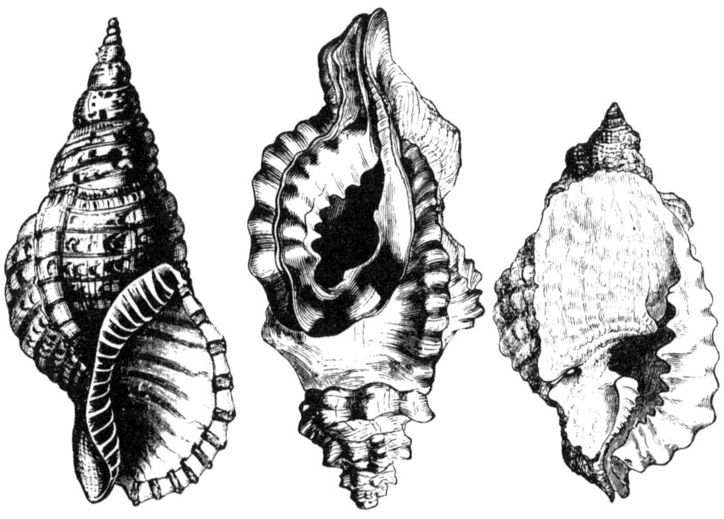

Fig. 280. Triton variegatum (Lam.) Fig. 281. Triton lotorium (Linn.) Fig. 282. Triton anus (Lam.)

in the Channel. Other species worthy of notice are found in the Mediterranean and the Adriatic, some of them, according to Cuvier and De Blainville, species which furnished the true Tyrian purple of the ancients; but our space prevents us from dwelling on them.

The *Tritons* are ranged beside the genus *Murex* in the system. Their shell is irregularly covered with scattered swelling excrescences, not, as in *Murex*, in longitudinal rows, but scattered all over the

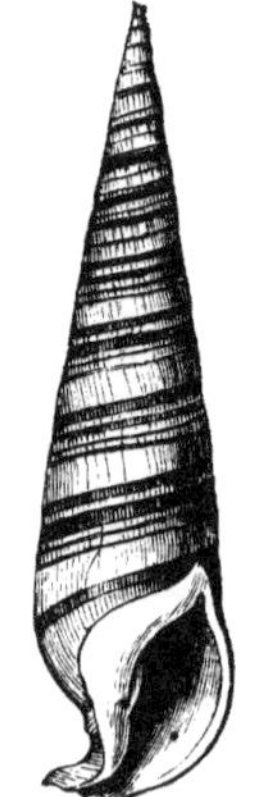

Fig. 283. Cerithium fasciatum (Brug.).

Fig. 284. Cerithium aluco (Linnæus).

Fig. 285. Cerithium giganteum (Lamarck).

surface. About forty species of Triton are known. They inhabit every sea, but more especially those in warm countries. *Triton variegatum*, vulgarly called the Marine Trumpet (Fig. 280), is a very large shell, which even attains a length of sixteen inches; it is enamelled with great elegance, in white, red, and tawny-brown. They come from the Indian Ocean, where they are very common. *Triton lotorium*

(Fig. 281) is of a reddish-brown externally and white within. The *Triton anus* (Fig. 282) is of a whitish colour, spotted with red.

Cerithium is a marine shell, which is found in muddy bottoms; on ships, and more frequently at the mouths of rivers, but rarely beyond the point to which the tide reaches. The genus is numerous in species. Such are *Cerithium fasciatum* (Fig. 283) and *Cerithium aluco* (Fig. 284).

The Giant Cerithium, *Cerithium giganteum* (Fig. 285), is the living analogue of a magnificent fossil species belonging to the tertiary

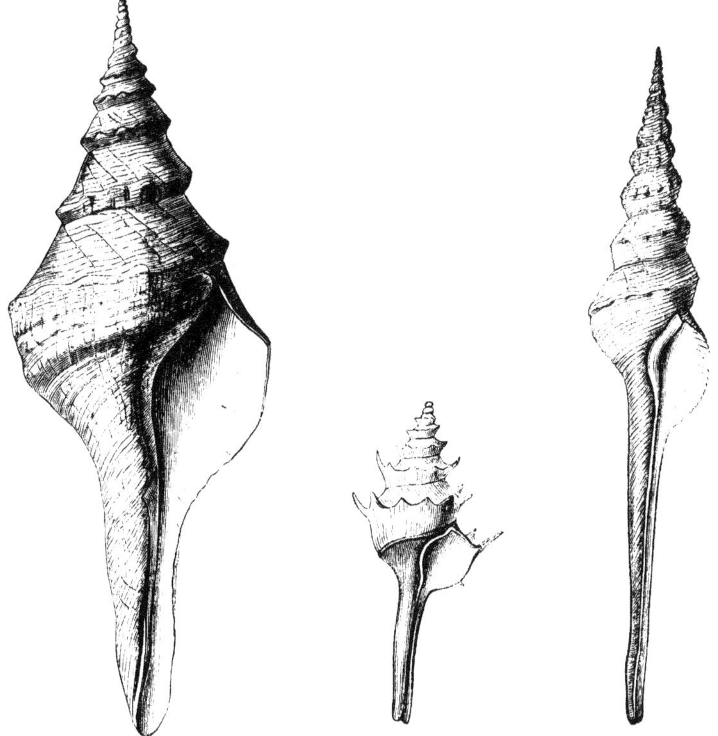

Fig. 286. Fusus proboscidiferus (Lam.). Fig. 287. Fusus pagodus (Lesson). Fig. 288. Fusus colus (Linnæus).

formation. The single known example of this species belongs to the Delessert Museum at Paris. A manuscript note by Lamarck, attached to this specimen, relates that this shell was first brought to Dunkirk in 1810 by an Englishman, one of the crew of an English ship.

The English sailor had drawn it up from the bottom of the sea with the sounding-lead from a bed of rocks off the coast of Australia.

The genus *Fusus*, or spindle shells, is distinguished by the elegance of its form rather than by the brilliancy of its colours. They are spindle-shaped, spire many whorled, canal long, operculum egg-shaped. Among the more remarkable species may be noted *Fusus proboscidiferus* (Fig. 286), *Fusus pagodus* (Fig. 287), and *Fusus colus* (Fig. 288).

The genus *Strombus* is a marine shell, belonging to Equatorial seas, of whose habits and manners very little is known. It is probable that they are long-lived, for their shells, when found perfect, have acquired a very considerable thickness and weight. They are even found

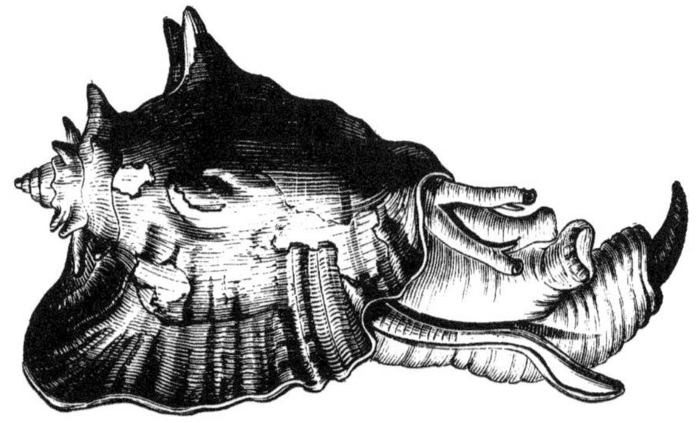

Fig. 289. Strombus gigas (Linnæus), with the animal.

encrusted in the interior with numerous layers of soft earthy sediment, and covered externally with small polypiers and other marine productions, as represented in *Strombus gigas* (Fig. 289).

Some species of *Strombus* attain great size and are placed as ornaments in halls and dining-rooms. In some of them the opening is brilliantly shaded, and those are chiefly sought after to decorate grottoes in gardens, or for collections of shells, where, from their size, they necessarily occupy a prominent place.

These shells are tun-bellied, terminating at their base by a short canal, notched or truncated; the right edge gets dilated with age; simple on one wing, lobed or cuneated in the upper part, and presenting in its lower part a groove or cavity separated from the canal or from the notch at the base.

The animal which inhabits this shell presents a distinct head, provided with a trunk or snout, and with two tentacles or horns, each bearing a large and vividly-coloured eye. The foot is compressed and

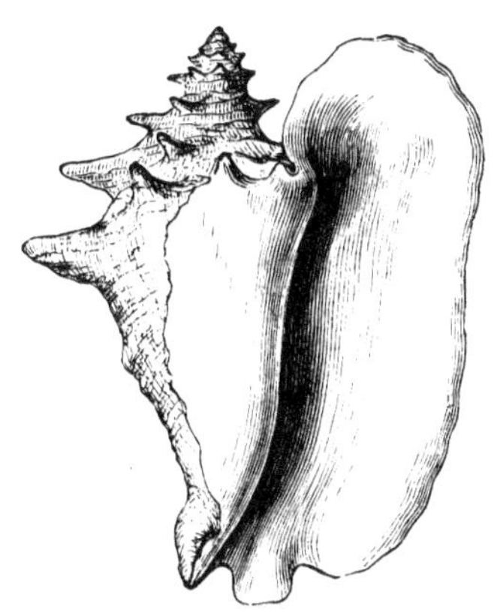

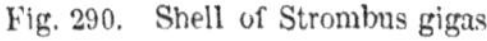

Fig. 290. Shell of Strombus gigas.

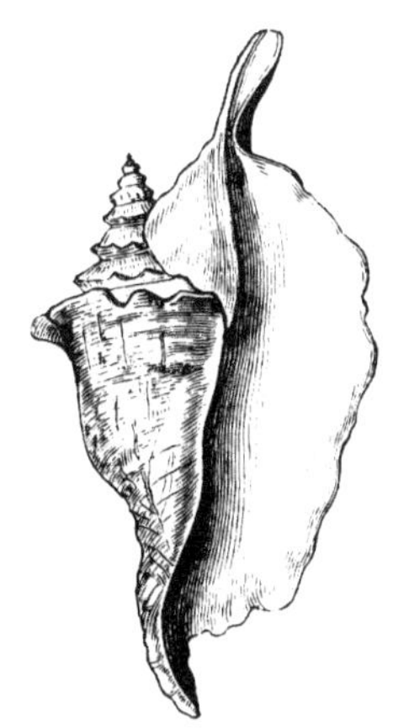

Fig. 291. Strombus gallus (Linn.).

divided into two portions, the posterior one, which is the longest, bearing a horny operculum—a true claw. In the eagle-winged *Strombus*, represented in Figs. 290 and 291, these several peculiarities are

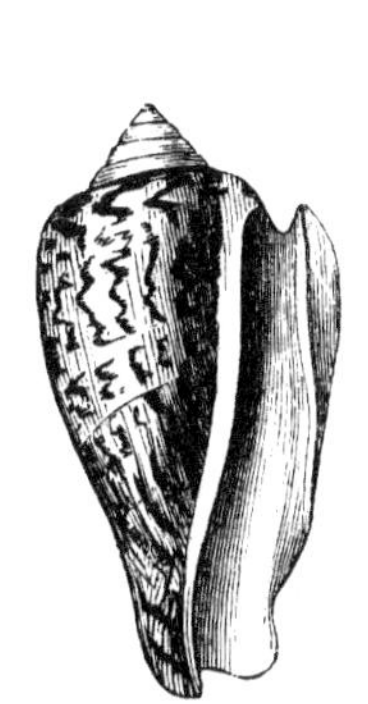

Fig. 292. Strombus luhuanus (Linnæus).

Fig. 293. Strombus cancellatus (Lamarck).

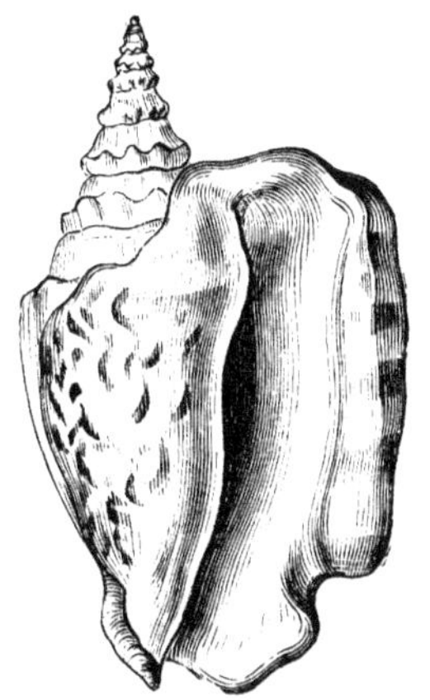

Fig. 294. Strombus thersites (Gray).

well developed. This shell is large, turbinate, distended in the middle, with an acutely-pointed spiral studded with conical tubercles, the right edge very broad, rounded off below. The opening is of a vivid rose purple fading into white. It is a native of the Antilles.

Strombus gallus, or the angel-winged (Fig. 291), veined with stripes of white and red, comes from the coasts of Asia and America. *Strombus luhuanus* (Fig. 292) is fawn-coloured, sown with white, and externally the right edge is red and striped; inside the columella is shaded purple and black.

Strombus cancellatus, the trellised Strombus (Fig. 293), is small in size and white in colour. *Strombus thersites* is also represented (Fig. 294).

Pterocera.

The Pterocera, from πτερὸν, wing, and κέρας, horn, in many respects resemble the Strombi. They are distinguished from them chiefly in this, that the right edge developes itself with age in long and slender digital spines more or less numerous, the numbers of which vary

Fig. 295. Pterocera scorpio (Linnæus).

Fig. 296. Pterocera millepeda (Linnæus).

according to the species. The Pteroceras are found in the seas of both hemispheres, their vulgar denomination being sea-spiders or scorpions. A glance at the illustrations (Fig. 295, *Pterocera scorpio*; Fig. 296, *P. millepeda*; Fig. 297, *P. chiragra*; and Fig. 298, *P. lambis*) will satisfy the reader as to the general correctness of this designation.

The family of Pterocera, whose remarkable form is so well calculated to excite our admiration, has yet another attraction: the colouring of the shell exhibits many shades, which are particularly varied

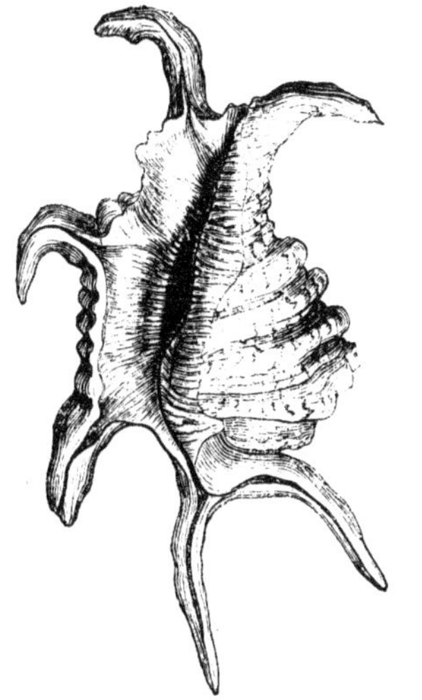

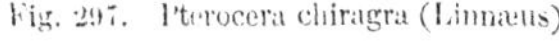

Fig. 297. Pterocera chiragra (Linnæus).

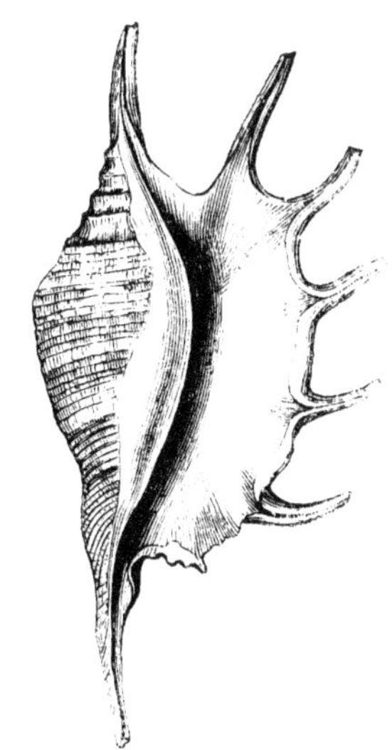

Fig. 298. Pterocera lambis (Linnæus).

towards the opening, where it is generally distinguished by great freshness and brilliancy, which, added to its other characters, render it the most interesting of all the Gasteropods.

Cyclobranchial Gasteropods.

The Cyclobranchial Gasteropods have the *branchiæ* in the form of leaflets or small pyramids, attached in one row on each side under the edge of the mantle. These are essentially marine animals, which form two families, viz. *Chitonidæ* and *Patellidæ*.

The *Chitons* are very singular creatures, destitute of eyes, of tentacles, and without jaws; they bear upon their back in place of a shell a cuirass composed of imbricated and movable scales. They have the power of elongating and contracting themselves like the snails. They roll themselves up into a ball like the woodlouse. They adhere with great force to the rocks, affecting those places most exposed to the beating waves. *Chiton magnificus* (Fig. 299) is found in all seas.

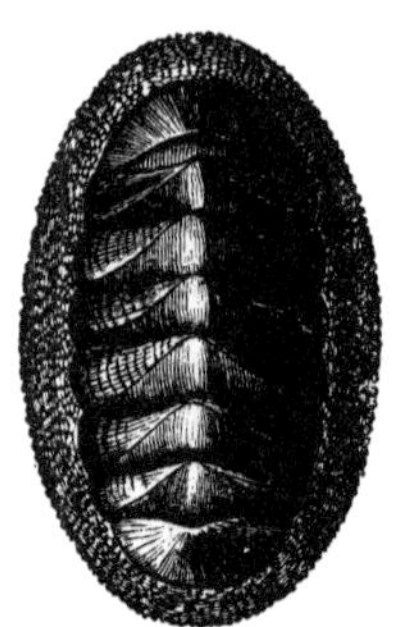
Fig. 299. Chiton magnificus (Deshayes).

The *Patellidæ*, or Limpets, constitute a very numerous family, distinguished at once by the form and structure of the animal, and by that of the shell. It was indebted to the ancients for its vulgar name of Limpet, which Linnæus changed to Patella, or little plate, although the majority of the species have little resemblance to a plate, large or small.

The shell of the Patellidæ is univalve, oval, or circular, non-spiral, but terminating in an elliptic cone, concave and simple beneath, non-pierced at the summit, entire and inclined anteriorly. It is smooth, or ornamented on the sides with ridges radiating from the summit, and often covered with scales; the edges are frequently dentate. The colours are vivid and much varied. The interior is very smooth, and remarkable for the brilliancy and vigour of its tints.

The head of the animal is furnished with two pointed tentacles or horns, having an eye at the external base of each. The body is oval and nearly circular, conical, or depressed. The foot is in the form of a thick fleshy disk. Certain lamellar branchiæ are arranged in series all round the body.

The Limpets dwell upon the sea shore, in the parts alternately covered and uncovered by the waves. They are almost always attached to rocks, or other submerged bodies, to which they adhere with great tenacity. If the Limpet is touched before any attempt is made to dislodge it, no human force, it is said, can remove it without breaking the shell. We are assured that a Limpet can sustain without yielding a weight of many pounds weight. It holds on by the great quantity of vertical fibres of the foot, which in raising the median part forms in the centre a sort of sucker. It is the celebrated experiment of the Magdeburg cups which these little molluscs realise by their vital action.

These animals bury themselves in the chalky rocks to the depth of two or three lines; when they are dispersed, they are observed constantly to return to the same place. Their movements are, besides, extremely slow; the advance of the Limpets being only perceived by watching the slow upheaval of the shell above the plane of its position. It is supposed, from the mouth being armed on its upper edge with a large semi-lunar, horny, cutting tooth, and in its lower part from having a tongue furnished with horny hooks, and from their inhabiting in great numbers places covered with marine plants, that their food is chiefly vegetable.

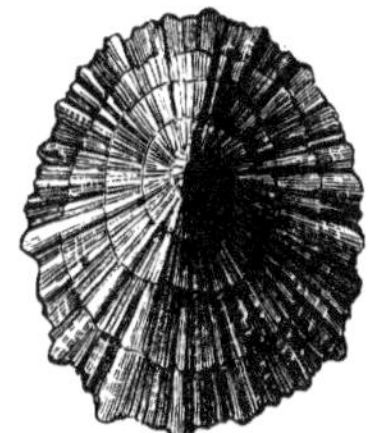

Fig. 300. Patella cærulea (Lamarck).

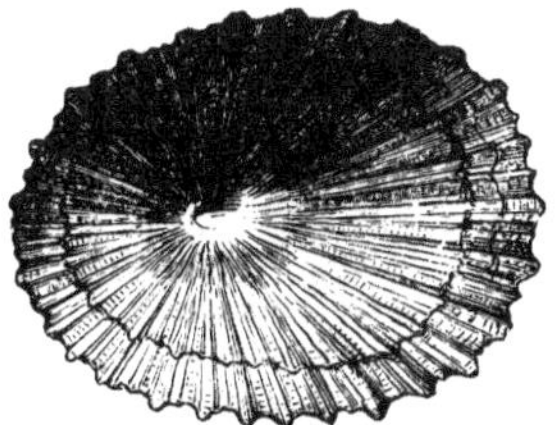

Fig. 301. Patella umbella (Gmel.).

The poorer inhabitants of the coast eat Limpets when they have nothing else, but their flesh is singularly coriaceous and indigestible.

Fig. 302. Patella granatina (Linnæus).

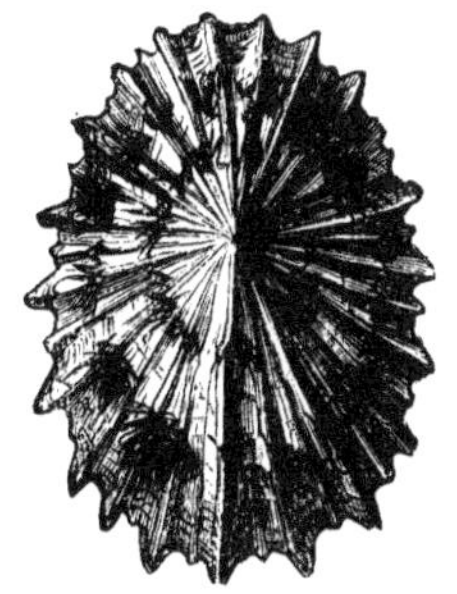

Fig. 303. Patella barbata (Lamarck).

They are found in every sea; but are, however, found to be larger as well as more numerous, and much richer in colour, in Equatorial seas, and especially in the southern hemisphere, than in European seas.

The common Limpet is thick, solid, oval, and nearly circular, generally conical, and covered with a great number of very fine stripes. Its colour is of a greenish grey, uniform above, and of a greenish yellow inside. It is abundant in the Channel and on Atlantic coasts.

The Blue Limpet, *Patella cærulea* (Fig. 300), from St. Helena, has an oval shell, broadest behind, moderately thick, depressed, flattened, covered with angular wrinkles, and dentate on the edge. It is of a spotted green outside and of a fine glossy blue within.

Other very elegant species are *Patella umbella* (Fig. 301), from the African coast. *Patella granatina* (Fig. 302), the ruby-eyed Limpet from the Antilles; *Patella barbata*, the bearded Limpet (Fig.

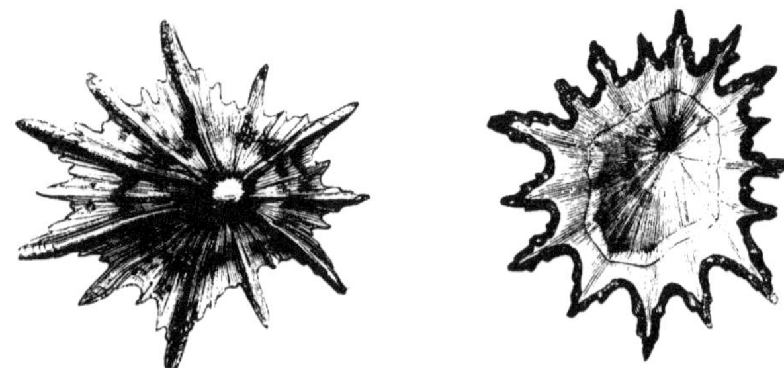

Figs. 304 and 305. Patella longicosta (Lamarck).

303), and the long-shore Limpet, *Patella longicosta* (Fig. 304), the outside of the shell, and Fig. 305 the inside.

CHAPTER XV.

MOLLUSCOUS PTEROPODS.

"Natura non facit saltus." LINNÆUS.

BETWEEN the Gasteropods and Cephalopods naturalists place a small group of marine animals very limited, both in genus and species, the principal characteristic of which is a membranous expansion situated on the right and left side of their head, from which they take their name of Pteropoda, from ποῦς-πτερὸς, winged feet.

Our space only permits us to notice the most remarkable of these curious creatures. To omit them would be to leave a gap in our history of molluscous animals.

The wings or flappers with which they are provided enable them to pass rapidly through the water, in which they feel about with rapid and continual movements, which can only be compared to those of a butterfly. Like these, the movements of the Pteropods are incessant, their flappers being not unlike the wings of the insect. They advance in this manner in a given direction, while the body or the shell remains in an oblique or vertical position.

These little molluscs may be seen to ascend to the surface very suddenly, turn themselves in a determinate space, or rather swim, without appearing to change their place while sustaining themselves at the same height. If anything alarms them they fold up their flappers, and descend to such a depth in their humid world as will give them the security they seek. They thus pass their lives in the open sea far from any other shelter, except that yielded by the gulf weed and other algæ. In appearance and habits, these small and sometimes microscopic creatures resemble the fry of some other forms of mollusca. They literally swarm both in Tropical and Arctic seas; sometimes so numerous as to colour the ocean for leagues. They are the principal food of whales and sea birds in high latitudes, rarely approaching the coast. Only one or two species have been accidentally taken on our shores, and those evidently driven thither by currents into which they have been entangled, or by tempests which have stirred the waters with a power beyond theirs. Dr. Leach states that in 1811, during a tour to the Orkneys, he observed on the rocks of the Isle of Staffa several mutilated specimens of *Clio borealis*. Some days after, having borrowed a large shrimp-net, and rowing along the coast of Mull when the sea, which had previously been extremely stormy, had become calm, he succeeded in catching one alive, which is now in the British Museum.

"In structure," Mr. Huxley tells us, "the Pteropods are most nearly related to the marine univalves, but much inferior to them. Their numerous ganglia are concentrated into a mass below the œsophagus; they have auditory vesicles containing otolithes, and are sensible of light and heat, and probably of odours, although at most they possess very imperfect eyes and tentacles. The true foot is small or obsolete; in *Cleodera lanceolata* (Fig. 310) it is combined with the fins; but in *Clio* it is sufficiently distinct, and consists of two elements or *spirals;* the superior portion of the foot supports an operculum. The fins are developed from the sides of the mouth or neck, and are the equivalents of the side-lappets (*Epipoda*) of the sea-snails. The mouth of *Pneumodermon* is furnished with two supporting miniature suckers; these organs have been compared to the dorsal arms of the cuttle-fishes; but it is doubtful whether their nature is the same. A more certain point of resemblance is the ventral flexure of the alimentary canal, which terminates on the under surface near the right side of the neck. The Pteropods have a muscular gizzard armed with gastric teeth, a liver, a pyloric cæcum, and a contractile renal organ opening into the cavity of the mantle. The heart consists of an auricle and a ventricle, and is essentially opisthobranchiatic, although sometimes affected by the general flexure of the body. The venous system is extremely incomplete. The respiratory organ, which is little more than a ciliated surface, is either situated at the extremity of the body, and unprotected by a mantle, or included in a branchial chamber with an opening in front. The shell when present is symmetrical, glassy, and translucent, consisting of a dorsal and a ventral plate united, with an anterior opening for the head, lateral slits for long filiform processes of the mantle, and terminated behind in one or three points; in other cases it is conical or spirally-coiled, and closed by a spiral operculum. The sexes are united, and the orifices situated on the right side of the neck. According to Vogt, the embryo Pteropod has deciduous vola like the sea-snails, before the proper locomotive organs are developed."

The Pteropods seem to be eminently sociable and gregarious, swarming together in great numbers; they present some analogical resemblances to the Cephalopodæ; but permanently they represent the larval stage of the sea-snails. De Blainville divides the group into two sections, *Thecosomata* and *Gymnosomata*, the first including the *Hyalœidæ* and *Lemacinidæ;* the second contains one family, the *Clionidæ.* The Hyalœidæ have small horny shells, very thin and transparent, globulous, or elongated, open anteriorly, cloven on the

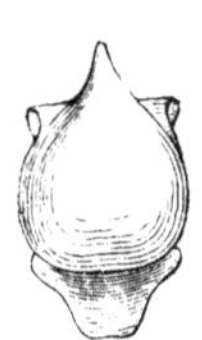
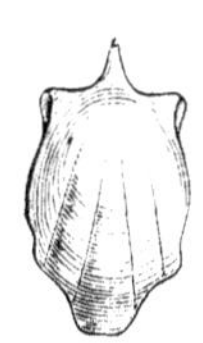

Figs. 306 and 307. Hyalea gibbosa (Rang.)

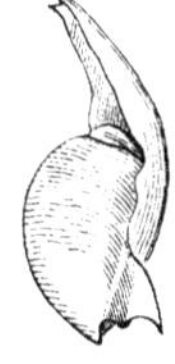
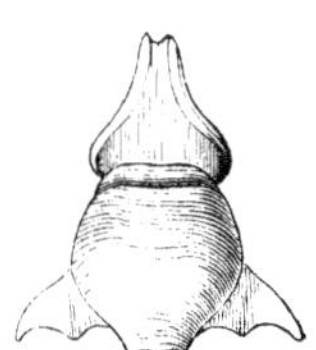

Figs. 308 and 309. Hyalea longirostris (Lesueur).

sides, and truncate at the posterior extremity. Their globular body is formed of two parts, the one including the head, bearing two very strong tentacles, and two large fins or flappers in the form of wings, springing from each side of the mouth.

These molluscs are small, and generally of a yellowish-blue or violet colour. They are inhabitants of the deep sea, and rarely seen out of what sailors call "blue water." They plough the waves with great rapidity by the aid of their formidable fins. Certain winds throw them sometimes in great numbers on the shores of the Mediterranean. These little creatures, so inoffensive, and which live together in vast numbers, seem to be an easy and ready-prepared prey, which the great marine animals may swallow by thousands. Twenty species of *Hyalea* are described as actually living in the Atlantic and Australian seas. Of these *Hyalea gibbosa* (Figs. 306, 307) and *Hyalea longirostris* (Figs. 308, 309) are here represented.

The great flappers of *Hyalea stridentata* are yellow, marked at their base with a fine violet spot. Its shell, plain above, convex beneath, is cloven on the side. The superior part is longer than the inferior, and the transverse line which unites them is furnished with three

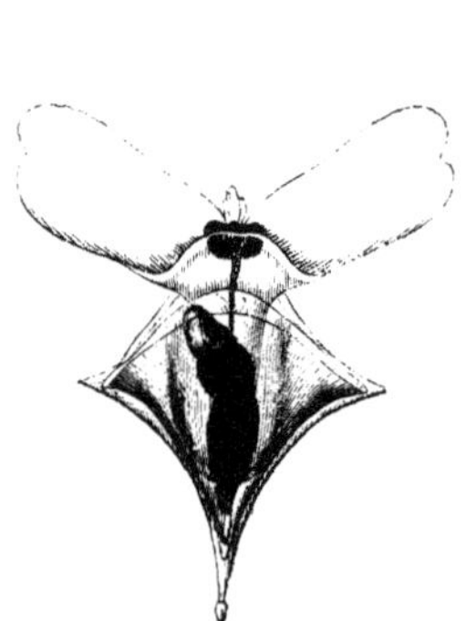

Fig. 310. Cleodora lanceolata (Lesueur).

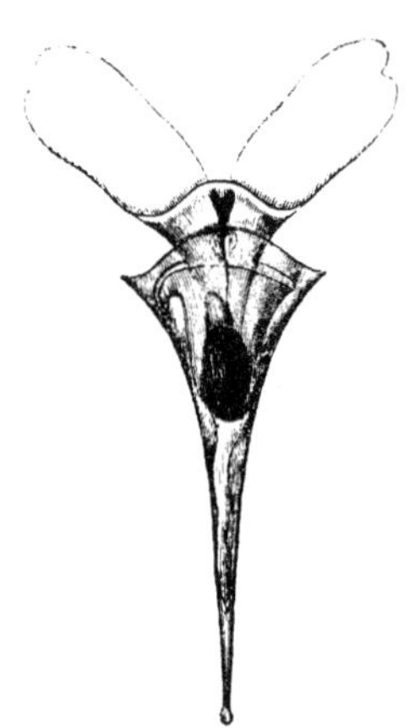

Fig. 311. Cleodora compressa (Eydoux and Souleyet).

teeth. This shell is yellow, and nearly translucent. When the animal swims, two expansions of its mantle issue from the lateral clefts in the shell.

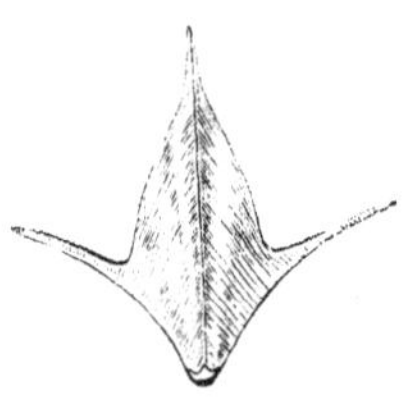

Fig. 312. Cleodora cuspidata (Bocc.).

The genus *Cleodora lanceolata* is a delicate and graceful creature; its body, of gelatinous appearance, has a distinct head, with its fins near the neck, notched in the form of a heart (Fig. 310); its posterior part is globulous, transparent, and luminous even in the dark. The animal which inhabits it sometimes shines through the shell like a light placed inside a lantern. This shell is triangular, as in *Cleodora cuspidata* (Fig. 312), thin, vitreous, and fragile, terminating in a long spine at the base.

CHAPTER XVI.

CEPHALOPODOUS MOLLUSCA.

"Monstrum, horrendum, informe, ingens." VIRGIL.

WE approach the more voluminous and perfect molluscs in the Cephalopods. Their name, as already stated, is taken from the position of the feet, which are inserted in the anterior part of the head: in Greek κεφαλὴ, head, and ποῦς-ποδὸς, foot.

The Cephalopodous Molluscs are greatly advanced in the scale of being, for they possess in a high degree the sense of sight, hearing, and touch. They appear with the first animals which present themselves on the earth, and they are numerous even now, although they are far from playing the important part assigned to them in the early ages of organic life upon our planet. The *Ammonites* and *Belemnites* existed by thousands among the beings which peopled the seas during the secondary epoch in the history of the globe.

This great class is divided into two orders: *Acetabuliferous*, or sucker-bearing, and *Tentaculiferous Cephalopods*, those furnished with strong fleshy tentacula.

ACETABULIFEROUS CEPHALOPODA.

To this group belong the cuttle-fish, squids, and argonauts, among existing species, and the Belemnites among the fossil species. Some of these creatures are large, and essentially flesh-eaters, or carnivorous; and, if we may believe all that has been written respecting them, very formidable ones. Listen to Michelet, while he paints the warlike humour of these inhabitants of the deep:—"The Medusæ and Molluscs," says this popular author, "are generally innocent creatures, and I have lived with them in a world of gentle peace. Few flesh-eaters among them; those even which are so, only kill to satisfy their wants, living for the most part on life just commenced—on gelatinous animals, which can scarcely be called organic. From this world grief was absent. No cruelty and no passion. Their little souls, if mild, were not without their ray of aspiration towards the light, and towards what comes to us from heaven, and towards that love, revelling in that changing flame which at night is the light of the deep. It is now, however, necessary to describe a much graver world: a world of rapine and of murder; from the very beginning, from the first appearance of life, violent death appeared; sudden refinement, useful but cruel, purification, of all which has languished, or which may linger or languish, of the slow and feeble creation whose fecundity had encumbered the globe.

"In the more ancient formations of the old world we find two murderous beasts—an eater and a sucker. The first is revealed to us by the imprint of the trilobite, a species now lost, the most destructive of extinct beings. The second subsists in one fearful fragment, a beak nearly two feet in length, which was that of a great sucker or cuttle-fish (*Sepia*). If we may judge from such a beak, this monster, if the other parts of the body are in proportion, must have been enormous; its ventose, invincible arms, of perhaps twenty or thirty feet, like those of some monstrous spider. The sucker of the world, soft and gelatinous! it is himself. In making war on the molluscs he remains mollusc also; that is to say, always an embryo. He presents the strange, almost ridiculous, if it was not also terrible, appearance of an embryo going to war; of a fœtus furious and cruel, soft and transparent, but tenacious, breathing with a murderous breath, for it is not for food alone that it makes war: it has the wish to destroy. Satiated, and even bursting, it still destroys. Without defensive armour, under its threatening murmurs there is no peace; its safety is to attack. It regards all creatures as a possible enemy. It throws about its long arms, or rather thongs, armed with suckers, at random." Such is the somewhat exaggerated picture which the eloquent historian and poet draws of the Molluscous Cephalopod, and it must be admitted that there is a basis of truth in this, as well as in the more recent one painted by Victor Hugo, in his eloquent book, "Les Travailleurs de la Mer." Where, however, there is so much of the fictitious floating about, it will be our endeavour to eliminate facts only.

The following fact is abbreviated from the "Natural History and Fishery of the Sperm Whale." Mr. Beale had been searching for shells among the rocks in Bonin Island, and was much astonished to see at his feet a most extraordinary-looking animal, crawling back towards the surf which it had just left. It was creeping on its eight legs, which, from their soft and flexible nature, bent considerably under the weight of its body, so that it was just lifted by an effort above the rocks. It appeared much alarmed, and made every attempt to escape. Mr. Beale endeavoured to stop it by putting his foot on one of its tentacles, but it liberated itself several times in spite of all his efforts. He then laid hold of one of the tentacles with his hand, and held it firmly, and the limb appeared as if it would be torn asunder in the struggle. To terminate the contest, he gave it a powerful jerk; it resisted the effort successfully, but the moment after the enraged animal lifted a head with large projecting eyes, and, loosing its hold of the rocks, suddenly sprang upon Mr. Beale's arm, which had been previously bared to the shoulder, and clung to it with its suckers, while it endeavoured to get the beak, which he could now see, between the tentacles, in a position to bite him. Mr. Beale describes its cold slimy grasp as extremely sickening, and he loudly called to the captain, who was also searching for shells, to come to his assistance. They hastened to the boat, and he was released by killing his tormentor with a boat-knife, when the arms were disengaged bit by bit. Mr. Beale states that this Cephalopod must have measured across its expanded arms about four feet, while its body was not bigger than a large hand clenched. It was the species called the rock-squid by whalers.

These formidable and curious Cephalopods, the Μαλάκια of Aristotle, *Mollia* of Pliny, and *Cephalophora* of De Blainville, have the mantle, according to Cuvier, united beneath the body, thus forming a muscular sac which envelopes the whole viscera. The body is soft and fleshy, varying much in form, being sub-spherical, sub-elliptical, and cylindrical, the sides of the mantle in many species extending into fleshy fins. The head protrudes from the muscular sac, and is distinct from the body; it is gifted with all the usual senses, the eyes in particular, which are either pedunculate or sessile, being large and well developed. The mouth is anterior and terminal, armed with a pair of horny or calcareous mandibles, which bear a strong resemblance to the bill of a parrot, acting transversely, one upon the other. Its position is the bottom of a sub-conical cavity, forming the base of numerous fleshy tentacular appendages which surround it, and which are termed arms by some writers. These appendages in the great majority of living species are provided with suckers, *acetabula* (cupping-glass-like appendages), by means of which the animal moves at the bottom of the sea, head downwards, or attaches itself to its prey. These suckers are armed or unarmed with a long, sharp, horny claw. In the unarmed acetabulum, the mechanism for adhesion is well described by Dr. Roget: "The circumference of the disk," says this writer, "is raised by a soft and turned margin; a series of long slender folds of membrane covering corresponding fascicula of muscular fibre converge from the circumference towards the centre of the sucker, at a short distance from which they leave a circular aperture; this opens into a cavity which widens as it descends, and contains a cone of soft substance rising from the bottom of the cavity, like the piston of a syringe. When the sucker is applied to the surface, for the purpose of adhesion, the piston, having previously been raised so as to fill the cavity, is retracted, and a vacuum produced, which may be still further increased by the retraction of the plicated portion of the disk." Here we have an excellent description of the apparatus for holding on. When the animal is disposed to let go his hold, according to Professor Owen, "the muscular arrangement enables the animal to push forward the piston, and thus in a moment destroy the vacuum which retraction had produced."

In the case of the armed Cephalopods (*Onychoteuthis*), Professor Owen remarks, "that there are circumstances in which even the remarkable apparatus described by Dr. Roget would be insufficient to fulfil the offices in the economy of Nature for which the Cephalopod was created, and that in species which have to contend with the agile mucous-clad fishes more powerful organs of prehension are superadded to the suckers, so that in the calamary the base of the piston is, he remarks, enclosed in a horny hoop, the outer and anterior margin of which is developed into a series of sharp curved teeth, which can be firmly pressed into the flesh of a struggling prey by the contraction of the surrounding transverse fibres, and can be withdrawn by the action of the retracting fibres of the piston. "Let the reader," the professor adds, "picture to himself the projecting weapon of the horny hoop developed into a long, curved, sharp-pointed claw, and these weapons clustered at the expanded terminations of the tentacles, and arranged in a double alternate series along the internal surface of the eight muscular feet, and he will have some idea of the formidable nature of the carnivorous cephalopod." The professor notices another structure which adds greatly to the prehensile powers of the uncinated Cephalopods. "At the extremities of the long tentacles a cluster of small, simple, unarmed suckers may be observed at the base of the expanded part. When these latter suckers are applied to one another, the tentacles are firmly locked together at that part, and the united strength of both the elongated peduncles can be applied to drag towards the mouth any resisting object which has been grappled by the terminal hooks. There is no mechanical contrivance which surpasses this structure; art has remotely imitated it in the fabrication of the obstetrical forceps, in which either blade can be used separately, or, by the interlocking of a temporary blade, be made to act in combination."—*Cyc. of Anat.*

Family of the Sepiadæ.

The body of the cuttle-fish (*Sepia*) is thus a very singular structure, somewhat reminding us of certain species of polypes. We find a body or abdominal mass, and a head, separated by compression, sufficiently marked. The body is covered by the mantle, which has the form of a sac opened only in front by a transverse cleft. The head has a projecting and well-developed eye on each side; it is surmounted by a sort of fleshy funnel, which is divided by four pairs of tentacles. At the bottom of this tentacular funnel is the mouth; and from the anterior opening in the mantle a tube issues, which is wide at its base.

If we study the general aspect of the animal more closely, we find that the tentacles—which serve at once as organs of locomotion for swimming, for creeping, and as prehensile organs for seizing and retaining its prey—are conical, very long, and all of the same form. Each of them has towards its axis a longitudinal canal, which encloses a great nerve, which is also surrounded with muscular fibres, arranged in rays. The suckers, already described, occupy all the internal surface of the eight tentacular arms, which are arranged in two rows, having the form very nearly of a semi-spherical capsule. Of these suckers, each arm of the cuttle-fish carries about two hundred and forty, the total number being nearly a thousand. The mouth we have already described, in Dr. Roget's words: "The teeth move vertically, much as the cutting edge of the two blades of a pair of scissors move upon each other, tearing the prey by the assistance of their hooked terminations."

The tongue is covered on its upper part by a thick horny bed, bristling in the centre with a series of recurving teeth, while its edge is armed with three other erect teeth, which are slender and hooked. The œsophagus is long and slender. At the abdomen the gullet expands into a sort of frill, to which succeeds a gizzard, with strong, fleshy walls; and, finally, a very short intestine, which directs itself forward, terminating on the median line of the body. Towards the anterior parts is a cavity, of which a few words must be said. It occupies the free space comprised between the exterior surface of the abdomen and the internal face of the mantle; and here the respiratory organs, namely, the *branchiæ*, are lodged. Here, also, are the reproductive and excretory organs.

The branchiæ, which are two in number, are voluminous, but short, tufted, and leaf-like. The branchial cavity can dilate and contract itself alternately. It communicates externally by two openings: the one, fashioned into a cleft, receives, while the other, which is prolonged into a tube, serves to eject, the water, and becomes a powerful organ of locomotion.

The inspiration of the animal is thus made by a cleft in the mantle, and expiration by the tube: the renewal of the respirable liquid acts as a sort of sucking and forcing pump, at the surface of the lamellar branchials. The cuttle-fish, in short, will be at no loss to reply to the question of the Don Diego of Corneille—

"Rodrique, as-tu du cœur?"

for they have three hearts. The two first are placed at the end of the branchiæ. With each beat of the pulse the venous blood is brought from all parts of the body, and propelled through each gill or branchiæ. Vivified by respiration in the internal tissue of the branchiæ, it is carried by the veins into the third heart, situated upon the median line of the body; and now the regenerated fluid is again distributed throughout the rest of the economy.

Not to oppress the reader with anatomical details, we shall just remark that the gaze of the cuttle-fish is decided and threatening. Its projecting eyes and golden-coloured iris are said to have something of fascination in them. The animal seems able even to economise the power of its glance, being able to cover its eyes from time to time by contracting the skin which surrounds them, and bringing the two translucent eyelids with which it is furnished closer together.

The cuttle-fishes are essentially aquatic and marine animals. We find them in every sea in all parts of the world; but they are most formidable in warm countries. They have a great predilection for the shore. During their youth they associate in flocks; but with age they fly from association, and retire into the clefts and hollows of the rocks. The old cuttle-fish is only found in rugged and rocky places, bristling with naked, pointed rocks, which have been worn by the waves, but generally in places only a few feet below the level of low water. "How often," says D'Orbigny, "have we not observed the cuttle-fish in his favourite retirement! There, with one of his arms cramped to the walls of its dwelling, it extends the other towards the animals which pass at its gate, embraces them, and by its power renders useless all their efforts to disengage themselves."

If we observe a cuttle-fish when it is what may be called walking, either on land or at the bottom of the sea, it will be seen to walk on one side, its head downwards, its mouth touching the ground, the arms extended and grappling some supporting object, and drawing the body forward; at the same time the arms at the opposite side are contracted and folded up, so as to assist by a contrary movement. On shore the movement of these animals is very slow. On the other hand, they swim very rapidly, assisted by all their arms, and aided by the water ejected from the locomotive tube, their movement being most frequently backwards, the body first, the six superior arms placed horizontally, the two others brought together above: the first help to sustain them in their horizontal position, the last to guide them, inclining to the right or left as the animal changes its direction.

The cuttle-fishes feed on crustaceans, fishes, and also on shelled molluscs—every kind of animal, in fact, which comes within their reach; so that it is readily taken by means of the flesh of fish or crustaceans, in which a strong hook is concealed. They live for five or six years, and reproduce by eggs, which are large, and generally found in clusters, known to fishermen under the name of *sea-raisins*.

Like the zoophytes, they possess the property of redintegration, already described, being able to reproduce any arm that may be destroyed. There is another singular peculiarity which the cuttle-fish shares with man. Under the influence of strong emotion the human face becomes pale, or blushes, and in some individuals it is said to become blue. This has always been supposed to be an attribute of humanity; but the cuttle-fish shares it with our race. Yielding to the impressions of the moment, the cuttle-fish suddenly changes colour, and, passing through various tints, it only resumes its familiar one when the cause of the change has disappeared. They are, in fact, gifted with great sensibility, which reacts immediately upon their tissues, these being extremely elastic and delicate. Sudden changes of colour are produced—changes which far exceed the same phenomena in man. Under the influence of passion or emotion man is born to blush, but under no sort of excitement does he cover himself with pustules; this the cuttle-fish does: it not only changes colour, but it covers itself with little warts. "Observe a poulpe in a pool of water," says D'Orbigny, "as it walks round its retreat—it is smooth, and of very pale colour. Attempt to seize it, and it quickly assumes a deeper tint, and its body becomes covered on the instant with warts and hairs, which remain there until its confidence is entirely restored."

The Cephalopods thus constituted—crowned with numerous fleshy arms bearing sucker disks, enveloped in a sac-like mantle, open in front, and sometimes enclosing a rudimentary shell, with a rudimentary brain and cartilaginous skeleton, breathing by gills, which are bathed in water passing beneath the mantle, and discharged through a tube—are divided by Dr. Leach into two families; namely, *Decapoda*, having two tentacles and movable eyes; and *Octopoda*, without tentacles, and eyes fixed.

The *Decapoda* includes the cuttle-fish, *Sepia*; the squids, *Soligodæ*; and the calmars, *Teuthidæ*. The Sepiadæ have eight arms rising from the crown of the head, armed with four rows of suckers, two long, slender tentacles, with broadly-expanding ends and stalked suckers, eyes moving in their sockets, body broadly ovate in *Sepia*; the body elongate, and a horny, flexible shell in *Soligo*, and conical in *Ommastrephos*, a pair of narrow fins bordering the whole length of the side; funnel large and short, closing with an internal valve; shell, or cuttle-bone, a broad, flat, calcareous substance, with horny edge, filled with layers of a spongy substance, supported by pillars.

The *Octopoda*, without tentacles, have eight long arms, united at the base by a web; the suckers in two rows, which are sessile; the eyes fixed; shell, two short stiles enclosed in the mantle; the body united to the head by a broad neck-band; no side-fins; shell internal and rudimentary in the British species; body oval, warty, and without fins, in *Octopus;* small and oblong, arms tapering and webbed, and suckers in a single row, in *Eledone* (Fig. 313).

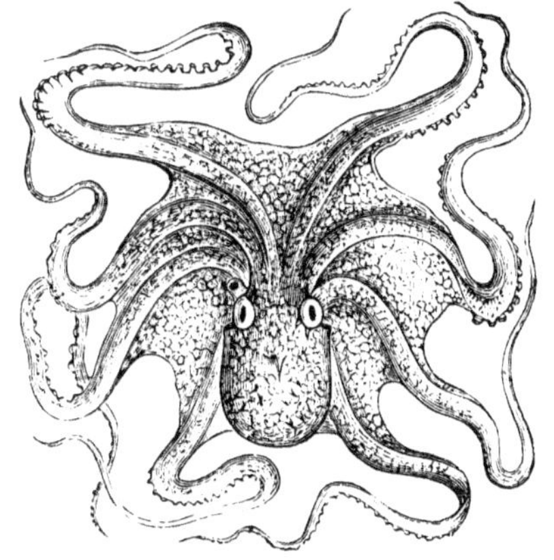

Fig. 313. Eledone, Octopus vulgaris (Lamarck).

In his great work, Professor Owen proposes to divide the Cephalopods into two groups, which he calls *Dibranchiata*, characterised by the presence of two branchiæ, which would bring together all the naked Cephalopods, including Sepia, Soligo, Octopus, Kassia, and Ommastrephos; and *Tetrabranchiata*, having four branchiæ, to which the *Nautilus*, and most of the fossil Cephalopods, such as the *Ammonites*, belong. Most of the first group are represented in the British seas, but the second are altogether absent.

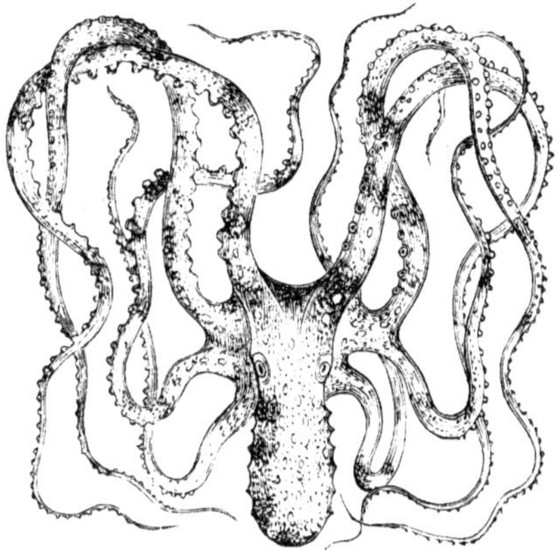

Fig. 314. Octopus macropus (Risso).

The *Decapoda* are of all sizes. Dr. Grant describes the body, or mantle, of *Sepiola vulgaris*, found on our coast, as measuring about six lines in length, and as much in breadth, while the head measures four lines in length, and, from the magnitude of the eyes, must be equal in breadth with the body. In

Onychoteuthis, distinguished for its uncinated suckers, they are found of the size of a man. In Cook's first voyages, the naturalists to the expedition, "Banks and Solander," to quote Professor Owen's account, "found the dead carcase of a gigantic species of this kind floating in the sea between Cape Horn and the Polynesian Islands, in 30° 44′ S. lat., and 110° 10′ W. long. It was surrounded by aquatic birds, which were feeding on its remains. From the parts of this specimen which are still preserved in the Hunterian Museum, and which have always strongly excited the attention of naturalists, it must have measured at least six feet from the end of the tail to the end of the tentacles."

The *Octopoda* include the genera *Octopus*, *Eledone*, *Philoxenis*. and *Argonauta*, which Professor Owen divides into *Testacea* and

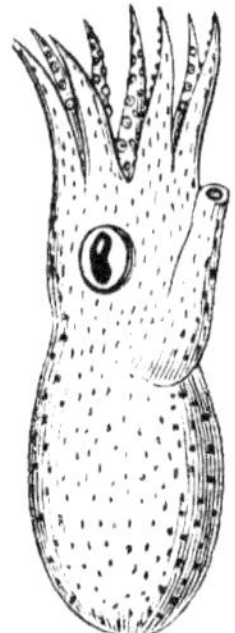

Fig. 315. Octopus brevisses (D'Orbigny).

Fig. 316. Octopus horridus (D'Orbigny).

Nuda, the first comprising the *Argonauta* and *Bellerophon*, the *Nuda* including the *Eledone* and *Octopus*.

In the genus *Eledone* the arms are reunited at their base by a very short membrane, with only a single row of suckers. The two best-known species of this group inhabit the Mediterranean. The one is *Eledone moschatus*, known in Italy under the name of Muscardino, from the strong odour of musk which it emits, even after death and desiccation; the other is *Eledone cirrhosus*, a small species, bluish grey on the back, and whitish under the belly.

The habits of *Eledone moschatus* have been carefully studied by M. Verany. The able naturalist of Nice preserved many of these animals during a month, in a great aquarium, noting their habits.

When in a state of tranquillity, the *Eledone* clung to the sides of the glass tank in which it was kept. Its head is then inclined forwards, with the sac hanging behind; the locomotive tube, turned upwards, presents the orifice between the arms. In this state the animal is yellowish in colour, its eyes dilated, its inspirations regular. But if irritated, a remarkable change takes place: its body assumes a fine maroon colour, and it is covered with numerous tubercles; the eye becomes contracted, a column of water is forcibly ejected from the locomotive tube at the aggressor, and the respiration becomes precipitate, jerky, and irregular. The creature would take a strong inspiration, and, having collected its force, suddenly throw a jet of water to a distance of more than three feet. This state of passion, which the slightest touch is sufficient to produce, endures for half an hour or more. When it ceases, the animal resumes its form and primitive colours; but the least shock impressed on the water is sufficient to give it a deeper tint, which passes like a flash of lightning over the skin of this singular proteus.

The Eledone sleeps by day as well as by night, attaching itself in its sleep to the walls of its prison, leaving its arms to float around, the two inferior ones extending backwards, and the sac inclining over them; its eyes are then contracted, and in part covered by the eyelids. Its respiration is regular and slow, and any ejection of water very rare; its colour is then of a livid grey, and vinous red below, with whitish spots, while the brown spots have now entirely disappeared. While still asleep, it is watchful and attentive to all the dangers which could surprise it. The extremities of the arms floating round its body are ready to announce the approach or contact of any other object. Even the most delicate touch is perceived immediately, and it shrinks from the hand which seeks to approach. Under every circumstance the Eledone exhales a strong odour of musk, which it preserves long after death.

When the Eledone swims, which it rarely does unless pressed by some urgent necessity, it carries the sac in advance, the arms floating behind—the six upper ones being on a horizontal line, the two others approaching each other below. Thus arranged, it presents, in consequence of its flattened form, a very large resisting surface to the water, its progress being due to the alternate dilatation and contraction of the body, which expels the water through the locomotive tube, and by reaction produces a rapid and jerking movement. Sometimes the arms aid the movement; the eyes of the animal are then much dilated, and its colour a clear livid yellow, finely shaded with red, and covered with bright spots.

It is a singular fact that the creature notably changes colour under any exertion, so that the animal at rest and in motion are two different beings. When walking under water the tube is directed behind, its arms are spread out, the head is raised, and the body slightly inclined forward; its mantle is then of a pearly grey, and the spots take the tint of wine-lees. When at rest the shades disappear.

The *Pinnoctopus* (Fig. 317), another genera of this family, have

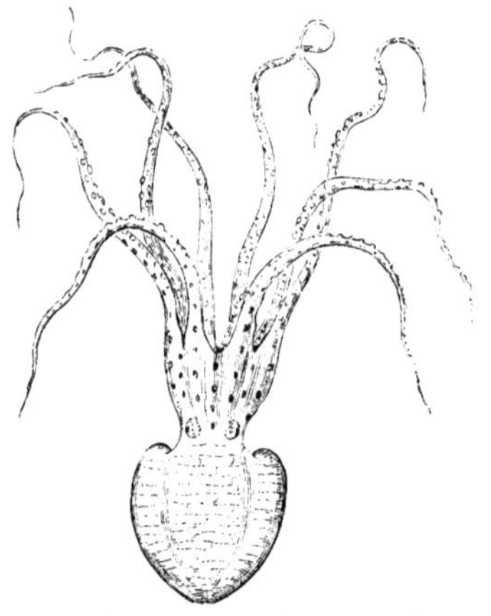

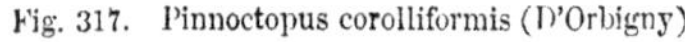

Fig. 317. Pinnoctopus corolliformis (D'Orbigny).

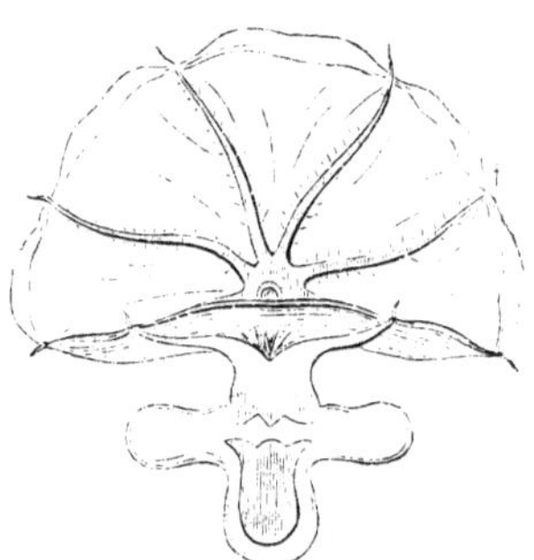

Fig. 318. Cirrotheutis Mülleri (Eschricht).

the body oblong, with lateral expansions, as represented in the accompanying figure.

In *Cirrotheutis* the arms are completely united in their whole extent by a thin membrane furnished with cirri, which alternate with certain suckers arranged in one row. Only one species of this genera is known as an inhabitant of northern seas, which is represented in Fig. 318.

It is no easy task to separate the real from the fabulous history of the Cephalopods. Aristotle and Pliny have alike assisted, by their marvellous relations, to throw that halo of wonder round it which the light of modern science has not altogether dispelled. Pliny the ancient relates the history of an enormous cuttle-fish which haunted the coast of Spain, and destroyed the fishing-grounds. He adds that this gigantic creature was finally taken, that its body weighed seven hundred pounds, and that its arms were ten yards in length. Its head came by right to Lucullus, to whose gastronomical privileges be all honour. It was so large, says Pliny, that it filled fifteen amphoræ, and weighed seven hundred pounds also.

Some naturalists of the Renaissance, such as Olaüs Magnus and Denis de Montfort, gave credit—which they are scarcely justified in doing—to the assertions of certain writers of the north of Europe, who believed seriously in the existence of a sea-monster of prodigious size which haunted the northern seas. This monster has received the name of the *Kraken.* The Kraken was long the terror of these seas; it arrested ships in spite of the action of the wind, sails, and oars, often causing them to founder at sea, while the cause of shipwreck remained unsuspected. Denis de Montfort gives a scientific description and representation of this Kraken, which he calls the Colossal Poulpe, in which the creature is made to embrace a three-masted ship in its vast arms. Delighted with the success which his representation met with, Denis laughed at the credulity of his contemporaries. "If my Kraken takes with them," he said, "I shall make it extend its arms to both shores of the Straits of Gibraltar." To another learned friend he said, "If my entangled ship is accepted, I shall make my Poulpe overthrow a whole fleet."

Among those who admitted the facetious history of the Kraken without a smile, there was at least one holy bishop, who was, moreover, something of a naturalist. Pontoppidan, Bishop of Bergen, in Norway, in one of his books assures us that a whole regiment of soldiers could easily manœuvre on the back of the Kraken, which he compares to a floating island. "Similior insulæ quam bestiæ," wrote the good Bishop of Bergen.

In the first edition of his "System of Nature," Linnæus himself admits the existence of this colossus of the seas, which he calls *Sepia microcosmos.* Better informed in the following edition, he erased the Kraken from his catalogue.

The statements of Pliny respecting the Colossal Poulpe, like those of Montfort about the Kraken, are evidently fabulous. It is, however, an undisputed fact that there exists in the Mediterranean and other seas cuttle-fish—a congenerous animal—of considerable size. A calmar has been caught in our own time, near Nice, which weighed upwards of thirty pounds. In the same neighbourhood some fishermen caught, twenty years ago, an individual of the same genus nearly six feet long, which is preserved in the Museum of Natural History at Montpelier. Péron, the naturalist, met in the Australian seas a cuttle-fish nearly eight feet long. The travellers Quoy and Gaimard picked up in the Atlantic Ocean, near the Equator, the skeleton of a monstrous mollusc, which, according to their calculations, must have weighed two hundred pounds. M. Rung met, in the middle of the ocean, a mollusc with short arms, and of a reddish colour, the body of which, according to this naturalist, was as large as a tun cask. One of the mandibles of this creature, still preserved in the Museum of the College of Surgeons, is larger than a hand.

In 1853 a gigantic cephalopod was stranded on the coast of Jutland. The body of this monster, which was dismembered by the fishermen, furnished many wheelbarrow loads, its pharynx, or back part of the mouth, alone being as large as the head of an infant. Dr. Steenstrup, of Copenhagen, who published a description of this creature under the name of *Architeuthis dux*, shows a portion of the arm of another cephalopod, which is as large as the thigh-bone of a man. But a well-authenticated fact connected with these gigantic cephalopods is related by Lieutenant Bayer, of the French corvette Alecton, and M. Sabin Berthelot, French Consul at the Canary Islands, by whom the report is made to the Académie des Sciences.

The steam-corvette Alecton was between Teneriffe and Madeira when she fell in with a gigantic calamary, not less—according to the account—than fifteen mètres (fifty feet) long, without reckoning its eight formidable arms, covered with suckers, and about twenty feet in circumference at its largest part, the head terminating in many arms of enormous size, the other extremity terminating in two fleshy lobes or fins of great size, the weight of the whole being estimated at four thousand pounds; the flesh was soft, glutinous, and of reddish-brick colour.

The commandant, wishing in the interests of science to secure the monster, actually engaged it in battle. Numerous shots were aimed at it, but the balls traversed its flaccid and glutinous mass without causing it any vital injury. But after one of these attacks the waves were observed to be covered with foam and blood, and, singular thing, a

Plate XXIV.—Gigantic Cuttle-fish caught by the French Corvette Alecton, near Teneriffe.

strong odour of musk was inhaled by the spectators. This musk odour we have already noticed as being peculiar to many of the Cephalopods.

The musket-shots not having produced the desired results, harpoons were employed, but they took no hold on the soft impalpable flesh of the marine monster. When it escaped from the harpoon it dived under the ship, and came up again at the other side. They succeeded at last in getting it to bite at the harpoon, and in passing a rope round the posterior part of the animal. But when they attempted to hoist it out of the water the rope penetrated deeply into the flesh, and separated it into two parts, the head with the arms and tentacles dropping into the sea and making off, while the fins and posterior parts were brought on board: they weighed about forty pounds.

The crew were eager to pursue, and would have launched a boat, but the commander refused, fearing that the animal might capsize it. The object was not, in his opinion, one in which he could risk the lives of his crew. Pl. XXIV. is copied from M. Berthelot's coloured representation of this scene. "It is probable," M. Moquin-Tandon remarks, commenting on M. Berthelot's recital, "that this colossal mollusc was sick or exhausted by some recent struggle with some other monster of the deep, which would account for its having quitted its native rocks in the depths of the ocean. Otherwise it would have been more active in its movements, or it would have obscured the waves with the inky liquid which all the Cephalopods have at command. Judging from its size, it would carry at least a barrel of this black liquid, if it had not been exhausted in some recent struggle."

"Is this mollusc a calmar?" asks the same writer. "If we might judge from the figure drawn by one of the officers of the Alecton during the struggle, and communicated by M. Berthelot, the animal had terminal fins, like the calmars; but it has eight equal arms, like the cuttle-fish. Now the calmars have ten, two of them being very long. Was this some intermediate species between the two? Or must we admit, with MM. Crosse and Fischer, that the animal had lost its more formidable tentacles in some recent combat?"*

* Is it necessary to say that even this account—apparently so well authenticated, not to speak of the representation drawn on the spot—should be taken "cum granum salis?"—Ed.

The Argonauta or Nautilus.

Floating gracefully on the surface of the sea, trimming its tiny sail to the breeze, just sufficient to ruffle the surface of the waves, behold the exquisite living shallop. The elegant little bark which thus plays with the current is no work of human hands, but a child of Nature: it is the Argonaut, whose tribes, decked in a thousand brilliant shades of colour, are wanderers of the night in innumerable swarms on the ocean's surface.

The marine shell which Linnæus called the Argonaut enjoyed great renown among the ancient Greeks and Romans. It was the subject of graceful legends; it had inspired great poets; it occupied the attention of Aristotle, who called it the *Nautilus* and *Nauticos*, and of Pliny, who called it *Pompylius*. Few animals, indeed, have been so celebrated, so anciently known. The Greek and Roman poets saw in it an elegant model of the ship which the skill and audacity of the man constructed who first braved the fury of the waves; in the words of the poet, "armour of triple oak and triple brass covered the heart of him who first confided himself in a frail bark to the relentless waves:"

> "Illi robur et æs triplex
> Circa pectus erat, qui fragilem truci
> Commisit pelago ratem
> Primus. . . . ."
>
> *Horace*, I. Car. iii. l. 9.

To meet the Pompylius was, according to the superstitious Roman, a favourable presage. This little oceanic wanderer, in spite of the capricious waves, was a tutelar divinity, who guarded the navigator in his course, and assured him of a happy passage. Listen to the immortal author of the first Natural History of Animals, the philosophical Aristotle. "The Nautilus Polyp," says the learned historian, "is of the nature of animals which pass for extraordinary, for it can float on the sea; it raises itself from the bottom of the water, the shell being reversed and empty, but when it reaches the surface it readjusts it. It has between the arms a species of tissue similar to that which unites the toes of web-footed birds. When there is a little wind, it employs this tissue as a sort of rudder, letting it fall into the water with the arms on each side. On the approach of the least danger it fills its shell with water, and sinks into the sea."

Pliny gives it the name of Pompylius, and, after the example of Aristotle, explains how it navigates, by elevating its two first arms, a membrane of extreme tenuity stretching between them, while it rows with the others, using its median arm as a rudder. The Greek poet, Oppian, who lived in the second century of our era, and to whom we are indebted for Poems on Fishing (*Halieutica*) and the Chase (*Cynegetica*), says of it: "Hiding itself in a concave shell, the Pompylius can walk on land, but can also rise to the surface of the water, the back of its shell upwards, for fear that it should be filled. The moment it is seen, it turns the shell, and navigates it like a skilful seaman: in order to do this, it throws out two of its feet like antennæ, between which is a thin membrane, which is extended by the wind like a sail, while two others, which touch the water, guide, as with a rudder, the house, the ship, and the animal. If danger approaches, it folds up its antennæ, its sail, and its rudder, and dives, its weight being increased by the water which it causes to enter the shell. As we see a man who is victor in the public games, his head circled by a crown, while vast crowds press around, so the Pompylius have always a crowd of ships following in their track, whose crews no longer dread to quit the land. O fish justly dear to navigators! thy presence announces winds soft and friendly: thou bringest the calm, and thou art the sign of it."

Oppian carried his admiration a long way. That the Argonaut is an animated skiff is agreed on all hands; but, in making it almost a bird—in according to it at once the faculty of gracefully navigating the sea and floating in the atmosphere as an inhabitant of the regions of air—he was passing the limits permissible to poetic license.

But the properties of the Nautilus has not alone struck the imagination of the Greeks and Romans; it also attracted the attention of the Chinese, who call it the boat-polyp. Rumphius informs us, that in India the shell fetches a great price (Fig. 319). Women consider it a great, a magnificent ornament. In their solemn fêtes, dancers carry one of these shells in the right hand, holding it proudly above their heads. Nor did it require the dithyrambic praises with which the ancients have surrounded it to recommend it to the admiration of modern naturalists. Without exaggerating the graceful attributes with which it is gifted, it is at once one of the most curious and elegant creations of Nature.

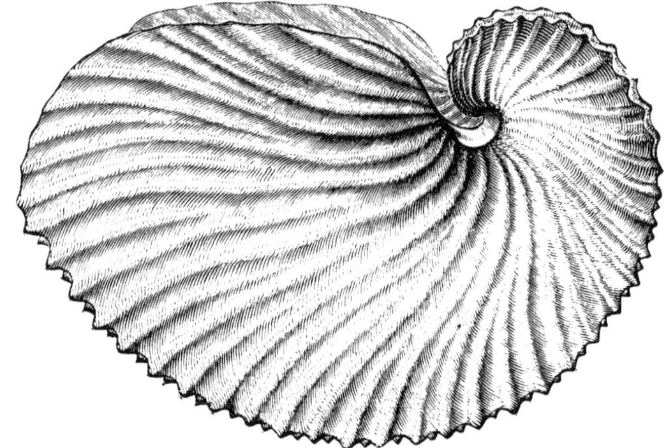

Fig. 319. Shell of Argonauta argo (Linnæus).

Its body (Fig. 320) is ovoid in form, and it is furnished with eight tentacles, covered with a double row of suckers. Of these tentacles, six are narrow and slender, tapering to a point towards the extremity, while two of them expand toward the extremity in the form of wings or sails. These are all folded up when in a state of repose. The body itself is contained in a thin, white, and fragile univalve shell, which is oval, flattened on the exterior, but rolled up in a spiral in the interior, the last turn of the shell being so large as to give it something of the form of an elegantly-shaped shallop. Singularly enough, the body of the animal does not penetrate to the bottom of the shell, nor is it attached to it by any muscular ligament; nor is the shell moulded exactly upon it, as is the case with most other testaceans.

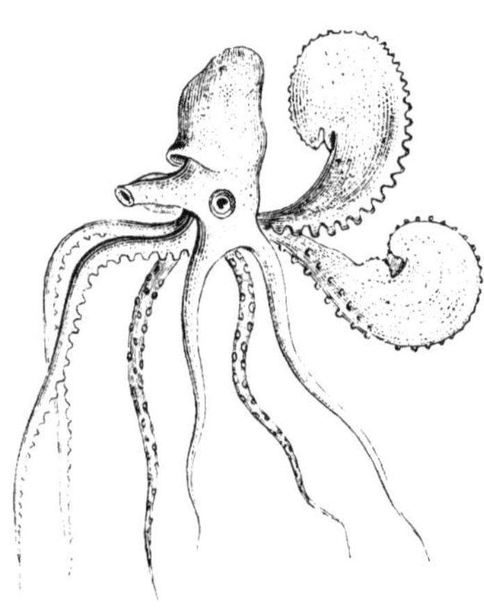

Fig. 320. The Argonauta argo (Linnæus).

What does all this imply? Is the Argonaut a parasite? a fraudulent disinheritor of the poor? a vile assassin, who, having surprised and killed the legitimate proprietor of the shell, has installed itself in its place, and in the proper house of its victim? Such crimes are not without example in the natural history of animals—witness the proceedings of the curious *hermit crab*, whose proceedings we shall glance at in a future chapter. The parasitic character of the Nautilus was long conceded by naturalists; but recent facts have corrected this opinion. We have collected their shells, of all dimensions and of all ages, inhabited always by the same animal, whose size is always proportioned to the volume of the shell. More than that, it is now known that in the egg of the Nautilus the rudiments of the shell exist. M. Chenu tells us, that under the microscope Professor Duvernoy discovered a distinct shell contained in the embryo. Sir Everard Home asserts the contrary; and no opportunity presented itself for the complete solution of the question, until Poli was placed by the King of Naples in a position to solve it. The piscina of Portici was placed at his disposal. He witnessed the curious mechanism by which the egg is expelled from the uterus, having a shell, and satisfied himself, by following their development day by day, that the shell existed in the embryo, and grew with the animal. He satisfied himself also that the opinion enunciated by Aristotle, that at no point did the animal adhere to the shell, was perfectly true.

Finally, in the curious series of experiments carried on by Madame Power, in the port of Messina, the fragments of the frail bark of the mollusc, which were broken off in taking it, were restored in a few days, having been reproduced. It is, therefore, quite demonstrated that the Nautilus, like other testaceous molluscs, itself secretes and constructs its shell—its diaphanous skiff. The reader, however, must not flatter himself that he can witness with his own eyes from the shore, in our narrow channel, the charming picture of the Nautilus painted by poets and natural historians: they never come near the shore. They are timid and cautious creatures, dwelling almost always in the open sea. They live in families, some hundreds of miles from the shore; and it is during the night, or at most in the fading light of sunset, that they assemble together to pursue their gambols on the surface of a tranquil sea.

However reluctant we may be to destroy the marvellous fictions of ancients and moderns, we are compelled to declare that there is no truth in the often-repeated statement that the Nautilus uses its palmated arms as oars or sails. In order to swim on the surface, it comports itself as all other Cephalopods do. It uses neither oars nor sails, and the palmate arms only serve to envelop and retain its hold on its frail

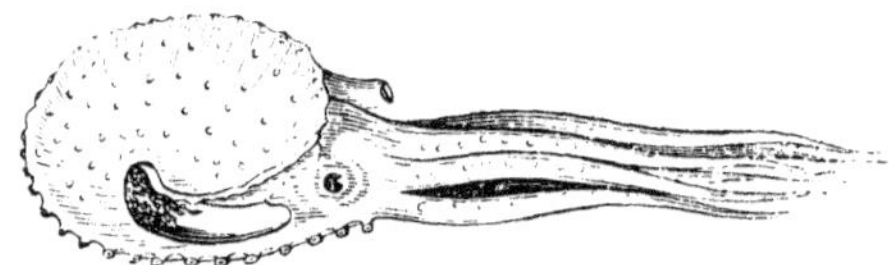

Fig. 321. Argonauta papyracea, as it swims by means of its locomotive tube.

shell. Its principal apparatus of progression is the *locomotive tube* with which it is furnished, in common with all Cephalopods, and which is in the Nautilus very long. Aided by this apparatus, it ejects the water after it has served the purpose of respiration, and, in doing so, projects itself against the liquid, as it were. While it advances through the water under this impulse, its pendent arms, elongated and reunited in bundles extending the whole length of the shell (Figs. 321 and 322), shows the position of the different parts of the animal when it thus breasts the waves. These arms are also powerful aids when the animal creeps on the ground at the bottom of the sea.

Fig. 322. Argonauta papyracea in its shell.

When the animal is disturbed it retires completely into its shell. From that moment, the equilibrium being changed, the shell is overturned, and the animal is nearly invisible. If frightened, it entirely submerges itself, and sinks to the bottom.

These little beings share with other Cephalopods the strange faculty of changing colour under the influence of some vivid impression; but their graceful and delicate organization redeems them from the charge we have brought against the cuttles. The Nautilus can blush, turn pale, and show through its transparent shell its body changing in sudden shades; but it never exhibits those bristling, unpleasant tubercles, the hideous inheritance of the larger and coarser Cephalopods—the tyrants of the sea.

The Nautilus carries its egg in the shell, and the little ones are also hatched in this floating cradle. Three species are at present known: the species described by Aristotle and Pliny, and the more ancient naturalists; namely, *A. argo*, or *Nautilus papyracea* (Figs. 319 and 320), which are inhabitants of the Mediterranean as well as the Indian Ocean and the Antilles. The two others, *A. tubercula*, belonging exclusively to the Indian Ocean, and *A. baillant*, which is met occasionally in the Pacific and Atlantic Ocean.

The poulpes and nautilus both belong to the family of Octopoda, and the class of Acetabuliferous Cephalopods, having, as the name indicates, eight feet, from ὀκτὼ, eight, and ποῦς, foot; at the same time the body is entirely fleshy, and without fins. The genera of Cuttles (*Sepia*) and Calmars (*Lolia*) belong to another family of the same class; namely, the Decapoda, because they have ten feet and a sort of internal osselet, with fins, &c.

The cuttles, *Sepia* (Fig. 323), have the body fleshy and depressed, continued into a sac, and bordered on all its length on both sides with a wing or narrow fin, the larger short and flat, broader than it is long, with two large eyes, covered by an expansion of the skin, which becomes transparent over a surface equal to the diameter of the iris, and furnished with inferior contractile eyelids.

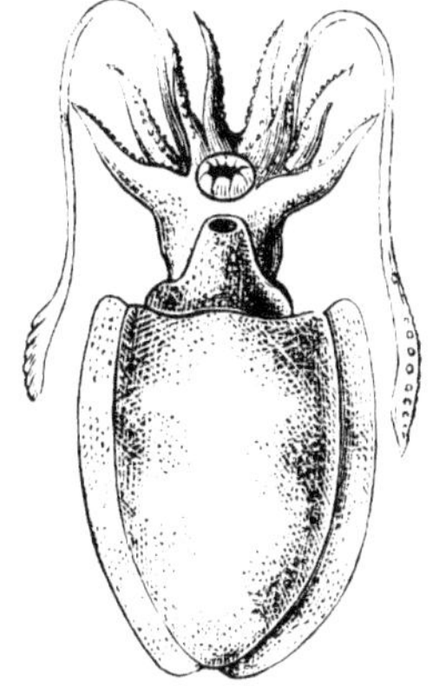

Fig. 323. Sepia officinalis (Linnæus).

This head is surmounted by ten tentacular arms or feet, eight of which are short and conical, and two long and slender, terminating in a sort of spatula. These arms are all armed with suckers, and are perfectly retractile. They surround a mouth armed with two horny jaws not unlike the beak of a parrot.

The skin of the cuttle-fish presents in one vast hollow, occupying all the extent of the back, a great calcareous part, the form and structure of which is quite characteristic of this genus. It is known as the cuttle-bone (Fig. 324). This bone is used for many purposes; among others, it is used in a powdered state as a dentifrice. It is sometimes suspended in the cage with captive birds, that they may whet their beaks on it, and collect carbonate of lime for the formation and repair of their bones. The osselet is oval or oblong, some provided with a slightly salient point. The upper part is surrounded with a horny or cretaceous margin, and presents in the centre a combination of spongy cells.

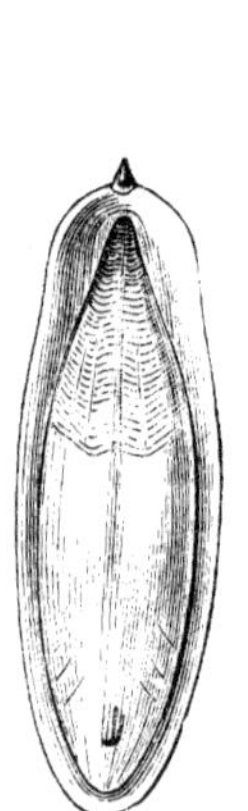

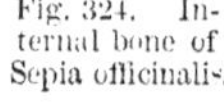

Fig. 324. Internal bone of Sepia officinalis.

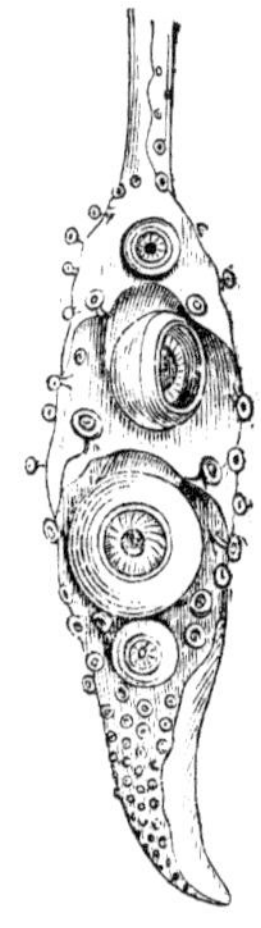

Fig. 325. Sepia tuberculosa (Lamarck).

Most of the Cephalopods secrete a blackish, inky fluid, to which some allusion has been made, but the uses of which, in the economy of the animals, is imperfectly known. The cuttles have considerable quantities of this liquor, which is contained in a sort of sac or ink-purse, placed low down in the abdomen. When the animal is pursued or threatened with danger it discharges a jet of the fluid, which renders the water thick and muddy, and permits it to escape in the obscurity from its pursuers. It appears that the cuttle-fish avails itself of this stratagem when left accidentally ashore. It is related of an English officer that, having dressed for dinner, and having some time to spare, he proceeded along the shore on his favourite search for objects of natural history. He reached a hollow rock in which a cuttle-fish had established its quarters; he soon detected the animal, which looked at him for some time with its great prominent eyes; in short, they watched each other with fixed attention. This mute contemplation came to a sudden and unexpected termination by the discharge of a voluminous jet of inky fluid, which covered the officer with the black liquid, which was the more unfortunate, since he was in his summer dress of white trousers.

The ink of the cuttle-fish is a favourite pigment, used in water-colour painting under the name of *sepia*. It is truly indestructible; and the hard and black substance found in the sac of fossil species of cuttle-fish when diluted with water produces a brilliant sepia. This property of the inky fluid was well known to the Romans, who used it in making ink. It was long supposed to be the chief ingredient in China ink; but a recent traveller, Mr. Seebold, who has visited the manufactory, and investigated the subject, has revealed the true process by which it is prepared.

The cuttle-fish affects the sea shore; they are along-shore molluscs. The flattened form of their bodies is favourable to a coasting life, by permitting them to rest easily on the bottom. Still they do not remain all the year round upon the coast. The cold in temperate regions, and the opposite reason in warm regions, leads them to withdraw from the shore, to which they only return in the spring. They are rarely seen in the Channel in winter, but with the vernal sun they appear in large shoals. What is the mechanism by which these animals are moved? When the cuttle-fish wishes to swim rapidly and backwards, they advance in the water by means of the locomotive tube, sending back the ambient liquid. When they wish to approach a prey slowly in order to seize it, they swim by the aid of their fins and arms. In order to swim backwards, they contract the arms provided with tentacles, and spread out horizontally the arms without tentacles.

The cuttles are flesh-eaters, and tolerably voracious. They feed themselves upon fishes, molluscs, and crustaceans. They are true aquatic brigands, who kill not to feed themselves, but for the sake of killing; and Nature, by a just equilibrium, applies to them the *lex talionis*. They fall victims, in their turn, to the vengeful jaws of the porpoises and dolphins. Such is the terrible harmony of Nature: some must die that others may live. Michelet gives us a glimpse of the manner in which the dolphins dispose of the cuttle-fish, in his "Livre de la Mer." "These lords of the ocean," he says, "are so delicate in their tastes that they eat only the head and arms, which are both tender and of easy digestion. They reject the hard parts, and especially the after-part of the body. The coast at Royan, for example, is covered with thousands of these mutilated cuttle-fish. The porpoises take most incredible bounds, at first to frighten them, and afterwards to run them down; in short, after their feast, they give themselves up to gymnastics."

In the spring the cuttle-fishes deposit their eggs, but without abandoning them. On the contrary, they exhibit a truly maternal care, taking much trouble to attach them to some submarine body, in which position the temperature of the water serves to hatch the eggs. *Sepia officinalis*, for example, chooses, at the moment of laying, a stem of *Fucus*, a foot of *Gorgonia*, or some other solid submarine body not less in dimensions than the little finger, and there it firmly attaches its eggs, which are pear-shaped, that is, pointed at one extremity, while a long *lanière* of a gelatinous nature, flat and black in appearance, with which they are provided, surrounds the solid body like a ring. Each female lays and attaches in this manner from twenty to thirty eggs, which are clustered together somewhat like a bunch of fine black grapes (Fig. 326). About a month after this the eggs are hatched.

The colours of *Sepia officinalis* vary considerably; but in general it may be remarked that the males are ornamented with deeper colours than the females. Transverse bands of a blackish brown furrow their backs, and diminish their breadth. Outside of these bands are small spots of a vivid white: very near the edge there is a white border, accompanied inside with a second edging of a beautiful violet. The median and anterior parts of the body are

Fig. 326. Sepia officinalis (Linnæus).

spotted here and there; beneath, a whitish tint with reddish speckles prevails.

The cuttle-fishes are found on every shore, and wherever they are found they are eaten, for their flesh is savoury. They are usually fried or boiled. They form an excellent bait for large bottom-fish, such as dog-fish, rays, and congers, which are fond of their flesh.

Thirty species are known, and they are chiefly characterised by the arrangement and form of the cupules of the arms. *Sepia officinalis* is common on the shores of the ocean from Sweden to the Canaries, and in all parts of the Mediterranean.

The *Calmars* were described by Aristotle under the name of Γείφις, and by Pliny under that of *Loligo*, which is still retained as the generic name. Their popular name of Calmar (calamar in old French) is taken from their resemblance to certain species of ink-holders. Oppian, who endowed the argonaut with wings, believed that the calmar also could take to the air, in order to avoid his enemies. Nevertheless, he was much puzzled how to give the form and functions of a bird to a fish. Themistocles, by way of insult to the Eretrians, likened them to calmars, saying they had swords and no hearts. Athenæus, a Greek physician before Galen, dwelt upon the nourishing properties of the flesh of the calmar.

Common enough in temperate regions, the calmars abound in the seas of the Torrid zone; they are gregarious, and live in numerous shoals, their bands taking every year the same direction, their emigration proceeding from temperate to warm regions—nearly the same course as that followed by the herrings and pilchards.

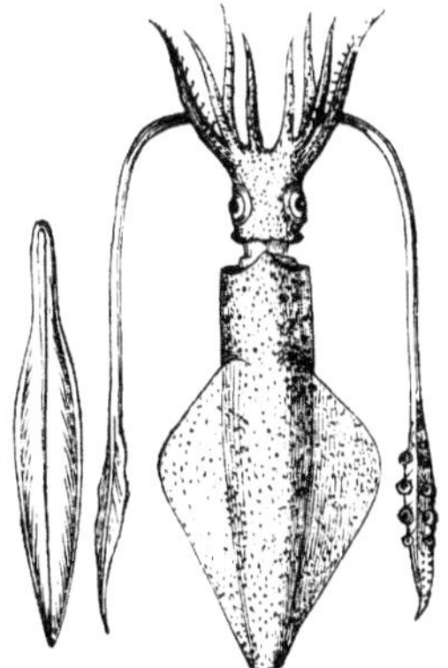

Fig. 327. Loligo vulgaris, with its feather, or internal bone (Lamarck).

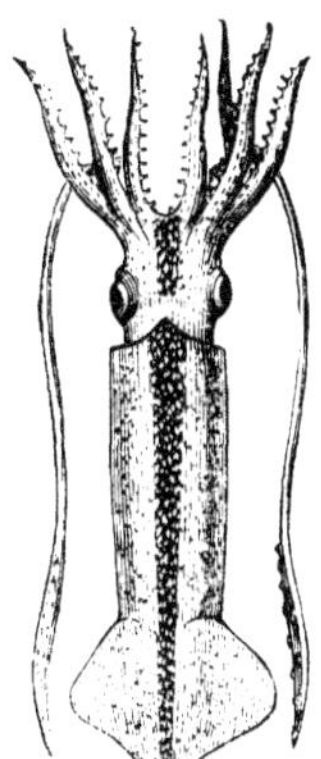

Fig. 328. Loligo Gahi (D'Orbigny).

The calmars, like the cuttles, propel themselves backwards through the water with great velocity, driving back the water by means of their locomotive tube, moving with such vigour and promptitude that they have been known to throw themselves out of the water, falling on the shore or on the deck of a vessel. They only appear momentarily on the shore, and only sojourn there to deposit their eggs, which are gelatinous in substance, about the level of the lowest tides. The body in the calmars is longer than in the cuttle-fish, cylindrical in shape, and terminating in a point, having two lateral fins, which occupy the lower half or third of its body.

In the common calmar, *Loligo vulgaris* (Fig. 327), and the *Loligo*

Gahi (Fig. 328), we have two extreme forms represented, both taken from the magnificent work of MM. D'Orbigny and Ferussac, on the *Cephalopodes acetabulifores*. These molluscs are whitish-blue and transparent, covered with spots of bright red. The osselet is lanceolate—that of the male elongated and somewhat resembling a feather, that of the female much broader and more obtuse. Their head is short, furnished with two large projecting eyes; the mouth is surrounded with ten arms, provided with suckers, two of these being much longer than the others, having peduncles or foot-stalks.

The internal bone of the calmar differs much from that of the cuttles; it is thin, horny, transparent, and somewhat resembling a feather, from a portion of which the *barbs* have been removed. Their food consists chiefly of small fishes and molluscs. With the greater fishes and cetaceæ they carry on constant war. They are caught and used for various purposes; along the coast they are eaten; the fishermen use them as bait, especially in fishing for cod.

Tentaculiferous Cephalopods.

In place of bearing simple suckers (*Acetabula*), like the first order of Cephalopods, this group is furnished with true organs of prehension, or tentacles. They differ from the first group chiefly in their more numerous arms, which are quite tentaculiferous, having neither suckers nor capsules, and by having an external shell. The number of living species is extremely limited; for this group of animals belong peculiarly to the earlier ages of our globe, is gradually becoming extinct, and presents in our days only some very rare species, when we compare them with the prodigious numbers of these beings which animated the seas of the ancient world. In fact, the only living type of the order is the nautilus, which has a singular resemblance in form to the argonaut.

The shell of this mollusc is a regular spiral, with contiguous turns, the last turn enclosing all the others. It is divided internally into numerous cells, formed by transverse partitions, concave in front and perforated towards the centre, and forming a kind of funnel, which gives passage to a respiratory siphon.

In the last cell of the shell (Fig. 329) is the animal, covered by its mantle, which covers the walls of the cells. When it contracts itself it is protected by a sort of triangular and fleshy hood. Numerous contractile tentacles, re-entering into the sheath, some of them furnished with numerous lamellæ, surround the head, which is, besides, scarcely distinguished from the body. The head bears two great projecting eyes, planted upon a peduncle.

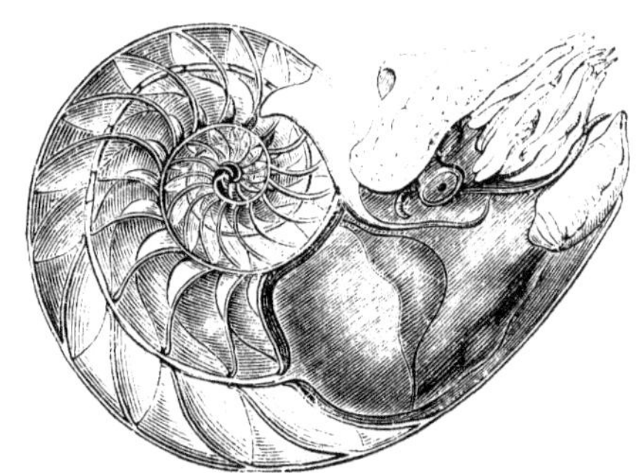

Fig. 329. Nautilus pompilius (Linnæus), showing the interior of the lower cell, to which the animal is fixed like a waterspout.

Like Sepia and Octopus, the mouth of the Nautilidæ is armed with mandibles, fashioned like the parrot's beak; the branchiæ are four in number. The circulating system consists of a ventricle and auricle, and the locomotive tube is protected in its whole length. The shell is secreted by the outer edge of the mantle, while its posterior extremity fashions the walls of the cells, which indicate the successive growth of the individual.

The siphon, which traverses all the chambers, receives and protects the ligament, by the aid of which the Cephalopod is retained in the last chamber of the shell.

Fig. 330 is the same section, with the last cell empty, and with the perforations through which the siphon passes.

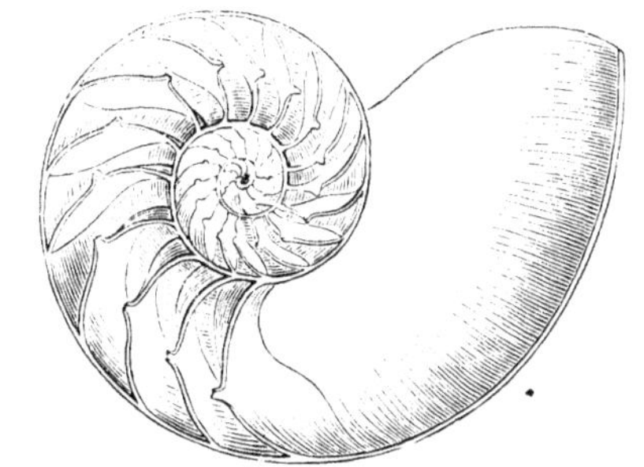

Fig. 330. Nautilus pompilius (Linnæus), showing the lower cell and the partition giving passage to the water-spout.

The Nautilidæ are inhabitants of the Indian Ocean and the sea round the Molucca Islands. In swimming, their head and tentacles are projected from out of the shell. In walking on rocks they drag themselves along the ground, the body upwards, the head and tentacles beneath. They betake themselves frequently to miry cavities frequented by fish. It is a much more common occurrence to find the empty than inhabited shells of the Nautilus at sea. This, probably, arises from its exposure to the attacks of crustaceans and other marine carnivora. This seems to be proved by the mangled appearance of the edges in the empty shells thus met with.

The Flaming Nautilus, *Nautilus pompilius* (Fig. 331), is so common on the Nicobar coast that the inhabitants salt and dry its flesh, and store them as provisions. Its shell attains about eight inches in its greatest height. It is nearly round, smooth, transversely blazed in its posterior part, and entirely white anteriorly. A very fine nacre is yielded by this mollusc, which is much used in ornamental cabinet-work. The Orientals make drinking-cups, on which they engrave designs and figures, which form graceful objects. Similar vases were formerly shaped in Europe, which found their way into great houses. In our days they are generally consigned to cabinets of curiosities and the shops of dealers in articles of vertù.

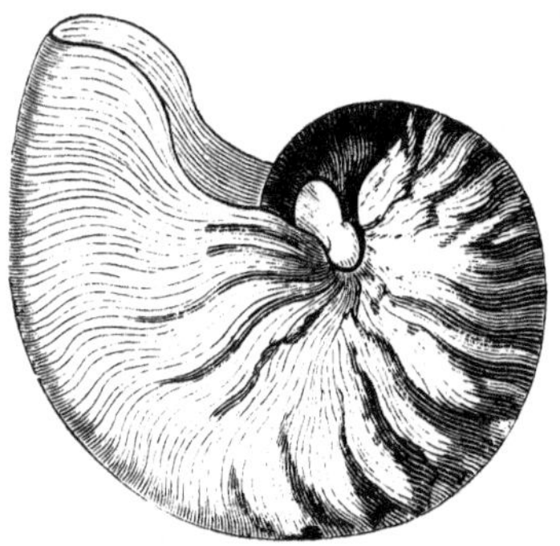

Fig. 331. Shell of Nautilus pompilius (Linnæus).

CHAPTER XVII.

CRUSTACEANS.

"Multa tamen lætus tristia pontus habet."

OVID.

PASSING OVER the vast numbers of beings which inhabit the debatable land—the *Annelids*, which were for ages confounded with the worms, because of their resemblance in form—a form which might be declared forbidding, but, as Aristotle has well said, Nature, in her domain, knows nothing low, nothing contemptible; the sea-leeches, whose condition was an impenetrable mystery to Pliny, "Omnia incerta ratione, et in naturæ majestate abdita;" and the singular cirripedes, one species of which, the barnacle (*Anatifa lævis*), was thought by old Gerard, the herbalist, and in his day by many others, to be the egg from which the barnacle goose was produced — passing over these ocean tribes, we reach the Crustaceans—the Insects of the Sea; but insects of greater size, force, and voracity than any land insect with which we are acquainted. Armed, also, at all points; for, in place of the coriaceous tunic, they are clothed in calcareous armour, both hard and strong, and bristling with coarse hairs, spiny tubercles—even armed spines. Stone is here substituted for a horny substance; the structure is in many respects the same, but the Creator has changed the materials.

The Crustaceans have nearly all of them claws, formidably hooked and toothed, which they employ as pincers both in offensive and defensive war. They have been compared to the heavily-armed knights of the middle ages—at once audacious and cruel; barbed in steel from head to foot, with visor and corslet, arm-pieces and thigh-pieces—nothing is wanting to realise its prototype.

These marine marauders live on the sea-coast, among the rocks, and near the shore. Some few of them frequent the deep waters, others hide themselves in the sand or under stones, while the common crab (*Carcinus mænas*, Leach) loves the shore almost as much as the salt water, and establishes itself accordingly under some moist cliff overhanging the sea, where it can enjoy both.

One of the necessary consequences of the condition of these animals, enclosed in a hard shell, is their power of throwing it off. The solidity of their calcareous carapace would effectually prevent their growth, but at certain determinate periods Nature despoils the warrior of his cuirass; the creature moults, and the calcareous crust falls off, and leaves it with a thin, pale, and delicate tunic. In this state the Crustacean is no longer worthy of its name—its skin has become vulnerable as that of the softest mollusc; but it has the instinct of weakness—it retires into lonely places, and hides its shame in some obscure crevice, until another vestment, more suitable for resistance, and adapted to its increased size, has been restored, and, along with it, its coat-armour and crustacean dignity.

The Crustacean has not, like the more advanced vertebrata, a vertebral column. In its nature it is altogether different from the internal skeleton; still its functions are the same. The tegumentary skeleton of the Crustacean consists of a great number of distinct pieces, connected together by means of portions of the epidermal covering which have not yet become hardened, in the same way as the bones in the internal skeleton of the vertebrata are connected by cartilages, the ossification of which only takes place in old age. The skeleton, or framework, consists of a series of rings varying in number, the normal number of the body-segments being twenty-one. Each ring is divisible into two arcs—one upper, or dorsal, the other lower, or ventral; and each arc may present four elementary pieces, two of which are united in the mesial line from the *tergum*, or back; the lower arc is a counterpart of this, while the others form the two side, or epimeral, pieces. Their skeleton, in short, is the stony envelope: the bone is not condensed within the body, but is accumulated on the circumference. The skin, therefore, performs the functions of the skeleton, so that the Crustaceans, as was said by Geoffroy Saint Hilaire, like the molluscs, live inside and not outside the bony column. There exists, then, among the vertebrata, animals with an interior—a *true skeleton;* and others with a dermal, or tegumentary skeleton.

The Crustaceans have a dark-grey iron colour, with a dash of steel-blue, like metal weapons forged for combat. Some few of them are red, or reddish-brown; others are of an earthy yellow, or of a livid blue.

"The integument," according to Milne Edwards, "consists of a *corium*, or true skin, and epidermis, with a pigmentary matter, which colours the latter. The corium is a thick, spongy, and vascular membrane, connected with the serous substance which lines the parietal walls of the cavities, as the serous membrane lines the internal cavities among the vertebrata." This pigment is less a membrane than an amorphous matter diffused through the outer layer of the superficial membrane, which changes to red in the greater number of species in alcohol, ether, acids, and water, at 212° Fahr.

The calcareous crust of the animal is thick, and in the dorsal region capable of great resistance; their members are also of remarkable hardness; but in the smaller species the shell is often thin, and of that crystalline transparency which permits of its digestion and circulation being observed. Many species, which are quite microscopic, contribute colour to the sea—red, purple, or scarlet: such are *Grimothea D'Urvillei* and *G. gregarea*.

Among the sea-spiders, which have no neck (*Cephalothorax*), the head gradually disappears in the breast, but the belly remains distinct; the middle of the body is compressed, the shape narrow and graceful. Among the Crustaceans which have neither neck nor shape, the head, the breast, and the belly form only one mass, often short, squat, athletic, and difficult to take, as in *Pisa tetraodon* (Fig. 332), the four-horned spider-crab.

Fig. 332. Pisa tetraodon.

Many of these animals have a powerful tail. consisting of a certain number of ciliated paddles, which it uses in swimming to beat the water, and to confuse its enemies.

The Crustaceans, so far as they are aquatic, respire by means of *branchiæ*, or gills. In the larger species these branchiæ are lamellous, or with filaments, whose supports are traversed by two canals, one of which leads the blood into the general economy, the other directs it towards the heart. These organs are enclosed in the body. In the smaller species the branchiæ often appear exteriorly, hanging in the water like a fungus. Sometimes these are at once swimming and breathing organs; in other cases the animal has no special organs of respiration.

Nearly all the Crustaceans are strong, hardy, and destructive, forming a horde of nocturnal brigands—merciless marauders, who recoil from no trap in which they can lie in wait for their prey. They fight *à l'outrance* not only with their enemies, but often among themselves, either for a prey or for a female, sometimes for the sake of the fight. The miserable creatures struggle audaciously with their claws. The carapace generally resists the most formidable blows; but the feet, the tail, and, above all, the antennæ, suffer frightful mutilation. Happily for the vanquished, the mutilated members sprout again after a few weeks of repose. This is the reason for the many Crustaceans met with having the talons of very unequal size: the smaller are those lost in battle replaced. Nature has willed that the Crustacean should not long remain an invalid. They soon return cured of their wounds. "We have seen lobsters," says Moquin-Tandon, "which have in an unfortunate rencounter lost a limb, sick and debilitated, reappear at the end of a few months with a perfect limb, vigorous, and ready for service. O Nature, how thou fillest our souls with astonishment and wonder!"

On the Spanish coast there is a species of crab, known, singularly enough, by the name of *Boccaccio;* it is caught for its claw, which is considered excellent eating. This is cut off, and the mutilated animal is thrown into the sea, to be taken at some future time when the claw has reappeared.

Crustaceans are nearly all carnivorous, and eat eagerly all other animals, whether living or dead, fresh or decomposed. Little think they of the quality or condition of their food. It is amusing to witness the address and gravity with which the common crab, when it has seized an unfortunate mussel, holds the valve open with one claw, while with the other it rapidly detaches the animal, carrying each morsel to the mouth, as one might do with the hand, until the shell is entirely empty. The crab does not kill its prey directly, like the lobster; it is swallowed also, but with greater appreciation.

M. Charles Lespés surprised upon the shore at Royan a shoal of crabs at their repast. This day they seemed to have dined in common, and "God knows the enjoyment," as the good Fontaines said. They were in rows, every head turned to the same side, and nearly on end on their eight feet. They seized the small objects on the shore, which were carried to the mouth, each hand in its turn in regular order: when the right hand reached the mouth the left was on the ground. Let us just figure to oneself a company of disciplined soldiers messing together from the same plate!

The Long-horned Corophius (*Corophium longicorne*), remarkable for its long antennæ, knows perfectly well how to cut the byssus by which the mussels suspend themselves, in order that the bivalve may fall on the weeds among them. Other Crustaceans, also great oyster-eaters, have the cunning or instinct to attack the mollusc without exposing themselves to danger. When the bivalve half opens its shell to enjoy the rays of the sun or take food, the evil-disposed Crustacean slips a stone between the valve. This done, it devours the poor inhabitant of the shell at its leisure.

The Corophius, respecting whom this question is hazarded, are extremely numerous on the shores of the Atlantic towards the end of summer and autumn. They make constant war upon certain marine worms. Off the coast of La Rochelle they may be seen in myriads beating the muddy bottom with their long antennæ in search of their prey. Sometimes they meet one of these Nereida or Arenicola many times their own size, when they unite in a body to attack it. In the oyster-beds of La Rochelle they are useful friends to the oyster by destroying these enemies, although they do not hesitate to attack the mollusc when it comes in their way. During the winter the mud of the bouchots gets piled up in unequal heaps, and when the warm season returns, it has become hard and unfit for the cultivation of the mollusc. It is necessary to level and dry these mud-heaps—a process which would be both difficult and costly. Well, the Corophia charge themselves with the task. They plough up annually many square leagues covered with these heaps. They dilute the mud, which is carried out by the ebbing tide, and the surface of the bay is left smooth, as it was in the preceding autumn.

We have said that the Crustaceans do not even respect each other; the larger of the same species often devour the smaller. *Rara concordia fratrum!* Mr. Rymer Jones relates that he had on one occasion introduced six crabs (*Platycarcinus pagurus*) of different size into an aquarium. One of them, venturing towards the middle of the reservoir, was immediately accosted by another a little larger, which took it with its claws as it might have taken a biscuit, and set about breaking its shell, and so found a way to its flesh. It dug its crooked claws into it with voluptuous enjoyment, appearing to pay no attention to the anger and jealousy of another of its companions, which was still stronger and as cruel, and advanced towards them. But, as Horace says—and he was not the first to say it—"No one is altogether happy in this lower world":

"Nihil est ab omni parte beatum."

Our ferocious Crustacean quietly continued its repast, when its companion seized it exactly as it had seized its prey, broke and tore it in the same fashion, penetrating to its middle, and tearing out its entrails in the same savage manner. In the meantime the victim, singularly enough, did not disturb itself for an instant, but continued to eat the first crab bit by bit, until it was itself entirely torn to pieces by its own executioner—a remarkable instance at once of insensibility to pain and of cruel infliction under the *lex talionis.* To eat and to be eaten seems to be one of the great laws of Nature.

Though essentially carnivorous, the Crustaceans sometimes eat marine vegetables. Many even seem to prefer fruit to animal food. Such is the tree-crab of the Polynesian Isles, which feeds almost exclusively on the cocoa-nut. This crab has thick and strong claws; the others are comparatively slender and weak. At first glance it seems impossible that it could penetrate a thick cocoa-nut surrounded by a thick bed of fibre and protected by its strong shell; but M. Liesk has often seen the operation. The crab begins by tearing off the fibre at the extremity where the fruit is, always choosing the right end. When this is removed, it strikes it with its great claws until it has made an opening; then, by the aid of its slender claws, and by turning itself round, it extracts the whole substance of the nut.

The Crustaceans have eyes of two kinds—simple and compound: the first are sessile and immovable, and very convex; the other borne on a short calcareous stem or peduncle, and formed of a number of small eyes symmetrically agglomerated—the reunion of all the microscopic cornea of a composite eye, resembling in shape a cap formed of facets. It is said, for instance, that the eye of the lobster consists of 2500 of these little facets. The simple eyes are *myopus*, or short-sighted—the compound eyes for more distant but perfect sight. They appear to have a strong sense of smell. Many of them cannot swim, but walk with more or less facility at the bottom of the water. It is said, for instance, that the cavalier of the Syrian coast, *Oxypoda cursor* (Fabricius), is named from the rapidity with which it traverses great distances; but it may be doubted if its pace equals that of a horse.

Many systems have been proposed by different writers for the arrangement of the Crustacea. That proposed by Mr. Milne Edwards recommends itself, being founded on anatomical examination and actual experiment made by himself and M. Audouin. He divides them into two great divisions:—I. Those in which the mouth is furnished with a certain number of organs adapted for the prehension or division of food. II. Those in which the mouth is surrounded by ambulatory extremities, the bases of which perform the part of jaws. The first includes the MAXILOSA or MANDIBULATA, again divided into *Decapoda*, having branchiæ attached to the sides of the thorax, and enclosed in special cavities. The *Decapoda* are divided into: 1. BRACHYURA, namely, the Crabs. *Cancer*, *Portumnus*, *Grapsus*, *Œcypodes*, and *Dorypes*, belong to this group. 2. ANOMOURA, including *Dromia*, *Pagurus*, *Porcellana*, and *Hippa*. 3. MACROURA, including the Lobsters, *Astacus*, *Palæmon*, the Craw-fish, *Palinurus*.

Stomapoda, with external branchiæ, sometimes rudimentary, sometimes none. Thoracic extremities prehensile, or for swimming generally, six or eight pairs. This division includes the Mysidæ, Phyllosoma, Squilla, &c.

The other divisions of Crustaceans we need not dwell upon. They are very obscure, and little known; some of them fresh-water Crustaceans, as in the *Entomostraca*; others are parasitic on the whale and various species of fish.

CRABS AND CRAW-FISH.

Crabs and lobsters may be regarded as the chiefs or lords of the Crustacean tribes. The crabs have very large claws and smooth backs; the last have small claws and the back covered with spines. Tiberius Cæsar had the face of a poor fisherman scratched by the rugged shell of a craw-fish.

Lobsters, especially, have an amazing fecundity, and yield an immense number of eggs, each female producing from 12,000 to 20,000 in the season. The crab is also very prolific. These eggs are, in the lobster, arranged in packets, which are attached to the lower surface of the tail, to which they are connected by a viscous substance. The manner in which the hen lobster disposes of her burden is curious and interesting. Whether she bends or stands erect she is able to hold it obscurely or expose it to the light. Sometimes, according to Coste, the eggs are left immovable, or simply submerged; at others they are subjected to successive washings by gently agitating the false claw which shelters them from right to left. When first exuded from the ovary the eggs are very small, but they seem to increase during the time they are borne about under the tail, and before they are committed to the sand or water they have attained the size of small shot. The evolution of the germ is in progress during six months. At the moment of exclusion the female extends the tail, impresses upon the eggs an oscillating motion, in order to destroy the shell and scatter the larvæ, delivering herself in two or three days of her entire burden (Coste). "As the young lie enclosed within the membrane of the egg," says Couch, "the claws are folded on each other, and the tail is flexed on them as far as the margin of the shield. The dorsal spine is bent backwards, and lies in contact with the dorsal shield, for the young when it escapes from the egg is quite soft; but it rapidly hardens and solidifies by the deposition of calcareous matter on what may be called its skin."

As soon as born, the young Crustaceans withdraw from the mother and ascend to the surface of the water, in order to gain the open sea. They swim in a circle; but this pelagic life is not of long duration; they quit it after their fourth moult, which takes place between the thirtieth and fortieth day, at which time they lose the transitory organs of natation which they have hitherto possessed. After this they are no longer able to maintain themselves on the surface, but drop to the bottom. Henceforth they are condemned to remain there, and such walking as they can exercise becomes their habitual mode of progres-

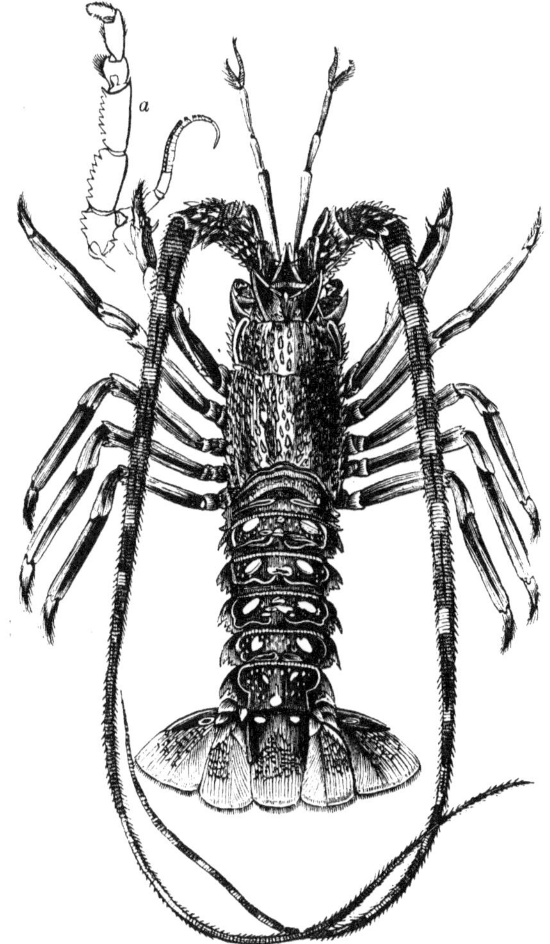

Fig. 333. Palinurus vulgaris. *a*, left outward jaw-foot

sion. As they increase in size they gradually approach the shore, which they had for the moment abandoned, and return to the places inhabited by the parent Crustaceans.

The form of the larvæ differs so much from that of the adult, that it would be difficult, except on the clearest evidence, to determine the species from which they proceed. Former naturalists considered the embryo cray-fish (*Palinurus*) to belong to a distinct genera, which they designated *Phyllosoma.* It is now known, however, that these are the young of the higher forms of Crustaceans undergoing metamorphosis. In the various forms of *Macroura* the metamorphosis is less decided than in the *Brachyura.* In the fresh-water cray-fish no change whatever takes place. Dissatisfied with the uncertainty of former experiments, Mr. Couch undertook a series of observations, which are recorded in the proceedings of the Cornwall Polytechnic Society, in which he established the fact that metamorphosis takes place in the following genera: Cancer, Zanthò, Pelumnus, Cacernus, Portumnus, Maia, Galathea, Hornarus, and Palinurus. "Metamorphosis has been demonstrated," says Dr. Bell, "in no less than seventeen genera of the Brachyurous order of Decapoda, in which it is most decided and obvious; in the Leptopodiadæ, Maiadæ, Canceridæ, Portumnidæ, Pinnotheridæ, and Grapsidæ. In the Anomourous order it is seen in the Pagurus, Porcellana, and Galathea, and in the Macrouran order in Homarus, Palinurus, Palæmon, and Crangon.

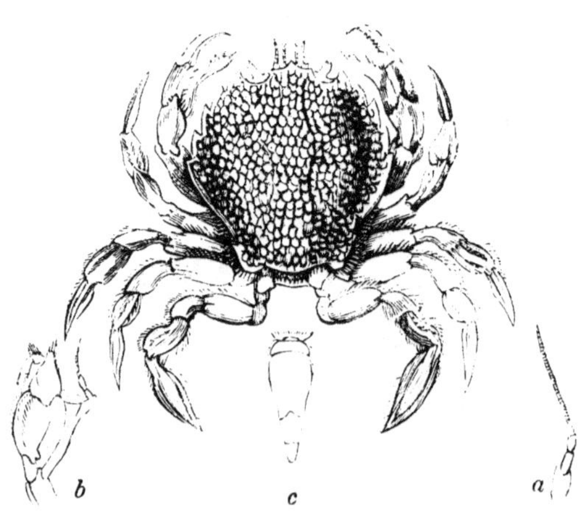

Fig. 334. Portumnus variegatus, male.
a, external antenna; *b*, external jaw-foot; *c*, tail or abdomen.

The swimming of these creatures is produced by flexions and expansions of the tail, and by repeated beating motions of the claws, the tail acting as a sort of vibratile oar, aided by which they maintain themselves in the water and facilitate their progress. As the shell becomes more solid they get less active, and finally return to the bottom to cast their shell and assume a new form.

According to the observations of M. Coste, the young lobster casts its shell from eight to ten times in the first year, from five to seven in the second, three to four times the third, and two or three times the fourth year. In the fifth year they attain the adult state. Whence it follows, that the small lobsters served at our tables have changed their calcareous vestment something like twenty-one times, and are now clothed in their twenty-second habit.

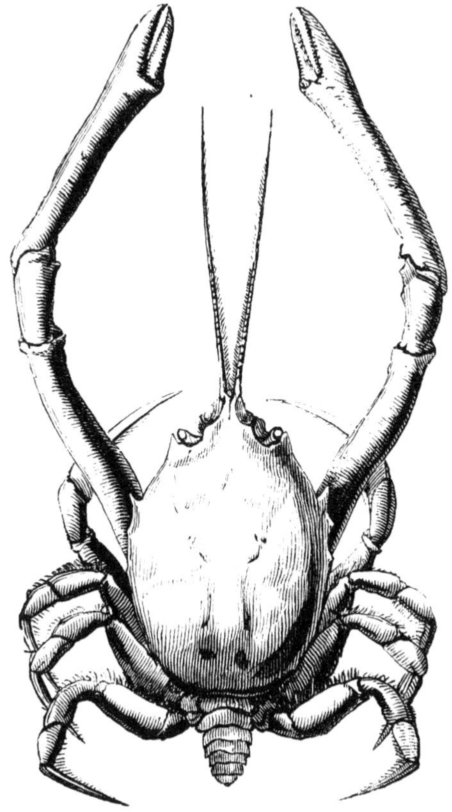

Fig. 335. Corystes Cassivelaunus, male.

The crabs are numerous in species and various in size. The long-clawed crab (*Corystes Cassivelaunus*) of Pennant and Leach (Fig. 335) is remarkable for its long antennæ, which considerably exceed the body. The jaw-feet have their third joint longer than the second, terminating in an obtuse point, with a notch on its interior edge; eyes wide apart, borne upon large peduncles, which are nearly cylindrical and short; anterior feet large, equal, twice the length of the body, and nearly cylindrical in the males; in the females (Fig. 336) about the length of the body, and compressed, especially towards the hand-claw. The other feet terminate in an elongated nail or claw, which is straight-pointed and channeled longitudinally: carapace oblong-oval, terminating in a rostrum anteriorly truncated and bordered posteriorly; the regions but slightly indicated, with the exception of the cordian region, the branchial or lateral regions being very much elongated.

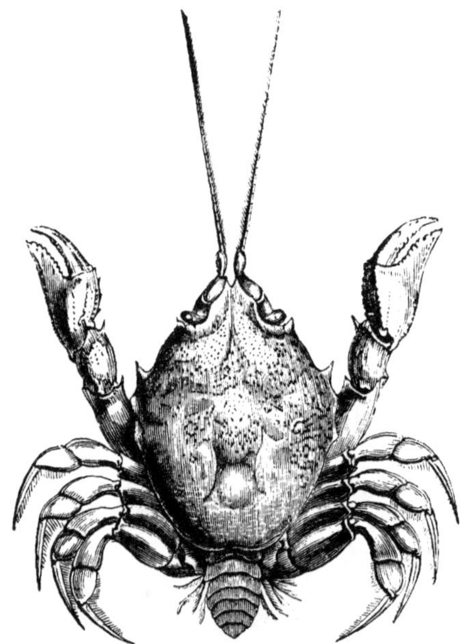

Fig. 336. Corystes Cassivelaunus, female.

Latreille gives the name of Corystes, which signifies a warrior armed, to this genus of Crustaceans, from κόρυς, a helmet, but it is perfectly inoffensive. Pennant had already conferred the name of *Cassivelaunus*, the chief of the ancient Britons, for the singular reason, according to Gosse, that the carapace, which is marked by wrinkles, bears, in old males especially, the strongest and most ludicrous resemblance to the face of an ancient man. Pennant's well-known sympathy with his British ancestry certainly never led him to caricature the grand old British warrior, as Mr. Gosse surmises. On the contrary, he saw in the Crustacean a creature armed at all points, and he named it after the hero of his imagination.

In this species the surface of the carapace is somewhat granulous, with two denticles between the eyes, and three sharp points directed forward on each side. The male has only five abdominal pieces, but the vestiges of the separation of the two others may be clearly remarked upon the outer mediate or third piece, which is the largest of all. The length of the antennæ are remarked on by Mr. Couch, in his Cornish Fauna. "These organs," he says, "are of some use beyond their common office of feelers; perhaps, as in some other Crustaceans, they assist in the process of excavation; and, when soiled by labour, I have seen the crab effect their cleaning by alternately bending the joints of their stalks, which stand conveniently angular for the purpose. Each of the long antennæ is thus drawn along the brush that fringes the internal face of the other, until both are cleared of every particle that adhered to them." On the other hand, Mr. Gosse suggests that the office of the antennæ is to keep a passage open for ejecting the deteriorated water after it has bathed and aerated the gills. "I have observed," he says, "that, when kept in an aquarium, these crabs are fond of sitting bolt upright, the antennæ placed close together, and pointing straight upwards from the head. This is doubtless the attitude in which the animal sits in its burrow, for the tips of the antennæ may often be seen just projecting from the sand. When the chosen seat has happened to be so close to the glass side of the tank as to bring the antennæ within the range of a pocket lens, I have minutely investigated these organs without disturbing the old warrior in his meditation. I saw on each occasion that a strong current of water was continuously pouring up from the points of the antennæ. Tracing this to its origin, it became evident that it was produced by the rapid vibration of the foot-jaws drawing in the surrounding water, and pouring it off upwards *between the united antennæ*, as through a tube. Then, on examining these organs, I perceived that the form and arrangement of their bristles did indeed constitute each antennæ a semi-tube, so that when the pair were brought face to face the tube was complete."

Among the numerous genera of *Brachyurous Crustaceans*, the Grapsidæ are distinguished by their less regularly quadrilateral form; the body nearly always compressed, and the sternal plastron but little or not at all curved backwards; the front strongly recurved, or, rather, bent downwards; the orbits oval-shaped and of moderate size; the lateral edges of the carapace slightly curving and trenchant; the ocular pedicles large, but short: their insertion beneath the front and the cornea occupies one half of their length.

The Hermit or Soldier Crab (*Pagurus Bernhardus*, Fabricius, Fig. 337) is, perhaps, the oddest and most curious of Crustaceans. It

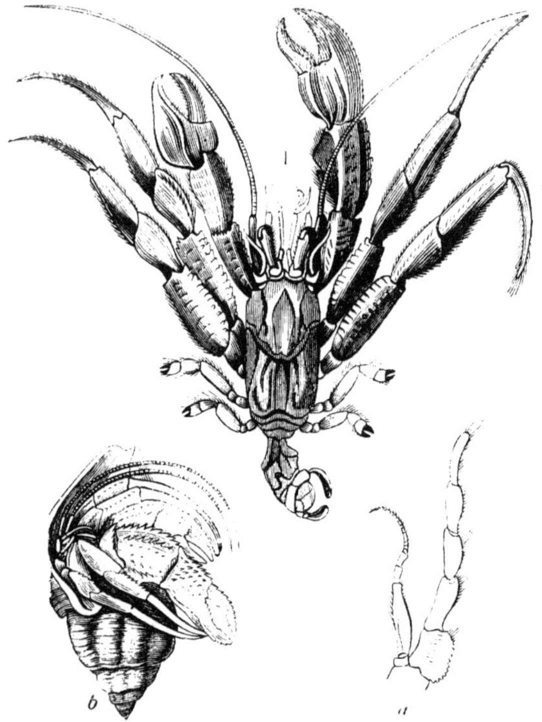

Fig. 337. Pagurus Bernhardus. 1, out of the shell; *a*, right jaw-foot; *b*, in the shell.

differs from most other Crustaceans in this: in place of having the body protected by a calcareous armour, more or less thick and solid, it has only a cuirass and head-piece to protect the head and breast; all the rest of the body is invested in a soft yielding skin; and this, the vulnerable part of the hermit crab, is the delicate morsel devoured by the gourmet. Nor is our somewhat evil-disposed Crustacean ignorant of the perfectly weak and defenceless state of its posterior quarters. Prudence or instinct makes it seek the shelter of some empty shell, of a shape and size corresponding to its own. When it fails to find one empty, it does not hesitate to attack some living testacean, which it kills without pity or remorse, and takes possession of its habitation without other form of process. Once master of the shell (Fig. 337), it introduces itself, stern foremost, and installs itself as in an entrenchment, where it is established so firmly that it moves about with it more or less briskly, according to its comparative size.

The Pagurians belong to the Anomourous family of Crustaceans, of which there are several genera, and a considerable number of species, the animal economy of which have been ably commented upon by Mr. Broderip. "Their backs," he says, "are towards the arch of the turbinated shell occupied by them, and their well-armed nippers and first two pairs of succeeding feet generally project beyond the mouth of it. The short feet rest upon the polished surface of the columella, and the outer surface of their termination, especially that of the first pair, is in some species most admirably rough-shod, to give 'the soldier' a firm footing when he makes his sortie, or to add to the resistance of the crustaceous holders at the end of his abdomen, or tail, when he is attacked, and wishes to withdraw into his castle. On passing the finger downwards over the terminations of these feet, they feel smooth; but if the finger be passed upwards, the roughness is instantly perceived. The same sort of structure (it is as rough as a file) is to be seen in the smaller caudal holders." In another species of Pagurus, from the Mauritius, which was nearly a foot in length, he found a great number of transverse rows, armed with acetabula, or suckers; these were visible without the aid of a glass, which must very much assist the hold of the *Pagurus*.

During the feeding and breeding-time, the hermit throws out his head and feet, and especially his great claws, and feels his way with his two antennæ, which are long and slender. When he walks he hooks on with his pincers to the nearest body, and draws his shell after him, as the snail does his. But the undefended parts of the body always remain under cover. At low water the hermits spread themselves over the rocky shore, and the spectator thinks he sees a great number of shells which move in all directions, with allurements different from that which belongs to their essentially slow and measured race. If they are touched they stop suddenly, and it is soon discovered that their shell is the dwelling of a crustacean, not a mollusc. The Bernhard lives alone in its little citadel, like the hermit in his cell or the sentinel in his box. Hence the name of *hermit* and *soldier*.

When our crustacean outgrows its borrowed habitation, it sets out in search of another shell, a little larger, and better suited for its increased size.

The hermit often avails itself, as we have said, of empty shells abandoned by their owners; when the tide retires these seldom fail them, and the hermit may be seen examining, turning, and re-turning, and even trying its new domicile. It glides slowly along on its abdomen, which is large and somewhat distorted, sometimes in one shell, sometimes in another, looking defiantly all round it, and returning very quickly to its ancient lodging if the new one does not turn out to be perfectly comfortable, often trying a great number, as a man might try many new clothes before suiting himself. In its successive removals the little sybarite chooses a hermitage more and more spacious, according to its taste or caprice in colour or architecture. The cunning little creature chooses its mansion, now grey or yellow, now red or brown, globular or cylindrical, in the form of a spiral or of a tun, toothed or crenulate, with trenchant edge or pointed terminations; but, as a rule, our crustacean Diogenes houses itself in spirals of considerable length, as in *Cerethium*, *Buccinum*, or *Murex*.

The hermit is very timid; at the least noise it shrinks into its shell and squats itself, without motion, drawing in its smaller claws and closing the door with its large ones, the latter being often covered with hairs, tubercles, or with teeth. In short, our prudent cenobite clings so closely to the bottom of its retreat, that we might pull it to pieces without getting it out entire; its tail is transformed into a sort of sucker, by the aid of which it attaches itself firmly to the walls of its habitation. It is at once strong and voracious, eating with much relish the dead fishes and fragments of molluscs and annelids which come in its way. Nor does it hesitate to attack and devour living animals. When introduced into an aquarium, it has sometimes thrown it into the utmost disorder by its insatiable rapacity. It has been possible sometimes to preserve harmony among many individuals inhabiting the same reservoir; but this has been owing rather to the impossibility of their attacking each other, in consequence of cunningly-devised barricades, than to their mildness of character or love of their neighbour. These animals, in short, are very quarrelsome. Two hermits cannot meet without exhibiting hostile intentions; each extends his long pincers, and seems to try to touch the other, much as a spider does when it seeks to seize a fly on its most vulnerable side, but each, finding the other armed in proof, and perfectly protected, though eager to fight, usually adopt the better part of valour, and prudently withdraw. They often have true passages of arms, nevertheless, in which claws are spread out, and displayed in the most threatening manner; the two adversaries tumbling head over heels, and rolling one upon the other, but they get more frightened than hurt. Nevertheless, Mr. Gosse once witnessed a struggle which had a more tragic end. A hermit crab met a brother Bernhard pleasantly lodged in a shell much more spacious than his own. He seized it by the head with his powerful claws, tore it from its asylum with the speed of lightning, and took its place not less promptly, leaving the dispossessed unfortunate struggling on the sand in convulsions of agony. "Our battles," says Charles Bonnet, "have rarely such important objects in view: they fight each other for a house."

A pretty little zoophyte, the Cloak Anemone (*Adamsia palliata*), loves to live with the hermit, and exhibits sympathies almost inexplicable. In aquariums this anemone attaches itself almost always to the shell which serves as the dwelling of the Crustacean; and it may be looked upon as certain that where the hermit is there will the anemone be found. These two creatures seem to live in perfect and intelligent harmony together, for Mr. Gosse's observations establish the existence of a cordial and reciprocal affection between them. This learned and intelligent observer describes the proceedings of a hermit which required a new habitation; he saw it detach, in the most deliberate but effective manner, its dear companion, the anemone, from the old shell, transport it with every care and precaution, and place it comfortably upon the new shell, and then with its large pincers give to its well-beloved many little taps, as if to fix it there the more quickly. Another species of Bernhardus makes a companion of the *mantled anemone.* "And we are assured," says Moquin-Tandon, "that when the crab dies its inconsolable friend is not long in succumbing also."

"Is there not here much more than what our modern physiologists call automatic movements, the results of reflex sensorial action?" says Gosse. "The more I study the lower animals, the more firmly am

I persuaded of the existence in them of psychical faculties, such as consciousness, intelligence, skill, and choice; and *that* even in those forms in which as yet no nervous centres have been detected."

LOBSTERS.

In a dietary, as well as commercial sense, the lobster far excels the crab; like the latter, they have an amazing fecundity, each female producing from twelve to twenty thousand eggs in a season; and wisely is it so arranged, otherwise the consumption would soon exhaust them.

In France the size of the marketable lobster is regulated by law, and fixed at twenty centimètres (eight inches) in length; all under that size are contraband. Every year the inhabitants of Blainville proceed to Chaussey to fish for lobsters. They are taken in baskets in the form of a truncated cone, the mouth of which is so arranged that the animal can enter, but cannot get out. The numbers caught by each fisherman and his family in a season may be estimated at a thousand or twelve hundred, which realise to the family thirteen or fourteen hundred francs, the season lasting about nine months.

Lobsters are collected all round our own coast for the London market. On the Scottish shore they are collected and kept in perforated chests floating on the water, until they can be taken away to market. From the Sutherland coast alone six to eight thousand lobsters are collected in a season. This process goes on all round the coast, and as far as Norway, whence an enormous supply of the finest lobsters are obtained, for which something like £20,000 per annum is paid, all these contributions being conveyed to the Thames and Mersey in welled vessels. But these old-fashioned systems are being rapidly superseded by the construction of artificial storing ponds, or basins. Of these ponds Mr. Richard Scovell has erected one at Hamble, near Southampton, in which he can store with ease fifty thousand lobsters, which will keep in good condition for six weeks. Mr. Scovell's tank is supplied from the coasts of France, Scotland, and Ireland, where fine lobsters abound. He employs three large and well-appointed smacks, each of which can carry from five thousand to ten thousand. On the coast of Ireland alone, it is said, ten thousand fine lobsters a week might be taken.

The Lobster (*Homarus*) is found in great abundance all round our coast; frequenting the more rocky shores and clear water, where it is of no great depth, about the time of depositing its eggs. Various are the modes in which they are taken: cone-shaped traps made of wicker-work, and baited with garbage, are perhaps the most successful. These are sunk among the rocks, and marked by buoys. Sometimes nets are sunk, baited by the same material. In other places a wooden instrument, which acts like a pair of tongs, is used for their capture.

Mr. Pennant, the naturalist, paid great attention to the lobsters, and their habits are well described in a letter from Mr. Travis, of Scarborough. "The larger ones," he says, "are in their best season from the middle of October to the beginning of May. Many of the smaller ones, and some few of the larger individuals, are good all the summer. If they are four and a half inches long from the top of the head to the end of the back shell, they are called sizeable lobsters; if under four inches, they are esteemed half-size, and two of them are reckoned for one of size. Under four inches they are called pawks, and these are the best summer lobsters. The pincers of one of the lobster's large claws are furnished with knobs, while the other claw is always serrated. With the former it keeps firm hold of the stalks of submarine plants; with the latter it cuts and masticates its food very dexterously. The knobbed or thumb claw, as the fishermen call it, is sometimes on the left, sometimes on the right, side, and it is more dangerous to be seized by the serrated claw than the other.

There is little doubt that the lobsters cast their shell annually, but the mode in which it is performed is not satisfactorily explained. It is supposed that the old shell is cast, and that the animal retires to some lurking-place till the new covering acquires consistence to contend with his armour-clad congeners. Others contend that the process is one of absorption, otherwise, if there were a period of moult, it would be shown by their shells. The most probable conjecture is that the shell sloughs off piecemeal, as it does in the cray-fish. The greatest mystery of all, perhaps, is the process by which the lobster withdraws the fleshy part of its claws from their calcareous covering. Fishermen say the lobster pines before casting its shell, so as to permit of its withdrawing its members from it.

The hen lobster does not seem to cast her shell the same year in which she deposits her ova, or, as the fishermen say, "is in berry."

When the ova first appears under the tail, they are small and very black, but before they are ready for deposition they are almost as large as ripe elderberries, and of a dark-brown colour. There does not seem to be any particular season for this act, as females are found in berry at all seasons, but more commonly in winter. In this state they are found to be much exhausted, and by no means fit for the table.

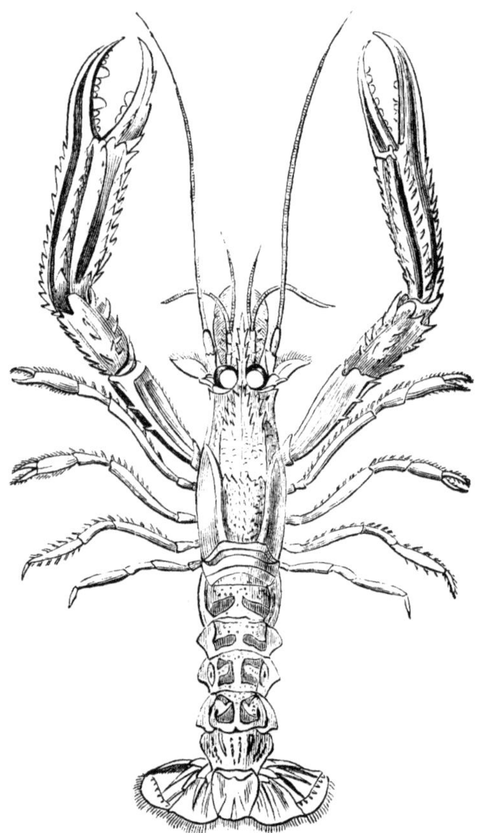

Fig. 338. Nephrops Norvegicus.

The generic name *Astacus* of Fabricius is now confined to the crawfishes, which have a depressed rostrum, one tooth on each side, and the last ring of the thorax movable. The lobsters (*Homarus*) have the eyes spherical, two rings of the thorax being soldered together The Norway Lobsters (*Nephrops Norvegicus*, Fig. 338) have the eyes uniform, and the two last rings of the thorax movable.

The last is one of the most beautiful of the larger Macrourans. Its general tint is pale flesh colour, with darker shades in parts, its pubescence light-brown. This is generally considered a northern species, but Mr. Bell states that he has received specimens from the Mediterranean. It is found plentifully on the coast of Norway, on the Scottish coast, and in the Bay of Dublin. It is considered the most delicate of all the Crustaceans.

FISHES.

Before speaking of the habits of the principal kinds of fishes, it is desirable to glance at their organization, and upon the manner in which they execute their physiological functions.

Fishes are intended to live always in water, and this circumstance has impressed its seal upon their organization. Nevertheless, their forms are very varied; they are generally oblong, compressed laterally. They have no neck, the head being merely a prolongation of the trunk. In the majority of instances, the body is covered with scales, generally a thin bony substance developed out of the skin and overlapping each other, like the tiles of a roof.

Nothing is more remarkable than the variety and brilliancy of colour in fishes; they present almost every gradation, from golden or silver, and other dazzling colours, mingling with shades of blue, green, red, and black.

Fishes are essentially formed for swimming (Fig. 339), and all their members are adapted for this purpose. The anterior members, which correspond with the arms in man and the wings in birds, are attached to each side of the trunk, immediately behind the head, and form the *pectoral fins*. The posterior members occupy the lower surface of the body, and form the *ventral fins*. The latter, which are always over the ventral line, may be before, beneath, or behind the former. Fishes possess, besides, fins in odd numbers. The fins which erect themselves on the back are called the back or *dorsal fins*, those at the end of the tail are the *caudal fins;* finally, there is frequently another attached to the lower extremity of the body, which is called the *anal fin*.

These fins are always nearly of the same structure, consisting generally of a fold of the skin, supported by slender, flexible, cartilaginous or osseous rays, connected by a thin membrane.

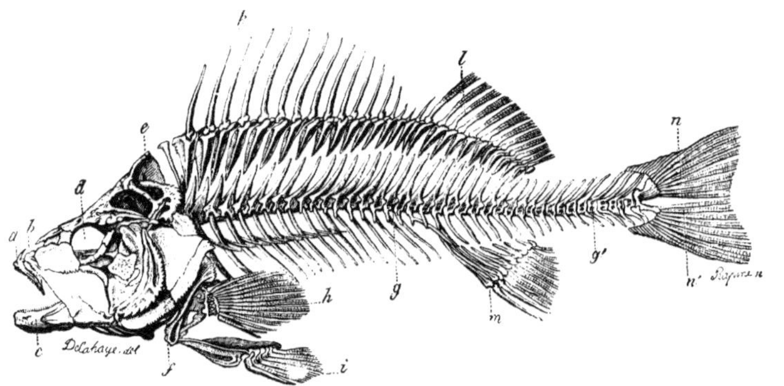

Fig. 339. Skeleton of the Common Perch.

a, the inter-maxillary bone; *b*, the maxillary bone; *d*, the gills; *c*, the under jaw; *f*, the inter-operculum; *g g'*, the vertebral column; *h*, the pectoral fin; *i*, the ventral fin; *k* and *l*, the dorsal fins; *m*, the anal fin; *n*, the caudal fin.

The muscles, which bind together the vertebral column, are so much developed in fishes as well as others of the superior animals, that they constitute in them alone the principal part of the body. The caudal, dorsal, and anal fins act as outlying oars; the pectoral and ventral fins assist in progression, at the same time that they help to maintain the equilibrium of the animal and guide and direct its movements, which are generally astonishing from their rapidity.

An organ, which belongs properly to fishes (Fig. 340), and which is usually considered as their chief aid in swimming, is a large bladder

Fig. 340. Swimming bladder of the Carp.

situated within the body, between the dorsal spine and the abdomen. This is usually called the *swimming bladder*. According to the volume this bladder assumes, the animal can increase or diminish the specific gravity of its body; that is, it can remain in equilibrium or ascend or descend in the bosom of the waters; it is, moreover, remarked that it is very small in those species which swim at the

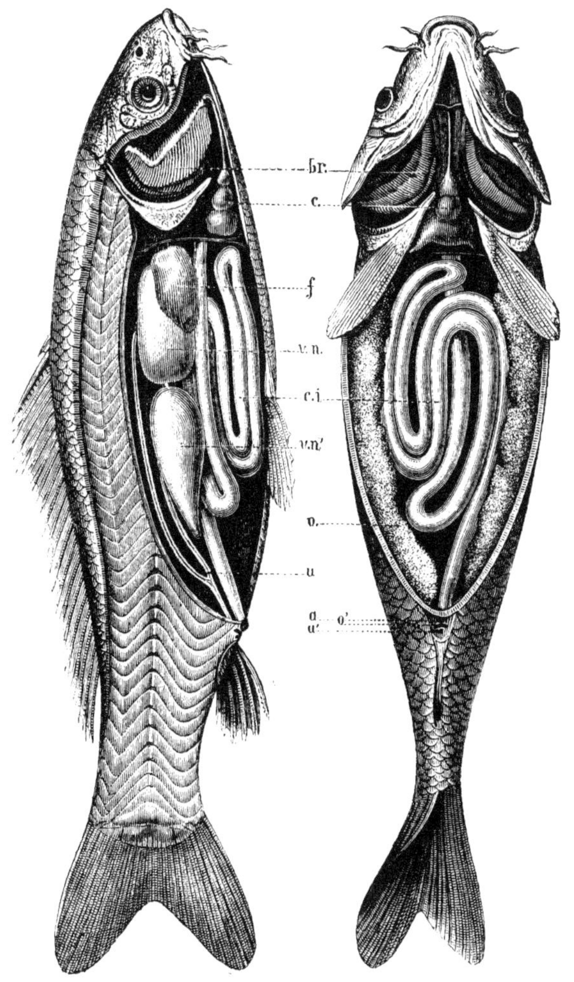

Fig. 341. Anatomy of the Carp.

br, the branchiæ, or gill openings; c, the heart; f, the liver; vn, swimming bladders; ci, intestinal canal; o, the ovarium; u, urethra; a, anus; o', oviduct.

bottom of the water, and Mr. Gosse says there is some reason for considering it to be the first rudimentary form of the air-breathing lung.

Immediately behind the head, two large openings are observed in fishes; these are the gill-openings. Their anterior edge is mobile, and they are raised or lowered to serve the purposes of respiration; under this species of covercle are the gills, or branchiæ. These usually consist of many rows of thin membranous plates, hung on slender arches of bone, placed on each side of the head, usually protected by a bony plate made up of several pieces, called the *gill-covers*. The breathing is produced by water taken in at the mouth, which passes over the gill-membranes, and is ejected through an orifice at the hind margin of the gill-covers. During the contact of the water with the gills, the blood which circulates in the train of this organ, and which communicates to them the red colour by which we recognise them, combines chemically with the oxygen of the air which the water holds in solution when it flows freely at the ordinary temperature in presence of the air. The blood is thus oxygenized, or made *arterial*.

The heart in fishes is placed between the inferior parts of the branchial arch, and consists of a ventricle and an auricle (Fig. 341). It corresponds with the right half of the heart in the Mammifera and birds, for it receives the venous blood from all parts of the body and sends it to the gills. From this organ the blood is delivered into one great artery, which creeps along the vertebral column.

The eye in fishes is generally very large—we may even say enormous relative to the size of the head—and without true eyelids; the skin usually passes over the ocular globe, and becomes from this point so transparent that the luminary rays traverse it. This light covering is all the eyelid belonging to fishes. The interior of the eye is covered by the membrane called *choroide*, the thin external leaf of which, in consequence of the presence of innumerable microscopic crystals, presents the appearance of a gold or silver-coloured coating, which gives to the iris that extraordinary brilliancy which

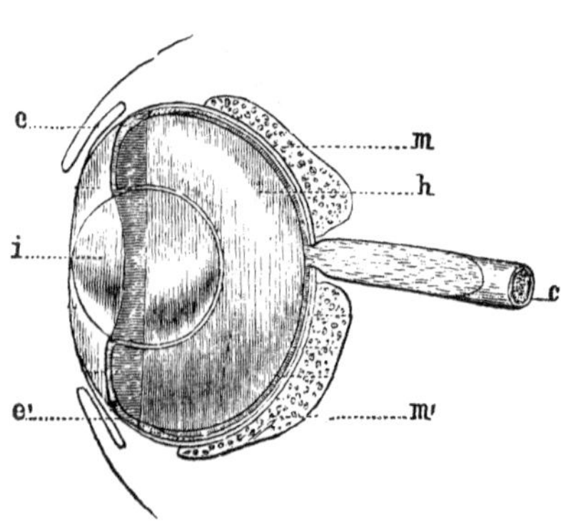

Fig. 342. The Fishes' Eye.
i, crystallized pupil; ee', cornea; mm', choroid; h, posterior chambers; c, optic nerve.

belongs to the fish's eye. The crystalline is voluminous, spherical, and diaphanous. When the fish is cooked, the crystalline constitutes that opaque and hard white substance which often comes under the teeth in eating fish of a certain size. Cuvier suspected, what anglers now know to be true, that those active chasseurs of the deep saw far and very clearly.

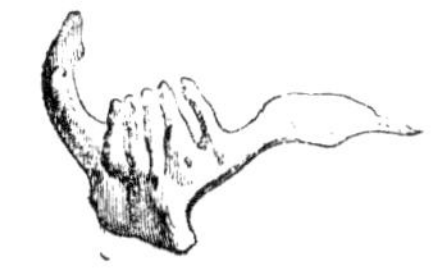
Fig. 343. Teeth of the Bream.

If fishes have great eyes, they have, on the other hand, very small ears. This organ, it is found, has no exterior opening. It forms a cavity in the interior of the cranium, which is far from presenting the complicated structure of the ear in Mammifers and birds. In spite, however, of the imperfect structure, fishes are sensible to the least noise. In consequence, silence is a rigorous law with the fisherman.

Fig. 344. Teeth of the Carp.

The dimensions of the mouth and teeth are very variable in fishes; these organs are in proportion to their voracity, which in many of these beings is very great. The form and development of the buccal pieces are also very various. Some species are toothless, but in most fishes the teeth are very numerous. They are sometimes attached not alone to the two jaws, but also to the palate, to the tongue, and upon the interior of the branchial arch, and even in the back mouth, that is to say, upon the ospharyngeal, which surrounds the mouth of the œsophagus.

Fig. 345. Teeth of the Trout.

The form of their teeth is very variable both in arrangement and position: some are in the form of an elongated cone, either straight or curved. When small and numerous, they are comparable to the points of the cards used in carding wool or cotton. Sometimes they are so slender and dense as to resemble the piles of velvet, and often, from their very minute size, their presence is more easily ascertained by the finger than the eye. In some members of the Salmonidæ, for instance, we

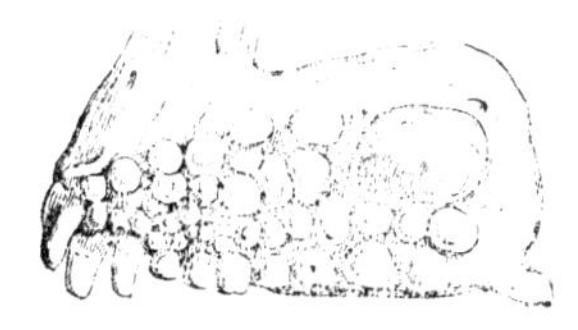
Fig. 346. Teeth of the Gold-fish Dorada.

find a row of teeth on the bone that forms the middle ridge of the palate, which is called the *vornex*. On each side of this is another row on the *palatine* bones, and outside these is a third pair of rows on the upper jaw-bones. Some fishes have flat teeth, with a cutting edge in front of the jaws, like a true incisor; others have them rounded or oval, adapted to bruise or crush the various substances on which they feed.

The œsophagus connected with the mouth is short in fishes; the stomach and intestines vary in form and dimensions. Digestion is very rapid with these beings. Most of them feed on flesh, but there are a few where the mouth is without teeth, which feed on vegetables.

The growth of fishes is slow or very rapid, according to the abundance of food; they can suffer a very long fast, but in that state they become diminutive in size, and finally perish of exhaustion. At certain seasons an irresistible impulse brings the two sexes together. Many species whose ordinary appearance is dull and unsightly now shine in the most brilliant colours. The female soon after lays her eggs, the number of which passes all imagination. Nature seems to have accumulated in the body of each female myriads of eggs—a wise provision, which is rendered necessary by the numerous causes of destruction which threaten them in their native element. The eggs, abandoned by the females to the mercy of the waves, are fecundated after being deposited by the melt of the males. Such is a very brief summary of the organization of fishes, which have been briefly described as vertebrate, cold-blooded animals, breathing by means of gills; living in water, moving through the water by means of their fins, and reproducing their kind by means of eggs, or spawn. And now a few words on their classification.

Fishes naturally divide themselves into two series, according to the composition of their internal skeleton. This is usually osseous; nevertheless, a whole group of them constantly retain the cartilaginous or fibro-cartilaginous state. With some this frame presents even less power of resistance, and remains membranous.

It is precisely upon this peculiarity of structure that we found the great division of the class of fishes into two great groups of CARTILAGINOUS and OSSEOUS fishes, the first being again subdivided into three orders: namely, I. *Cyclostomata*. II. *Selachia*. III. *Sturiona*. The second into four orders: I. *Plectognathii*. II. *Lophobranchii*. III. *Malacopterygii*. IV. *Acanthopterygii*.

CHAPTER XVIII.

CARTILAGINOUS FISHES.

CARTILAGINOUS FISHES are generally animals of considerable size, their structure ranging from ordinary fishes to eels. They are chiefly sea-fishes, only a few species being river-fishes. Naturalists divide them into two orders; namely, those having the gills free on the outer edge (the gilled *Chondropterygeans*), and those having these organs fixed on both edges. The first order comprehend three families: I. *Cyclostomata*, or Eels, Lampreys, &c., in which the mouth forms a sucker; II. *Selachians*, including Raias and Sharks, in which the mouth is furnished with jaws; III. *Sturonia*, or Sturgeons, which have the gills free.

I. CYCLOSTOMATA.

The first are characterised by the singular conformation of the mouth, which is formed for suction. The body is elongated, naked, and viscous, reminding us of serpents in their external form; they have neither pectoral nor ventral fins; their vertebræ is reduced to simple cartilaginous rings, scarcely perceptible one from the other, traversed by tendons, and covered by a second and more solid series of rings, which surround the soft cartilaginous spine. Their gills, in place of presenting the comb-like appearance of other fishes, have something of the form of a purse. The lampreys may be considered as the type of this family.

The Lampreys (*Petromyzon*) are cylindrical, with seven gill-openings on each side of the neck, forming two longitudinal lines; mouth round, armed with many teeth. The Sea Lamprey, *P. marinus* (Fig. 347), belongs to the Mediterranean. In the spring it ascends the rivers, where it is sometimes caught in abundance. Full-grown it is about three feet long, marbled brown upon yellow; the dorsal fins are separated by long intervals; its mouth is circular and surrounded by a fleshy lip, furnished with cirri, having a cartilaginous plate for support; it is provided on its internal surface with many circular rows of strong teeth, some single, the others double.

The Lamprey feeds on worms, molluscs, and small fishes; its mouth is a powerful sucker, by the aid of which it attaches itself to fishes often of great size, and sucks them like a leech. It is taken by hook and line, and speared by a sort of barbed harpoon, like the trident of

Fig. 317. The Lamprey (Petromyzon marinus).

the mythological Neptune, which is thrown, javelin fashion, at the animal when seen at the bottom of the water; the flesh is fat and delicate. In the twelfth century one of our kings, Henry I., surfeited himself at Elbeuf by partaking too royally of the Lamprey. The river-lamprey resembles the above in its general conformation, but is much smaller, and differs in the armature of the mouth, having only a single circular row of teeth. It is blackish above, silvery beneath, and is common in the markets of London and Paris, being frequently taken in the Seine. A smaller species, about ten inches in length, never leaves the fresh waters. It resembles the last species in colour, but its two dorsal fins are continuous; it is found in most European rivers and brooks. In some of the English rivers they are frequently taken in the eel-pots, weighing two and three pounds. They frequent stony bottoms, where they find small animals on which they feed. In its larva state it was long considered to be a distinct species of *Ammocetta*; it is now, however, ascertained that it only acquires its perfect form at the end of its second or third year.

II. Selachia.

The Selachians include a great number of cartilaginous fishes, varying much in form, including the rays, dog-fish, skate, torpedo, hammer-fish, sharks, and saw-fish; they have pectoral and ventral fins. On each side of the neck, on the lower surface, are five gill-openings, in form of a slit to each gill. Many of the species have two *blow-holes* in the upper part of the head. The order is divided into Raiadæ and Squalidæ.

RAIADÆ.

Of the Raiadæ there are several genera, and many species. In *Cephaloptera* the head is truncated, with large, lateral eyes. In *Myliobates* it is projecting, the pectoral fins extending like wings. In *Trygon* it is enclosed by the pectorals. In the Skate (*Raia*) the body is rhomboidal, tail without spine, but two small dorsals near the top. In the *Torpedo* the body is nearly round, the tail short and fleshy, with two dorsals and a caudal fin.

The White Ray, *Raia batis* (Fig. 348), reminds us of the lozenge shape, the point of the muzzle forming the lower angle, the longest ray of each pectoral forming the lateral angles, while the summit of the tail forms the last angle; the whole surface seems flat, but a swelling is distinguishable towards the head, on the upper surface, which bears, as it were, the contour of the body, properly so called, namely, the three cavities of the head, the throat, and the belly, which occupy the centre of the lozenge, beyond which the pectoral fins extend. These fins, though covered with a thick skin, permit the cartilaginous rays, with their articulations, to be very distinctly seen.

The head of the white ray, which terminates in a muzzle slightly pointed, is attached behind to the cavity of the breast. The mouth, placed in the lower part of the head and far from the extremity of the muzzle, is elongated; its edges are cartilaginous, and furnished with many rows of hooked and pointed teeth; the nostrils are placed in front of the mouth. The eyes, which open in the upper part of the head, are half projecting, and protected in part by a continuation of the soft, elastic, and retractile skin, which covers the head. Immediately behind the eyes are two blow-holes, which communicate with the interior of the mouth. The animal is able to open and close these holes at pleasure, by means of an extensible membrane, which

Fig. 318. The White Ray (Raia batis).

acts as a sort of valve. Through these holes it ejects the superabundant water beyond what is necessary for respiration. In its general colour the animal is ashy grey on its upper surface; white, with rows of black spots, below.

Its tail is long, flexible, and slender, acting at once as a rudder and a weapon of offence or defence. When lying in ambush, nearly buried in mud at the bottom of the sea, and it has no desire to change its position, a rapid and sudden stroke of this formidable weapon, armed with hooked bones on its upper surface, arrests its victim by wounding or killing it, without disturbing the mud or sea-weed by which it is covered. This species sometimes attains a very considerable size, and their flesh is firm and nourishing; but the larger specimens rarely approach inhabited shores, even when the female desires to lay her eggs. These eggs have a very singular shape, differing from almost every other fish, and particularly from those of all other osseous fishes. They are quadrangular, a little flat, each of the four corners terminating in a small cylindrical cowl—a kind of pocket formed of a strong and transparent membrane.

Fig. 349. The Lump-fish (Raia clavata).

The Lump-fish, *R. clavata* (Fig. 349), so called in consequence of its armature, inhabits every European sea; sometimes it attains the length of twelve feet, and, being excellent eating, is much sought after by fishermen. It is frequently seen with the skate in European markets. A ray of great curving spines occupies the back and extends to the end of the tail; two similar spines are above, and two below the point of the muzzle. Two others are placed before, and three behind the eyes. Each side of the tail is furnished with a row of shorter spines; the whole surface, in short, bristles with larger or smaller spines, justifying the name of buckler-fish; for these are not given by way of ornament, but defence. The colour of the upper surface is generally brown, with whitish spots. The tail, which exceeds the body in length, presents towards the end two small dorsals, terminating in a caudal fin.

Ray-fish of all kinds are inhabitants of the deep sea, but they change according to the seasons. While stormy weather prevails, they hide themselves in the depth of the ocean, where they lie in ambush, creeping along the bottom But they do not always live at the bottom. They rise occasionally to the surface far from the shore, eagerly chasing other inhabitants of the deep, lashing the water with

Fig. 350. The Cramp-fish (Torpedo marmorata).

their formidable tails and fins, springing out of the water, and making it foam again under their gambols.

When pursuing their prey the rays deploy their great pectoral fins, which resemble wings, and are aided by a very delicate and mobile tail; they beat the waters in order to fall unexpectedly upon their prey, as the eagle stoops upon its victim. It may thus be called the king of fishes, as the eagle is the king of birds.

The Cramp-fish, *Torpedo marmorata* (Fig. 350), has considerable analogy with the Raia. Its flattened body forms a roundish disk, beyond which its rays form large pectoral fins; but the humeral girdle which carries them, carries also, in a great hollow, a most singular organic apparatus, which possesses the property of producing violent electrical commotions. This apparatus is placed in the interval between the end of the muzzle and the extremity of the fin, and completes the rounded disk of the body. The mouth is small, the slit crosswise; the jaws bare; the teeth in squares of five. The eyes are small; behind them are two star-like spout-holes. On the lower surface of the breast are two rows of small transverse slits, openings of the gill pouches, like those of the rays. The tail is thick, short, and conical, carrying part of the ventral, and terminating in a sort of caudal fin. On the back are two small, soft, and adipose fins. The skin is smooth; its colour varies with the species; generally it is reddish-brown, with eye-like spots of a deep blue in the centre; sometimes azure, and surrounded by a great brownish circle; the spots being five or six. These curious fishes are found in the Channel and on the shores of the Mediterranean.

The electrical effects produced on the fisherman who seizes them were noted from early times; but Redi, the Italian naturalist of the seventeenth century, was the first who studied them scientifically. Having caught and landed one of them with every precaution, "I had scarcely touched and pressed it with my hand," says the Italian naturalist, "than I experienced a tingling sensation, which extended to my arms and shoulders, which was followed by a disagreeable trembling, with a painful and acute sensation in the elbow joint, which made me withdraw my arm immediately."

Réaumur also made some observations upon the Torpedo. "The benumbing influence," he says, "is very different from any similar sensation. All over the arm there is a commotion which it is impossible to describe, but which, so far as comparison can be made, resembles the sensation produced by striking the tender part of the elbow against a hard substance." Redi remarks, besides, that the pain and trembling sensation resulting from the touch diminishes as the death of the Torpedo approaches, and that it ceases altogether when the animal dies.

In the seventeenth century, the fishermen affirmed that the sensation was even communicated through the line by which it was caught, and even by the water. Redi does not deny this phenomenon, neither does he confirm it. He states that the action of the animal is never more energetic than when it is strongly pressed by the hand, and makes violent efforts to escape. Neither Redi nor Réaumur, however, could explain the cause of the strange phenomenon. It was reserved for Dr. Walsh, a member of the Royal Society of London, to demonstrate the fact that the power was electrical in its nature. This he did by numerous experiments, which he made in the Isle of Ré. The following are some of his experiments:—

He placed a living torpedo upon a clean wet towel; from a plate he suspended two pieces of brass wire by means of silken cord, which served to isolate them. Round the torpedo were eight persons, standing on isolating substances. One end of the brass wire was supported by the wet towel, the other end being placed in a basinfull of water. The first person had a finger of one hand in this basin, and a finger of the other in a second basin, also full of water. The second person placed a finger of one hand in this second basin, and a finger of the other hand in a third basin. The third person did the same, and so on, until a complete chain was established between the eight persons and nine basins. Into the ninth basin the end of the second brass wire was plunged, while Dr. Walsh applied the other end to the back of the torpedo, thus establishing a complete conducting circle. At the moment when the experimenter touched the torpedo, the eight actors in the experiment felt a sudden shock, similar in all respects to that communicated by the shock of a Leyden jar, only less intense.

When the torpedo was placed on an isolated supporter, it communicated to many persons similarly placed from forty to fifty shocks in a minute and a half. Each effort made by the animal, in order to give them, was accompanied by the depression of its eyes, which were slightly projecting in their natural state, and seemed to be drawn within their orbits, while the other parts of the body remained immovable.

If only one of the two organs of the torpedo is touched it happens that, in place of a strong and sudden shock, only a slight sensation is experienced—a numbness, or start, rather than a shock. The same result followed with every experiment tried. The animal was tried with a non-conducting rod, and no shock followed; glass, or a rod covered with wax, produced no effect; touched with a metallic wire, a violent shock followed. Melloni, Matteucci, Becquerel, and Breschet have all made the same experiments with the same results—Matteucci having ascertained that the shock produced by the torpedo is comparable to that given by a voltaic pile of a column of a hundred to a hundred and fifty couples.

The organ which produces this curious result is formed like a half moon; it is double, and placed on each side of the mouth of the respiratory organs. It consists of a multitude of small prisms arranged parallel the one to the other and perpendicularly to the surface; twelve hundred and sixty-two of these prisms have been counted in one of the two organs of a torpedo, three feet in length. Without entering into the anatomical descriptions which have been given by Stannius, Max Schultze, Breschet, and others, we may mention here that all the small parallelopipedes, which enter into their structure, are separated one from the other by walls of cellular tissue, in which are distributed the vessels and nerves. The nervous threads which each apparatus receives are divided into four principal trunks. According to modern authors, the electricity is elaborated in the brain under the influence of the will. It is afterwards transferred by means of the nervous threads into the principal organ, where it serves the purpose of charging the numerous little voltaic piles which constitute the organ of commotion.

It is, nevertheless, necessary to receive our comparisons of the apparatus of the torpedo with the voltaic pile of our laboratories with caution. The apparatus resembles a good conducting body, which is capable of being strongly electrified; it is sufficient to touch one of the surfaces in order to receive the shock. But if the little prisms composing it were charged like our voltaic piles, it would be necessary to touch both their surfaces in order to receive the shock. No real analogy can therefore exist between this natural apparatus and the scientific instrument named after Volta.

It is possible by the aid of heat to restore the extinct or suspended electrical functions of the torpedo. Retained in a tank of sea-water, a yard in height by a third of that in diameter, and at 22° Centigrade in temperature, a torpedo preserved its faculties during five or six hours; another, which remained during ten hours in a very small quantity of sea-water at a temperature of 10° to 11° Cent., and which seemed dead, revived a little when placed in water at 20° Cent., and gave shocks during an hour. If held firmly by the tail and pressed both above and below by a platinum rod to gather the true electricity, the animal contracts itself violently; but its movements are not always accompanied by electrical discharges, which demonstrate that the jets of electrical matter are not the result simply of the muscular contractions, but that they are subject to the will of the animal, and evidently given for resisting its enemies, and benumbing its prey. How wonderful and varied are the resources which Nature grants to her creatures in order to secure their existence!

SQUALIDÆ.

This family approaches more to the Raias than any other fish; but all the species have a lengthened body, merging into a thick tail, pectorals moderate in size, gill-openings on the sides of the neck, and not beneath the body as in the Raia; eyes lateral, and the roughness of their skin is a protection from their enemies. The family comprehends the *Sharks, Dog-fishes, Hammerheads, and Saw-fish.*

Fig. 351. The Shark (Carcharius vulgaris).

The sharks are said to attain the length of twenty and even thirty feet; but its size is not its worst attribute. It has received, besides, strength and terrible arms. Ferocious, voracious, impetuous, and unsatiable, spread over almost every climate, an inhabitant of every sea, and recently not seldom seen on our own shores, the shark rabidly pursues every fish, which fly at its approach; and threaten with its wide gullet the unfortunate victims of shipwreck, shutting them out from all hope of safety.

The body of the shark is long, and its skin is studded with small tubercles: this skin becomes so hard, and takes so high a polish, that it is employed for various ornamental purposes. This resisting power protects the shark from the bites of every inhabitant of the sea, if there be any daring enough to approach it with that view.

The back and sides of the Shark, *Carcharius vulgaris* (Fig. 351), are of an ashy brown; beneath it is faded white. The head is flat, and terminates in a muzzle slightly rounded. Its terrible mouth is in the form of a semicircle, and of enormous size; the contour of the upper jaw of a shark of ten yards length being about two yards wide, and its throat being of a proportionate diameter to this monstrous opening. When the throat of the animal is open we see beyond the lips, which are straight and of the consistence of leather, certain plates of teeth, which are triangular, dentate, and white as ivory. If the shark is an adult it has in the upper as in the lower jaw six rows of these murderous arms, an arsenal ready to tear and rend its victim. These teeth take different motions according to the will of the animal; and obedient to the muscles round their base, by means of which it can erect or retract its various rows of teeth, it can even erect a portion of any row, while the others remain at rest in their bed. Thus this far-seeing tyrant of the ocean knows how to measure the number and power of the arms necessary to destroy its prey: for the destruction of the weak and defenceless one row of teeth suffices; for the more formidable adversary it has a whole arsenal at command.

The eyes of the shark are small, and nearly round; the iris of a deep green, the eyeball, shaped in a transversal slit, is bluish; its scent is very subtle; its fins are strong and rough.

The pectoral fins are triangular, and much larger than the others, extending on each side, and giving powerful aid in swimming. The caudal fin is divided into two very unequal lobes, the upper extending in a sloping direction to twice the length of the other. This tail is possessed of immense power, and is capable of breaking the limb of a robust man by a single stroke.

During the hot season the male and female seek each other; they approach the coast roving in company, forgetting their ferocity for the time. The eggs are hatched at several periods in the ovary, from which the little ones issue two or three at a time.

The shark, when scarcely born, becomes the scourge of the sea. He seizes all that come near him. He eats the cuttle-fish, molluscs, and fishes; among others flounders and cod-fish. But the prey which has the greatest charm for him is man; the shark loves him dearly, but it is with the affection of the gourmand. It even manifests, according to some authors, a preference for certain races. If we may believe some travellers, when several varieties of human food comes in its way, the shark prefers the European to the Asiatic, and both to the negro. Still, whatever may be the colour, he seeks eagerly for human flesh, and haunts the neighbourhood where it hopes to find the precious morsel. He follows the ship in which his instinct tells him it is to be found, and makes extraordinary efforts to reach it. He has been known to leap into a boat in order to seize the frightened fishermen; he throws himself upon the ship, cleaving the waves at full speed to snap up some unhappy sailor who has shown himself beyond the bulwarks. He follows the course of the slaver, watching for the horrors of the middle passage, ready to engulf the negroes' corpses as they are thrown into the sea. Commerson relates a significant fact bearing on the subject. The corpse of a negro had been suspended from a yard-arm twenty feet above the level of the sea. A shark was seen to make many efforts to reach the body, and it finally succeeded in seizing it, member by member, undisturbed by the cries of the horror-stricken crew assembled on deck to witness the strange spectacle. In order that an animal so large and heavy should be able to throw itself to this height, the muscles of the tail and posterior parts of the body must have an astonishing power.

The mouth of the shark being placed in the lower part of the head, it becomes necessary to turn itself round in the water before it can seize the object which is placed above him. He meets with men bold enough to profit by this conformation, and chase this formidable and ferocious creature. On the African coast the negroes attack the shark in his own element, swimming towards him, and seizing the moment when he turns himself to rip up his belly with a sharp knife. This act of courage and audacity cannot, however, be said to be shark-fishing. The fishing operation is conducted as follows:—Choosing a dark night, a hook is prepared by burying it in a piece of lard, and attaching it to a long and solid wire chain: the shark looks askance at this prey, feels it, then leaves it; he is tempted by withdrawing the bait, when he follows, and swallows it gluttonously. He now tries to sink into the water, but, checked by the chain, he struggles and fights. By-and-by he gets exhausted, and the chain is drawn up in such a manner as to raise the head out of the water. Another cord is now thrown out with a running knot or loop, in which the body of the shark is caught about the origin of the tail. Thus bound, the captured shark is soon

Plate XXV.—Shark Fishing.

hoisted on deck, as represented in Pl. XXV. On the quarter-deck of the ship he is put to death, not without great precaution, however, for he is still a formidable foe from his terrible bites and from the still dangerous blows of his tail. Moreover, he dies hard, and long resists the most formidable wounds.

Captain Basil Hall gives a spirited sketch of the appearance and capture of one of those dreaded fishes; a capture in which the whole ship's company, captain, officers, young gentlemen inclusive, shout in triumphant exultation as the body of the shark flounders in impotent rage on poop or forecastle.

"The sharp, curved, dorsal fin of a huge shark was seen rising about six inches above the water, and cutting the glazed surface of the sea by as fine a line as if a sickle had been drawn along it. 'Messenger, run to the cook for a piece of pork,' cried the captain, taking the command with as much glee as if an enemy's cruiser had been in sight. 'Where's your hook, quartermaster?' 'Here, sir, here,' cried the fellow, feeling the point, and declaring it was as sharp as any lady's needle, and in the next instant piercing with it a huge junk of pork weighing four or five pounds. The hook, which is as large as one's little finger, has a curvature about as large as a man's hand when half closed, and is six or eight inches in length, while a formidable line, furnished with three or four feet of chain attached to the end of the mizen topsail haulyard, is now cast into the ship's wake.

"Sometimes the very instant the bait is cast over the stern, the shark flies at it with such eagerness that he actually springs partially out of the water. This, however, is rare. On these occasions he gorges the bait, the hook, and a foot or two of the chain, without any mastication, and darts off with the treacherous prize with such prodigious velocity that it makes the rope crack again as soon as the coil is drawn out. Much dexterity is required in the hand which holds the line at this moment. A bungler is apt to be too precipitate, and jerk away the hook before it has got far enough into the shark's maw. The secret of the sport is to let the monster gulp down the whole bait, and then to give the line a violent pull, by which the barbed point buries itself in the coat of the stomach. When the hook is first fixed, it spins out like the log line of a ship going twelve knots.

"The suddenness of the jerk with which the poor devil is brought up often turns him quite over. No sailor, however, thinks of hauling a shark on board merely by the rope fastened to the hook. To prevent the line breaking, the hook snapping, or the jaw being torn away, a running bowline is adopted. This noose is slipped down the rope and passed over the monster's head, and is made to join at the point of junction of the tail with the body: and now the first part of the fun is held to be completed. The vanquished enemy is easily drawn up over the taffrail, and flung on deck, to the delight of the crew."

The flesh of the shark is leathery, of bad taste, and difficult to digest. Nevertheless, the negroes of Guinea feed upon it, but not until it has been made tender and eatable by long preservation. In many parts of the Mediterranean coast small sharks are taken from their mother's belly and eaten. The under parts of adult sharks is also eaten by the fishermen after the bad parts have been removed. In Norway and Iceland this part of the animal is dried in the air during the most part of the twelve months. The Icelanders also use the fat of the animal; the liver of one of them, according to Pontoppidan, will furnish two tons and a half of oil.

We have thus, with the care it deserves, painted the portrait of the shark. The original is by no means beautiful; but, frightful as it may be, our description would be incomplete if we did not add that divine honours have been granted to this monster of the waters. Man worships force: he knows the hand which crushes, the teeth which rend. He respects the master or the king who strikes, and he venerates the shark. The inhabitants of several parts of the African coast worship the shark: they call it their *joujou*, and consider its stomach the road to heaven. Three or four times in the year they celebrate the festival of the shark, which is done in this wise:—

They all move in their boats to the middle of the river, where they invoke, with the strangest ceremonies, the protection of the great shark. They offer to him poultry and goats in order to satisfy his sacred appetite. But this is nothing: an infant is every year sacrificed to the monster, which has been reared for the purpose from its birth; it is fêted and nourished for the sacrifice from its birth to the age of ten. On the day of the fête it is bound to a post on a sandy point at low water; as the tide rises, the child may utter cries of horror, but it is abandoned to the waves, and the sharks arrive. The mother is not far off; perhaps she weeps, but she dries her tears and thinks that her child has entered heaven through this horrible gate.

The Dog-fish, *Acanthias vulgaris* (Fig. 352), which sometimes attains the length of between three and four feet, is exceedingly voracious. It feeds upon other fish, of which it destroys great quantities; it does not hesitate to attack the fishermen, and especially bathers in the sea. It places itself in ambush, like the Raias, in order to attack its prey. The flesh of the dog-fish is hard, smells of musk, and is rarely eaten; but the skin becomes an article of commerce, and is known as *shagrin*, being, like the skin of the shark, used for making spectacle-cases and for other ornamental purposes, for which its green colour and high polish recommend it. There is a smaller species than the preceding, which haunts rocky shores, where it lies in wait for its prey. Its spots are larger and more scattered, and its ventral fins are nearly square. It feeds on molluscs, crustaceans, and small fishes.

Fig. 352. The Dog-fish (Acanthias vulgaris).

The Hammerhead, *Zygæna malleus* (Fig. 353), is chiefly distinguished by the singular conformation of its head, which is flattened horizontally, truncate in front, and the sides prolonged transversely, giving it the appearance of the head of a hammer. The eyes of this fish are placed at the extremity of the lateral prolongations of the head: they are grey, projecting, and the iris is gold-coloured. When the animal is irritated, the colours of the iris become like flame, to the horror of the fishermen who behold them.

Beneath the head and near to the junction of the trunk is the mouth, which is semicircular, and furnished on each jaw with three or four rows of large teeth pointed and barbed on two sides.

The most common species in our seas is long and slender in the body, which is grey, the head blackish. It usually attains the length of eleven or twelve feet, weighing occasionally nearly five hundred

Fig. 353. The Hammerhead (*Zygæna malleus*).

pounds. Its boldness and voracity, and craving for blood, are more remarkable than its size. If the hammerhead has not the strength of the shark, it surpasses it in fury; few fishes are better known to sailors in consequence of its striking conformation. Its voracity often brings it round ships even in roadsteads, and near the coast. Its visits impress themselves on the memory of the sailor, and he loves to relate his hairbreadth escape from the meeting.

The saw-fish is distinguished from all other known fishes by the formidable arm which it carries in its head. This weapon is a prolongation of the muzzle, which, in place of being rounded off or reduced to a point, forms a long, strong, straight, sword-like termination, flat on both sides, but on the two edges it is furnished with numerous strong teeth of considerable length, which are prolongations of the hard, bony substance which forms the muzzle—forming, in short, a sword-blade deeply toothed on each edge.

Thus armed, the saw, or sword-fish, as it is sometimes called, the length of which is from twelve to fifteen feet, fearlessly attacks the most formidable inhabitants of the sea. With its threatening weapon, sometimes two yards in length, it dares to measure its strength with the whale. All fishermen who visit the northern seas assert that the meeting of these ocean potentates is always followed by a combat of the most singular kind, in which the activity of the sword-fish is a match for the formidable strength of the whale. Occasionally it dashes itself with such force against the sides of a ship, that its sword is broken in the timber. In the Museum of Natural History of Paris, the blade of a sword-fish may be seen which was thus implanted in the side of a whale.

III. Sturiona.

In the second division of cartilaginous fishes, or sturgeons, the gills are free, as in the ordinary fishes. In the sturgeon the gill-openings are a single, very wide orifice, with an operculum, but without radiating membrane. They are fishes of great size, living in the sea, but ascending the larger rivers in the spawning season. Our space only permits us to notice the Chimæra and Sturgeon.

The naturalists Clusius and Aldrovandus compared the fish, to which they gave the name of *Chimæra arctica*, to the chimæra, a monster of mythological antiquity, which is represented with the body of a goat, the head of a lion, the tail of a dragon, and a gaping throat which vomited flames. The strange form of this fish, the manner in which it moves, the different parts of its muzzle, its mode of showing its teeth, its ape-like contortions and grimaces, its long tail, which acts with such rapidity,—reminding one not a little of a reptile,—are well calculated to strike the imagination. At a later period mediæval naturalists were contented to see in it a fish with a lion's head, and as the lion was then regarded as the king of animals, so the chimæra became the *Herring* king.

The king of the herrings (Fig. 354) is from five to six feet in length, of a general silvery colour, spotted with brown. It inhabits the North Sea, living on molluscs and crustaceans; occasionally, as if to justify the title which has been given it, levying heavy contributions upon the herrings. Another species, *C. antarctica*, is found in the southern hemisphere, which greatly resembles, in its conformation and habits, the northern species. In both the end of the muzzle terminates in a cartilaginous appendage, which projects forward, curving afterwards over the mouth. This extension assimilates to a crest.

Fig. 354. The Arctic chimæra.

The Sturgeons (*Acipenser*) are among the largest fishes known. On this account, as well as from their exterior conformation, they approach the *Squalidæ*. Their muscles, however, are less firmly knit, their flesh more delicate, and their muscular strength consequently infinitely smaller. Neither is their mouth armed with so many rows of teeth. Moreover, they are less voracious, and their habits altogether less ferocious.

The sturgeons are sea-fishes which periodically ascend the larger rivers. A great many species are known in Europe. They abound in the Black Sea and Sea of Azof, but they are chiefly known as frequenting the Volga and the Danube. The enormous consumption of caviare in Russia leads to a deadly pursuit of the common sturgeon in all the great European rivers, and this species is in a fair way of disappearing altogether.

The Common Sturgeon, *Acipenser sturio* (Fig. 355), abounds in the North Sea and the Mediterranean, and occasionally it appears in the Thames, the Rhine, the Seine, the Loire, and the Gironde. It is usually about two yards to seven feet long, but has been known to attain the length of ten or twelve feet. Its general colour is yellow

Fig. 355. The Common Sturgeon (Acipenser sturio).

with a white belly. It is rendered remarkable by the number and form of the osseous plates or scales, which cover the body like so many bucklers. Upon the back and belly are no less than twelve to fifteen of these rough bony plates, relieved by projections, which are pointed in the young, and soften down with age. On each side is a row of thirty to thirty-five of these triangular plates, separated from each other by considerable intervals. The head is broad at the base, gradually contracting towards the point, and terminating in a conical muzzle. The mouth is large and considerably behind the extremity of the muzzle, and its jaws, in place of teeth, are furnished with cartilages. Between the mouth and the muzzle are four slender and very elastic barbs, or wattles, like so many little worms. It is pretended that these wattles attract small fishes to the jaws of the animal, while it conceals itself among the roots of aquatic plants.

In the sea the sturgeon feeds on herrings, mackerel, cod-fish, and other fishes of moderate size. In the rivers it attacks the salmon which ascend them about the same time. Mingling with them, however, it seems a giant. It deposits its eggs in great quantity, which are gathered and made into caviare. Its flesh is delicate, and in countries where they are caught in quantities it is dried and preserved. The rivers which enter the Black and Caspian seas contain, besides the common sturgeon, many other species of the same genus, the flesh of which is even more delicate and *recherché* than the common sturgeon. Among the ancients this fish was held in unusual esteem. In Rome, in the time of the emperors, we read of sturgeons borne in triumph to the sound of instruments, and laid upon tables fastidiously covered and decorated with flowers.

The Great Sturgeon, which sometimes exceeds a thousand pounds, is only found in the rivers which flow into the Caspian and Black seas. The Volga, the Don, and the Danube produce the largest species.

We are indebted to the Russian naturalist Pallas for the information we possess respecting the mode of taking the sturgeon in the Volga and other Asiatic rivers. Stakes are placed across the river, leaving just sufficient space between each pile to permit the animal to pass. Towards the centre this dike forms an angle opposed to the current, and, consequently, opposed to the fish which ascend the river towards the summit of this angle. At this point there is an opening which leads into a kind of enclosure, consisting of fillets towards the end of winter, and of osier-hurdles during summer. The fishermen establish themselves upon a sort of scaffold placed over the opening. When the fish is engaged in the reservoir, the men upon the scaffold drop a gate, which prevents his return to the sea. The movable bottom of the chamber is now raised, and the fishes easily taken, as represented in Pl. XXVI.

The fishermen are informed during the day of the approach of the sturgeons to the great enclosure by the movement they communicate to cords suspended to small floating substances in the water. During the night the sturgeons enter the enclosure, agitating by their move-

Plate XXVI.—Sturgeon Fishing on the Volga.

ments other cords arranged round the hurdles. The agitation communicated to the cord is sufficient to shut the gates behind; they are thus imprisoned by the dropping of the gate, which in falling sounds a bell to wake the watching fisherman on the scaffold, should he be asleep. The sturgeon-fisheries of the Volga are thus admirably organized. Gmelin describes with some minuteness the sturgeon-fishing, during the winter, in the caverns and hollows of the river-banks near Astrakhan, in the estuary of the Volga. A great number of fishermen are assembled there with their boats. The flotilla approaches the retreats to which the fishes have betaken themselves, the nets are skilfully arranged all round them, and all at once the whole mass of fishermen join in a great cry, at which the frightened fishes rush from their concealment and throw themselves into the nets spread for them.

The size of the fish, the nourishing properties of its flesh, its healthy and agreeable taste, and the immense quantity of eggs produced, have a wonderful power in exciting the commerce and industry of the inhabitants of these countries. In order to give some idea of the abundance of the eggs of the sturgeon, it is stated that the weight of two ovaries equalled nearly a third of the weight of the whole animal; in other words, these ovaries weighed nearly eight hundred pounds in a female whose weight was two thousand and eight hundred pounds.

It is with these eggs chiefly, but not altogether, that caviare is prepared, and the article is more or less relished according to the state of the eggs. The display of caviare, as exhibited at the Universal Exposition of Paris during the year 1867, will remain to those who have visited it one of the most lasting recollections.

CHAPTER XIX.

OSSEI, OR BONY FISHES.

UNDER this denomination is comprehended many of the fishes which are most familiar to us. They are characterised, as we have said elsewhere, as a group of animals having a solid skeleton. They are divided into six orders; founded, however, it is necessary to add, on characteristics of little organic importance, and the names bestowed upon them are of a most barbarous description. These names are, I. *Plectognathi*, namely, fishes in which the upper jaw is attached to the cranium, from πλεκτὸς, interlaced, and γνάθος, jaw.

Afterwards those in which the upper jaw is movable, and the gills arranged in circles, like rounded hoops. These are, II. the *Lophobranchii*, from λόφος, crested, or aigrette, βράγχια, gill.

In the other orders the gills are arranged in a comb-like form. These are divided into two great groups. In the first, the rays of the fins are soft, except occasionally the first of dorsal or pectoral fins. These are, III. the *Malacopterygians*, from μαλακὸς, soft, and πτερύγιον, fins — the third group of osseous fishes. In a later group the fish have bony rays to the anterior dorsal fins, some osseous rays, and the anal fin and generally one of the ventral fins. These are, IV. the *Acanthopterygians*, from ἄκανθα, spiny, and πτερύγιον, finned, which form the last group of bony fishes.

I. PLECTOGNATHI.

From their organization the fishes of this order establish the passage from *cartilaginous* to the *osseous* fishes. Their skeleton, which remains for some time more or less soft, becomes finally hard. The chief characteristic of the order is that the maxillary is firmly attached to the side of the intermaxillary bone which forms the jaw, and the arch of the palate is united to the skull in such a manner as to be motionless. The operculum and rays of the gills are hidden under a thick skin, which leaves externally only a small branchial slit. These fishes have no true ventral fin, and have only vestiges of side fins.

This order comprehends two natural families characterised by the armature of their jaws. They are the *Gymnodonta* and the *Sclerodermata.*

Fig. 356. The Globe-fish (Orthagoriscus), and Sun-fish (Tetraodon).

In the family of *Gymnodonta* the jaws have no apparent teeth, but they are furnished with a species of beak in ivory, which represents them. The Sun-fish, *Tetraodon* (Fig. 356), belong to the family.

The Globe-fish are so named from their large head and bony salient jaws, which are each divided in front by a sort of vertical slit in two portions, which simulate two teeth. These four portions of bony jaw, which project beyond the lips, somewhat resemble the hard and dentate jaws of the turtle. Their anterior part is sometimes prolonged, like the mandibles of the beak of the parrot. They are perfectly arranged to crush the shells of the molluscs, as well as the resisting envelope of the crustaceans on which they feed. The skin of these fishes bristles with small slightly projecting spines, the number of which compensate for their brevity, which repel their enemies, and even wound the hand that would grasp them. They enjoy, besides, a singular faculty; they can inflate the lower part of their body, and give it an extension so considerable that it becomes like an inflated ball, in which the real shape of the animal is lost. This result is obtained by the introduction of an immense quantity of air into the stomach when it wishes to ascend to the surface. The species of globe-fish are numerous. Some of them are common in the Nile, where they are frequently left ashore during the annual inundations.

The Globe-fish (*Orthagoriscus mola*), in the upper part of the engraving, is easily distinguished from the *Tetraodons* by its compressed spineless body; being very round in its vertical contour, it has been compared to a disk, and more poetically to the moon—whence its popular names—to the great circular surface of which the dazzling silvery white disk bears some resemblance. But it is especially during the night that it justifies the name given to it. Then it shines brightly, from its own phosphorescent light, at a little distance beneath the surface. On very dark nights, the globe-fish is sometimes seen swimming in the soft light which emanates from its body, the rays rendered undulating by the rippling of the water which it traverses, so as to resemble the trembling light of the moon half-veiled in misty vapours. When many of these fishes rove about together, mingling their silvery trains, the scene suggests the idea of dancing stars. The moon-fish is common in the Mediterranean, and sometimes reaches the markets of Paris. It is about thirty inches in length, and its weight is considerable. Its flesh is fat and viscous, and by no means pleasant to eat.

The *Diodons* (Fig. 357) only differ from the globe-fish in the form of their bony jaws, each forming only one piece. They seem to have two teeth, whence their name from δίς, two, ὀδοὺς, teeth. They differ also in their spines, which are much larger than those of the globe-fish. These fishes may be said to be the hedgehogs and porcupines of the sea. Like the globe-fish, they can erect their spines and inflate their bodies.

They are numerous in species—*Diodon pilosus*, represented in Fig. 357, being typical of the others.

Fig. 357. Diodon pilosus.

The Sclerodermes are distinguished by their conical or pyramidal muzzle, terminating in a little mouth armed with true teeth; their

Fig. 358. The File-fish (Balistes).

skin is generally stiff and covered with hard scales. The File-fish, *Balistes* and *Coffres*, are selected for notice. The File-fish (Fig. 358) have the body compressed; the jaws are furnished with eight teeth, arranged in a single row on each jaw, and covered with true lips; the eyes are nearly level with the skin; the mouth is small, and the body enveloped in very hard scales, which are connected in groups and distributed into compartments more or less regular, and strongly connected by means of a thick skin. The animal is thus protected by a sort of cuirass and casque very difficult to penetrate.

With the exception of one species, the Balistes are inhabitants of Tropical seas. They are generally brilliantly coloured; they herd together in great numbers, and in their gambols produce curious combinations of brilliant colouring in the Equatorial seas. Their flesh is

Fig. 359. The Coffre, or Ostracion.

held in slight estimation, and at certain periods of the year is even said to be dangerous.

The Coffres, or Ostracions (Fig. 359), are without scales, but covered with regular osseous compartments, which are so jointed the one to the other that the body is, as it were, enclosed in a kind of box or long coffer, which only reveals the external organs of locomotion—namely, the fins and a portion of tail. In some the body is triangular, in others quadrangular, with or without spines.

These singular fishes are found in the Indian Ocean and in the American seas. They are of moderate size, and of little value as food for man.

II. Lophobranchii.

The Lophobranchii comprehend a few types, but are numerous in species. Here the gills are divided into small round tufts, and arranged in pairs along the branchial arches; a structure quite peculiar, of which we have no examples in any other fishes. These gills are enclosed under a large cover, or operculum, attached on all sides by a membrane, which leaves only a small hole for the escape of water which has served the purposes of respiration.

These little cuirassed fishes consist of two genera, *Syngnathus* and *Hippocampus*. The Syngnathes, or pipe-fishes, possess a very curious

Fig 360. The Trumpet Pipe-fish (Syngnathus).

organic peculiarity. Their bodies are long, slender, and slightly tapering, covered with plates set lengthwise, without ventrals; the skin, in swelling, forms under the belly or under the tail, according to the species, a pouch into which the eggs glide to be hatched, and which is afterwards a shelter for the young. Most of the species are strangers to European seas, but some few are found in the Channel. The Trumpet Pipe-fish (Fig. 360) has the head small, the muzzle long, nearly cylindrical, slightly raised at the end, and terminating in a very small mouth without teeth. The animal is about twenty inches long; its skin is of a yellowish colour varied with brown. It lives in the Atlantic and Mediterranean, where it is largely used by the fishermen in baiting their hooks.

The Sea-horse (*Hippocampus*) is a small creature about the size of the engraving (Fig. 361); its head has a singular resemblance to that of the horse. The rings which constitute the integument of the body and tail have a close resemblance to the rings of some caterpillars. This curious combination of forms originated the name, Hippocampus, from ἵππος, horse, and κάμπος, fish, adopted in very ancient times to designate this creature. It is found in the Atlantic, round the coast

Fig. 361. The Sea-horse (Hippocampus).

of Spain, the south of France, in the Mediterranean, and in the Indian Ocean. Mr. Lukis, who raised two females in captivity, describes their habits as follows:—"When they swim," he says, "they preserve a vertical position, but their tail seems on the alert to seize whatever it meets with in the water, clasping the stem of the rushes. Once fixed, the animal seems to watch attentively all the surrounding objects, and darts on any prey presenting itself with great dexterity. When one of them approaches the other, they interlace their two tails, and it is only after a struggle that they can separate again, attaching themselves by the lower part of the chin to some rush in order to release themselves. They have recourse to the same manœuvre when they wish to raise the body, or when they wish to wind their tail to some new object. Their two eyes seem to move independently of each other, like those of the chameleon. The iris is bright and edged with blue."

The sea-horses have the pectoral fins so formed as easily to sustain the body, not only in the water, but even in the air; they are, in fact, winged fishes, and probably originated the famous winged courser of mythology, after which they are sometimes named. They rarely exceed four inches in length; the body is covered with triangular scales, commonly of a bluish colour. They live on worms, fishes' eggs, and fragments of organic substances which they find in the far land at the bottom of the sea.

III. Malacopterygii.

The principal character of the fishes of this order is that the rays of the fins are soft, except sometimes the first ray of the dorsal or pectorals. They inhabit either sea or fresh water, and include fishes of the utmost importance as human food, such as the herring, the cod, the salmon, carp, pike, and many others. Modern naturalists, following Cuvier, subdivide them into three orders:—1. *Apoda*, without ventrals; 2. *Sub-branchiati*, ventrals under the pectorals; 3. *Abdominales*, having ventrals behind the pectorals.

1. APODA.

A single family composes this order, which comprehends great numbers both in genera and species; they are anguilliform or snake-like, elongated in form, the skin thick and soft, and have no ventral fins. In this order are included the *Ammodytes*, *Gymnotes*, *Muræнas*, and *Anguilla*, or eels.

The Ammodytes have the body elongated and serpent-like, having a continuous fin extending along the greater part of the back, with another at the opposite side, and a third or forked fin at the end of the tail. The muzzle is also long; the lower jaw longer than the upper. *A. lancea* (Fig. 362) buries itself in the sand; hence it is called the sand-eel; it hollows out a burrow for itself in the sand with its muzzle to the depth of fifteen or twenty inches, where it hunts out worms, on which it feeds, while it shelters itself from the jaws of many voracious fishes, which eagerly pursue it for its delicate flesh. In appearance the *Ammodytes lancea* is silvery blue, brighter on the lower parts than on the upper, the radiating fins on the abdomen being alternately white and bluish in colour.

Fig. 362. The Lance (A. lancea).

The Gymnotes are long, nearly cylindrical, and also serpent-like, the tail being long in comparison to the other parts of the body. Beneath the tail is a long swimming fin, the only locomotive organ,

Fig. 363. The Gymnotus Electricus, or Electrical Eel.

and it is this nakedness of the back which confers its designation of γυμνὸς, naked, νῶτος, back.

The Gymnotes are fresh-water fishes of South America, where they attain a great size. There are several species; but the most remarkable, from its singular physical properties, is the Electrical Eel, *Gymnotus electricus* (Fig. 363). These properties enable the gymnotus to arrest suddenly the pursuit of an enemy, or the flight of its prey, to suspend on the instant every movement of its victim, and subdue it by an invisible power. Even the fishermen themselves are suddenly struck and rendered torpid at the moment of seizing it, while nothing external betrays the mysterious power possessed by the animal.

The electrical properties of the gymnotus were reported for the first time by Van Berkal. The astronomer Richer, who had been sent to Cayenne in 1671 by the Academy of Sciences of Paris, on the Geodesic Survey, first made known the singular properties of the American fish. "I was much astonished," says this author, "to see a fish some three or four feet in length, and resembling an eel, deprive of all motion for a quarter of an hour the arm and neighbouring parts which touched it. I was not only an ocular witness of the effect produced by its touch; but I have myself felt it, on touching one of these fishes still living, though wounded by a hook, by means of which some Indians had drawn it from the water. They could not tell what it was called; but they assured me that it struck other fishes with its tail in order to stupefy them and devour them afterwards, which is very probable when we consider the effect of its touch upon a man."

The observations of Richer made little impression at the time on the *savants* of Paris, and matters remained in this state for seventy years, when the traveller Condamine spoke in his "Voyage en Amérique" of a fish which produced the effects described by Richer. In 1750 a physician named Ingram furnished some new views respecting this fish, which he thought was surrounded by an electric atmosphere. In 1755 another physician, the Dutch Dr. Gramund, writes: "The effect produced by this fish corresponds exactly with that produced by the Leyden jar, with this difference, that we see no tinsel on its body, however strong the blow it gives; for if the fish is large, those who touch it are struck down, and feel the blow on their whole body."

Many experiments followed these; but we are indebted to Alexander von Humboldt for the first precise account of this very curious fish. The celebrated naturalist read to the Institute of France an important memoir upon the electrical eel from Bonpland's observations, the substance of which we shall give here.

Plate XXVII.—Fishing for Electrical Eel (Gymnotus) on the Orinoco.

In traversing the Llanas of the province of Caracas, in order to embark at San Fernando de Apure on his voyage up the Orinoco, M. Bonpland stopped at Calabozo. The object of this sojourn was to investigate the history of the gymnotus, great numbers of which are found in the neighbourhood. After three days' residence in Calabozo some Indians conducted them to the Cano de Bera, a muddy and stagnant basin, but surrounded by rich vegetation, in which *Clusia rosea*, *Hymenœa courbaril*, some grand Indian figs, and some magnificent flowering odoriferous mimosas, were pre-eminent. They were much surprised when informed that it would be necessary to take thirty half-wild horses from the neighbouring Savannahs in order to fish for the gymnotus.

The idea of this fishing, called in the language of the country *embarbascar con caballos* (intoxicating by means of horses), is very odd. The word *barbasco* indicates the roots of the *Lacquinia*, or any other poisonous plant, by contact of which a body of water acquires the property of killing, or, at least, of intoxicating or stupefying, the fishes. These come to the surface when they have been poisoned in this manner. The horses chasing them here and there in a marsh has, it seems, the same effect upon the alarmed fishes. While our hosts were explaining to us this strange mode of fishing, the troop horses and mules had arrived, and the Indians had made a sort of battue, pressing the horses on all sides, and forcing them into the marsh. The Indians, armed with long canes and harpoons, placed themselves round the basin, some of them mounting the trees, whose branches hung over the water, and by their cries, and still more by their canes, preventing the horses from landing again. The eels, stunned by the noise, defended themselves by repeated discharges of their batteries. For a long time it seemed as if they would be victorious over the horses. Some of the mules especially, being almost stifled by the frequency and force of the shock, disappeared under the water, and some of the horses, in spite of the watchfulness of the Indians, regained the bank, where, overcome by the shocks they had undergone, they stretched themselves at their whole length. The picture presented was now indescribable. Groups of Indians surrounded the basin; the horses with bristling mane, terror and grief in their eyes, trying to escape from the storm which had surprised them; the eels, yellow and livid, looking like great aquatic serpents swimming on the surface of the water, and chasing their enemies, were objects at once appalling and picturesque. In less than five minutes two horses were drowned. An eel, more than five feet long, glided under one horse, discharged its apparatus through its whole extent, attacking at once the heart, the viscera, and the plexus of the nerves of the animal, probably benumbing and finally drowning it.

When the struggle had endured a quarter of an hour, the mules and horses appeared less frightened, the manes became more erect, the eyes expressed less terror, the eels shunned in place of attacking them; at the same time approaching the bank, when they were easily taken by throwing little harpoons at them attached to long cords, the harpoon, sometimes hooking two at a time, being landed by means of the long cord. They were drawn ashore without being able to communicate any shock.

Having landed the eels, they were transported to little pools dug in the soil, and filled with fresh water; but such is the terror they inspire, that none of the people of the country would release them from the harpoon—a task which the travellers had to perform themselves, and receive the first shock, which was not slight—the most energetic surpassing in force that communicated by a Leyden jar, completely charged. The gymnotus surpasses in size and strength all the other electric fishes. Humboldt saw them five feet three inches long. They vary in colour according to age, and the nature of the muddy water in which they live. Beneath, the head is of a fine yellow colour mixed with red; the mouth is large, and furnished with small teeth arranged in many rows.

The gymnotus makes its shock felt in any part of its body which is touched, but the excitement is greater when touched under the belly, and in the pectoral fin. The gymnotus gives the most frightful shocks without the least muscular movement in the fins, in the head, or any other part of the body. The shock, indeed, depends upon the will of the animal, and in this respect differs from a Leyden jar, which is discharged by communicating with two opposite poles. It happens sometimes that a gymnotus, seriously wounded, only gives a very weak shock, but if, thinking it exhausted, it is touched fearlessly and at once, its discharge is terrible. Indeed, the phenomena depends so much upon the will of the animal, that, according to Von Humboldt, if it is touched by two metallic rods, the shock is communicated some-

Plate XXVIII.—Natives Fishing for Halibut on the Greenland Coast.

times by one, sometimes by the other wand, though their extremities are close together.

The experiments already related in connection with the torpedo were repeated here. If we place ourselves upon an isolated support, and take hold of a metallic rod, a shock is received; but no shock is received, on the other hand, if the fish is touched with a glass-rod, or one covered with wax. Humboldt and Bonpland repeated this experiment many times, with decisive results. The electric organ has been carefully described by these observers. The organs extend from under the tail, occupying nearly one-half of the thickness. It is divided into four longitudinal bundles of muscles, the upper ones large, the two smaller below, and against the base of the anal fin. Each bundle consists of many parallel membranous plates, placed closely together and very nearly horizontal. These plates abut in one part on the skin, in another, on the mean vertical plane of the fish. They are united to each other by an infinity of smaller plates, placed either vertically or transversely. The smaller prismatic and transversal canal, intercepted by these two orders of plates, are filled with gelatinous matter. All this organic apparatus receives many nerves, and presents, in many respects, an arrangement nearly analogous to that of the torpedos.

The Sea-Eels (*Muræna Helena*) are serpent-like fishes, of cylindrical form and delicate proportions, but strong, flexible, and active, swimming in waving, undulating movements in the water, just as a serpent creeps on dry land. The muræuas have no pectoral fin; the dorsal and anal fin are reunited in the tail fin. A bronchial opening is observable on each side of the body. The sea-eels are numerous in species. *Muræna Helena* (Fig. 364), which is an inhabitant of the Mediterranean, has only a single row of teeth upon each jaw. It attains the length of forty to fifty inches. It loves to bask in the hollows of rocks, approaching the coast in spring-time. It feeds on crabs and small fishes, seeking eagerly for polypes. The voracity of these fishes is such that when other food fails they begin to nibble at each other's tails.

The sea-eels are caught with rod and line, or by lines and ground-bait, but their instinct is such that they often escape. When they have swallowed a hook they often cut the line with their teeth, or they turn upon it and try, by winding it round some object, to strain or break it. When caught in a net, they quickly choose some mesh through which their body can glide.

Those who have studied the classics will remember the passionate love with which the Roman gourmet regarded these fishes. In the days of the Empire enormous sums were expended in keeping up the ponds which enclosed them, and the fish themselves were multiplied to such an extent that Cæsar, on the occasion of one of his triumphs, distributed six thousand among his friends. Licinius Crassus was celebrated among wealthy Romans for the splendour of his eel-ponds. They obeyed his voice, he said, and when he called them, they darted towards him in order to be fed by his hands. The same Licinius Crassus, and Quintus Hortensius, another wealthy Roman patrician,

Fig. 364. The Sea-Eel (Muræna Helena).

wept the loss of their murænas on one occasion, when they all died in their ponds from some disease. This, however, was only a matter of taste, passion, or fashion; sometimes, however, accompanied by cruelty, and gross corruption.

It was thought among the Romans that murænas fed with human flesh were the most delicately-flavoured. A rich freedman, named Pollion, who must not, however, be confounded with the orator of the name, had the cruelty to order such of his slaves as he thought deserving of death, and sometimes even those who had done nothing to excite his anger, to be thrown to them. On one occasion, when he entertained the Emperor Augustus, a poor slave who attended had the misfortune to break a precious vase; Pollion immediately ordered him to be thrown to the eels. But the indignant emperor gave the slave his freedom, and, in order to manifest his indignation with Pollion, he ordered his attendants to break every vase of value which the freedman had collected in his mansion.

In the present day sea-eels are little esteemed in a gastronomic point of view. Nevertheless they are still sought for on the coast of Italy, and the fishermen avoid with great care the bites of their acrid teeth.

The Eels (*Anguilla*) have pectoral fins, under which are the gill-openings on each side; the dorsal and anal fins extending up to the tail, mingling with this last, which terminates in a point at the extre-

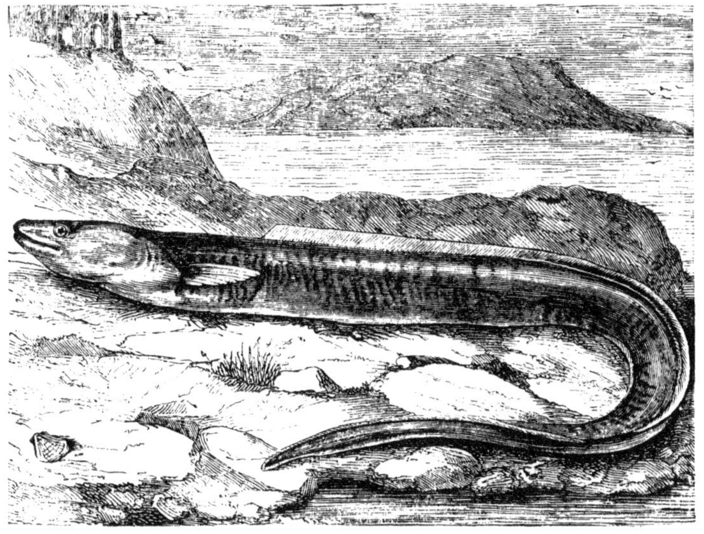

Fig. 365. The Common Conger (Anguilla Conger).

mity. The eels are divided into two groups: 1. The Eels (*Anguilla*), properly so called; and, 2. The *Congers*. The first inhabit most European rivers, except in the spawning season, when, according to some naturalists, they betake themselves to the sea. During the greater part of their existence, therefore, they have no connection with the ocean. The *Conger*, on the other hand, are fishes of great size, which inhabit the seas of warm countries, as well as those of Northern Europe. The type of this family is the Common Conger, *Anguilla Conger* (Fig. 365), which differs from the true eels chiefly in the dorsal fins, which commence very near to the pectorals; and also in their upper jaw being longer than their under one. They attain the thickness of a man's leg, and are sometimes two yards in length. The conger-eel is frequently found in salt marshes, but its flesh is held in little esteem.

2. SUB-BRANCHIATI.

The fishes of this order are characterised by vertical fins being attached under the pectorals, and immediately suspended to the shoulder bone. Exclusively marine fishes, they inhabit every region of the globe. The order comprehends three families:—I. *Discobolidæ;* II. *Pleuronectidæ,* or flat fishes; III. the *Gadidæ.*

I. DISCOBOLIDÆ.

The family of Discobolidæ consists of a small number of species characterised by their ventral fins being discoform, as in the sea-snails

Fig. 366. The Sea-Snail (Liparis).

(*Liparis*), in which the lengthened mucous body is without scales, but with one long dorsal fin; the pectoral and ventrals forming one disk, as in Fig. 366, or the Suckers (*Lepidogaster*), where the pectorals and ventrals form two disks.

In the Lump-fish, *Cyclopteris* (Fig. 367), the disk formed by the ventrals forms a sort of sucker, by which the fish attaches itself to the rocks; while the *Echineis* is remarkable for the disk-like sucker with which it is provided.

The *Echineis remora* is an inhabitant of the Mediterranean. It is furnished with a flat disk, which covers its head, as represented in

Fig. 368, which is formed of a number of transverse and movable

Fig. 367. The Lump-fish (Cyclopteris).

cartilaginous plates. Aided by this organ, it attaches itself firmly

Fig. 368. Echineis remora.

to rocks, and even to ships and larger fishes, such as the Dog-fish

(*Acanthius*), which it meets with in its wanderings. Its adhesion to those objects is so strong that the strength of a man fails to separate them. It sometimes attaches itself to the belly of the shark, and makes long voyages on this monstrous locomotive animal, and that without fatigue or danger, for its enemies are kept at a distance by the formidable monster which carries it.

II. PLEURONECTIDÆ.

The Flat-fishes (*Pleuronectidæ*) have the body flat and greatly compressed, but in a direction different from that of the *Raias* and other analogous beings. In the case of the Raia the body is flattened horizontally, while in the Pleuronectidæ they are compressed laterally. The head of fishes of this order is not symmetrical; the two eyes are placed on the same side; the two sides of the mouth are unequal.

To these peculiarities of structure we shall return when we come to observe the several types more clearly. In inaction, as in motion, the flat-fishes are always turned upon their side, and the side turned towards the bottom of the sea is that which has no eye. This habit of swimming on their side is that to which they owe their name of πλευρὰ, side, and νέχτος, swimmers.

Their chief organ of natation is the caudal fin, but they are distinguished from all other fishes by the manner in which they use this oar. When turned upon their side this organ is not horizontal, but vertical, and strikes the water vertically up and down. They advance through the water but very slowly, compared to the motion of other fishes. They ascend or descend in the water with greater promptitude, but they cannot turn to the right or left with the same facility as other fishes. This property of rising or sinking in the water with facility is the more useful to them inasmuch as the greater part of their existence is passed at the greatest depths, where they draw themselves along the sands at the bottom of the sea, and often hide themselves from their enemies. Among the *Pleuronectidæ*, soles, turbot, flounders, and plaice may be noted.

Soles (*Solea*) have the body oblong, the side opposite to the edges generally furnished with shaggy, soft hairs; the muzzles round, nearly always in advance of the mouth, which is twisted to the left side, and furnished with teeth on one side only, while the eyes are on the right side. The dorsal fin commences about the mouth, and extends up to the caudal or terminal fin. The Common Sole, *Solea vulgaris* (Fig. 369), is plentiful in the Channel, along the Atlantic coasts, and especially in the Mediterranean. It is brown on the right, and whitish on the opposite side. Its pectoral fins are spotted black; the scales rugged and denticulate; its size seems to vary according to the coast it frequents. Off the mouth of the Seine soles are sometimes

Fig. 369. The Common Sole (*Solea vulgaris*).

taken eighteen and twenty inches in length. There are several modes of taking them, but for commercial purposes it is taken by the trawl-net. When the ground-hook is employed it is baited with fragments of small fish. Every one knows the delicate flavour of the flesh of the sole. According to Lacepede, its flesh may be kept many days, not only without corruption, but it acquires even a finer taste.

The Turbot, *Rhombus maximus* (Fig. 370), resembles in its general form a lozenge, whence its name of *rhombus*. Its under jaw is more advanced than the upper jaw, and is furnished with many rows of small teeth. Its fins are yellow, with brownish spots. The left side is marbled brown and yellow; the right side, which is the inferior, white with brownish spots and points. The true turbot is the special delight of the epicure, and fabulous sums are said to have been given at different times by rich persons in order to secure a fine turbot. The fish used to be taken largely on our own coasts, but now we have to rely upon more distant fishing-grounds for a large portion of our supply—large quantities coming from Holland. The turbot spawns

Fig. 370. The Turbot (Rhombus maximus).

during the autumn, and is in fine condition during spring and early summer. Mr. Yarrell says that it spawns in spring. Dr. Bertram doubts this, although he is not quite sure of it, inasmuch as "there will, no doubt, be individuals of the turbot kind, as there are of all other kinds of fish, that will spawn all the year round." The turbot abounds on our west coast, round Torbay, and off the mouth of the Seine and the Somme, from whence comes most of the fish consumed in London and Paris. The flounders, plaice, and halibut form an important section of the Pleuronectidæ.

The Flounders and Plaice (*Platessa*) inhabit the northern seas of Europe. They have their eyes placed on the right side; the dorsal as well as the anal fin extending from over the eyes to the caudal, both stretching out to a point towards the centre, giving a rhombic form to the fish. In *Platessa* the jaws are furnished with a single row of obtuse teeth.

The Common Plaice, *P. vulgaris* (Fig. 371), attains the length of ten or twelve inches; it is brown above, spotted with red or orange. On the eye-side of the head are some osseous tubercles. The body, which is somewhat lozenge-shaped, is smooth.

Fig. 371. The Common Plaice (Platessa vulgaris).

The Flounders (*P. flessus*) are fresh-water fishes of small size, abundant in the Thames and many other rivers; they are only second in importance to the soles and turbot among the Pleuronectidæ; the numbers of brill, flounders, dab, and plaice required being close upon a hundred million for the supply of London alone.

The usual mode of capturing flat-fish is by means of a trawl-net, but many varieties of these may be caught with a hand-line. "A day's sea-fishing," says Dr. Bertram, in his "Harvest of the Sea," "will be chequered by many little adventures. There are various minor monsters of the deep that will vary the monotony of the day by occasionally devouring the bait. A tadpole fish, better known as the sea-devil, or angler, may be hooked; or a visit from a hammer-headed shark, or a pile-fish, will add greatly to the excitement; and if the 'dogs' should be at all plentiful, it is a chance if a single fish be got out of the sea in its integrity. So voracious are these Squalidæ, that I have often enough pulled a mere skeleton into the boat, instead of a plump cod of ten or twelve pounds weight."

The Dab, *P. limanda* (Fig. 372), is very common in the markets of Paris, where it is held in great esteem. It takes its name from the hard and dentate scales on its body. The Platessa have the jaws furnished with a single row of obtuse teeth; the dorsal fin only extends in front to a line with the eye, leaving an interval between it and the caudal. The form of the body is rhomboidal, as in the turbot, and the eyes are usually on the right side. The flounder, the plaice, and the dab, are all examples of this group of fishes.

Fig. 372. The Dab (Platessa limanda).

The Halibut, *Hippoglossus vulgaris* (Fig. 373), is a large fish, inhabiting the seas of Northern Europe and Greenland, where it is occasionally caught, measuring seven feet, and weighing from three to four hundred pounds. A fish of this species was brought to Edinburgh market in April, 1828, measuring seven feet and a half in length and three feet broad, weighing three hundred and twenty pounds. The body of the halibut is more elongated than that of the plaice or flounder, the jaws and pharyngeans being armed with strong and pointed teeth.

Great quantities of this fish are caught on the Greenland and Norway coasts, and other northern regions. According to Lacepede, the natives fish for this with an implement which they call *gang-naed*. It is composed of a hempen cord five or six hundred yards in length, to which are attached some thirty smaller cords, each furnished with a barbed hook at its extremity. The larger cord is attached to floating planks, which act as trimmers, indicating the place of this formidable engine of destruction.

The Greenlanders usually replace the hempen cords by thongs of whalebone or narrow bands of sharks' skin. At the end of twenty

Fig. 373. The Halibut (Hippoglossus vulgaris).

hours these lines are drawn home, and it is not at all unusual to find five or six large halibut caught on the hooks. Pl. XXVIII. represents the native mode of fishing for halibut in the Greenland Seas.

Another mode of capturing this and other flat-fish is to spear them on their sandy beds. "No rule can be laid down," says Dr. Bertram, "for this method of fishing. It is carried on successfully by means of a common pitchfork, but some gentlemen go the length of fine spears made for the purpose, very long, and with very sharp prongs. Others, again, use a three-pronged farmyard graip, which has been known to do as much real work as more elaborate single points contrived for the purpose. The simplest directions I can give is just to spear every fish they see." M. Figuier adds, as a caution, that before attacking these fishes, body to body, it is necessary to wait till they are somewhat exhausted, otherwise they might overturn both bark and fisherman.

The Greenlanders cut the animal up, and salt the pieces; then expose them to the air, in order to dry them preparatory to a long voyage.

In its fresh state the halibut is not very delicate, although it is frequently taken for such by those not conversant with the qualities of fish. We may add that, notwithstanding its great size, the halibut has deadly enemies in the dolphins, as well as in the birds which prey upon fishes on the shore. It is itself a voracious fish, devouring crabs, cod-fish, and even the *Raiadæ*, not even sparing its own species; they attack each other, nibbling at the tail or fins.

III. GADIDÆ.

The Gadidæ embrace the whole of the Linnæan genus *Gadus.* They are found mostly in the seas of cold or temperate regions in both hemispheres, and are the objects of pursuit for which the great fisheries of Europe and America are established. They are known by the position of the ventral fin under the throat, and by the pointed character of those fins. The body is long and slightly compressed; the head well proportioned. Their fins are soft, and their scales are small and soft. The jaws and front of the *os vomer* have unequal pointed teeth of moderate size, and disposed in several rows. The gill-covers are large, and consist of seven rays. Most of the species have the dorsal fin, and contain two others besides—a fin behind the vent, and a distant caudal fin. The stomach is large, and the intestine long. The air-bladder large and strong, and in some cases notched on the margin. The flesh of most of the species yields white, healthy, and agreeable food, easily separable into flakes when cooked, and easy of digestion. The family includes the several genera:—MORRHUA, to which belongs the Common Cod-fish, *M. callarias;* the Haddock, *M. æglefinus.*—The MERLANGUS, or Whiting, *M. vulgaris,* and *M. albus;* the Coal-fish, *M. carbonarus;* and the Pollack, *M. pollachius.* —The MERLUCIUS, or Hakes.—The LOTA, or Ling, *L. molva.*—

MOTELLA, or Rock Ling, and Silver Gade, *M. argenteola*; and other genera of less importance.

The head of the Cod (*Morrhua callarias*) is compressed; the eyes placed on the side, close to each other, and veiled by a transparent membrane, a conformation which, according to Lacepede, enables the animal to swim on the surface of the water in northern regions in the midst of mountains of ice and under banks covered with snow, without being dazzled by the brilliant light; but this opinion is unsupported by any other naturalist of note.

Fig. 374. The Cod-fish (Morrhua callarias).

The jaws of the cod-fish are unequal, and among the rows of teeth with which it is armed many are mobile, and can be hidden in their cavities or raised, according to the will of the animal. The dorsal fins, three in number, are in clusters, as in Fig. 374; anal fins are two; pectoral fins narrow, and terminating in a point; caudal fin slightly forked. Its colour is of an ashy grey, spotted with yellow on the back; white and sometimes reddish beneath.

The cod-fish is provided with a vast stomach, and is very voracious, feeding on fishes, crabs, and molluscs. It is so gluttonous and indiscriminating, that it will even swallow pieces of wood and other similar objects. This is essentially a sea-fish: it is never seen in fresh-water streams or rivers, remaining during the greater part of the year in the depths of the sea. Its habitual sojourn is in the portion of the Northern Ocean lying between the fortieth and sixty-sixth degrees of latitude.

In the vast range thus frequented by the cod, two large spaces are pointed out which it seems to prefer. The first extends to the coast of Greenland, and the other is limited by Iceland, Norway, the Danish coast, Germany, Holland, and the east and north coast of Great Britain and the Orkney Isles, comprehending the Doggerbank, Vell-bank, and Cromer coast, together with salt-water lakes and arms of the sea, such as the Gairloch, Portsoy, and the Moray Firth, which indent the west coast of Scotland, and attract considerable shoals of cod-fish.

The second range, less generally known, but more celebrated among sailors, includes the coast of New England, Cape Breton, Nova Scotia, and, above all, the island of Newfoundland, on the south coast of which is the famous sand-bank called the *Great Bank*, having a length of nearly two hundred leagues, with a breadth of sixty-two, over which flows from ten to fifty fathoms of water. Here the cod-fish swarm, for here they meet shoals of herrings and other animals on which they feed. Such is, according to Lacepede, the geographical distribution of the cod-fish.

The English, French, Dutch, and Americans give themselves up to the cod-fishery on the bank of Newfoundland with inconceivable ardour. This island was discovered and visited by the Norwegians in the tenth and eleventh centuries, long before the discovery of America; but it was only in 1497, after the discoveries of Columbus, that the navigator, John Cabot, having visited these regions, gave it the name by which it has since been known, and called attention to the swarms of cod-fish which inhabited the surrounding sea. Immediately after, the English and some other nations hastened to reap these fruitful fields of living matter. In 1578, France sent a hundred and fifty ships to the great bank, Spain a hundred and twenty-five, Portugal fifty, and England forty.

During the first half of the eighteenth century, England and her colonies, with the French, cultivated the cod-fishery.

From 1823 to 1831 France sent three hundred and forty-one ships, with seven thousand six hundred and eighty-five men, which carried into port over fifty million pounds of fish, an average of about six millions annually. Two thousand English ships of various sizes, manned by thirty thousand seamen, are now employed in this important branch of industry.

On the coast of Norway, from the frontiers of Russia to Cape Lindesnæs, the cod-fishery is an important branch of trade, in which a maritime population of twenty thousand fishermen are employed, with five thousand boats.

The cod is taken either by net or line. The net is chiefly employed at Newfoundland. The net used is rectangular, and furnished with lead at the lower edge, and cork buoys on the upper edge. One of the extremities is fixed on the coast; the other is carried seaward, following a curve taken by the boats, and the fish are attracted by drawing upon both extremities of the net; and by one stroke many boat-loads are sometimes taken.

The modern cod-smack is clipper-built, with large wells for carrying the fish alive, its cost being about £1500. The crew usually consists of ten to twelve men and boys, including the captain. The line is also used for taking cod and haddocks. "Each man," says Bertram, "has a line of fifty fathoms in length, and attached to each of these lines are a hundred 'snoods,' with hooks already baited with mussels, pieces of herring, or whiting. Each line is laid 'clear,' in a shallow basket, and so arranged as to run freely as the boat shoots ahead. The fifty-fathom line with a hundred hooks is in Scotland called a 'taes.' If there are eight men in a boat, the length of the line will be four hundred fathoms, with eight hundred hooks, the lines being tied to each other before setting. On arriving at the fishing-ground, the fishermen heave overboard a cork buoy, with a flagstaff about six feet in height attached to it. This buoy is kept stationary by a line, called the 'pow end,' reaching to the bottom of the water, where it is held by a stone or a grapnel fastened to the lower end. To the 'pow end' is also fastened the fishing line, which is then paid out as fast as the boat sails, which may be from four to five knots an hour. Should the wind be unfavourable for the direction in which the crew wish to set the line, they use the oars. When the line or 'taes' is all out, the end is dropped and the boat returns to the buoy. The 'pow' line is hauled up with the anchor and fishing line attached to it. The fishermen then haul in the line, with the fish attached to it. Eight hundred fish might be taken, and often have been, by eight men in a few hours by this operation; but many fishermen say now, that they consider themselves fortunate when they get a fish on every fifth hook on an eight-lined 'taes'-line."

Hungry cod-fish will seize almost any kind of bait, and this is used either fresh or salted. The fresh bait is furnished by the herring, whiting, and capelan, a little fish which in the spring descends from the North Sea in shoals, pursued by the cod-fish. In the terror caused by the innumerable bands of their enemies, the capelans spread themselves in all the seas round Newfoundland in masses so thick that the waves throw them ashore, and they accumulate occasionally in heaps upon the sandy beach.

The principal fishery for capelan intended for bait takes place on the coast of Newfoundland. The inhabitants of these regions carry their booty to the fishermen, who make Saint-Pierre their rendezvous, with whom they find ready purchasers.

The schooners, with a fair provision of bait, leaving Saint-Pierre and other ports, take a north-easterly direction towards the great bank, and, having chosen their fishing-ground, cast anchor in fifty or sixty fathoms, and forthwith the crews give their sole attention to the lines; some of them watch the lines, which are raised every instant, the captured fish removed, and the hooks re-baited; others subject the captured fishes to a first preparation for preserving them; they are opened, the entrails removed, and the fish split in two, and piled one on the other, and covered with salt. This labour goes on as long as the fishing lasts. The sailor is on deck night and day, covered with oil and blood, and surrounded with all sorts of offal and fish-like smells. But this alone is insufficient. Boats, manned by crews of two or three sailors, are continually moving about, attending to the more distant lines or "taes," which radiate round the ship in all directions.

One portion of the cod caught is despatched to Europe in a fresh state, without other preparation than the salting which they receive on the deck of the schooner. But much the greater portion are carried on shore and subjected to further preparation. Saint-Pierre and Miquelon Islands, which are granted to the French fishermen on condition that no fortifications are erected on them, is resorted to for the purpose by the French fleet; St. John's, the capital, by the English. The Comte de Gobineau gives an animated picture of the whole process of curing the cod-fish in the "Tour du Monde for 1863." "The French houses which pursue this branch of trade," he says, "belong principally to the Ports of Granville and St. Breuc; and the crews of their ships consist of two very distinct elements; the smaller portion, being specially raised among the fishermen properly so called, they form the aristocracy on board; to these are added a larger number of mere labourers, who are landed on the arrival of the vessel at her port. Their functions are limited to receiving the fish from the boats, opening it, washing off the glutinous matter in the *chauffant*, putting the liver apart, and laying out the split fish between the layers of salt; finally, subjecting it to the different phases of the drying process on the strand.

"The *chauffant* is a shed raised upon piles, standing one half in the water and one half on shore; it is constructed of planks and posts, through which the air is suffered to circulate freely, but covered in with some of the ship's sails. Here the process of separating the intestines from the body of the fish, and the salting process, are carried on, in the midst of an atmosphere charged with all manner of disgusting smells, for the labourer is by no means delicate, and never thinks of removing the disgusting impurities which he is creating. There he stands, knife in hand, tearing and cutting out intestines and separating vertebræ, his only care being to avoid cutting himself, which is the chief danger he runs, in the midst of odours sufficient to produce suffocation.

"Connected with the platform on which this rough operation is performed is a cauldron, sunk in the earth, to receive the oil pressed out of the liver. This cauldron is surmounted by a roof some nine feet in height, in the form of an inverted cone. Here the oil which flows from the open way above is suffered to ferment, after which it is drawn off into casks.

"The drying sheds, formerly of wood, are now constructed of stone, and in places well exposed to the sun, and especially to the wind, artificial or otherwise. The sun, it is said, does not dry, but scorches; the wind, on the other hand, marvellously fulfills the purpose, and in order to avoid the one and court the other, an apparatus has been invented, consisting of long movable branches, which can be inclined so as to bring the wind directly upon the row of cod, in connection with the sun's rays, which are, indeed, not very formidable in this foggy region."

The cod-fish thus dried at Newfoundland are forwarded for consumption to all parts of the world; but only a small part of the products of the fishery are thus prepared. More than half the produce of the French fleet are sent to France merely salted, by ships which carry salt, bringing back fish in return to Rochelle, Bordeaux, and Cette, where the process of curing is completed. In our home fisheries, to abbreviate slightly Dr. Bertram's account, the greater part of the cod taken are eaten fresh, but considerable quantities of the cod and ling taken on the coast are sent to market cured. The process pursued is very simple: they are brought on shore quite fresh, and are at once split from head to tail, and by copious washings thoroughly cleansed from all particles of blood; a piece of the backbone is cut away; they are drained, and afterwards laid down in long vats, where they are covered with salt, and kept under heavy weights. By-and-by the fish are taken out of the vats; they are once more drained, and carefully brushed, to remove any impurity, and bleached by being spread out singly on the sandy beach, or on the rocks; when thoroughly bleached, they are collected into heaps technically called *steeples*, and when the *bloom*, or whitish appearance, comes out on the fish, they are ready for the market.

The cod is one of our best-known fishes, and was at one time much more plentiful and cheap. It is a deep-water fish, found in all northern seas, and in the Atlantic, but never in the Mediterranean. It is extremely voracious, greedily eating up the smaller denizens of the ocean. It grows to a large size, and is very prolific, as most fishes are. A cod-roe has been found more than once to be half the gross weight of the fish, and specimens of the female cod have been caught with upwards of eight millions of eggs. The fish spawn in midwinter: but here our information ceases; when it becomes reproductive is unknown. Dr. Bertram thinks that it is at least three years old before it is endowed with breeding power.

The growth of the cod is supposed to be very slow; Dr. Bertram quotes the authority of a rather learned fisherman of Buckie, who had seen a cod which had got enclosed in a large rock pool, and he found that it did not grow at a greater rate than eight to twelve ounces per annum, though it had abundance of food.

On our own coast two modes of fishing are in common use: one by deep sea lines, on each of which hooks are fastened at distances twelve feet apart by means of short lines six feet long, called on the Cornish coast "snoods." Buoys, ropes, or grapnels, are fixed to each end of the long line, to keep them from entanglement with each other. The hooks are baited with capelan, launce, or whelks, and the lines are shot across the tide about the time of slack water, in from forty to fifty fathoms, and are hauled in for examination after six hours.

An improvement has been introduced upon this mode of fishing by Mr. Cobb. He fixes a small piece of cork about twelve inches above the hook, which suspends the bait, and exhibits it more clearly to the fish by the motion of the wave. The fishermen, when not engaged in hauling, shooting, or baiting the long lines, fish with hand-lines, holding one in each hand, each armed with two hooks, kept apart by a strong piece of wire. A heavy weight attached to the lower end of each line keeps it steady near the ground, where the fish principally feed. Enormous quantities of cod, haddock, whiting, and coal-fish, with pollack, hake, ling, and torsk, are taken in this way all round our coast. Of cod-fish alone four hundred to five hundred and fifty have been taken in ten hours by one man, and eight men have taken eighty score of cod in one day, fishing off the Doggerbank in five and twenty fathoms water. Latterly the Norfolk and Lincoln, and even the Essex, coasts, have yielded a large supply of fish, which are caught as described, and are stowed in well-boats, in which they are carried to Gravesend, whence they are transhipped into market-boats, and sent up to Billingsgate by each evening tide; the store-boats not being allowed to come up higher, as the fresh water would kill the fish.

The Haddock (*Morrhua æglefinus*) is common in our markets; it is much smaller than the cod, but in other respects not unlike it. It frequents the same localities, and is caught with long lines baited with pieces of herring and sand-larvæ. On the north-east coast of Scotland the haddock, cured over a juniper fire, is one of the principal adjuncts to the celebrated Scottish breakfast.

The Whiting, *Merlangus vulgaris* (Fig. 375), by some amateurs considered the most delicate of all the Gadidæ, is plentiful all round our coast. It spawns in March, and the eggs are quickly hatched. It prefers a sandy shore, and is usually found some miles from the coast. It is a small fish, rarely exceeding twelve inches, and seldom reaching two pounds in weight. The whiting is long in the body, clothed with very small, thin, and round scales; its dorsal fins are, like the cod, three in number; it is without barbellary appendage; its upper jaw projects over the lower; it is of a silvery white, sometimes relieved by an olive tint, which is contrasted upon the back by the blackish tint which distinguishes the pectoral and caudal fins, and by a black spot which some individuals have at the junction of the pectorals with the body.

Fig. 375. The Whiting (Merlangus vulgaris).

The whiting inhabits the seas which wash the whole European coast, often approaching the shore in shoals, which are taken annually in great numbers.

3. ABDOMINALES.

The fishes belonging to this order have the ventral fins under the abdomen placed behind, and not attached to the bones of the shoulder. It is much the most numerous and important of the great division of the Malacopterygeans. It includes most of our fresh-water fishes, a great number of marine species, and many like the salmon, which betake themselves to the rivers in the spawning season to deposit their ova. We shall limit our remarks to the species which are essentially marine, such as the *Salmonidæ*, the *Clupeadæ*, and a few others.

SALMONIDÆ.

The fishes of this family are graceful in shape, and have the body clothed in scales; they have two dorsals, the first with soft rays, followed by a second, which is smaller, formed without rays, and adipose—that is, formed simply of a skin filled with fatty matter, unsupported by osseous rays. They inhabit the seas of temperate and northern regions; ascending the rivers at certain seasons, and, in some instances, living exclusively in the great rivers and watercourses. They are found even in the most elevated mountain brooks. The grayling or shad, guiniad, sprat, trout, and the salmon, the type of the family, belong to the group.

The genus *Salmo* includes three species, namely, *Salmo salor*, *S. croix*, and *S. trutta*, the trout. Of these, *S. salor* (Fig 376) has the

Fig. 376. Adult Salmon.

body long, the muzzle roundish, but more so in the male than in the female, the upper jaw provided with a fossette, into which the point of the lower jaw penetrates; the back is a slaty blue, the sides and lower part of the body of a silvery diaphanous white, with great black spots scattered round the upper part of the head, round the upper edge of the eye and over the operculum or covering. Some brownish irregular spots, variable both in form and size, are sprinkled over the sides. In other respects their colours are subject to variations according to circumstances. Before assuming the characters here indicated, however, the

Fig. 377. The Young Salmon.

salmon has passed through three stages, each of which are marked by peculiarities worthy of being noted. The young salmon (Fig. 377) is greyish and striped with black. At the end of a year it has acquired

Fig. 378. Salmon, or Parr, a year old.

a fine metallic hue. "The other parts," according to Mr. Blanchard, "are of a dazzling steel-blue; eight or ten large spots of the same brilliant blue cover it as with a silvery mantle on the sides; between these spots a reddish or, rather, brightish-rusty iron colour prevails; a black spot is usually observable in the middle of the speculum. The belly is of a fine diaphanous blue in the parr" (Fig. 378).

Dr. Bertram gives a very clear and intelligible account of the early days of the salmon, which was at one time veiled in mystery: "The spawn, deposited by the parent fish in October, November, and December, lies in the river till about April or May, when it quickens into life. I have already described the changes apparent in the salmon's egg, from the time of its fructification till the birth of the fish. The infant fry are of course very helpless, and are seldom seen during the first week or two of their existence, when they carry about with them, as a provision for food, a portion of the egg from whence they emanated. At that time the fish is about half an inch in size, and presents such a singular appearance that no person seeing it would ever believe that it would grow into a fine grilse or salmon. About fifty days is required for the animal to assume the shape of a perfect fish; before that time it might be taken for anything else than a young salmon. At the end of two years it has changed into a smolt. After eating up its umbilical bag, which it takes a period of twenty to forty days to accomplish, the young salmon may be seen about its birthplace, timid and weak, hiding about the stones, and always apparently of the same colour as the surroundings of its sheltering place. The transverse bars of the parr, however, speedily become apparent, and the fish begins to grow with considerable rapidity, especially if it is to be a twelvemonth smolt, and this is very speedily seen at such a place as the Stormouthfield ponds. The young fish continue to grow for a little longer than two years before the whole number make the change from parr to smolt, and seek the salt water. Half the number of any one hatching begin to change at a little over twelvemonths from the date of their coming to life. And thus there is the extraordinary anomaly of fish of the same hatching being at one and the same time parr of half an ounce in weight, and grilse weighing four pounds. The smolts of the first year return from the sea, while their brothers and sisters are timidly disporting in the breeding shallows of the upper streams."

It thus appears that, in its first stage, the Young Salmon (Fig. 377) is called a *parr*: during the second it is a *smolt*. While they continue in the state of parr they lead a secluded life, totally unable to endure salt water, which would kill them. When they have become smolts the fish betake themselves in bands to the sea. The sea feeding being favourable, and the fish strong enough for the salt water, a rapid growth is the consequence. Arrived at the spot where the tide stops, they stop a few days in the brackish water, as if to accustom themselves to the new element. After that they disappear, spreading themselves over the wide world of the ocean. At the end of two months of a life mysterious and so far unknown, these fishes reappear in the rivers, returning to their native pools; but how changed! *Quantum mutati!* The smolt, which has lived in the river two or three years, and only attained the length of six or eight inches, returns at the end of a two months' sojourn in the sea, weighing three to four pounds. It is now a grilse.

After depositing their eggs the grilse remain some time in the fresh water, when they again go to the sea. This second sojourn, of about two months, is sufficient to send it back weighing from six to twelve pounds. It is now an adult salmon. Each new visit to the sea brings the salmon back increased in size in proportion to the duration of the voyage. In the month of March, 1845, the Duke of Athole took a salmon in the Tay after it had deposited its eggs; he marked it by attaching a metal label to it. It weighed ten pounds. The same individual with its metal label was again fished up after five weeks and three days' absence. It now weighed twenty-one pounds, having in the meantime travelled forty miles down the river to the sea.

In most circumstances, according to Mr. Blanchard, to whom we are indebted for much information relative to the development and migration of these fishes, salmon of various ages, which have nevertheless sojourned in the sea as grilse, adult salmon, and others intermediate between them, whose first sojourn at sea has extended to eight or ten months, ascend the rivers together in an order no less varied, the older individuals heading the column, the youngest bringing up the rear.

When the period for depositing their eggs approaches, a male and female pair off, as it were; seeming to choose, by a common accord, the place intended to receive the egg. Here both male and female employ themselves in hollowing out a nest in the strand, some eight or nine inches deep, wherein the female deposits her eggs, which the male fertilizes by shedding a milky fluid over them, sheltering the eggs afterwards by a covering of sand.

The salmon only ascends the rivers to spawn. They eagerly return afterwards to salt water. When enjoying themselves in the water they swim slowly, floating near the surface; but in pursuit of any object, or if threatened with danger, they dart out of the water with extraordinary promptitude. The tail is, in fact, a true oar moved by powerful muscles; a waterfall, or lofty cataract, is to the salmon no serious obstacle when it is impelled to ascend to its breeding-place. Curving its vertebral column, it forms itself into a sort of elastic spring; the arc of which, being suddenly unbent, strikes the water with great force with the tail, and in the rebound it leaps to the height of four or five yards, clearing waterfalls of considerable height. If it falls without accomplishing its object, it repeats the manœuvre until it is at last successful. It is especially when the leader of the band makes a successful leap that the others, acquiring new spirit from its example, throw themselves upwards until their emulation is rewarded by success.

Fig. 379. Salmon Leap at Kilmorack.

Some of the British waterfalls are celebrated for their salmon leaps. Wales, Scotland, and Ireland have each their celebrated leaps; in Pembrokeshire, Argyleshire, and at Ballyshannon, in county Donegal, and at Leixlip. The cataract of Leixlip is upwards of twenty feet high, and the country people make a holiday in order to see the salmon clear its height. These acrobat fishes frequently fall before they finally succeed, and it is not unusual for the people to place osier baskets to trap them in their fall. At the cataract of Kilmorack, in Inverness-shire (Fig. 379), the inhabitants living near the river have a practice of fixing branches of trees on the edge of the rocks. By means of these branches they contrive to catch the fishes which have failed in their leap; it is even asserted that sportsmen have been known to kill them on the wing, as it were, in their leap. But the exploit, attributed to Lord Lovat by Dr. Franklin, is perhaps the nearest approach to the fabulous which we have met with.

Having remarked that great numbers of salmon failed in their efforts to surmount the Falls of Kilmorack, and that they generally fell on the bank at the foot of the fall, Lord Lovat conceived the idea of placing a furnace and a frying-pan on a point of rock overhanging the river. After their unsuccessful effort some of the unhappy salmon would fall accidentally into the frying-pan. The noble lord could thus boast that the resources of his country were so abundant that, on placing a furnace and frying-pan on the banks of their rivers, the salmon would leap into it of their own accord, without troubling the sportsman to catch them. It is more probable, however, that Lord Lovat knew that the time to enjoy salmon in perfection is to cook it when fresh from the water, and before the richer parts of the fish have ceased to curd.

We have seen how rapidly the young salmon increase in size in the sea. We can only conjecture what is the nature of their food at this stage of their existence: we are better informed as to their manner of living in fresh water. During their first stage they live chiefly on insects, and the spawn of small fishes; from the time when they attain a certain size—that is, from the grilse to the adult state—they devour a multitude of these small fishes themselves.

The British rivers in which the salmon abound are the Severn, the Wye, the Tweed, the Tay, the Don, and the Dee, with many of their tributaries, and in Ireland, the Shannon. Besides these, many of the watercourses of lesser note adjoining the coast have been renowned for their salmon fisheries. Some of the Scottish rivers, especially, are famous for the size and quality as well as numbers of salmon. In days not very distant from ours, farm servants made it a condition of their hiring that salmon should not be served to them more than three days in the week. These times are changed. In the districts in which this condition was the most stringently insisted on, the riverains derive a princely revenue from this source alone. The Tay fisheries yield a revenue of seventeen thousand pounds per annum. The Spey, for its length the richest in Scotland, produces twelve thousand pounds per annum. The river is only a hundred and twenty miles from its source to the sea, and its picturesque banks are celebrated in a local ballad which says, not very harmoniously, that

> "Dipple, Dundurcus, Dandaleith, and Dulocq,
> Are the bonniest haughs of the run of the Spey";

but there's "no standing water in the Spey!" The river drains thirteen hundred miles of mountains, many of whose bases are more than a thousand feet above the level of the sea. The Tweed, which has been "poached" and plundered, by its proprietors using unfair implements until there was scarcely a fish in its upper waters, is slowly recovering under legislative enactments, and its rental is now seven thousand five hundred pounds.

Salmon abounds in the Loire and its affluents, but is much more rare in the Seine and Marne. They enter the Rhine and the Elbe, and most of the great rivers of the north of Europe. In France they were formerly found in the rivers of Brittany, and in the Gironde. They are now very rare in these rivers. The coast of Picardy is well furnished, but they are rare in Upper and Lower Normandy. In Norway, especially in the district of Drontheim, the salmon fishery is conducted on a large scale on the sea-shore as well as in the interior waters. The Baltic is rich in salmon. Considerable fisheries are carried on in the waters of the Gulf of Finland and Bothnia, as well as in the waters of Swedish Laponia.

The modes of procedure in salmon fishery are very various. Lines, bow-nets, hooks, and tridents, or spears, are employed, but especially nets—namely the hoop-net or tremail, a net which is thrown quite across a river; it is made with thickish string, and is about a hundred fathoms in length by eighteen inches in height, the meshes being from four to five inches square.

ESOCIDÆ.

This family includes the *Pike*, which, being a fresh-water fish, need not now occupy our attention; it includes also the singular genus *Stomias*, and the Flying-fish, *Exocœtus*.

The *Stomias* have a body much elongated, the muzzle being very short, the mouth very deeply cleft, the opercula reduced to small membranous laminæ; the maxillarius fixed to the cheek; the intermaxillary palatine and maxillary bones are rather sparingly furnished with teeth, and those are long and hooked. Similar teeth are observable on the tongue. The ventral fins are placed far back, and the dorsal fin is placed opposite the anal fin, on the hinder extremity of the body.

Only two species of this genus are known: the one of the Mediterranean, *Stomia bea* (Fig. 380), the other of the Atlantic Ocean, *S.*

Fig. 380. Stomia bea.

barbatus, so called from the long barbula on the chin. Both species are black in colour, with numerous small silvery spots on the abdomen. The body of *S. bea* is thin, compressed, covered with little thin scales of blackish blue, much spotted on the back and abdomen, a little brighter on the sides—the head, in some respects, recalling that of a serpent.

Flying is so much associated in our minds with the usual denizens of the air, that the idea of flying-fishes seems to be a contradiction. Nevertheless, some fishes possess that power, the fins being transformed into wings, which they are enabled to raise for a few seconds. These wings, however, are neither long nor powerful, for it rather acts the part of a parachute than wings. The distinguishing character of the *Exocœtus*, or flying-fish, are the pectoral fins, nearly the length of the body, the head flattened above and on the sides, the lower part of the body furnished with a longitudinal series of carinated scales on each side, the dorsal fin placed above the anal, the eyes large, and the jaws furnished with small pointed teeth.

The Flying-fishes (Fig. 381) in their own element are harassed by attacks of other inhabitants of the ocean, and when under the excitement of fear they take to the air, they are equally exposed to the attacks of aquatic birds, especially the various species of gulls. We

Fig. 381. The Flying-fish (E. exiliens).

have said that, in their leap from the water, their fins sustain them rather as parachutes than wings, with which they beat the air. Mr. Bennett's description is pretty clear on this point. "I have never," he says, "been able to see any percussion of the pectoral fins during flight; and the greatest length of time I have seen this volatile fish on the fly has been thirty seconds by the watch, and the longest flight, mentioned by Captain Basil Hall, has been two hundred yards, but he thinks that subsequent observation has extended the space.

The usual height of their flight, as seen above the surface of the water, is from two to three feet, but I have known them come on board at the height of fourteen feet and upwards. And they have been well ascertained to come into the chains of a line-of-battle ship, which is considered to be upwards of twenty feet. But it must not be supposed that they have the power of raising themselves into the air after having left their native element; for on watching them I have often seen them fall much below the elevation at which they first rose from the water; nor have I ever in any instance seen them rise from the height to which they first sprang, for I conceive the elevation they take depends on the power of the first spring."

The most common species is *E. volitans*. Its brilliant colouring would seem designed to point it out to its enemies, against whom it is totally defenceless. A dazzling silvery splendour pervades its surface. The summit of its head, its back, and its sides, are of azure blue; this blue becomes spotted upon the dorsal fin, the pectoral fin, and the tail. This fish is the common prey of the more voracious fishes, such as the shark and the sea-birds; its enemies abound in the air and water. If it succeeds in escaping the Charybdis of the water, the chances are in favour of its coming to grief in the Scylla of the atmosphere;—if it escapes the jaws of the shark, it will probably fall to the share of the sea-gull. The dolphin is also a formidable enemy to the much-persecuted flying-fish. Captain Basil Hall gives a very animated description of their mode of attack.* He was in a prize, a low Spanish schooner, rising not above two feet and a half out of the water. "Two or three dolphins had ranged past the ship in all their beauty. The ship in her progress through the water had put up a shoal of these little things (flying-fish), which took their flight to windward. A large dolphin which had been keeping company with us abreast of the weather gangway at the depth of two or three fathoms, and as usual glistening most beautifully in the sun, no sooner detected our poor dear friends take wing than he turned his head towards them, darted to the surface, and leaped from the water with a velocity little short, as it seemed to us, of a cannon-ball. But though the impetus with which he shot himself into the air gave him an initial velocity greatly exceeding that of the flying-fish, the start which his fated prey had got enabled them to keep ahead of him for a

* "Lieutenant and Commander," by Captain Basil Hall. Bell & Daldy, London.

considerable time. The length of the dolphin's first spring could not be less than ten yards, and after he fell we could see him gliding like lightning through the water for a moment, when he again rose, and shot upwards with considerably greater velocity than at first, and of course to a still greater distance. In this manner the merciless pursuer seemed to stride along the sea with fearful rapidity, while his brilliant coat sparkled and flashed in the sun quite splendidly. As he fell headlong in the water at the end of each leap, a series of circles were sent far over the surface, for the breeze, just enough to keep the royals and topgallant studding-sails extended, was hardly felt as yet below.

"The group of wretched flying-fishes, thus hotly pursued, at length dropped into the sea; but we were rejoiced to observe that they merely touched the top of the swell, and instantly set off again in a fresh and even more vigorous flight. It was particularly interesting to observe that the direction they took now was quite different from the one in which they had set out, implying but too obviously that they had detected their fierce enemy, who was following them with giant steps along the waves and was gaining rapidly upon them. His pace, indeed, was two or three times as swift as theirs, poor little things! and the greedy dolphin was fully as quick-sighted; for whenever they varied their flight in the smallest degree, he lost not the tenth part of a second in shaping his course so as to cut off the chase; while they, in a manner really not unlike that of the hare, doubled more than once upon the pursuer. But it was soon plainly to be seen that the strength and confidence of the flying-fish were fast ebbing; their flights became shorter and shorter, and their course more fluttering and uncertain, while the leaps of the dolphin seemed to grow more vigorous at each bound. Eventually this skilful sea-sportsman seemed to arrange his springs so as to fall just under the very spot on which the exhausted flying-fish were about to drop. This catastrophe took place at too great a distance for us to see from the deck what happened; but on our mounting high on the rigging, we may be said to have been in at the death; for then we could discover that the unfortunate little creatures, one after another, either popped right into the dolphin's jaws as they lighted on the water, or were snapped up instantly after."

Unhappy Exocœtus! Nature has cruelly expiated the double

privilege she has granted thee; she has taken with both hands what she has awarded with one!

THE CLUPEADÆ,

Of which the herring is the graceful, useful, and well-known type, and to which also the pilchard, the shad, and the anchovy belong. The Clupea have the body longish and compressed, especially at the belly, where it comes to an edge; it is clothed with large scales, forming towards the belly a saw-like edge, which is very thin and easily

Fig. 382. The Herring (Clupea harengus).

removed. One dorsal fin without spinous rays, and one ventral, both placed near the middle of the body, are its locomotive characteristics.

The Herring, *Clupea harengus* (Fig. 382), is too well known to require description; its appearance is magnificent; but we shall only remark here that its back, which in the fish after death is of an indigo bluish colour, is green during life; the other parts vary considerably in their colours and markings, sometimes representing written characters, which ignorant fishermen have considered to be words of mystery. In November, 1587, two herrings were taken on the coast of Norway, on the bodies of which were markings resembling Gothic printed characters. These herrings had the signal honour of being presented to the King of Norway, Frederick II. This superstitious prince turned pale at sight of this supposed prodigy. On the back of these innocent inhabitants of the deep he saw certain cabalistic characters, which he thought announced his death and that of his queen. Learned men were consulted. Their science, as reported, enabled them to read distinctly words expressing the sentiment, " Very soon you will cease to fish herrings, as well as other people." Other *savants* were assembled who gave another explanation; but in 1588 the king died, and the people were firmly convinced that the two herrings were celestial messengers charged to announce to the Norwegian people the approaching end of the monarch.

This fish abounds throughout the entire Northern Ocean in immense shoals, which are found in the bays of Greenland, Lapland, and round the whole coast of the British islands. Great shoals of them occupy the Gulfs of Sweden, of Norway, and of Denmark, the Baltic and the Zuyder Zee, in the Channel, and along the coast of France up to the Loire, beyond which they never appear to be found.

The herrings are gregarious fishes, and live in great shoals closely packed together; shoals to be counted not by thousands, but by millions and thousands of millions, in every shore and bay. It was the favourite theory, not very long ago, that herrings emigrated to and from the arctic regions. It was asserted, by the supporters of this theory, that in the inaccessible seas of high northern latitudes herrings existed in overwhelming numbers, an open sea within the arctic circle affording a safe and bounteous feeding-ground. At the proper season vast bodies gathered themselves together into one great army, which, in numbers exceeding the powers of imagination, departed for more southern regions. This great *Heer*, or army, was subdivided, by some instinct, as they reached the different shores, led, according to the ideas of fishermen, by herrings of more than ordinary size and sagacity, one division taking the west side of Britain, while another took the east side, the result being an adequate and well divided supply of herrings, which penetrated every bay and arm of the sea round our coast, from Wick to Yarmouth. Closer observation, however, shows that this theory has no existence in fact. Lacepede denies that those periodical journeyings take place. Valenciennes also rejects them. It is true that the herrings have disappeared in certain neighbourhoods in which they were formerly very plentiful; but it is also certain that, in many of the fishing stations, fish are taken all the year round. Moreover, the discovery that the herring of America is a distinct species from that of Europe, and that they do not even spawn in the same waters, is fatal to the theory. In short, there is a total absence of proof of their pretended migrations to high northern latitudes, and recent discoveries all tend to show that the herring is native to the shores on which it is taken.

"It has been demonstrated," says Dr. Bertram, "that the herring is really a native of our immediate seas, and can be caught all the year round on the coast of the three kingdoms. The fishing begins at the island of Lewis, in the Hebrides, in the month of May, and goes on as the year advances, till in July it is being prosecuted off the coast of Caithness; while in autumn and winter we find large supplies of herrings at Yarmouth; there is a winter fishery in the Firth of Forth. Moreover, this fish is found in the south long before it ought to be there, according to the emigration theory. It has been deduced, from a consideration of the annual takes of many years, that the herring exists in distinct races, which arrive at maturity month after month. It is well known that the herrings taken at Wick in July are quite different from those caught at Dunbar in August and September; indeed I would go further, and say that even at Wick each month has its changing shoal, and that as one race appears for capture another disappears, having fulfilled its mission. It is certain that the herrings of these different seasons vary considerably in size and appearance; localities are marked by distinctive features. Thus the well known Loch Fyne herring is essentially different from that of the Firth of Forth; and those differ again, in many particulars, from those caught off Yarmouth. In fact, the herring never ventures far from the shore where it is taken; and its condition, when it is caught, is just an index of the feeding it has enjoyed in its particular locality. The superiority of flavour of the herring taken in our great land-locked salt-water lochs is undoubted. Whether or not resulting from the depth and body of water, from more plentiful marine vegetation, or from the greater variety of land food likely to be washed into these inland seas, has not yet been determined, but it is certain that the herrings of our western sea-lochs are infinitely superior to those captured in the more open sea." "Moreover," he adds, "it is now known, from the inquiries of the late Mr. Mitchell and other authorities on the geographical distribution of the herring, that the fish has never been noticed as being at all abundant in the arctic regions."

The herring feeds on small crustaceans, fishes just hatched, and even on the fry of its own species. On the other hand, its enemies are the most formidable inhabitants of the ocean; the whales destroy them by thousands, but man, above all, carries on a war which threatens to be one of extermination. In fact, the herring-fishery has been to certain nations the great cause of their prosperity. It was the foundation of Dutch independence. Silk manufacture, coffee, tea, spices, which are productive of great commercial movements, address themselves only to the wants of luxury or fashion. The produce of the herring-fishery, on the contrary, is one of necessity to the people; and Holland would have languished and quickly disappeared, with its fictitious territory, if the sea had not added to its commercial industry this inexhaustible mine of wealth. That vast field it has worked with persevering ardour. Struggling for an existence, it has conquered. Every year numerous vessels leave the coast of Holland for this precious marine harvest. The herring-fishery is, for the Dutch people, the most important of maritime expeditions. It is with them known as the "great fishery." Whaling is known as the "small fishery." The great fishery is a golden mine to Holland; it is, besides, a very ancient occupation with ourselves. We find it flourishing in the twelfth century; for, in 1195, according to the historians, the city of Dunwich, in the county of Suffolk, was obliged to furnish the king with twenty-four thousand herrings. We also find mention made of the herring-fishery in a chronicle of the Monastery of Evesham in the year 709.

Towards the year 1030 the French sent vessels into the North Sea from Dieppe for this fishing, nearly a century before the Dutch made the attempt; but as early as the thirteenth century that enterprising people employed two thousand boats in this industry. The Danes, Swedes, and Norwegians also threw themselves into this trade at an early period. The French, Danes, and Swedes furnish at the present time only sufficient for home consumption. The monopoly of foreign trade belongs to the English, Dutch, and Norwegians. "The quantity of herrings gathered every year by our neighbours beyond the Channel," says Moquin-Tandon, "is truly enormous. In Yarmouth alone four hundred ships, of from forty to sixty tons, are equipped, the largest being manned by twelve men. The revenue derived from this fleet is about seven hundred thousand pounds. In 1857 three of these fishing-boats, belonging to the same proprietors, carried home three millions seven hundred and sixty-two thousand fishes."

Since the beginning of this century the Scottish fishermen have emulated the zeal of the English. In a paper communicated to the British Association in 1854, Mr. Cleghorn, who has paid great attention to the subject, states "that there are nine hundred and twenty Wick boats engaged in the fishing, and that the produce was ninety-five thousand six hundred and eighty barrels" in one week alone, this being, however, a falling off of sixty-one thousand barrels from the previous year. The cause of this immense falling off was ascribed to a storm which had swept along the coast at the height of the season; but Mr. Cleghorn was inclined to ascribe it mainly to over-fishing, which had gradually diminished the number of herrings captured.

The boats employed by the French and Dutch in the herring-fishery are about sixty tons burden. They generally depart for the Orkney and Shetland isles. They afterwards betake themselves to the German Ocean, and fish the Channel in November and December. These boats carry up to sixteen hands, according to their size. Arrived at their fishing-ground, they cast their nets, as seen in Pl. XXIX.

The lines of the Dutch fishermen are five hundred feet in length, composed of fifty or sixty different nets. The upper parts of these nets are supported by empty barrels or cork-buoys, the lower edge being weighted with lead or stones, which are kept at a convenient depth by shortening or lengthening the cords by which the buoys are attached. The size of the mesh of the nets is such that the herrings of a certain size are caught in it by the gills and pectoral fins. If the first mesh is too large to hold them they pass through, and get caught by the next or succeeding mesh, which is smaller. The herring-fishery is regulated by Act of Parliament, and the legal mode of capture is by means of what is called a drift-net. The drift-net is made of fine twine, marked with squares of an inch each to allow for the escape of the young fish. The nets are measured by the barrel bulk, a net measuring fifty feet long by thirty-two deep, and each holding half a barrel. The drift is composed of many separate nets fastened together by means of a back

Plate XXIX.—The Herring Fishery.

rope, and each separate net of the series is marked off by a bladder or empty cask. The process is that described by Dr. Bertram in an article published in the "Cornhill Magazine." The writer had made his arrangement for a night at the herring-fishery under the auspices of Francis Sinclair, a very gallant-looking fellow, who sails his own boat from Wick, and takes his own venture. Bounding over the waves with a good capful of wind, they had left the shore and beetling cliffs far behind them; they reached their fishing-ground, where they tacked up and down, eagerly watching for the oily phosphorescent gleam which is indicative of herrings. "At last, after a lengthened cruise," he says, "our commander, who had been silent for half an hour, jumped up and called to action. 'Up, men, and at them!' was the order of the night. The preparations for shooting the nets at once began by lowering sail. Surrounding us on all sides was to be seen a moving world of boats; many with sails down, their nets floating in the water, and their crews at rest. Others were still flitting uneasily about, their skippers, like our own, anxious to shoot in the right place. By-and-by we were ready; the sucker goes splash into the water; the 'dog,' a large inflated bladder to mark the far end of the train, is heaved overboard, and the nets, breadth after breadth, follow as fast as the men can pay them out, till the immense train is all in the water, forming a perforated wall a mile long, and many feet in depth; the 'dog' and the marking bladder floating and dipping in long zigzag lines, reminding one of the imaginary coils of the great sea serpent. After three hours of quietude beneath a beautiful sky, the stars—

'The eternal orbs that beautify the night'—

began to pale their fires, and, the grey dawn appearing, indicated that it was time to take stock. We found that the boat had floated quietly with the tide till we were a long distance from the harbour. The skipper had a presentiment that there were fish in his net; and the bobbing down of a few of the bladders made it almost a certainty, and he resolved to examine the drifts. By means of the swing rope the boat was hauled up to the nets. 'Hurrah!' exclaimed Murdoch of Skye; 'there's a lot of fish, skipper, and no mistake.' Murdoch's news was true; our nets were silvery with herrings—so laden, in fact, that it took a long time to haul them in. It was a beautiful sight to see the shimmering fish as they came up like a sheet of silver from the water, each uttering a weak death-chirp as it was flung into the bottom of the boat. Formerly the fish were left in the meshes of the net till the boat arrived in the harbour; but now, as the net is hauled on board, they are at once shaken out. As our silvery treasure showers into the boat we roughly guess our capture at fifty cranes—a capital night's work."

But there is a reverse to this medal. Wick Bay is not always rippled by the land-breeze as on this occasion. "The herring fleet has been more than once overtaken by a fierce storm, where valuable lives have been lost, and thousands of pounds worth of netting and boats destroyed, and the gladdening sights of the herring-fishery have been changed to wailing and sorrow."

The Yarmouth boats are decked vessels of from fifty to eighty tons, with attendant boats, costing about one thousand pounds, and having stowage for about fifty lasts; nominally, ten thousand, but, counted fisherwise, thirteen thousand, herrings, besides provision for a five or six days' voyage. Leaving a hand or two in charge of the vessel, the majority of the crew are out in the smaller boats fishing.

The Dutch herring-fishery is usually pursued during the night. When the nets are in the water the boat is left, as we have seen in Dr. Bertram's excursion, to drift in the meantime. Each boat is furnished with a lantern, which serves the double purpose of attracting the shoals of fish, and preventing collisions with other boats. The herring-fishery is extremely capricious in its results; one or two boats have been known to carry into port the whole takings of a night. Valenciennes witnessed the capture of a hundred and ten thousand herrings in less than two hours. The nets are hauled in when moderately charged with fish by the crew; but it is often necessary to have recourse to the capstan in the process. Some of the hands are stationed to detach the fish from the nets; others detach the nets from the buoys; while others again fold up and stow away the nets for future use.

On the coast of Norway the electric telegraph is applied to the herring-fishery, being employed to announce to the inhabitants of the fishing towns the approach of the shoals of fish. In the fiords of Norway, where the produce of the herring-fishery is the principal means of excitement to nearly the entire population, it often happened that the fish made its appearance at the most unexpected times, and on some parts of the coast the shoals could only be met by one or two boats. Before the boats from the bays and fiords could take part in the fishery the herrings had deposited their spawn, and returned to the open sea.

To prevent these disappointments, often repeated with great loss to the fishermen, the Norwegian government established, in 1857, a submarine electric cable, along the coast frequented by the herrings, of a hundred miles, with stations on shore at intervals conveniently placed for communicating with the villages inhabited by the fishermen. As soon as a shoal of herrings is known to be in the offing, and they can always be perceived at a considerable distance by the wave they raise, a telegraph is despatched along the coast, which makes known in each village the approach to the bay in which the herrings have established themselves.

This important branch of industry has only assumed its real character since the fourteenth century, and its sudden and prodigious extension is due to the discovery of a simple Dutch fisherman, George Benkel, who died in 1397. To this man Holland owes much of its wealth. He discovered, in short, the art of curing the herring so as to preserve it for an indefinite time. From that moment the herring-fishery assumed an unexpected importance, and became the source of much wealth to Holland and its industrious and enterprising people. Two hundred years after his death the Emperor Charles V. solemnly ate a herring on Benkel's tomb; it was a small homage paid to the memory of the creator of a new industry which had enriched his native land.

The Shad (*Alosa*), which have the body round and more plump than the herring, are still more distinguishable by the arrangement of their teeth. More than twenty species of this genus are known, varying considerably in size. They inhabit the seas which wash the coasts of Europe, Africa, India, and America. One type is the Common Shad, *Alosa communis* (Fig. 383), which is found in the Channel, the North Sea, and all round our coast. It is of a silvery tint generally, greenish on the back, with one or two black spots behind the gills. The shad approaches the mouths of rivers and great estuaries, and habitually ascends them in the spring for the purpose of depositing its ova, and is found at this season in the Rhine, the Seine, the Garonne, the Volga, the Elbe, and many of our own rivers. In some of the Irish rivers the masses of shad taken in the seine-net have been so great that no amount of exertion has been sufficient to land them. It sometimes attains a very considerable size, weighing as much as from four to six pounds. The shad taken at sea are less delicate in their flesh than those caught in fresh water. The habits of the shad are very imperfectly known. Two species are found on the British coast, namely, the Twaite Shad of Yarrell (*Alosa finta*), which is about fourteen inches in length, brownish green on the back, inclining to blue in certain lights, the rest of the body silvery white, with five

Fig. 383. The Shad (Alosa communis).

or six dusky spots on each side arranged longitudinally. The jaws are furnished with distinct teeth; the tail deeply forked.

The second species, the Common or Allise Shad (*C. communis*), is considerably larger, sometimes attaining twelve and even fifteen inches in length, having only one spot on each side of the body near the head; the jaws without teeth, the scales small in proportion. This species is plentiful in the Severn, but rare in the Thames.

The shad is found in the Severn and Thames in considerable quantities about the second week in July. They reach the fresh water about May, deposit their spawn, and return to salt water in July. Their scales are large.

The Sprat (*C. spratus*) has been the subject of a great controversy like the parr—one party contending that it is the young of the herring; another, that it is a distinct species. Pennant, Yarrell, and many eminent naturalists adopt the first view: its specific characters, according to Pennant, being "greater depth of body than the young herring, gill-covers not veined; teeth of the lower jaw so small as to be scarcely visible to the touch; the dorsal fin placed far back, and the sharp edge of the abdomen more acutely serrated than in the herring." Like the herring, they inhabit the deep water during the summer, following the shoal to the sea-shore in autumn. The sprat-fishing commences in November and continues during the winter months, when they are caught in such numbers that in some localities they have been used as manure.

In support of the individuality of the sprat, the serrated belly and relative position of the fins are dwelt upon, together with the instance detailed by Mr. Mitchell, the Belgian consul at Leith, who exhibited a pair of sprats, having the roe and milt fully developed.

On the other hand, the abundance of the sprat has been adduced as a reason for its being the young herring. In addition to this, anatomists declare their anatomy shows no difference but size. "As to the serrated belly," says Bertram, "we may look on that as we do on the back of a child's frock, namely, as a provision for growth." If this is so, Dr. Bertram supplies material at once for thought and legislation. "The slaughter of sprats," he says, "is as decided a case of killing the goose with the golden eggs as the grilse slaughter carried on in our salmon rivers."

The Pilchard, *Clupea pilchardus* (Fig. 384), sometimes called the gipsy herring, visits our coasts all the year round. It was at one time thought, as the herring was, to be migratory, but, like that fish, it is now found to be a native of our own seas, and a constant inhabitant of our shores. It has been known to spawn in May, but the usual time is October, and authorities like Mr. Couch think it breeds only once a year. Its visit to shallow water causes immense excitement; persons watch night and day from the lofty cliffs along the Cornwall coast, and the watchers (locally called "huers") signal the boats at sea beneath them the moment they see indications of the approach of a shoal. Mr. Wilkie Collins gives an animated picture of the "huer:" "A stranger in Cornwall, taking his first walk along the cliffs in August, could not advance far without witnessing what would strike him as a very singular and even alarming phenomenon. He would see a man standing on the extreme edge of a precipice just over the sea, gesticulating in a very remarkable manner, with a bush in his hand, waving it to the right and to the left, brandishing it over his head, sweeping it past his feet; in short, acting the part apparently of a maniac of the most dangerous description. It would add considerably to the stranger's surprise if he were told that the insane individual before him was paid for flourishing the bush at the rate of a guinea a week. And if he advanced a little, so as to obtain a nearer view of the madman, and observed a well-manned boat below turning carefully to the right and left, as the bush turned, his mystification would

Fig. 384. The Pilchard (Clupea pilchardus).

probably be complete, and his ideas as to the sanity of the inhabitants would be expressed with grievous doubt.

"But a few words of explanation would make him alter his opinion. He would learn that the man was an important agent in the pilchard-fishery of Cornwall, that he had just discovered a shoal swimming towards the land, and that the men in the boats were guided by his gesticulations alone in their arrangements for securing the fish on which so many depend for a livelihood."

The pilchard, which is the sardine of commerce, where its place is not usurped by the sprat, is taken chiefly in the Channel, on the coasts of Brittany and Cornwall, and in the Mediterranean, and on the coast of Sardinia, whence its commercial name. In Brittany floating-nets are employed. The fishing is conducted in boats, each carrying five men;

thousands of these boats may sometimes be seen engaged at the same time three or four leagues from the coast, the nets being only drawn when they are fully charged, when the fish are arranged bed upon bed in osier baskets, each boat returning habitually to port when it has secured twenty-five thousand fishes. The fishery extends over five or six months, the produce being about six hundred millions of sardines.

The Basque fishermen employ a net in the form of a sack, with rings at each corner.

On the coast of Cornwall, as we have hinted, it is one of the staple industries, and pursued systematically. Where they come from, and whither they go, seems alike unknown. All that is certain is, that they are met with in shoals swimming past the Scilly Islands as early as July. In August the inshore fishing begins, and they appear on various parts of the coast as far north as Devonshire and the south coast of Ireland up to October and November; no doubt those which have escaped the innumerable nets spread for them.

"The first sight from the cliffs of a shoal of pilchards," says Mr. Collins, in the work already quoted, "is not a little interesting. They produce on the sea the appearance of the shadow of a dark cloud, which approaches until you can see the fish leaping and playing on the surface by hundreds at a time, all huddled close together, and so near the shore that they can be caught in fifty or sixty feet of water. Indeed, when the shoals are of considerable magnitude, the fish behind have been known literally to force the fish in front up to the beach, so that they could be taken in baskets, or even with the hand.

"With the discovery of the first shoal, the active duties of the look-out, or huer, on the cliffs begin. Each fishing village places one or more of these men on the watch all round the coast. He is, therefore, not only paid his guinea a week while he is on the watch, but a percentage on the produce of all the fish taken under his auspices. He is placed at his post, where he can command an uninterrupted view of the sea some days before the pilchards are expected.

"The principal boat used is, at least, of fifteen tons burden, and carries a large net called the 'seine,' which measures a hundred and ninety fathoms in length, and costs a hundred and twenty pounds—sometimes more. It is simply one long strip from eleven to thirteen fathoms in breadth, composed of very small meshes, and furnished all along its length with cork at one edge and lead at the other. The men who cast this net are called 'shooters,' and receive eleven shillings and sixpence a week, and one basket of fish out of every haul.

"As soon as the 'huer' discerns a shoal he waves his bush. The signal is conveyed to the beach by men and boys watching near him. The 'seine'-boat, accompanied by another, to assist in casting the net, is rowed out to where he can see it; then there is a pause and hush of expectation. Meanwhile the devoted pilchards press on—a compact mass of thousands on thousands of fish—swimming to meet their doom. All eyes are fixed on the 'huer;' he stands watchful and still, until the shoal is thoroughly embayed in water which he knows to be within the depth of the 'seine.' Then, as the fish begin to pause in their progress and gradually crowd closer and closer together, he gives the signal, and the 'seine' is cast or 'shot' overboard.

"The grand object is now to enclose the entire shoal. The leads sink one side of the net perpendicularly to the bottom, the corks buoy the other to the surface of the water. When it has been taken all round the shoal, the two extremities are made fast, and the fishes are imprisoned within an oblong barrier of netting. The art is how to let as few of the pilchards escape as possible while the process is being completed. Whenever the 'huer' observes that they are startled, and separating at any particular point, he waves his bush, and thither the boat is steered, and there the net is shot at once; the fish are thus headed and thwarted in every direction with extraordinary address and skill. This labour completed, the silence of intense expectation that has hitherto prevailed is broken—there is a shout of joy on all sides—the shoal is secured.

"The 'seine' is now regarded as a great reservoir of fish. It may remain in the water a week or more; to secure it against being moved from its position, in case a gale should come on, it is warped by two or three ropes to points of land in the cliff, and is at the same time contracted in circuit by its opposite ends being brought together and passed lightly over its breadth for several feet. While these operations are being performed, another boat, another set of men, and another net, are approaching the scene of action.

"The new net is called the 'tuck;' it is smaller than the 'seine;' inside which it is to be let down for the purpose of bringing the fish close to the surface. The men who manage this net are called 'regular sewers.' The boat is first of all rowed inside the seine-net, and laid close to the seine-boat, which remains stationary outside. To its bows one rope at the end of the tuck-net is fastened. The tuck-boat now slowly makes the inner circle of the seine, the smaller net being dropped overboard, and attached to the seine at intervals as she goes. To prevent the fish from getting between the two nets during the operation, they are frightened into the middle of the enclosure by beating the water with oars, and stones fastened to ropes. When the 'tuck' has at length travelled round the whole circle of the 'seine,' and is securely fastened to the seine-boat at the end as it was at the beginning, everything is prepared for the great event of the day—hauling the fish to the surface.

"Now all is excitement on sea and shore; every little boat in the place puts off, crammed with idle spectators; boys shout, dogs bark, and the shrill voices of the former are joined by the deep voices of the 'seiners.' There they stand, six or eight stalwart, sun-burnt fellows, ranged in a row in the seine-boat, hauling with all their might at the 'tuck'-net, and roaring out the nautical 'Yo, heave ho!' in chorus. Higher and higher rises the net; louder and louder shout the boys and the idlers; the 'huer,' so calm and collected hitherto, loses his self-possession, and waves his cap triumphantly. 'Hooray! hooray! Yoy—hoy, hoy! Pull away, boys! Up she comes! Here they are!' The water boils and eddies; the 'tuck'-net rises to the surface; one teeming, convulsed mass of shining, glancing, silvery scales; one compact mass of thousands of fish, each one of which is madly striving to escape, appears in an instant. Boats as large as barges now pull up, in hot haste, all round the nets, baskets are produced by dozens, the fish are dipped up in them, and shot out, like coals out of a sack, into the boats. Presently the men are ankle-deep in pilchards; they jump upon the benches, and work on till the boats can hold no more. They are almost gunwale under before they leave for the shore."

In the process of curing, the scene becomes doubly picturesque, but this is shore-work, with which our space forbids us to deal.

"Some idea of the almost incalculable multitude of pilchards caught on the Cornwall shores," says Mr. Collins, "may be gathered from the following data: At the small fishing cove of Trereen six hundred hogsheads were taken in little more than a week, during August,

1850. Allowing two thousand four hundred fish only to each hogshead (three thousand would be the highest calculation), we have a result of one million four hundred and forty pilchards caught by the inhabitants of one little village alone, on the Cornish coast, at the commencement of the season's fishing."

The Anchovy (*Engraulis*) is chiefly taken in the Mediterranean, and is much sought after for its delicate flavour when salted and cured. It is a small, slender fish, about four to four and a half inches in length; head pointed, mouth very wide, gill-openings large, abdomen smooth; when living, it is greenish on the back, silvery beneath; after death it changes to a bluish black. The fishery which gives the most abundant results takes place on the shores of the Mediterranean, principally on the coast of Sicily, the isles of Elba, Corsica, Antibes, Frejus, Saint-Tropez, and Cannes. They are also taken on the Dalmatian coast, and in the neighbourhood of Ragusa.

The anchovy is only fit for food after being preserved and salted. The process of curing commences by throwing it into a strong brine; then, the head and entrails being removed, they are arranged in rows in barrels or boxes of tin, in alternate layers of salt and fish; finally, after some days of exposure, they are hermetically closed and despatched to market. Those prepared on the Provençal coast were formerly carried to the fair of Beaucaire, whence they found their way all over France, and to many parts of Europe. Now, the anchovies cured at Marseilles, and other Provençal ports, are sent direct to the various markets of Europe.

The Acanthopterygeans

Include the Perch family, which is altogether a fresh-water fish, and, however interesting in itself, foreign to our present purpose. It includes also the cat-fish, which is also known as the *bar*, and more commonly the wolf-fish, in Bas-Languedoc and Provence. It is common in the Mediterranean, and in many of the great rivers which empty themselves into it. The Cat-fish (Fig. 385) has the appearance of an elongated perch: its colour, in the adult state, is of a uniform silvery hue, marked with brown and yellow spots in the young.

The Weevers (*Trachinus*), forming another division of this family, are characterised by their very compressed head and the strong spines of the operculum. They are elongated in shape, with short muzzles; they have a habit of burying themselves in the sand, and are formidable

Fig. 385. The Cat-fish.

to fishermen, from the dangerous wounds they inflict with their spines. *Trachinus communis* (Fig. 386) is widely diffused in the Atlantic and Mediterranean.

Fig. 386. The Weever-fish (Trachinus communis).

The genus *Uranoscopus*, so named from the position of their eyes, which are directed towards the sky, from *οὐρανὸς*, the heavens, and *σκοπέω*, I regard. From this peculiar arrangement, they can only see above them. They are closely connected with the cat-fish. *Uranoscopus vulgaris* (Fig. 387) belongs to the Mediterranean, and is remarkable for its thick cubical head and erect spiny dorsal fins.

The Mullets (*Mullus*) have the body thick and oblong, the profile of the head approaching the vertical line; scales large, two dorsal fins, widely separated—the rays of the first spinous, of the second, flexible; two cirri at the lower jaw. Two species are known, both inhabitants of our west and south-west coasts: the Red or Striped

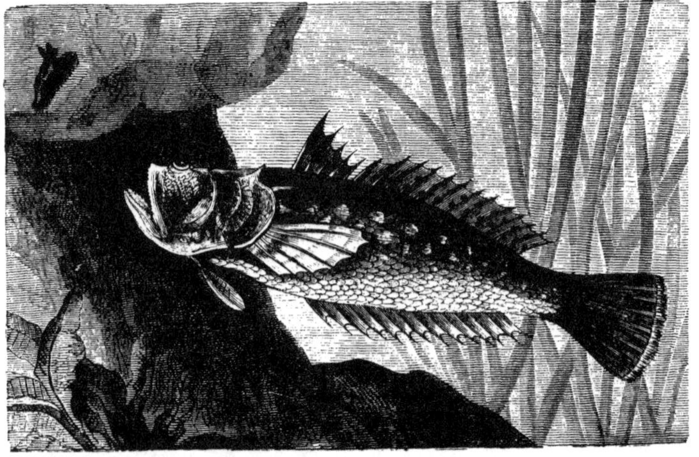

Fig. 387. Uranoscopus vulgaris.

Surmullet (*Mullus surmulus*), and the Red Mullet (*M. barbatus*). The first is a fine bright vermilion red, with three dominating yellow lines; the throat, breast, ventral, and lower surface of the tail are white, slightly tinged with rose; the fins have their rays more or less red, the iris of the eyes a pale gold colour, just touched with red; the head bears two barbels. This beautiful fish is plentiful in the Mediterranean and sometimes in the Channel, common in the gulfs of Gascony, and is frequently served on the table at Bordeaux and Bayonne, where it is known as the barbel; its flesh is a little flaky, of an agreeable flavour, but less esteemed than the red mullet.

The Red Mullet (*Mullus barbatus*) is clothed in brilliant colours of bright red, mingling with silvery tints upon the side and belly; it presents fine indistinct reflections, but none of the yellow lines which occur in the preceding species. It is to its brilliant colouring that the red mullet owes much of its celebrity. When we add that its flesh is white, firm, and agreeable to the taste, the estimation in which it was held by the ancients is sufficiently explained. With the Romans the mullet was an object of luxury on which they expended fabulous sums; they cultivated the fish in their fish-ponds not only as a delicacy of the table, but for the beauty of form and colour. This fierce love of beauty, however, too often approached to cruelty. Seneca and Pliny both give us to understand that the rich patricians of Rome gave themselves the barbarous pleasure of seeing the mullet expire under their eyes, in order to witness the various shades of purple, violet, and blue which succeed each other—from cinnabar red to the palest white, as the animal gradually loses its strength, and expires by a slow and cruel death. The great rival of Cicero, the advocate Hortensius, who attracted crowds of people to the Forum by his eloquent and elegant discourses, had an inordinate passion for this kind of enjoyment. These little inhabitants of the waters were led by a small canal which was carried under the festive table, and his great enjoyment was to witness the agonies of the unhappy fish just taken from its native element and carried to the table, palpitating with its dying convulsions, as it perished beneath his eyes, he in the meanwhile enjoying a sumptuous banquet. The possession of these poor creatures had, in short, become the rage, a furious passion, and their price soon became excessive. A fish of three pounds produced a considerable sum to the fortunate fisherman, while one of four and a half pounds was simply ruinous, says Martial. Asinius Gelius purchased one for eight thousand sesterces (upwards of sixty pounds). Under Caligula, according to Suetonius, three mullets cost thirty thousand sesterces (about two hundred and forty pounds). Although it is no longer the object of ferocious enjoyment, on the one hand, or prodigal expenditure on the other, it is still much sought after, both for its beauty of form and excellent table qualities. It is found in many seas, but particularly in the Mediterranean, where it is taken all round the coast, usually in muddy bottoms; it is fished for both by line and net.

The Gurnards (*Trigla*) are remarkable for the singular manner in which the head is mailed and cuirassed; the operculum and shoulder-bones are armed with spines, having trenchant blades, which give them a disagreeable, even a hideous, physiognomy, and has procured them various names, such as sea-frog, sea-scorpion, sea-devil, and sundry other equally significant names. With this forbidding appearance, however, the gurnards are among the most resplendent inhabitants of the sea. Nothing can exceed the beauty of their markings; but the brilliancy with which Nature has gifted them is their misfortune; it betrays them to their enemies, which are found in the air as well as in the water, and without their prodigious fecundity this species would long since have disappeared.

Fig. 388. The Red Gurnard (Trigla pini).

Twelve species of Trigla are known. In the British seas the commonest species is the Grey Gurnard (*Trigla gurnardus*), a silvery-grey fish, more or less clouded with brown and speckled with black. A rare species with us, but very common in the Mediterranean, is the Red Gurnard, *Trigla pini* (Fig. 388). It is of a fine bright rose-red colour,

Plate XXX.—Agony of a Red Mullet at the Feast of Hortensius.

paler beneath and more vivid about the fins, of which there are two distinct dorsal and one ventral. Beneath the pectorals are three detached rays; both jaws and front of the lower palate are armed with fine velvety teeth. The Perlon, or Sapharine Gurnard (*T. hirundo*), is a large and handsome fish, remarkable for the lively green and blue hues of the inner surface of its large pectoral fins.

The Flying Gurnard (*Dactylopterus volitans*) somewhat resembles the Triglas, but differs in having the fin-rays of the pectorals connected by membranes, by which it is enabled to support itself some time in the air, like the flying-fish; the pectorals, when extended,

Fig. 389. The Flying Gurnard (Dactylopterus volitans).

forming a sort of parachute (Fig. 389), which sustains it when it leaps out of the water. Several species are known.

All nature seems to conspire against these singular creatures, while they have been gifted with the double power of swimming and flying. The flying-fish only escapes from the Bonitas, and other voracious fishes which pursue it on the bosom of the sea, to expose itself to the attacks of the inhabitants of the air. A crowd of sea-fowls, such as frigate-birds, the albatross, and the gulls, carry on a bloody war with them when they venture on flight. War thus pursues the unhappy fish whatever element it betakes itself to. Nevertheless it passes from one element to the other, with an energy which frequently defeats the attacks of its enemies. When it leaps from the sea to the height of five or six feet, it sustains itself for several hundred feet, changing its direction. In its flight it may be compared to that of the flying dragon; the popular name given to it is said to be derived from the grunting noise they make on being taken out of the water.

LABYRINTHIFORM PHARYNGEANS.

In the fishes of this order the superior pharyngeal bones are divided into numerous and irregular little leaflets, which intersect the cellules situated under the operculum, which again serve to retain a certain quantity of water. This water preserves the gills, however, when the animal is dry, which permits them to live on shore, where they frequently contrive to creep over great distances in search of water. The genus *Anabas*, from *ἀναβαίνω*, to ascend, possess this peculiarity of organization in a remarkable degree; it enables them to leave the rivers and marshes and little watercourses of Borneo and Java, and other islands of the Indian Archipelago, and creep through the herbage or along the ground by means of the inflexions of their bodies, the dentation of their opercules, of their spines and fins. This fact, although only recently known to modern naturalists, was well known to the ancients, and has been recorded by Theophrastus.

The family of the SCOMBEROIDES is the most important group in the order, comprehending some of the fishes most useful to man, from their size, the excellence of their flesh, and their abundance. The Tunny (*Thynnus*, Cuv.), the Mackerel (*Scomber scombrus*), and the Bonita (*Thynnus pelamys*), have yielded, from the remotest antiquity, immense resources as human food, both in the fresh and preserved state.

The tunny, while resembling the mackerel in many respects in its general form, is rounder, and attains a much larger size, being sometimes found eight and nine feet in length, and weighing three to four hundred pounds. The upper part of the body is a bluish-black; the belly is grey, with silvery spots. These fishes sometimes present themselves in the Atlantic, but in the Mediterranean they are very abundant. At some periods of the year they approach the coast in innumerable shoals, and in numerous serried ranks, forming a vast battalion, which conceals itself under the waves, and only betrays itself on the exterior by the motion of the sea, caused by such vast numbers travelling rapidly through the water. In many localities the shoals of tunnies show themselves in the spring, pursuing their way towards the east, and in the autumn we find them pursuing an opposite direction. We see the same thing on the coast of Provence. Upon the coast of La Ciotat a first fishing takes place from the months of March to July, and a second again from July to October. But at other points of the coast they arrive at the same time from very different directions. Besides, finally, it is only in winter that they are found.

The tunny-fishing goes back to the remotest antiquity. The Phœnicians, the first navigators known, carried it on on the coast of Spain. In our days the fishing is carried on with great activity on the coasts of Provence, of Sardinia, and Sicily.

The fishing is carried on by the tunny-net, and in Provence it is fished with a net in the enclosure called the *madrague.*

The tunny-net consists of a combination of nets, which is quickly cast into the sea in order to head the tunnies at the moment of their passage. When the sentinels, posted for the purpose, as in the pilchard-fishery, have signaled the approach of a shoal of tunnies and its direction, by the indications of a flag which points to the spot occupied by the finny tribe, the fishing-boats are immediately directed to the designated spot, and ranged in curved lines, forming with the light floating net a half circular enclosure, turned towards the shore, the interior of which is called the *garden.* The tunnies thus enclosed in this garden, between the coast and the net, become agitated with terror. As they advance towards the shore they press upon the enclosure, or rather a new interior enclosure is formed with other nets held in reserve. In this second enclosure an opening is left, through which the tunnies have to pass. In continuing thus to diminish the space by successive enclosures, each occupies a smaller diameter, in which the fish are enclosed in about a fathom and a half of water. At this moment a species of seine-net is thrown into the garden. This net is hauled into shallow water by force of arms, and the small tunnies are taken by the hand, the larger by hooks. The boats are charged with them, and they are carried ashore. A single day's fishing will sometimes produce as many as sixteen thousand tunnies, each from twenty to five and twenty pounds weight.

When the park, in place of being established for a single fishery, is a permanent construction in the sea, it is called, in Provence, a madrague. The madrague is a vast enclosure. The netting which forms the partitions of its chambers are sustained by buoys of cork on the surface, and kept down by heavy stones and other weights on the lower edge, and maintained in this position by cords, one extremity of which is attached to the net, and the other is moored to an anchor. The madrague is intended to arrest the shoals of tunnies at the moment when they abandon the shore in order to return to the open sea. For this purpose a long alley or run is established between the sea-shore and the park or madrague. The tunnies follow this alley, and, after passing from chamber to chamber, betake themselves at last to the body of the park.

In order to force them into the madrague they are pressed towards the shore by means of a long net, which is extended in their rear attached to two boats, each of which sustain one of the upper angles of the net. When the fishes come to the last compartment, the fishermen raise a horizontal net, which makes a sort of plate of this compartment, in which the fishes are gradually raised to the surface of the water. This operation occupies the whole night.

In the morning the tunnies are collected in a very narrow space, and at varying distances from the shore; and now the carnage commences. The unhappy creatures are struck with long poles, boat-hooks, and other weapons. The tunny-fishing presents a very sad spectacle at this its last stage; fine large fish perish under the blows of a multitude of fishermen, who pursue their bloody task with most dramatic effect. The sight of the poor creatures, some of them wounded and half dead, trying in vain to struggle with their ferocious assailants, is very painful to endure. The sea, red with blood, long preserves traces of this frightful carnage, of which an illustration is attempted in Pl. XXXI.

The flesh of the tunny is much esteemed, being firm and wholesome. It is called the salmon of Provence. "For our part," says M. Figuier, "we put it far above the salmon. Nothing is comparable to the fresh tunny thrown into a hot frying-pan, and sprinkled with vinegar and salt. When properly cooked, nothing can be more firm or savoury. In short, nothing of the kind can rival, or even be compared, with the tunny, as we find it at Marseilles and Cette."

Plate XXXI.—Fishing for Tunny at Madrigue, on the Coast of Provence.

The tunny is greatly celebrated among the Greeks and other inhabitants on the shores of the Mediterranean, of the Propontus, and the Black Sea. The Romans attached great value to certain parts of this fish, as the head and the lower part of the belly. The neighbouring parts were in little esteem with them. They cut them into pieces and preserved them in vases filled with salt. They are now preserved with oil and salt after being cooked; this preparation is in great request at Cette, Montpellier, and Marseilles. With a pot of marine tunny, salted in the vinegar of Lunel, a household is pretty well prepared for any event.

The Mackerel (*Scomber scombrus*) is too well known to require description. Who has not admired these fishes, with their steel-blue

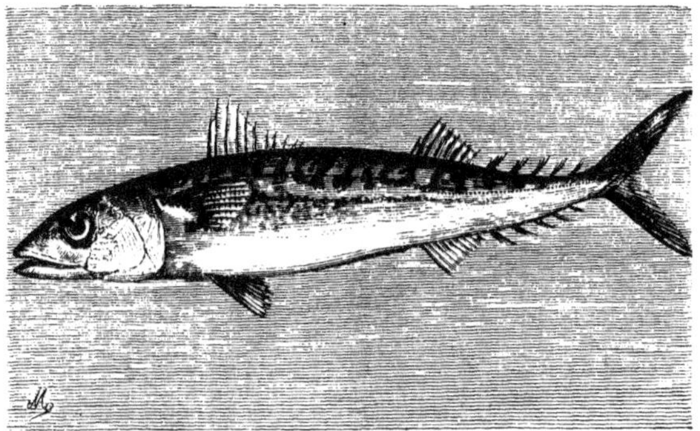

Fig. 390. The Mackerel (Scomber scombrus).

back, and changing iridescent sides of gold and purple and green, relieved by fine waving lines of deeper black, as they appear on the market-stalls, or as they are emptied in the early morning from the fishing-boat? The head is blue above, with black markings, the rest of the body being raised with iridescent shades of gold and purple.

There are two species of mackerel—that of the Atlantic and of the Channel, which has no swimming-bladder, *Scomber scombrus* (Fig. 390), and the mackerel of the Mediterranean, *Scomber coleas,* which has the swimming-bladder, and which is a very rare fish in our seas.

The mackerel is common to all European seas: being the *Veirat* of the Bay of Languedoc; the *Aurion* of Provence; the *Bretal* in some parts of Brittany; the *Macarello* of the modern Romans; the *Scombro* of the Venetians; the *Lacesto* of the Neapolitans; the *Cavallo* of the

Spaniards; the well-known Mackerel of our own shores, and the *Makril* of the Swedes; it is found on the coast of North America, and as far south as the Canary Islands. It is a wandering, unsettled fish, supposed to be migratory, but individuals are always found on our coast. They are supposed to remain during the winter in the North Sea, and afterwards on the coast of Scotland and Ireland in January and February, on their way to the Atlantic. There their great army is divided into two: one branch passes along the Spanish and Portuguese coasts, while the other enters the Channel. In May they appear on the coasts of England and France. In June they reach Holland. In July one portion of them returns to the Baltic, while another skirts the coast of Norway on its way to winter quarters.

Lacepede estimated that this migration, which is so regular, and its stages so rigorously indicated, was irreconcilable with a great number of very precise observations; and he arrived at the conclusion that the mackerel passes the winter at the bottom of the sea, more or less remote from the coast, which they again approach in the spring. At the commencement of the fine season they advance towards the shore which best agreed with them, showing themselves often on the surface, like the tunny, traversing the sea in courses more or less direct or sinuous, but never following the periodical circle which has been so ingeniously traced out for them.

Mr. Milne Edwards also remarks that, if these legions of fishes ascended from the Polar seas, they ought to visit the Orkneys before they appeared in the Channel, and enter the Mediterranean later in the season; but he is assured that they appear at the Orkneys late in the season. It appears, in short, that there are different varieties which haunt the several neighbourhoods in which they abound.

The largest mackerel are taken at the entrance of the Channel, but they are considered less delicate than the smaller fishes. The shoals of mackerel, it appears, never enter the Gulf of Gascony, but they abound along the shores of Brittany up to the North Sea. It is about the month of April that they begin to be met with, but they are still small and without milt or roe. In the months of June and July the fish is in its most perfect state. Towards the end of September and October mackerel of the same year's birth are taken; finally, in November and December, the fishermen still fish them, and send them to market, but this is an irregularity, and the fishermen of

Lowestoft and Yarmouth take their great harvest in May and June. In the Firth of Forth, and on the north coast of Scotland, at a few weeks later.

As mackerel are very voracious, they greedily devour all sorts of bait, but they are chiefly taken by the drift-net. The drift-net is twenty feet deep and a hundred and twenty feet long, well buoyed at the upper edge, but without weights at the bottom. The meshes, made of fine twine tanned to a reddish colour for preservation, are calculated to admit the head of the fish and catch it by the gills, so as to prevent its withdrawal. A fleet of mackerel-boats dragging these large nets, which are extended vertically in the sea, or float between the two tides, are well represented in Pl. XXXII.

The flesh of the mackerel is fat and melting. Among the ancients a liquid was extracted from this fat called *garum*, which was considered a very nourishing preparation. The price of this liquid was very high; in modern measures it was valued at about sixteen shillings the pint. It was acrid, half putrefied, and very nauseous, but it had the property of rousing the appetite and stimulating the digestive organs. Garum played the part of a condiment at a period when the exciting array of Indian spices were unknown. Seneca charges it, as we do pepper and other hot spices taken in excess, with destroying the stomach and health of gourmands. This garum is spoken of by the traveller Pierre Belon, writing in the sixteenth century, as being held in great estimation at Constantinople in his time. Rondelet, the author of a very remarkable book published in 1554, who ate garum at the table of William Pellicier, Bishop of Maguelonne, thought he could trace the liquid not to the mackerel, but to one of the Sparoïdes (*Sparus smaris*).

The mackerel possesses phosphorescent properties which cause it to shine in the dark, especially after death, when decomposition has commenced, for it is of an oily consistence.

The mackerel is not only voracious, but, in spite of their small size, they have the hardihood to attack fishes much larger and much stronger than themselves. It is even said that they love human flesh. According to the naturalist bishop, Pontoppidan, who lived in the sixteenth century, a sailor belonging to a vessel which had cast anchor in one of the Norwegian ports, when bathing one day in the sea, was assailed by a shoal of mackerel. His companions came to his relief;

the eager band were repulsed with great difficulty, but not till it was too late: the unfortunate sailor was so exhausted that he died a few hours after. By a fair enough retaliation Nature has surrounded the mackerel with numerous enemies; the larger inhabitants of the ocean eagerly devour them. Certain fishes, in appearance very weak, such as the muræna, fight them with great advantage.

Closely connected with the mackerel and other Scombridæ, we have the Bonita of the Tropics. This is a fish of considerable size,

Fig. 391. The Sword-fish (Xiphias gladius).

celebrated by its pursuit in great shoals of the flying-fish, of which we have already spoken. The Bonita (*Thynnus pelamys*) is not unlike the mackerel in shape, but less compressed, and upwards of twenty-five to thirty inches long. It is occasionally found on our coast, but only as an accidental visitor, for its true home is the Tropics. It is a beautiful fish of a fine blue colour.

The Sword-fish, *Xiphias gladius* (Fig. 391), so called from the upper jaw being elongated into a formidable spear or sword, was known to the ancients, and has borne the name which recalls its salient characteristic from very early times. In short, it is recog-

Plate XXXII.—Fishing for Mackerel off the Cornwall Coast.

nised at a glance from its organic structure, and from the resemblance of its prolonged horizontal and trenchant muzzle to the blade of a sword. With the ancients it was Ξιφίας, and *Gladius;* with the moderns it is the sword-fish, the *Dart*, the *Spece spada*, and *l'Espadon épée*.

This fish attains a great size, being found in the Mediterranean and Atlantic, in company with the tunny, from five to six feet in length. Its body is lengthy, and covered with minute scales, the sword forming three-tenths of its length. On the back it bears a single long dorsal fin; the tail is keeled, the lower jaw is sharp, the mouth toothless, the upper part of the fish bluish-black, merging into silver beneath. It seems to have a natural desire to exercise towards and against all the arm with which Nature has furnished it; it darts with the utmost fury upon the most formidable moving bodies; it attacks the whale; and there are numerous and well authenticated instances of ships being perforated by the jaw of this powerful creature.

In 1725, some carpenters having occasion to examine the bottom of a ship, which had just returned from the Tropical seas, found the lance of a sword-fish buried deep in the timbers of the ship. They declared that, to drive a pointed bolt of iron of the same size and form to the same depth, would require eight or nine blows of a hammer weighing thirty pounds. From the position of the weapon it was evident that the fish had followed the ship while under full sail; it had penetrated through the metal sheathing, and three inches and a half beyond, into the solid frame.

The sword-fish has obstinate combats with the saw-fish, and even the shark, and it is supposed that when he attacks the bottom of a vessel he takes that sombre mass for the body of an enemy. But this terrible jouster, this Paladin of the abyss, often becomes himself the prey of a most contemptible enemy. A miserable little parasite, the *Pennatula filesa*, penetrates its flesh, and almost drives it mad with pain.

The flesh of the young sword-fish is white, compact, and of excellent taste; that of adults resembles the tunny. It is the object of a fishery of some importance in the Straits of Messina. The fishermen of Messina and Reggio join in this fishery with a great number of boats, carrying brilliant flambeaus, while one of the crew is stationed at the mast-head to announce the approach of the sword-fish. At a given signal the boats rush on to attack them with the harpoons (Fig. 392). During this fishery the sailors sing a peculiar melody, but without words.

The family of *Pediculate Pectorals* is so named from the fishes of which it is composed bearing their pectoral fins on a species of arm which forms a prolongation of the carp bone; it includes the Frog-fish, remarkable for the excessive circumference of the head and shoulders as compared to the rest of the body, the immense opening of a jaw, armed with pointed teeth, and the cutaneous jagged stripes

Fig. 392. Fishing for Sword-fish in the Straits of Messina.

of various lengths with which it bristles at many points. Its skin is soft, smooth, and without scales or other asperities; the members which support the pectorals, and other peculiarities, combine to render it a hideous and forbidding object, well calculated in ignorant and superstitious times to frighten the multitude. The remains of this fish, prepared in such a manner as to be transparent and rendered luminous by a lamp enclosed in its interior, has often helped to deceive and frighten the timid by its fantastic appearance.

The Frog-fish, *Lophius piscatorius*—Linn. (Fig. 393), which attains the length of five or six feet, lives in the sand, or sunk in the mud, leaving the long and movable filaments with which the head is furnished to float in the water; the shreds which terminate them act as natural bait when they float about in different directions, from their resemblance to worms and other living creatures. The fishes which swim above them, and which they see very well by the assistance of their two eyes placed on the summit of the head, are attracted by these deceitful decoys. When the prey arrives near to the enormous

Fig. 393. The Frog-fish (Lophius piscatorius).

jaws, which are almost always wide open, it is engulfed and torn to pieces by its strongly-hooked teeth.

This manner of lying in ambush, and fishing, as it were, with a hook and line for fishes which its conformation does not permit it to pursue, has acquired for it the name of the frog-fish, which is sometimes given to it. It is found more or less in all parts of the Mediterranean and in many parts of the Atlantic, being frequently taken both in the Gulf of Gascony and in the Channel.

The family of *Labridæ* comprehends: I. The Wrasse (*Labrus*), a genus of fishes decked in the most lively colours; for the yellow, green, blue, and red, forming bands of spots, give the body the appearance of being enriched with brilliant metallic reflections. II. The *Julis*, of Risso, the Mediterranean species of which is remarkable for its fine violet colour, relieved on each side by an orange band.

Of the *Labridæ* we represent here, as a type of the family, the adult Green and Red Labrus (Fig. 394), varieties of the commonest species, called the sea-parrot, the body of each being oblong, clothed with large scales: a dorsal fin, frequently with membranous appendages, thick

Fig. 394. Adult Green and Red varieties of Labrus communis.

fleshy lips, and large conical teeth; cheeks and gill-covers clothed with scales; gill-covers smooth at the edges; three spines in the anal fin. In *Julis* the cheeks and gill-covers are without scales; in other respects they resemble *Labrus*.

Among the acanthopterygeous fishes we shall only notice the singular family of *Fistulariadæ*, or Pipe-fishes, so called from the extreme elongation of the fore part of the head, forming a tube, at the extremity of which is the mouth. Of this family, *Fistularia tabacaria*

(Fig. 395) may be considered the type. The tube of the muzzle is long and flat, and from the caudal fin springs a terminal filament nearly as long as the body. This species of pipe-fish is common at

Fig. 395. The Pipe-fish (*Fistularia tabacaria*).

the Antilles; it attains the length of about three feet, but its flesh is leathery and insipid. It feeds upon crustaceans and small fishes, which it drags from the interstices of the rocks and stones by means of its long and taper pipe.

We close our abbreviated history of the Ocean and such of the inhabitants with which it swarms as seemed most likely, from their habits and other peculiarities, to interest the readers, conscious of its many imperfections. Where every creature which moves and breathes in the watery world is so full of interest, it will not surprise the reader to learn that one of the editor's chief difficulties has been that of selection, his most painful task that of rejecting the vast mass of interesting matter he had necessarily to pass in review.

We have shown in the first chapter of this work that nearly three-fourths of the surface of the earth is bathed by the sea. Struck with this vast extent of ocean, a witty French writer says, "One is almost tempted to believe that our planet was specially created for fishes." They are, indeed, a very important part of creation; they form, as it were, a bond uniting the vertebrate to invertebrate animals. They have a more complicated organization than the other oceanic inhabitants, as they are also the most numerous, the most varied in form, and by far the most brilliant in colour, and the most active in their movements.

Pliny, the naturalist, describes ninety-four species of fishes. Linnæus has characterised four hundred and seventy-eight. The naturalists of the present day know upwards of thirteen thousand, a tenth of which are fresh-water fishes.

INDEX.

Abdominales, 552.
Acalephæ, or Sea Nettles, 197.
Acanthopterygians, 578.
Acclimatizing sponges, 116.
Acephalous Molluscs, 319.
Acetabuliferous Cephalopods, 445.
Achatina zebra, 401.
Actiniaria, 183.
——— dianthus, 191.
Æquerea violacea, 200.
Agalma rubra, 241. Its graceful appearance, 241. Its interior, 242.
Alcyonaria, 121.
Alcyonaria proper, 146.
Alcyonium digitatum, 146, 153.
Alise Shad, 572.
Alternate generation in the Biphora, 317.
Alveolina oblonga, 87.
Ambulacral appendages, 265.
Amiba diffluens, 77.
——— princeps, 77.
Ammodytes lancea, 529.
Anabas, 584.
Analysis of sea water, 17, 20.
Anatomy of the Carp, 495.
Anchovy (Engraulis), 578.
Ancient trilobite, 446.
Animalcules, their action, 12.
Antarctic Ocean, 5. Discoveries, 48, 54.
Antipathidæ, 150, 151.
Apiocrinus pentacrinus, 273.
Aplysia depilans, shell and animal, 408.
Apoda, 528.
Apolemia contorta, 243. Parts magnified, 244.
Aporous Madrepores, 152.
Appearance of the sea, 63.
Aquarium, the, 69.
Arctic Ocean, 11.
Argonauta, fables concerning it, 460. Aristotle's description, 460. Oppian's description, 461. His mistakes, 461. Rumphius, 461. Real history, 463. Madame Power's experiments, 463. Locomotive organs, 464.
Argonauta argo, shell and animal, 462.
——— papyracea, animal and shell, 464.
Aristotle's Lantern, 289, 291.
Ascidians, simple, social, and composite, 312.
Ascidia microcosmus, 312.
——— pedunculata, 313.
Aspergillum vaginiferum, 389.
Asteracanthion glacialis, 266.
Asterias, 262.
——— aurantiaca, 264.
——— rubens, 263.
Asterophyton verrucosum, 281.
Astrea punctifera, 157.
Atlantic Ocean, 4.
Atmospheric currents, 33.
Atolls and Atollons, 168.
Aurelia aurita, 201.
Azoic rocks, 64.

Bacterium termo, 100.
Baffin's Bay discovered, 48.

Baltic Sea, 8.
Barentz's discoveries, 48.
Barren reefs, 175.
Beale's adventure with a Cuttle-fish, 447.
Bed of coral, 130.
Behring's Straits, 48.
Beröe Forskahli, 257.
Berthelot's representation of the capture of a Cephalopod, 459.
Biphora, 316.
Birth of coralline larvæ, 135.
Bivalves, how united, 321.
Blue minyade, 195.
Bonitas, 583, 590.
Bonpland's account of the Electrical Eel, 531.
Boring Pholades, 380.
Botrylla, 313, 314.
Branch of Virgularia magnified, 145.
Branchial infusoria, 99.
Breathing in Molluscs, 307.
Brooke's sounding apparatus, 7.
Bryozoare Polypes, 136. Their organization, 307.
Buccinum senticosum, and B. undatum, 429.
Bulimus sultanus, 400, 401.
Bulla ampulla, B. oblonga, and B. nebulosa, 409.

Cabot's discoveries, 47, 546.
Calmar, the, 468.
Callianira, 259.
Campanulariæ, 230.
Cancale Oysters, 327.
Cape Horn, 4.
Cape Race, 10.
Carcharius vulgaris (the Shark), 508. Its description, 508. Destructive habits, 509. Immense power, 510. Its flesh coarse, 512. Superstitious devotions to, 512, 513.
Cardium hians, and C. Greenlandicum, 374.
Cardium aculeatum, C. edulis, and C. costatum, 375, 376.
Carnivorous Cephalopods, 449.
Cartilaginous fishes, 499.
Caryophillia cyathus, 153.
Cassidulina, 83.
Cassiopea Andromeda, 224.
Cassis glauca, C. rufa, C. canaliculata, and C. Madagascariensis, 425.
Cassis undata, 426.
Cat-fish, 579.
Celebrated Oyster eaters, 332.
Cephalopodous Mollusca, 445.
Cephalous Mollusca, 391.
Cerithium fasciatum, C. aluco, and C. giganteum, 432.
Cestidæ, 260.
Chancellor's discoveries, 47.
Chart of the Atlantic, 9.
Charybdis, whirlpool of, 46.
Chimæra arctica, 515.
Chiton magnificus, 438.
Chrysaora Gaudichaudi, 220.
Ciliate Infusoria, 103.
Circulating tubes in the Coral, 133.
Circulation of the ocean, 27.
Cirrotheutis Mülleri, 456.
Classic feast on the Corniche du Prado, at Marseilles, 293.
Cleodara cuspidata, 444.
——— lanceolata and C. compressa, 444.
Clupeadæ, 564.
Clypeaster rosaceus, 289.
Cocos Island, 171, 173.
Cod-curing, 548.
Cod-fish (Morrhua callarius), 545.
Cod-fisheries, 547.
Coffres (Ostracion), 525.
Colour of the sea, 13. Local causes of, 14. Effects of animalcules, 14. Algæ of rivers, 16.
Comatulæ, 277.
Comatula Mediterranea, 278.
Complicated organization of a polypier, 139.
Condylostoma patens, 105.
Conger Eels (Anguilla conger), 535.
Contents of a drop of water, 89.

Conus, principal forms of, 417.
Cook's discoveries, 48, 55.
Coral and living polypus, 131.
Coral fisheries, 139.
Coral islands, 22. Reefs, 23.
Coralline spicula, 132.
Corallines, 121.
Cornularia cornucopia, 146.
Corpuscles from which young polypiers emanate, 138.
Corystes cassivelaunus, male, 483. Female, 484.
Cothurnia pyxidiformis, 103.
Crabs, their habits, mode of attacking cocoa-nuts, 478. Travelling Crabs, 479. Propagation, 480.
Cramp-fish (Torpedo marmorata), 504.
Crinoïdea, 272.
Cruelty to Oysters, 334.
Crustaceans, 473. Their organization, 474. Breathing apparatus, 476. Destructive habits, 476.
Crystatella mucedo, 309.
Ctenophora, 200, 256.
Cultivation of Oysters, 337.
Currents of the ocean, their causes, 27, 31, 32. Bifurcation of currents, 37.
Cuttle-fish, 446. Described, 465. Its pigments, 464. Habits, 467.
Cyclobranchial gasteropods, their organization, 437.
Cyclones, 36.
Cyclopteris, 536.
Cyclostoma, 499.
Cydippa pilens, 259.
Cypræa, principal forms of, 418.
——— capensis, C. testudinaria, C. nucleus, and C. pantherina, 421.
Cypræa coccinella, 419.
——— tigris and animal, 419.
——— undata, C. zigzag, C. moneta, and C. Madagascariensis, 420.
Cytherea, principal forms of, 378.
——— geographica, 379.

Dab (Platessa limanda), 542.
Dactylopora cylindracea, 87.
Darwin's observations at Tierra del Fuego, 172.
——— theory of Coral islands, 24.
——— theory of subsidence, 172.
Daughter of the sea, 139.
Davis's discoveries, 47.
Dead men's fingers, 146.
Death in the ocean, 64.
Decapoda, their organization, 452.
Decomposition of Infusoria, 99.
De Haven's search for Franklin, 61.
Delphinula sphærula, 415.
Dendrophylla ramea, 162. Magnified, 163.
Density of salt water, 18.
Dentalina communis, 82.
Depth of the sea, 3.
Depths of oceanic storms, 66.
Diodon pilosus, 524.
Diphydæ, 244.
Disaster of the San Francisco, 36.
Discobolidæ, 536.
Discophora, 200.
Distribution of land and water, 3.
Dog-fish (Acanthias vulgaris), 513.
Donax trunculus, 323.
——— rugosus and D. denticulatus, 377.
Drag-net employed in Oyster fishing, 336.
Dujardin's discoveries, 81.
D'Urville's voyages, 48, 55. Adelia's Land, 56.
Dykes of Holland undermined, 385.

Early animal life, 64.
Echineis remora, 536, 537.
Echinodermata, 261.
Echinoidæ, 282. Armament, 282. Skeleton and masticating apparatus, 290.
Echinus esculentus, 286.
——— mamillatus, without spines, 284.
Echinus mamillatus, with spines, 283.
Edible Snails, 393.
Edwardsia calimorpha, 193.
Effects of hurricanes, 44.
Eggs of Sepia officinalis, 467.

Electrical Eel, 529.
Electrical properties of the Cramp-fish, 505. Organs described, 507.
Eledone moschatus, its habits, 454.
Encrinites, or Stone-lilies, 272.
Encrinus liliformis, 273.
Enderby's Land, 48.
Equinoctial currents, 34.
Eschara, 310.
Esocidæ, 559.
Euglenia viridis, 103.
European pentacrinus, 275.
Euryalina, 281.
Evaporation, 19. Its effects on the sea, 19.
Exocœtus exiliens, 561.
Expanding Coral, 137.
Experiments on the Physalia, 252.
Exuberance of life in the ocean, 65.

Fabularia descolithes, 87.
Falkland Islands, 168.
Fan Gorgon, magnified, 124.
Faujasina, 83.
File-fish (Balistes), 524.
First Oyster-eater, 330.
Fishes, their organization, 493. Locomotive apparatus, 494. Swimming bladder, 494. Breathing apparatus, 495. Sight, 496. Propagation, 498. Classification, 498.
Fishes' eye, 496.
——— teeth, 497.
Fishing for Coral, 140.
——— Electrical Eels with horses, 531.
Fishing for Halibut, 543.
——— Sponges, 115.
Flabellum pavoninum, 155.
Flaming Nautilus, 472.
Flat fishes, their organization, 538. Special properties, 538.
Flight of the Flying-fish, 562.
Flounders (Platessa flessus), 541.
Flustra foliacea, 310.
Flux of the waves, 41.
Flying-fish, 559, 561.
Flying Gurnard, 583.
Fog-banks, 30.
Foraminifera, 78.
Franklin's discoveries, 51.
Fringing reefs, 175, 176.
Frog-fish (Lophius), 593.
Fungia agariciformis, 160.
——— echinata, 159.
Fusus proboscidiferus, F. pagodus, and F. colus, 433.

Gadidæ, 544.
Galeolaria aurantiaca, 246.
Gathering of the waters, 13.
Generation of Star-fishes, 269.
Geographical distribution of Oysters, 329.
Gigantic Cephalopod stranded on the coast of Jutland, 458.
Globe-fish (Orthagoniscus mola), 522.
Gorgonia flabellum, 123.
——— verticellata, 125.
Gorgonidæ, 123.
Gosse's description of the Sea-urchin, 284.
Great barrier reef, 23.
Gulf of Mexico, 11.
Gulf Stream, 34.
Gurnards (Trigla), 582.
Gymnotus, its electrical properties, 530. Effect of its shock, 532.

Haddock (Morrhua æglefinus), 551.
Halibut, 543.
Hammerhead (Zygæna malleus,) 513, 514.
Hammerhead mollusc, 352.
Harpa imperialis, and H. articularis, 430.
——— ventricosa, 429.
Harpooning Holothuria, 297.
Helix citrina, and H. Stuartia, 400.
Hermit Crab, 486.
Herring, the, 564. Habits, 565. Fisheries, 567. Scotch fisheries, 568. Dutch fisheries, 568. A night at the herring fishery, 569. Norwegian fisheries, 570.
Holothuria lutea, 295.
——— fishery, 297.
Humboldt's researches, 533.
Hyalea gibbosa, and H. longirostris, 443.

Indian Ocean, 4.
Industrial occupation on the sea-shore, 67.
Inequalities of the sea basin, 11.
Infusoria, 89. Their numbers, 89. In the Ganges, 89. Species, 89. In blocks of ice, 90. Reproduction, 95.
Infusorial parasites, 97.
Isis corolloïdis, 126.
Isis hippuris, 127.

Jan Mayen's Island, 48.

Kane's, Dr., discoveries, 29, 53.
Kerguelen Island, 48.
Kraken, marvellous stories concerning, 457.

Labridæ, 594.
Labrus communis, 594.
Labyrinthiform Pharyngeans, 584.
Land and water, 3.
Legend of the first Mussel-fisher, 364.
——————— Sea-urchin, 282.
Life in the ocean, 63.
Limax rufus, 403.
Limpets, 438.
Lobsters, 490.
Loligo vulgaris, and L. Gahi, 469.
Lophias piscatorius, 593.
Lophobranchii, 526.
Luidia fragillissima, 271.
Lump-fish (Cyclopteris), 537.
————— (Raia clavata), 503.
Lunar tides, 39.
Lymnea stagnalis, 405.
Lymneans, 404. Their habits, 404. Organization, 404.

Mackerel, 587. Do they migrate, 588.
M'Clintock's discoveries, 52.
M'Clure's discoveries, 52.
Madreporidæ, 161.
Madrepora plantaginea, 164.
Madrique, a combination of nets, 586.
Maelström whirlpool, 46.
Malacopterygii, 528.
Malleus alba, 352.
——— vulgaris, 352.
Mantle in Molluscs, its uses, 321.
Marennes Oysters, 342.
Masticating apparatus, 290.
Mean depth of the sea, 3, 5.
Meandrina cerebriformis, 158.
Mediterranean Sea, 8.
Medusadæ, 197, 215.
Medway Oyster-beds, 330.
Meleagrina margaritifera, 353.
Metamorphoses in Infusoria, 98.
Microscopic forms of life, 65.
Millepora alcicornis, 166.
Milne Edwards' study, 68.
Minyadinians, 195.
Mitra episcopalis and M. papalis, 424.
Molluscoïda, 305. Organization, 306. Generation, 307.
Molluscs, 301. Their characteristics, 317.
Monade Lentille, 101.
Monodonta Australis, and M. labio, 415.
Monsoons, 37.
Montfort, Denis de, on the Kraken, 457.
Mounts Erebus and Terror, 59.
Mullet (Mullus), 580. A Roman luxury, 581.
Muræna, 533.
———— ponds, a passion with Roman patricians, 534.
Murex scorpio, and M. erinaceus, 431.
——— tenuispina, and M. haustellum, 430.
Muschelkalk rocks, 274.
Mussels, 361. Organization of, 362. Habits, 362. Localities, 363.
Mussels of Aiguillon Bay, 364
Mussel-piles in Aiguillon Bay, 366.
——————, with basket work, 367.
——— punt of Aiguillon, 365.
Mutilation of Infusoria, 99.
Mytilus edulus, 361.

Nacre, its composition, 353.
Nadir points, 40.
Nautilus pompilius, section with animal and without, 471.
Nephtys, 147.

New Caledonia, 176.
Noctiluca miliaris, 88.
Non-pulmonary Gasteropods, 407. Their organization, 407.
Nummulites, 80.
Nummulitis lenticularis, 83.
———— Rouaulti, 85.

Occulina flabelliformis, 155.
Octopus brevisses, and O. horridus, 454.
——— macropus, 453.
——— vulgaris, 453.
Olaüs Magnus on the Kraken, 457.
Oldhamia, 64.
Oliva erythrostoma, O. porphyria, O. irisans, and O. Peruviana, 423.
Operculina, 83.
Ophiocoma Russei, 280.
Ophiuradæ, 279.
Orbulina universa, 82.
Organization of Foraminiferæ, 88.
———— Infusoria, 92.
———— Sponges, 118.
———— Star-fishes, 262.
Ossei, or Bony fishes, 521.
Ostend Oysters, 329.
Ostreadæ (the Oyster), 324.
Oyster (Ostrea), 324. Its organization, 324. Reproduction, 326. Incubation, 327.
Oyster beds of France, 340.
——— beds on Lake Fusaro, 338, 339.
——— claires of Marennes, 342.
——— cultivation, 337.
——— eaters, 332.
——— farms at Whitstable, 344.
——— fishing, 335.
——— of different ages, 329.
Oyster packing system, 340.
Ovula oviformis, and O. cornea, 422.
—— volva, 423.

Pacific Ocean, 5.
Pagurus Bernhardus, 486.
Palinurus vulgaris, 481.
Pallas on Alcyonia, 147.
Pandore Oyster beds, 330.
Paramecium aurelia and its parasites, 97.
Paramecium Bursaria, 104.
Parr, or young Salmon, 554.
Parry's discoveries, 49.
Patella cærulea, P. umbella, P. granatina, and P. barbata, 439.
Patella longicosta, 440.
Paulin's submarine apparatus, 68.
Pearl fisheries, 354. Value of, 357.
Pearl Oyster, 353.
Pecten glaber, 347.
——— Japonica, 349.
——— opercularis, 348.
——— plica, 349.
——— pseudamussium, 347.
Pectenidæ, 345.
Pelagia noctiluca, 202.
Pelagic plants and animals, 66.
——— rivers, 34.
Pennatula spinosa, 143.
Pennatulidæ, 141.
Pentacrinus, 273.
———— caput Medusæ, 274.
———— Europæus, 276.
———— fasciculosus, 273.
Pectunculatis aureflua, 349.
———— delessertii, 349.
———— pectiniformis, 350.
———— scriptus, 351.
Perforated madrepores, 152.
Peyssonnel's discoveries, 128.
Phallusia grossularia, 313.
Pholades, or borers, 380.
Pholas crispata, 382.
——— papyracea and P. melanoura, 383.
Phosphorescence of the sea, 14. Causes of, 15.
Phosphorescent chain of Salpæ, 317.
Phyllactis prætexta, 194.
Physa castanea, 406.
Physalia, 246. Its poisonous properties, 250.
Physical properties of water, 28.
Physophora hydrostatica, 236.
Pilchards, 573. Cornwall "huers," The pilchard fishery, 574.
Pina bullata and P. nobilis, 370.

Pina radis and P. nigrina, 369.
Pinnoctopus corolliformis, 456.
Pintadine pearls, 353.
Pipe-fish (Syngnathus), 526.
Pipe-fishes (Fistularia), 595.
Plaice (Platessa vulgaris), 541.
Planorbis corneus, 405.
Pleuronectidæ, 538.
Plumatella cristallina, 308.
Polar seas, 47. Expeditions to, 47.
Polype and branch, 133.
Polypidum, 146.
Polypier and Polypi defined, 107.
Polypifera, 107.
Polypiferous crust in Gorgons, 151.
Pomotouan Archipelago, 171.
Porcelain shells, 418.
Porites, 164.
——— astroïdes, 149.
——— furcata, 165.
Porpila pacifica, 235.
Porpitæ, 234.
Portion of the disk of Physophora hydrostatica, 238.
Portumnus variegatus, 482.
Poulpe: Marvellous stories of the ancients concerning, 457. Mandibles preserved in the College of Surgeons, 458.
Praya diphys, 245.
Primitive generation, 98.
Principal forms of Anodonta, 370.
Principal species of Sea-anemones, 189.
Propagation of Infusoria, 96.
——— of Sea-urchins, 292.
Protozoa, 74. Leuwnhoek's discoveries, 74.
Pteroceras, their origin, 436.
——— chiragra and P. lambis, 437.
——— scorpio, and P. millepeda, 436.
Pteropoda, 441. The organization, wings, or flappers, 441.
Pulmonary Gasteropods, 393, 404.
Pupa uva, 401.
Pure water, 17.
Purpura, its reputation with the ancients, 427.
——— consul, 428.
Purpura lapillus and patula, 428.
Pyrosoma, 314.

Raiadæ, 501.
Rarefaction in Polar seas, 62.
Rataria, 234.
Ravages of the Teredo, 385.
Ray-fish, 504.
Recuperative powers of Holothuria, 295.
Red Sea Corals, 177.
Reflux of tides, 41.
Reign of law, 64.
Rhizopods, 75.
Rhizostoma Aldrovandi, 223.
——— Cuvieri, 222.
Rock covered with young Coral Polypes, 137.
Roman indifference to life, 534.
Rose aurelia, 227.
Ross's (Sir James) discoveries, 50, 51, 58.
Rotation of the earth, 40.
Rotella Zealandica, 412.
Rudimentary forms of life, 64.
Rugous madrepores, 150.

Sagartia viduata, 191.
Salmonidæ, 553.
Salmon leaps, 557. Falls of Kilmorack, 557. Anecdote of Lord Lovat, 558.
Salpa maxima, 316.
Saltness of the sea, 18. Its source, 25.
Salt water at the Poles, 21. At the Equator, 21.
Salt-water lakes, 18.
Sarcoda, 92.
Sargasso Sea, 35.
Saw-fish, 514.
Scallop shell, 346.
Scomberoïdes, 584.
Scoresby's account of the Polar seas, 60.
Scottish pearls, 372.
Scylla and Charybdis, 46.
Sea Anemone, 184. Organization, 185. Toxological properties, 188.
Sea Cucumber, 293.
Sea Eel (Muræna Helena), 533.
Sea Eggs, 293.

Sea Horse (Hippocampus), 527.
Sea Lampreys, 499.
Sea Level, 12.
Sea Mussels, 361.
Sea Nettles, 197.
Sea Palm, 274.
Sea Pen, 141—146.
Sea Slug, 402.
Sea Snail (Liparis), 536.
Sea Stars (Astrea), 157.
Sea Urchins, 283.
Sea water, its components, 17.
Section of a Coral branch, 134.
Section of Atlantic Telegraph, 10.
Seine Net, 576.
Selachians, 501.
Sepia (Cuttlefish), 446. Its Suckers, 447, 448.
Sepia officinalis, 465.
Sepia tuberculosa, and bone of S. officinalis, 466.
Sertulariadæ, 213.
Shad, the (Alosa), 572.
Shallow water, its temperature, 29.
Shark (Carcharius vulgaris), 508.
Shark fishing, 510.
Shell of the Mollusca, 319. Is it a skeleton? 320. How built up, 321.
Shell of the Strombus, 435.
Ship-worm and its ravages, 385. Its organization, 386. Reproduction, 387. Its boring hood, 389.
Siderolites calcitrapoides, 86.
Silver in the sea, 24.
Siphonophora, 230.
Skeleton Echinus, 290.
Skeleton of the Perch, 494.
Smolt, 555.
Snails: Form and characteristics, 394. Their organization, 395. Breathing, 395. Circulation, 395. Sight, 396. Reproduction, 396. Shell, 396. Their reputation with the Classics, 397.
Solarium perspecticum, and S. variegatum, 413.
Solar-lunar tides, 41.
Soles (Solea vulgaris), 539.
Sophonophora, 200.
Spearing Halibut, 543.
Spey Salmon, 558.
Spherical form of the Earth, 12.
Spiroloculina, 84.
Spondylus, various, 350.
Spongia, half natural size, 112.
Spongia, 109. Their generation, 110. Organization, 111. Localities, 111 Varieties of, 117.
Spontaneous division of Infusoria, 96.
Spontaneous generation, 97.
Squalidæ, 508.
Star-fishes, 157, 262. Their metamorphoses, 269. Dismemberment, 270. Suicidal propensities, 270.
Star-fishes and Oysters, 268.
Stentor Mülleri, 106.
Stinging apparatus of Physophora hydrostatica, 240.
Stinging tentacles of Physalia, 249.
Stomach of Infusoria, 94.
Stomia bea, 560.
Strombus gigas, shell and animal, 434.
Stone lilies, 278.
Stormouthfield fish-ponds, 555.
Straits of Gibraltar, 38.
Sturgeon (Acipenser sturio), 517.
——— fishing in the Volga, 518.
Sturiona, 515.
Stylaster flabelliformis, 156.
Sub-branchiata, 536.
Submarine currents, 37.
Subsidence, theory of Coral islands, 180.
Suckers of Star-fishes, 266. Suicidal tendency of Star-fishes, 271.
Swimming bladder, 494.
Sword-fish (Xiphias), 590. Warlike habits, 591. Fishing, 592.
Symphynota, 355.
Synapta duvernea, 301.
Succinea putris, 401.

Tabulate madrepores, 165.
Teeth of the Bream, 497.
——— Carp, 497.
——— Gold-fish. 497.

Teeth of the Trout, 497.
Tellina radiata, 377.
——— sulphurea, and T. donacina, 378.
——— virgata, 377.
Temperature of the sea, 26.
Tentacles of Molluscs, 304.
Tentaculiferous Cephalopods, 470. Their suckers (Acetabula), 470.
Teredo navalis, its ravages, 385, 386.
Testacella haliotidea, 403.
Textilaria, 83.
Thalassianthidæ, 193.
Thames Oyster beds, 330.
Thermal lines of sea temperature, 27.
Thynnus pelamys (the Bonito), 584, 590.
Tidal wave, 41. Its height in different seas, 42. Of the Atlantic, 29.
Tides, 39.
Torpedo marmorata, 504.
Trachinus communis, 579.
Trade-winds, their origin, 33.
Trembley's discoveries, 109.
Tridacna gigas, 372.
——— squamosa, 373.
Triton variegatum, T. lotorium, and T. anus, 431.
Trochus agglutinans, T. stellaris, 412.
——— inermis, T. Cookii, T. imbricatus, and T. agglutinans, 411.
Trochus niloticus, and T. virgatus, 410.
Tubelaridæ, 228.
Tubipora musica, 122.
Tubiporinæ, 122.
Tubulous madrepores, 152.
Tunicata, 311.
Tunny fish (Thynnus), 584.
——— fishing, 585.
——— net, 586.
Turbinolia, 152.
Turbo imperialis, 414.
——— margaritaceus and T. argyrostomus, 413.
Turbo undulatus, 414.
Turbot (Rhombus), 539.

Ultima Thule, 47.
Umbellularia Greenlandica, 145.
Unio littoralis, and U. pictorum, 371.
Uranoscopus vulgaris, 580.
Uses of salt in the sea, 29.

Vastness of the oceanic fields of observation, 67.
Vegetable life, 67.
Venus verrucosa, 378.
Veretillum cynomorium, 146.
Vetrina fasciata, 402.
Vibracule in molluscs, 304.
Vibrion baguette, 100.
Vilelladæ, 231.
——— limbosa, 231.
Virgularia, 144.
——— mirabilis, 145.
Volvox globator, 102.

Walsh's, Dr., experiments with the Torpedo, 506.
Water, 3.
Watering-pot, the, 389.
Water-lilies, 308.
Waves off Cape Horn, 45.
Weddell's discoveries, 48, 55.
Weevers (Trachinus), 579, 580.
Weight of the waters of the sea, 13.
——— of equatorial waters, 32.
Whence comes the salt of the sea? 25.
Whirlpools, 46. Scylla, 46. Charybdis, 46.
White Ray (Raia batis), 502.
Whiting (Merlangus vulgaris), 551, 552.
Whorled Gorgon, magnified, 126.
Wilkes' expedition, 48, 55.
Willoughby's discoveries, 47.
Winds, 43. Effect on tides, 43.
Wrasse (the), Labrus, 594.

Young Oysters, 328.
Young Polype attached to a rock, 137.

Zenith points, 40.
Zoantharia, 149, 161.
Zoantha thalassanthos, 150.
Zoanthus socialis, 195.
Zone of Calms, 34.
Zoophytes, 71. Its derivation, 72.

LONDON:
PRINTED BY WILLIAM CLOWES AND SONS, STAMFORD STREET
AND CHARING CROSS.

CHARLES DICKENS.

Illustrated Library Edition of Mr. Charles Dickens's Works.

Beautifully printed in Post 8vo., and carefully revised by the Author. With the Original Illustrations.

1.	Pickwick Papers	43 Illustrations	2 vols.	16*s.*
2.	Nicholas Nickleby	40 ditto	2 vols.	16*s.*
3.	Martin Chuzzlewit	40 ditto	2 vols.	16*s.*
4.	Dombey and Son	40 ditto	2 vols.	16*s.*
5.	David Copperfield	40 ditto	2 vols.	16*s.*
6.	Bleak House	40 ditto	2 vols.	16*s.*
7.	Little Dorrit	40 ditto	2 vols.	16*s.*
8.	Old Curiosity Shop and Reprinted Pieces	36 ditto	2 vols.	16*s.*
9.	Barnaby Rudge and Hard Times	36 ditto	2 vols.	16*s.*
10.	Sketches by Boz	40 ditto	1 vol.	8*s.*
11.	Oliver Twist	24 ditto	1 vol.	8*s.*
12.	Christmas Books	17 ditto	1 vol.	8*s.*
13.	A Tale of Two Cities	16 ditto	1 vol.	8*s*
14.	Great Expectations	8 ditto	1 vol.	
15.	Pictures from Italy and American Notes	8 ditto	1 vol.	
16.	Our Mutual Friend	40 ditto	2 vols.	